D0423362

SPEECH INDEX

An Index to Collections of World Famous Orations and Speeches for Various Occasions

Fourth Edition
Supplement, 1966-1980

by

CHARITY MITCHELL

The Scarecrow Press, Inc.
Metuchen, N.J., & London 1982

Library of Congress Cataloging in Publication Data

Mitchell, Charity.
    Speech index.

    Rev. ed. of: Speech index. Fourth edition supple-
ment / by Roberta Briggs Sutton and Charity Mitchell.
1972-1977.
    Includes indexes.
    1. Speeches, addresses, etc.--Indexes. 2. Orations--
Indexes. 3. American orations--Indexes. I. Sutton,
Roberta Briggs. Speech index. Fourth edition supplement. II. Sutton, Roberta Briggs. Speech index.
4th ed. III. Title.
AI3.S85 1966 Suppl. 2   081   81-23282
ISBN 0-8108-1518-4   AACR2

Dedicated to

Roberta Briggs Sutton

CONTENTS

PREFACE

This supplement cumulates the 1966-1970 and 1971-1975 supplements to the fourth edition of Roberta Sutton's Speech Index. It also includes speeches in books published between 1975 and 1980 and in earlier publications listed in the Library of Congress Subject Catalog between 1970 and 1980. It indexes 115 titles (176 volumes) published mostly between 1966 and 1980.

The Speech Index is an index to monographs; periodicals have not been included. For speeches published in Vital Speeches and other periodicals, the Readers' Guide and other periodical indexes should be consulted.

Each title was indexed for speeches only. Small selections have been excluded. The List of Books Indexed indicates the coverage of the indexing of each title. Since many editors of anthologies do not state whether they have used a speech in its entirety or have just included selections, extracts are not indicated. It would be extremely difficult to ascertain the completeness of each speech except by comparing each speech word for word with the complete works of each orator. To help the user identify speeches, the date and place of the presentation of the speech is included, if known, in the author entry for books indexed in the last two supplements.

To ensure that as far as possible all the entries for one speech are listed together, cross-references have been made from variant titles to the title which was first indexed. A speech appearing only once is entered as stated in the source.

Some speeches are known better by title than by orator; therefore there is a selective title listing with an explanation at the end of the main index.

The following sources were checked as authorities for subject headings: Library of Congress Subject Headings, 7th--9th editions; Readers' Guide; and the Social Sciences Index. Names were checked in the National Union Catalog, British Museum Catalogue, OCLC, various Who's Who books, and the Dictionary of National Biography. Some subject headings have been changed to bring them into line with current Library of Congress practice.

LIST OF BOOKS INDEXED

KEY TO SYMBOLS

*Books with this symbol have been indexed for speeches only.

ACC   The accused and the accusers; the famous speeches of the eight Chicago anarchists in court. Introduction by Leon Stein and Philip Taft. New York, Arno, 1969. (American labor)

ALA   Aly, Bower and Lucile F.
     American short speeches; an anthology selected and edited by Bower Aly and Lucile Folse Aly. New York, Macmillan, 1968.

ALS
PN 6122
, A48   Aly, Bower and Lucile F.
     Speeches in English. New York, Random House, 1968.

AND   Andrews, James R.
     A choice of worlds; the practice and criticism of public discourse. New York, Harper & Row, 1973. *

ANN   Annals of America. Chicago, Encyclopaedia Britannica, 1970. 20 vol. *

ARN   Arnold, Carroll C.
     Criticism of oral rhetoric. Columbus, Ohio, Charles E. Merrill Pub. Co., 1974. *

ARS   Arnold, Carroll C.
     The speaker's resource book. 2d ed. Glenview, Ill., Scott, Foresman and Co., 1966. *

BA   Baird, Albert Craig, comp.
     Representative American speeches, 1965-1980. 15 vols. New York, H. W. Wilson, 1965-1980.

BAAE   Baird, Albert Craig
     Essentials of general speech communication. 4th ed. New York, McGraw-Hill, 1973. *

BAAGB   Baird, Albert Craig
     General speech communication. 4th ed. New York, McGraw-Hill, 1971. *

BAD   Bagnall, Joseph
      Depression dialogue. Dubuque, Iowa, W. C.
    Brown, 1965. *

BAP   Barrett, Harold
      Practical methods in speech. 2d ed. New York,
    Holt, 1968. *

BAPR   Barrett, Harold
      Practical methods in speech. 3rd ed. San Fran-
    cisco, Rinehart Press, 1973. *

BAPRR Barrett, Harold
      Practical uses of speech communication. 4th ed.
    New York, Holt, 1977. *

BAS   Barker, Thoburn V.
      Speech; its structure and composition. New York,
    American Book Co., 1968.

BEN   Benedict, Stewart H.
      Famous American speeches. New York, Dell,
    1967.

BLY   Blyton, Gifford
      Speaking out: 2 centuries of Kentucky orators,
    by Gifford Blyton and Randall Capps. Winston-Salem,
    N. C., Hunter Pub. Co., 1977.

BNH   Bolding, Amy
      Handy introduction and replies and other helps for
    speakers. Grand Rapids, Michigan, Baker Book
    House, 1968. *

BON   Bolding, Amy
      New welcome speeches. Grand Rapids, Michigan,
    Baker Book House, 1971.

BOORA Boorstin, Daniel J., ed.
      American primer. Chicago, University of Chicago
    Press, 1966. 2 volumes. *

BOS   Bolding, Amy
      Simple welcome speeches and other helps. Grand
    Rapids, Michigan, Baker Book House, 1968. * (In-
    dexed for speeches or parts of speeches only.)

BOSC   Bosmajian, Haig A. and Hamida Bosmajian
      Rhetoric of the Civil Rights Movement. New York,
    Random House, 1969. *

BOSR   Bosmajian, Haig A.
      Rhetoric of the speaker: speeches and criticism.
    Boston, D. C. Heath and Co., 1967. *

BOST   Bosmajian, Hamida
                This great argument: the rights of women, edited
                by Hamida Bosmajian and Haig Bosmajian. Reading,
                Mass., Addison-Wesley Pub. Co., 1972. *

BREWE   Brewer, David J.
                World's best orations. Metuchen, N.J., Mini-
                Print Corporation, 1970 rep. of 1901. 10 vols. in 2.

BREWW   Brewer, Robert S.
                Winning FFA speeches; principles of speech prep-
                aration and presentation, by Robert S. Brewer and
                Dan B. Curtis. Danville, Ill., Interstate Printers
                & Publishers, 1976.

BRN   Brandes, Paul Dickerson
                The rhetoric of revolt. Englewood Cliffs, N.J.,
                Prentice-Hall, 1971. *

BRP   Braden, Waldo W.
                Public speaking: the essentials. New York,
                Harper, 1966. * (Indexed for speeches and sugges-
                tions for preparation of types of speeches.)

BRR   Brockway, Thomas P., ed.
                Language and politics. Boston, D. C. Heath
                and Co., 1965. *

BRYF   Bryant, Donald C.
                Fundamentals of public speaking, by Donald C.
                Bryant and Karl R. Wallace. 5th ed. Englewood
                Cliffs, N.J., Prentice-Hall, 1976. *

BRYH   Bryant, Donald C., ed.
                Historical anthology of select British speeches
                edited by Donald C. Bryant, Carroll C. Arnold,
                Frederick W. Haberman, Richard Murphy, and Karl
                R. Wallace. New York, Ronald Press Co., 1967.

BRYO   Bryant, Donald C.
                Oral communication: a short course in speaking,
                by Donald C. Bryant and Karl R. Wallace. 4th ed.
                Englewood Cliffs, N.J., Prentice-Hall, 1976. *

BURT   Burton, Arthur
                Mr. Toastmaster: the basic principles of better
                listening-thinking-talking through effective public
                speaking. New York, William-Frederick Press,
                1967. *

CAPB   Capp, Glenn Richard
                Basic oral communication. 3rd ed. Englewood
                Cliffs, N.J., Prentice-Hall, 1971. *

CAPG   Capp, Glen R.
            Great society; a sourcebook of speeches. Bel-
            mont, California, Dickenson Pub. Co., 1967.

CLAYP   Clarke, William
            Political orations, from Wentworth to Macaulay. .
            London, W. Scott, 1889. (The Camelot series)

COG   Connor, W. Robert
            Greek orations. Ann Arbor, University of Michi-
            gan Press, 1966.

CROCK   Crocker, L. G.
            Rhetorical analysis of speeches. Boston, Allyn,
            1967.

CUB   Culp, Ralph Borden.
            Basic types of speech. Dubuque, Iowa, Wm. C.
            Brown Co., 1968. (Speech communication series)*

CUR   Current, Richard N., ed.
            Reconstruction (1865-1877). Englewood Cliffs,
            N.J., Prentice-Hall, 1965. *

CURM   Curry, Horace C.
            Masterpieces in Philippine oratory and lessons in
            public speaking, edited by Horace C. Curry in col-
            laboration with T. Uewaki. Manila, Novel Publishing
            Co., 1970. Reprint of the 1939 ed. *

DAVF   Davis, David Brion
            The fear of conspiracy. Ithaca, N.Y., Cornell
            University Press, 1971. *

ECH   Echoes from the South; comprising the most impor-
            tant speeches, proclamations and public acts emanat-
            ing from the South during the late war. Westport,
            Conn., Negro Universities Press, 1970. (Reprint of
            1866 edition.)*

EHN   Ehninger, Douglas
            Principles and types of speech communication, by
            Douglas Ehninger, Alan H. Monroe, and Bruce E.
            Gronbeck. 8th ed. Glenview, Ill., Scott, Foresman,
            1978. *

EMP   Emerson, Rupert, ed.
            Political awakening of Africa, edited by Rupert
            Emerson and Martin Kilson. Englewood Cliffs, N.J.,
            Prentice-Hall, 1965. *

ERP   Ericson, Jon L.
            Public speaking as dialogue. Dubuque, Iowa,
            Kendall/Hunt, 1970. *

FON   Foner, Philip S.
                      The voice of Black America, major speeches by
Negroes in the United States, 1797-1971. New York,
Simon and Schuster, 1972.

FRIP   Frisch, Morton J.
                      The political thought of American statesmen.
Edited by Morton J. Frisch and Richard G. Stevens.
Itasca, Ill., F. E. Peacock Publishers, 1973. *

GRG   Graham, John
                      Great American speeches, 1898-1963. Texts and
studies. New York, Appleton-Century-Crofts, 1970. *

HAW   Hawken, Henry A.
                      Trumpets of glory: Fourth of July orations, 1786-
1861. Granby, Conn., Salmon Brook Historical So-
ciety, 1976.

HNWM   Hobbs, Herschel H.
                      More welcome speeches and emergency addresses
for all occasions. Grand Rapids, Mich., Zondervan
Publishing House, 1968.

HNWSN   Hobbs, Herschel
                      New welcome speeches. Grand Rapids, Michigan,
Zondervan Publishing House, 1975.

HOR   Horn, Francis H.
                      Go forth, be strong: advice and reflections from
commencement speakers. Carbondale, Southern Illi-
nois University Press, 1978.

HOW   Howe, Daniel Walker
                      The American Whigs. New York, Wiley, 1973. *

HURD   Hurd, Charles
                      A treasury of great American speeches. New and
revised edition. Selected by Charles Hurd. Revised
and edited by Andrew Bauer. New York, Hawthorn
Books, 1970.

HURH   Hurd, Charles
                      A treasury of great American speeches. Selected
by Charles Hurd. New ed., rev. by Andrew Bauer.
New York, Hawthorn Books, 1970.

HURS   Hurst, Charles G.
                      Effective expression, by Charles G. Hurst and
Lewis H. Fednerson. Columbus, Ohio, Merrill, 1966.

JAE   Jackman, Sydney W., ed.
                      English reform tradition, 1790-1910. Magnolia,
Mass., P. Smith, 1967. *

JAM   Jamieson, Kathleen M.
                     Critical anthology of public speeches.   Palo Alto,
Calif., Science Research Associates, 1978.

JEF   Jeffrey, Robert Campbell
                     Speech.   New York, Harper, 1971. *

JEFF   Jeffrey, Robert Campbell
                     Speech.   2nd ed.   New York, Harper & Row,
1975. *

JON   Jones, Phyllis M.
                     Salvation in New England; selections from the
sermons of the first preachers.   Edited by Phyllis
M. Jones and Nicholas R. Jones.   Austin, Univ. of
Texas Press, 1977.

KEO   Kendall, H. Bruce and Stewart, C. J.
                     On speech and the speakers.   New York, Holt,
1968. *

LAA   Lafeber, Walter
                     America in the cold war.   New York, Wiley,
1969.   (Problems in American History series.)*

LINR   Linkugel, Wil A.
                     Contemporary American speeches.   2d ed.   Bel-
mont, Calif., Wadsworth Publishing Company, 1969.

LINRS   Linkugel, Wil A.
                     Contemporary American speeches.   3rd ed.   Bel-
mont, Calif., Wadsworth Publishing Company, 1972.

LINRST   Linkugel, Wil A.
                     Contemporary American speeches.   4th ed.   Du-
buque, Iowa, Kendall/Hunt Pub. Co., 1978.

LINS   Linsley, William A.
                     Speech criticism: methods and materials.   Du-
buque, Iowa, William C. Brown Company, 1968. *

LYI   Lyle, Guy R. and Guinagh, Kevin.
                     I am happy to present.   2d ed.   New York, H. W.
Wilson Co., 1968.

MAC   McCroskey, James C.
                     Introduction to rhetorical communication.   Engle-
wood Cliffs, N.J., Prentice-Hall, 1968. *

MACR   McCroskey, James C.
                     An introduction to rhetorical communication.   2nd
ed.   Englewood Cliffs, N.J., Prentice-Hall, 1972. *

MACS   McIntyre, W. David
            Speeches and documents on New Zealand history,
            ed. by W. David McIntyre and W. J. Gardner.   Ox-
            ford, Clarendon Press, 1971. *

MAES   Maestas, John A.
            Contemporary native American address.   Provo,
            Utah, Brigham Young University, 1976.

MCA   McLeod, A. L.
            Australia speaks; an anthology of Australian
            speeches.   Sydney, Wentworth Press, 1969.

MCB   McBath, James H.
            British public addresses, 1828-1960.   Edited by
            James H. McBath and Walter R. Fisher.   Boston,
            Houghton Mifflin, 1971.

MDT   Mathews, Donald G.
            Agitation for freedom.   New York, Wiley, 1972. *

MDV   Matson, Floyd W., ed.
            Voices of crisis: vital speeches on contemporary
            issues.   New York, The Odyssey Press, 1967.

MDYG   May, Derwent, ed.
            Good talk: an anthology from BBC radio.   New
            York, Taplinger Publishing Company, 1969.

MILS   Miller, Melvin H.
            Special occasion speeches.   Skokie, Illinois,
            National Textbook Company, 1965. *   (Indexed for
            suggestions on preparation of types of speeches for
            various occasions.)

MONS   Morais, John Victor, ed.
            Selected speeches; a golden treasury of Asian
            thought and wisdom.   Kuala Lumpur, Printed by
            Rajiv Printers, 1967.

MONSA   Morais, John Victor, ed.
            Selected speeches; a golden treasury of Asian
            thought and wisdom.   New ed.   Petaling Jaya,
            Malaysia, 1971.

MOP   Monroe, Alan Houston
            Principles of speech communication.   6th ed.
            Glenview, Ill., Scott, Foresman, 1969. *

MOPR   Monroe, Alan H.
            Principles of speech communication, by Alan H.
            Monroe and Douglas Ehninger.   7th brief ed.   Glen-
            view, Ill., Scott, Foresman, 1975. *

MUS   Mudd, C. S.
      Speech; content and communication. 2d ed. San
      Francisco, Chandler, 1969.

NOB   Nobel Prize Library
      New York, Alexis Gregory, 1971. 20 vol. *

NOL   Nobel Lectures
      Literature, 1901-1967. Edited by Horst Frenz.
      Amsterdam, Elsevier, 1969. *

NOLC   Nobel Lectures
      Chemistry, 1901-1970. Amsterdam, Elsevier,
      1966-1972. 4 vols. *

NOLM   Nobel Lectures
      Physiology or medicine, 1901-1970. Amsterdam,
      Elsevier, 1967-1972. 4 vols. *

NOLP   Nobel Lectures
      Peace, 1901-1970. Edited by Frederick W.
      Haberman. Amsterdam, Elsevier, 1972. 3 vols. *

NOLPH   Nobel Lectures
      Physics, 1901-1970. Amsterdam, Elsevier, 1967-
      1972. 4 vols. *

OE   O'Neill, Daniel Joseph
      Speeches by Black Americans. Encino, Calif.,
      Dickenson Publishing Company, 1971.

OLIS   Oliver, Robert T., ed.
      Selected speeches from American history, edited
      by Robert T. Oliver and Eugene E. White. Boston,
      Allyn and Bacon, 1966.

PAE   Painter, Margaret
      Educator's guide to persuasive speaking. Engle-
      wood Cliffs, N.J., Prentice-Hall, 1966. *

PAF   Parsons, Lucy Eldine (Gonzalez)
      Famous speeches of the eight Chicago anarchists.
      New York, Arno, 1969. (Mass violence in American
      History series). Reprint of 1910.

POC   Potter, David and Thomas, Gordon L.
      Colonial idiom. Carbondale, Southern Illinois
      University Press, 1970. (Landmarks of rhetoric
      and public address)

PRS   Prochnow, Herbert V.
      Successful toastmaster by Herbert V. Prochnow
      and Herbert V. Prochnow, Jr. New York, Harper

and Row, 1966. * (Indexed for complete speeches only.)

REID   Reid, Loren Dudley, 1905-   .
              Speaking well. 3d ed. New York, McGraw-Hill, 1977. *

REIR   Rein, Irving J.
              Relevant rhetoric: principles of public speaking through case studies. Free Press, 1969.

              Representative American speeches see Baird, Albert Craig, comp. Representative American speeches.

ROD   Rollins, Alfred B., Jr., ed.
              Depression, recovery, and war: 1929-1945. New York, McGraw-Hill, 1966. (Documentary History of American life, vol. 7)*

SAG   Saunders, A. N. W.
              Greek political oratory. Harmondsworth, Penguin, 1970.

SCHW   Schrier, William, ed.
              Winning Hope College orations, 1941-1966. Holland, Hope College, 1966.

SIN   Singer, Aaron
              Campaign speeches of American Presidential candidates, 1928-1972. New York, Ungar, 1976.

SMHR   Smith, Arthur L.
              Rhetoric of Black revolution. Boston, Allyn and Bacon, 1969.

SMHV   Smith, Arthur L.
              The voice of Black rhetoric: selections, edited by Arthur L. Smith and Stephen Robb. Boston, Allyn and Bacon, 1971.

STAT   State of the Union Messages of the Presidents from Washington to Johnson. Introduction by Arthur Schlesinger, Jr. Robert Hector Publishers, 1966. 3 volumes.

STOT   Stewart, Charles J.
              On speech communication; an anthology of contemporary writing and messages. New York, Holt, Rinehart and Winston, 1972. *

STRM   Strother, David B., ed.
              Modern British eloquence. New York, Funk and Wagnalls, 1969.

TAC

Tacey, William S.
Business and professional speaking. 2nd ed.
Dubuque, Iowa, Brown, 1975. *

THOMS

Thomas, William B.
Shall not perish; nine speeches by three great
Americans; selected and edited by William B.
Thomas. Copenhagen, Gyldendal, 1968.

USINAU

United States. 91st Congress, 1st Session, House
Document 142
Inaugural addresses of the Presidents of the
United States from George Washington, 1789 to
Richard Milhous Nixon, 1969. Washington, D.C.,
United States Govt. Print. Off., 1969.

USINAUG

United States. 93rd Congress, 1st Session, House
Document 93-208
Inaugural addresses of the Presidents of the
United States from George Washington, 1789 to
Richard Milhous Nixon, 1973. Washington, United
States Govt. Print. Off., 1974.

VER

Verderber, Rudolph F.
The challenge of effective speaking. 2nd ed.
Belmont, Calif., Wadsworth Publishing Company,
1973. *

VERD

Verderber, Rudolph F.
The challenge of effective speaking. 3rd ed.
Belmont, Calif., Wadsworth Publishing Company,
1976. *

VI

Vietnam War: Christian perspectives, ed. by Michael
P. Hamilton. Grand Rapids, Eerdmans, 1967. *

WALE

Wallack, Morton A.
Eulogies. New York, Jonathan David, 1965.

INDEX TO SPEECHES

1

Abzug, Bella Savitsky
A new kind of Southern strategy
(Nashville, Tenn. , Feb. 12,
1972). BA 1971-72:37

ACADEMIC DEGREES See Ac-
ceptance speeches--Degrees,
Academic; Presentation
speeches-Degrees, Academic

ACADEMIC FREEDOM See
Teaching, Freedom of

ACCEPTANCE SPEECHES
Ford, G. R.
Acceptance speech.
BA 1973-74:193
King, Mrs. M. L. , Jr.
We need to be united.
FON:1169
Quezon, M. L.
On Spain's contribution to the
Philippines. CURM:24

---- DEGREES, ACADEMIC
Churchill, W. L. S.
Sinews of peace (speech at
Fulton, Missouri).
ANN 16:365; MCB:541
Humphrey, H. H. , Jr.
Open door (21st anniversary
of Churchill's "Iron Curtain"
speech). LINR:236
Kennedy, J. F.
Intellectual and the politician.
BAP:285; LINR:236
Romulo, C. P.
The mind of a new common-
wealth. CURM:267
Sampson, E. S.
Choose one of five.
MOP:386
Stevenson, A. E.
Today's most fateful fact (ac-
cepting honorary degree of
Doctor of Laws). OLIS:272
Washington, B. T.
Address delivered at the Har-
vard Alumni dinner in 1896.
HURH:144

---- GIFTS
Acceptance of a gift (3 examples).
BNH:87
Suggestions for preparation of a
speech accepting a gift or an
award. MILS:10
Suggestions for preparation of

acceptance speeches. With
examples of. PAE:181

---- JOURNALISM AND JOURNAL-
ISTS
Gallagher, W.
Upon acceptance of the 1967
William Allen White Founda-
tion Award for Journalistic
Merit. JEF:327; JEFF:311

---- MEDALS
Glenn, J. H.
Accepting the Distinguished
Service Medal (outline of
speech). CUB:65

---- MILITARY COMMISSIONS
Washington, G.
Acceptance of military com-
mission. POC:164

---- NOMINATIONS
Bryan, W. J.
Imperialism (accepting Demo-
cratic nomination for Presi-
dency, 1900). ANN 12:345
Dewey, T. E.
Acceptance speech, Chicago,
Illinois, June 28, 1944.
SIN:205
Acceptance speech, Philadel-
phia, Pennsylvania, June 24,
1948. SIN:229
Eisenhower, D. D.
Acceptance speech, Chicago,
Illinois, July 11, 1952.
SIN:242
Acceptance speech, San Fran-
cisco, California, August 23,
1956. SIN:265
Ford, G. R.
Republican National Convention
acceptance speech.
LINRST:349
Goldwater, B. M.
Extremism in defense of liberty
(accepting nomination for presi-
dency, July 17, 1964).
MAC:251; MACR:292; MDV:115;
SIN:337
Hoover, H. C.
Acceptance speech, Constitution
Hall, Washington, D.C., Aug-
ust 11, 1932. SIN:88
Accepting the nomination for
presidency. SIN:4

Luthuli, A. J.
  Africa and freedom.   MDV:79;
  NOLP 3:217
MacArthur, D.
  Farewell to the cadets (ac-
  cepting Sylvanus Thayer award
  for service to his nation,
  West Point, May 12, 1962).
  LINR:264; LINRS:283;
  LINRST:357; MDV:20;
  MUS:332
McNamara, R. S.
  Searching for new solutions
  to poverty.   BA 1976-77:91
Mann, T.
  Acceptance [of the Nobel Prize
  for Literature, 1929].
  NOB 12:225; NOL:263
Mathias, C. M.
  The First Amendment: free-
  dom and responsibility.
  BA 1977-78:134
Mauriac, F.
  Acceptance [of the Nobel Prize
  for Literature, 1952].
  NOB 13:7; NOL:481
Mistral, G.
  Acceptance [of the Nobel Prize
  for Literature, 1945].
  NOB 14:170; NOL:408
Osborne, L.
  Acceptance [of the Nobel Prize
  for Peace for Cordell Hull, Dec.
  10, 1945].   NOLP 2:318
Peirce, H. H. D.
  Acceptance [of the Nobel Prize
  for Peace for Theodore
  Roosevelt, Dec. 10, 1906].
  NOLP 1:99
Perse, S.
  Acceptance [of the Nobel
  Prize for Literature, 1960].
  NOB 20:7; NOL:556
Pirandello, L.
  Acceptance [of the Nobel Prize
  for Literature, 1934].
  NOB 20:77; NOL:324
Quasimodo, S.
  Acceptance [of the Nobel Prize
  for Literature, 1959].
  NOB 20:285; NOL:537
Royster, V. C.
  What the people grant, they
  can take away.
  BA 1978-79:191
Russell, B. A. W.
  What desires are politically
  important?   NOL:452

Sachs, L. N.
  Acceptance [of the Nobel Prize
  for Literature, 1966].
  NOB 16:5; NOL:619
Schmedeman, A. G.
  Acceptance [of the Nobel Prize
  for Peace for Woodrow Wilson,
  1919, Dec. 10, 1920].
  NOLP 1:294
Seferis, G.
  Acceptance [of the Nobel Prize
  for Literature, 1963].
  NOB 17:5; NOL:582
Sienkiewicz, H.
  Acceptance [of the Nobel Prize
  for Literature, 1905].
  NOL:45; NOB 17:183
Stanton, F.
  Remarks on government regula-
  tion of broadcasting (accepting
  Printers' Ink gold medal).
  MDV:277
Steinbeck, J.
  Acceptance [of the Nobel Prize
  for Literature, 1962].
  NOB 19:205; NOL:575
Suggestions for preparation of a
  speech accepting a gift or
  award.   MILS:10
Torata, Count de
  Acceptance [of the Nobel Prize
  for Literature for Jacinto
  Benavente, 1922].   NOL:191
Truman, H. S.
  Campaign speech, Harlem,
  New York, October 29, 1948.
  SIN:226
Undset, S.
  Acceptance [of the Nobel Prize
  for Literature, 1928].
  NOB 18:167; NOL:255
Vallotton, H.
  Acceptance [of the Nobel Prize
  for Literature for Hermann
  Hesse, 1946].   NOB 9:237;
  NOL:416
Wauters, C. C. M. A.
  Acceptance [of the Nobel Prize
  for Literature for Maurice
  Maeterlinck, 1911].   NOL:114
Yalow, R. S.
  "Let us join hands, hearts and
  minds. " BA 1977-78:181
Yeats, W. B.
  Acceptance [of the Nobel Prize
  for Literature, 1923].
  NOB 18:263; NOL:199

ACETIC ACID
  Lynen, F.
    The pathway from "activated
    acetic acid" to the terpenes
    and fatty acids.   NOLM 4:103

Acheson, Dean G.
  Ethics in international relations
    today.   ARS:229
  Marshall Plan; relief and re-
    construction are chiefly
    matters of American self-
    interest.   LAA:55
  North Atlantic Pact.   ANN 16:587
  Strategy of freedom.   ANN 17:42

ACHIEVEMENT See Success

ACKNOWLEDGMENTS See Ac-
  ceptance speeches; Thanks

Acton, Harold See Sykes, C.,
  jt. auth.

Adams, Charles Francis, 1807-
  1886
  States and the Union.
    BREWE 1:25

Adams, Charles Francis, Jr.,
  1835-1915
  Battle of Gettysburg.
    BREWE 1:31

Adams, E. J.
  These are revolutionary times.
    (Charleston, S.C., March
    19, 1867).   FON:342

Adams, John
  First annual address.
    STAT 1:40
  Fourth annual message.
    STAT 1:52
  Inaugural address.   BREWE 1:39;
    USINAU:7; USINAUG:7
  On the Boston Massacre.
    BREWE 1:45; POC:108
  Second annual address.
    STAT 1:44
  Speech in defence of the sol-
    diers. Same as his On the
    Boston Massacre
  Third annual message.
    STAT 1:49

ADAMS, JOHN
  Everett, E.

  Adams and Jefferson.
    HURH:64
  Webster, D.
    Eulogy on Adams and Jefferson.
    BREWE 10:3848
  Wirt, W.
    Death of Jefferson and Adams.
    BREWE 10:3905

Adams, John Quincy
  Declaration and the Constitution.
    Same as his Jubilee of the
    Constitution (50th)
  First annual message (Dec. 6,
    1825).   ANN 5:185; HOW:11;
    STAT 1:232
  Fourth annual message.
    STAT 1:278
  Fourth of July oration, 1828.
    HAW:94
  Inaugural address.   ANN 5:138;
    USINAU:47; USINAUG:47
  Jubilee of the Constitution (50th).
    ANN 6:470; BREWE 1:85
  Life and character of Lafayette.
    BREWE 1:79
  On participating in a congress of
    American nations.   ANN 5:188
  Oration at Plymouth (commemora-
    tion of the landing of the Pil-
    grims).   (Plymouth, Mass.,
    Dec. 22, 1802).   HURH:51
  Oration at Plymouth (commemora-
    tion of the landing of the Pil-
    grims).   BREWE 1:65
  Policy for internal improvements.
    Same as his First annual mes-
    sage
  Second annual message.
    STAT 1:249
  State of the Union Message.
    Same as his First annual mes-
    sage
  "Think of your forefathers and of
    your posterity." Same as his
    Oration at Plymouth (commem-
    oration of the landing of the
    Pilgrims)
  Third annual message.
    STAT 1:264

Adams, Samuel
  American independence.
    BREWE 1:94; HURH:31
  "We have no other alternative
    than independence." Same as
    his American independence

Addams, Jane
  Foreign-born children in the
    primary grades. ANN 12:130
  "...one who has looked through
    the confusion of the moment
    and has seen the moral issue
    involved." Same as her
    Washington's birthday
  Washington's birthday (Chicago,
    Feb. 23, 1903). HURH:163

ADDAMS, JANE
  Koht, H.
    Presentation [of the Nobel
    Prize for Peace to Jane Ad-
    dams and Nicholas Murray
    Butler, Dec. 10, 1931].
    NOLP 2:125

Adler, Kurt
  Diene synthesis and related
    reaction types (Nobel Lec-
    ture, Dec. 12, 1950).
    NOLC 3:267

ADLER, KURT
  Fredga, A.
    Presentation [of the Nobel
    Prize for Chemistry to Otto
    Paul Hermann Diels and
    Kurt Adler, Dec. 12, 1950].
    NOLC 3:255

Adler, Morris
  Rare spirit. WALE:3

Adrian, Edgar Douglas
  The activity of the nerve
    fibres (Nobel Lecture,
    Dec. 12, 1932).
    NOLM 2:293

ADRIAN, EDGAR DOUGLAS
  Liljestrand, G.
    Presentation [of the Nobel
    Prize for Physiology or
    Medicine to Sir Charles
    Scott Sherrington and Edgar
    Douglas Adrian, Dec. 12,
    1932]. NOLM 2:273

ADULT EDUCATION See
  Education, Adult

ADVERTISING
  Myers, N. J.
    Moppet manipulation. ARS:123
  Rokeach, M.

Images of the consumer's
  changing mind on and off Madison Avenue. ARS:115

Aelfric
  Sermon on the sacrifice on Easter-
    Day. BRYH:14

Aelred, Saint
  Farewell. BREWE 1:110
  On manliness. BREWE 1:113
  Sermon after absence.
    BREWE 1:111

Aeschines
  Against Ctesiphon. BREWE 1:114;
    COG:120
  Debate on the crown. Same as
    his Against Ctesiphon

AFRICA
  Bacon, L.
    Plea for Africa. HAW:60
  Blyden, E. W.
    Africa's service to the world.
    EMP:26
    The African problem and the
    methods of its solution.
    FON:540
  Casely-Hayford, J. E.
    Leadership and African cooper-
    ation. EMP:49
  Houphouet-Boigny, F.
    French Africa and the French
    Union. EMP:73
  Johnson, J. W.
    Africa at the Peace Table and
    the descendants of Africans
    in our American democracy.
    FON:730
  Legum, C.
    Pan-Africanism, the Commun-
    ists, and the West. ARS:255
  Luthuli, A. J.
    Africa and freedom. MDV:79;
    NOLP 3:217
  Nkrumah, F. N. K.
    African history through African
    eyes. EMP:22
    Freedom and unity as Africa's
    salvation. EMP:145
  Palmer, J.
    Africa: continent of change.
    LINRS:33
    New Africa: continent of
    change. LINR:32
  Pitt, W., 1759-1806
    Indicts the slave trade and

foresees a liberated Africa.
BREWE 8:3208; CLAYP:138;
JAE:12; STRM:91
Robeson, P.
Anti-imperialists must defend
Africa. FON:833

AFRICA, SOUTH See South Africa

AFTER DINNER SPEECHES
Burton, S.
You (male) should wear long
hair. BAS:200 (outline only)
Clemens, S. L.
Horrors of the German lan-
guage. BEN:204
"The ladies. " BEN:201
New England weather.
HURH:128
Curtis, G. W.
Liberty under the law.
BAS:141 (outline only);
LINS:249
Dear Old Dad. BURT:172
Executive. BURT:27
Frustrated toastmaster.
BURT:160
Good old days. BURT:158
Grady, H. W.
New South (speech to the
New England Society).
ANN 11:240; BAS:121 (outline
only); BOORA 1:465; LINS:254
Hazlitt, W.
On wit and humor.
BREWE 7:2449
Hypochondriac. BURT:106
Investor. BURT:175
Landis, F.
Witty after-dinner speech on
Will Hayes. LYI:224
Police. BURT:32
Schurz, C.
Old world and the new.
HURH:135
Sickness. BURT: 7
Suggestions for the preparation
of an after-dinner speech.
MILS:13
What makes Sammy laugh?
BURT:60

AGE See Old age; Youth; Youth-
Adult relationship

Agnew, Spiro
Address before the Midwest
Regional Republican Com-

mittee. BA 1969-70:59
Responsibility and television news.
Same as his Television news
coverage; network censorship
Television news coverage; network
censorship (Des Moines, Iowa,
Nov. 13, 1969). ARN:367;
BRYF:467; ERP:153; LINRS:191;
LINRST:221; MACR:331;
STAT:274
Television news media. Same as
his Television news coverage;
network censorship
Thoughts on broadcast journalism.
Same as his Television news
coverage; network censorship
Vice President Agnew on televised
news. Same as his Television
news coverage; network censor-
ship

AGNEW, SPIRO
Stanton, F.
Reply to the Vice President.
STOT:282

Agnon, Shmuel Yosef
Acceptance [of the Nobel Prize
for Literature, 1966].
NOB 1:5; NOL:614

AGNON, SHMUEL YOSEF
Österling, A.
Presentation [of the Nobel
Prize for Literature to Shmuel
Yosef Agnon and Leonie Nelly
Sachs, 1966]. NOB 1:3;
NOB 16:3; NOL:611

AGRICULTURAL ADMINISTRATION
- UNITED STATES
Truman, H. S.
First annual message.
STAT 3:2900

AGRICULTURAL INNOVATIONS
Howell, W.
A new century in agriculture.
BREWW:211
Morrison, H. C.
In the pursuit of excellence.
BREWW:61

AGRICULTURAL LAWS AND LEGIS-
LATION See Agriculture

AGRICULTURAL RESEARCH
Grass, F.

The sky's the limit.
BREWW:115

AGRICULTURE
Benson, E. T.
Price supports and farm sur-
pluses.   ANN 17:383
Blizzard, E.
Not just a farmer.
BREWW:49
Borah, W. E.
Western farming and the
tariff.   ANN 15:28
Brooks, T. J.
Antitrust laws as applied to
farmers.   ANN 13:331
Cobden, R.
Effects of protection in agri-
culture.   MCB:189
Effects of Corn Laws in
agriculture.   STRM:246
Coolidge, C.
Vetoing the farmer: Non-
planning as a way of life.
ANN 14:568
Cram, R. A.
What is a free man?
ANN 15:498
Davidson, G.
Farmer, heal thyself!
BREWW:165
Herink, R.
A succession of goals.
BREWW:141
Ivens, M.
I still believe in the future
of farming.   BREWW:195
Lincoln, A.
Labor, education, and the
American farmer.   ANN 9:121
Madison, J.
Agriculture and conservation.
ANN 4:503
Madrid, S.
I am proud to be a part of it.
BREWW:153
Mathias, T.
Is agriculture on its way out?
BREWW:64
May, C.
The American farmer.
LINSR:117
Muench, A.
Rural families and welfare.
ANN 15:462
Price, S.
Agriculture--the real answer
to starvation.   BREWW:161

Roosevelt, F. D.
Fireside chat: AAA and NRA,
July 24, 1933.   ANN 15:210
Roosevelt, T.
Seventh annual message.
STAT 3:2240
Roper, B.
A fable come true.
BREWW:201
Smith, E. R.
United we stand, divided we
fall.   BREWW:134
Stratton, T.
Agriculture--America's great-
est tool.   BREWW:109
Wallace, H. A.
Declaration of interdependence.
ANN 15:220
New Farm Act--balanced
abundance for farm and city.
BAD:37
Pigs and pig iron.   ANN 15:336
Wilson, W.
First annual message.
STAT 3:2544

---- EDUCATION - MALAYSIA
Aziz, U.
Scientific concepts of external
aid for agricultural education.
MONSA:161

---- EXPERIMENTATION
Morse, D.
Lab farms in vocational agri-
culture.   BREWW:144

AGRICULTURE AS A PROFESSION
Morelli, L.
Vocational agriculture, the
FFA, and our free enterprise
system.   BREWW:78
Morse, D.
Lab farms in vocational agri-
culture.   BREWW:144
Spray, C.
A new crisis in agriculture.
BREWW:71

Ahmad, Ungku Omar   See   Ungku
Omar Ahmad

Ahmad bin Mohamed Ibrahim   See
Ibrahim, Ahmad M.

Aiken, Frederick A.
Defense of Mrs. Mary E. Surratt.
BREWE 1:120

Aiken, George D.
    Either impeach ... or get off
        his back. (Washington, D.C.,
        Nov. 7, 1973). BA 1973-74:66

AIR - POLLUTION
    Schalliol, G.
        Strangler.   LINR:246;
        LINRS:260; LINRST:298

Akerman, J.
    Presentation [of the Nobel Prize
        for Physiology or Medicine
        to Alexis Carrel, Dec. 11,
        1912]. NOLM 1:437

Akintola, Samuel Ladoke and oth-
        ers (A. T. Balewa)
    Nigeria debates self-govern-
        ment. EMP:65

ALASKA
    Roosevelt, T.
        Annual message, December
        6, 1905. STAT 2:2105
    Seward, W. H.
        Promise of Alaska.
        ANN 10:193

Alatas, Syed Hussein
    Sheep and lions in trade unions
        (Johore Bharu, Oct. 22,
        1970). MONSA:179 selections
    Universities: discrepancy be-
        tween ideal and reality takes
        alarming turn (Kuala Lum-
        pur, Aug., 1970).
        MONSA:177

Albert, Carl See Burger, W.
    E., jt. auth.

Albertus Magnus, bp. of Ratisbon
    Blessed dead.   BREWE 1:149
    Meaning of the crucifixion.
        BREWE 1:147

ALCOHOLISM
    Karos, P. A.
        Haven of the defeated.
        ARS:148

Alconcel, Douglas
    Aquaculture--an answer to the
        food crisis.   BREWW:88

Aldrin, Edwin E. See
    Armstrong, Neil, jt. auth.

Alfvén, Hannes
    Plasma physics, space research
        and the origin of the solar
        system (Nobel Lecture, Dec.
        11, 1970). NOLPH 4:306

ALFVEN, HANNES
    Gustafsson, T.
        Presentation [of the Nobel
        Prize for Physics to Hannes
        Alfvén and Louis Néel, Dec.
        11, 1970]. NOLPH 4:303

ALICYCLIC COMPOUNDS
    Wallach, O.
        Alicyclic compounds.
        NOLC 1:178

ALIEN AND SEDITION LAWS, 1798
    Alien, J. and others
        Debate on the Sedition Act.
        ANN 4:53
    Dickerson, M.
        Alien and Sedition Acts of the
        Adams administration.
        BREWE 5:1836
    Gallatin, A.
        Constitutional liberty and exe-
        cutive despotism.
        BREWE 6:2209
    Livingston, E.
        On the Alien Bill.   ANN 4:49
    Marshall, J.
        Address on constitutionality of
        Alien and Sedition Laws.
        FRIP:99

Allen, Ethan
    Call to arms (1861).
        BREWE 1:150

Allen, James
    The Naval Defence Bill, 1908
        (New Zealand House of Repre-
        sentatives, Sept. 30, 1908).
        MACS:270 sel.

Allen, John and others (A. Gallatin)
    Debate on the Sedition Act.
        ANN 4:53

Alphand, Hervé
    Responds to introductions.
        PRS:159; 198

ALSCHULER, ALFRED S.
    Shulman, C. E.
        Alfred S. Alschuler. WALE:299

Alsop, John
  Responds to an introduction.
    PRS:154

Altgeld, John Peter
  Children of toil.   ANN 11:445
  Choice before labor-organiza-
    tion or annihilation.   Same
    as his Children of toil

Alunan, Rafael R.
  Mindanao, the land of promise
    (University of the Philip-
    pines, Dec. 7, 1937).
    CURM:108

Alvarez, Luis W.
  Recent developments in particle
    physics (Nobel Lecture, Dec.
    11, 1968).   NOLPH 4:241

ALVAREZ, LUIS W.
  Friesen, S. V.
    Presentation [of the Nobel
    Prize for Physics to Luis
    W. Alvarez, Dec. 11, 1968].
    NOLPH 4:239

Aly, Bower
  Remarks on Jefferson Day.
    BAP:273

AMERICA See United States

AMERICAN COLONIZATION
    SOCIETY
  Blyden, E. W.
    The African problem and the
    methods of its solution.
    FON:540

AMERICAN INDIAN MOVEMENT
  Bellecourt, V.
    American Indian Movement.
    MAES:66
  Trudell, J.
    Commitment.   MAES:83
  Wilson, D.
    Real Indian leaders condemn
    A. I. M.   MAES:63

AMERICAN LEGION
  Stevenson, A. E.
    Speech to the American
    Legion, August 27, 1952.
    BEN:129

AMERICAN WAY See United
    States - Economic policy

AMERICANISM See Citizenship;
    National characteristics -
    American; Nationalism -
    United States

AMERICANS FOR INDIAN OPPOR-
    TUNITY
  Harris, L.
    American Indian education and
    pluralism.   MAES:96

AMERICANS IN FOREIGN COUNTRIES
  Kuiper, D. R.
    "You're an American, aren't
    you?" SCHW:186

Ameringer, Oscar
  Overproduction and undercon-
    sumption.   ANN 15:129

Ames, Fisher
  Jay Treaty.   BREWE 1:156
  On the British Treaty.   Same as
    his Jay Treaty

AMMONIA
  Bosch, C.
    The development of the chemi-
    cal high pressure method dur-
    ing the establishment of the
    new ammonia industry.
    NOLC 2:197
  Haber, F.
    The synthesis of ammonia
    from its elements.
    NOLC 1:326

ANAPHYLAXIS
  Richet, C. R.
    Anaphylaxis.   NOLM 1:473

ANARCHISM AND ANARCHISTS
  Abbott, L.
    Cure for anarchism.
    ANN 12:441
  Goldman, E.
    Anarchy vs. patriotism.
    HURH:166
  Lawson, J.
    The remedy for anarchy.
    FON:639
  Sanford, E. T. and others
    Gitlow v. New York: opinion
    for the court and dissenting
    opinion.   ANN 14:476

---- See also Chicago Haymarket
    Square Riots

Andelson, Robert V.
  Campus unrest; the erosion of
    excellence. (Union Academy,
    Dadeville, Ala., May 29,
    1970). LINRS:204

Anderson, Carl David
  The production and properties
    of positrons (Nobel Lecture,
    Dec. 12, 1936).
    NOLPH 2:365

ANDERSON, DILLON
  Tweed, H.
    Presents Dillon Anderson.
    LYI:125

Andino, Judy and others (Gary
    Pandora, Karen Brown,
    Jerry Pursley)
  How can the government best
    protect the American con-
    sumer? EHN:462; MOPR:387

Andrić, Ivo
  Acceptance [of the Nobel Prize
    for Literature, 1961].
    NOB 1:121; NOL:565

ANDRIC, IVO
  Österling, A.
    Presentation [of the Nobel
    Prize for Literature to Ivo
    Andrić, 1961.] NOB 1:117;
    NOL:562

Andrus, Cecil D.
  The inaugural address (governor
    of Idaho). (Boise, Idaho,
    January 4, 1971).
    BA 1970-71:137

Angell, Norman
  Peace and the public mind
    (Nobel Lecture for 1934,
    June 12, 1935). NOLP 2:153

ANGELL, NORMAN
  Lange, C. L.
    Presentation of the Nobel
    Prize for Peace, 1933, to
    Norman Angell, Dec. 10,
    1934. NOLP 2:147

ANIMAL HUSBANDRY See
  Agriculture

ANIMALS
  Hughes, T.
    Capturing animals. MDYG:191

---- See also Monkeys

Anjain, John
  Speech before the Senate Commit-
    tee on Energy and Natural Re-
    sources, June 16, 1977.
    JAM:12

Annerstedt, Claes
  Presentation [of the Nobel Prize
    for Literature to Selma Ottili-
    ana Lovisa Lagerlöf, 1909].
    NOB 10:279; NOL:90

ANNIVERSARIES
  Adams, J. Q.
    Jubilee of the Constitution
    (50th). ANN 6:470;
    BREWE 1:85
  Aly, B.
    Remarks on Jefferson Day.
    BAP:273
  Beecher, H. W.
    Success of American democ-
    racy (anniversary of attack on
    Fort Sumter). OLIS: 191
  Brown, H. A.
    Dangers of the present.
    BREWE 2:685
    One century's achievement
    (Valley Forge centennial).
    BREWE 2:683
  Burger, W. E.
    Bicentennial of American inde-
    pendence. BA 1976-77:185
  Choate, R.
    On American nationality (82nd
    anniversary of American inde-
    pendence). ANN 9:54
  Church, B.
    Boston Massacre oration (third
    anniversary). POC:255
  Clay, C. M.
    The man died, but his memory
    lives. BLY:109
  Constitution, right or wrong (out-
    line of speech celebrating Con-
    stitution Day). CUB:80
  Douglass, F.
    I denounce the so-called eman-
    cipation as a stupendous fraud.
    FON:520
  Elizabeth II, Queen of England

Toast to President Ford and
to the American people.
JAM:22

Everheart, W. E.
We hold these truths.
BA 1975-76:27

Ford, G. R.
Toast to Queen Elizabeth.
JAM:21

Frankfurter, F.
The Zeitgeist and the Judiciary. FRIP:3 40

Fuller, Z.
Tree of liberty (George Wash-
ington Birthday address).
ANN 5:355

Gannon, A. I.
A Catholic college, yesterday
and tomorrow. HOR:78

Graham, W. F.
Our bicentennial.
BA 1975-76:34

Hancock, J.
Boston Massacre. BRN:26;
HURH:24
Boston Massacre oration
(third anniversary).
BREWE 6:2393; POC:262

Harper, F. E. W.
Address at the centennial
anniversary of the Pennsylvania Society for Promoting
the Abolition of Slavery.
FON:430

Howard, J. A.
"... our sacred honor."
BA 1975-76:9

Hughes, C. E.
150th anniversary of the
First Congress. HURH:237

Hugo, V. M.
On the centennial of Vol-
taire's death. BREWE 7:2550

Humphrey, H. H., Jr.
Open door (21st anniversary
of Churchill's "Iron Curtain"
speech). LINR:236

Hunt, E. L.
Lincoln's rhetorical triumph
at Cooper Union (centennial
speech). BA 1969-70:189

Johari, M. K.
Malaysian Brothers (diamond
jubilee of Y. M. C. A. of
Kuala Lumpur). MONS:150

Johnson, L. B.
As the days dwindle down.
BA 1972-73:138

Kerr, C.
Urban-grant university (centen-
nial meeting of City College).
BA 1967-68:86

Kirk, G.
Responsibilities of the educated
man (at centennial of University
of Denver). LINR:143

Langston, J. M.
Equality before the law (anni-
versary of adoption of Fifteenth
Amendment). FON:409

Lee Kuan Yew
Brighter future for all peoples
of Singapore if.... MONSA:239

Lewis, W. D.
Founder's Day remarks.
BAS:164 (outline only)

McGill, R. E.
Meaning of Lincoln today (cen-
tennial of Lincoln's speech at
Cooper Institute). LINS:360

McGill, W. J.
Science and the law.
BA 1977-78:83

Mayhew, J.
Discourse on the anniversary
of the death of Charles I.
ANN 1:481; POC:508

Oppenheimer, J. R.
Prospect in the arts and sciences (at Columbia University
bicentennial anniversary celebration). HURH:319;
HURS:211

Potter, H. C.
Washington and American
aristocracy (100th anniversary
of Washington's first inauguration). BREWE 8:3225

Quincy, J., 1772-1864
At the second centennial of
Boston. BREWE 9:3272

Razak, T. A.
UMNO'S twentieth milestone
(20th anniversary of United
Malay National Organization).
MONS:53

Reed, T. B.
Immortality and good deeds
(semi-centennial of Girard
College). BREWE 9:3307

Sandburg, C.
On Lincoln (at 150th anniver-
sary of Lincoln's birth).
GRG:101; HURH:347

Sayre, F. B.
The tall ships.

BA 1976-77:181
Schrier, W.
    Address to the 60th Anniver-
    sary Oratorical Banquet,
    March 1, 1957. SCHW:226
Seward, W. H.
    Fourth of July oration, 1840.
    HAW:183
Smith, G.
    Lamps of fiction (at centenary
    of Sir Walter Scott).
    BREWE 9:3465
Suggestions for preparation of
    the anniversary speech.
    MILS:5
Toh Chin Chye
    The beginnings of the city
    state and its achievement.
    MONSA:288
Urey, H. C.
    Science and society (at 100th
    anniversary Academic Con-
    vocation of Cooper Union for
    the Advancement of Science
    and Art). ARS:78
Webster, D.
    Plymouth oration.
    BREWE 10:3846
Wiesner, J. B.
    Science in the affluent soci-
    ety (centennial celebration of
    National Academy of Sci-
    ences). ANN 18:186
Young, O. D.
    How we meet ourselves
    (semi-centennial of Hendrix
    College). HURH:227

---- See also Birthdays; Com-
    memorative addresses.
    Also names of special days,
    e.g. Fourth of July

---- GOLDEN
McNally, J.
    "Terrible beauty is born"
    (golden jubilee of St. Joseph's
    Novitiate and silver jubilee
    of Rev. Brother Michael in
    Penang). MONS:334

---- SILVER
McNally, J.
    "Terrible beauty is born"
    (golden jubilee of St. Joseph's
    Novitiate and silver jubilee
    of Rev. Brother Michael in
    Penang). MONS:334

ANNOUNCEMENTS
    Announcements of things to come.
    (10 examples). BNH:88
    Suggestions for preparation of an-
    nouncements. With examples
    of. PAE:183
Trumbull, L.
    Announcing the death of Douglas.
    BREWE 9:3654

ANNUAL ADDRESSES See Anniver-
    saries; Also under names of
    United States Presidents

Anselm, Saint
    Sea of life. BREWE 1:168

Anspach, Charles L.
    Responds to an introduction.
    PRS:138

Anthony, Susan B.
    Enfranchisement of women. (New
    York, 1873). HURH:123
    "The only question left to be set-
    tled now is: Are women per-
    sons?"--Same as her Enfran-
    chisement of women

ANTHONY, SUSAN B.
Holtzman, E.
    In celebration of the inaugura-
    tion of the Susan B. Anthony
    coin. BA 1979-80:174

ANTI-AMERICAN PROPAGANDA
    See Propaganda, Anti-Amer-
    ican

ANTI-BALLISTIC MISSILES SYSTEM
    See Guided missiles - De-
    fenses

ANTI-TRUST LAWS See Trusts,
    Industrial

ANTONY, MARK
Cicero, M. T.
    Fourth Philippic.
    BREWE 3:1201

APATHY
Estep, P. M.
    Apathy. ARS:164

Appleton, Sir Edward Victor
    The ionosphere (Nobel Lecture,
    Dec. 12, 1947). NOLPH 3:79

APPLETON, SIR EDWARD VICTOR
  Hulthén, E.
    Presentation [of the Nobel
    Prize for Physics to Sir Ed-
    ward Victor Appleton, Dec.
    12, 1947]. NOLPH 3:75

Appling, Howell, Jr.
  Responds to an introduction.
  PRS:144

APPRECIATION See Thanks

AQUACULTURE
  Alconcel, D.
    Aquaculture--an answer to
    the food crisis. BREWW:88

Aquino, Benigno S.
  The Church and the State must
    never mixi (National As-
    sembly, April 26, 1938).
    CURM:129

ARAB COUNTRIES - 20TH CEN-
    TURY
  Eagleton, T. F.
    1977: year of opportunity
    in the Middle East?
    LINRST:124

ARCHIAS
  Cicero, M. T.
    For the poet Archias.
    BREWE 3:1189

ARCHITECTURE
  Banham, R.
    Fourth monument.
    MDYG:216
  Sullivan, L.
    Characteristics and ten-
    dencies of American archi-
    tecture. ANN 11:40
    Young architect. ANN 12:385
  Wright, F. L.
    Art and the machine.
    ANN 12:409
    On architecture. HURH:241

ARGON
  Rayleigh, J. W. S.
    The density of gases in the
    air and the discovery of
    argon. NOLPH 1:90

ARGUMENTATIVE SPEAKING See
  Debates and debating

ARISTOCRACY
  Deniehy, D. H.
    On the Constitution Bill.
    MCA:26

ARIZONA
  Taft, W. H.
    Veto of Arizona Enabling Act.
    ANN 13:272

Arm, Milton
  Vial of fragrant ointment.
  WALE: 13

ARMAMENTS See Disarmament;
  Munitions

ARMED FORCES DAY
  Welcome to military personnel.
  HNWM:25

ARMISTICE DAY See Unknown sol-
    dier; Veterans Day

Armstrong, Lebbeus
  Masonry proved to be a work of
    darkness (1830). (New York,
    1830). DAVF:82

Armstrong, Neil and others (Neil
    Armstrong and Michael Collins)
  Moon rendezvous. (Congress,
    Sept. 16, 1969). BAAGB:404

ARMY
  Pulteney, W.
    Against standing armies.
    BREWE 8:3244

---- See also Armed Forces Day;
    Conscription; Soldiers; Also
    Names of countries, subhead
    Army, e.g. United States -
    Army

ARMY APPROPRIATION ACT
  Hayes, R. B.
    Veto of the Army Appropriation
    Act. ANN 10:449

Arnold, Carroll C.
  Speech as a liberal study. ARS:2

Arnold, Matthew
  Literature and science. (Cam-
    bridge Univ., June 14, 1882).
    MCB:388

ARNOLD, MATTHEW
Holmes, O. W.
Introduces Matthew Arnold.
LYI:44

Arnold, Thomas
Realities of life and death.
BREWE 1:173

Arnoldson, Klas Pontus
World referendum (Nobel Lec-
ture, Dec. 10, 1908).
NOLP 1:175

ARNOLDSON, KLAS PONTUS
Løvland, J. G.
Presentation [of the Nobel
Prize for Peace to Klas
Pontus Arnoldson, Dec. 10,
1908]. NOLP 1:173

Arrhenius, Svante August
Development of the theory of
electrolytic dissociation
(Nobel Lecture, Dec. 11,
1903). NOLC 1:45
Presentation of the Nobel Prize
for Physics for 1921 to Al-
bert Einstein, July 11, 1923.
NOLPH 1:482
Presentation [of the Nobel Prize
for Physics to Niels Bohr,
Dec. 11, 1922]. NOLPH 2:3

ARRHENIUS, SVANTE AUGUST
Törnebladh, H. R.
Presentation [of the Nobel
Prize for Chemistry to
Svante August Arrhenius,
Dec. 11, 1903]. NOLC 1:43

ART AND ARTISTS
Cousin, V.
Eloquence and the fine arts.
BREWE 4:1419
Dondero, G. A.
Modern art shackled to com-
munism. DAVF:302
Gladstone, W. E.
Commercial value of artistic
excellence. BREWE 6:2283
Morris, W.
Art, wealth, and riches.
BRYH:422
Oppenheimer, J. R.
Prospect in the arts and sci-
ences (at Columbia University
bicentennial anniversary

celebration). HURH:319;
HURS:211
Wright, F. L.
Art and the machine.
ANN 12:409

---- See also Negro artists

Arthur, Chester A.
First annual message.
STAT 2:1424
Fourth annual message.
STAT 2:1492
Inaugural address. BREWE 1:180
Second annual message.
STAT 2:1452
Third annual message.
STAT 2:1474

Ascoli, Max
Scarcity of ideas. ARS:201

ASEAN DECLARATION
Abdul Rahman, T.
Can ASEAN meet the challenge
of the 70's? MONSA:61

Ashley, Leonard R. N.
A guided tour of gobbledygook.
REID:408

Ashmore, Harry Scott
Presents J. William Fulbright.
LYI:205

ASIA
Goh Keng Swee
Elite combat party (Communist
Party). MONS:394
Some delusions of the decade
of development. MONS:385
Lee Kuan Yew
Democratic socialism under
stress in Asia. MONS:345
Lim Kim San
Three major problems of de-
veloping countries. MONS:412
Muhammad Ghazali bin Shafie
Malaysia and the Asian per-
spective. MONS:222
Rajaratnam, S.
Asia's unfinished revolution.
MONS:425

---- See also Malaysia; Singapore

---- INDUSTRIES
Rajaratnam, S.

Asia needs the spirit of
Sisphyus to succeed.
MONSA:303

---- SOUTHEASTERN
Abdul Kadir bin Yusof
Now is the era of real awaken-
ing in Southeast Asia.
MONSA:351
Lee Kuan Yew
Problems of leadership.
MONS:371
Muhammad Ghazali bin Shafie
Power politics and nation-
building (Malaysia).   MONS:232
Narayanan, P. P.
Role of trade unions in South-
East Asia.   MONS:295
Rahman, Dr. I. bin A.
New era of regional cooper-
ation.   MONS:103
Razak, T. A.
Crucial cross-roads of his-
tory.   MONS:64
Most unfortunate of conflicts.
MONS:69

---- FOREIGN RELATIONS
Razak, T. A.
Hopes and anxieties of the
countries of Southeast Asia.
MONSA:47

Asquith, Herbert Henry   See
Oxford and Asquith, Herbert
Henry, 1st Earl of

ASSER, TOBIAS MICHAEL CAREL
Løvland, J. G.
Presentation [of the Nobel
Prize for Peace to Tobias
Michael Carel Asser, Dec.
10, 1911].   NOLP 1:233

ASSETS   See   Success

ASSOCIATIONS   See   Club speeches

Aston, Francis William
Mass spectra and isotopes
(Nobel Lecture, Dec. 12,
1922).   NOLC 2:7

ASTON, FRANCIS WILLIAM
Söderbaum, H. G.
Presentation [of the Nobel
Prize for Chemistry to
Francis William Aston,
Dec. 12, 1922].   NOLC 2:3

ASTRONOMY
Rittenhouse, D.
Oration, &c.   POC:142

Asturias, Miguel Angel
Acceptance [of the Nobel Prize
for Literature, 1967].
NOB 2:7; NOL:626

ASTURIAS, MIGUEL ANGEL
Österling, A.
Presentation [of the Nobel
Prize for Literature to Miguel
Angel Asturias, 1967].
NOB 2:3; NOL:624

Atcitty, Thomas E.
The future is at hand.   MAES:160

Atcitty, Wilbur R.
Remarks.   MAES:38

Athanasius, Saint
Divinity of Christ.   BREWE 1:182

ATHENS
Hypereides
Funeral oration.   COG:210
Isocrates
Panegyric.   COG:27; SAG:99
Lysias
Funeral orations.   COG:9
Pericles
On those who died in the war.
ARS:191; BAS:133 (outline only);
BREWE 8:3169; SAG:33

---- See also Greece, Ancient

ATHLETICS
Welcome and introduction of coach
of athletic team at awards
banquet.   HNWM:34

---- See also Sports

Atkinson, Harry
Proposal for a National Insurance
scheme, 1882 (New Zealand
House of Representatives, July
10, 1882).   MACS:186 sel.

Atkinson, Henry and others (Sir
George Grey)
The abolition of the provinces,
1876 (New Zealand House of
Representatives, Sept. 19,
1876).   MACS:111 sel.

ATLANTA RIOTS, 1906
  Washington, B. T.
    We must be a law-abiding
    and law-respecting people.
    FON:652

ATLANTIS
  DeBeer, G.
    Atlantis. MDYG:272

ATOMIC AGE
  Van Voorst, B.
    Clock. SCHW:74

ATOMIC BOMB
  Truman, H. S.
    Announcement of the first use
    of the atomic bomb.
    ANN 16:334

ATOMIC ENERGY
  Anjain, J.
    Speech before the Senate
    Committee on Energy and
    Natural Resources, June 16,
    1977. JAM:12
  Baruch, B. M.
    International control of
    atomic energy. ANN 16:360;
    HURH:279
  Eisenhower, D. D.
    International control of atomic
    power for peaceful purposes.
    ANN 17:211
  Nixon, R. M.
    Campaign speech, Toledo,
    Ohio, October 27, 1960.
    SIN:319

ATOMIC POWER See Atomic
  energy

ATOMIC WARFARE
  Hatfield, M. O.
    If we fall down in the land
    of peace. BA 1979-80:67
  Hiatt, H. H.
    Prevention of the last epi-
    demic. BA 1979-80:56
  Kennedy, J. F.
    Step toward peace.
    ANN 18:192
  McNamara, R. S.
    Nuclear strategy.
    ANN 18:527
  Wald, G.
    Generation in search of a
    future. BA 1968-1969:33

ATOMIC WEAPONS AND DISARMA-
  MENT
  Carter, J.
    Our common responsibility and
    our common challenge.
    BA 1977-78:59

ATOMIC WEIGHTS
  Richards, T. W.
    Atomic weights. NOLC 1:280

ATOMS
  Bohr, N.
    The structure of the atom.
    NOLPH 2:7
  Hertz, G.
    The results of electron-impact
    tests in the light of Bohr's
    theory of atoms. NOLPH 2:112
  Siegbahn, K. M. G.
    The x-ray spectra and the
    structure of the atoms.
    NOLPH 2:81
  Stark, J.
    Structural and spectral changes
    of chemical atoms.
    NOLPH 1:427

Attlee, Clement R.
  A common endeavour. Same as
  his Speech in Commons on the
  United Nations charter.
  The Labour programme. (BBC
  Broadcast, June 5, 1945).
  MCB:471
  Speech in Commons on the United
  Nations charter. (Jan. 10,
  1946). MCB:536

---- See Baldwin, S. B., jt. auth.

Attwood, Thomas
  Chartist movement. JAE:68

Aubert, Jean-Marie
  Vietnam and world peace. VI:104

AUCKLAND RIOT, 1932
  Lee, J. A.
    The Auckland Riot, 1932.
    MACS:312 sel.

Augustine, Saint
  On our Lord's prayer.
  BREWE 1:188

AUSTRALIA
  Evatt, H. V.

Australia and the United Nations charter.   MCA:161
Payne, J. R.
Australia and the Vietnam War.   VI:75

---- COLONIES
Parkes, H.
New constellation.   MCA:37

---- CONSTITUTION
Deakin, A.
For the Federal Constitution.   MCA:84

---- FOREIGN RELATIONS - UNITED STATES
Curtin, J.
We are fighting mad.
MCA:154

---- IMMIGRATION AND EMIGRATION See Immigration and emigration - Australia

---- POLITICS AND GOVERNMENT
Deniehy, D. H.
On the Constitution Bill.
MCA:26
Hughes, W. M.
Australian Judas.   MCA:125

---- See also Labor Party (Australia)

AUTHORS AND AUTHORSHIP
See Literature; Poetry and poets

AUTOBIOGRAPHY
Cutforth, R.
Illuminations.   MDYG:35

AUTOMOBILE DRIVERS
Lorge, B.
Great auto rally (outline).
REIR:93

AUTOMOTIVE INDUSTRY AND TRADE
Cole, E. N.
Two myths and a paradox.
BA 1971-72:93
Curtice, H.
Automotive research at General Motors.   ANN 17:379

AUXILIARIES See Club speeches

Avebury, John Lubbock, 1st Baron
Hundred best books.
BREWE 7:2820

AWARDS See Acceptance speeches - Rewards (Prizes); Presentation speeches - Rewards (Prizes)

Axelrod, Julius
Noradrenaline: fate and control of its biosynthesis (Nobel Lecture, Dec. 12, 1970).
NOLM 4:444

AXELROD, JULIUS
Uvnäs, B.
Presentation [of the Nobel Prize for Physiology or Medicine to Julius Axelrod, Ulf Von Euler, and Bernhard Katz, Dec. 12, 1970].   NOLM 4:441

Ayer, A. J. and others (R. Kee; O. Todd)
What are philosophers for?
MDYG:101

Aziz, Ungku
Languages: anguish and confusion (Univ. of Malaya).   MONSA:167
Scientific concepts of external aid for agricultural education (Copenhagen, July 28-Aug. 8, 1970).   MONSA:161

Azmi, Bin Haji Mohamed
Duty of a lawyer.   MONS:97

- B -

Babbidge, Homer D.
On thinking big (Univ. of Connecticut, May 18, 1975).
HOR:121

BABIES See Children

BACCALAUREATE ADDRESSES
Brewster, K., Jr.
Due process radicalism.
HOR:37
Heuss, J.
Introduction to baccalaureate

sermon. PRS:55
Lindsley, P.
  Dangers of a sectarian col-
  lege. ANN 5:310
Pusey, N. M.
  Thanksgiving and entreaty, a
  President's valedictory.
  HOR:26

BACHELORS
  Long live the bachelors.
  BURT:71

BACKACHES
  Ragan, D. O.
    Backaches.   MOP:366;
    MOPR:358

Backhouse, Margaret A.
  The international service of the
  Society of Friends (Nobel
  Lecture, Dec. 12, 1947).
  NOLP 2:380

Bacon, Francis, Viscount of St.
  Albans
  Against dueling.   BREWE 1:199;
    BRYH:96
  Upon the motion of subsidy
    (November 15, 1598 speech).
    BRYH:90

Bacon, Leonard
  Plea for Africa (Boston, July 5,
    1824). HAW:60
  Sermon from Mark XII, 34
    (Boston, July 4, 1824).
    HAW:57

Bacon, Wallace A.
  Language and the lived world
    (Knoxville, Tenn., April 18,
    1977). BA 1976-77:174
  The seacoast of Bohemia: truth
    in literature (Washington,
    Dec. 2, 1977).
    BA 1977-78:170

BACTERIA
  Jacob, F.
    Genetics of the bacterial cell.
    NOLM 4:148

BACTERIAL DISEASES
  Domack, G. J. P.
    Further progress in chemo-
    therapy of bacterial infec-
    tions. NOLM 2:490

BAECK, LEO
  Dreyfus, A. S.
    Leo Baeck. WALE:207

Bajer, Fredrik
  The organization of the Peace
    Movement (Nobel Lecture,
    1908, May 18, 1909).
    NOLP 1:190

BAJER, FREDRIK
  Løvland, J. G.
    Presentation [of the Nobel
    Prize for Peace to Fredrik
    Bajer, Dec. 10, 1908].
    NOLP 1:188

Baker, Richard
  Crime of Mrs. Douglass in teach-
    ing colored children to read.
    ANN 8:224

Balch, Emily Greene
  Toward human unity or beyond
    nationalism (Nobel Lecture for
    1946, April 7, 1948).
    NOLP 2:333

BALCH, EMILY GREENE
  Jahn, G.
    Presentation of the Nobel Prize
    for Peace to Emily Greene
    Balch, Dec. 10, 1946.
    NOLP 2:325

Baldwin, H. C. See Warner, A.
  J., jt. auth.

Baldwin, James
  The American dream is at the
    expense of the American Negro.
    FON:1012

Baldwin, Roger S.
  Executive prerogative in foreign
    policy. ANN 7:423

Baldwin, Stanley Baldwin, 1st Earl
  of Bewdley
  Goodwill in industry. (H. of
    Commons, March 6, 1925).
    MCB:243; STRM:433
  Industrial peace. Same as his
    Goodwill in industry

---- and others (Edward VIII; C.
    Attlee; A. Sinclair; W. L. S.
    Churchill; J. Maxton; W.

Gallacher; G. Buchanan; C.
Stephen; W. Thorne; J.
Simon; A. Chamberlain)
Debate in the House of Com-
mons on the abdication of
Edward VIII. BRYH:491

Balewa, Sir Aubbaker Tafawa See
Akintola, S. L. , jt. auth.

Ball, George W.
Issue in Vietnam. BA 1965-66:43

Ball, John
Bondmen and freemen: address
to the rebels at Blackheath.
BRYH:42
Let us go to the King. Same
as his We have the pain and
travail
Speech at the Peasants' rising.
Same as his Bondmen and
freemen: address to the
rebels at Blackheath
We have the pain and travail.
BRYH:42

Ballance, John
The 1890 election: the opposition case (Wanganui, Sept.
23, 1890). MACS:201
selections
A land tax of a halfpenny in
the pound on land exceeding
£500 in value, 1878 (New
Zealand House of Representatives, Aug. 6, 1878).
MACS:184 selections

BALLOT See Blacks - Politics
and suffrage; Elections;
Women - Suffrage

BALZAC, HONORE DE
Hugo, V. M.
Oration on Honoré de Balzac.
BREWE 7:2546

Bancroft, George
Fourth of July oration, 1826.
(Northampton, Mass. , July
4, 1826). HAW:75

Banham, Reyner
Fourth monument. MDYG:216

BANK OF THE UNITED STATES,
1816-1836 See Banks and
banking

BANKRUPTCY
Webster, D.
For a uniform bankruptcy law.
ANN 6:561

Banks, Nathaniel P. See Butler,
B. F. , jt. auth.

BANKS AND BANKING
Benton, T. H.
Against the United States Bank.
ANN 5:430; BREWE 2:425
Clay, H.
Bank and the power of the
executive. ANN 6:46
Crockett, D.
Fourth of July oration, 1834.
HAW:136
Jackson, A.
Fifth annual message.
STAT 1:373
Fourth annual message.
STAT 1:358
Seventh annual message.
ANN 6:164; STAT 1:415
Sixth annual address.
STAT 1:389
Veto message of July 10, 1832.
ANN 5:524
La Follette, R. M.
A small group of men hold in
their hands the business of
this country (1908).
DAVF:200
Lee, H. H. S.
Great Institution (Central Bank
of Malaya). MONS:164
Peel, R.
Bank charter--the currency.
STRM:213
Robinson, R.
A Jacksonian attack on monop-
oly (1834). DAVF:69
Tyler, J.
Second annual message.
STAT 1:581
Van Buren, M.
First annual message.
STAT 1:472
Webster, D.
For the Bank Renewal Bill.
ANN 5:535

---- MALAYSIA
Ismail bin Mohammed Ali
The central Bank--the "financial conscience" of the government. MONSA:189

BANQUETS See After dinner
    speeches; Announcements;
    Club speeches; Toastmas-
    ters; Also types of speeches
    e. g. Introductions; Toasts;
    Welcoming addresses, etc.
    Also types of banquets e. g.
    Fathers and sons; Mothers
    and daughters

Banting, Frederick Grant
    Diabetes and insulin (Nobel
    Lecture for 1923, Sept. 15,
    1925). NOLM 2:50

BANTING, FREDERICK GRANT
    Sjöquist, J.
        Presentation [of the Nobel
        Prize for Physiology or
        Medicine for 1923 to Fred-
        erick Grant Banting and
        John James Richard Mac-
        leod, 1925]. NOLM 2:45

BAPTIST CHURCH See Church

BAR See Law and lawyers

Barany, Robert
    Some new methods for func-
        tional testing of the vesti-
        bular apparatus and the
        cerebellum (Nobel Lecture
        for 1914, Sept. 11, 1916).
        NOLM 1:500

Barbour, James
    Treaties as supreme laws.
        BREWE 1:209

Bard, George M.
    Introduces Alexander Rorke,
        Jr. PRS:69
    Introduces Arthur Godfrey.
        PRS:45
    Introduces Dr. Deane W.
        Malott, President of
        Cornell University. PRS:115
    Introduces Dr. Henry A. Kis-
        singer. PRS:124
    Introduces George Ratterman.
        PRS:62
    Introduces Gilbert W. Fitz-
        hugh. PRS:17
    Introduces Walter W. Heller,
        chairman of the President's
        Council of Economic Ad-
        visers. PRS:33

Introduces William F. Buckley,
    Jr., columnist. PRS:57

Bardeen, John
    Semiconductor research leading
        to the point contact transistor
        (Nobel Lecture, Dec. 11, 1956).
        NOLPH 3:318

Barger, Robert Newton
    Theology and amnesty. (Peoria,
        Ill., Nov. 11, 1973).
        BA 1973-74:177

Bark, Dale R.
    World food crisis. BREWW: 219

Barkla, Charles Glover
    Characteristic Röntgen radiation
        (Nobel Lecture for 1917, June
        3, 1920). NOLPH 1:392

Barkley, Alben W.
    Record of Democratic Party.
        (Philadelphia, July 12, 1948).
        BLY:233

Barlow, Earl J.
    Education on Indian terms.
        MAES:90
    If a man loses something; ad-
        dress at the 5th annual state
        Indian Education Conference,
        College of Great Falls, Mon-
        tana, April 3, 1975. MAES:343
    Multicultural education: its effec-
        tive management. MAES:110

Barlow, Joseph
    Unfinished revolution. ANN 3:90

Barnard, Daniel D.
    American experiment in govern-
        ment. ANN 6:353
    The social system. (House of
        Convocation of Trinity Col-
        lege, Hartford, Conn., 1848).
        HOW:106

Barnard, Sir John See Walpole,
    R., jt. auth.

Barnave, Antoine Pierre Joseph
    Marie
    Commercial politics.
        BREWE 1:221
    Representative democracy against
        majority absolutism.
        BREWE 1:218

Barnett, Ferdinand L.
  Race unity. (Nashville, Tenn.,
    May 6-9, 1879). FON:461

Barton, Bruce
  Which knew not Joseph (New
    York, 1923). BRYF:554;
    BRYO:228

Barton, Derek H. R.
  The principles of conforma-
    tional analysis (Nobel Lec-
    ture, Dec. 11, 1969).
    NOLC 4:298

BARTON, DEREK H. R.
  Fredga, A.
    Presentation [of the Nobel
    Prize for Chemistry to
    Derek H. R. Barton and
    Odd Hassel, Dec. 11, 1969].
    NOLC 4:295

Barrett, B. F.
  The unreasonable prejudices
    against people of color in
    Philadelphia. (Philadel-
    phia, Sept. 23, 1866).
    FON:337

Barrow, Isaac
  Slander. BREWE 1:224

Baruch, Bernard M.
  Choice between the quick and
    the dead. Same as his
    International control of
    atomic energy
  International control of atomic
    energy (United Nations,
    June 14, 1946). ANN 16:360;
    HURH:279
  "We are here to make a choice
    between the quick and the
    dead. " Same as his Inter-
    national control of atomic
    energy (June 14, 1946)

Barzun, Jacques
  Place and the price of excel-
    lence. ARS:28

Basil the Great, Saint
  On a recreant nun.
    BREWE 1:235

BASIL THE GREAT, SAINT
  Gregory of Nazianzur

Eulogy on Basil of Baesarea.
  BREWE 6:2336

Basov, Nikolai G.
  Semiconductor lasers (Nobel Lec-
    ture, Dec. 11, 1964).
    NOLPH 4:89

BASOV, NIKOLAI G.
  Edlén, B.
    Presentation [of the Nobel
    Prize for Physics to Charles
    H. Townes, Nikolai G. Basov,
    and Alexander M. Prochorov,
    Dec. 11, 1964]. NOLPH 4:55

Bates, Darrell
  Bride-price. MDYG:59

Bathurst, Henry See Walpole, R.,
  jt. auth.

Baxter, Richard
  Unwillingness to improve.
    BREWE 1:242

BAY OF PIGS See United States -
  Foreign relations - Cuba

Bayard, James Asheton
  Commerce and naval power.
    BREWE 1:262
  Federal Judiciary. BREWE 1:249

Bayard, Thomas F.
  Plea for conciliation in 1876.
    BREWE 1:265

Beaconsfield, Benjamin Disraeli,
  1st Earl of
  Against democracy for England.
    BREWE 1:296
  Against repeal of the Corn Laws.
    Same as his Third reading of
    the Corn Importation Bill
  Assassination of Lincoln.
    BREWE 1:295
  Conservative and liberal princi-
    ples. Same as his Meaning
    of conservatism
  Conservative versus liberal.
    Same as his Meaning of con-
    servatism
  Meaning of conservatism (Crystal
    Palace, London, June 24,
    1872). BREWE 1:309;
    BRYF:534; MCB:431
  Reform Bill of 1867 (Edinburgh

speech, October 29, 1867).
STRM:296
Third reading of the Corn Im-
portation Bill (H. of Com-
mons, May 15, 1846).
BRYH:371; MCB:211
Tory democracy.   JAE:139

BEACONSFIELD, BENJAMIN
    DISRAELI, 1st EARL OF
Gladstone, W. E.
    On Lord Beaconsfield.
    BREWE 6:2291

Beadle, George Wells
    Genes and chemical reactions
    in Neurospora (Nobel Lec-
    ture, Dec. 11, 1958).
    NOLM 3:587

BEADLE, GEORGE WELLS
Caspersson, T.
    Presentation [of the Nobel
    Prize for Physiology or
    Medicine to George Wells
    Beadle, Edward Lawrie
    Tatum, and Joshua Leder-
    berg, Dec. 11, 1958].
    NOLM 3:583

BEATNIKS
Brown, J. M.
    "Beat" generation. HURH:341

Beaudin, John A.
    Testimony to the Senate Educa-
    tion Committee May 6, 1975
    at the State Capitol concern-
    ing Senate Bill 145. MAES:245

BEAUTY, PERSONAL
Flaxman, J.
    Physical and intellectual
    beauty. BREWE 6:2167

Becker, Arie
    To make a commonplace won-
    drous. WALE:15

BECKETT, SAMUEL
Gierow, K. R.
    Presentation address [of the
    Nobel Prize for Literature
    to Samuel Beckett, 1969].
    NOB 3:3

Becquerel, Antoine Henri
    On radioactivity, a new property

of matter (Nobel Lecture, Dec.
11, 1903).   NOLPH 1:52

BECQUEREL, ANTOINE HENRI
Törnebladh, H. R.
    Presentation [of the Nobel
    Prize for Physics to Antoine
    Henri Becquerel, Pierre Curie
    and Marie Sklodowska-Curie,
    Dec. 11, 1903]. NOLPH 1:47

Bede (The Venerable)
    Meeting of mercy and justice.
    BREWE 1:340
    On the nativity of St. Peter and
    St. Paul. BRYH:9
    Sermon for any day.
    BREWE 1:343
    Torments of hell. BREWE 1:344

Beecher, Henry Ward
    Effect of the death of Lincoln.
    BREWE 1:365
    "Hold each other in true fellow-
    ship. Same as his On fellow-
    ship
    Liverpool speech, October 16,
    1863. LINS:229
    On fellowship. (Plymouth, Mass.,
    Nov. 18, 1869). HURH:118
    Raising the flag over Fort Sum-
    ter. BREWE 1:347
    Success of American democracy
    (anniversary of attack on Fort
    Sumter). OLIS:191

Beecher, Lyman
    A plea for the West. (Delivered
    several times, 1835). HOW:133

BEERNAERT, AUGUSTE MARIE
    FRANÇOIS
Løvland, J. G.
    Presentation [of the Nobel
    Prize for Peace to Auguste
    Marie François Beernaert,
    Dec. 10, 1909]. NOLP 1:211

Begin, Menachem See Carter, J.,
    jt. auth.

BEHAVIOR
    Getting along with difficult people.
    BURT:109
Nies, N.
    Warrior and the woman.
    SCHW:10
Roosevelt, T.

Strenuous life.   BEN:189;
HURH:150
Wycliffe, J.
Rule for decent living.
BREWE 10:3918

Behring, Emil Adolf Von
Serum therapy in therapeutics
and medical science (Nobel
Lecture, Dec. 12, 1901).
NOLM 1:6

BEHRING, EMIL ADOLF VON
Mörner, K. A. H.
Presentation [of the Nobel
Prize for Physiology or
Medicine to Emil Adolf
Von Behring, Dec. 12, 1901].
NOLM 1:3

Bekesy, Georg Von
Concerning the pleasures of observing, and the mechanics
of the inner ear (Nobel Lecture, Dec. 11, 1961).
NOLM 3:722

BEKESY, GEORG VON
Bernhard, C. G.
Presentation [of the Nobel
Prize for Physiology or
Medicine to Georg Von
Bekesy, Dec. 11, 1961].
NOLM 3:719

Belhaven, John Hamilton, 2d Baron
Plea for the national life of
Scotland.   BREWE 1:371

Bell, David E.
Responds to introduction.
PRS:94

Bell, Francis H. D.
The defence of the Empire in
the Great War (July 12,
1917).   MACS:273 selections

Bell, Griffin B.
Notes on the situation: a critique (Lawrence, Kan., Jan.
25, 1979).   BA 1978-79:93

Bell, John
Against extremists, North and
South.   BREWE 1:384
Trans-continental railroads.
BREWE 1:390

Bellecourt, Vernon
American Indian Movement.
MAES:66

Belloc, Hilaire See Shaw, G. B.,
jt. auth.

BELMONT, ELEANOR ROBSON
Lamont, T. W.
Presents Eleanor Robson Bel-
mont.   LYI:23

Beloff, Max
Americanisation of British intellectual life.   MDYG:114

Belson, Richard S.
What really counts.   WALE:18

BENAVENTE, JACINTO
Hallström, P.
Presentation [of the Nobel
Prize for Literature to Jacinto
Benavente, 1922].   NOB 2:179;
NOL:186
Torata, Count de
Acceptance [of the Nobel Prize
for Literature for Jacinto
Benavente, 1922].   NOL:191

Benchley, Robert C.
Treasurer's report.   (New York,
1930).   HURH:211

Benedict, Donald L.
Remarks in Chicago on urban imperatives.   BA 1967-68:78

Benezet, Louis T.
Acceleration or direction?
BA 1966-67:105
The educator's leap of faith
(Hebrew Union College, Los
Angeles, June 13, 1 969).
HOR:107

Benham, William J.
An Indian education resources
center.   MAES:114

Benitez, Jaime
Acceptance [of the Nobel Prize
for Literature for Juan Ramón
Jiménez, 1956].   NOB 10:7;
NOL:517

Benjamin, Judah Philip
Farewell to the Union.

BREWE 1:399
Slavery as established by law.
BREWE 1:406

Bennett, John C.
Issue of peace: the voice of
religion.   BA 1965-66:142

Bennett, Robert
The fall and rise of Indian
sovereignty.   MAES:11

BENNY, JACK
Jessel, G.
Presents Jack Benny.   LYI:30

Benson, Ezra Taft
Price supports and farm sur-
pluses.   ANN 17:383

Benton, Thomas Hart
Against the United States Bank.
ANN 5:430; BREWE 2:425
Mischiefs of a national bank.
Same as his Against the
United States Bank
Political career of Andrew
Jackson.   BREWE 2:411
There is East; there is India.
BREWE 2:429

BENTON, THOMAS HART
Blair, F. P.
Character and work of Benton.
BREWE 2:509
Deathbed of Benton.
BREWE 2:514

Benton, William
For the expulsion of Senator
McCarthy.   ANN 17:108

Bergius, Friedrich
Chemical reactions under high
pressure (Nobel Prize for
Chemistry for 1931, May 21,
1932).   NOLC 2:244

BERGIUS, FRIEDRICH
Palmaer, W.
Presentation [of the Nobel
Prize for Chemistry for
1931 to Carl Bosch and
Friedrich Bergius, May 21,
1932].   NOLC 2:189

Bergson, Henri
Acceptance [of the Nobel Prize
for Literature, 1927].
NOB 2:273; NOL:246

BERGSON, HENRI
Hallström, P.
Presentation [of the Nobel Prize
for Literature to Henri Bergson,
1927].   NOB 2:267; NOL:242

Bergstrand, H.
Presentation [of the Nobel Prize
for Physiology or Medicine
to Max Theiler, Dec. 11,
1951].   NOLM 3:347

Bergstrom, S.
Presentation [of the Nobel Prize
for Physiology or Medicine to
Konrad Bloch and Feodor Ly-
nen, Dec. 11, 1964].
NOLM 4:75

BERI-BERI
Eijkman, C.
Antineuritic vitamin and beri-
beri.   NOLM 2:199

Berkeley, William
Speech to the Virginia House of
Burgesses.   POC:169

Berle, Adolf A., Jr.
Emerging common law of free
enterprise.   ANN 16:573

BERLIN QUESTION, 1945-
Kennedy, J. F.
Berlin crisis.   THOMS:22
Ich bin ein Berliner.   ALA:129;
AND:79; LINR:294; LINRS:293

Bernard, Saint
Advice to young men.
BREWE 2:433
Against luxury in the Church.
BREWE 2:434
On the Canticles.   BREWE 2:435
Preaching the Crusade.   Same as
his Why another crusade
Second crusade.   Same as his
Why another crusade
Why another crusade?   BAS:43
(outline only); BREWE 2:432

Bernard, Sir Francis
Speech to the Council and House
of Representatives.   POC:227

Bernhard, C. G.
Presentation [of the Nobel Prize
for Physiology or Medicine to
Georg Von Bekesy, Dec. 11,
1961].   NOLM 3:719

Presentation [of the Nobel Prize
for Physiology or Medicine to
Ragnar Granit, Haldan Kef-
fer Hartline, and George
Wald, Dec. 12, 1967].
NOLM 4:251

Bernstein, Leonard
American musical comedy.
KEO:274
World of jazz. (Telecast:
October 16, 1955). ARN:320;
ARS:67

Berrien, John M.
Conquest and territorial organ-
ization. BREWE 2:436
Effect of the Mexican conquest.
BREWE 2:439

Berryer, Pierre Antoine
Censorship of the press.
BREWE 2:443

Bersin, Alan
Open letter to my middle-aged
father. REIR:215

Bertonneau, Arnold
Every man should stand equal
before the law. (Boston,
April 12, 1864). FON:303

Besdin, Abraham R.
Life's struggle. WALE:20

Bethe, Hans Albrecht
Energy production in stars
(Nobel Lecture, Dec. 11,
1967). NOLPH 4:215

BETHE, HANS ALBRECHT
Klein, O.
Presentation [of the Nobel
Prize for Physics to Hans
Albrecht Bethe, Dec. 11,
1967]. NOLPH 4:211

Betjeman, John See Sykes, C.,
jt. auth.

Bevan, Aneurin
Change the direction of the war.
(H. of Commons, July 2,
1942). MCB:524
National Health Service Bill.
STRM:445

Beveridge, Albert J.
In support of an American empire.
Same as his Philippine ques-
tion
March of the flag. ANN 12:198;
BOORA 2:622; GRG:14;
LINS:276
Philippine question. ANN 12:336;
BRR:29
Philippines are ours forever.
Same as his Philippine ques-
tion
Taste of empire. Same as his
March of the flag

Bevin, Ernest
Testimony at the "Docker's Inquiry." STRM:423

Bial, Morrison D.
Light from the stones. WALE:21

BIBLE
Damiani, P.
New Testament history as alle-
gory. BREWE 4:1606

BIBLE SCHOOLS See Religious
education

BICENTENNIAL SPEECHES See
Anniversaries

Biddle, Nicholas
Princeton commencement address.
(Sept. 30, 1835). HOW:123

Bigelow, Jacob
Future of the arts and sciences.
ANN 4:449

BILE
Wieland, H. O.
The chemistry of the bile
acids. NOLC 2:94

Bilheimer, Robert S.
Christian conscience and the
Vietnam War. VI:15

BILL OF RIGHTS (UNITED STATES)
See United States - Constitution

Billings (District Judge)
Labor and the antitrust laws.
Same as his United States v.
Workingmen's Amalgamated

Billington, Ray A.
Council of New Orleans, 1893
United States v. Workingmen's
Amalgamated Council of New
Orleans, 1893. ANN 11:435

Billington, Ray A.
Cowboys, Indians, and the land
of promise: the world image
of the American frontier
(San Francisco, Aug. 22,
1975). BA 1975-76:176

Bingham, John A.
Against the assassins of President Lincoln. BREWE 2:445

---- See also Butler, B. J., jt. auth.

Binney, Barnabas
Valedictory oration. POC:51

BIOLOGICAL RESEARCH
Tatum, E. L.
A case history in biological
research. NOLM 3:602

BIOLOGY
Delbrück, M.
A physicist's renewed look
at biology--twenty years
later. NOLM 4:404

Birenbaum, William M.
Time for reconstruction.
BA 1969-70:154

Birkenhead, Lord See Sykes,
C., jt. auth.

BIRKETT, SIR NORMAN
Daniels, J.
Presents Sir Norman Birkett.
LYI:135
Lusty, R.
Presents Sir Norman Birkett.
LYI:54

BIRTHDAYS
Holmes, O. W., Jr.
"Live-I am coming:" re-
sponse to birthday greeting.
GRG:48; HURH:215

Bishop, Joey
Responds to introduction (when
substituting for Sir Cedric
Hardwicke). PRS:119

Bismarck, Otto von
Plea for imperial armament.
BREWE 2:456

Bittner, John R.
The news media and campus unrest. (Indiana Speech Association meeting - Indianapolis,
Oct. 4, 1969). STOT:290

Bjorklund, Jan
Nice people. EHN:158;
MOPR:246

Bjørnson, Bjørnstjerne Martinus
Acceptance [of the Nobel Prize
for Literature, 1903]. NOL:16;
NOB 3:81
Introduction [presenting the Nobel
Prize for Peace to Bertha von
Suttner, 1905, April 18, 1906].
NOLP 1:81

BJØRNSON, BJØRNSTJERNE MAR-
TINUS
Wirsen, C. D. af
Presentation [of the Nobel
Prize for Literature to
Bjørnstjerne Martinus Bjørn-
son, 1903]. NOL:14; NOB 3:77

Black, Hugo L.
Need to share what we have.
ROD:75
United States v. Lovett, Watson,
and Dodd: opinion for the
court. ANN 16:404

---- and others (F. Frankfurter, F.
Murphy, R. H. Jackson)
Korematsu v. United States:
opinion for the court and dissenting opinion. ANN 16:234

---- See also Brennan, W. J., Jr.,
jt. auth; Jackson, R. H., jt.
auth.

Black, Jeremiah Sullivan
Corporations under eminent domain. BREWE 2:471

BLACK ARTISTS
Hansberry, L.
A challenge to artists.
FON:954

BLACK AUTHORS
Hughes, L.
Negro writers have been on
the blacklist all their lives.
FON:916
Killens, J. O.
White liberals and the Black
revolution.   FON:1001

BLACK-ENGLISH DIALECTS
Taylor, O. L.
African origins of Black
English. JEF:443

BLACK MUSLIMS
Little, M.
Prospects for freedom.
SMHV:250

BLACK NATIONALISM
Little, M.
Black revolution. SMHV:235
Prospects for freedom.
SMHV:250

BLACK PANTHER PARTY
Cleaver, E.
Farewell address.
SMHV:284
Political struggle in Amer-
ica. SMHR:166
Revolution in the white mother
country and national libera-
tion in the black colony.
FON:1101
Hulett, J.
We've decided to stop beg-
ging. FON:1019
Newton, H. P.
The transformation of the
Black Panther Party.
FON:1182
Seale, B.
Free Huey.   MACR:322;
SMHR:175

BLACK PANTHERS
Garry, C. R.
In defense of Huey Newton.
ERP:161

BLACK POWER
Brown, H. R.
The Third World and the
ghetto. FON:1088
Carmichael, S.
Black power. FON:1033;
SMHV:264

Power and racism. BOSC:101
Speech at Morgan State Col-
lege, January 16, 1967.
BOSC:109
Clark, K. B.
The present dilemma of the
Negro. FON:1091
Cleaver, E.
Revolution in the white mother
country and national liberation
in the black colony. FON:1101
Forman, J.
Black manifesto. FON: 1156;
OE:235
Karenga, M. R.
The Black community and the
university; a community or-
ganizer's perspective.
LINRS:255
Killens, J. O.
White liberals and the black
revolution. FON:1001
King, M. L., Jr.
Where do we go from here?
FON:1068
McKissick, F. B.
Speech at the National Confer-
ence on Black Power, July 21,
1967. BOSC:127; FON:1065
Simmons, B.
As time runs out.   LINRS:251

BLACK STUDENTS
Carmichael, S.
Speech at Morgan State College,
January 16, 1967. ARN:343;
BOSC:109

BLACK SUFFRAGE See Blacks -
Politics and suffrage

Blackett, Patrick Maynard Stuart
Cloud chamber researches in nuclear physics and cosmic radiation (Nobel Lecture, Dec. 13,
1948). NOLPH 3:97

BLACKETT, PATRICK MAYNARD
STUART
Ising, G.
Presentation [of the Nobel Prize
for Physics to Patrick Maynard
Stuart Blackett, Dec. 13, 1948].
NOLPH 3:93

BLACKS
Abbott, R. S.
A message to youth. FON:778

Baldwin, J.
The American dream is at
the expense of the American
Negro. FON:1012
Barnett, F. L.
Race unity. FON:461
Blyden, E. W.
The African problem and
the method of its solution.
FON:540
Breitman, G.
Myths about Malcolm X:
another view. LINR:120
Brockett, J. A.
Reply to Grady. ANN 11:250
Brown, D. P.
The state of the country
from a Black man's point
of view. FON:617
Brown, E. E.
Importance of race pride.
FON:514
Brown, J.
Don't terrorize--but organize.
BRYF:495
Browne, R. S.
A case for separation.
FON:1121
---- and others
Separation or integration:
which way for America?
BA 1968-69:143
Bruce, J. E.
Negro plea for organized re-
sistance to white men.
ANN 11:214; FON:536
Bryant, M. E.
How shall we get our rights?
FON:510
Clark, K. B.
The present dilemma of the
Negro. FON:1091
Cleage, A.
Myths about Malcolm X.
LINR:108
Costley, W.
A plan for a defense move-
ment. FON:640
Davis, B. J.
The Negro people on the
march. FON:902
Delany, M. R.
Advice to ex-slaves.
FON:318
Douglas, S. A.
Reply to Lincoln at Chicago,
July 9, 1858. ANN 9:4;
BAS:45 (outline only);

OLIS:133
Douglass, F.
The abilities and possibilities
of our race. FON:326
The claims of the Negro ethno-
logically considered. FON:144
Color line in America.
ANN 10:584; FON:491
I denounce the so-called eman-
cipation as a stupendous fraud.
FON:520
"Men of color, to arms!"
OE:49
There is a better day coming.
CUR:173
What the Black man wants.
MDT:175
DuBois, W. E. B.
Behold the land. FON:837
Shall the Negro be encouraged
to seek cultural equality?
FON:772
The value of agitation. FON:663
Evers, C.
We are going to make it better
for Blacks and Whites.
FON:1167
Farmer, J.
The "Movement" now.
FON:1040
---- and others
Debate at Cornell University,
March 7, 1962. BOSC:59;
OE:248
Feldmann, M. H.
Eyes of the whole world.
SCHW:156
Florence, F.
Meaning of Black power.
SMHR:161
Ford, J. W.
The right of revolution for the
Negro people. FON:800
Fortune, T. T.
It is time to call a halt.
FON:556
Garvey, M.
The principles of the Universal
Negro Improvement Associa-
tion. FON:748; OE:103;
SMHV:100
We are mostly subject peoples
all over the world. FON:790
Graham, D. A.
Some facts about Southern
lynchings. FON:613
Green, J. P.
These evils call loudly for

redress. FON:499

Greener, R. T.
Emigration of colored citizens
from the southern states.
FON:466

Grimke, A. H.
Shame of America, or the
Negro's case against the
Republic. FON:764

Hamilton, W.
A defense of the Negro.
FON:26
Why a Negro convention is
necessary. FON:56

Hayden, L.
Deliver us from such a
Moses. FON:334

Holland, J. H.
Options along the pathway
of community involvement.
HOR:8

Holly, J. T.
The Negro race, self-government and the Haitian revolution. FON:169

Hood, W. R.
Uncle Tom is dead!
FON:843

Hope, J.
We are struggling for equality. FON:594

Hughes, L.
Negroes speak of war.
FON:787

Humphreys, B. G.
Justice but not equality for
the Negro. ANN 9:626

James, D.
"Given time we'll get it
together." BA 1974-75:135

Johnson, M. W.
Faith of the American Negro
(at Harvard commencement).
FON:742

Jones, W. N.
Why Negroes should support
the Communists.
FON:785

Jordan, V. E., Jr.
The Black agenda for the
1980s. BA 1979-80:87
The Black and Jewish com-
munities. VERD:273
Under the hammer: free-
dom, justice, and dignity.
LINRST:215

Kane, A.
Glory of notoriety.

REIR:223

King, M. L., Jr.
"I have a dream." AND:50;
ANN 18:156; ARS:154; BRR:78;
CAPG:83; FON:971; GRG:117;
HURH:366; LINR:290;
LINRS:289; LINRST:362;
LINS:379; MAC:247; MACR:288;
MDV:156; MUS:336; OE:152;
OLIS:289; SMHV:182; THOMS:94
Nonviolence and social change.
OE:157
Where do we go from here?
FON:1068

Little, M.
To young people. FON:1004

Lynch, J.
Colored men standing in the
way of their own race.
FON:316

McDuffie, G.
Natural slavery of the Negro.
ANN 6:191

McGowan, E. D.
Stop the foes of Negro freedom. FON:860

McKissick, F. B.
Speech at the National Conference on Black Power, July
21, 1967. BOSC:127; FON:1065

Miller, K.
The Brownsville affair.
FON:654

Morris, C. S.
The Wilmington massacre.
FON:604

Pennington, J. W. C.
The position and duties of the
colored people. FON:271

Pickens, W.
Kind of democracy the Negro
race expects. FON:601

Pinchback, P. B. S.
The whole race must protest.
FON:596

Powell, A. C.
Can any good thing come out
of Nazareth? FON:1027;
SMHR:154

Randolph, A. P.
The crisis of the Negro and
the Constitution. FON:816
March on Washington address.
OE:113
The task of the Negro people.
FON:807

Remond, C. L.
Rights of colored citizens in

travelling. ANN 7:74;
FON:72
Rustin, B.
A way out of the exploding
ghetto. FON:1078
Sampson, B. K.
To my white fellow citizens.
FON:347
Smith, J. M.
On the fourteenth query of
Thomas Jefferson's Notes
on Virginia. FON:215
Spottswood, S. G.
The Nixon administration's
anti-Negro policy. FON:1173
Steffens, G.
Law of the land. SCHW:132
Stephens, A. H.
On the Confederate Consti-
tution. ECH:77
Tilton, T.
The Negro: a speech.
MDT:161
Trotter, W. M.
How I managed to reach the
Peace Conference. FON:740
Turner, H. M.
How long? How long, O
Heaven? FON:445
Justice or emigration should
be our watchword. FON:561
Reasons for a new political
party. FON:504
Walters, A. and others
Two contrasting Black
voices. FON:611
Washington, B. T.
Address at the opening of
the Atlanta Exposition.
ANN 12:9; BAPRR:255;
BAS:77 (outline only);
BRYF:492; FON:577;
LINS:263; OE:82; SMHV:94
There is still much to be
done. FON:707
We must be a law-abiding
and law-respecting people.
FON:652
Watkins, W. J.
Our rights as men. FON:130
Weaver, R. C.
Negro as an American.
MDV:162; SMHV:129
White, G. H.
Defense of the Negro race.
FON:635
I raise my voice against one
of the most dangerous evils

in our country. FON:624
Wilkins, R.
Keynote address to the NAACP
annual convention, Los Ange-
les, July 5, 1966. OE:166;
AND:101
Williams, F.
Duty of colored men in the
present national crisis.
FON:281
Williams, P.
A tribute to Captain Paul
Cuffe. FON:28
Young, W. M., Jr.
A strategy for the seventies:
unity, coalition, negotiation.
STOT:331

---- See also Black Panther Party;
Black Power; Civil Rights;
Civil Rights Act (1866); Civil
Rights Act of 1964; Discrimination; Emancipation Proclamation; Integration; National Association for the Advancement
of Colored People; Race problems; Segregation; Segregation,
Resistance to; Segregation in
education; Slavery in the United
States; Voting Rights Law of
1965. Also headings under this
subject

---- ECONOMIC CONDITIONS
Bond, J.
A new movement and a new
method. FON:1161

---- EDUCATION
Baker, R.
Crime of Mrs. Douglass in
teaching colored children to
read. ANN 8:224
Grisham, G. N.
The functions of the Negro
scholar. FON:599
Smith, C. S.
The fallacy of industrial educa-
tion as the solution of the race
problem. FON:607

---- HISTORY
Clarke, J. H.
The meaning of Black history.
FON:1138

---- POLITICS AND SUFFRAGE
Adams, E. J.

These are revolutionary times.
FON:342
Bertonneau, A.
Every man should stand equal
before the law. FON:303
Bruce, B. K.
Speech delivered in March,
1876 when it became neces-
sary for the Senate to intro-
duce a resolution appointing
a committee to investigate
election practices in Mis-
sissippi. ANN 10:350
DuBois, W. E. B.
Politics and industry.
FON:673
Gray, W. H.
Justice should recognize no
color. FON:353
Holmes, O. W., Jr.
Nixon v. Herndon: opinion
for the court. ANN 14:534
Johnson, L. B.
Voting Rights Law of 1965--
a victory for freedom.
CAPG:97
King, M. L., Jr.
Give us the ballot--we will
transform the South.
FON:919
Langston, J. M.
Equality before the law.
FON:409
Little, M.
The ballot or the bullet.
AND:135; FON:985; REIR:47;
SMHV:214
Miller, T. E.
A plea against the dis-
franchisement of the Negro.
FON:582
Morton, O. P.
Reasons for Negro suf-
frage. BREWE 8:3079
Stevens, T.
Radical view of recon-
struction. BREWE 9:3529;
CUR:58
Still, W.
A defense of independent
voting. FON:398
Taylor, G. E.
Revolution by the ballot.
FON:647
Tilden, S. J.
Negro suffrage. ANN 10:122
Turner, H. M.
I claim the rights of a man.

FON:357
Wears, I. E.
The Ku Klux of the North.
FON:378

---- UNEMPLOYED See Unemployed - Blacks

BLACKS AS BUSINESSMEN
DuBois, W. E. B.
Politics and industry.
FON:673
Goodloe, J. W.
A Black-operated firm.
VER:253

BLACKS AS SOLDIERS
Campbell, J. P.
Give us equal pay and we will
go to war. FON:300
Cornish, D. T.
A warrior against fate.
BA 1975-76:207
Green, A. M.
Let us take up the sword.
FON:249
Johnson, J. W.
Africa at the Peace Table and
the descendants of Africans in
our American democracy.
FON:730
Miller, G. F.
They are all heroes. FON:719

BLACKS IN AFRICA
Bruce, J. E.
Reasons why the colored Amer-
ican should go to Africa.
FON:459

BLACKS IN THE PERFORMING ARTS
Robeson, P.
The Negro artist looks ahead.
FON:849

Blaine, James Gillespie
"He trod the wine-press alone."
Same as his Life and character
of J. A. Garfield
Life and character of J. A. Gar-
field (Washington, Feb. 27,
1882). BREWE 2:482;
HURH:137

BLAINE, JAMES GILLESPIE
Ingersoll, R. G.
Nominating Blaine.
BREWE 7:2578; HURH:154

Blair, Austin
  Military government.
    BREWE 2:504

Blair, Francis Preston
  Character and work of Benton.
    BREWE 2:509
  Deathbed of Benton.
    BREWE 2:514
  On the 15th Amendment.
    BREWE 2:516

Blake, Eugene Carson
  Ecumenism and peace.
    VI:132

Blakely, Robert J.
  Presents Stephen Hayes Bush.
    LYI:77

Bland, Richard P.
  Parting of the ways.
    BREWE 2:530

Blizzard, Eddie
  Not just a farmer.   BREWW:49

Bloch, Felix
  The principle of nuclear in-
    duction (Nobel Lecture,
    Dec. 11, 1952).
    NOLPH 3:203

BLOCH, FELIX
  Hulthén, E.
    Presentation [of the Nobel
    Prize for Physics to Felix
    Bloch and Edward Mills
    Purcell, Dec. 11, 1952].
    NOLPH 3:199

Bloch, Konrad
  The biological synthesis of
    cholesterol (Nobel Lecture,
    Dec. 11, 1964).   NOLM 4:78

BLOCH, KONRAD
  Bergstrom, S.
    Presentation [of the Nobel
    Prize for Physiology or
    Medicine to Konrad Bloch
    and Feodor Lynen, Dec.
    11, 1964].   NOLM 4:75

BLOOD
  Landsteiner, K.
    On individual differences in
    human blood.   NOLM 2:234

---- DISEASE
  Zimmerman, R.
    Mingled blood.   ARS:98;
    LINR:199

Blough, Roger M.
  Responds to an introduction on an
    occasion when he is given an
    award.   PRS:129

Blue, Brantley
  Thinking out loud (American Indian
    Prayer Breakfast Group, Au-
    gust 20, 1976).   MAES:419

Blue Spruce, George
  Needed: Indian health profession-
    als.· MAES:171

Blumenschein, Carl M.
  Introduces Smith Hempstone.
    PRS:23

Blyden, Edward Wilmot
  The African problem and the
    methods of its solution.
    (Washington, D. C., Jan. 19,
    1890).   FON:540
  Africa's service to the world.
    EMP:26

Bocobo, Jorge C.
  Love of country (University of the
    Philippines, June 7, 1937).
    CURM:149

BOER WAR See South African
    War, 1899-1902

Bohr, Niels
  The structure of the atom (Nobel
    Lecture, Dec. 11, 1922).
    NOLPH 2:7

BOHR, NIELS
  Arrhenius, S. A.
    Presentation [of the Nobel Prize
    for Physics to Niels Bohr, Dec.
    11, 1922].   NOLPH 2:3

Boissier, Leonard L.
  Some aspects of the mission of
    the International Committee of
    the Red Cross (Nobel Lecture,
    Dec. 11, 1963).   NOLP 3:301

Bolinbroke, Henry Saint-John, 1st
    Viscount
  Misfortune and exile.

BREWE 2:541
Patriotism.   BREWE 2:550

Bolton, Thomas
Oration (burlesque of Warren's
second Boston Massacre
oration).   POC:301

Bonaventura, Saint
Life of service.   BREWE 2:552

Bond, Julian
A new movement and a new
method. (New York-Lex-
ington Democratic Club
Annual Dinner - May, 1969).
FON:1161

Bonner, James _See_ Sevareid,
E., jt. auth.

BONUS BILL, 1816
Madison, J.
On the commerce clause.
ANN 4:462

Böök, Fredrik
Presentation [of the Nobel Prize
for Literature to Thomas
Mann, 1929]. NOB 12:221;
NOL:260

BOOK REVIEWS
Crooks, J.
Defense of "The death of a
President." REIR:182
Suggestions for preparation of
book reviews. PAE:190

BOOKS AND READING
Gallup, G.
Mass information or mass
entertainment. ANN 17:215

---- _See also_ Booksellers and
Bookselling; Literature

BOOKSELLERS AND BOOKSELL-
ING
Textbooks and all that: an
inquiry into the operation
of the college bookstore
(outline). CUB:28
You get what you ask for
(outline of speech). CUB:31

BOOMS _See_ Business cycles

Boorstin, Daniel J.
Beginnings (Washington, Nov. 9,
1976). BA 1976-77:138
Dissent, dissension and the news.
BA 1967-68:125; JEF:187;
JEFF:181; LINR:203
An historian adapts his introduc-
tion to an audience of journal-
ists.   Same as his Dissent,
dissension and the news

Booth, Arch N.
Responds to an introduction.
PRS:146

Borah, William E.
League of Nations. (Washington,
Nov. 19, 1919).   HURH:190
"Peace upon any other basis than
rational independence ... is fit
only for slaves." Same as his
League of Nations
Release of political prisoners.
ANN 14:405
Western farming and the tariff.
ANN 15:28

BORDET, JULES
Petterson, A.
Presentation [of the Nobel Prize
for Physiology or Medicine to
Jules Bordet, 1919].
NOLM 1:519

Borlaug, Norman Ernest
The green revolution, peace, and
humanity (Nobel Lecture, Dec.
11, 1970). NOLP 3:454

BORLAUG, NORMAN ERNEST
Lionaes, A.
Presentation [of the Nobel
Prize for Peace to Norman
Ernest Borlaug, Dec. 10,
1970]. NOLP 3:445

Born, Max
The statistical interpretation of
quantum mechanics (Nobel Lecture, Dec. 11, 1954).
NOLPH 3:256

BORN, MAX
Waller, I.
Presentation [of the Nobel Prize
for Physics to Max Born and
Walther Bothe, Dec. 11, 1954].
NOLPH 3:253

BORROMEO, ANDRES
   Malcolm, G. A.
      Judge Andres Borromeo did
      his duty! CURM:183

Borsch, Reubin A.
   Introduces Irish Deputy Prime
      Minister William Norton.
      PRS:41
   Introduces Selwyn Lloyd,
      former British Secretary
      of State for Foreign Affairs.
      PRS:39

Bosch, Carl
   The development of the chemical
      high pressure method during
      the establishment of the new
      ammonia industry (Nobel
      Lecture for 1931, May 21,
      1932). NOLC 2:197

BOSCH, CARL
   Palmaer, W.
      Presentation [of the Nobel
      Prize for Chemistry for
      1931 to Carl Bosch and
      Friedrich Bergius, May 21,
      1932]. NOLC 2:189

Bosley, Harold
   Is God really dead?
      BA 1965-66:157

Bosman, Robert A.
   Witch hunt. SCHW:128

Bossuet, Jacques Benigne, bp.
   Funeral oration over the
      Prince of Condé.
      BREWE 2:557

BOSTON
   Hale, E. E.
      Boston's place in history.
      BREWE 6:2355
   Mather, C.
      "Boston Ebenezer."
      POC:395
   Quincy, J. 1772-1864
      At the second centennial of
      Boston. BREWE 9:3272

BOSTON MASSACRE, 1770
   Adams, J.
      On the Boston Massacre.
      BREWE 1:45; POC:108
   Bolton, T.

      Oration (burlesque of Warren's
      second Boston Massacre ora-
      tion). POC:301
   Church, B.
      Boston Massacre oration (third
      anniversary). POC:255
   Hancock, J.
      Boston Massacre. BRN:26;
      HURH:24
   Lovell, J.
      Boston Massacre oration.
      POC:231
   Quincy, J., 1744-1775
      Defence of British soldiers,
      1770. BREWE 9:3269; POC:25
   Rock, J. S.
      I will sink or swim with my
      race. FON:203
   Thatcher, P.
      Boston Massacre oration,
      March 5, 1776. POC:272
   Warren, J.
      Boston Massacre (March 5,
      1772). ANN 2:211; POC:237
      Oration on the Boston Massacre
      (March 5, 1775). POC:245

BOSTON TEA PARTY, 1773
   Quincy, J., 1744-1775
      "Let us look to the end."
      POC:295

Bothe, Walther
   The coincidence method (Nobel
      Lecture, 1954). NOLPH 3:271

BOTHE, WALTHER
   Waller, I.
      Presentation [of the Nobel Prize
      for Physics to Max Born and
      Walther Bothe, Dec. 11, 1954].
      NOLPH 3:253

Boucher, Jonathan
   Civil liberty and nonresistance.
      ANN 2:343; POC:552

Boudinot, Elias
   Mission of America.
      BREWE 2:581

Bourdaloue, Louis
   Passion of Christ. BREWE 2:581

BOURGEOIS, LEON VICTOR AU-
   GUSTE
   Buen, A. J.
      Remarks [presenting the Nobel

Prize for Peace to Leon
Victor Auguste Bourgeois,
Dec. 10, 1920]. NOLP 1:304

Bourguiba, Habib
Responds to an introduction.
PRS:136

Boutwell, George Sewall
President Johnson's "High
crimes and misdemeanors."
BREWE 2:604

Bovet, Daniel
The relationships between isosterism and competitive
phenomena in the field of
drug therapy of the auto-
nomic nervous system and
that of the neuromuscular
transmission (Nobel Lec-
ture, Dec. 11, 1957).
NOLM 3:552

BOVET, DANIEL
Uvnäs, B.
Presentation [of the Nobel
Prize for Physiology or
Medicine to Daniel Bovet,
Dec. 11, 1957]. NOLM 3:549

Bowdoin, James
Encouragement of knowledge.
ANN 2:540

Bowen, William G.
Commitment to scholarship
and research (Washington,
March 7, 1979).
BA 1978-79:41

BOY SCOUTS
Welcome to Boy Scout troop
(or Boys' Brigade).
HNWM:49

BOYCOTTING
Parnell, C. S.
At Ennis (boycotting defined
and defended). MCB:296;
STRM:346

Boyd Orr, John
Science and peace (Nobel Lec-
ture, Dec. 12, 1949).
NOLP 2:415

BOYD ORR, JOHN
Jahn, G.
Presentation [of the Nobel Prize
for Peace to Lord Boyd Orr of
Brechin, Dec. 10, 1949].
NOLP 2:407

BOYS' BRIGADE
Welcome to Boy Scout troop (or
Boys' Brigade). HNWM:49

Bozeman, Mike
Soil--America's lifeblood.
BREWW:85

Brackenridge, Henry M.
Vindication of civil rights for
Jews. ANN 4:552

BRADEEN, JOHN
Rudberg, E. G.
Presentation [of the Nobel Prize
for Physics to William Shockley, John Bardeen and Walter
Houser Brattain, Dec. 11,
1956]. NOLPH 3:315

Brademas, John
Eulogy for Robert Kennedy (June
9, 1968). JAM:43

Braden, Waldo W.
Has TV made the public speaker
obsolete? EHN:309; MOPR:360

Bradlaugh, Charles
Appeal for justice. JAE:142

Bradley, Joseph P. and others
(J. M. Harlan)
Civil rights cases: opinion for
the court and dissenting opinion. ANN 10:577

Bragg, Lawrence
Art of talking about science.
MOP:358

Bragg, William Lawrence
The diffraction of x-rays by cry-
stals (Nobel Lecture for 1915,
Sept. 6, 1922). NOLPH 1:370

Brandeis, Louis Dembitz
Ashwander rules. ANN 15:350
Business as a profession.
ANN 13:342

Curse of bigness. BOORA 2:759
Danger of inaction: dissenting
opinion for the Supreme
Court on New State Ice Co.
v. Liebmann, 1931.
ROD:73
Law and the laboring classes.
ANN 13:23

---- See Sutherland, G., jt. auth.

Brandli, Wilbur
Taps and reveille. SCHW:30

Branting, Karl Hjalmar
Fraternity among nations
(Nobel Lecture for 1921,
June 19, 1922). NOLP 1:324

Brattain, Walter Houser
Surface properties of semicon-
ductors (Nobel Lecture,
Dec. 11, 1956).
NOLPH 3:377

BRATTAIN, WALTER HOUSER
Rudberg, E. G.
Presentation [of the Nobel
Prize for Physics to Wil-
liam Shockley, John Bardeen
and Walter Houser Brattain,
Dec. 11, 1956].
NOLPH 3:315

Braun, Carl Ferdinand
Electrical oscillations and
wireless telegraphy (Nobel
Lectures, Dec. 11, 1909).
NOLPH 1:226

BRAUN, CARL FERDINAND
Hildebrand, H.
Presentation [of the Nobel
Prize for Physics to Gug-
lielmo Marconi and Carl
Ferdinand Braun, Dec. 11,
1909]. NOLPH 1:193

Bray, Charles W.
De-mystifying anti-American-
ism (Washington, Jan. 17,
1980). BA 1979-80:38

Breckenridge, John C.
Dred Scott decision, Decem-
ber 1859. BREWE 2:615
Removal of the United States
Senate. (Washington, 1858).
BLY:122

Breitman, George
Myths about Malcolm X: another
view. LINR:120

Brennan, William J., Jr.
Baker v. Carr: opinion for the
Supreme Court. ANN 18:130
Conciliation between the press
and the law (Newark, N.J.,
Oct. 17, 1979).
BA 1979-80:119

---- and others (H. Black and W. O.
Douglas)
Ginzburg et al. v. United States:
opinion for the court and dissenting opinion. ANN 18:350

Brewer, David J.
In Re Debs: opinion for the
court. ANN 12:18
Independent judiciary as the salvation of the nation. ANN 11:423

Brewster, Kingman, Jr.
The decade of shortcuts. (Yale
University, Sept. 11, 1972).
BA 1972-73:176
Due process radicalism (Yale
College, June 7, 1970).
HOR:37

Briand, Aristide
Acceptance of the Nobel Prize for
Peace, Dec. 10, 1926.
NOLP 2:3

BRIAND, ARISTIDE
Nansen, F.
Speech at Award Ceremony
presenting Nobel Prize for
Peace to Aristide Briand and
Gustav Stresemann, Dec. 10,
1926. NOLP 2:3

Bridgman, Percy Williams
General survey of certain results
in the field of high-pressure
physics (Nobel Lecture, Dec.
11, 1946). NOLPH 3:53

BRIDGMAN, PERCY WILLIAMS
Lindh, A. E.
Presentation [of the Nobel
Prize for Physics to Percy
Williams Bridgman, Dec. 11,
1946]. NOLPH 3:53

Bright, John
  The angel of death.   Same as
    his Russia: negotiations
    at Vienna, House of Com-
    mons, February 23, 1855
  Morality and military greatness
    (Birmingham, Oct. 29, 1858).
    BREWE 2:637; MCB:23
  On punishment of death.
    BRYH:398
  On the foreign policy of Eng-
    land.   Same as his Morality
    and military greatness
  Russia: negotiations at Vienna,
    House of Commons, Febru-
    ary 23, 1855.   AND:61
  Trent affair.   STRM:271
  Will the United States subjugate
    Canada?   BREWE 2:620

Bristol, George Digby, 2d Earl of
  Army in domestic politics.
    BREWE 5:1865
  Grievances and oppressions un-
    der Charles I.
    BREWE 5:1861

BRITISH COMMONWEALTH See
  Commonwealth of Nations

BRITISH EMPIRE See Great
  Britain

Brockett, Joshua A.
  Reply to Grady.   ANN 11:250

Bronowski, Jacob
  Protest-past and present.
    BA 1969-70:119

Brooke, Edward W.
  The cause of civil rights.
    (Boston, 1967).   FON:1058
  Crisis in the two-party system
    (Boston, Jan. 5, 1966).
    BA 1965-66:170; SMHV:143
  Responsibilities inherent in a
    constitutional democracy.
    (Milwaukee, Wisc., Feb.
    27, 1974).   BA 1973-74:74

Brooks, Edward
  Report on Vietnam and East
    Asia.   BA 1966-67:23

Brooks, Phillips, Bp.
  Character of Abraham Lincoln.
    BREWE 2:644

Lincoln as a typical American.
  Same as his Character of Ab-
  raham Lincoln
Power over the lives of others.
  BREWE 2:651

Brooks, Preston S.
  Assault on Sumner.   BREWE 2:654

Brooks, Sidney H.
  God's grief.   WALE:23

Brooks, T. J.
  Antitrust laws as applied to
    farmers.   ANN 13:331

Brorby, Melvin
  Introduces Arnold J. Toynbee,
    professor, author and historian
    of Great Britain.   LYI:86

BROTHERLINESS
  Men's brotherhood (for laymen's
    group).   HNWM:23

Brougham and Vaux, Henry Peter
    Brougham, 1st Baron
  Against Pitt and war with Amer-
    ica.   BREWE 2:661
  Closing argument for Queen
    Caroline.   BREWE 2:665
  Present state of the law (1828).
    STRM:153
  Speech on Parliamentary reform.
    Same as his Supports the Re-
    form Bill
  Supports the Reform Bill.
    BRYH:322

BROUN, HEYWOOD
  Nizer, L.
    Presents Heywood Broun.
    LYI:105

Brown, Benjamin Gratz
  Prophecy.   BREWE 2:675

Brown, D. P.
  The state of the country from a
    Black man's point of view.
    (New England Conference of
    the African Episcopal Church,
    August, 1899).   FON:617

Brown, Edmund G.
  State of the state address (Jan.
    7, 1976).   JAM:13
  Proposals for change: an in-

augural address (Sacramento,
Calif., Jan. 8, 1979).
BA 1978-79:103

BROWN, EDMUND G.
Zumwalt, E.
Introduction to Edmund G.
Brown, Jr.   JAM:33

Brown, Edward Everett
Importance of race pride.
(National League of Boston,
March 5, 1888).   FON:514

BROWN, GEORGE ALFRED
Cavanagh, J. P.
Presents George Alfred
Brown.   LYI:203

Brown, H. Rap
Colonialism and revolution.
Same as his The Third
World and the ghetto.
The Third World and the ghetto
(Detroit, Oct., 1967).
FON:1088; SMHV:304

Brown, Harrison S.
Science, technology, and world
development.   ARS:83
Social responsibility of science.
BAP:280

Brown, Henry Armitt
Dangers of the present.
BREWE 2:685
One century's achievement
(Valley Forge centennial).
BREWE 2:683
Plea of the future.
BREWE 2:686

Brown, Henry B. and others
(J. M. Harlan)
Plessy v. Ferguson: opinion
for the court and dissenting
opinion.   ANN 12:92

Brown, James
Don't terrorize--but organize.
(1968).   BRYF:495

Brown, James E.
Acceptance [of the Nobel Prize
for Literature for Eugene
Gladstone O'Neill, 1936].
NOB 19:131; NOL:336

Brown, Joan and others (Peggy Way
and Helen Fannings)
Liberation struggle generates
tension on race, sex issues.
BOST:265

Brown, John
Courtroom speech.   Same as his
Last speech at Charleston,
West Virginia
"I feel no consciousness of guilt."
Same as his Last speech at
Charleston, West Virginia
Last speech at Charleston, West
Virginia (Nov. 2, 1859).
ALA:21; ANN 9:143; BOS:44;
HURH:103
To free the slaves.   Same as his
Last speech at Charleston,
West Virginia

BROWN, JOHN
Garrison, W. L.
On the death of John Brown.
BREWE 6:2238
Moore, S.
A Southern response to John
Brown and black republicanism
(1859).   DAVF:146
Phillips, W.
John Brown and the spirit of
"59."   BREWE 8:3181
Roosevelt, T.
New nationalism (at dedication
of John Brown Memorial Park,
Osawatomic, Kansas).
ANN 13:250; BOORA 2:711
Thoreau, H. D.
Plea for Captain John Brown.
ANN 9:136

Brown, John Mason
"Beat" generation.   (Groton,
Mass., 1958).   HURH:341
"I am sick and tired of the
snivelers, the defeated and
the whiners."   Same as his
"Beat" generation

Brown, Karen   See   Andino, Judy

Brown, Millard
Famine: a reality, not just a
threat.   BREWW:168

Brown, William Wells
Slavery as it is, and its influence
upon the American people.

(Salem, Mass. Female Anti-
slavery Society, Nov. 4,
1847). FON:90

Browne, Robert S.
A case for separation.
(Plenary Session of the Na-
tional Jewish Community
Relations Advisory Councils,
June 30, 1968). FON:1121

---- and others (B. Rustin)
Separation or integration:
which way for America?
BA 1968-69:143

Brownlow, William Gannaway
Grape shot and hemp.
BREWE 2:690
Value of the American Union.
BREWE 2:690

Bruce, Blanche K.
A call for a change in our
Indian policy. (Washington,
April 7, 1880). FON:471
Negro hopes for assimilation.
Same as his Speech deli-
vered in March, 1876, etc.
Speech delivered in March,
1876 when it became necessary for the Senate to intro-
duce a resolution appointing
a committee to investigate
election practices in Mis-
sissippi. ANN 10:350

Bruce, John E.
Negro plea for organized re-
sistance to white men (Oct.
5, 1889). ANN 11:214;
FON:536
Organized resistance is our
best remedy. Same as his
Negro plea for organized
resistance to white men
Reasons why the colored Amer-
ican should go to Africa.
(Philadelphia, Oct. 1877).
FON:459

Brunsting, Lucille
Kid dreams. SCHW:49

Bryan, William Jennings
Cross of gold (Chicago, 1896).
ANN 12:100; BAS:50 (outline
only); BEN:52; BOORA 2:575;

BREWE 2:694; HURH:147;
LINS:268; OLIS:207
Imperialism (accepting Democratic
nomination for Presidency,
1900). ANN 12:345
Naboth's Vineyard. GRG:11
Paralyzing influence of imperialism. Same as his Imperialism
(accepting Democratic nomination for Presidency, 1900)
"You shall not crucify mankind
upon a cross of gold." Same
as his Cross of gold

BRYAN, WILLIAM JENNINGS
Depew, C. M.
Presents William Jennings
Bryan. LYI:227

Bryant, M. Edward
How shall we get our rights?
(Selma, Ala., Dec. 4, 1887).
FON:510

Bryant, William Cullen
Greatness of Burns. Same as
his To the Burns Club
To the Burns Club. BREWE 2:702

BRYCE, JAMES
Choate, J. H.
Presents James Bryce.
LYI:237

Brzezinski, Zbigniew
Our China policy in a wider context (Washington, Jan. 15,
1979). BA 1978-79:150

Buchan, John
Novel and the fairy tale. ARS:54

Buchanan, Colin
Planning and public opinion.
MDYG:130

Buchanan, David
Eulogy of Garibaldi. MCA:78

Buchanan, George See Baldwin,
S. B., jt. auth.

Buchanan, James
First annual message.
STAT 1:942
Fourth annual message.
ANN 9:209; STAT 1:1025
Impending disruption of the Union.

Buchanan, John G.

Same as his Fourth annual
message
Inaugural address.
BREWE 2:707; USINAU:111;
USINAUG:111
Second annual message.
STAT 1:969
Third annual message.
STAT 1:1001

Buchanan, John G.
Presents Augustus N. Hand.
LYT:133

Buchner, Eduard
Cell-free fermentation (Nobel
Lecture, Dec. 11, 1907).
NOLC 1:103

BUCHNER, EDUARD
Mörner, K. A. H.
Presentation [of the Nobel
Prize for Chemistry to
Eduard Buchner, Dec. 11,
1907]. NOLC 1:99

Buchwald, Art
Parody of political speeches
(Washington Post, Jan. 13,
1976). JAM:27

Buck, Pearl
Acceptance [of the Nobel Prize
for Literature, 1938].
NOB 3:157; NOL:359
The Chinese novel (Nobel lec-
ture, Dec. 12, 1938).
NOL:361

BUCK, PEARL
Hallström, P.
Presentation [of the Nobel
Prize for Literature to
Pearl Buck, 1938].
NOB 3:149; NOL:354

Buckley, F. R.
La Folle epoque. MDYG:181

Buckley, James
The Equal Rights Amendment:
the legislative aspect
(Washington, March 22,
1972). LINRST:271

Buel, David, Jr. See Sanford,
N., jt. auth.

Buen, A. J.
Remarks [presenting the Nobel
Prize for Peace to Leon Victor
Auguste Bourgeois, Dec. 10,
1920]. NOLP 1:304

BUILDINGS, DEDICATION OF See
Dedication addresses, subheads
Buildings; Churches, Corner-
stones, Libraries

Buisson, Ferdinand Edouard
Changes in concepts of war and
peace (Nobel Lecture, 1927,
May 31, 1928). NOLP 2:35

BUISSON, FERDINAND EDOUARD
Stang, F.
Presentation of the Nobel Prize
for Peace to Ferdinand Edouard
Buisson and Ludwig Quidde,
Dec. 10, 1927. NOLP 2:29

Bulkeley, Peter
City set upon a hill. ANN 1:211
The gospel-covenant (1638 or
1639). JON:30

Bulkley, William L.
Race prejudice as viewed from an
economic standpoint. (National
Negro Conference-1909).
FON:680

Bullock, Hugh
Presents Lester B. Pearson.
LYI:207

Bunche, Ralph J.
Barriers of race can be sur-
mounted. CAPG:66
Human relations in world perspective. (Dillard University
- spring 1954). FON:882
Some reflections on peace in our
time (Nobel Lecture, Dec. 11,
1950). NOLP 2:443

BUNCHE, RALPH J.
Jahn, G.
Presentation of the Nobel Prize
for Peace to Ralph Johnson
Bunche, Dec. 10, 1950.
NOLP 2:435

BUNDY, McGEORGE
Martin, C.

Presents McGeorge Bundy.
LYI:88

Bunin, Ivan Alekseevich
Acceptance [of the Nobel Prize
for Literature, 1933].
NOB 3:291; NOL:314

BUNIN, IVAN ALEKSEEVICH
Hallström, P.
Presentation [of the Nobel
Prize for Literature to Ivan
Alekseevich Bunin, 1933].
NOB 3:285; NOL:309

Bunting, James E.
The pay is good. (California
State Univ., Hayward).
BAPR:364; BAPRR:271

Bunting, Mary Ingraham
Their questions (Amherst Col-
lege, May 28, 1965).
HOR:93

Bunyan, John
Heavenly footman.   BREWE 2:716

BUREAUCRACY
Bell, G. B.
Notes on the situation: a
critique.   BA 1978-79:93

---- UNITED STATES
Hart, G.
Big government: real or
imaginary?   LINRST:100

Burger, Warren E.
How long can we cope?
(Washington, Sept. 21, 1978).
BA 1978-79:81
State of the Judiciary. (St.
Louis, Mo., Aug. 10, 1970).
BA 1970-71:13

---- and others
Bicentennial of American in-
dependence (Washington,
July 2, 1976). BA 1976-77:185

Burges, Tristam
Supreme Court.   BREWE 2:729

Burgess, W. Randolph
Presents Paul H. Douglas.
LYI:231

Burke, Edmund
Against coercing America.   Same
as his Conciliation with Amer-
ica
Age of chivalry.   BREWE 2:817
Conciliation with America (March
22, 1775).   ALS:29 (with an-
alysis); ANN 2:312;
BREWE 2:806; CLAYP:50;
STRM:39
Declining the poll.   Same as his
On declining the election at
Bristol, September 9, 1780
Marie Antoinette.   Same as his
Age of chivalry
On conciliation with the colonies.
Same as his Conciliation with
America
On declining the election at Bris-
tol, September 9, 1780.
BRYH:243
Principle in politics: speech at
Bristol, previous to the elec-
tion, 1780 (defends his Parlia-
mentary conduct).
BREWE 2:812; BRYH:211
Speech on moving resolutions for
conciliation with the American
colonies, March 22, 1775.
Same as his Conciliation with
America
To his Constituents.   Same as
his Principle in politics:
speech at Bristol, previous to
the election, 1780 (defends his
Parliamentary conduct)

Burke, Yvonne Brathwaite
"Aspirations ... unrequited."
(Los Angeles, March 10, 1975).
BA 1974-75:143

Burlingame, Anson
Massachusetts and the Sumner
assault.   BREWE 2:820

Burnet, Sir Frank Macfarlane
Immunological recognition of self
(Nobel Lecture, Dec. 12,
1960). NOLM 3:689

BURNET, SIR FRANK MACFARLANE
Gard, S.
Presentation [of the Nobel
Prize for Physiology or Medi-
cine to Sir Frank Macfarlane
Burnet and Peter Brian Meda-

war, Dec. 12, 1960].
NOLM 3:685

Burns, John L.
Responds to an introduction.
PRS:150

BURNS, ROBERT
Bryant, W. C.
To the Burns Club.
BREWE 2:702
Emerson, R. W.
Memory of Burns.   HURH:106

BURR, AARON
Randolph, E.
In defence of Aaron Burr,
1807.   BREWE 9:3284
Wirt, W.
Burr and Blennerhasset (at
trial of Burr).
BREWE 10:3908

Burrows, John Lansing
Opposition to the theater in
time of war.   ANN 9:402

Burstein, Abraham
Power of memory.   WALE:25

Burton, Steven
You (male) should wear long
hair.   BAS:200 (outline only)

Bush, George
Views of US foreign policy in
the future (Washington,
Jan. 25, 1979).
BA 1978-79:159

BUSH, STEPHEN HAYES
Blakely, R. J.
Presents Stephen Hayes
Bush.   LYI:77

BUSH, VANNEVAR
Trippe, J. T.
Presents Vannevar Bush.
LYI:177

Bushnell, Horace
Dignity of human nature.
BREWE 3:825

BUSINESS
Abdul Rahman, T.
Tunku's recipe for success:
how to get things done.

MONSA:67
Berle, A. A., Jr.
Emerging common law of free
enterprise.   ANN 16:573
Brandeis, L. D.
Business as a profession.
ANN 13:342
Carpenter, C. U.
Justification of big business.
ANN 13:327
Goodman, S. J.
Raising the fallen image of
business.   BA 1973-74:160
McGraw, H. W.
Business's responsibility in an
information society.
BA 1977-78:121
Marshall, J.
Trustees of Dartmouth College
v. Woodward: opinion for the
Supreme Court.   ANN 4:522
Moorehead, J. R.
Plight of small business.
ANN 13:322
Roosevelt, F. D.
What the New Deal has done for
business (campaign speech in
Chicago, October 14, 1936).
ANN 15:379
Sulzberger, A. O.
Business and the press: is the
press anti-business? EHN:387
Taylor, F. W.
On scientific management.
BOORA 2:740

BUSINESS CYCLES
Grant, U. S.
Sixth annual message.
STAT 2:1275

BUSINESS DEPRESSION See Business cycles; United States -
Economic conditions

BUSINESS ETHICS
Marcus, S.
Can free enterprise survive
success? BA 1975-76:152

BUSING See School integration

Buteyn, Donald P.
Invisible abutments.   SCHW:44

Butler, Benjamin F.
"Article Ten, " (Impeaching A.
Johnson).   BREWE 3:832

---- and others (R. P. Spalding;
    N. P. Banks; S. Shellabarger;
    J. Mullins; W. E. Robinson;
    J. A. Bingham; H. Maynard;
    G. W. Woodward)
  Congressional debate on Haiti
    and Santo Domingo, January
    13, 1869. ANN 10:143

Butler, Joseph
  Government of the tongue.
    BREWE 3:842

Butler, Joseph T. See Lodge,
    H. C., jt. auth.

Butler, Nicholas Murray
  Presents Wilbur L. Cross.
    LYI:97
  Radio address (Nobel Lecture,
    Dec. 12, 1931). NOLP 2:136

BUTLER, NICHOLAS MURRAY
  Koht, H.
    Presentation [of the Nobel
    Prize for Peace to Jane
    Addams and Nicholas Murray
    Butler, Dec. 10, 1931].
    NOLF 2:125

BUYING AND MARKETING See
    Business; Sales talks and
    salesmanship

Butz, Earl Laver
  Feast or famine: the key to
    peace. (Des Moines, Dec.
    10, 1974). BA 1974-75:81

BYRNES, JAMES F.
  Fraser, L.
    Presents James F. Byrnes.
    LYI:218

                    - C -

Cadbury, Henry J.
  Quakers and peace (Nobel Lec-
    ture, Dec. 12, 1947).
    NOLP 2:391

Cadwell, Darius
  Oration (Andover, Ohio, July
    4, 1847). HAW:319

Caesar, Caius Julius
  On the conspiracy of Catiline.
    BREWE 3:846

Cahill, Daniel W.
  Last judgment. BREWE 3:851

Caird, John
  Art of eloquence. BREWE 3:855

Calhoun, John C.
  Against general resolutions on
    foreign affairs. ANN 7:336
  Compromise of 1850. Same as
    his On the slavery question
  Danger of abolitionist petitions
    (February, 1837). ANN 6:346
  Denouncing Andrew Jackson.
    BREWE 3:919
  Either slavery or disunion. Same
    as his On the slavery question
  Force Bill. BREWE 3:866
  "... the greatest and gravest
    question that ever can come
    under your consideration: how
    can the Union be preserved?"
    Same as his On the slavery
    question
  Individual liberty. BREWE 3:925
  On internal improvement, 1817.
    ANN 4:457
  On territorial expansion.
    ANN 7:87
  On the slavery question (Washing-
    ton, March, 1850). ANN 8:16;
    HURH:77; OLIS:93
  Replying to Henry Clay (from "In-
    dependent treasury debate").
    BREWE 3:921
  Roadways and waterways. Same
    as his On internal improve-
    ment, 1817
  Self-government and civilization.
    BREWE 3:924

---- See also Niles, J., jt. auth.

Califano, Joseph A.
  Federal support of science and
    medicine (Ann Arbor, Mich.,
    Dec. 18, 1977). BA 1977-78:99
  A tribute to the man of the people
    (Washington, Nov. 1, 1977).
    BA 1977-78:197

CALIFORNIA
  Polk, J. K.

Fourth annual message.
STAT 1:731
Seward, W. H.
On the admission of California
to the Union. ANN 8:29

---- BUDGET
Brown, E. G., Jr.
Proposals for change: an
inaugural address.
BA 1978-79:103

---- ECONOMIC CONDITIONS
Brown, E. G.
State of the state address.
JAM:13

---- POLITICS AND GOVERNMENT
Brown, E. G.
State of the state address.
JAM:13

Calvin, John
Necessity for courage.
BREWE 3:928

Calvin, Melvin
The path of carbon in photo-
synthesis (Nobel Lecture,
Dec. 11, 1961).
NOLC 3:618

CALVIN, MELVIN
Myrbäck, K.
Presentation [of the Nobel
Prize for Chemistry to Mel-
vin Calvin, Dec. 11, 1961].
NOLC 3:615

CAMBODIA
Nixon, R. M.
Cambodia. LINRS:236

Cambon, Pierre Joseph
Crisis of 1793. BREWE 3:931

CAMBRIDGE UNIVERSITY
D'Ewes, S.
Antiquity of Cambridge.
BREWE 5:1818

CAMPAIGN FUNDS
Nixon, R. M.
Apologia. MAC:258;
MACR:269; REIR:191

CAMPAIGN SPEECHES
Attlee, C. R.

The Labour programme.
MCB:471
Ballance, J.
The 1890 election: the opposi-
tion case. MACS:201 selections
Barkley, A. W.
Record of Democratic Party.
BLY:233
Beveridge, A. J.
March of the flag. ANN 12:198;
BOORA 2:622; GRG:14;
LINS:276
Brougham and Vaux, H. P. B.
Against Pitt and war with
America. BREWE 2:661
Bryan, W. J.
Naboth's Vineyard. GRG:11
Buchwald, A.
Parody of political speeches.
JAM:27
Carter, J.
Speech at the Martin Luther
King, Jr. Hospital. JAM:25
Chisholm, S.
Economic injustice in America
today. BA 1971-72:27
Churchill, Sir W. L. S.
The Conservative programme.
MCB:464
Coates, J. G.
The 1925 election: the Coates
campaign. MACS:307 sel.
Cockran, W. B.
An answer to William J. Bryan.
BREWE 4:1339
Costley, W.
A plan for a defense movement.
FON:640
Coughlin, C. E.
Money changers in the temple.
ANN 15:388
Dewey, T. E.
Acceptance speech, Chicago,
Illinois, June 28, 1944.
SIN:205
Acceptance speech, Philadelphia,
Pennsylvania, June 24, 1948.
SIN:229
Campaign speech, Des Moines,
Iowa, September 20, 1948.
SIN:232
Corporate state not an American
system (campaign speech, Octo-
ber 7, 1944). ROD:333
Opening campaign speech in
Philadelphia (Sept. 7, 1944).
SIN:210
Douglas, S. A.

Fifth joint debate at Galesburg, October 7, 1858.
ANN 9:22
Lincoln-Douglas joint debate at Alton, October 15, 1858.
ANN 9:30
Opening speech of Lincoln-Douglas debate, Ottawa, August 21, 1858. ANN 9:8
Reply to Lincoln at Chicago, July 9, 1858. ANN 9:4;
BAS:45 (outline only);
OLIS:133
Reply to Lincoln, Freeport, August 27, 1858. ANN 9:17;
BREWE 5:1912; HURH:94
Reply to the Jonesboro speech. ANN 9:20

Eisenhower, D. D.
Acceptance speech, Chicago, Illinois, July 11, 1952.
SIN:242
Acceptance speech, San Francisco, California, August 23, 1956. SIN:265
Campaign speech, Cleveland, Ohio, October 1, 1956.
SIN:275
Crusade for peace.
ANN 17:199

Ford, G. R.
Presidential remarks with question-and-answer session.
BA 1975-76:133
Republican National Convention acceptance speech.
LINRST:349
The third presidential debate.
BA 1976-77:30

Gladstone, W. E.
Campaign speech (at Perth, December 1, 1879).
BRYH:415

Goldwater, B. M.
Campaign speech, Washington, D.C., October 21, 1964.
SIN:345
Extremism in defense of liberty (accepting nomination for presidency, July 17, 1964). MAC:251; MACR:292;
MDV:115; SIN:337
Why we must be stronger militarily. BAS:92 (outline only); LAA:8

Harding, H. F.
Matter of doubt and grave concern. BA 1968-1969:121

Hoover, H. C.
Acceptance speech, Constitution Hall, Washington, D.C., August 11, 1932. SIN:88
Accepting the nomination for presidency. SIN:4
Against the proposed New Deal (October 31, 1932). ANN 15:188
Campaign speech, Madison Square Garden, New York City, October 31, 1932. SIN:103
In defense of tradition (Detroit, 1932). ROD:39
Speech at New York City, October 22, 1928. ANN 14:595;
BOORA 2:803: SIN:21

Humphrey, H. H., Jr.
Acceptance speech, Chicago, Illinois, August 29, 1968.
SIN:372
Campaign speech, Salt Lake City, Utah, September 30, 1968. SIN:380

Johnson, L. B.
Acceptance speech, Atlantic City, New Jersey, August 27, 1964. SIN:329
Campaign speech, Washington, D.C., October 7, 1964.
SIN:334

Jordan, B. C.
Keynote address to the Democratic National Convention.
BA 1976-77:11; JAM:7;
LINRST:334

Kennedy, J. F.
New frontier. CAPG:8;
HURH:353; SIN:298
Religion in government.
ANN 17:589; SIN:303

Landon, A. M.
Acceptance speech, Topeka, Kansas, July 23, 1936.
SIN:136
Action challenged. ROD:162
Campaign speech, New York City, October 29, 1936.
SIN:145
Federal and family finances.
BAD:62

Lemke, W.
Introduction of the aims of the Union Party of the United States. BAD:117

Lincoln, A.
First joint debate at Ottawa, August 21, 1858. ANN 9:11
Lincoln-Douglas joint debate at

Alton, October 15, 1858.
ANN 9:26
Reply to Douglas at Chicago.
OLIS:150
Second joint debate at Free-
port, August 27, 1858.
ANN 9:15; BREWE 7:2785
Speech at Charleston, Sep-
tember 18, 1858. ANN 9:21
Speech at Galesburg, October
7, 1858. ANN 9:23
Speech at Jonesboro, Sep-
tember 15, 1858. ANN 9:19
McGovern, G.
Acceptance speech, Miami
Beach, Florida, July 14,
1972. SIN:408
Campaign speech, Washing-
ton, D.C., August 5, 1972.
SIN:413
Muskie, E. S.
Election eve address.
STOT:262
Nixon, R. M.
Acceptance speech, Miami
Beach, Florida, August 8,
1968. SIN:356
Acceptance speech, Miami
Beach, Florida, August 23,
1972. SIN:392
Bridges to human dignity.
LINR:255
Campaign speech, radio
broadcast, September 19,
1968. SIN:366
Campaign speech, Toledo,
Ohio, October 27, 1960.
SIN:319
Campaign speech, White
House, Washington, D.C.,
November 2, 1972. SIN:402
It is time to speak up for
America. SIN:307
---- and others.
Opening statements: the
fourth debate. GRG:106
Percy, C. H.
Chicagoan goes South.
BA 1956-66:106
Reagan, R.
Time for choosing. CAPG:48
Roosevelt, F. D.
Acceptance of renomination
for the presidency, June 27,
1936. SIN:125
Acceptance speech, Chicago,
Illinois, July 2, 1932.
SIN:68

Acceptance speech on renomina-
tion for president, July 20,
1944. SIN:194
Acceptance speech via radio to
convention, Washington, D.C.,
July 19, 1940. SIN:156
Action defended (campaign
speech, October 31, 1936).
ROD:168
Address to the Commonwealth
Club, September 23, 1932.
ANN 15:158; ROD:31; SIN:77
American business is moving
ahead. BAD:1
Call for federal responsibility
(October 13, 1932). ANN 15:185
Campaign speech, Chicago, Il-
linois, October 14, 1936.
SIN:129
Campaign speech, Cleveland,
Ohio, November 2, 1940.
SIN:164
Facing Communism: the true
conservative is liberal. BAD:15
Opening campaign speech at
dinner of International Brother-
hood of Teamsters. LINS:330;
SIN:198
Philosophy of social justice
through social action (campaign
speech in Detroit October 2,
1932). ARS:135
Republican leadership and na-
tional defense. ANN 15:379
What the New Deal has done
for business (campaign speech
in Chicago, October 14, 1936).
ANN 15:379
Roosevelt, T.
Issues of the coming election.
ANN 11:170
Smith, A. E.
Acceptance speech, Albany,
New York, August 22, 1928.
SIN:34
Campaign speech, Oklahoma
City, Sept. 20, 1928. SIN:52
Religion and politics.
HURH:209
Stevenson, A. E.
Acceptance speech, Chicago,
Illinois, August 17, 1956.
SIN:282
Agrees to run for President.
ANN 17:196; BEN:123; GRG:96;
HURH:302; LINS:345; SIN:251
Campaign speech, Academy of
Music, Brooklyn, New York,

October 31, 1952. SIN:255
Campaign speech, Minneap-
olis, Minnesota, September
29, 1956. SIN:288
The speaker seeks a favorable
hearing. JEF:189; JEFF:182
Speech to the American Le-
gion, August 27, 1952.
BEN:129
Tilden, S. J.
Negro suffrage. ANN 10:122
Truman, H. S.
Acceptance speech, Demo-
cratic Party National Con-
vention. OLIS:262; SIN:220
Campaign speech, Harlem,
New York, October 29,
1948. SIN:226
Willkie, W. L.
Acceptance speech. ANN
16:27; SIN:171
Campaign speech, St. Louis,
Missouri, October 17, 1940.
SIN:183
Consensus established.
ROD:174
Wilson, W.
Fear of monopoly.
ANN 13:356
New call to duty. ALA:77
What is progress? BEN:62
Zumwalt, Elmo
Introduction to Edmund G.
Brown, Jr. JAM:33

Campbell, Alexander
Mind the master force.
BREWE 3:935

Campbell, Bill
On the banks of the Wabash
(Purdue Univ., 1966).
KEO:226; STOT:266

Campbell, J. P.
Give us equal pay and we will
go to war. (Baltimore,
Feb. 29, 1864). FON:300

Camus, Albert
Acceptance [of the Nobel Prize
for Literature, 1957].
NOB 4:7; NOL:524

CAMUS, ALBERT
Österling, A.
Presentation [of the Nobel
Prize for Literature to

Albert Camus, 1957]. NOB 4:3;
NOL:522

CANADA
Bright, J.
Will the United States subjugate
Canada? BREWE 2:620
Laurier, W.
Canada, England and the United
States in 1899. BREWE 7:2737
Macdonald, J. A.
On the treaty of Washington.
BREWE 8:2891
Prerogative and public right.
BREWE 8:2895
Mackintosh, J.
Canada and the autonomy of
British colonies.
BREWE 8:2909
Quincy, J., 1772-1864
Against the conquest of Canada.
BREWE 9:3274
Stevenson, A. E.
Today's most fateful fact (ac-
cepting honorary degree of
Doctor of Laws). OLIS:272
Thompson, D.
Hitler's plans for Canada and
the United States. HURH:257

CANALS
Adams, J. Q.
Fourth of July oration, 1828.
HAW:94
Clinton, D.
Address at the Licking Summit
near Newark, Ohio. HAW:119
Wolcott, O.
Address at state line between
Southwick, Massachusetts and
Granby, Connecticut, July 4,
1825. HAW:122

CANCER
Fibiger, J. A. G.
Investigations on Spiroptera
carcinoma and the experimental
induction of cancer.
NOLM 2:122
Huggins, C. B.
Endocrine-induced regression
of cancers. NOLM 4:235
Rous, P.
The challenge to man of the
neoplastic cell. NOLM 4:220

CANDIDATES
Burke, E.

Canning, George

On declining the election at
Bristol, September 9, 1780.
BRYH:243
Nixon, R. M.
Apologia (Television, Sept.
23, 1952). MAC:258;
MACR:269; REIR:191

Canning, George
Christianity and oppression.
BREWE 3:944
England in repose.
BREWE 3:941
Hate in politics. BREWE 3:946

CAPILLARIES
Krogh, A.
A contribution to the physi-
ology of the capillaries.
NOLM 1:536

CAPITAL AND LABOR See
Industrial relations

CAPITAL PUNISHMENT
Bright, J.
On punishment of death.
BRYH:398
Darrow, C.
Against capital punishment.
BEN:149
Robespierre, M.
Against capital punishment.
BREWE 9:3326

CAPITALISM
Carlat, Janice
Green parrot. LINR:46
Carleton, William G.
Effective speech in a
democracy. ARS:5
Carlyle, Thomas
Edinburgh address. Same
as his Inaugural address
at Edinburgh
Debs, E. V.
The issue. LINR:46
Fortune, T. T.
The present relations of
labor and capital. FON:506
Friedman, M.
The future of capitalism.
LINRST:243

Capp, Al
Is this your university?
(Franklin Pierce College,
Rindge, N. H., April 27,
1969). STOT:297

CARBOHYDRATES
Haworth, W. N.
The structure of carbohydrates
and of vitamin C. NOLC 2:414

CARBON
Calvin, M.
The path of carbon on photo-
synthesis. NOLC 3:618

CARDIAC CATHETERIZATION
Forssmann, W. T. O.
The role of heart catheterization and angiocardiography in
the development of modern
medicine. NOLM 3:506
Richards, D. W.
The contributions of right heart
catheterization to physiology
and medicine, with some observations on the physiopathology of pulmonary heart disease. NOLM 3:513

Cardozo, Francis L.
Break up the plantation system.
(Charleston, S. C.-Constitution-
al Convention of South Carolina,
1868). FON:350

CARDUCCI, GIOSUE
Wirsén, C. D. af
Presentation [of the Nobel Prize
for Literature to Giosuè
Carducci, 1906]. NOB 5:3;
NOL:48

Carlat, Janice
Green parrot (Univ. of Kansas,
1967). LINR:46; LINRS:59

Carlyle, Thomas
Heroic in history. BREWE 3:962
Inaugural address at Edinburgh.
BREWE 3:951

Carmichael, Stokely
Black power (Univ. of California,
Berkeley, Nov. 16, 1966).
FON:1033; SMHV:264
Power and racism. BOSC:101
Speech at Morgan State College,
January 16, 1967. ARN:343;
BOSC:109

Carnot, Lazare N. M.
Against imperialism in France.
BREWE 3:967

CAROLINE AMELIA ELIZABETH,
CONSORT OF GEORGE IV,
KING OF GREAT BRITAIN
Brougham and Vaux, H. P. B.
Closing argument for Queen
Caroline. BREWE 2:665

Carpenter, C. U.
Justification of big business.
ANN 13:327

Carpenter, Edna
We are involved in the world
food crisis. BREWW:223

Carpenter, Liz
Faces and voices of American
women (Houston, Nov. 19,
1977). BA 1977-78:184

Carpenter, Matthew Hale
In favor of universal suffrage.
BREWE 3:978
Louisiana Returning Board.
BREWE 3:976
Replying to the Grand Duke
Alexis (response to Duke's
toast "To the President of
the United States").
BREWE 3:974

Carrel, Alexis
Suture of blood-vessels and
transplantation of organs
(Nobel Lecture, Dec. 11,
1912). NOLM 1:442

CARREL, ALEXIS
Akerman, J.
Presentation [of the Nobel
Prize for Physiology or
Medicine to Alexis Carrel,
Dec. 11, 1912].
NOLM 1:437

Carson, Alexander
Glories of immortality.
BREWE 3:981

Carson, Sir Edward See Oxford
and Asquith, Herbert Henry
Asquith, 1st Earl of, jt.
auth.

Carson, Hampton L.
American liberty.
BREWE 3:985

Carstairs, Paddy See Sykes, C.,
jt. auth.

Carter, Jimmy
Address to the citizens of the
world. Same as his Inaugural
address
Energy address to the nation (April 18, 1977). EHN:327
Energy and the national goals
(Washington, July 15, 1979).
BA 1979-80:76
Energy problems (Washington,
April 18, 1977).
BA 1976-77:117
Fireside chat: unity on U. S.
goals (Washington, Feb. 2,
1977). LINRST:340
The inaugural address (Washington, Jan. 20, 1977).
BA 1976-77:18; JAM:38
Inauguration address. (Atlanta,
Ga., Jan. 12, 1971).
BA 1970-71:142
My good friend Hubert Humphrey
(Washington, Dec. 2, 1977).
BA 1977-78:200
Our common responsibility and
our common challenge (New
York, Oct. 4, 1977).
BA 1977-78:59
Speech at the Martin Luther King,
Jr. Hospital. (Los Angeles,
June 1, 1976). JAM:25
Universal declaration of human
rights (Washington, Dec. 6,
1978). BA 1978-79:52

---- and others (Anwar El-Sadat and
Menachem Begin)
Announcing the Camp David accords (Washington, Sept. 17,
1978). BA 1978-79:142

---- See Ford, G. R., jt. auth.

CARTER, JIMMY
Moore, P.
A biblical faith for a president.
BA 1976-77:24

Carty, John J.
Pure science and industrial research. ANN 14:9

CASABLANCA CONFERENCE
Roosevelt, F. D.

Address at the annual gathering of the White House Correspondents' Association, February 12, 1943.
ANN 16:130

Casely-Hayford, Joseph Ephraim
Leadership and African cooperation. EMP:49

Caspersson, T.
Presentation [of the Nobel Prize for Physiology or Medicine to George Wells Beadle, Edward Lawrie Tatum, and Joshua Lederberg, Dec. 11, 1958]. NOLM 3:583
Presentation [of the Nobel Prize for Physiology or Medicine to Hermann Joseph Muller, Dec. 12, 1946]. NOLM 3:149

Cass, Lewis
American progress and foreign oppression. BREWE 3:989

---- and others (J. C. Jones)
Suitability of moral declaration in foreign policy. ANN 8:167

Cassin, Rene-Samuel
The charter of human rights (Nobel Lecture, Dec. 11, 1968). NOLP 3:394

CASSIN, RENE-SAMUEL
Lionaes, A.
Presentation of the Nobel Prize for Peace to René-Samuel Cassin, Dec. 10, 1968. NOLP 3:385

Castelar, Emilio
In the Camp Santo of Pisa. BREWE 3:1003
Plea for Republican institutions. BREWE 3:998

Castro, Fidel
Cuba is no longer an American colony. LAA:127 (Summary)
Give me liberty or give me death! (Civic Plaza, Havana, May 1, 1960). BRN:136

CATALYSIS
Ostwald, W.
On catalysis. NOLC 1:150

CATHODE RAYS
Lenard, P. E. A. V.
On cathode rays. NOLPH 1:105

CATHOLIC CHURCH See Roman Catholic Church

CATHOLICS IN THE UNITED STATES
Kennedy, J. F.
Religion in government. ANN 17:589; SIN:303
Smith, A. E.
Campaign speech, Oklahoma City, Sept. 20, 1928. SIN:52

Catiline
Before defeat in battle. Same as his To his soldiers
To his soldiers. BAS:37 (outline only)

CATILINE
Caesar, C. J.
On the conspiracy of Catiline. BREWE 3:846
Cato, M. P.
Against the accomplices of Catiline. BREWE 3:1007
Cicero, M. T.
First oration against Catiline. BREWE 3:1159
Second oration against Catiline. BREWE 3:1171

Cato, Marcus Porcius, known as Uticensis
Against the accomplices of Catiline. BREWE 3:1007

CATO, MARCUS PORCIUS, KNOWN AS UTICENSIS
Cicero, M. T.
Cato and the Stoics. BREWE 3:1182

Catt, Carrie Chapman
Political parties and women voters (Chicago, Feb. 14, 1920). BRYF:506

CATTLE
Fishburn, P.
Land of cattle, land of America. BREWW:105
Hayes, K.
Crossbreeding beef cattle: progress or regression? BREWW:214

CATTO, OCTAVIUS V.
  Wears, I. C.
    The Ku Klux of the North.
    FON:378

Catton, Bruce
  Response to introduction.
    PRS:88

CATTON, BRUCE
  Shull, M. A.
    Presents Bruce Catton.
    LYI:203

Cavanagh, Jerome P.
  Presents George Alfred Brown.
    LYI:203

Caveny, Charles C.
  Greets Joey Bishop, substituting
    for Sir Cedric Hardwicke.
    PRS:118
  Introduces David E. Bell, di-
    rector of the Bureau of
    the Budget.   PRS:92
  Introduces Dr. George W.
    Beadle, chancellor of the
    University of Chicago.
    PRS:50
  Introduces Dr. Jonas E. Salk.
    PRS:88
  Introduces Henry J. Taylor,
    former United States Am-
    bassador to Switzerland.
    PRS:25
  Introduces Leonard E. Read.
    PRS:98
  Introduces Ogden Nash.
    PRS:106
  Introduces Robert E. Brooker,
    president of Whirlpool Cor-
    poration.   PRS:9
  Introduces Senator John G.
    Tower of Texas.   PRS:111
  Introduces Senator Kenneth
    B. Keating.   PRS:27

Cavour, Camillo Benso, Conte di
  Rome and Italy.
    BREWE 3:1012

Cecil, Robert
  The future of civilization
    (Nobel Lecture for 1937,
    June 1, 1938).   NOLP 2:246

CECIL, ROBERT
  Lange, C. L.

Presentation of the Nobel Prize
  for Peace to Viscount Cecil
  of Chelwood, Dec. 10, 1937.
  NOLP 2:235

Cecil of Salisbury, Robert Arthur
  Talbot Gascoyne-Cecil, 3d
  Marquis See Salisbury,
  R. A. T. G.-C.

Cederblom, J. E.
  Presentation [of the Nobel Prize
    for Chemistry to Sir William
    Ramsay, Dec. 12, 1904].
    NOLC 1:65
  Presentation [of the Nobel Prize
    for Physics to Lord Rayleigh,
    Dec. 12, 1904].   NOLPH 1:87

CELEBRATIONS See Anniversaries

CELL NUCLEI
  Kossel, A.
    The chemical composition of
    the cell nucleus.   NOLM 1:394

CELL PHYSIOLOGY
  Ehrlich, P.
    Partial cell functions.
    NOLM 1:304

Celler, Emanuel See Griffiths,
  Martha W.

CELLS
  Lwoff, A.
    Interaction among virus, cell,
    and organism.   NOLM 4:186
  Monod, J.
    From enzymatic adaptation to
    allosteric transitions.
    NOLM 4:188

CENSORSHIP
  Agnew, S.
    Television news coverage; net-
    work censorship.   ARN:367;
    BRYF:467; ERP:153; LINRS:191;
    LINRST:221; MACR:331;
    STAT:274
  Berryer, P. A.
    Censorship of the press.
    BREWE 2:443
  Brennan, W. J., Jr. and others
    Ginzburg et al. v. United
    States: opinion for the court
    and dissenting opinion.
    ANN 18:350

Krug, J. F.
In defense of liberty: extremism and other vices.
BA 1975-76:193
Royer-Collard, P. P.
Against press censorship.
BREWE 9:3347
Stanton, F.
Reply to the Vice President.
STOT:282
Woolsey, J. M.
Opinion December 6, 1933
(Ulysses case-freedom of
reading). ANN 15:236

CENSURE See Prosecution

CENTENNIAL CELEBRATIONS
See Anniversaries

CENTRAL INTELLIGENCE AGENCY
Donovan, W. J.
Call for a Central Intelligence Agency. ANN 16:391

CENTRIFUGES
Svedberg, T.
The ultracentrifuge.
NOLC 2:67

CEREBELLUM
Barany, R.
Some new methods for functional testing of the vestibular apparatus and the cerebellum.
NOLM 1:500

Cerenkov, Pavel Aleksejevič
Radiation of particles moving
at a velocity exceeding that
of light, and some of the
possibilities for their use
in experimental physics
(Nobel Lecture, Dec. 11,
1958). NOLPH 3:423

CEYLONESE IN MALAYSIA
Thuraisingham, E. E. S. C.
Call to Ceylonese to have
one and only loyalty to rulers
of Malaysia. MONSA:185

Chadwick, James
The neutron and its properties
(Nobel Lecture, Dec. 12,
1935). NOLPH 2:339

CHADWICK, JAMES
Pleijel, H.
Presentation [of the Nobel Prize
for Physics to James Chadwick, Dec. 12, 1935].
NOLPH 2:333

CHAFFEE, ROGER B.
Sevareid, E.
Eulogy for the astronauts.
MOP:189

Chain, Ernst Boris
The chemical structure of the
penicillins (Nobel Lecture for
1945, March 20, 1946).
NOLM 3:110

CHAIN, ERNST BORIS
Liljestrand, G.
Presentation [of the Nobel Prize
for Physiology or Medicine to
Sir Alexander Fleming, Ernst
Boris Chain, and Sir Howard
Walter Florey, Dec. 11, 1945].
NOLM 3:77

CHAIRMEN See Officers, presiding;
Toastmasters; Toasts

Challemel-Lacour, Paul Amand
Humboldt and the Teutonic intellect. BREWE 3:1018

Chalmers, Thomas
Use of living. BREWE 3:1025
War and truth. BREWE 3:1024
When old things pass away.
BREWE 3:1023

Chamberlain, Sir Austen See
Baldwin, S. B., jt. auth.

Chamberlain, Daniel Henry
Present hour in South Carolina
(inaugural address of would-be
governor). CUR:158

Chamberlain, Joseph
Acceptance [of the Nobel Prize
for Peace for 1925, Dec. 10,
1926]. NOLP 1:394
Empire and home rule. (Birmingham, May 15, 1903).
MCB:60; STRM:387
Imperial preference. Same as his
Empire and home rule
Imperial union and tariff reform.

Same as his Empire and
home rule
Manhood suffrage. Same as his
Megaphone and manhood suffrage
Megaphone and manhood suffrage. BREWE 3:1026

CHAMBERLAIN, JOSEPH
Nansen, F.
Speech at Award Ceremony
[presenting the Nobel Prize
for Peace to Joseph Austen
Chamberlain and Charles
Gates Dawes for 1925, Dec.
10, 1926]. NOLP 1:383

Chamberlain, Owen
The early antiproton work
(Nobel Lecture, Dec. 11,
1959). NOLPH 3:489

CHAMBERLAIN, OWEN
Hulthén, E.
Presentation [of the Nobel
Prize for Physics to Emilio
Gino Segrè and Owen
Chamberlain, Dec. 11, 1959].
NOLPH 3:487

Chambers, Merritt M.
Higher education who should
pay? CAPG:125

Champion, George
Consensus complex vs. the
free market. BA 1965-66:187

Chandler, A. B.
Address to the General Assem-
bly, Frankfort, Kentucky,
April 20, 1936. BLY:258

Chandler, Marvin
Introduces Roscoe Drummond.
PRS:122
Quest for peace. SCHW:180

Chandler, Zachariah
On Jefferson Davis.
BREWE 3:1030

Chaney, Fannie Lee
Ben is going to take his big
brother's place. (New
York, 1965). FON:1017

CHANEY, JAMES
Chaney, F. L.
Ben is going to take his big
brother's place. FON:1017

Channing, William Ellery
Attack on orthodox Calvinism.
Same as his Unitarian Chris-
tianity
Man above the state.
BREWE 3:1032
Unitarian Christianity. ANN 4:544

Chapin, Edwin Hubbell
Peaceful industry.
BREWE 3:1037
Rectitude higher than morality.
BREWE 3:1040
Scientia Liberatrix.
BREWE 3:1039
Source of modern progress.
BREWE 3:1038
Sovereignty of ideas.
BREWE 3:1036

Chapman, John Ray
Coatesville. ARS:163

Chapuisat, Edouard
The activity of the International
Committee of the Red Cross
during the War, 1939-1945
(Nobel Lecture for 1944, Dec.
11, 1945). NOLP 2:295

CHARACTER
Moody, D. L.
On Daniel and the value of
character. BREWE 8:3057

CHARITIES
Winthrop, J.
Modell of Christian charity.
BOORA 1:10

CHARLES I, KING OF ENGLAND
Mayhew, J.
Discourse on the anniversary
of the death of Charles I.
ANN 1:481; POC:508

CHARTISM
Attwood, T.
Chartist movement. JAE:68

CHASE, HARRY WOODBURN
Nizer, L.

Presents Harry Woodburn
Chase. LYI:91

CHASE, ILKA
Mulroy, T. R.
Presents Ilka Chase. LYI:17

Chase, Salmon P.
Thomas Jefferson and the
colonial view of manhood
rights. BREWE 3:1044
Three great eras.
BREWE 3:1056

---- and others (J. R. Giddings)
Opposition to the Kansas-
Nebraska Bill (January 1854).
ANN 8:251

CHASE, SAMUEL
Harper, R. G.
Defending Judge Chase.
BREWE 6:2425

Chateaubriand, François Auguste
René, Viscomte de
Has one government the right
to intervene in the internal
affairs of another?
BREWE 3:1060

Chatham, William Pitt, 1st Earl
of See Pitt, W., 1708-
1778

Chauncy, Charles
Caveat against enthusiasm.
POC:488
Good news from a far country
(repeal of Stamp Act).
BREWE 3:1090

Cheek, James E.
A promise made, a promise to
keep: Whitney Young and
the nation. (Washington,
D. C., March 19, 1971).
BA 1970-71:131

CHEMICAL BONDS
Hassel, O.
Structural aspects of inter-
atomic charge-transfer
bonding. NOLC 4:312
Mulliken, R. S.
Spectroscopy, molecular or-
bitals, and chemical bonding.
NOLC 4:131

CHEMICAL COMPOUNDS
Werner, A.
On the constitution and configuration of higher-order compounds. NOLC 1:256

CHEMICAL EQUILIBRIUM
Hoff, J. H. V.
Osmotic pressure and chemical
equilibrium. NOLC 1:5

CHEMICAL REACTIONS
Eigen, M.
Immeasurably fast reactions.
NOLC 4:170

CHEMISTRY
Nernst, W. H.
Studies in chemical thermo-
dynamics. NOLC 1:353
Pauling, L. C.
Modern structural chemistry.
NOLC 3:429

CHEMOTHERAPY
Bovet, D.
The relationships between isosterism and competitive phenomena in the field of drug
therapy of the autonomic nervous system and that of the
neuromuscular transmission.
NOLM 3:552

CHEROKEE INDIANS
Marshall, J.
Cherokee Nation v. State of
Georgia: opinion for the
Supreme Court. ANN 5:427
Swimmer, R. O.
Cherokee history. MAES:314

Chertoff, Mordecai S.
Benjamin A. Lichter. WALE:205
Go thou in peace. WALE:27

CHESAPEAKE & OHIO CANAL
Adams, J. Q.
Fourth of July oration, 1828.
HAW:94

Chesterfield, Philip Dormer Stan-
hope, 4th Earl of
Against revenues from drunkenness and vice. BREWE 3:1095

Chesterton, Gilbert Keith See
Shaw, G. B., jt. auth.

Cheves, Langdon
In favor of a stronger navy.
BREWE 3:1101

CHEVRILLON, ANDRE
Phelps, W. L.
Presents André Chevrillon.
LYI:52

Chew, Samuel
Speech, &c.   POC:77

Chiang, Mei-Ling (Sung) Mme.
Chiang Kai Shek
Japan is first U. S. foe.
CROCK:46

CHICAGO - WORLD'S COLUMBIAN
EXPOSITION, 1893
Depew, C. M.
Columbian oration.
BREWE 5:1769

CHICAGO HAYMARKET SQUARE
RIOTS
Engel, G.
Address at trial, Chicago,
October 7-9, 1886.
ACC:43; PAF:37
Fielden, S.
Address at trial, Chicago,
October 7-9, 1886. ACC:49;
PAF:41
Fischer, A.
Address at trial, Chicago,
October 7-9, 1886.
ACC:36; PAF:32
Lingg, L.
Address at trial, Chicago,
October 7-9, 1886. ACC:39;
PAF:34
Neebe, O.
Address at trial, Chicago,
October 7-9, 1886. ACC:29;
PAF:28
Parsons, A. R.
Address at trial, Chicago,
October 7-9, 1886. ACC:90;
PAF:65
Schwab, M.
Address at trial, Chicago,
October 7-9, 1886. ACC:24;
PAF:25
Spies, A.
Address at trial, Chicago,
October 7-9, 1886. ACC:1;
ANN 11:117; PAF:11

CHICANOS See Mexicans in the
United States

Chiel, Samuel
Seder of life.   WALE:29

Chifley, Joseph Benedict
Things worth fighting for.
MCA:166

CHILD LABOR
Cobbett, W.
Factory Bill (1833). STRM:191
Roesch, G. F.
Constitutionality of a New York
child labor law: opinion for the
court. ANN 12:571
Shaftesbury, A. A. C.
Employment of children.
JAE:81

CHILDREN
Geiman, C. K.
Are they really "unteachable"?
LINR:94
Jones, J. L.
"Let's bring back Dad": a
solid value system. LINRST:254
Kingsley, C.
Human soot: address at Liver-
pool in behalf of the Kirkdale
Ragged Schools. BREWE 7:2645
Myers, N. J.
Moppet manipulation. ARS:123
Nixon, R. M.
Remarks at the White House
Conference on Children.
BA 1970-71:37
Stowe, L.
Children, peanuts-and you.
MOP:263

CHILDREN'S DAY
Children on Children's Day (wel-
come address). HNWM:15
Welcome to mothers on Children's
Day. HNWM:7

CHILDREN'S RIGHTS
Lonnquist, K.
Ghosts. LINRST:176

Chillingworth, William
False pretenses. BREWE 3:1106

CHINA
Clemens, S. L.

Public Education Association.
GRG:21
Cushing, C.
England and America in
China. BREWE 4:1583
McKinley, W.
Fourth annual message.
STAT 2:1971

CHINESE IN MALAYSIA
Tan Siew Sin
Malays and Chinese must
co-exist. MONSA:85
The role of M.C.A. and the
loyalty of Malaysian Chinese.
MONSA:78

CHINESE IN THE UNITED STATES
Meade, E. R.
Chinese immigration to the
United States. ANN 10:386

CHINESE LITERATURE
Buck, P.
The Chinese novel. NOL:361

Chino, Wendell
Indian affairs--what has been
done and what needs to be
done. BA 1969-70:179

Chisholm, Shirley
Economic injustice in America
today (Newark College of
Engineering, April 15, 1972).
BA 1971-72:27
In support of the Equal Rights
Amendment (Washington,
Aug. 10, 1970). BOST:243;
EHN:364; MOPR:372
It is time for a change (March
26, 1969-Congress).
FON:1152
It is time to reassess our na-
tional priorities.
BA 1968-1969:68
Representative Shirley Chisholm
speaks in support of the
Equal Rights Amendment.
Same as her In Support of
the Equal Rights Amendment
Women in politics (Houston,
Feb. 9, 1973).
BA 1972-73:79

Chiu Ban It
Be strong and of good courage
(enthronement sermon).
MONS:456

CHIVALRY
Burke, E.
Age of chivalry. BREWE 2:817

CHLOROPHYLL
Fischer, H.
On haemin and the relationships
between haemin and chlorophyll.
NOLC 2:165

Choate, Joseph Hodges
Bench and bar. (New York, Dec.
22, 1880). HURH:133
Farragut. BREWE 3:1109
Presents James Bryce. LYI:237
"You cannot live without lawyers,
and certainly you cannot die
without them." Same as his
Bench and bar

Choate, Rufus
Books and civilization in America.
BREWE 3:1120
Heroism of the early colonists.
Same as his Puritan and Spartan
heroism
Necessity of compromises in
American politics.
BREWE 3:1127
On American nationality (82nd
anniversary of American inde-
pendence). ANN 9:54
Preservation of the Union. (Bos-
ton, Mass., 1850). HURH:80
Puritan and Spartan heroism.
BREWE 3:1135
State and mental culture.
ANN 7:235
"There are influences that never
sleep." Same as his Preserva-
tion of the Union

CHOIRS See Music and musicians

CHOLESTEROL
Bloch, K.
The biological synthesis of
cholesterol. NOLM 4:78

CHRISTIAN ETHICS
Winthrop, J.
Modell of Christian charity.
BOORA 1:10

CHRISTIANITY
Canning, G.
Christianity and oppression.
BREWE 3:944

Unitarian Christianity.
ANN 4:544
Dix, J. A.
Christianity and politics.
BREWE 5:1883
Ethelbert
Coming of Christianity.
BRYH:3
Hare, J. C.
Children of light.
BREWE 6:2402
Nation, C. A.
Spiritual authority for my
Christian work. BLY:183
selections
Newman, J. H., Cardinal
Christianity and scientific
investigation. MCB:361
Ockenga, H. J.
Evangelical Christianity.
ANN 16:115
Parker, T.
Transient and permanent in
Christianity. LINS:178
Shepard, T.
The parable of the ten vir-
gins. JON:133
Söderblom, N.
The role of the church in
promoting peace (Nobel Lec-
ture, Dec. 11, 1930).
NOLP 2:93
Thomas, J. B.
"Light of the world."
SCHW:110
Vander Werf, N.
Mistaken enemy. SCHW:171
Van Tatenhove, J. E.
Echo or a voice? SCHW:115

CHRISTIANITY AND ECONOMICS
Herron, G. D.
Christianity and the use of
private property.
ANN 12:226

CHRISTMAS
Christmas prayer. BNH:75
Paul VI
Key to peace. BAS:150
(outline only)

CHROMATOGRAPHY
Martin, A. J. P.
The development of partition
chromatography. NOLC 3:359
Synge, R. L. M.
Applications of partition
chromatography. NOLC 3:374

Chrysostom, John, Saint, Patriarch
of Constantinople
Avarice and usury.
BREWE 3:1141
Blessing of death.
BREWE 3:1138
Heroes of faith. BREWE 3:1139

Church, Benjamin
Boston Massacre oration (third
anniversary). POC:255

Church, Frank
Foreign policy and the generation
gap (St. Louis, Dec. 3, 1970).
BA 1970-71:49
Rediscovering America (San Fran-
cisco, Oct. 20, 1975).
BA 1975-76:124
War without end. BA 1969-70:27
The yen to make a mark with the
dollar (Provo, Utah, Dec. 12,
1978). BA 1978-79:168

CHURCH
Bernard, Saint
Against luxury in the Church.
BREWE 2:434
Korteling, M.
Renascence. SCHW:39
Parker, T.
Critique of American churches.
ANN 7:486
Welcome to Baptist Training Union
officers (Christian Endeavor,
etc.). HNWM:27
Welcome to church officials
(Deacons, Stewards, Elders,
etc.). HNWM:26
Welcome to guest speaker at a
stewardship banquet (3 exam-
ples). HNWM:60
Welcome to new Christians (3
examples). HNWM:62
Welcome to new church member
by transfer. HNWM:63
Welcome to new members of
church staff and family.
HNWM:64
Welcome to visitors at church
service (3 examples).
HNWM:52
Welcome to visitors at Men-of-the-
Church dinner (3 examples).
HNWM:39

---- See also Dedication addresses -
Churches

CHURCH AND STATE
Colman, B.
Piety and duty of rulers to comfort and encourage the ministry of Christ. POC:142
Grant, U. S.
Separation of church and school. ANN 10:365
Harris, J. G.
The prayer amendment. BA 1971-72:143
Henry, J.
On religion and elective office. ANN 4:239; BOORA 1:220
Kahn, R. I.
Vote against prayer and for God. KEO:300
Madison, J.
Civil and religious functions of government. ANN 4:287
Wilkinson, H. C.
How separate should government and God be? LINR:98

---- PHILIPPINE ISLANDS
Aquino, B. S.
The Church and the State must never mix! CURM:129

CHURCH COLLEGES
Stendahl, K.
Faith that enlivens the mind. BA 1976-77:168

Churchill, Lord Randolph Henry Spencer
Administration of Chips. STRM:355
Age of action. BREWE 3:1144
Financial reform: the administration of "Chips." Same as his Administration of Chips
Gladstone's Egyptian inconsistencies. BREWE 3:1148
"Trust the people" speech. (Birmingham, April 16, 1884). MCB:441

---- See also Sykes, C. , jt. auth.

Churchill, Sir Winston Leonard Spencer
Acceptance [of the Nobel Prize for Literature, 1953]. NOB 4:183; NOL:493
Address to Congress, December 26, 1941. ALS:223;

AND:120; ARN:301; BRR:51; CROCK:29; JEF:190; JEFF:184
Be ye men of valour. (BBC Broadcast, May 19, 1940). MCB:495
"Blood, sweat and tears." (H. of Commons, May 13, 1940). ALA:99; MCB:493
Blood, toil, tears, and sweat. Same as his "Blood, sweat and tears"
A British prime minister addresses Congress. Same as his Address to Congress, December 26, 1941
The Conservative programme. (BBC Broadcast, June 4, 1945). MCB:464
Dunkirk. (H. of Commons, June 4, 1940). MCB:498
Government policy (October 5, 1938 speech). STRM:468
Iron curtain. Same as his Sinews of peace
Never in the field of human conflict. (H. of Commons, Aug. 20, 1940). MCB:514
On the Munich Agreement (October 5, 1938). BRYH:521
Parliament in the air raids (September 17, 1940 speech). STRM:481
Sinews of peace (Westminster College, Fulton, Missouri, March 5, 1946). ANN 16:365; MCB:541
Solemn hour (May 19, 1940 broadcast). BRYH:534
"Their finest hour." (H. of Commons, June 18, 1940). MCB:506

---- See also Baldwin, S. B. , jt. auth.

CHURCHILL, SIR WINSTON LEONARD SPENCER
Clemens, S. L.
Presents Winston Churchill. LYI:198
Menzies, R. G.
Eulogy of Churchill. MCA:151
Siwertz, S.
Presentation [of the Nobel Prize for Literature to Sir Winston Leonard Spencer Churchill, 1953]. NOB 4:177; NOL:488
Stevenson, A. E.
Address at the memorial serv-

ice for Sir Winston Churchill.
LINR:305; LINRS:307;
LINRST:373
Truman, H. S.
Presents Winston Churchill.
LYI:211
Vincent, J.
Churchill's early achieve-
ments. MDYG:50

Cicero, Marcus Tullius
Catiline's departure. Same as
his Second oration against
Catiline
Cato and the Stoics.
BREWE 3:1182
Crucifixion of Gavius. Same
as his First oration against
Verres
First oration against Catiline.
BREWE 3:1159
First oration against Verres.
BREWE 3:1174
For the poet Archias.
BREWE 3:1189
Fourth Philippic. BREWE 3:1201
Second oration against Catiline.
BREWE 3:1171
Supernatural justice.
BREWE 3:1178

CITIES AND TOWNS
Benedict, D. L.
Remarks in Chicago on urban
imperatives. BA 1967-68:78
Church, F.
Rediscovering America.
BA 1975-76:124
Dinwoodie, S. D.
Inner city--our shame.
ARS:216
Ely, R. T.
Needs of the city. ANN 11:234
Kingsbury, F. J.
In defense of the city.
ANN 12:61
Lindsay, J. V.
Reality and rhetoric.
BA 1967-68:79
Olmsted, F. L.
Unplanned growth of cities.
ANN 10:224
Stevenson, A. E.
City--a cause for statesman-
ship. ARS:219
Stuart, J. D.
What can I do that matters?
BRYF:512

Thani Nayagam, X.
Town versus gown. MONS:183
Whitney, F. L.
Total redevelopment of cities.
ANN 18:338
Wilson, W. H.
Interaction of country and city.
ANN 14:4
Young, W. M., Jr.
Crisis of the city: the danger
of the ghetto. BA 1966-67:82;
OE:177; SMHV:160

CITIZEN ACTION See Local government - citizen participation

CITIZENSHIP
Curtis, G. P.
Public duty of educated men.
ALS:179
Farber, W. O.
Changing concepts of public
service. ARS:208
Gardiner, R. K.
Citizenship and political lib-
eralism. EMP:106
Marshall, D. S.
Duty of citizens. MONS:448
Warren, E.
Perez v. Brownell: dissenting
opinion. ANN 17:499

---- See also Suffrage

---- NEW ZEALAND
Parry, W. E.
New Zealand citizenship, 1948.
MACS:294 sel.

CIVIL DISOBEDIENCE See Government, Resistance to

CIVIL LIBERTY See Democracy;
Liberty; United States -
Economic policy

CIVIL RIGHTS
Barrett, B. F.
The unreasonable prejudices
against people of color in
Philadelphia. FON:337
Brackenridge, H. M.
Vindication of civil rights for
Jews. ANN 4:552
Bradley, J. F. and others
Civil rights cases: opinion for
the court and dissenting opinion.
ANN 10:577

Brooke, E. W.
    The cause of civil rights.
    FON:1058
Bruce, J. E.
    Negro plea for organized
    resistance to white men.
    ANN 11:214
Carter, J.
    Universal declaration of
    human rights. BA 1978-79:52
Cassin, R. S.
    The charter of human rights
    (Nobel Lectures, Dec. 11,
    1968). NOLP 3:394
Chase, S. P.
    Thomas Jefferson and the
    colonial view of manhood
    rights. BREWE 3:1044
Collins, L.
    Rout the forces of hate.
    ARS:157
Cushing, C.
    Primordial rights of the
    universal people.
    BREWE 4:1577
Douglass, F.
    Color line in America.
    ANN 10:584; FON:491
Dunn, O. J.
    We ask an equal chance in
    the race of life. FON:355
Eisenhower, D. D.
    Federal Court orders must
    be upheld. ANN 17:457
Farmer, J. and others
    Debate at Cornell Univer-
    sity, March 7, 1962.
    BOSC:59; OE:248
Goldberg, A. J.
    Human rights and détente.
    BA 1977-78:71
Gregory, D.
    Let your son fight for free-
    dom. FON:981
Grimke, F. J.
    Equality of rights for all
    citizens, black and white,
    alike. FON:668
Hannah, J. A.
    Civil rights and the public
    universities. BA 1965-66:93
Hatcher, R. G.
    Which is the path of change?
    FON:1110
James, D.
    "Given time we'll get it
    together." BA 1974-75:135
Johnson, L. B.

Address to a Joint Session of
    Congress, March 15, 1965.
    AND:81; BOORA 2:919;
    CROCK:164; MDV:144; REIR:143
    Voting Rights Law of 1965--a
    victory for freedom. CAPG:97
Jordan, V. E., Jr.
    Blacks and the Nixon adminis-
    tration: the next four years.
    BA 1972-73:39
    Survival. BA 1971-72:49
Katzenbach, N.
    Civil Rights Act of 1964: re-
    spect for law. CAPG:88
Kennedy, J. F.
    Negro and the American prom-
    ise. ANN 18:152
    Special message to the Con-
    gress on Civil Rights.
    THOMS:50
Kennedy, R. F.
    Law Day address--University
    of Georgia. CAPG:73;
    THOMS:120
King, M. L., Jr.
    "I have a dream." AND:50;
    ANN 18:156; ARS:154; BRR:78;
    CAPG:83; FON:971; GRG:117;
    HURH:366; LINR:290;
    LINRS:289; LINRST:362;
    LINS:379; MAC:247; MACR:288;
    MDV:156; MUS:336; OE:152;
    OLIS:289; SMHV:182; THOMS:94
    I see the promised land.
    FON:1108
    A long way to go. SMHV:188
    Nonviolence and social change.
    OE:157
    Where do we go from here?
    FON:1068
Lewis, J.
    We are in a serious revolution.
    FON:975
Little, M.
    Black revolution. SMHV:235
Macdonald, J. A.
    Prerogative and public right.
    BREWE 8:2895
McGill, W. J.
    Simple justice and existential
    victims. BA 1978-79:23
Marshall, T.
    In praise of the sit-in strikes.
    FON:930
    The legal attack to secure civil
    rights. OE:123
Muhammad, E.
    We must have justice.

FON:969
Nixon, R. M.
Bridges to human dignity.
LINR:255
Patterson, W. L.
"Free by '63." FON:924
Percy, C. H.
Chicagoan goes South.
BA 1965-66:106
Price, J. C.
The race problem stated.
SMHV:78
Randolph, A. P.
March on Washington ad-
dress. OE:113
Rowan, C. T.
New frontiers in racial re-
lations. OE:201
Russell, R. and others
Pro's and con's of civil
rights. BRR:73
Steffens, G.
Law of the land. SCHW:132
Stephens, A. H.
Civil rights in the Con-
federacy. ANN 9:493
Truman, H. S.
Campaign speech, Harlem,
New York, October 29,
1948. SIN:226
Civil Rights, February 2,
1948. ANN 16:510
Vance, C. R.
Human rights and the foreign
policy. BA 1976-77:127
Warren, E.
Brown et al v. Board of
Education of Topeka et al:
opinion for the court.
ANN 17:253; BOORA 2:904
---- and others
Miranda v. Arizona: opinion
for the court and dissenting
opinion. ANN 18:427
Weaver, R. C.
Negro as an American.
MDV:162
Wilkins, R.
Keynote address to the
NAACP annual convention,
Los Angeles, July 5, 1966.
AND:101; BOSC:89; OE:166
Young, W. M., Jr.
Crisis of the city: the
danger of the ghetto.
BA 1966-67:82; OE:177;
SMHV:160
The social revolution:

challenge to the nation.
FON:961
A strategy for the seventies:
unity, coalition, negotiation.
STOT:331

---- See also Free speech; Liberty
of the press; Negroes; Religious liberty; Segregation in
education

---- RUSSIA
Griffin, R. P.
When freedom dies in its sleep.
BA 1978-79:60

CIVIL RIGHTS ACT (1866)
Elliott, R. B.
Civil Rights Bill. FON:384;
OE:55
Johnson, A. and others
Debate on civil and states'
rights. ANN 10:11
Rapier, J. T.
Civil Rights Bill. FON:418

CIVIL RIGHTS ACT OF 1964
Katzenbach, N.
Civil Rights Act of 1964: re-
spect for law. CAPG:88
Wallace, G. C.
Civil Rights Bill: fraud, sham
and hoax. MDV:175

CIVIL SERVICE
Arthur, C. A.
First annual message.
STAT 2:1424
Second annual message.
STAT 2:1452
Burger, Warren E.
How long can we cope?
BA 1978-79:81
Cleveland, G.
First annual message (first
term). STAT 2:1514
Hayes, R. B.
First annual message.
STAT 2:1334
Fourth annual message.
STAT 2:1395
Schurz, C.
Necessity and progress of Civil
Service reform. ANN 11:493

---- MALAYSIA
Suffian bin Hashim
Important factors for ensuring

efficient, loyal public serv-
ice. MONSA:132
Tan Slew Sin
The need for dedicated serv-
ice by civil servants.
MONSA:89 selections

CIVIL SERVICE REFORM
Bell, G. B.
Notes on the situation: a
critique. BA 1978-79:93

CIVILIZATION
Calhoun, J. C.
Self-government and civili-
zation. BREWE 3:924
Choate, R.
Books and civilization in
America. BREWE 3:1120
Guizot, F. P. G.
Civilization and the individual
man. BREWE 6:2344
Pennings, B.
New men for a new world.
SCHW:153

Claesson, S.
Presentation [of the Nobel
Prize for Chemistry to
Lars Onsager, Dec. 11,
1968]. NOLC 4:269

Clark, Champ
Courage of leadership.
BREWE 3:1207

Clark, Edwin M.
Responds to an introduction.
PRS:139

Clark, Kenneth B.
Beyond the dilemma.
BA 1969-70:168
The present dilemma of the
Negro. (Second Carter
G. Woodson Memorial
Luncheon, Greensboro,
N. C., Oct. 14, 1967).
FON:1091

Clark, Peter H.
Socialism: the remedy for
the evils of society. (Cincinnati, July 22, 1877).
FON:451

Clark, Thomas C.
Sheppard v. Maxwell, warden:

opinion for the court.
ANN 18:402

CLARK, THOMAS C.
Lewe, J. C.
Presents Thomas C. Clark
(Attorney General of the
United States). LYI:137

Clarke, John Henrik
The meaning of Black History.
(Jewish Currents Conference -
New York, Feb. 15, 1969).
FON:1138

CLASS DAY ADDRESSES See
Commencement addresses;
Farewell addresses; Valedictory
addresses; Welcoming ad-
dresses

Clay, Cassius Marcellus
America as a moral force.
BREWE 3:1213
Aspirations for the Union.
BREWE 3:1212
The man died, but his memory
lives. (Yale College, Feb. 22,
1832). BLY:109
Rhapsody. BREWE 3:1211

Clay, Clement C., Sr.
Subtreasury Bill of 1837.
BREWE 3:1216

Clay, Henry
Against the growing power of the
executive. ANN 6:565
American industry, 1824.
ANN 5:114
American system (U.S. Senate,
Feb. 2nd, 3rd, 6th, 1832).
BREWE 4:1249; HOW:32
Bank and the power of the execu-
tive. ANN 6:46
Compromise of 1850 (Washington,
Feb. 5 & 6, 1850). ANN 8:1;
BREWE 4:1273; HURH:83;
OLIS:66
Compromise resolutions. Same
as his Compromise of 1850
Dictators in American politics
(Washington, April 30, 1834).
BLY:33; BREWE 4:1224
Emancipation of South American
Republics. ANN 4:488;
BREWE 4:1240
Expunging Resolution.

BREWE 4:1233
For a vigorous prosecution of
the war. Same as his On
the War of 1812
Free trade and seamen's rights.
BREWE 4:1264
Greek Revolution.
BREWE 4:1268
In favor of a paternal policy of
internal improvements.
BREWE 4:1260
Internal improvements and the
power of Congress.
ANN 4:482
"Let us look to our country and
our cause, elevate ourselves
to the dignity of pure and
disinterested patriots."
Same as his Compromise of
1850 (February 5 & 6, 1850
speech)
Manufacturing and a protective
tariff. ANN 4:612
Noblest public virtue.
BREWE 4:1271
On the Seminole War.
BREWE 4:1236
On the War of 1812. ANN 4:327
Protective tariff. Same as
his American industry,
1824
Recognition for Latin American
governments. Same as his
Emancipation of South Amer-
ican Republics
Sixty years of sectionalism.
Same as his Compromise
of 1850
Slavery and expansion, May 13
and May 21, 1850.
ANN 8:36
System of real reciprocity.
ANN 5:392

CLAY, HENRY
Crittenden, J. J.
Henry Clay and the nine-
teenth-century spirit.
BREWE 4:1472

Clay, Laura
Laws of the states affecting
women. (Women's Club
of Central Kentucky, ca.
1894). BLY:199

CLAY COMPROMISE See Slavery
in the United States

Clayton, John M.
Clayton-Bulwer treaty and expansion. BREWE 4:1283
Justice the supreme law of nations. BREWE 4:1290

Cleage, Albert
Myths about Malcolm X.
LINR:108

Cleaver, Eldridge
Farewell address (San Francisco,
Nov. 22, 1969). SMHV:284
Meditation on the assassination of
Martin Luther King, Jr.
(April, 1968). OE:229
Political struggle in America.
SMHR:166
Revolution in the white mother
country and national liberation
in the black colony. (Rich-
mond, Calif., March 16, 1968).
FON:1101

Clemens, Jeremiah
Cuba and "manifest destiny."
BREWE 4:1292

Clemens, Samuel Langhorne
Accident insurance--etc.
MUS:291
Horrors of the German language.
BEN:204
"The ladies." BEN:201
New England weather. (New
York, Dec. 22, 1876).
HURH:128
Presents Henry M. Stanley.
LYI:117
Presents Joseph B. Hawley.
LYI:148
Presents Winston Churchill.
LYI:198
Public Education Association.
GRG:21
"There is a sumptuous variety
about the New England weather
that compels the stranger's
admiration--and regret."
Same as his New England
weather

Cleon
Democracies and subject colonies.
Same as his On the punishment
of the Mytileneans
On the punishment of the Mytile-
neans. BREWE 4:1298

CLERGY
  Edwards, J.
    Farewell-sermon.   POC:443
  Introductions for evangelists
    (19 examples).   BNH:13
  Introductions for ministers
    (16 examples).   BNH:9
  Reply to an introduction by a
    former pastor (4 examples).
    BNH:82
  Stoddard, S.
    Defects of preachers re-
    proved.   POC:430
  Tennent, G.
    Danger of an unconverted
    ministry.   POC:469
  Welcome to a new pastor and
    family (2 examples).
    BNH:49
  Welcome to guest minister at
    church service (4 examples).
    HNWM:59
  Welcome to minister as speaker
    at a civic club (3 examples).
    HNWM:43
  When a pastor has to say good-
    bye (2 examples).   BNH:83
  Words by a young man about
    to be ordained as a minis-
    ter.   BNH:90

Cleveland, Grover
  American interests in the
    Cuban Revolution.   Same
    as his Fourth annual mes-
    sage (second term)
  Controversy over Hawaii
    (against annexation).
    ANN 11:480
  First annual message (first
    term).   STAT 2:1514
  First annual message (second
    term).   STAT 2:1736
  First inaugural address.
    BREWE 4:1301; USINAU:149;
    USINAUG:149
  Fourth annual message (first
    term).   STAT 2:1598
  Fourth annual message (second
    term).   ANN 12:119;
    STAT 2:1824
  On tariff revision.   ANN 11:154;
    STAT 2:1587
  Second annual message (first
    term).   STAT 2:1555
  Second annual message (second
    term).   STAT 2:1762
  Second inaugural address.
    USINAU:163; USINAUG:163

  Skeptical view of pension legisla-
    tion.   ANN 11:90
  Surplus revenues and the tariff.
    Same as his On Tariff revision
  Third annual message (first term).
    Same as his On Tariff revision
  Third annual message (second
    term).   STAT 2:1794

Clevenger, Theodore
  To have lived without reason.
    (Baylor University, 1951).
    CAPB:373

Clifford, Clark M.
  We must renew our confidence.
    (Philadelphia, Nov. 1, 1972).
    BA 1972-73:109

Clinton, De Witt
  Address at the Licking Summit
    near Newark, Ohio, July 4,
    1825.   HAW:119
  Against the military spirit.
    BREWE 4:1309
  Federal power and local rights.
    BREWE 4:1306

CLOTHING AND DRESS
  MacColl, R.
    Borrowed plumage.   MDYG:174
  Wesley, J.
    On dressing for display.
    BREWE 10:3880

CLOUD CHAMBER
  Blackett, P. M. S.
    Cloud chamber researches in
    nuclear physics and cosmic
    radiation.   NOLPH 3:97

CLUB SPEECHES
  Bryant, W. C.
    To the Burns Club.
    BREWE 2:702
  Nine examples of brief thanks to
    special committees.   BNH:46
  Welcome to new members in civic
    club (3 examples).   HNWM:46

Coates, Dandeson
  Missionary opposition to the New
    Zealand Company (House of
    Lords Committee on New Zea-
    land, May 14, 1838).
    MACS:4 selections

Coates, J. Gordon
  The 1925 election: the Coates

campaign (Christchurch, Oct.
13, 1925). MACS:307 sel.
Support for the Singapore
Naval Base, 1927 (New
Zealand House of Repre-
sentatives, Sept. 21, 1927).
MACS:278 selections

Cobb, Howell
"Fifty-four forty or fight."
BREWE 4:1317
Speech of Howell Cobb, at
Atlanta, Georgia, May 22.
ECH:182

Cobbett, William
Factory Bill (1833). STRM:191
Man on the tower (defending
himself against a charge
of libel). BREWE 4:1321

Cobden, Richard
Effects of Corn Laws in agri-
culture. STRM:246
Effects of protection in agri-
culture. (H. of Commons,
March 13, 1845). MCB:189
Free trade with all nations.
BREWE 4:1326
Need for improved education.
JAE:124
Small states and great achieve-
ments. BREWE 4:1336

COBDEN, RICHARD
Palmerston, H. J. T.
On the death of Cobden.
BREWE 8:3131

Cockcroft, Sir John Douglas
Experiments on the interaction
of high-speed nucleons with
atomic nuclei (Nobel Lec-
ture, Dec. 11, 1951).
NOLPH 3:167

COCKCROFT, SIR JOHN DOUGLAS
Waller, I.
Presentation [of the Nobel
Prize for Physics to Sir
John Douglas Cockcroft and
Ernest Thomas Sinton Wal-
ton, Dec. 11, 1951].
NOLPH 3:163

Cockran, William Bourke
An answer to William J. Bryan.
BREWE 4:1339

Coffin, William Sloane, Jr.
Vietnam: a sermon. VI:64

Coffman, Lotus Delta
Adult education for the unemployed. ANN 15:98

Coke, Edward
Prosecuting Sir Walter Raleigh.
BREWE 4:1348

Cole, Albert L.
Responds to introduction. PRS:97

Cole, Edward N.
Two myths and a paradox.
(Warren, Michigan, Feb. 10,
1972). BA 1971-72:93

Colepeper, John, 1st Baron
Against monopolies.
BREWE 4:1494

Coleridge, John Duke Coleridge, 1st
Baron
Sacredness of matrimony.
BREWE 4:1355

Coles, Robert
A "larger vision" of the humanities (Washington, Oct. 18,
1977). BA 1977-78:163

Colfax, Schuyler
Confiscation of rebel property.
BREWE 4:1361

COLLECTIVISM
Hoover, H. C.
Road to freedom. ANN 15:384
Welch, R.
More stately mansions (1964).
DAVF:327

COLLEGE EDUCATION See Colleges and universities; Education, Higher; Knowledge, Theory of; Learning and scholarship

COLLEGE STUDENTS See Students

COLLEGES AND UNIVERSITIES
Birenbaum, W. M.
Time for reconstruction.
BA 1969-70:154
Crosby, G. A.
The uses of adversity.

BA 1976-77:156
Damrin, D. E.
  The James Scholars and the
  university. BRYF:528;
  BRYO:243
Hannah, J. A.
  Civil rights and the public
  universities. BA 1965-66:93
Henry, D. D.
  Perceptions of the university.
  HOR:70
Horner, M. S.
  Opportunity for educational
  innovation. BA 1972-73:184
Karenga, M. R.
  The Black community and
  the university; a community
  organizer's perspective.
  LINRS:255
Kerr, C.
  Urban-grant university (cen-
  tennial meeting of City
  College). BA 1967-68:86
Lewis, W. D.
  Founder's Day remarks.
  BAS:164 (outline only)
Lindsley, P.
  Dangers of a sectarian col-
  lege. ANN 5:310
McGill, W. J.
  Requiem for Joe College.
  BA 1969-70:139
Norton, E. H.
  In pursuit of equality in
  academe: new themes and
  dissonant chords.
  BA 1976-77:65
Randolph, J.
  Japanese "Lunchbox" univer-
  sities. REIR:15
Reinert, P. C.
  America, America, how
  does your garden grow?
  HOR:82
Reston, J.
  Remarks at the Centennial
  Charter Day Convocation,
  the Ohio State University,
  March 22, 1970. BAAE:285
Shaw, G. B.
  Universities and education.
  KEO:237
Sutton, P. M.
  Liberal arts in an agricul-
  tural college. ANN 11:18
Tappan, H. P.
  Call for a secularized uni-
  versity. ANN 9:79

Turner, J. B.
  Industrial university for Illinois.
  ANN 8:157
Washington, G.
  Eighth annual message.
  ANN 3:604; STAT 1:31

---- See also Education, Higher;
  Educators; Students. Also
  names of universities, e.g.
  Dartmouth College; Harvard
  University; Oxford University;
  University of Malaya

---- AUSTRALIA
  Wentworth, W. C.
    For the University Bill.
    MCA:17

---- ENTRANCE REQUIREMENTS
  Howe, H. II
    Changing the pecking order.
    BA 1967-68:111

---- MALAYSIA
  Alatas, S. H.
    Universities: discrepancy be-
    tween ideal and reality takes
    alarming turn. MONSA:177
  Hamzah Sendut
    Some new approaches to uni-
    versity education. MONSA:168
  Suffian bin Hashim
    University should slow down:
    call to education planners
    (Univ. of Malaya, June 20,
    1970). MONSA:144

---- SINGAPORE
  Toh Chin Chye
    The role of the university in a
    multi-racial society.
    MONSA:291

Collins, LeRoy
  Rout the forces of hate. ARS:157

Collins, Michael See Armstrong,
  Neil, jt. auth.

COLLOIDS
  Zsigmondy, R. A.
    Properties of colloids.
    NOLC 2:45

Colman, Benjamin
  Piety and duty of rulers to comfort and encourage the ministry
  of Christ. POC:412

COLONIALISM
  Romulo, C. P.
    Bandung address.
    CROCK:141

COLONIZATION
  Cotton, J.
    God's promise to his planta-
    tions. ANN 1:107

---- NEW ZEALAND
  Vogel, J.
    Colonization by public works
    and immigration.
    MACS:42 sel.

COLOR PHOTOGRAPHY
  Lippmann, G.
    Colour photography.
    NOLPH 1:186

COMBUSTION
  Semenov, N. N.
    Some problems relating to
    chain reactions and to the
    theory of combustion.
    NOLC 3:487

COMMEMORATIVE ADDRESSES
  Adams, J. Q.
    Oration at Plymouth (com-
    memoration of the landing
    of the Pilgrims).
    BREWE 1:65; HURH:51
  Chapman, J. R.
    Coatesville. ARS:163
  Frankfurter, F.
    John Marshall and the judi-
    cial function, September
    22, 1955. FRIP:353
  Suggestions for preparation of
    commemorative speech.
    MILS:3

COMMENCEMENT ADDRESSES
  Alunan, R. R.
    Mindanao, the land of
    promise. CURM:108
  Andelson, R. B.
    Campus unrest; the erosion
    of excellence. LINRS:204
  Babbidge, H. D.
    On thinking big. HOR:121
  Benezet, L. T.
    The educator's leap of faith.
    HOR:107
  Biddle, N.
    Princeton commencement

address. HOW:123
Brandeis, L. D.
  Business as a profession.
  ANN 13:342
Brown, J. M.
  "Beat" generation. HURH:341
Bunche, R. J.
  Barriers of race can be sur-
  mounted. CAPG:66
Bunting, M. I.
  Their questions. HOR:93
Califano, J. A.
  Federal support of science and
  medicine. BA 1977-78:99
Curtis, G. W.
  Public duty of educated men.
  ALS:179
Dewey, T. E.
  Public service. ANN 16:471
Eisenhower, M. S.
  A new historical perspective,
  interdependence. HOR:157
Gannon, A. I.
  A Catholic college, yesterday
  and tomorrow. HOR:78
Goheen, R. F.
  Sorting it out. HOR:21
Golden, J. L.
  Moments to remember (com-
  mencement address-John Glenn
  High School). BRP:236
Graduates at commencement time.
  HNWM:16
Hammarskjöld, D.
  Values of nationalism and in-
  ternationalism (Stanford Univer-
  sity commencement address).
  HURS:206
Hancher, V. M.
  Art of contemplation.
  CROCK:132
Hartzog, G. B., Jr.
  Finding America.
  BA 1972-73:194
Henry, D. D.
  Perceptions of the university.
  HOR:70
Hesburgh, T. M.
  The problems and opportunities
  on a very interdependent planet.
  HOR:142
  Service to others.
  BA 1979-80:180
Holland, J. H.
  Options along the pathway of
  community involvement.
  HOR:8
Howard, J. A.

HOR:3
White, R.
The educated man in the age
of Aquarius. BAAE:271
Wilson, L.
Education for adequacy.
HOR:16
Wilson, W.
New call to duty. ALA:77

COMMERCE
Barnave, A. P. J. M.
Commercial politics.
BREWE 1:221
Bayard, J. A.
Commerce and naval power.
BREWE 1:262
Morgenthau, H., Jr.
Roosevelt monetary program.
BAD:23

COMMON LAW See Law and
lawyers

COMMONWEALTH OF NATIONS
Lee Kuan Yew
The moral for Common-
wealth members and Britain.
MONSA:259
A new relevance and a fresh
validity for Commonwealth.
MONSA:272
Macmillan, H.
"The wind of change."
MCB:75

COMMUNICATION
Ashley, L. R. N.
A guided tour of gobbledy-
gook. REID:408
Bacon, W. A.
Language and the lived world.
BA 1976-77:174
Bittner, J. R.
The news media and campus
unrest. STOT:290
Goldhaber, G. M.
Organizational communica-
tion. LINRST:44
Lundy, R. F.
World divided by three
(politics, science, and reli-
gion). MONS:489
McGraw, H. W.
Business's responsibility in
an information society.
BA 1977-78:121
Nail, W. A.

What did you say? VER: 272
Oliver, R. T.
Culture and communication.
ARS:19

COMMUNICATION IN SCIENCE
Root, T. C.
The failure of scientists to
communicate. BA 1977-78:110

COMMUNICATIONS SATELLITES
Stasheff, E.
What will the satellites say?
KEO:262

COMMUNION
Frelinghuysen, T.
Revivalist sermon. ANN 1:344

COMMUNISM
Bosman, R. W.
Witch hunt. SCHW:128
Davis, A.
I am a black revolutionary
woman. FON:1177
Dondero, G. A.
Modern art shackled to com-
munism. DAVF:302
Eisenhower, D. D.
State of the Union (January 9,
1958). STAT 3:3076
Ford, J. W.
The right of revolution for the
Negro people. FON:800
Goh Keng Swee
Elite combat party (Communist
Party). MONS:394
Some delusions of the decade
of development. MONS:385
Goldwater, B.
Total victory in the Cold War.
ANN 18:42
Why we must be stronger mili-
tarily. BAS:92 (outline only);
LAA:8
Harriman, W. A.
Challenges to peace and free-
dom. ANN 18:328
Hoover, J. E.
Menace of the Communist Par-
ty. ANN 16:451
Jones, W. N.
Why Negroes should support
the Communists. FON:785
Legum, C.
Pan-Africanism, the Commun-
ists, and the West. ARS:255
McCarthy, J. R.

Annual Kansas Day Republican banquet speech. BOSR:53
Communists in the State Department. ANN 17:16
A conspiracy of blackest infamy (1951). DAVF:304
Muhammad Ghazali bin Shafie
Malaysia and the Asian perspective. MONS:222
Power politics and nation-building (Malaysia). MONS:232
Roosevelt, F. D.
Facing Communism: the true conservative is liberal. BAD:15
Truman, H. S.
Veto of the Internal Security Act. ANN 17:35
Vander Werf, N.
Mistaken enemy. SCHW:171
Youngdahl, L.
United States v. Lattimore. ANN 17:300

---- See also Russia

---- GUATEMALA
Dulles, J. F.
Why the Arbenz government was overthrown in Guatemala. LAA:117

---- RUSSIA
Dulles, J. F.
Containment or liberation? ANN 17:204

COMMUNIST PARTY OF AMERICA
Dondero, G. A.
Communism in our schools (1946). DAVF:296
Jackson, R. H.
The Communist Party is a secret conclave. DAVF:282
To secure the existing order against revolutionary radicalism (1950). DAVF:294

COMPROMISE (ETHICS)
Watterson, H.
The compromises of life. BLY:158

COMPROMISE OF 1850 See Slavery in the United States

Compton, Arthur Holly
X-rays as a branch of optics (Nobel Lecture, Dec. 12, 1927). NOLPH 2:174

COMPTON, ARTHUR HOLLY
Siegbahn, K. M. G.
Presentation [of the Nobel Prize for Physics to Arthur Holly Compton and Charles Thomson Rees Wilson, Dec. 12, 1927]. NOLPH 2:169

COMPUTERS
Sargent, F. W.
The computer and civil liberties. BA 1973-74:141

Conant, James Bryant
Education for a classless society. ANN 16:22
Responds to an introduction. PRS:153
Role of the state in education. CAPG:131
Science and spiritual values. ARS:88

CONDE, LOUIS II DE BOURBON
Boussuet, J. B.
Funeral oration over the Prince of Condé. BREWE 2:557

CONDUCT OF LIFE See Behavior; Character; Charities; Conscience; Courage; Ethics; Honesty; Justice; Life; Love; Man; Patience; Patriotism; Success; Truthfulness and falsehood

CONFEDERATE STATES OF AMERICA
Davis, J.
Final exhortation to the Confederate people. ANN 9:557
Inaugural address of 1861. ANN 9:238; BREWE 5:1656; ECH:137
Stephens, A. H.
Civil rights in the Confederacy. ANN 9:493
On the Confederate Constitution. BREWE 9:3517; ECH:77
Toombs, R.
Robert Toombs' address, to the people of Georgia. ECH:103

CONFERENCE SPEECHES See
    Congresses and conven-
    tions; Debates and debating

CONFLICT OF GENERATIONS
    See Youth-adult relationship

CONFORMATIONAL ANALYSIS
    Barton, D. H. R.
        The principles of conforma-
        tional analysis.
        NOLC 4:298

CONGRATULATIONS
    Brief words of congratulations
    on special occasions (9
    examples). BNH:92

CONGRESSES AND CONVENTIONS
    Suggestions for preparation
    of reports on conventions.
    PAE:188

Conkling, Roscoe
    Against Senator Sumner.
        BREWE 4:1374
    Nomination of U. S. Grant
    for a third term.
        BREWE 4:1366
    Stalwart standpoint.
        BREWE 4:1369

Connally, Thomas T. and others
    (C. Glass)
    Censure of Senator Nye.
        BRR:69

Connolly, Cyril See Sykes,
    C., jt. auth.

Connor, John T.
    Impact on the American econ-
    omy of the Vietnamization
    program. BA 1969-70:47

CONSCIENCE
    Leenhouts, T.
        Men of conscience.
        SCHW:119
    Morgan, C., Jr.
        Time to speak. KEO:308

CONSCRIPTION
    Cry on the campus. BURT:102
    Howarth, D.
        2S Draft deferment should
        be retained. REIR:130
    Mannix, D.

Case against conscription.
    MCA:134
Webster, D.
    Against conscription. ANN 4:355
Wirtz, W. W.
    Address at Catholic University
    of America. BA 1966-67:177

CONSERVATION OF NATURAL RE-
    SOURCES
    Dubos, R.
        Theology of the earth.
        BA 1969-70:83
    Hill, J. J.
        Natural wealth of the land and
        its conservation. ANN 13:153
    Madison, J.
        Agriculture and conservation.
        ANN 4:503
    Roosevelt, T.
        Annual message, December 6,
        1904. STAT 2:2105
        Eighth annual message.
        STAT 3:2296
        Fifth annual message.
        ANN 13:1; STAT 3:2144
        First annual message.
        ANN 12:433; STAT 2:2014
        "I took the Canal Zone."
        STAT 2:2073
        Public domain: the people's
        heritage. ANN 13:161
        Seventh annual message.
        STAT 3:2240
    Schurz, C.
        Need for a rational forest poli-
        cy. ANN 11:200

CONSERVATISM
    Coolidge, C.
        Have faith in Massachusetts
        (on being elected President of
        Massachusetts Senate).
        BOORA 2:752

CONSERVATIVE PARTY (GREAT
    BRITAIN)
    Beaconsfield, B. D.
        Meaning of conservatism.
        MCB:431
    Churchill, Lord R. H. S.
        Trust the people speech.
        MCB:441
    Churchill, Sir W. L. S.
        The Conservative programme.
        MCB:464

---- See also Great Britain - Politics
    and government

Cook, Joseph
    Ultimate America.
    BREWE 4:1381

Coolidge, Calvin
    Destiny of America.   ANN 14:409
    Fifth annual message.
    STAT 3:2710
    First annual message.
    STAT 3:2642
    Fourth annual message.
    STAT 3:2690
    Have faith in Massachusetts
    (on being elected President
    of Massachusetts Senate).
    BOORA 2:752.
    Inaugural address.
    USINAU:215; USINAUG:215
    Intervention in Nicaragua.
    ANN 14:519
    Second annual message.
    STAT 3:2655
    Sixth annual message.
    STAT 3:2727
    Third annual message.
    STAT 3:2669
    Veto of the McNary-Haugen
    Bill. Same as his Vetoing
    the farmer: Nonplanning
    as a way of life
    Vetoing the farmer: Nonplan-
    ning as a way of life.
    ANN 14:568

COOLIDGE, CALVIN
    Rogers, W.
    Nominating Calvin Coolidge.
    BAP:298; BAPR:366

Cooper, Lady Diana See Sykes,
    C., jt. auth.

COOPERATION
    Casely-Hayford, J. E.
    Leadership and African co-
    operation. EMP:49
    Everett, E.
    Universal and uncoerced
    cooperation. BREWE 6:2115

Copely, James S.
    Responds to an introduction.
    PRS:152

Corbin, Francis
    Answering Patrick Henry.
    BREWE 4:1394

Cordiner, Ralph J.
    Responds to an introduction.
    PRS:137

Cori, Carl Ferdinand and others
    (Gerty Theresa Cori-Radnitz)
    Polysaccharide phosphorylase
    (Nobel Lecture, Dec. 11,
    1947). NOLM 3:186

CORI, CARL FERDINAND
    Theorell, H.
    Presentation [of the Nobel Prize
    for Physiology or Medicine to
    Carl Ferdinand Cori, Gerty
    Theresa Cori-Radnitz, and
    Bernardo Alberto Houssay,
    Dec. 11, 1947]. NOLM 3:179

Cori-Radnitz, Gerty Theresa See
    Cori, Carl Ferdinand

CORI-RADNITZ, GERTY THERESA
    Theorell, H.
    Presentation [of the Nobel Prize
    for Physiology or Medicine to
    Carl Ferdinand Cori, Gerty
    Theresa Cori-Radnitz, and
    Bernardo Alberto Houssay, Dec.
    11, 1947]. NOLM 3:179

CORN LAWS
    Beaconsfield, B. D.
    Third reading of the Corn Im-
    portation Bill. BRYH:371;
    MCB:211
    Cobden, R.
    Effects of Corn Laws in agri-
    culture. STRM:246
    Effects of protection in agri-
    culture. MCB:189
    Peel, R.
    On the repeal of the Corn
    Laws. BREWE 8:3148; JAE:102

Cornish, Dudley T.
    A warrior against fate (Pittsburg,
    Kansas, Nov. 16, 1975).
    BA 1975-76:207

CORPORATIONS
    Black, J. S.
    Corporations under eminent
    domain. BREWE 2:471

CORRUPTION See Civil service;
    Crime and criminals; Elections
    - Corrupt practices; Watergate

CORTISONE
  Hench, P. S.
    The reversibility of certain
    rheumatic and nonrheumatic
    conditions by the use of
    cortisone or of the pituitary
    adrenocorticotropic hormone.
    NOLM 3:311
  Kendall, E. C.
    The development of cortisone
    as a therapeutic agent.
    NOLM 3:270

Corwin, Thomas
  Against dismembering Mexico.
    Same as his War with
    Mexico
  War with Mexico. (Senate,
    Feb. 11, 1847).   HOW:203;
    BREWE 4:1405

COSMIC PHYSICS
  Powell, C. F.
    The cosmic radiation.
    NOLPH 3:144

COSMIC RAYS
  Hess, V. F.
    Unsolved problems in physics:
    tasks for the immediate fu-
    ture in cosmic ray studies.
    NOLPH 2:360

Costley, William
  A plan for a defense movement.
    (San Francisco, Sept. 1902).
    FON:640

Costo, Rupert
  Indian history--fact or fiction.
    MAES:321

Cotton, John
  Divine right to occupy the
    land.   Same as his God's
    promise to his plantations
  God's promise to his planta-
    tions.   ANN 1:107
  A treatise of the covenant of
    grace (Boston, 1630's).
    JON:48
  Viall I: the powring out of
    the seven vials or An ex-
    position, with an application
    of the 16th Chapter of
    Revelation.   POC:363
  The way of life (1627-1630).
    JON:121

Coughlin, Charles E.
  The menace of the World Court
    (1935). (Radio address, Jan.
    27, 1935).   DAVF:249
  Money changers in the temple.
    ANN 15:388

Coulter, Thomas H.
  Introducing Marguerite (Maggie)
    Higgins to the Executives'
    Club of Chicago.   LYI:113

COUNTRY LIFE See Rural life

COURAGE
  Calvin, J.
    Necessity for courage.
    BREWE 3:928
  Leenhouts, T.
    Men of conscience.   SCHW:119

Cournand, André Frederic
  Control of the pulmonary circula-
    tion in man with some remarks
    on methodology (Nobel Lec-
    ture, Dec. 11, 1956).
    NOLM 3:529

COURNAND, ANDRE FREDERIC
  Liljestrand, G.
    Presentation [of the Nobel Prize
    for Physiology or Medicine to
    André Frederic Cournand,
    Werner Theodor Otto Forssmann,
    and Dickinson Woodruff Rich-
    ards Jr., Dec. 11, 1956].
    NOLM 3:501

COURTS
  Brewer, D. J.
    Independent judiciary as the
    salvation of the nation.
    ANN 11:423
  Burger, W. E.
    State of the Judiciary.
    BA 1970-71:13
  Roosevelt, T.
    Eighth annual message.
    STAT 3:2296
  Thomson, T. J. B.
    Spirit of humanity (opening of
    Federal Court of Malaysia).
    MOND:285
  Warren, E.
    Federal court congestion.
    ANN 17:487

---- See also Law and lawyers;
Also names of courts e.g.
United States - Supreme
Court

---- PHILIPPINE ISLANDS
Osias, C.
Justice and separation of
powers. CURM:190
Yamzon, V.
The lawyer shall never re-
treat. CURM:323

Cousin, Victor
Eloquence and the fine arts.
BREWE 4:1419
Foundations of law.
BREWE 4:1428
Liberty an inalienable right.
BREWE 4:1426
True politics. BREWE 4:1431

COWARDICE
Davies, S.
Curse of cowardice.
ANN 2:23; POC:534

Cox, Archibald
Can the dream survive? (Bos-
ton, Mass., July 4, 1979).
BA 1979-80:157
Creative in law and government.
(Amherst, Mass., Jan. 22,
1974). BA 1973-74:49

Cox, Harvey See Sevareid, E.,
jt. auth.

Cox, Samuel Sullivan
Against the ironclad oath.
BREWE 4:1436
Sermon on the Mount.
BREWE 4:1446
Stephen A. Douglas and his
place in history.
BREWE 4:1449

Coxe, Tench
Prospects for American manufacturing. ANN 3:196

Cragg, Richard T.
Introduces Judge Lester H.
Loble of Juvenile Court
of Helena, Montana.
PRS:38
Presents Chet Huntley.
LYI:109

Presents Cyril Northcote.
LYI:45
Cram, Ralph Adams
What is a free man? ANN 15:498

Cramer, John See Sanford, N.,
jt. auth.

Cranmer, Thomas
Against the fear of death.
BREWE 4:1458
Forgiveness of injuries.
BREWE 4:1459
Speech at the stake.
BREWE 4:1455; BRYH:60

Crary, Daniel R.
Plague of people. LINR:220

Crawford, Frederick C.
Jobs, freedom, and opportunity.
ANN 16:132

Crawford, William Harris
Issue and control of money under
the Constitution.
BREWE 4:1462

CRAWLEY, SIR FRANCIS
Waller, E.
Tyrant's plea, necessity (im-
peaching Justice Crawley).
BREWE 10:3709

CREATION
Helmholtz, H. L. F.
Mystery of creation.
BREWE 7:2465

CREDIT
Witherspoon, J.
Public credit under the Con-
federation. BREWE 10:3912

Cremer, William Randal
The progress and advantages of
international arbitration (Nobel
Lecture for 1903, Jan. 15,
1905). NOLP 1:46

CREMER, WILLIAM RANDAL
Løvland, J. G.
Welcome [presenting the Nobel
Prize for Peace, 1903, to
William Randal Cremer, Jan.
15, 1905]. NOLP 1:45

Crichton, John
  Consumer protection: what
    Johanna won't read.
    BA 1965-66:210

Crick, Francis Harry Compton
  On the genetic code (Nobel
    Lecture, Dec. 11, 1962).
    NOLM 3:811

CRICK, FRANCIS HARRY COMP-
    TON
  Engström, A.
    Presentation [of the Nobel
      Prize for Physiology or
      Medicine to Francis Harry
      Compton Crick, James
      Dewey Watson, and Maurice
      Hugh Frederick Wilkins,
      Dec. 11, 1962].
      NOLM 3:751

CRIME AND CRIMINALS
  Barry, R.
    Sentencing of "Ned" Kelly.
      MCA:74
  Bingham, J. A.
    Against the assassins of
      President Lincoln.
      BREWE 2:445
  Chew, S.
    Speech, &c. POC:77
  Darrow, C.
    Crime and criminals.
      ARS:142
  Izenbart, L.
    Real criminal. SCHW:101
  Marvin, R.
    Man's other society.
      MOP:377
  Murphy, P. V.
    What the police expect of
      the citizenry. BA 1970-71:122
  Roosevelt, T.
    Sixth annual message.
      STAT 3:2194
  Stanmeyer, W. A.
    Urban crime: its causes
      and control. LINRST:303
  Why go second class? (Outline
    of speech to persuade City
    of Del Norte it should estab-
    lish a Juvenile Court).
    CUB:42
  Woodmason, C.
    You are to take these free
      booters and desperadoes.
      POC:548

CRIMEAN WAR, 1853-1856
  Bright, J.
    Russia: negotiations at Vienna,
      House of Commons, February
      23, 1855. AND:61
  Lyndhurst, J. S. C.
    Russia and the Crimean War.
      BREWE 7:2842

Crispi, Francesco
  At the unveiling of Garibaldi's
    statue. BREWE 4:1467
  Socialism and discontent.
    BREWE 4:1469

CRITICISM
  Howard, J. A.
    The new furies: skepticism,
      criticism, and coercion.
      LINRST:146

Crittenden, John Jordan
  Against warring on the weak.
    BREWE 4:1477
  Compromise resolutions. Same
    as his On the Crittenden Com-
    promise
  Henry Clay and the nineteenth
    century spirit. BREWE 4:1472
  On the Crittenden Compromise.
    ANN 9:221; BLY:71
  Speech on his resolution. Same
    as his On the Crittenden Com-
    promise
  Union at any price. ANN 9:246

Crittenden, Thomas T.
  Trade and commerce for the
    southwestern states. ANN 11:16

Croarkin, Walter
  Presents Frank F. Rosenthal.
    LYI:165
  Presents William David O'Brien.
    LYI:163

Crockett, David
  Fourth of July oration, 1834
    (Philadelphia, July 4, 1834).
    HAW:136
  Raccoon in a bag. BREWE 4:1482

Crockett, George W.
  Racism in the law. (Wayne State
    Univ., Detroit, Oct. 15, 1968).
    FON:1131

Cromwell, Oliver
  Address to Parliament, Septem-
    ber 4, 1654. BRYH:144
  Debating whether or not to be-
    come King of England.
    BREWE 4:1485
  On the dissolution of Parlia-
    ment (First Protectorate
    Parliament). (Jan. 22,
    1655). CLAYP:14
  Speech on the dissolution of
    the First Protectorate Parlia-
    ment, January 22, 1655.
    Same as his On the dissolu-
    tion of Parliament (First
    Protectorate Parliament)
  Speech to the First Protector-
    ate Parliament. Same as
    Address to Parliament,
    September 4, 1654

CROMWELL, RICHARD
  Vane, H.
    Against Richard Cromwell.
    BREWE 10:3684

Cronbach, Abraham
  Of Earth, earthy and of
    Heaven, heavenly. WALE:30

Crooks, John
  Defense of "The death of a
    President." REIR:182

Crosby, Glenn A.
  The uses of adversity (Pullman,
    Wash., March 8, 1976).
    BA 1976-77:156

CROSS, WILBUR L.
  Butler, N. M.
    Presents Wilbur L. Cross.
    LYI:97

Crosswaith, Frank R.
  The Negro labor committee.
    (March 6, 1952). FON:857

CRUCIFIXION
  Albertus Magnus
    Meaning of the crucifixion.
    BREWE 1:147

Crummell, Alexander
  The Black woman of the
    South: her neglects and
    her needs. (Ocean Grove,
    N. J., August 15, 1883).
    FON:479

CRUSADES
  Bernard, Saint
    Why another crusade? BAS:43
    (outline only); BREWE 2:432

CTESIPHON
  Aeschines
    Against Ctesiphon.
    BREWE 1:114; COG:120

CUBA
  Castro, F.
    Cuba is no longer an American
    colony. LAA:127
    Give me liberty or give me
    death! BRN:136
  Clemens, J.
    Cuba and "manifest destiny."
    BREWE 4:1292
  Cleveland, G.
    Fourth annual message (second
    term). ANN 12:119;
    STAT 2:1824
  Garnet, H. H.
    A plea in behalf of the Cuban
    revolution. FON:380
  Giddings, J. R.
    Slavery and the annexation of
    Cuba. BREWE 6:2258
  Lodge, H. C.
    For intervention in Cuba.
    ANN 12:85
  McKinley, W.
    First annual message.
    ANN 12:161; STAT 2:1858
    Second annual message.
    STAT 2:1881
    Third annual message.
    STAT 2:1922

---- See also United States - For-
    eign relations - Cuba

CUFFE, PAUL
  Williams, P.
    A tribute to Captain Paul Cuffe.
    FON:28

Cullman, Howard S.
  Presents Roger L. Stevens.
    LYI:29

Culpeper, John See Colepeper,
  John

CULTURAL RELATIONS
  Thayer, R. H.
    America's cultural relations
    abroad. ANN 17:545

CULTURE
  Choate, R.
    State and mental culture.
    ANN 17:545
  Huxley, T. H.
    Science and culture.
    MCB:376
  Oliver, R. T.
    Culture and communication.
    ARS:19
  Tan Siew Sin
    Meeting place of cultures.
    MONS:115
  Thomas, D.
    Life among the culture vul-
    tures. ANN 17:239
  Young, O. D.
    How we meet ourselves
    (semi-centennial of Hendrix
    College). HURH:227

Curie, Marie
  Radium and the new concepts
    in chemistry (Nobel Lec-
    ture, Dec. 11, 1911).
    NOLC 1:202

CURIE, MARIE
  Dahlgren, E. W.
    Presentation [of the Nobel
    Prize for Chemistry to
    Marie Sklodowska Curie,
    Dec. 11, 1911].
    NOLC 1:199
  Harding, W. G.
    Presents Marie S. Curie.
    LYI:179
  Törnebladh, H. R.
    Presentation [of the Nobel
    Prize for Physics to Antoine
    Henri Becquerel, Pierre
    Curie and Marie Sklodowska-
    Curie, Dec. 11, 1903].
    NOLPH 1:47

Curie, Pierre
  Radioactive substances, espe-
    cially radium (Nobel Lec-
    ture for 1903, June 6,
    1905). NOLPH 1:73

CURIE, PIERRE
  Törnebladh, H. R.
    Presentation [of the Nobel
    Prize for Physics to Antoine
    Henri Becquerel, Pierre
    Curie and Marie Sklodowska-
    Curie, Dec. 11, 1903].
    NOLPH 1:47

Curran, John Philpot
  Against pensions. BREWE 4:1543
  Diversions of a Marquis.
    BREWE 4:1539
  England and English liberties--in
    the case of Rowan.
    BREWE 4:1546
  Farewell to the Irish Parliament.
    BREWE 4:1552
  For Peter Finnerty and free
    speech. BREWE 4:1537
  In the case of Justice Johnson--
    Civil liberty and arbitrary ar-
    rests. BREWE 4:1499
  Liberties of the indolent.
    BREWE 4:1550
  On government by attachment.
    BREWE 4:1557

CURRENCY See Money

CURRENCY QUESTION See Silver

Curtice, Harlow
  Automotive research at General
    Motors. ANN 17:379

Curtin, John
  We are fighting mad. MCA:154

Curtis, Benjamin Robbins
  Defense of President Johnson.
    BREWE 4:1563

Curtis, George William
  Duty of the American scholar.
    ANN 8:411
  Eulogy on Wendell Phillips.
    BREWE 4:1571
  His sovereignty under his hat.
    BREWE 4:1570
  Liberty under the law. BAS:141
    (outline only); LINS:249
  Public duty of educated men.
    ALS:179
  Puritan principle: liberty under
    law. Same as his Liberty un-
    der the law
  Wendell Phillips as a history-
    maker. Same as his Eulogy
    on Wendell Phillips

Curzon of Kedleston, George and
    others (Earl of Halsbury, Mar-
    quess of Landsdowne, Viscount
    Morley, and Earl of Rosebery)
  Debate on the Parliament Bill.
    (H. of Lords, August 9-10,
    1911). MCB:169

Cushing, Caleb
England and America in China.
BREWE 4:1583
Extermination of the Indians.
BREWE 4:1584
Primordial rights of the uni-
versal people.
BREWE 4:1577

CUSTER, GEORGE A.
Tanner, B. T.
The Sioux's revenge.
FON:443

Cutforth, René
Illuminations.   MDYG:35

CYCLOTRON
Lawrence, E. O.
The evolution of the cyclotron.
NOLPH 2:430

Cyprian, Saint, Bp. of Carthage
Unshackled living.
BREWE 4:1588

Cyril, Saint, Bp. of Jerusalem
Infinite artifices of nature.
BREWE 4:1594

- D -

D-DAY See World War, 1939-
1945 - Campaigns - Western
front

Dabney, Virginius
Facts and the founding fathers.
(Williamsburg, Va., Feb.
8, 1975). BA 1974-75:168

Dahlgren, E. W.
Presentation [of the Nobel Prize
for Chemistry to Marie
Sklodowska Curie, Dec. 11,
1911]. NOLC 1:199
Presentation [of the Nobel Prize
for Physics to Wilhelm
Wien, Dec. 11, 1911].
NOLPH 1:271

DAKOTA INDIANS
Tanner, B. T.
The Sioux's revenge.
FON:443

Dale, Sir Henry Hallett
Some recent extensions of the
chemical transmission of the
effects of nerve impulses
(Nobel Lecture, Dec. 12, 1936).
NOLM 2:402

DALE, SIR HENRY HALLETT
Liljestrand, G.
Presentation [of the Nobel Prize
for Physiology or Medicine to
Sir Henry Hallett Dale and Otto
Loewe, Dec. 12, 1936].
NOLM 2:397

Dale, James
Rehearsing with George Bernard
Shaw. MDYG:44

DALEN, NILS GUSTAF
Söderbaum, H. G.
Presentation [of the Nobel Prize
for Physics to Nils Gustaf
Dalen, 1912]. NOLPH 1:293

Dallas, George M.
Pennsylvania idea.
BREWE 4:1599

Dam, Henrik
The discovery of vitamin K, its
biological functions and therapeutical application (Nobel Lecture for 1943, Dec. 12, 1946).
NOLM 3:8

Damiani, Peter, Saint
New Testament history as allegory.
BREWE 4:1606
Secret of true greatness.
BREWE 4:1605

Damrin, Dora E.
The James Scholars and the university (Univ. of Illinois, Dec. 4,
1964). BRYF:528; BRYO:243

DAMS
Brandeis, L. D.
Ashwander rules. ANN 15:350
Roosevelt, F. D.
President reminds Congress of
the comprehensive program of
the Tennessee Valley Authority.
BAD:21

Daniel, John Warwick
Dedication of the Washington

monument. BREWE 4:1608
Was Jefferson Davis a traitor?
BREWE 4:1615

Daniels, Josephus
Presents Sir Norman Birkett.
LYI:135

Danton, George Jacques
Against imprisonment for debt.
BREWE 5:1628
Education, free and compulsory.
BREWE 5:1629
Freedom of worship.
BREWE 5:1631
How can France be saved?
(National Convention, Salle
du Manege, Paris, March
27, 1793). BRN:56
Let France be free.
BREWE 5:1626
Squeezing the sponge.
BREWE 5:1631
To dare again, ever to dare.
BREWE 5:1625

D'Arcy, Martin · See Sykes, C.,
jt. auth.

Darrow, Clarence
Against capital punishment.
BEN:149
Crime and criminals. ARS:142
Defense of Richard Loeb and
Nathan Leopold. (Chicago,
1924). HURH:196
"I am pleading that we over-
come cruelty with kindness
and hatred with love."
Same as his Defense of
Richard Loeb and Nathan
Leopold
To the jury; self-defense.
GRG:31

DARTMOUTH COLLEGE
Marshall, J.
Trustees of Dartmouth Col-
lege v. Woodward: opinion
for the Supreme Court.
ANN 4:522
Plumer, W.
State control of Dartmouth
College. ANN 4:420
Webster, D.
Dartmouth College case.
ANN 4:477; BREWE 10:3860

Dato Azmi See Azmi, Bin Haji
Mohamed

Dato David S. Marshall See Marshall, David Saul

Dato Sir Clough Thuraisingham See
Thuraisingham, Ernest Emmanuel
Sir Clough

DAUGHTERS OF THE AMERICAN
REVOLUTION
Roosevelt, F. D.
Immigrants and revolutionists.
ALA:93

Davenport, John
Responds to an introduction.
PRS:155
The saint's anchor-hold (1661).
JON:147

David, John K.
Responds to an introduction at a
Newcomen Society dinner.
PRS:151

Davidson, Gregg
Farmer, heal thyself!
BREWW:165

Davies, Samuel
Curse of cowardice. ANN 2:23;
POC:534

Davis, Angela
I am a black revolutionary woman.
(Dec., 1970 and Jan. 5, 1971-
2 statements). FON:1177
The legacy of George Jackson.
(August, 1971). FON:1191

Davis, Benjamin J.
The Negro people on the march.
(New York, June 23, 1956).
FON:902

Davis, Chester R.
Presents Will Durant. LYI:56

Davis, David
Ex parte Milligan, 1866: opinion
for the court. ANN 10:31
On appeal from the caucus.
BREWE 5:1634

Davis, George R.
Vietnam War: a Christian perspective. VI:46

Davis, Henry Winter
   Constitutional difficulties of re-
      construction. BREWE 5:1647
   Reasons for refusing to part
      company with the South.
      BREWE 5:1642

Davis, Jefferson
   Against Clay and compromise.
      BREWE 5:1660
   Announcing the secession of
      Mississippi. Same as his
      On withdrawing from the
      Union
   Final exhortation to the Con-
      federate people. ANN 9:557
   "If you will have it thus, we
      will invoke the God of our
      fathers." Same as his On
      withdrawing from the Union
   Inaugural address in 1861.
      ANN 9:238; BREWE 5:1656;
      ECH:137
   Message to Congress, April
      29, 1861. ANN 9:259
   On withdrawing from the Union
      (Washington, Jan. 21, 1861).
      BAS:71 (outline only);
      BREWE 5:1651; ECH:72;
      HURH:109
   Speech of President Davis at
      Richmond, June 1st, 1861.
      ECH:146
   War message. Same as his
      Message to Congress, April
      29, 1861

DAVIS, JEFFERSON
   Chandler, Z.
      On Jefferson Davis.
      BREWE 3:1030
   Daniel, J. W.
      Was Jefferson Davis a traitor?
      BREWE 4:1615

Davis, John W.
   Presents Lester B. Pearson.
      LYI:220

Davis, Ossie
   Malcolm was our manhood, our
      living black manhood.
      (Harlem, Feb. 27, 1965).
      FON:1010

Davis, Samuel H.
   We must assert our rightful
      claims and plead our own

cause. (Buffalo, N.Y., August
   15-19, 1843). FON:77

Davisson, Clinton Joseph
   The discovery of electron waves
      (Nobel Lecture, Dec. 13, 1937).
      NOLPH 2:387

DAVISSON, CLINTON JOSEPH
   Pleijel, H.
      Presentation [of the Nobel Prize
      for Physics to Clinton Joseph
      Davisson and George Paget
      Thomson, Dec. 13, 1937].
      NOLPH 2:387

Davitt, Michael
   Ireland a nation, self-chartered and
      self-ruled. BREWE 5:1666

Dawes, Charles Gates
   Acceptance [of the Nobel Prize for
      Peace, 1925, Dec. 10, 1926].
      NOLP 1:399

DAWES, CHARLES GATES
   Nansen, F.
      Speech at Award Ceremony
      [presenting the Nobel Prize for
      Peace to Joseph Austen Cham-
      berlain and Charles Gates
      Dawes for 1925, Dec. 10,
      1926]. NOLP 1:383

Dawes, Henry Laurens
   Tariff Commission of 1880.
      BREWE 5:1671

Dawson, Mathew
   My profession. (Baylor Univer-
      sity). CAPB:363

Day, James E.
   Introduces G. Keith Funston,
      president New York Stock Ex-
      change. PRS:10
   Introduces John L. Lewis, Amer-
      ican Labor leader. LYI:61

DAY, JAMES R.
   Milburn, J. G.
      Presents James R. Day.
      LYI:90

Day, William R. See McKenna, J.,
   Jt. auth.

Dayton, William L.
  Arraigning President Polk.
    BREWE 5:1676
  Issues against slavery forced
    by the Mexican War.
    BREWE 5:1679

DDT
  Neal, J.
    DDT: friend or foe?
    BREWW:183

Deakin, Alfred
  For a white Australia.
    MCA:88
  For the Federal Constitution.
    MCA:84

DEAKIN, ALFRED
  Hughes, W. M.
    Australian Judas. MCA:125

Dean, Vera Micheles
  Minds of the non-western world.
    ARS:234

DEATH
  Albertus Magnus.
    Blessed dead. BREWE 1:149
  Arnold, T.
    Realities of life and death.
    BREWE 1:173
  Chrysostom, J.
    Blessing of death.
    BREWE 3:1138
  Cranmer, T.
    Against the fear of death.
    BREWE 4:1458
  Everybody dies. BURT:178
  Trumbull, L.
    Announcing the death of
    Douglas. BREWE 9:3654

DEATH OF GOD THEOLOGY
  Bosley, H.
    Is God really dead?
    BA 1965-66:157

DEBATES AND DEBATING
  Eliezer, C. J.
    Democratic societies and
    debating societies.
    MONS:262
  Ford, G. R.
    The third presidential debate.
    BA 1976-77:30
  Goodman, J. B.
    Broadcast journalism: serv-

ing the democratic process.
  BA 1976-77:52
Klayton, R. J.
  Bureau of Forests and Waters
    should control pests by biologi-
    cal means rather than pesti-
    cides. BAS:188 (outline only)
Macios, M. A.
  Model studies of structural de-
    sign and construction should be
    conducted prior to the building
    of structure rather than on the
    site studies made after the
    completion of the project.
    BAS:193 (outline only)
  Suggestions for group discussion.
    PAE:192
Weicker, L. P.
  Televised debates.
    BA 1976-77:61
Zwerling, J. C.
  Federal Government should con-
    tinue its present housing pro-
    gram for low-income groups
    rather than change to the pro-
    posed rent subsidy plan.
    BAS:196 (outline only)

DeBeer, Sir Gavin
  Atlantis. MDYG:272

DeBow, James D. B.
  That feeling of hostility. CUR:52

DeBroglie, Louis
  The wave nature of the electron
    (Nobel Lecture, Dec. 12,
    1929). NOLPH 2:244

DE BROGLIE, LOUIS
  Oseen, C. W.
    Presentation [of the Nobel Prize
    for Physics to Louis-Victor de
    Broglie, Dec. 12, 1929].
    NOLPH 2:241

Debs, Eugene V.
  Capitalism and socialism. Same
    as his The Issue
  "I am prepared to receive your
    sentence." Same as his On
    receiving sentence
  The issue. ANN 13:137
  On receiving sentence. (Chicago,
    Sept. 1918). HURH:183

DEBS, EUGENE V.
  Brewer, D. J.

In Re Debs: opinion for the court. ANN 12:18

DEBTS
Danton, G. J.
Against imprisonment for debt. BREWE 5:1628

Debye, Petrus Josephus Wilhelmus
Methods to determine the electrical and geometrical structure of molecules (Nobel Lecture, Dec. 12, 1936). NOLC 2:383

DEBYE, PETRUS JOSEPHUS WILHELMUS
Westgren, A.
Presentation [of the Nobel Prize for Chemistry to Petrus Josephus Wilhelmus Debye, Dec. 12, 1936]. NOLC 2:379

DECISION-MAKING
Rusk, D.
Formulating foreign policy. ANN 18:20

DEDICATION ADDRESSES
Dedication of a musical instrument. BNH:65
Greetings to people on day of dedication. BOS:67
Quirino, E.
Commemorating a national event. CURM:239
Suggestions for preparation of a speech of dedication. MILS:7

---- BRIDGES
Roosevelt, F. D.
Quarantining the aggressors. ANN 15:502; BEN:93; BOORA 2:847; ROD:263

---- BUILDINGS
Brennan, W. J., Jr.
Conciliation between the press and the law. BA 1979-80:119
Califano, J. A.
A tribute to the man of the people. BA 1977-78:197
Cornish, D. T.
A warrior against fate. BA 1975-76:207

Curtice, H.
Automotive research at General Motors. ANN 17:379
Dedication services of a building. BNH:61
Dedication services of a Christian home. BNH:59
Dedications of a building. BOS:61
Holmes, O. W., Jr.
Path of the law. BOORA 2:593
Lee Kuan Yew
Lesson we have to learn (opening new Science Tower at University of Singapore). MONS:361
Livingston, H. J.
Responds to an introduction and speaks briefly at the dedication of a new manufacturing plant. PRS:130

---- CEMETERIES
Lincoln, A.
Gettysburg address. See Lincoln, A. Gettysburg address

---- CHURCHES
Appreciation on a day of dedication (3 examples). BNH:68
Dedication of a Christian home. BOS:59
Dedication of a pastor's study and church office. BNH:66
Greetings to people on day of dedication (2 examples). BNH:67
Hildebert of Lavardin
Rebecca at the well. BREWE 7:2502

---- CORNERSTONES
Roosevelt, T.
Man with the muck-rake. ARS:102; GRG:24; HURH:291; LINS:283; OLIS:217
Seward, W. H.
Prosperity and education. ANN 6:140

---- EXHIBITIONS
Washington, B. T.
Address at the opening of the Atlanta Exposition. ANN 12:9; BAPRR:255; BAS:77 (outline only); BRYF:492; FON:577; LINS:263; OE:82; SMHV:94

---- LIBRARIES
Dedication of a library (2 examples). BNH:64
Dedications of a library.
BOS:64
Nixon, R. M.
Campus revolutionaries.
BAAGB:386

---- MONUMENTS
Abdul Rahman, T.
Lest we forget (at unveiling ceremony of National monument in Kuala Lumpur).
MONS:34
Blair, F. P.
Deathbed of Benton.
BREWE 2:514
Daniel, J. W.
Dedication of the Washington monument.   BREWE 4:1608
Douglass, F.
Address for the unknown dead. ALA:51
Oration in memory of Abraham Lincoln (at unveiling of Freedman's monument, Washington, D.C.).
FRIP:242
Evangelista, T.
The needs of a nation.
CURM:160
McKinley, W.
American patriotism (at dedication of Cuyahoga County Soldiers' and Sailors' monument in Cleveland).
BREWE 8:2899
Grant (at dedication of Grant monument in New York City).   BREWE 8:2905
Webster, D.
Bunker Hill monument.
BREWE 10:3828; HURH:62;
LINS:145

---- MUSICAL INSTRUMENTS
Dedications of a musical instrument. BOS:65

---- PARKS
Roosevelt, T.
New nationalism (at dedication of John Brown Memorial Park, Osawatomic, Kansas).
ANN 13:250; BOORA 2:711

---- PASTOR'S STUDY
Dedications of a pastor's study and church office. BOS:66

---- SCULPTURE
Haydon, H.
Testimony of sculpture.
MOP:384

---- STATUES
Blair, F. P.
Character and work of Benton.
BREWE 2:509
Choate, J. H.
Farragut. BREWE 3:1109
Crispi, F.
At the unveiling of Garibaldi's statue. BREWE 4:1467
Depew, C. M.
Unveiling the Statue of Liberty.
BREWE 3:1782

DEFEAT
Houston, S.
On his defeat as a Union candidate. BREWE 7:2530

DEFECTORS, POLITICAL
Ward, E. J.
Petrov case. MCA:196

DEFENSE, SPEECHES OF
Adams, J.
On the Boston Massacre.
BREWE 1:45; POC:108
Aiken, F. A.
Defense of Mrs. Mary E. Surratt. BREWE 1:120
Andocides
On the mysteries. SAG:61
Bernard, F.
Speech to the Council and House of Representatives. POC:227
Brougham and Vaux, H. P. B.
Closing argument for Queen Caroline. BREWE 2:665
Brown, J.
Last speech at Charleston, West Virginia. ALA:21;
ANN 9:143; BOS:44; HURH:103
Burke, E.
Principle in politics: speech at Bristol, previous to the election, 1780 (defends his Parliamentary conduct).
BREWE 2:812; BRYH:211
Cicero, M. T.
For the poet Archias.

BREWE 3:1189
Cobbett, W.
Man on the tower (defending
himself against a charge of
libel). BREWE 4:1321
Cranmer, T.
Speech at the stake.
BREWE 4:1455; BRYH:60
Crooks, J.
Defense of "The death of a
President." REIR:182
Curran, J. P.
England and English liberties
--in the case of Rowan.
BREWE 4:1546
In the case of Justice John-
son--civil liberty and ar-
bitrary arrests.
BREWE 4:1499
Curtis, B. R.
Defence of President Johnson.
BREWE 4:1563
Darrow, C.
Defense of Richard Loeb and
Nathan Leopold. HURH:196
To the jury; self-defense.
GRG:31
Debs, E. V.
On receiving sentence.
HURH:183
Demosthenes
On the crown. BREWE 5:1686;
COG:151
Deseze, R.
Defending Louis XVI.
BREWE 5:1811
Dexter, S.
"Higher law" of self-defense.
BREWE 5:1825
Emmet, R.
Protest against sentence as
a traitor. BREWE 6:2030
Engel, G.
Address at trial, Chicago,
October 7-9, 1886.
ACC:43; PAF:37
Erskine, T.
Free speech and fundamental
rights: defense of Tom
Paine. BREWE 6:2069;
CLAYP:166
Homicidal insanity (J. Had-
field). BREWE 6:2058;
BRYH:294
In defense of Thomas Hardy.
BREWE 6:2066
Speech in behalf of John
Stockdale. BREWE 6:2050

Evarts, W. M.
Weakest spot in the American
system (defense at impeachment
of A. Johnson). BREWE 6:2082
Fielden, S.
Address at trial, Chicago, Oc-
tober 7-9, 1886. ACC:49;
PAF:41
Fischer, A.
Address at trial, Chicago, Oc-
tober 7-9, 1886. ACC:36;
PAF:32
Garry, C. R.
In defense of Huey Newton.
ERP:161
Gibbons, J.
Defense of the Knights of Labor.
ANN 11:131
Grattan, H.
Invective against Corry.
BREWE 6:2330
Hamilton, W.
A defense of the Negro.
FON:26
Hampden, J.
Patriot's duty defined: against
own impeachment.
BREWE 6:2385
Harper, R. G.
Defending Judge Chase.
BREWE 6:2425
Harrison, T.
Speech on the scaffold.
BREWE 6:2421
Holborne, R.
In defense of John Hampden.
BREWE 7:2524
Houston, S.
His defense at the Bar of the
House. BREWE 7:2532
Johnson, L. B.
A president defends his policies
by argument from authorities.
JEF:331; JEFF:316
Kamin, L.
Defense of the Jew.
CAPB:366
Langston, C. H.
Should colored men be subject
to the pains and penalties of
the Fugitive Slave Law?
FON:208
Lewis, D.
His speech on the scaffold.
BREWE 7:2772
Lingg, L.
Address at trial, Chicago, Oc-
tober 7-9, 1886. ACC:39;

PAF:34
Logan, John, Chief of the
Mingoes
On the murder of his family.
ALA:9; BOORA 1:62;
BREWE 7:2569
Luther, M.
Before the Diet of Worms.
BREWE 7:2829
MacArthur, D.
Defends his conduct of the
war in Korea. ALS:243;
ANN 17:79; ARS:279; BAS:82
(outline only); BEN:113;
BOSR:22; GRG:88; HURH:293;
HURS:214; LINS:337
Mackintosh, J.
In behalf of free speech: on
the trial of Jean Peltier ac-
cused of libelling Napoleon
Bonaparte. BREWE 8:2919
Mirabeau, H. G. R.
Against the charge of treason.
BREWE 8:3039
More, T.
Speech when on trial for life.
BREWE 8:3062
Morse, W. L.
Rejoiner to Joseph Alsop's
attack. BRR:72
Verbiage of defense and at-
tack. BRR:71
Neebe, O.
Address at trial, Chicago,
October 7-9, 1886. ACC:29;
PAF:28
Nixon, R. M.
Apologia. MAC:258;
MACR:269; REIR:191
Parsons, A. R.
Address at trial, Chicago,
October 7-9, 1886.
ACC:90; PAF:65
Phillips, W.
Murder of Lovejoy.
ALS:161; HURH:74
Quincy, J., 1744-1775
Defence of British soldiers,
1770. BREWE 9:3269;
POC:95
Raleigh, W.
Speech on the scaffold.
BREWE 9:3280; BRYH:104
Randolph, E.
In defence of Aaron Burr,
1807. BREWE 9:3284
Robespierre, M.
Defense from the charge

of tyranny. BREWE 9:3341
His defense of terrorism.
BREWE 9:331
Rumbold, R.
Against booted and spurred
privilege. BREWE 9:3352
Sacco, N. and Vanzetti, B.
Proclaim their innocence.
ALA:85; ANN 14:527
Schwab, M.
Address at trial, Chicago, Oc-
tober 7-9, 1886. ACC:24;
PAF:25
Sidney, A.
Governments for the people and
not the people for government
(scaffold speech). BREWE 9:3454
Socrates
On being declared guilty.
BAS:67 (outline only);
BREWE 9:3493
Spies, A.
Address at trial, Chicago, Oc-
tober 7-9, 1886. ACC:1;
ANN 11:117; PAF:11
Strafford, T. W.
Defense before the House of
Lords. BREWE 9:3540;
BRYH:131
Talfourd, T. N.
Queen against Moxon-Shelley
as a blasphemer.
BREWE 9:3565
Taylor, F. W.
On scientific management.
BOORA 2:740
Tooke, J. H.
On the "Murders at Lexington
and Concord" (at his trial for
libel). BREWE 9:3633
Vane, H.
At his trial for high treason.
BREWE 10:3685
Walpole, R.
On patriots (at motion to dis-
miss him from Council).
BREWE 10:3724
White, G. H.
Defense of the Negro race.
FON:635
Zola, E.
Appeal for Dreyfus. BAS:110
(outline only); BREWE 10:3931

DeGaulle, Charles
France: the third world power.
MDV:38

DeGeer, G.
Presentation [of the Nobel Prize
for Chemistry to Walther
Hermann Nernst, 1920,
Dec. 12, 1921]. NOLC 1:349

DEGREES, ACADEMIC See Ac-
ceptance speeches - De-
grees, Academic

Delany, Martin Robinson
Advice to ex-slaves. (St.
Helena Island, South Caro-
lina, July, 1865). FON:318

Delbrück, Max
A physicist's renewed look at
biology--twenty years later
(Nobel Lecture, Dec. 10,
1969). NOLM 4:404

DELBRÜCK, MAX
Gard, S.
Presentation [of the Nobel
Prize for Physiology or
Medicine to Max Delbrück,
Alfred D. Hershey, and
Salvador E. Luria, Dec.
10, 1969]. NOLM 4:401

DELEDDA, GRAZIA
Schück, H.
Presentation [of the Nobel
Prize for Literature to
Grazia Deledda, 1926].
NOB 5:117; NOL:232

De Leon, Daniel
Aims of socialism. ANN 12:106
Political power of labor.
ANN 13:19

DEMENTIA PARALYTICA
Wagner-Jauregg, J.
The treatment of dementia
paralytica by malaria
inoculation. NOLM 2:159

Demmert, William G.
Tribal chartered education.
MAES:156

DEMOCRACY
Barnave, A. P. J. M.
Representative democracy
against majority absolutism.
BREWE 1:218
Beaconsfield, B. D.

Against democracy for England.
BREWE 1:296
Beecher, H. W.
Success of American democracy
(anniversary of attack on Fort
Sumter). OLIS:191
Brooke, E. W.
Responsibilities inherent in a
constitutional democracy.
BA 1973-74:74
Cleon
On the punishment of the My-
tileneans. BREWE 4:1298
Desmoulins, C.
Live free or die.
BREWE 5:1815
Douglas, W. O.
Function of democracy.
BAP:275
Jefferson, T.
First inaugural: democracy
defined. AND:116; ANN 1:143;
BOORA 1:212; BREWE 7:2612;
HURH:48; LINS:140; OLIS:28;
USINAU:13; USINAUG:13
Johnson, J. W.
Our democracy and the ballot.
FON:757
Jordan, B. C.
Keynote address to the Demo-
cratic National Convention.
BA 1976-77:11; JAM:7;
LINRST:334
Lilienthal, D. E.
My faith in democracy.
ALA:111
Lowe, R.
Coming of democracy.
MCB:138
Monroe, J.
Federal experiments in history.
BREWE 8:3041
Parker, T.
Present crisis in American af-
fairs. ANN 8:372
Pickens, W.
Kind of democracy the Negro
race expects. FON:601
Razak, T. A.
Crucial cross-roads of history.
MONS:64
Democracy and development in
Malaysia. MONS:80
Roosevelt, F. D.
Address at University of Penn-
sylvania, September 20, 1940.
FRIP:324
Address to White House

Correspondents' Association
dinner, March 15, 1941.
CROCK:11
Fireside chat on party pri-
maries, June 24, 1938.
FRIP:324
Third inaugural address.
USINAU:244
Stevenson, A. E.
Prospects for democracy
around the world.   LINS:350
Tyndall, J.
Democracy and higher in-
tellect.   BREWE 9:3668
Willkie, W. L.
Loyal opposition.   GRG:63;
HURH:243
Wilson, W.
Eighth annual message.
STAT 3:2608
The nature of democracy in
the United States.   FRIP:270

---- SINGAPORE
Lee Kuan Yew
Leaders' responsibility in
sustaining a democratic
system.   MONSA:269

DEMOCRATIC CONVENTIONS
See   Political Conventions,
Democratic

DEMOCRATIC PARTY
Barkley, A. W.
Record of Democratic Party.
BLY:233
Doolittle, J. R.
In favor of re-union.
BREWE 5:1894
Jordan, B. C.
Keynote address to the
Democratic National Con-
vention.   BA 1976-77:11;
JAM:7; LINRST:334
Schwellenbach, L. B.
First seven years of the
New Deal: let's view the
record.   BAD:47

Demosthenes
First Olynthiac oration.
SAG:199
First Philippic.   COG:40;
SAG:188
For Megalopolis.   Same as
his Oration for the
Megalopolitans

On the Chersoneus.   SAG:235
On the crown.   BREWE 5:1688;
COG:151
Oration for the Megalopolitans.
SAG:173
Oration on the liberty of the
Rhodians.   SAG:180
Oration on the peace.
BREWE 5:1759; SAG:223
Second Olynthiac.   BREWE 5:1754;
COG:56; SAG:205
Second Philippic.   BREWE 5:1763;
SAG:228
Third Olynthiac.   SAG:212
Third Philippic.   COG:91;
SAG:249

DEMOSTHENES
Aeschines
Against Ctesiphon.
BREWE 1:114; COG:120
Dewey, O.
Genius of Demosthenes.
BREWE 5:1822
Lytton, E. G. E. L.
Demosthenes and the nobility
of the classics.   BREWE 8:2869

Deniehy, Daniel Henry
On the Constitution Bill.   MCA:26

Dennis, David Worth   See   Jordan,
B. C., jt. auth.

DEOXYRIBONUCLEIC ACID
Hershey, A. D.
Idiosyncrasies of DNA structure.
NOLM 4:417
Kornberg, A.
The biologic synthesis of
deoxyribonucleic acid.
NOLM 3:665

DEPARTMENT STORES
Wanamaker, J.
On the department store.
BOORA 2:632

Depew, Chauncey M.
Columbian oration.   BREWE 5:1769
England and America since the
Spanish War.   BREWE 5:1790
Liberty enlightening the world.
Same as his Unveiling the
Statue of Liberty
Military spirit in America.
BREWE 5:1785
"A perfect woman, nobly planned,

to warm, to comfort, and
command. " Same as his
Woman
Poetry and politics in Britain.
BREWE 5:1796
Presents William Jennings
Bryan. LYI:227
Unveiling the Statue of Liberty.
BREWE 5:1782
Woman. (New York, Dec. 22,
1875). HURH:125

DEPRESSIONS, BUSINESS See
Business cycles; United
States - Economic conditions

Depta, Mark
Aims and purposes of the FFA.
BREWW:157

Derby, Edward George Villiers
Stanley, 17th Earl of
Emancipation of British Negroes.
BREWE 5:1800

DERELICTS
Karos, P. A.
Haven of the defeated.
ARS:148

Dering, Sir Edward
For the encouragement of
learning. BREWE 5:1805
Religious controversy in Parliament. BREWE 5:1808

Deseze, Raymond
Defending Louis XVI.
BREWE 5:1811

Desmoulins, Camille
Live free or die.
BREWE 5:1815

De Sola Pool, David
Man's advocate. WALE:33

De Tuncq, Darlyne
UN: symbol or reality?
SCHW:165

DEUTERIUM
Urey, H. C.
Some thermodynamic properties of hydrogen and deuterium. NOLC 2:339

DeVries, Calvin
Standards that stand. SCHW:15

D'Ewes, Sir Simon
Antiquity of Cambridge.
BREWE 5:1818

Dewey, John
School and social progress.
ANN 12:255

Dewey, Orville
Genius of Demosthenes.
BREWE 5:1822
Rust of riches. BREWE 5:1823

Dewey, Thomas E.
Acceptance speech, Chicago, Illi-
nois, June 28, 1944. SIN:205
Acceptance speech, Philadelphia,
Pennsylvania, June 24, 1948.
SIN:229
Campaign speech, Des Moines,
Iowa, September 20, 1948.
SIN:232
Campaign speech, Philadelphia,
Pennsylvania, September 7,
1944. Same as his Opening
campaign speech in Philadel-
phia
Corporate state not an American
system (campaign speech, Oc-
tober 7, 1944). ROD:333
Opening campaign speech in Phila-
delphia (Sept. 7, 1944).
SIN:210
Public service. ANN 16:471

Dexter, Samuel
"Higher law" of self-defense.
BREWE 5:1825

DIABETES
Banting, F. G.
Diabetes and insulin.
NOLM 2:50
Houssay, B. A.
The role of the hypophysis in
carbohydrate metabolism and
in diabetes. NOLM 3:210

DIAMONDS
Koblish, C. F.
Diamonds, their mining, sell-
ing, perfecting, and the deter-
mining of their quality.
BAS:206 (outline only)

Diaz, Porfirio
  Mexican progress.
    BREWE 5:1832

Dickerson, Mahlon
  Alien and Sedition Acts of the
    Adams administration.
    BREWE 5:1836

Dickey, John Sloan
  Betrayal of idealism (convoca-
    tion address).
    BA 1967-68:136

Dickinson, Daniel S.
  Rebuking Senator Clemens
    of Alabama.   BREWE 5:1844

DICKINSON, JACOB M.
  Lewis, J. H.
    Introduction of Jacob M.
    Dickinson.   LYI:217

Dickinson, John
  Before the Pennsylvania As-
    sembly, March 24, 1764.
    POC:182
  Declaration of the Colonies on
    taking up arms.
    BREWE 5:1849
  Speech against independence.
    ANN 2:438
  Speech against the petition
    to change the form of gov-
    ernment.   Same as his
    Before the Pennsylvania
    Assembly, March 24, 1764

DICTATORS AND DICTATORSHIP
  LaFollette, P. F.
    Party of our time.   BAD:120
  Roosevelt, F. D.
    Address to White House
    Correspondents' Association
    dinner, March 15, 1941.
    CROCK:11
    Message to Congress, Janu-
    ary 4, 1939.   STAT 3:2842

Didon, Henri
  Christ and higher criticism.
    BREWE 5:1856

Diels, Otto Paul Hermann
  Description and importance of
    the aromatic basic skeleton
    of the steroids (Nobel Lec-
    ture, 1950).   NOLC 3:259

DIELS, OTTO PAUL HERMANN
  Fredga, A.
    Presentation [of the Nobel Prize
    for Chemistry to Otto Paul Her-
    mann Diels and Kurt Adler,
    Dec. 12, 1950].   NOLC 3:255

DIENE SYNTHESIS
  Adler, K.
    Diene synthesis and related re-
    action types.   NOLC 3:267

Digby, Lord See Bristol, G. D.

DIGESTION
  Pavlov, I. P.
    Physiology of digestion.
    NOLM 1:141

Dilke, Charles Wentworth
  America.   BREWE 5:1873
  Omphalism.   BREWE 5:1880

Dinwoodie, S. David
  Inner city--our shame.   ARS:216

Dirac, Paul Adrien Maurice
  Theory of electrons and positrons
    (Nobel Lecture, Dec. 12, 1933).
    NOLPH 2:320

DIRAC, PAUL ADRIEN MAURICE
  Pleijel, H.
    Presentation [of the Nobel Prize
    for Physics for 1932 to Werner
    Heisenberg and for 1933 to Er-
    win Schrodinger and Paul Adrien
    Maurice Dirac, Dec. 11, 1933].
    NOLPH 2:283

Dirksen, Everett
  Presents Robert A. Taft.   LYI:210
  Responds to introduction.
    PRS:122

DISARMAMENT
  Eisenhower, D. D.
    First steps in disarmament.
    ANN 17:330
  Noel-Baker, P. J.
    Peace and the arms race (Nobel
    Lecture, Dec. 11, 1959).
    NOLP 3:186
  Quidde, L.
    Security and disarmament
    (Nobel Lecture, Dec. 10, 1927).
    NOLP 2:47

DISCRIMINATION
  Brockett, J. A.
    Reply to Grady. ANN 11:250
  Bunche, R. J.
    Human relations in world
      perspective. FON:882
  Deakin, A.
    For a white Australia.
      MCA:88
  Douglass, F.
    Color line in America.
      ANN 10:584
  Hains, J.
    Lamp of freedom. SCHW:6
  Hood, W. R.
    Uncle Tom is dead!
      FON:843
  Humphreys, B. G.
    Justice but not equality for
      the Negro. ANN 9:626
  Randolph, A. P.
    Liberty, justice and democ-
      racy. SMHV:110
  Rylaarsdam, J.
    Undesirable one. SCHW:1
  Wright, T. S.
    Prejudice against the colored
      man. FON:61

DISCRIMINATION IN EMPLOYMENT
  Bulkley, W. L.
    Race prejudice as viewed
      from an economic stand-
      point. FON:680

DISCUSSIONS See Debates and
    debating

Disraeli, Benjamin See Beacons-
    field, Benjamin Disraeli,
    1st Earl of

DISSENTERS
  Boorstin, D. J.
    Dissent, dissension and the
      news. BA 1967-68:125;
      JEF:187; JEFF:181; LINR:203
  Bronowski, J.
    Protest-past and present.
      BA 1969-70:119
  Griswold, E. N.
    Dissent, protest, and dis-
      obedience. ANN 18:670;
      BA 1967-68:141; JEF:196
  Smith, M. C.
    Declaration of conscience--
      twenty years later.
      BA 1969-70:133

Ditzen, Lowell Russell
  The right ticket but the wrong
    train (Washington). REID:404

DIVORCE
  Rogers, J.
    Day before Christmas.
      KEO:232; STOT:269
  Stanton, E. C.
    Address on the Divorce Bill,
      1861. BOORA 1:367

Dix, John Adams
  Christianity and politics.
    BREWE 5:1883

Dixon, Owen
  Law and the scientific expert.
    MCA:176

Dod, Albert B.
  Value of truth. BREWE 5:1885

DOGS
  Vest, G. G.
    Man's best friend--his dog.
      ALA:45; HURH:161

Dohrer, Jean
  Our forgotten man. (Aberdeen,
    S.D., Feb. 1971). LINRS:269

Domack, Gerhard Johannes Paul
  Further progress in chemotherapy
    of bacterial infections (Nobel
    Lecture for 1939, Dec. 12,
    1947). NOLM 2:490

Domiano, Paul
  Break down at United (Swimming
    Pool Company). REIR:38

DOMINICAN REPUBLIC
  Grant, U. S.
    For annexation (of Dominican
      Republic). ANN 10:231
  Sumner, C.
    Against annexation (of the Dom-
      inican Republic). ANN 10:233

---- See also United States - Foreign
    Relations - Dominican Republic

Dondero, George A.
  Communism in our schools (1946).
    (Washington, June 14, 1946).
    DAVF:296
  Modern art shackled to communism.

(Washington, August 16,
1949). DAVF:302

Donne, John
   Man immortal, body and soul.
      BREWE 5:1888
   Sermon preached at St. Paul's
      (Easter Day, 1625).
      BRYH:109

Donner, Frederic G.
   Responds to an introduction.
      PRS:150

Donovan, Hedley
   Presents Henry R. Luce.
      LYI:103

Donovan, William J.
   Call for a Central Intelligence
      Agency. ANN 16:391

Doolittle, James R.
   Attitude of the West in the
      Civil War. BREWE 5:1891
   In favor of re-union.
      BREWE 5:1894

Dorr, Thomas
   People's right to remake their
      constitution. ANN 7:56

Dorset, Edward Sackville, 4th
      Earl of
   In favor of slitting Prynne's
      nose. BREWE 5:1899

Dougherty, Daniel
   "Hancock the superb."
      BREWE 5:1904

Douglas, Lewis W.
   Presents Lord Halifax. LYI: 222

Douglas, Paul H. See Russell,
   R., jt. auth.

DOUGLAS, PAUL H.
   Burgess, W. R.
      Presents Paul H. Douglas.
      LYI:231

Douglas, Stephen A.
   Campaign speech for United
      States Senate--Chicago,
      July 9, 1858. Same as his
      Reply to Lincoln at Chicago,
      July 9, 1858

Defense of the Kansas-Nebraska
   Bill (January 30, 1854).
   ANN 8:254
"Expansion" and co-operation with
   England. BREWE 5:1918
Fifth joint debate at Galesburg,
   October 7, 1858. ANN 9:22
First debate with Lincoln. Same
   as his Reply to Lincoln at
   Chicago, July 9, 1858
Issues of 1861. BREWE 5:1929
John Brown raid. BREWE 5:1926
Kansas and "Squatter sovereignty."
   BREWE 5:1924
"Leave the people free to do as
   they please." Same as his
   Reply to Lincoln, Freeport,
   August 27, 1858
Lincoln-Douglas joint debate at
   Alton, October 15, 1858.
   ANN 9:30
Opening speech of Lincoln-Douglas
   debate, Ottawa, August 21,
   1858. ANN 9:8
Reply to Lincoln at Chicago, July
   9, 1858. ANN 9:4; BAS:45
   (outline only); OLIS:133
Reply to Lincoln, Freeport, August
   27, 1858. ANN 9:17;
   BREWE 5:1912; HURH:94
Reply to the Jonesboro speech.
   ANN 9:20

DOUGLAS, STEPHEN A.
   Cox, S. S.
      Stephen A. Douglas and his place
      in history. BREWE 4:1449
   Trumbull, L.
      Announcing the death of Douglas.
      BREWE 9:3654

Douglas, William O.
   Function of democracy. BAP:275
   Responds to an introduction.
      PRS:161

---- See also following jt. auths.
   Brennan, W. J.; Jackson, R.
   H.

Douglass, Frederick
   The abilities and possibilities of
      our race. (Baltimore, Oct. 1,
      1865. Opening of the Douglass
      Institute). FON:326
   Address for the unknown loyal
      dead. ALA:51
   The claims of the Negro ethno-

logically considered. (Western Reserve College, July
12, 1854). FON:144
Color line in America (Louis-
ville, Ky., Sept. 24, 1883).
ANN 10:584; FON:491
Fourth of July. Same as his
Slavery: speech at Rochester, July 5, 1852
Fourth of July oration. Same
as his What to the slave is
the Fourth of July?
I denounce the so-called eman-
cipation as a stupendous
fraud. (Washington, D.C.,
April 16, 1888). FON:520
If there is no struggle there
is no progress. (Canan-
daigua, N.Y., August 4,
1857). FON:197
Lecture on slavery no. 1.
Same as his Nature of
slavery (speech at Roches-
ter, New York, December
1, 1850)
The meaning of July fourth for
the Negro. Same as his
Slavery: speech at Roches-
ter, July 5, 1852
"Men of color, to arms!"
(March 2, 1863). OE:49
The mission of the war.
(Cooper Institute, N.Y.,
January 13, 1864). FON:283
Nature of slavery (speech at
Rochester, New York,
December 1, 1850).
BOSR:113; FRIP:222
Oration in memory of Abraham
Lincoln (at unveiling of
Freedmen's monument,
Washington, D.C.).
FRIP:242
Plea for free speech in Boston
(Boston, Dec. 3, 1860).
BREWE 5:1906; FON:244
Reception speech at Finsbury
Chapel, Moorsfield, Eng-
land. (May 12, 1846).
OE:30; SMHV:31
Reception speech in England.
Same as his Reception speech
at Finsbury Chapel, Moors-
field, England
Slavery: speech at Rochester,
July 5, 1852. FON:104;
SMHR:125
Speech on the Declaration of

Independence. Same as his
What to the slave is the Fourth
of July?
There is a better day coming.
CUR:173
What is my duty as an anti-slavery
voter? (April 25, 1856).
FRIP:229
What the black man wants.
(Mass. Anti-Slavery Society,
1865). MDT:175
What to the slave is the Fourth
of July? (July 4, 1852).
JAM:19; OE:41
Woman suffrage. (Washington,
D.C. International Council of
Women, April, 1888).
FON:517

Douglass, H. Ford
I do not believe in the antislavery
of Abraham Lincoln. (Fram-
ingham, Mass., July 4, 1860).
FON:232

DOUGLASS INSTITUTE
Douglass, F.
The abilities and possibilities
of our race. FON:326

Dow, Lorenzo, Jr.
Hope and despair.
BREWE 5:1934
Improvement in America.
BREWE 5:1933

Dowling, Alexander
Constitutionality of a compulsory
school law: opinion for the
court. ANN 12:417

Downing, George T.
May Hungary be free. (New
York, Dec. 9, 1851).
FON:102

DRAFT See Conscription

DRAFT RIOTS, 1863
Pennington, J. W. C.
The position and duties of the
colored people. FON:271

Drake, Charles D.
Against "Copperheads."
BREWE 5:1936

DRAMA - IRELAND
    Yeats, W. B.
        The Irish dramatic move-
        ment. NOL:201

Drayton, William Henry
    Charge to the Grand Juries,
        November 5 & 15, 1774.
        POC:297

Drazin, Nathan
    From the summit. WALE:34

DRED SCOTT DECISION
    Breckenridge, J. C.
        Dred Scott decision, Decem-
        ber 1859. BREWE 2:615
    Lincoln, A.
        Dred Scott Decision.
        ANN 8:459
    Taney, R. B.
        Dred Scott Case: opinion
        for the Supreme Court.
        ANN 8:440

Dreier, Alex
    Introduces the Honorable Wil-
        liam Proxmire, United
        States Senator from Wiscon-
        sin. PRS:34

DRESS See Clothing and dress

Dreyfus, A. Stanley
    Leo Baeck. WALE:207

DREYFUS, ALFRED
    Labori, P.
        Conspiracy against Dreyfus.
        BREWE 7:2684
    Zola, E.
        Appeal for Dreyfus.
        BAS:110 (outline only);
        BREWE 10:3931

Driberg, Tom See Sykes, C.,
    jt. auth.

Drier, Alex
    Introduces James T. Quirk.
        PRS:18

DRUGS
    Rindo, J. P.
        Life, librium, and the pur-
        suit of happiness.
        LINRST:230

Drumm, Streuby L.
    War on prosperity. CAPG:185

Drummond, Henry
    Greatest thing in the world.
        BREWE 5:1941
    Preparation for learning.
        BREWE 5:1959
    Talk on books. BREWE 5:1964

Drummond, Roscoe
    Responds to introduction. PRS:123

DuBois, W. E. Burghardt
    Address to the National Negro
        Convention. (May 31, 1909).
        OE:88
    Behold the land. (Columbia, S.C.,
        Oct. 20, 1946). FON:837
    The great migration north.
        (1918). FON:721
    Politics and industry. (New York,
        May 31 and June 1, 1909).
        FON:673
    Shall the negro be encouraged to
        seek cultural equality? (Chi-
        cago, March 17, 1929).
        FON:772
    The value of agitation. (1906).
        FON:663

DUBOIS, W. E. BURGHARDT
    King, M. L., Jr.
        Honoring Dr. DuBois.
        SMHR:204

Dubos, René
    Humanizing the earth. (December
        29, 1972). BA 1972-73:149
    Social attitudes and technological
        civilization (Harvard Univ.,
        June 6, 1978). BA 1978-79:11
    Theology of the earth.
        BA 1969-70:83

Ducommun, Elie
    The futility of war demonstrated
        by history (Nobel Lecture for
        1902, Oslo, May 16, 1904).
        NOLP 1:17

DUCOMMUN, ELIE
    Løvland, J. G.
        Toast to E. Ducommun.
        NOLP 1:15

DUELING
    Against dueling. BREWE 1:199;
        BRYH:96

Duffey, Joseph D.
    General education: the rule of
    the humanities (Univ. of
    Rhode Island, Oct. 24, 1977).
    BA 1977-78:146

DUFFIELD, EDWARD D.
    Hedges, J. E.
        Presents Edward D. Duf-
        field. LYI:69

DuGard, Roger Martin
    Acceptance [of the Nobel Prize
    for Literature, 1937].
    NOB 14:9; NOL:348

DUGARD, ROGER MARTIN
    Hallström, P.
        Presentation [of the Nobel
        Prize for Literature to
        Roger Martin DuGard, 1937].
        NOB 14:3; NOL:342

Dulles, John Foster
    Containment or liberation?
        ANN 17:204
    "The fact is that today any
        problem in any part of the
        world ramifies into almost
        every part of the world."
        Same as his Modern foreign
        policy
    Modern foreign policy. (Wash-
        ington, April 11, 1955).
        HURH:324
    Peace through law. ANN 17:528
    Strategy of massive retaliation.
        ANN 17:250
    Why the Arbenz government was
        overthrown in Guatemala.
        LAA:117

DULUTH
    Knott, J. P.
        Glories of Duluth. BLY:135;
        BREWE 7:2653

Dumper, Anthony Charles
    Church in a secular state.
    MONS:485

Dunbar, Roxanne
    Women's liberation: where
    the movement is today and
    where it's going. (Nat.
    Org. for Women, May,
    1970). STOT:311

DUNKIRK
    Churchill, Sir W. L. S.
        Dunkirk. MCB:498

Dunlap, David E.
    The world needs our help.
    BREWW:98

Dunn, Oscar J.
    We ask an equal chance in the
    race of life. (Louisiana, July
    31, 1868). FON:355

DuPont, Henry B.
    Greatest invention of them all.
    ANN 17:530

DURANT, WILLIAM J. (WILL)
    Davis, C. R.
        Presents Will Durant. LYI:56

Durfee, Job
    Influence of scientific discovery
    and invention on social and
    political progress. ANN 7:128
    Science and political progress.
    Same as his Influence of sci-
    entific discovery and invention
    on social and political progress

DuVall, W. O.
    Presents Billy Graham. LYI:160

Dwight, Timothy
    On the duty of Americans at the
    present crisis. ANN 4:33
    Pursuit of excellence.
    BREWE 5:1968

- E -

Eagleton, Thomas F.
    1977: year of opportunity in the
    Middle East? (Manhattan,
    Kan., Dec. 8, 1976).
    LINRST:124

EAR
    Bekesy, G. V.
        Concerning the pleasures of
        observing, and the mechanics
        of the inner ear. NOLM 3:722

EAST HARLEM
    Dinwoodie, S. D.
        Inner city-our shame. ARS:216

EAST INDIA BILL
  Fox, C. J.
    On the East India Bill.
    BREWE 6:2189

EASTER
  Aelfric
    Sermon on the sacrifice on
    Easter-day. BRYH:14
  Donne, J.
    Sermon preached at St. Paul's
    (Easter Day, 1625).
    BRYH:109
    Prayer for Easter. BNH:76

Eban, Abba
  Responds to an introduction.
  PRS:159

Eccles, John Carew
  The ionic mechanism of post-
  synaptic inhibition (Nobel
  Lecture, Dec. 11, 1963).
  NOLM 4:6

ECCLES, JOHN CAREW
  Granit, R.
    Presentation [of the Nobel
    Prize for Physiology or
    Medicine to John Carew
    Eccles, Alan Lloyd Hodgkin,
    and Andrew Fielding Huxley,
    Dec. 11, 1963]. NOLM 4:3

Eccles, Marriner S.
  Government spending is sound.
  BAD:29

ECHEGARAY, JOSE DE
  Wirsén, C. D. af
    Presentation [of the Nobel
    Prize for Literature to
    Frédéric Mistral and José
    de Echegaray y Eizaguirre,
    1904]. NOL:23; NOB 13:119

ECOLOGY
  Dubos, R.
    Theology of the earth.
    BA 1969-70:83
  Jones, A. L.
    A question of ecology: the
    cries of wolf. LINRST:115
  Muskie, E. S.
    Environment: can man pros-
    per and survive?
    BA 1969-70:98

ECONOMIC ASSISTANCE, AMERICAN
  Gaud, W. S.
    Why foreign aid?
    BA 1967-68:179
  Truman, H. S.
    Point Four Program.
    ANN 16:595

ECONOMIC OPPORTUNITY ACT OF
    1964
  Wirtz, W. W.
    Economic Opportunity Act of
    1964. CAPG:165

ECONOMIC PLANNING See United
    States - Economic policy

ECONOMIC POLICY
  Rogers, W.
    Morgenthau's plan. GRG:55

ECONOMICS See Capitalism; Free
    trade and protection; Industry

Edberg, Rolf
  Acceptance [of the Nobel Prize
  for Peace for Dag Hammarskjöld, Dec. 10, 1961].
  NOLP 3:248

Eddy, Edward D., Jr.
  Student involvement in educational
  policy. BA 1965-66:221;
  LINR:251

Edlén, B.
  Presentation [of the Nobel Prize
  for Physics to Charles H.
  Townes, Nikolai G. Basov, and
  Alexander M. Prochorov, Dec.
  11, 1964]. NOLPH 4:55

Edmunds, George F.
  Constitution and the Electoral
  Commission. BREWE 5:1971

EDUCATION
  Addams, J.
    Foreign-born children in the
    primary grades. ANN 12:130
  Brewster, K., Jr.
    The decade of shortcuts.
    BA 1972-73:176
  Choate, R.
    State and mental culture.
    ANN 7:235
  Clemens, S. L.
    Public Education Association.

GRG:21

Conant, J. B.
Education for a classless society. ANN 16:22
Role of the state in education. CAPG:131

Danton, G. J.
Education, free and compulsory. BREWE 5:1629

Dewey, J.
School and social progress. ANN 12:255

Dowling, A.
Constitutionality of a compulsory school law: opinion for the court. ANN 12:417

Eliezer, C. J.
Ideology and education. MONSA:231

Euwema, B.
Excellence in teaching. ARS:48

Gardner, J. W.
Education. BA 1972-73:119

Geiman, C. K.
Are they really "unteachable"? LINR:94

Howe, H. II
Changing the pecking order. BA 1967-68:111
Public education for a humane society. BA 1972-73:161

Hutchins, R. M.
All our institutions are in disarray. BA 1974-75:117
The institutional illusion. BA 1971-72:161
Where do we go from here in education? CROCK:110

Irwin, H.
The true aim of education. CURM:167

Johnson, L. B.
Education opportunity message. CAPG:112

Lee Kuan Yew
Hong Kong and Singapore: a tale of two cities. MONSA:264

Lindsley, P.
Education of every child of the Republic. ANN 5:157

Macaulay, T. B.
Popular education. BREWE 8:2883

McElwee, R.
A plea for universal education in the South. FON:477

Mann, H.
The necessity of education in a Republican government. HOW:148

Montalembert, C. F. R.
For freedom of education. BREWE 8:3046

Myers, N. J.
Moppet manipulation. ARS:123

Rogers, W.
Education and wealth. HURH:200

Rosten, L.
Myths by which we live. KEO:240

Seward, W. H.
Prosperity and education. ANN 6:140

Shapp, M. J.
The educational process. VER:267

Spencer, S. R., Jr.
A call for new missionaries. BA 1971-72:172

Stevens, T.
Education as a public duty. ANN 6:136

Thio Chan Bee
Inspired education through inspired educators. MONS:463

Warren, P.
Bring forth the children. BRYF:485; MOPR:368

Wellington, J. K.
A look at the fundamental school concept. LINRST:314

White, R.
The educated man in the age of Aquarius. BAAE:271

Willkie, W. L.
Education determines civilization; the importance of liberal education policies. CROCK:93

Winter, R. A.
This I believe. SCHW:87

Wright, F.
Of existing evils and their remedy. ANN 5:290

---- See also Colleges and universities; Commencement addresses; Educators; Learning and scholarship; Religious education; Segregation in education; Students; Teachers; Veterans - Education. Also this subject with subheads Educa-

tion, Adult; Education, Higher; Education of women

---- FINANCE
Chambers, M. M.
Higher education who should
pay? CAPG:125

EDUCATION, ADULT
Coffman, L. D.
Adult education for the un-
employed. ANN 15:98

---- HIGHER
Andelson, R. B.
Campus unrest; the erosion
of excellence. LINRS:204
Barzun, J.
Place and the price of ex-
cellence. ARS:28
Benezet, L. T.
Acceleration or direction?
BA 1966-67:105
The educator's leap of faith.
HOR:107
Curtis, G. W.
Public duty of educated men.
ALS:179
Eddy, E. D., Jr.
Student involvement in edu-
cational policy.
BA 1965-66:221; LINR:251
Eliot, C. W.
Inaugural address as presi-
dent of Harvard. ANN 10:201
Everett, E.
Plea for support of an Ohio
college. ANN 6:26
State funds for Harvard.
ANN 7:502
Fawcett, N. G.
Direction for destiny.
BA 1970-71:106
Ferris, W. H.
Education and the Triple
Revolution. MDV:216
Goheen, R. F.
Sorting it out. HOR:21
Griswold, A. W.
On conversation--chiefly
academic. CROCK:75
Hesburgh, T. M.
Higher education begins the
seventies. BA 1970-71:85;
BAAE:277
Howard, J. A.
The innovation mirage.
BA 1970-71:94

Hutchins, R. M.
Message to the younger genera-
tion. MDV:198
Kirk, G.
Responsibilities of the educated
man (at centennial of Univer-
sity of Denver). LINR:143
McBath, J. H.
The vital university.
BA 1974-75:127
McGill, W. J.
The public challenge and the
campus response.
BA 1971-72:182
Requiem for Joe College.
BA 1969-70:139
Meyerson, M.
The ivory tower of Babel.
HOR:99
Morgan, E. S.
What every Yale freshman
should know. ARS:35
Nixon, R. M.
Campus revolutionaries.
BAAGB:386
Peel, R.
Plea for higher education (in-
stallation speech as Lord
Rector of University of Glas-
gow). BREWE 8:3153
Romney, G.
From the bottom to the top.
CAPG:140
Shaw, G. B.
Universities and education.
KEO:237
Syed Hussein Alatas
Primary aim of a university.
MONS:475
Wentworth, W. C.
For the University Bill.
MCA:17
Wilson, L.
Education for adequacy.
HOR:16
Wong, L. K.
Intelligentsia in a nation of
immigrants (Singapore).
MONS:476

---- MALAYA
Thuraisingham, E. E. C.
Milestones in Malayan educa-
tion. MONS:173
Spirit of teaching. MONS:169

---- MALAYSIA
Hamdan bin Sheikh Tahir, H.

Education for service--to
society, the nation and our
creator. MONSA:149
Problems of national educa-
tion. MONSA:155 selections
Johari, M. K.
All schools are the same.
MONS:145
Key to open the doors to all
hearts and minds.
MONS:141
Successful teacher. MONS:146
Lim Ching Yah
Teaching profession and na-
tion building (Malaysia).
MONS:317
Syed Hussein Alatas
Malaysia and its intellectual
revolution. MONS:469
Tan Chee Khoon
The teachers' dilemma: the
government gets the blame.
MONSA:180

---- SINGAPORE
Ong Pang Boon
Educational pyramid.
MONS:436
Wong, L. K.
Intelligentsia in a nation of
immigrants (Singapore).
MONS:476

EDUCATION AND STATE
Cobden, R.
Need for improved education.
JAE:124
Conant, J. B.
Role of the state in educa-
tion. CAPG:131
Johnson, L. B.
Education opportunity mes-
sage. CAPG:112
Kennedy, J. F.
Federal aid to education.
ANN 18:8
Romney, G.
From the bottom to the top.
CAPG:140

EDUCATION DAY
Welcome to parents and ladies
of the Woman's Missionary
Society on Education Day.
HNWM:21
Welcome to students on Edu-
cation Day. HNWM:20
Welcome to teachers on Edu-
cation Day. HNWM:18

EDUCATION OF WOMEN
Rush, B.
Thoughts on female education.
ANN 3:207
Stevenson, A. E.
Trained intelligence: education
and womanpower (Radcliffe
College commencement ad-
dress). MDV:205

EDUCATORS
Lim Chong Yah
Teaching profession and nation
building (Malaysia). MONS:317
Welcome to a new educational
director (2 examples). BNH:50

---- See also Inaugural addresses;
Teachers

Edward VIII, King of England (ab-
dicated)
Farewell of former King Edward
VIII. BRYH:517
See also Baldwin, S. B., jt. auth.

EDWARD VIII, KING OF ENGLAND
(ABDICATED)
Baldwin, S. B. and others
Debate in the House of Com-
mons on the abdication of Ed-
ward VIII. BRYH:491

Edwards, George
Murder and gun control. (Wash-
ington, D.C., May 3-7, 1971).
BA 1971-72:101

Edwards, Jonathan
Eternity of Hell torments.
BREWE 5:1977
Farewell--sermon. POC:443
Sinners in the hands of an angry
God (Enfield, Conn., July 8,
1741). ANN 1:423;
BREWE 5:1982; HURH:21;
LINS:121
Wrath upon the wicked to the ut-
termost. BREWE 5:1979
"You are thus in the hands of an
angry God." Same as his
Sinners in the hands of an
angry God

Edwards, Ludy (Ludwika)
Libbing. BRYF:489

Edwin, King of Northumbria
 On the flight of a sparrow and
   the life of man. BRYH:5

EFFICIENCY IN BUSINESS
 See Business

EGYPT - FOREIGN RELATIONS
   - ISRAEL
 Carter, J.
   Announcing the Camp David
   accords. BA 1978-79:142

EGYPT AND SUDAN CAMPAIGNS,
 1882-1900
 Churchill, R. H. S.
   Gladstone's Egyptian inconsistencies. BREWE 3:1148

Ehrlich, Paul
 Partial cell functions (Nobel
   Lecture, Dec. 11, 1908).
   NOLM 1:304

EHRLICH, PAUL
 Mörner, K. A. H.
   Presentation [of the Nobel
   Prize for Physiology or
   Medicine to Elie Metchnikoff
   and Paul Ehrlich, Dec. 11,
   1908]. NOLM 1:277

Eigen, Manfred
 Immeasurably fast reactions
   (Nobel Lecture, Dec. 11,
   1967). NOLC 4:170

EIGEN, MANFRED
 Olander, H. A.
   Presentation [of the Nobel
   Prize for Chemistry to
   Manfred Eigen, R. G. W.
   Norrish and George Porter
   Dec. 11, 1967].
   NOLC 4:165

Eijkman, Christiaan
 Antineuritic vitamin and beri-
   beri (Nobel Lecture, Dec.
   11, 1929). NOLM 2:199

EIJKMAN, CHRISTIAAN
 Liljestrand, G.
   Presentation [of the Nobel
   Prize for Physiology or
   Medicine to Christiaan Eijk-
   man and Sir Frederick
   Gowland Hopkins, Dec.
   11, 1929]. NOLM 2:193

Eilberg, Joshua See Jordan, B. C.,
 jt. auth.

Einstein, Albert
 Fundamental ideas and problems
   of the theory of relativity
   (Nobel Lecture for 1921, July
   11, 1923). NOLPH 1:482

EINSTEIN, ALBERT
 Arrhenius, S.
   Presentation [of the Nobel Prize
   for Physics for 1921 to Albert
   Einstein, July 11, 1923].
   NOLPH 1:482
 My friend Albert. BURT:145
 Nizer, L.
   Presents Albert Einstein.
   LYI:176

Einthoven, Willem
 The string galvanometer and the
   measurement of the action currents of the heart (Nobel Lecture for 1924, Dec. 11, 1925).
   NOLM 2:94

Eisenhower, Dwight D.
 Acceptance speech, Chicago, Illi-
   nois, July 11, 1952. SIN:242
 Acceptance speech, San Francis-
   co, California, August 23,
   1956. SIN:265
 Atoms for peace. Same as his
   International control of atomic
   power for peaceful purposes
 Campaign speech, Cleveland, Ohio,
   October 1, 1956. SIN:275
 Campaign speech, Detroit, Michi-
   gan, October 24, 1952. Same
   as his Crusade for peace
 Crisis in the Middle East.
   ANN 17:411
 Crusade for peace (Detroit, Octo-
   ber 24, 1952). ANN 17:199;
   SIN:245
 Dangers of the military-industrial-
   university complex in America.
   Same as his Farewell address,
   January 17, 1961
 Eighth annual message.
   STAT 3:3096
 Faith in the individual. CAPG:31
 Farewell address, January 17,
   1961. ANN 18:1; JAM:36;
   LAA:209; MDV:132
 Federal Court orders must be
   upheld. ANN 17:457
 Fifth annual message.

STAT 3:3068
First annual message.
    STAT 3:3012
First inaugural address. (Wash-
    ington, Jan. 20, 1953).
    HURH:304; USINAU:257;
    USINAUG:257
First steps in disarmament.
    ANN 17:330
Fourth annual message.
    STAT 3:3052
"History does not long entrust
    the care of freedom to the
    weak or the timid." Same
    as his First inaugural ad-
    dress
I shall go to Korea. Same
    as his Crusade for peace
International control of atomic
    power for peaceful pur-
    poses. ANN 17:211
Little Rock School crisis.
    Same as his Federal Court
    orders must be upheld
Ninth annual message.
    STAT 3:3107
Open skies proposal to Russia.
    Same as his First steps in
    disarmament
Order of the day (June 6, 1944).
    Same as his Order of the
    Day to the Allied troops in-
    vading France
Order of the Day to Allied
    troops invading France.
    GRG:74
Price of peace: second in-
    augural address.
    USINAU:263; USINAUG:263
Responds to an introduction.
    PRS:152
Second annual message.
    STAT 3:3026
Second inaugural address.
    Same as his Price of
    Peace: second inaugural
    address
Seventh annual message.
    STAT 3:3086
Sixth annual message. Same
    as his State of the Union
    (January 9, 1958)
Spirit of Geneva. BEN:136
State of the Union (January 9,
    1958). STAT 3:3076
Third annual message.
    STAT 3:3038
U-2 incident (May 25, 1960).

ANN 17:550
Veto of Natural Gas Bill.
    ANN 17:370

EISENHOWER, DWIGHT D.
    Reid, C. T.
        Tribute to Dwight D. Eisen-
        hower. BA 1968-69:165

Eisenhower, Milton S.
    A new historical perspective, in-
    terdependence (Johns Hopkins
    Univ., June 13, 1967).
    HOR:157

Ekstrand, A. G.
    Presentation [of the Nobel Prize
    for Chemistry to Fritz Haber,
    1918, June 2, 1920].
    NOLC 1:321
    Presentation [of the Nobel Prize
    for Physics to Charles-Edouard
    Guillaume, Dec. 11, 1920].
    NOLPH 1:441
    Presentation [of the Nobel Prize
    for Physics for 1919 to Johannes
    Stark, June 3, 1920].
    NOLPH 1:423
    Presentation [of the Nobel Prize
    for Physics for 1918 to Max
    Planck, June 2, 1920].
    NOLPH 1:405

ELECTION - ACCEPTANCE See
    Offices - Acceptance

ELECTION DISTRICTS
    Brennan, W. J., Jr.
        Baker v. Carr: Opinion for
        the Supreme Court. ANN 18:130

ELECTION LAWS
    Johnson, L. B.
        Address to a Joint Session of
        Congress, March 15, 1965.
        AND:81; BOORA 2:919;
        CROCK:164; MDV:144; REIR:143

ELECTIONS
    Bayard, T. F.
        Plea for conciliation in 1876.
        BREWE 1:265
    Curran, J. P.
        Liberties of the indolent.
        BREWE 4:1550
    Davis, D.
        On appeal from the caucus.
        BREWE 5:1634

Jarrow, C.
  Case for the non-voter.
  KEO:229
Johnson, J. W.
  Our democracy and the ballot.
  FON:757
LaFollette, R. M.
  Which shall rule, manhood
  or money? HURH:158
Macaulay, T. B.
  Reform Bill. CLAYP:295;
  MCB:110
Root, E.
  Invisible government: Short
  Ballot Amendment.
  ANN 13:528
Russell, J. R.
  Reform of the franchise.
  MCB:87
Shepard, T.
  Election sermon. POC:355
West, S.
  Election sermon. POC:578

---- CORRUPT PRACTICES
Carpenter, M. H.
  Louisiana Returning Board.
  BREWE 3:976

---- PRIMARY See Primaries

ELECTORAL COLLEGE
Lodge, H. C., Jr.
  For abolishing the Electoral
  College. ANN 17:2

ELECTRIC WAVES
Kastler, A.
  Optical methods for studying
  Hertzian resonances.
  NOLPH 4:186

ELECTRICITY
Thomson, J. J.
  Carriers of negative elec-
  tricity. NOLPH 1:145

ELECTROLYTES
Arrhenius, S. A.
  Development of the theory
  of electrolytic dissociation.
  NOLC 1:45

ELECTRONS
Davisson, C. J.
  The discovery of electron
  waves. NOLPH 2:387
De Broglie, L.

The wave nature of the electron.
NOLPH 2:244
Dirac, P. A. M.
  Theory of electrons and posi-
  trons. NOLPH 2:320
Franck, J.
  Transformations of kinetic en-
  ergy of free electrons into ex-
  citation energy of atoms by
  impacts. NOLPH 2:98
Kusch, P.
  The magnetic moment of the
  electron. NOLPH 3:298
Lorentz, H. A.
  The theory of electrons and the
  propagation of light.
  NOLPH 1:14
Millikan, R. A.
  The electron and the light-quant
  from the experimental point of
  view. NOLPH 2:54
Thomson, G. P.
  Electronic waves.
  NOLPH 2:397

ELECTROPHORESIS
Tiselius, A. W. K.
  Electrophoresis and adsorption
  analysis as aids in investigations of large-molecular weight
  substances and their breakdown.
  NOLC 3:195

Eliezer, Christie Jayaratnam
  Democratic societies and debating
  societies. MONS:262
  Educated man with a sense of ur-
  gency (presenting Doctor of
  Laws degree). MONS:275
  Ideology and education (Kuala
  Lumpur, Jan. 5, 1968).
  MONSA:231
  Mathematics the queen of the arts.
  MONS:265
  Toast to Oxford. MONS:271

Eliot, Charles W.
  Elective curriculum. Same as
  his Inaugural address as
  president of Harvard
  Harvard and Yale. (New York,
  Dec. 22, 1877). HURH:130
  Inaugural address as president of
  Harvard. ANN 10:201
  "You can not build a university
  on a sect at all; you must
  build it upon the nation." Same
  as his Harvard and Yale

Eliot, Sir John
  On the Petition of Right.
    BREWE 5:1986; BRYH:123

Eliot, Thomas Stearns
  Acceptance [of the Nobel Prize
    for Literature, 1948].
    NOB 5:267; NOL:435

ELIOT, THOMAS STEARNS
  Österling, A.
    Presentation [of the Nobel
    Prize for Literature to
    Thomas Stearns Eliot,
    1948]. NOB 5:261; NOL:431
  Trilling, L.
    Presents T. S. Eliot.
    LYI:35

Elizabeth I, Queen of England
  Queen and the royal succes-
    sion. BRYH:69
  Speech at the dissolution of
    Parliament. BRYH:75
  Speech at the proroguing of
    Parliament. BRYH:77
  Speech on marriage and suc-
    cession, to a delegation
    from the Lords and Com-
    mons. Same as her Queen
    and the royal succession

Elizabeth II, Queen of England
  Toast to President Ford and
    to the American people
    (1976). JAM:22

ELIZABETH II, QUEEN OF
    ENGLAND
  Ford, G. R.
    Toast to Queen Elizabeth.
    JAM:21
  Garran, R. R.
    Royal visit. MCA:191

Elleson, Jim
  The imbalance of power (West
    Allis, Wisc., 1977).
    LINRST:135

Elliott, Janice
  There's always a mongoose.
    MDYG:223

Elliott, Robert Browne
  Civil Rights' Bill. (Washington,
    Jan. 6, 1874). FON:384;
    OE:55

Ellsworth, Oliver
  Union and coercion.
    BREWE 5:1993

El-Sadat, Anwar See Carter, J.,
    jt. auth.

Elson, Edward L. R.
  Freaks for Jesus' sake. (Wash-
    ington, D.C., June 27, 1971).
    BA 1971-72:151

Ely, Richard T.
  Needs of the city. ANN 11:234

EMANCIPATION OF NEGROES See
    Slavery in the United States

EMANCIPATION PROCLAMATION
  Bryant, M. E.
    How shall we get our rights?
    FON:510
  Gibbs, J. C.
    Freedom's joyful day. FON:262
  Lincoln, A.
    Third annual message.
    ANN 9:473; STAT 2:1084
  Phillips, W.
    The proclamation, how to make
    it efficient. MDT:148
  Purvis, R.
    The good time is at hand.
    FON:266

EMBARGO
  Jefferson, T.
    Eighth annual message.
    STAT 1:94

EMBRYOLOGY
  Spemann, H.
    The organizer-effect in em-
    bryonic development.
    NOLM 2:381

Emerson, Ralph Waldo
  American scholar. ANN 6:367;
    ARS:39; BAS:156 (outline only);
    BOORA 1:283; BREWE 5:2003;
    LINS:162; OLIS:47
  Greatness of a plain American.
    BREWE 5:1999
  Man the reformer.
    BREWE 5:2008
  Memory of Burns. (Boston, Jan.
    25, 1859). HURH:106
  On the Fugitive Slave Law.
    ANN 8:261

"No man existed who could look
down on Burns." Same as
his Memory of Burns
Uses of great men.
BREWE 5:2012
Young American. ANN 7:182

Emmet, Robert
Protest against sentence as a
traitor. BREWE 6:2030

EMMET, ROBERT
Plunket, W. C.
Prosecuting Robert Emmet.
BREWE 8:3213

EMPLOYMENT
Taft, R. A.
Should the government
guarantee employment?
ANN 16:263

Enche Arshad bin Ayub
The value of the English lan-
guage--intensive study urged
(Kuala Lumpur, April 7,
1970). MONSA:194 selections

Enders, John Franklin (and others)
The cultivation of the polio-
myelitis viruses in tissue
culture (Nobel Lecture,
Dec. 11, 1954).
NOLM 3:448

ENDERS, JOHN FRANKLIN
Gard, S.
Presentation [of the Nobel
Prize for Physiology or
Medicine to John Franklin
Enders, Thomas Huckle
Weller, and Frederick Chap-
man Robbins, Dec. 11,
1954]. NOLM 3:443

ENERGY CONSERVATION
Carter, J.
Energy problems.
BA 1976-77:117

ENERGY CRISIS See Power resources

ENERGY INDUSTRIES
Sawhill, J. C.
Energy and the job market.
BA 1975-76:102

ENERGY POLICY
Carter, J.
Energy address to the nation.
EHN:327
Goodall, C. H.
Energy statement. TAC:219
Sawhill, J. C.
Energy and the job market.
BA 1975-76:102
Wydler, J. W.
Science and the public trust.
BA 1979-80:139

Engel, George
Address at trial, Chicago, Octo-
ber 7-9, 1886. ACC:43;
PAF:37

ENGINEERING AND ENGINEERS
Holley, A. L.
Theory and practice in industrial
engineering. ANN 10:366
Macios, M. A.
Model studies of structural design and construction should be
conducted prior to the building
of structure rather than on the
site studies made after the
completion of the project.
BAS:193 (outline only)

ENGLAND See Great Britain;
World War, 1939-1945 - Great
Britain

ENGLISH LANGUAGE
Abdul Rahman, T.
English language must continue.
MONS:7
Enche Arshad bin Ayub
The value of the English lan-
guage--intensive study urged.
MONSA:194 selections

---- DIALECTS - BLACKS See
Black-English dialects

Engman, Lewis A.
Federal Trade Commission (De-
troit, April 29, 1974).
TAC:214

Engström, A.
Presentation [of the Nobel Prize
for Physiology or Medicine to
Francis Harry Compton Crick,
James Dewey Watson, and

Maurice Hugh Frederick
Wilkins, Dec. 11, 1962].
NOLM 3:751

ENTERTAINMENT See Introductions; Music and musicians;
Theater, Wit and humor

ENTERTAINMENT, SPEECHES OF
See After-dinner speeches

ENTHUSIASM
Chauncy, C.
Caveat against enthusiasm.
POC:488

ENVIRONMENT
Dubos, R. J.
Humanizing the earth.
BA 1972-73:149
Mead, M.
The planetary crisis and the
challenge to scientists.
BA 1973-74:97
Muskie, E. S.
Environment: can man
prosper and survive?
BA 1969-70:98
Ransley, M.
The life and death of our
lakes. LINRS:63
Ruckelshaus, W. D.
The environment revolution.
BA 1971-72:125
Seaborg, G. T.
Positive power of science.
BA 1969-70:108
Swearingen, J. E.
Environmental pollution: a
national problem.
BAAGB:392

ENVIRONMENTAL PROTECTION
Speth, G.
Environmental regulation and
the immobilization of truth.
BA 1979-80:145

ENZYMES
Northrop, J. H.
The preparation of pure
enzymes and virus proteins.
NOLC 3:124
Sumner, J. B.
The chemical nature of
enzymes. NOLC 3:114
Theorell, A. H. T.
The nature and mode of ac-

tion of oxidation enzymes.
NOLM 3:480

EQUAL RIGHTS AMENDMENT
Buckley, J.
The Equal Rights Amendment:
the legislative aspect.
LINRST:271
Chisholm, S.
In support of the Equal Rights
Amendment.   BOST:243;
EHN:364; MOPR:372
Furay, M.
Statement [before the] Subcom-
mittee on Constitutional Amend-
ments of the Committee on the
Judiciary of the U.S. Senate.
BOST:219
Goldman, E. and others
Statement [before the] Subcom-
mittee on Constitutional Amend-
ments of the Committee on the
Judiciary of the U.S. Senate.
BOST:215
Green, E.
Representative Edith Green
speaks in support of the Equal
Rights Amendment.   BOST:237
Griffiths, M. W. and others
House debates the Equal Rights
Amendment.   BOST:230
Holtzman, E.
Women and equality under the
law.   BA 1976-77:80
Springen, P. J.
The dimensions of the oppres-
sion of women.   LINRS:109;
LINRST:130
Witter, J.
Statement [before the] Subcom-
mittee on Constitutional Amend-
ments of the Committee on the
Judiciary of the U.S. Senate.
BOST:203
Wolfe, H. B.
The backlash phenomenon.
LINRST:85

EQUALITY
Norton, E. H.
In pursuit of equality in aca-
deme.   BA 1976-77:65
Thibeault, M. L.
The hazards of equity.
VERD:265

---- See also Democracy

Erickson, Donald J.
  Presents W. E. Whitehead.
    LYI:63

Erlanger, Joseph
  Some observations on the re-
    sponses of single nerve
    fibers (Nobel Lecture for
    1944, Dec. 12, 1947).
    NOLM 3:50

Erskine, Thomas
  Against Paine's "The Age of
    Reason." Same as his
    Against Thomas Williams
    for the publication of Paine's
    Age of Reason
  Against Thomas Williams for
    the publication of Paine's
    Age of Reason. BREWE 6:2038
  "Dominion founded on violence
    and terror." Same as his
    Speech in behalf of John
    Stockdale
  Free speech and fundamental
    rights: defense of Tom
    Paine (Court of King's
    Bench, Dec. 18, 1792).
    BREWE 6:2069; CLAYP:166
  Homicidal insanity (J. Hadfield).
    BREWE 6:2058; BRYH:294
  In behalf of Hadfield. Same as
    his Homicidal insanity (J.
    Hadfield)
  Speech in behalf of John Stock-
    dale. BREWE 6:2050
  Speech in behalf of Thomas
    Paine. Same as his Free
    speech and fundamental
    rights: defense of Tom
    Paine

ESKIMOES
  Sara, M. J.
    Do not refuse us.
    BA 1969-70:148

ESPIONAGE
  Donovan, W. J.
    Call for a Central Intelli-
      gence Agency. ANN 16:391

Essrig, Harry
  Lordly cedar. WALE:35

Estep, Phyllis M.
  Apathy. ARS:164

Ethelbert
  Coming of Christianity. BRYH:3
  On Augustine's mission to England
    (597). Same as his Coming of
    Christianity

ETHICS
  Acheson, D. G.
    Ethics in international relations
      today. ARS:229
  Chapin, E. H.
    Rectitude higher than morality.
      BREWE 3:1040
  DeVries, C.
    Standards that stand. SCHW:15
  Hoover, H. C.
    Moral standard in an industrial
      era. ANN 14:428
  Jeffrey, R. C.
    Ethics in public discourse.
      BA 1973-74:119
  Jones, J. L.
    Who is tampering with the soul
      of America? LINR:211;
      LINRS:220
  Lerner, D.
    Comfort and fun: morality in a
      nice society. ARS:168
  Lewis, C. S.
    Social morality. ARS:177
    Three parts of morality.
      ARS:175
  Mount, A.
    The Playboy philosophy--pro.
      LINRS:157; LINRST:181
  Parson, M. J.
    Idealism: what's wrong with it?
      BA 1975-76:166
  Pinson, W. M., Jr.
    The Playboy philosophy--con.
      LINRS:170
  Powell, L. F., Jr.
    The eroding authority.
      BA 1972-73:101
  Spiritual patterns. BURT:124

---- See also Behavior; Character;
    Charities, Christian ethics;
    Courage; Crime and criminals;
    Friendship; Honesty; Justice;
    Liberty; Love; Patience; Patriot-
    ism; Peace; Sin; Social prob-
    lems; Success; Truthfulness and
    falsehood

Ettelson, Harry W.
  God be with thee. WALE:38

Look above and beyond!
WALE:41
Parting is such sweet sorrow.
WALE:44

Eucken, Rudolf
Naturalism or idealism?
(Nobel Lecture, March 27,
1909). NOL:74

EUCKEN, RUDOLF CHRISTOPH
Hjärne, H.
Presentation [of the Nobel
Prize for Literature to
Rudolf Christoph Eucken,
1908]. NOB 6:3; NOL:67

Euler, Hans Von
Fermentation of sugars and
fermentative enzymes
(Nobel Lecture for 1929,
May 23, 1930).
NOLC 2:144

EULER, HANS VON
Söderbaum, H. G.
Presentation [of the Nobel
Prize for Chemistry to
Arthur Harden and Hans
Karl August Simon von
Euler-Chelpin, Dec. 12,
1929]. NOLC 2:127

EULOGIES
Adler, M.
Bare spirit. WALE:3
Teacher's spiritual dimen-
sions. WALE:6
Arm, M.
Vial of fragrant ointment.
WALE:13
Becker, A.
To make a commonplace
wondrous. WALE:15
Beecher, H. W.
Effect of the death of Lin-
coln. BREWE 1:365
Belson, R. S.
What really counts.
WALE:18
Besdin, A. R.
Life's struggle. WALE:20
Bial, M. D.
Light from the stones.
WALE:21
Blaine, J. G.
Life and character of J. A.
Garfield. BREWE 2:482;

HURH:137
Brademas, J.
Eulogy for Robert Kennedy.
JAM:43
Brooks, S. H.
God's grief. WALE:23
Buchanan, D.
Eulogy of Garibaldi. MCA:78
Burstein, A.
Power of memory. WALE:25
Califano, J. A.
A tribute to the man of the
people. BA 1977-78:197
Carter, J.
My good friend Hubert Humph-
rey. BA 1977-78:200
Chaney, F. L.
Ben is going to take his big
brother's place. FON:1017
Cheek, J. E.
A promise made, a promise to
keep: Whitney Young and the
nation. BA 1970-71:131
Chertoff, M. S.
Benjamin A. Lichter.
WALE:205
Go thou in peace. WALE:27
Chiel, S.
Seder of life. WALE:29
Cleaver, E.
Meditation on the assassination
of Martin Luther King, Jr.
OE:229
Cronbach, A.
Of Earth, earthy and of Heaven,
heavenly. WALE:30
Curtis, G. W.
Eulogy on Wendell Phillips.
BREWE 4:1571
Davis, A.
The legacy of George Jackson.
FON:1191
Davis, O.
Malcolm was our manhood, our
living Black manhood. FON:1010
De Sola Pool, D.
Man's advocate. WALE:33
Drazin, N.
From the summit. WALE:34
Dreyfus, A. S.
Leo Baeck. WALE:207
Essrig, H.
Lordly cedar. WALE:35
Ettelson, H. W.
God be with thee. WALE:38
Look above and beyond!
WALE:41
Parting is such sweet sorrow.

Eulogy on Adlai E. Stevenson. BA 1965-66:227

Malcolm, G. A.
Judge Andres Borromeo did his duty! CURM:183

Mansfield, M. J.
Eulogy for John F. Kennedy. ANN 18:202

Mays, B. E.
Eulogy on Dr. Martin Luther King, Jr. BA 1967-68:161; BAAGB:399; SMHV:296

Menzies, R. G.
Eulogy of Churchill. MCA:151

Milgrom, J.
He cannot be replaced. WALE:132

Minda, A. G.
He died climbing. WALE:134
Vision that looks beyond. WALE:137

Mondale, W. F.
A time to celebrate life. BA 1977-78:205

Nussbaum, M.
Al Jolson. WALE:225

Parker, T.
Discourse on the death of Daniel Webster. BREWE 8:3137

Pearl, C.
Seal of truth. WALE:140

Percy, C. H.
Eulogy for Robert Kennedy. JAM:42

Phillips, W.
Toussaint L'Ouverture. OLIS:170

Pollak, G.
Light from sorrow. WALE:143

Poplack, A. M.
Preparation for eternity. WALE:146

Rackovsky, I.
Loom of time. WALE:147

Rainey, J. H.
Eulogy on Charles Sumner. FON:403

Ransom, R. C.
William Lloyd Garrison: a centennial oration. SMHV:66

Raskas, B. S.
Physician's prayer. WALE:149

Roosevelt, T.
First annual message. ANN 12:433; STAT 2:2014

Rosenthal, N. L.
My son, my son. WALE:152

Routtenberg, M. J.
Crown of a good name. WALE:154

Rubel, C. M.
Beauties of Japheth and the glory of Shem. WALE:157

Rudin, J. P.
Shadows in the sun. WALE:160

Rusk, D.
Eulogy of Lyndon Baines Johnson. BA 1972-73:132

Salkowitz, S.
King's answer. WALE:163

Sevareid, E.
Eulogy for the astronauts. MOP:189; MOPR:165
Eulogy for Wernher Von Braun. EHN:373

Shtull, J.
Man of deed. WALE:164

Shulman, C. E.
Alfred S. Alschuler. WALE:229

Silver, S. M.
Come back. WALE:166

Simon, E. Y.
Heavenly glow. WALE:169
Two arks. WALE:172

Simon, R.
This was a man! WALE:174
Upward climb. WALE:175

Stanley, A. O.
Address in honor of Robert E. Lee. BLY:216

Stanley, J.
Tribute to a fallen Black soldier. FON:268

Stern, H. J.
Work of art. WALE:178

Stevenson, A. E.
Address at the memorial service for Sir Winston Churchill. LINR:305; LINRS:307; LINRST:373
Eulogy on Eleanor Roosevelt. BRP:230
Farewell to a friend (Lloyd Lewis). ALA:119

Stiskin, M. N.
Man is a soul. WALE:179

Suggestions for the preparation of eulogistic speeches. MILS:6

Swarensky, M. E.
  Bridge of love. WALE:181
  Spiritual portrait.
  WALE:183
Teller, M.
  What the Lord requires.
  WALE:185
Thomson, T. J. B.
  Brightness is darkened
  (eulogy on Tuanku Abdul
  Rahman Ibni Al-Marhum
  Tuanku Mohammed, first
  King of Malaysia).
  MONS: 281
  Let these be his epitaph
  (eulogy on Sultan Hissa-
  muddin Alam Shah Ibni-
  Marhum Sultan Ala'iddin
  Sulaiman Shah). MONS:283
Thoreau, H. D.
  Plea for Captain John
  Brown. ANN 9:136
Tomsky, M. B.
  Bitter and the sweet.
  WALE:187
  Righteous shall flourish like
  the palm-tree. WALE:188
  Symphony of life. WALE:190
Turitz, L. E.
  Measure of greatness.
  WALE:192
Wallack, M. A.
  And thou shalt choose life.
  WALE:197
  Living presence. WALE:194
Wears, I. C.
  The Ku Klux of the North.
  FON:378
Webster, D.
  Eulogy on Adams and Jef-
  ferson. BREWE 10:3848
Weinberger, S.
  Cheerful spirit. WALE:198
Weinstein, J. J.
  One of the thirty-six.
  WALE:200
Whipper, W.
  Eulogy on William Wilber-
  force. FON:49
Williams, P.
  A tribute to Captain Paul
  Cuffe. FON:28
Wirt, W.
  Death of Jefferson and
  Adams. BREWE 10:3905

EUROPE - HISTORY - 20TH
    CENTURY
Nansen, F.

The suffering people of Europe
(Nobel Lecture, Dec. 19, 1922).
NOLP 1:361

EUROPEAN WAR, 1914-1918
Johnson, J. W.
  Africa at the Peace Table and
  the descendants of Africans in
  our American democracy.
  FON:730
La Follette, R. M., Sr.
  Against war with Germany.
  ANN 14:104
  Soldier's pay. GRG:36
Lloyd George, David
  Appeal to the nation. MCB:483
Mannix, D.
  Case against conscription.
  MCA:134
Norris, G. W.
  Opposition to Wilson's War
  Message. ANN 14:101
Root, E.
  European War and the preserva-
  tion of America's ideals.
  ANN 14:70
Wilson, W.
  "Eyes of the people opened."
  STAT 3:2580
  Fourteen points (January 8,
  1918). BOORA 2:773; FRIP:291;
  GRG:42; HURH:180; OLIS:228
  Neutrality message to the Sen-
  ate, August 19, 1914.
  ANN 13:491
  Peace without victory.
  ANN 14:65; FRIP:286; HURH:173
  Second annual message.
  STAT 3:2551
  Sixth annual message.
  STAT 3:2587
  Speech opening campaign for
  fourth liberty loan. FRIP:295
  Third annual message.
  STAT 3:2560
  War message to Congress, Ap-
  ril 2, 1917. ANN 14:77;
  HURH:177; LINS:291

---- See also Peace; Peace Confer-
     ence, 1919; Unknown soldier

---- NEW ZEALAND
  Bell, F. H. D.
    The defence of the Empire in
    the Great War. MACS:273

Euwema, Ben
  Excellence in teaching. ARS:48

Evangelista, Teodora
    The needs of a nation (Rizal,
    Dec. 3, 1933). CURM:160

EVANGELISTS See Clergy

Evans, Theodore H., Jr.
    Application of love. VI:90

Evarts, William M.
    Weakest spot in the American
    system (defense at im-
    peachment of A. Johnson).
    BREWE 6:2082

Evatt, Herbert Vere
    Australia and the United Nations
    charter. MCA:161

Everett, Edward
    Adams and Jefferson.
    (Charlestown, Mass., Aug.
    1, 1826). HURH:64
    Circumstances favorable to
    the progress of literature
    in America. ANN 5:118
    "The fabric of American free-
    dom ... may crumble into
    dust. But the cause in
    which these our fathers
    shone is immortal." Same
    as his Adams and Jefferson
    History of liberty.
    BREWE 6:2092
    Moral forces which make
    American progress.
    BREWE 6:2112
    Plea for support of an Ohio
    college. ANN 6:26
    State funds for Harvard.
    ANN 7:502
    Universal and uncoerced co-
    operation. BREWE 6:2115

Everheart, William E.
    We hold these truths (Kansas
    City, Mo., Jan. 22, 1976).
    BA 1975-76:27

Evers, Charles
    We are going to make it better
    for Blacks and Whites.
    (New York, May, 1969).
    FON:1167

EVIL See Sin

EVOLUTION
    Müller, F. M.

    Impassable barrier between
    brutes and man. BREWE 8:3086

EXCITATION
    Huxley, A. F.
    The quantitative analysis of ex-
    citation and conduction in nerve.
    NOLM 4:52

EXECUTIVE POWER - UNITED
    STATES
    Polk, J. K.
    Fourth annual address.
    STAT 1:731

EXECUTIVES
    Business leaders of tomorrow.
    BURT:37
    Executive. BURT:27

EXHIBITIONS
    McKinley, W.
    At the Pan-American Exposition.
    ANN 12:428
    Washington, B. T.
    Address at the opening of the
    Atlanta Exposition. ANN 12:9;
    BAPRR:255; BAS:77 (outline
    only); BRYF:492; FON:577;
    LINS:263; OE:82; SMHV:94

EXPLANATION AND INSTRUCTION,
    SPEECHES OF See Informa-
    tive speeches

EXPUNGING RESOLUTION
    Clay, H.
    Expunging Resolution.
    BREWE 4:1233

EXTREMISM See Right and left
    (Political science)

EYE
    Granit, R.
    The development of retinal
    neurophysiology. NOLM 4:255
    Gullstrand, A.
    How I found the mechanism of
    intracapsular accommodation.
    NOLM 1:414
    Hartline, H. K.
    Visual receptors and retinal
    interaction. NOLM 4:269
    Wald, G.
    The molecular basis of visual
    excitation. NOLM 4:292

- F -

Fabunmi, Larry
  Black and white keys.
  SCHW:206

FAILURE See Success

FAITH
  Bulkeley, P.
    The gospel-covenant.
    JON:30
  Fosdick, H. E.
    Power to see it through.
    CROCK:58

---- See also Religion

Falkland, Lucius Cary, 2nd Vis-
    count
  Ship-money-impeaching Lord
    Keeper Finch.
    BREWE 6:2123

FAME
  Conwell, R. H.
    Acres of diamonds.
    ANN 11:271; BEN:159;
    HURH:202
  Damiani, P.
    Secret of true greatness.
    BREWE 4:1605
  Emerson, R. W.
    Uses of great men.
    BREWE 5:2012
  Kane, A.
    Glory of notoriety. REIR:223

FAMILY
  Jones, J. L.
    "Let's bring back Dad": a
    solid value system.
    LINRST:254
  Muench, A.
    Rural families and welfare.
    ANN 15:462

FAMINES
  Brown, M.
    Famine: a reality, not just
    a threat. BREWW:168
  Price, S.
    Agriculture--the real answer
    to starvation. BREWW:161

FANEUIL, PETER
  Lovell, J.
    Funeral oration. POC:138

Fannings, Helen See Brown, Joan

FAR EAST See Orient; United
    States - Foreign Relations -
    East (Far East)

Farber, Seymour M.
  Why national concern for biomedi-
    cal communication?
    BA 1966-67:118

Farber, William O.
  Changing concepts of public serv-
    ice. ARS:208

FAREWELL ADDRESSES
  Aelred, Saint
    Farewell. BREWE 1:110
  Benjamin, J. P.
    Farewell to the Union.
    BREWE 1:399
  Cleaver, E.
    Farewell address. SMHV:284
  Curran, J. P.
    Farewell to the Irish Parlia-
    ment. BREWE 4:1552
  Edward VIII
    Farewell of former King Ed-
    ward VIII. BRYH:517
  Edwards, J.
    Farewell-sermon. POC:443
  Eisenhower, D. D.
    Farewell address, January 17,
    1961. ANN 18:1; JAM:36;
    LAA:209; MDV:132
  Hutchins, R. M.
    Message to the younger genera-
    tion. MDV:198
  Jackson, A.
    Farewell address, 1837.
    ANN 6:298
  Jones, H. M.
    Farewell to the English Depart-
    ment. REIR:232
  Lee, R. E.
    To the Army of Northern Vir-
    ginia. ECH:188
  Lincoln, A.
    Farewell to Springfield (outline
    of speech). REIR:232
  MacArthur, D.
    Farewell to the cadets (accept-
    ing Sylvanus Thayer award for
    service to his nation, West
    Point, May 12, 1962).
    LINR:264; LINRS:283;
    LINRST:357; MDV:20; MUS:332
  Parting word from the pastor's
    wife (2 examples). BNH:84

Roxas, M.
A farewell to the Assembly.
CURM:282
Sevareid, E.
Parting thoughts.
BA 1977-78:143
Washington, G.
Farewell address.   ANN 3:606;
BEN:18; BOORA 1:194;
BREWE 10:3740; HURH:44
When a pastor has to say good-
bye (2 examples).   BNH:83
Words of farewell.   BON:53

Farley, James A.
Responds to an introduction.
PRS:145

Farmer, James
The "Movement" now. (American Studies Conference at
Lincoln Univ., Pa., Feb.
25, 1967).   FON:1040

---- and others (Malcolm X)
Debate at Cornell University,
March 7, 1962.   ROSC:59;
OE:248
Debate on the solution to Amer-
ica's race problem.   Same
as his Debate at Cornell
University, March 7, 1962

FARMERS
Gould, J. C.
My responsibility as an agri-
cultural citizen.
BREWW:147

---- See also Agriculture

---- NEW ZEALAND
Massey, W. F.
Repeal of income tax on
farmers, 1923.   MACS:304
sel.

FARMINGTON CANAL
Wolcott, O.
Address at state line between
Southwick, Massachusetts
and Granby, Connecticut,
July 4, 1825.   HAW:122

FARRAGUT, DAVID GLASGOW
Choate, J. H.
Farragut.   BREWE 3:1109

Farrar, Frederick William
Funeral oration on General Grant.
BREWE 6:2128

Farwell, Jane See Scott, Richard

FATHERS
Dear old Dad.   BURT:172
Overhill, J.
Regular snob.   MDYG:75

FATHERS AND SONS
Berson, A.
Open letter to my middle-aged
father.   REIR:215
Welcome to fathers at Father-Son
banquet.   HNWM:37
Welcome to sons at Father-Son
banquet.   HNWM:38

FATHER'S DAY
Boy and his Dad (welcome address
on Father's Day).   HNWM:12
Forgotten man (welcome address
on Father's Day).   HNWM:10
He's somebody special (welcome
address on Father's Day).
HNWM:11
What is in a name (welcome ad-
dress on Father's Day)?
HNWM:13

Faulkner, William
On accepting the Nobel Prize, ex-
horts the young writers of the
world (Stockholm, Dec. 10,
1950).   ALA:125; ANN 17:33;
ARS:52; BOORA 2:988;
GRG:86; HURH:291; MOPR:379;
NOB 19:7; NOL:444
Writer's duty.   Same as his On
accepting the Nobel prize

FAULKNER, WILLIAM
Hellström, G.
Presentation [of the Nobel Prize
for Literature for 1949 to
William Faulkner].   NOB 19:3;
NOL:440

Fawcett, Novice G.
Direction for destiny. (Ohio State
University, March 13, 1971).
BA 1970-71:106
Introduces E. W. Ingram, presi-
dent, White Castle, Inc.
PRS:6

Fazakerly, Nicholas See Wal-
    pole, R., jt. auth.

FEAR
  Gaustad, E. S.
    The beginning of wisdom.
    CAPB:370
  Hall, R. O.
    Fear and faith. VI:98

Featherston, Isaac
  The demand for responsible
  government (Wellington,
  April 18, 1853). MACS:84
  sel.

---- and others (William Fox)
  "Provincialism" 1856 (New
  Zealand House of Repre-
  sentatives, May 2, 1856).
  MACS:96 sel.

Fedder, Abraham H.
  Three ways to mourn.
  WALE:47

FEDERAL AID TO EDUCATION
  See Education and state

FEDERAL AID TO RESEARCH
  Califano, J. A.
    Federal support of science
    and medicine.
    BA 1977-78:99

FEDERAL GOVERNMENT
  Atkinson, H.
    The abolition of the prov-
    inces, 1876. MACS:111
    sel.
  Church, F.
    Rediscovering America.
    BA 1975-76:124
  Hamilton, A.
    On an act granting to Con-
    gress certain imposts and
    duties. ALS:133
  Hoover, H. C.
    Reassuring touch: President
    Hoover speaks, 1931.
    ROD:15
  Marshall, J.
    McCulloch v. Maryland:
    opinion for the Supreme
    Court. ANN 4:530;
    BOORA 1:241

---- See also United States -
  Politics and government

Feibelman, Julian B.
  Life's victor. WALE:49

Feldmann, Margaret
  Eyes of the whole world.
  SCHW:156
  Of mice and women. SCHW:64

FELLOWSHIP See Friendship

FEMINISM
  Edwards, L.
    Libbing. BRYF:489
  Pogrebin, L. C.
    Commencement address.
    TAC:242

---- See also Women

Fénelon, François de Salignac de la
  Mothe
  Nature as a revelation.
  BREWE 6:2142
  Simplicity and greatness. Same
  as his True and false simplic-
  ity
  True and false simplicity.
  BREWE 6:2137

FENTON, WALTER S.
  Simmons, D. A.
    Presents Walter S. Fenton.
    LYI:131

Ferguson, Jane
  Witch trials. (Baylor University,
  1955). CAPB:377

Ferguson, Virginia
  Women in agriculture.
  BREWW:122

FERMENTATION
  Buchner, E.
    Cell-free fermentation.
    NOLC 1:103
  Euler, H. V.
    Fermentation of sugars and
    fermentative enzymes.
    NOLC 2:144
  Harden, A.
    The function of phosphate in al-
    coholic fermentation.
    NOLC 2:131

Fermi, Enrico
  Artificial radioactivity produced by
  neutron bombardment (Nobel

Lecture, Dec. 12, 1938).
NOLPH 2:414

FERMI, ENRICO
Pleijel, H.
Presentation [of the Nobel
Prize for Physics to En-
rico Fermi, Dec. 12, 1938].
NOLPH 2:409

Ferrell, Dianne
Young men with visions.
(Baylor University, 1969).
CAPB:385

Ferris, W. H.
Education and the Triple Revolution. MDV:216

Feynman, Richard P.
The development of the space-
time view of quantum
electrodynamics (Nobel Lecture, Dec. 11, 1965).
NOLPH 4:155

FEYNMAN, RICHARD P.
Waller, I.
Presentation [of the Nobel
Prize for Physics to Sin-
Itiro Tomonaga, Julian
Schwinger, and Richard P.
Feynman, Dec. 11, 1965].
NOLPH 4:123

FFA See Future Farmers of
America

Fibiger, Johannes Andreas Grib
Investigations on Spiroptera
carcinoma and the experi-
mental induction of cancer
(Nobel Lecture, Dec. 12,
1927). NOLM 2:122

FIBIGER, JOHANNES ANDREAS
GRIB
Wernstedt, W.
Presentation of the Nobel
Prize for Physiology or
Medicine for 1926 to Johannes
Andreas Grib Fibiger, Dec.
12, 1927. NOLM 2:119

FICTION See Literature

Field, David Dudley
Cost of "Blood and Iron."

BREWE 6:2157
In re Milligan--martial laws as
lawlessness. BREWE 6:2147
In the case of McCardle--neces-
sity as an excuse for tyranny.
BREWE 6:2155

Field, Stephen J. See following jt.
auths. Miller, S. F.; Terry,
D. S.; Waite, M. R.

Fielden, Samuel
Address at trial, Chicago, Octo-
ber 7-9, 1886. ACC:49;
PAF:41

Fillmore, Millard
First annual message. ANN 8:109;
STAT 1:792
Golden rule for foreign affairs.
Same as his First annual mes-
sage
Second annual message.
STAT 1:808
Third annual message.
STAT 1:834

FINANCE - UNITED STATES
Coolidge, C.
Third annual message.
STAT 3:2669
Landon, A. M.
Federal and family finances.
BAD:62
Taft, W. H.
Fourth annual message: part
II, December 6, 1912.
STAT 3:2511
Third annual message: part
IV, December 21, 1911.
STAT 3:2469

---- See also Tariff; Annual messages under name of each
President, i.e. Hayes, Rutherford B. First annual message

FINANCIERS See Banks and banking

Finch, Sir Heneage See Nottingham, H. F.

FINCH OF FORDWICH, JOHN
FINCH, 1st BARON
Falkland, L. C.
Ship-money-impeaching Lord
Keeper Finch. BREWE 6:2123

FINE ARTS See Art and artists

Finkle, Jesse J.
Brief sojourn. WALE:51

Finley, Charles O.
Responds to introduction.
PRS:115

FINSEN, NIELS RYBERG
Mörner, K. A. H.
Presentation [of the Nobel
Prize for Physiology or
Medicine to Niels Ryberg
Finsen, 1903]. NOLM 1:123

FIREMEN
Welcome to a Fire Chief as
speaker of a civic club.
HNWM:42

Fischer, Adolph
Address at trial, Chicago,
October 7-9, 1886.
ACC:36; PAF:32

Fischer, G.
Presentation [of the Nobel Prize
for Physiology or Medicine
to Paul Hermann Müller,
Dec. 11, 1948].
NOLM 3:227

Fischer, Hans
On haemin and the relationships
between haemin and chlorophyll (Nobel Lecture, Dec.
11, 1930). NOLC 2:165

FISCHER, HANS
Söderbaum, H. G.
Presentation [of the Nobel
Prize for Chemistry to Hans
Fischer, Dec. 11, 1930].
NOLC 2:161

Fischer, Hermann Emil
Syntheses in the purine and
sugar group (Nobel Lec-
ture, Dec. 12, 1902).
NOLC 1:21

FISCHER, HERMANN EMIL
Théel, H.
Presentation [of the Nobel
Prize for Chemistry to
Hermann Emil Fischer,
Dec. 12, 1902]. NOLC 1:17

Fischer-Hjalmars, Inga
Presentation [of the Nobel Prize
for Chemistry to Robert S.
Mulliken, Dec. 12, 1966].
NOLC 4:127

Fishburn, Phillip
Land of cattle, land of America.
BREWW:105

Fisher, Charles T., Jr.
Presents George C. Kenney.
LYI:150

Fisher, John
Jeopardy of daily life.
BREWE 6:2164

Fisk, Theophilus
War of capital against labor.
ANN 6:118

Fitch, Thomas
A fervent appeal for free silver
(1889). (National Silver Convention at St. Louis, Nov.
1889). DAVF:190

Flack, Gene
Responds to an introduction.
PRS:191

FLAG DAY
Beecher, H. W.
Raising the flag over Fort
Sumter. BREWE 1:347

FLAGS
Beveridge, A. J.
March of the flag. ANN 12:198;
BOORA 2:622; GRG:14;
LINS:276
Jackson, R. H.
Court broadens the rights of
citizens: the Second Flag
Salute Case, 1943. ROD:214
---- and others
West Virginia Board of Educa-
tion et al v. Barnette et al:
opinion for the court and dis-
senting opinion. ANN 16:148

Flaxman, John
Physical and intellectual beauty.
BREWE 6:2167

Flechier, Esprit
Death of Turenne.
BREWE 6:2174

Fleming, Sir Alexander
  Penicillin (Nobel Lecture,
    Dec. 11, 1945).
    NOLM 3:83

FLEMING, SIR ALEXANDER
  Liljestrand, G.
    Presentation [of the Nobel
    Prize for Physiology or
    Medicine to Sir Alexander
    Fleming, Ernst Boris Chain,
    and Sir Howard Walter
    Florey, Dec. 11, 1945].
    NOLM 3:77

Fleming, Mrs. Ian See Sykes,
  C., jt. auth.

Florence, Franklin
  Meaning of Black power.
    SMHR:161

Florey, Sir Howard Walter
  Penicillin (Nobel Lecture, Dec.
    11, 1945). NOLM 3:96

FLOREY, SIR HOWARD WALTER
  Liljestrand, G.
    Presentation [of the Nobel
    Prize for Physiology or
    Medicine to Sir Alexander
    Fleming, Ernst Boris Chain,
    and Sir Howard Walter
    Florey, Dec. 11, 1945].
    NOLM 3:77

Flowers, Walter See Jordan,
  B. C., jt. auth.

FLYING SAUCERS
  Sonberg, H. A.
    Unidentified flying objects;
    their history, and various
    explanations which have been
    given concerning their na-
    ture. BAS:203 (outline only)

FOCH, FERDINAND
  Pepper, G. W.
    Introducing Ferdinand Foch.
    LYI:145

FOLK LITERATURE
  Buchan, J.
    Novel and the fairy tale.
    ARS:54

FOOD
  Boyd Orr, J.

Science and peace (Nobel Lec-
    ture, Dec. 12, 1949).
    NOLP 2:415
Butz, E. L.
  Feast or famine: the key to
    peace. BA 1974-75:81
Hannah, J. A.
  Meeting world food news.
    BA 1976-77:103
Hatfield, M. O.
  Global interdependence: "Life,
    Liberty, and the Pursuit of
    Happiness" in today's world.
    BA 1974-75:89
Kissinger, H. A.
  Address before the World Food
    Conference. BA 1974-75:62

FOOD SUPPLY
  Bark, D. R.
    World food crisis.
    BREWW:219
  Borlaug, N. E.
    The green revolution, peace,
    and humanity (Nobel Lecture,
    Dec. 11, 1970). NOLP 3:454
  Brown, M.
    Famine: a reality, not just a
    threat. BREWW:168
  Carpenter, E.
    We are involved in the world
    food crisis. BREWW:223
  Dunlap, D. E.
    The world needs our help.
    BREWW:98
  Grappe, A.
    The age of food. BREWW:112
  Kubicek, K.
    Global crisis. BREWW:128
  Rush, W.
    Feeding the hungry world.
    BREWW:91
  Stratton, R. D.
    Food: a world crisis.
    BREWW:81
  Sullivan, J. H.
    The United States and the com-
    ing world food crisis.
    BA 1979-80:46
  Trafton, C.
    The moral dimensions of the
    world food problem.
    BREWW:206

FOOTE'S RESOLUTIONS See
    Foot's Resolution

FOOT'S RESOLUTION
  Hayne, R. Y.

On Foot's Resolution (January 21, 1830). BREWE 7:2441
Webster, D.
Reply to Hayne. ANN 5:347; BEN:35; BREWE 10:3758; BRR:23; HOW:53

Forbes, George W.
The Public Safety Conservation Bill, 1932. (New Zealand House of Representatives, April 19, 1932). MACS:314 sel.

FORCED LABOR
White, W. F.
"Work or fight" in the South. FON:724

Ford, Gerald R.
Acceptance speech. (Washington, D.C., Dec. 6, 1973). BA 1973-74:193
First presidential address. (Washington, Aug. 9, 1974). BA 1974-75:50
Presidential remarks with question-and-answer session (Peoria, Ill., March 5, 1976). BA 1975-76:133
Republican National Convention acceptance speech (Kansas City, Mo., Aug. 19, 1976). LINRST:349
State of the Union address (Jan. 15, 1975). JAM:31
Toast to Queen Elizabeth (1976). JAM:21

---- and others (Jimmy Carter)
The third presidential debate (Williamsburg, Va., Oct. 22, 1976). BA 1976-77:30

---- See Burger, W. E., jt. auth.

FORD, GERALD R.
Elizabeth II, Queen of England
Toast to President Ford and to the American people. JAM:22
Kaunda, K.
Toast to President Ford. JAM:23
Nelson, G. A.
Against the nomination of Gerald R. Ford.

BA 1973-74:188
Percy, C. H.
For the nomination of Gerald R. Ford. BA 1973-74:189

Ford, Guy Stanton
Presents Christopher Morley. LYI:55

Ford, Henry, II
Presents Elmo Roper. LYI:73

Ford, James W.
The right of revolution for the Negro people (Harlem, 1935). FON:800

FOREFATHERS' DAY
Prentiss, S. S.
On New England's Forefathers' Day. BREWE 8:3233

FOREIGN AID PROGRAM See Economic assistance, American; World War, 1939-1945 - United States - Aid to Great Britain

FOREIGN POPULATION See Immigration and emigration

FOREIGN TRADE See Commerce

Forman, James
Black manifesto. (Detroit, April 25, 1969). FON:1156; OE:235

Forssmann, Werner Theodor Otto
The role of heart catheterization and angiocardiography in the development of modern medicine (Nobel Lecture, Dec. 11, 1956). NOLM 3:506

FORSSMANN, WERNER THEODOR OTTO
Liljestrand, G.
Presentation [of the Nobel Prize for Physiology or Medicine to André Frederic Cournand, Werner Theodor Otto Forssmann, and Dickinson Woodruff Richards Jr., Dec. 11, 1956]. NOLM 3:501

Forten, James and others (R. Perrott)
Address to the humane and benev-

olent inhabitants of the
city and county of Philadelphia. (Philadelphia, Aug.
10, 1817). OE:14

An appeal against the colonization movement.... Same
as his Address to the hu-
mane and benevolent in-
habitants of the city and
county of Philadelphia

Fortune, T. Thomas
It is time to call a halt.
(Chicago, Jan., 1890).
FON:556
The present relations of labor
and capital. (Brooklyn,
April 20, 1886). FON:506

FORTUNES See Wealth

Fosdick, Harry Emerson
Christian conscience about
war. OLIS:237
Fundamentalist controversy.
Same as his Shall the
Fundamentalists win?
Power to see it through.
CROCK:58
Shall the Fundamentalists win?
ANN 14:325
Unknown soldier. LINS:312

FOSDICK, HARRY EMERSON
Gossett, W. T.
Presents Harry Emerson
Fosdick. LYI:157

FOUNDERS' DAY See Anniversaries

FOUR-H CLUBS
Welcome to Four H club members. HNWM:49

FOURTH OF JULY
Adams, J. Q.
Fourth of July oration,
1828. HAW:94
Bacon, L.
Plea for Africa. HAW:60
Sermon from Mark XII, 34.
HAW:57
Bancroft, G.
Fourth of July oration,
1826. HAW:75
Barlow, J.
Unfinished revolution.

ANN 3:90
Boudinot, E.
Mission of America.
BREWE 2:581
Burger, W. E.
Bicentennial of American inde-
pendence. BA 1976-77:185
Cadwell, D.
Oration. HAW:319
Carson, H. L.
American liberty.
BREWE 3:985
Choate, R.
On American nationality (82nd
anniversary of American inde-
pendence). ANN 9:54
Clinton, D.
Address at the Licking Summit
near Newark, Ohio. HAW:119
Cook, J.
Ultimate America.
BREWE 4:1381
Cox, A.
Can the dream survive?
BA 1979-80:157
Crockett, D.
Fourth of July oration, 1834.
HAW:136
Douglass, F.
I do not believe in the anti-
slavery of Abraham Lincoln.
FON:232
Slavery: speech at Rochester,
July 5, 1852. FON:104;
SMHR:125
What to the slave is the Fourth
of July? JAM:19; OE:41
Dwight, T.
On the duty of Americans at
the present crisis. ANN 4:33
Everett, E.
History of liberty.
BREWE 6:2092
Garrison, W. L.
Dangers of slavery.
ANN 5:303; MDT:26
Hecker, F. K. F.
Liberty in the New Atlantis.
BREWE 7:2457
King, T. S.
Fourth of July oration, 1860.
HAW:231
The two declarations of inde-
pendence: 1776 and 1861.
HAW:260
McCorkle, S.
A sermon for the anniversary
of American independence,

July 24th, 1786. HAW:292
Mack, E.
    Fourth of July oration,
    1838. HAW:164
Mason, J., Jr.
    Oration delivered on the 4th
    of July, 1818 at Williams-
    burg, Virginia. HAW:300
Meek, A. B.
    Oration. HAW:307
Osborne, P.
    It is time for us to be up
    and doing. FON:47
Phillips, W.
    Fourth of July oration.
    HAW:223
Rantoul, R., Jr.
    On the barbarity of the com-
    mon law. ANN 6:262
Robbins, A.
    Fourth of July oration,
    July 4, 1834. HAW:160
Robinson, F.
    A Jacksonian attack on
    monopoly (1834). DAVF:69
    Labor as the source of
    reform. ANN 6:69
Rush, R.
    Fourth of July oration,
    1812. HAW:16
Seward, W. H.
    Fourth of July oration,
    1840. HAW:183
Sumner, C.
    True grandeur of nations.
    BREWE 9:3548
Thoreau, H. D.
    Fourth of July oration,
    1854. HAW:200
Wallace, G. C.
    Civil Rights Bill: fraud,
    sham, and hoax. MDV:175
Webster, D.
    Fourth of July oration,
    1800. HAW:1
Whitney, A. G.
    Oration. HAW:329
Williams, P.
    Slavery and colonization.
    FON:43
Wolcott, O.
    Address at state line be-
    tween Southwick, Massachu-
    setts and Granby, Connecti-
    cut, July 4, 1825. HAW:122

Fox, Charles James
    Address on the King's speech

(protesting the call-up of the
militia). STRM:121
Against Warren Hastings.
    BREWE 6:2192
Character of the Duke of Bedford.
    BREWE 6:2182
In favor of Mr. Grey's motion
    for Parliamentary reform.
    BRYH:254
On electoral reform. Same as
    his In favor of Mr. Grey's
    motion for Parliamentary re-
    form
On the East India Bill.
    BREWE 6:2189
On the rejection of Napoleon's
    overtures. (H. of Commons,
    Feb. 3, 1800). CLAYP:232
Speech in the debate in Parlia-
    ment on the French overtures
    for peace, February 3, 1800.
    Same as his On the rejection
    of Napoleon's overtures

Fox, William See Featherston,
    Isaac, jt. auth.

France, Anatole
    Acceptance [of the Nobel Prize
    for Literature, 1921].
    NOB 6:93; NOL:181

FRANCE, ANATOLE
    Karlfeldt, E. A.
        Presentation [of the Nobel Prize
        for Literature to Anatole
        France, 1921]. NOB 6:85;
        NOL:174

FRANCE
    Carnot, L. N. M.
        Against imperialism in France.
        BREWE 3:967
    DeGaulle, C.
        France: the third world power.
        MDV:38
    Hugo, V. M.
        Liberty tree in Paris.
        BREWE 7:2548
    Pitt, W., 1759-1806
        Against French Republicanism.
        BREWE 8:3202
    ---- and others
        Deliverance of Europe (contains
        his Against French Republican-
        ism speech). BRYH:281

---- FOREIGN RELATIONS -
    AFRICA
Houphouet-Boigny, F.
    French Africa and the French
    Union. EMP:73

---- ---- MEXICO
Theirs, L. A.
    Mexico and Louis Napoleon's
    policies. BREWE 9:3610

---- HISTORY
Gambetta, L.
    France after German con-
    quest. BREWE 6:2217

---- ---- REVOLUTION, 1789-1799
Cambon, P. J.
    Crisis of 1793. BREWE 3:931
Danton, G. J.
    How can France be saved?
    BRN:56
    Let France be free.
    BREWE 5:1626
    To dare again, ever to dare.
    BREWE 5:1625
Dwight, T.
    On the duty of Americans
    at the present crisis.
    ANN 4:33
Guadet, M. E.
    Reply to Robespierre.
    BREWE 6:2244
Mackintosh, J.
    In behalf of free speech: on
    the trial of Jean Peltier
    accused of libelling Napoleon
    Bonaparte. BREWE 8:2919
Mirabeau, H. G. R.
    Defying the French aristoc-
    racy. BREWE 8:3033
    Justifying revolution.
    BREWE 8:3038
    On Necker's project "And yet
    you deliberate."
    BREWE 8:3024
    Reason immutable and sov-
    ereign. BREWE 8:3036
Robespierre, M.
    Defense from the charge of
    tyranny. BREWE 9:3341
    Demanding the King's death.
    BREWE 9:3338
    His defense of terrorism.
    BREWE 9:3331
    Moral ideas and Republican
    principles. BREWE 9:3334
Sheridan, R. B.

On the French Revolution.
    BREWE 9:3438
    Patriotism and perquisites.
    BREWE 9:3439
Tappan, D.
    A warning to Harvard seniors
    against world revolution (1798).
    DAVF:49
Vergniaud, P. V.
    Reply to Robespierre.
    BREWE 10:3692
    To the camp. BREWE 10:3690

---- ---- REVOLUTION, 1848
Lamartine, A. M. L.
    Revolution of 1848.
    BREWE 7:2702

---- POLITICS AND GOVERNMENT
Barnave, A. P. J. M.
    Representative democracy against
    majority absolutism.
    BREWE 1:218

FRANCHISE See Citizenship; Elec-
    tions; Suffrage; Woman suffrage

Francis, Hal
    Our three goals. BREWW:131

Franck, James
    Transformations of kinetic energy
    of free electrons into excitation
    energy of atoms by impacts
    (Nobel Lecture for 1925, Dec.
    11, 1926). NOLPH 2:98

FRANCK, JAMES
Oseen, C. W.
    Presentation [of the Nobel Prize
    for Physics for 1925 to James
    Franck and Gustav Hertz, Dec.
    11, 1926]. NOLPH 2:95

Frank, Il'ja Michajlovič
    Optics of light sources moving in
    refractive media (Nobel Lec-
    ture, Dec. 11, 1958).
    NOLPH 3:442

FRANK, IL'JA MICHAJLOVIC
Siegbahn, K.
    Presentation [of the Nobel Prize
    for Physics to Pavel Alekse-
    jevič Cerenkov, Il'ja Michaj-
    lovič Frank and Igor' Evgen'evič
    Tamm, Dec. 11, 1958].
    NOLPH 3:423

Frankfurter, Felix
John Marshall and the judicial
function, September 22,
1955. (Conf. on Govt. un-
der Law--Harvard Law
School in commemoration
of the 200th anniversary
of John Marshall's birth).
FRIP:353
The judicial process and the
Supreme Court, April 22,
1954. (American Philo-
sophical Society). FRIP:345
The Zeitgeist and the Judiciary. (25th anniversary
dinner of the Harvard Law
Review in 1912). FRIP:340

---- See following jt. auths.
Black, H. L.; Jackson,
R. H.

Franklin, Barbara Hackman
Consumer safety and health
(Boston, Mass., Nov. 29,
1978). BA 1978-79:133

Franklin, Benjamin
Address to the Federal Con-
vention. Same as his
Disapproving and accepting
the Constitution
Dangers of a salaried bureauc-
racy. BREWE 6:2199
Disapproving and accepting the
Constitution (Philadelphia,
Sept. 17, 1787). ALA:13;
AND:99; BOORA 1:78;
BREWE 6:2197; HURH:34;
REID:393
"The older I grow, the more
apt I am to doubt my own
judgment of others." Same
as his Disapproving and
accepting the Constitution
On signing the Constitution.
Same as his Disapproving
and accepting the Constitu-
tion
On the Constitution. Same as
his Disapproving and accept-
ing the Constitution
Plea to the Constitutional Con-
vention. Same as his Dis-
approving and accepting the
Constitution

FRANKLIN, BENJAMIN
Mirabeau, H. G. R.

Announcing the death of Franklin. BREWE 8:3035

Franklin, John Hope
America's window to the world:
her race problem. (New
York, Oct. 26, 1956). FON:907
Martin Luther King and American
traditions. BA 1968-69:45

Franks, Brian See Sykes, C., jt.
auth.

Fraser, Leon
Presents James F. Byrnes.
LYI:218

Fraser, Peter
Universal collective security--
amendments to the United Na-
tions Charter, 1945 (San
Francisco, May 3, 1945).
MACS:378 sel.

---- and others
The adoption of the Statute of
Westminster (New Zealand
House of Representatives, Nov.
7 and 11, 1947). MACS:286
sel.

FRATERNITY See Brotherliness

Fredga, A.
Presentation [of the Nobel Prize
for Chemistry to Derek H. R.
Barton and Odd Hassel, Dec.
11, 1969]. NOLC 4:295
Presentation [of the Nobel Prize
for Chemistry to Hermann
Staudinger, Dec. 11, 1953].
NOLC 3:393
Presentation [of the Nobel Prize
for Chemistry to Karl Ziegler
and Giulio Natta, Dec. 12,
1963]. NOLC 4:3
Presentation [of the Nobel Prize
for Chemistry to Otto Paul
Hermann Diels and Kurt Adler,
Dec. 12, 1950]. NOLC 3:255
Presentation [of the Nobel Prize
for Chemistry to Robert Burns
Woodward, Dec. 11, 1965].
NOLC 4:97
Presentation [of the Nobel Prize
for Chemistry to Sir Alexander
Robertus Todd, Dec. 11, 1957].
NOLC 3:519
Presentation [of the Nobel Prize

for Chemistry to Sir Robert
Robinson, Dec. 12, 1947].
NOLC 3:166
Presentation [of the Nobel Prize
for Chemistry to Vincent
du Vigneaud, Dec. 12,
1955]. NOLC 3:443

FREE PRESS See Liberty of
the press

FREE SPEECH
Constant, B.
Free speech necessary for
good government.
BREWE 4:1376
Curran, J. P.
England and English liberties
--in the case of Rowan.
BREWE 4:1546
For Peter Finnerty and free
speech. BREWE 4:1537
Douglass, F.
Plea for free speech in
Boston. BREWE 5:1906;
FON:244
Erskine, T.
Against Thomas Williams for
the publication of Paine's
Age of Reason.
BREWE 6:2038
Free speech and fundamental
rights: defense of Tom
Paine. BREWE 6:2069;
CLAYP:166
Speech in behalf of John
Stockdale. BREWE 6:2050
Gallagher, W.
Free just free.
BA 1973-74:132
Hamilton, A.
In the case of Zenger--for
free speech in America.
BREWE 6:2373
Holmes, O. W., Jr.
Dissenting opinion on Abrams
v. United States.
ANN 14:244; BOORA 2:666
Kennedy, R. F.
Fruitful tension.
BA 1966-67:138
LaFollette, R. M., Sr.
Free speech in wartime.
CUB:53 (outline only)
Mackintosh, J.
In behalf of free speech:
on the trial of Jean Peltier ac-

cused of libelling Napoleon
Bonaparte. BREWE 8:2919
Milton, J.
For the liberty of unlicensed
printing. BREWE 8:3017
Phillips, W.
Murder of Lovejoy. ALS:161;
HURH:74
Royer-Collard, P. P.
Against press censorship.
BREWE 9:3347
Sanford, E. T. and others
Gitlow v. New York: opinion
for the court and dissenting
opinion. ANN 14:476

---- See also Dissenters

FREE TRADE AND PROTECTION
Beaconsfield, B. D.
Third reading of the Corn Im-
portation Bill. MCB:211
Clay, H.
Free trade and seamen's rights.
BREWE 4:1264
Cobden, R.
Effects of protection in agricul-
ture. MCB:189; STRM:246
Free trade with all nations.
BREWE 4:1326

---- See also Corn laws; Tariff

---- NEW ZEALAND
Marshall, J. R.
NAFTA, 1965. MACS:448 sel.

FREEDMEN'S BUREAU, 1865
Johnson, A.
Veto of Freedmen's Bureau
Bill. ANN 10:3

FREEDOM See Liberty; Religious
liberty; Teaching, Freedom of

FREEDOM OF INFORMATION
Krug, J. F.
In defense of liberty: extremism
and other vices. BA 1975-76:193

FREEDOM OF SPEECH See Free
speech

Frehof, Solomon B.
David Glick. WALE:210

FREEMASONS

Address of the United States Anti-
Masonic Convention (1830).
DAVF:73

An anti-Masonic call for per-
severance (1834).
DAVF:83

Armstrong, L.
Masonry proved to be a work
of darkness (1830).
DAVF:82

Debates at the Anti-Masonic
Convention (1830). DAVF:79

Hall, P.
Pray God give us the
strength to bear up under
all our troubles. FON:13

Frelinghuysen, Theodore
The Cherokee lands. (Con-
gress, April 9, 1830).
HOW:189

In favor of universal suffrage.
BREWE 6:2203

Revivalist sermon. ANN 1:344

FRIED, ALFRED HERMANN
Løvland, J. G.
Presentation [of the Nobel
Prize for Peace to Alfred
Hermann Fried, Dec. 10,
1911]. NOLP 1:238

Fried, Paul
Price of peace. SCHW:35

Friedman, Milton
The future of capitalism
(Los Angeles, Feb. 9,
1977). LINRST:243

FRIENDS, SOCIETY OF
Backhouse, M. A.
The international service
of the Society of Friends
(Nobel Lecture, Dec. 12,
1947). NOLP 2:380

Cadbury, M. J.
Quakers and peace (Nobel
Lecture, Dec. 12, 1947).
NOLP 2:391

Jahn, G.
Presentation [of the Nobel
Prize for Peace to the
Friends Service Council and
the American Friends Service Committee, Dec. 10,
1947]. NOLP 2:373

FRIENDSHIP
Beecher, H. W.
On fellowship. HURH:118
Welcome to old friends (2 exam-
ples). BNH:52

Friesen, S. Von
Presentation [of the Nobel Prize
for Physics to Luis W. Alvarez, Dec. 11, 1968].
NOLPH 4:239

Fry, Franklin Clark See Sevareid,
E., jt. auth.

FUGITIVE SLAVE BILL See
Slavery in the United States

Fulbright, James William
Arrogance of power. ANN 18:362
Foreign policy--old myths and
new realities (Washington,
March 25, 1964). ANN 18:225;
HURH:374
Great Society is a sick society.
LAA:10
Intervention in Santo Domingo;
we are much closer to being
the most unrevolutionary nation
on earth. LAA:165
"The neglect of the song." (Na-
tional Press Club, Washington,
D.C., Dec. 18, 1974).
BA 1974-75:109
Old myths and new realities.
Same as his Foreign policy--
old myths and new realities
Press and politicians. ERP:159
Two Americas. BA 1965-66:115
Violence in the American char-
acter. ANN 18:206
"We are clinging to old myths in
the face of new realities."
Same as his Foreign policy--
old myths and new realities

FULBRIGHT, JAMES WILLIAM
Ashmore, H. S.
Presents J. William Fulbright.
LYI:205

Fuller, Melville Weston and others
(J. M. Harlan)
United States v. E. C. Knight
Company, 1895: opinion for
the Supreme Court and dissent-
ing opinion. ANN 12:23

Fuller, Zelotes
Tree of liberty (George Wash-
ington birthday address).
ANN 5:355

FUNDAMENTALISM See Religion

FUNERAL SERMONS
Bossuet, J. B.
Funeral oration over the
Prince Condé. BREWE 2:557
Brooks, P.
Character of Abraham Lin-
coln. BREWE 2:644
Emerson, R. W.
Greatness of a plain Amer-
ican. BREWE 5:1999
Flechier, E.
Death of Turenne.
BREWE 6:2174
Hugo, V. M.
Oration on Honoré de Balzac.
BREWE 7:2546
Hypereides
Funeral oration. COG:210
Ingalls, J. J.
Undiscovered country.
BREWE 7:2574
Lee, H.
Funeral oration on Washing-
ton. BREWE 7:2744
Lovell, J.
Funeral oration. POC:138
Lysias
Funeral oration. COG:9
Morris, G.
Oration over Hamilton.
BREWE 8:3075; HURH:54
Morton, P.
Oration at the reinternment
of Warren. POC:320
Pericles
On those who died in the
war. ARS:191; BAS:133
(outline only); BREWE 8:3169;
SAG:33
Stanley, A. P.
Palmerston and the duty of
England (funeral oration).
BREWE 9:3506

Funston, G. Keith
Responds to an introduction.
PRS:135

Furay, Mortimer
Statement [before the] Subcommittee on Constitutional

Amendments of the Committee
on the Judiciary of the U. S.
Senate. BOST:219

Furuseth, Andrew
Work is worship. ANN 14:561

FUTURE
Brown, H. A.
Plea of the future.
BREWE 2:686
Mather, L.
Discourse concerning the uncer-
tainty of the times of men.
POC:377

FUTURE FARMERS OF AMERICA
Depta, M.
Aims and purposes of the FFA.
BREWW:157
Francis, H.
Our three goals. BREWW:131
Harrison, R.
Leadership--a goal for us all.
BREWW:150
Herink, R.
A succession of goals.
BREWW:141
Madrid, S.
I am proud to be a part of it.
BREWW:153
Morelli, L.
Vocational agriculture, the
FFA, and our free enterprise
system. BREWW:78
Slabach, D.
Five hundred miles south.
BREWW:208

- G -

Gage, Patty
The Oahe Project--yes or no?
BREWW:191

Gaitskell, Hugh
Labour, politics and democratic
socialism. (Blackpool, Nov.
28, 1959). MCB:250

Galamison, Milton A.
Integration must work--nothing
else can. (New York, March
27, 1963). FON:959

Galbraith, John Kenneth
On history, political economy, and

Vietnam (Memphis State University, May 30, 1975).
BA 1975-76:78

Gale, James
Great American institution.
REIR:161

Gallacher, William See Baldwin, S. B., jt. auth.

Gallagher, Buell G.
Memorial convocation address (on Martin Luther King, Jr.). BA 1967-68:169

Gallagher, Wes
The credibility gap: argument by specific instances. Same as his Upon acceptance of the 1967 William Allen White Foundation Award for Journalistic Merit
Free just free. (Saint Bonaventure, N. Y., May 14, 1973).
BA 1973-74:132
Upon acceptance of the 1967 William Allen White Foundation Award for Journalistic Merit. BA 1966-67:148; JEF:327; JEFF:311

Gallatin, Albert
Constitutional liberty and executive despotism.
BREWE 6:2209

---- See also Allen, J., jt. auth.

Galloway, Joseph
Speech for the petition to change the form of government. POC:200

Gallup, George
Mass information or mass entertainment. ANN 17:215

GALSWORTHY, JOHN
Österling, A.
Presentation [of the Nobel Prize for Literature to John Galsworthy, 1932].
NOB 6:277; NOL:302

Gambetta, Leon
France after German conquest.
BREWE 6:2217

GAMBLING
Thuraisingham, E. E. C.
Lotteries: Hell, Hitler, and Bernard Shaw. MONS:167

GANDHI, INDIRA
Hayes, A.
Presents Indira Gandhi. LYI:99

Gandhi, Mohandas Karamchand
I live under no illusion. Same as his Speech in London (1931)
Speech in London (1931) (Second Round Table Conference, London, Nov. 28, 1931). BRN:109

Gannon, Ann Ida
A Catholic college, yesterday and tomorrow (Ursuline College, Cleveland, May 22, 1972).
HOR:78

Gard, S.
Presentation [of the Nobel Prize for Physiology or Medicine to François Jacob, André Lwoff, and Jacques Monod, Dec. 11, 1965]. NOLM 4:143
Presentation [of the Nobel Prize for Physiology or Medicine to John Franklin Enders, Thomas Huckle Weller, and Frederick Chapman Robbins, Dec. 11, 1954]. NOLM 3:443
Presentation [of the Nobel Prize for Physiology or Medicine to Max Delbrück, Alfred D. Hershey, and Salvador E. Luria, Dec. 10, 1969].
NOLM 4:401
Presentation [of the Nobel Prize for Physiology or Medicine to Sir Frank Macfarlane Burnet and Peter Brian Medawar, Dec. 12, 1960]. NOLM 3:685

GARDENS
Hirschler, P.
How to beautify your farm.
BREWW:124

Gardiner, Robert K.
Citizenship and political liberalism.
EMP:106

Gardner, Henry J.
New England nativism.
ANN 8:484

Gardner, John William
Education. (Austin, Jan. 1972).
BA 1972-73:119
In behalf of a troubled nation.
BA 1967-68:102
People power. (New Orleans,
April 3, 1975--Public Af-
fairs Research Council).
BA 1974-75:158

Garfield, James A.
Conflict of ideas in America.
BREWE 6:2231
Inaugural address.
USINAU:141; USINAUG:141
Revolution and the logic of
coercion. BREWE 6:2226

GARFIELD, JAMES A.
Blaine, J. G.
Life and character of J. A.
Garfield. BREWE 2:482;
HURH:137

GARIBALDI, GIUSEPPE
Buchanan, D.
Eulogy of Garibaldi.
MCA:78
Crispi, F.
At the unveiling of Garibaldi's
statue. BREWE 4:1467

Garnet, Henry Highland
Address to the slaves of the
United States of America.
(Buffalo, N.Y., National
Convention of Negro Citi-
zens, August, 1843).
FON:81; OE:20; SMHV:21
Let the monster perish.
(Washington, D.C., Feb.
12, 1865). FON:307
A plea in behalf of the Cuban
revolution. (New York,
Dec. 13, 1872). FON:380

Garran, Robert Randolph
Royal visit. MCA:191

Garrison, William Lloyd
Address delivered before the
Old Colony Anti-Slavery
Society, July 4, 1839.
Same as his Dangers of
slavery
At Charleston, South Carolina,
1865. BREWE 6:2241
Beginning a revolution.

BREWE 6:2237
Dangers of slavery (July 4, 1839).
ANN 5:303; MDT:26
On the death of John Brown.
BREWE 6:2238
Union and slavery. BREWE 6:2240

GARRISON, WILLIAM LLOYD
Mill, J. S.
A tribute to William Lloyd Gar-
rison. REID:395 selections
Ransom, R. C.
William Lloyd Garrison: a
centennial oration. SMHV:66

Garry, Charles R.
In defense of Huey Newton.
ERP:161

Garsek, Isadore
Do not judge this violent death.
WALE:52
Highest attainment. WALE:54
Sorrow but not tragedy.
WALE:57

Garvey, Marcus
The principles of the Universal
Negro Improvement Association. (New York, Nov. 25,
1922). FON:748; OE:103;
SMHV:100
UNIA movement. Same as his The
principles of the Universal Negro Improvement Association
We are mostly subject peoples all
over the world. (7th International Convention of the Negro
Peoples of the World, St.
Andrew, Jamaica, August,
1935). FON:790

GASES
Norrish, R. G. W.
Some fast reactions in gases
studied by flash photolysis and
kinetic spectroscopy.
NOLC 4:206
Ramsay, Sir W.
The rare gases of the atmos-
phere. NOLC 1:68
Rayleigh, J. W. S.
The density of gases in the air
and the discovery of argon.
NOLPH 1:90
Waals, J. D. V. D.
The equation of state for gases
and liquids. NOLPH 1:254

Gasser, Herbert Spencer
  Mammalian nerve fibers (Nobel
  Lecture for 1944, Dec. 12,
  1945). NOLM 3:34

Gaud, William Steen
  Why foreign aid?
  BA 1967-68:179

Gaustad, Eddie S.
  The beginning of wisdom.
  (Baylor University, 1947).
  CAPB:370

Geiman, Carolyn Kay
  Are they really "unteachable"?
  LINR:94

Gell-Mann, Murray
  Symmetry and currents in
  particle physics (Nobel Lecture, 1969). NOLPH 4:299

GELL-MANN, MURRAY
  Waller, I.
    Presentation [of the Nobel
    Prize for Physics to Murray
    Gell-Mann, 1969].
    NOLPH 4:295

GENERAL MOTORS CORPORATION
  Curtice, H.
    Automotive research at
    General Motors. ANN 17:379

GENERATION GAP See Youth-
  adult relationship

GENETIC ENGINEERING
  McGill, W. J.
    Science and the law.
    BA 1977-78:83

GENETICS
  Crick, F. H. C.
    On the genetic code.
    NOLM 3:811
  Lederberg, J.
    A view of genetics.
    NOLM 3:615
  Morgan, T. H.
    The relation of genetics
    to physiology and medicine.
    NOLM 2:313
  Nirenberg, M. W.
    The genetic code.
    NOLM 4:370

GENEVA CONFERENCE, 1955
  Eisenhower, D. D.
    Spirit of Geneva. BEN:136

GENIUS
  Reynolds, J.
    Genius and imitation.
    BREWE 9:3313
  Wirt, W.
    Genius as the capacity of work.
    BREWE 10:3910

George III, King of Great Britain
  Speech to Parliament (Nov. 11,
  1800). JAM:32

George, Dan
  Brotherhood and understanding.
  MAES:393
  My people, the Indians (Yakima,
  Washington). MAES:397

GEORGE, GRACE
  Taylor, D.
    Presents Grace George.
    LYI:19

Geren, Paul
  The lie of war. (Baylor University, 1935). CAPB:359

German, Obadiah
  Unprepared for war with England.
  ANN 4:319

GERMAN LANGUAGE
  Clemens, S. L.
    Horrors of the German lan-
    guage. BEN:204

GERMANY
  Bismarck, O.
    Plea for imperial armament.
    BREWE 2:456
  Stresemann, G.
    The new Germany (Nobel Lec-
    ture for 1926, June 29, 1927).
    NOLP 2:8

GERSHWIN, GEORGE
  Nizer, L.
    Presents George Gershwin.
    LYI:15

Gerstein, Israel
  Candle of the Lord. WALE:60
  Man is a soldier. WALE:60

GETTYSBURG, BATTLE OF,
1863
Adams, C. F., Jr.
Battle of Gettysburg.
BREWE 1:31

GETTYSBURG NATIONAL CEME-
TERY See Lincoln, A.
Gettysburg address

Ghali, Waguih
Egyptian in Israel. MDYG:152

Giauque, William Francis
Some consequences of low-
temperature research in
chemical thermodynamics
(Nobel Lecture, Dec. 12,
1949). NOLC 3:227

GIAUQUE, WILLIAM FRANCIS
Tiselius, A. W. K.
Presentation [of the Nobel
Prize for Chemistry to
William Francis Giauque,
Dec. 12, 1949].
NOLC 3:221

Gibbons, James, Cardinal
Defense of the Knights of
Labor. ANN 11:131
Progress of the Catholic
Church in America.
ANN 11:148
To the Parliament of Religions.
BREWE 6:2248

Gibbs, Jonathan C.
Freedom's joyful day.
(Philadelphia, Jan. 1,
1863). FON:262

Gibson, John Bannister
Against judicial review: dissenting opinion on Eakin
v. Raub. ANN 5:174

Giddings, Joshua Reed
Slavery and the annexation
of Cuba. BREWE 6:2258
Texas and slavery.
ANN 7:201

---- See also Chase, S. P., jt.
auth.

Gide, André
Acceptance [of the Nobel

Prize for Literature, 1947].
NOB 7:7; NOL:426

GIDE, ANDRE
Österling, A.
Presentation [of the Nobel Prize
for Literature to André Gide,
1947]. NOB 7:3; NOL:422

GIDEONSE, HARRY D.
Sellers, R. Z.
Presents Harry D. Gideonse.
LYI:80

Gierow, Karl Ragnar
Presentation address [of the Nobel
Prize for Literature to Alek-
sandr Solzhenitsyn, 1970].
NOB 18:3
Presentation address [of the Nobel
Prize for Literature to Samuel
Beckett, 1969]. NOB 3:3

GIFTS See Acceptance speeches -
Gifts; Presentation speeches -
Gifts

Ginna, Robert
Responds to an introduction at a
Newcomen Society dinner.
PRS:156

GIRARD COLLEGE
Reed, T. B.
Immortality and good deeds
(semi-centennial of Girard
College). BREWE 9:3307

GIRL SCOUTS
Welcome to Girl Scouts (or
Pioneer Girls, etc).
HNWM:50

Gittings, Robert
Exploring the known. MDYG:207

Gladstone, William Ewart
Campaign speech (at Perth, De-
cember 1, 1879). BRYH:415
Commercial value of artistic
excellence. BREWE 6:2283
Destiny and individual aspiration.
BREWE 6:2288
First Home Rule Bill. Same as
his Home Rule, June 7, 1886
Fundamental error of English
colonial aggrandizement.
BREWE 6:2266

Home Rule, June 7, 1886.
(H. of Commons). MCB:301
Home rule and autonomy.
BREWE 6:2278
On domestic and foreign af-
fairs. (West Calder, Nov.
27, 1879). MCB:39;
STRM:316
On Lord Beaconsfield.
BREWE 6:2291
Principles of foreign policy.
Same as his On domestic
and foreign affairs
Use of books. BREWE 6:2289

GLADSTONE, WILLIAM EWART
Churchill, R. H. S.
Gladstone's Egyptian in-
consistencies.
BREWE 3:1148
Laurier, W.
Character and work of Glad-
stone. BREWE 7:2732

Glaser, Donald Arthur
Elementary particles and bubble
chambers (Nobel Lecture,
Dec. 12, 1960).
NOLPH 3:529

GLASER, DONALD ARTHUR
Siegbahn, K.
Presentation [of the Nobel
Prize for Physics to Donald
Arthur Glaser, Dec. 12,
1960]. NOLPH 3:525

Glass, Carter See Connally,
T. T., jt. auth.

Glenn, John H.
Accepting the Distinguished
Service Medal. (Outline
of speech). CUB:65
Address before the Joint Meeting of Congress. (Wash-
ington, Feb. 26, 1962).
HURH:362
"What we have done so far but
small building blocks in a
huge pyramid to come."
Same as his Address before
the Joint Meeting of Con-
gress

GLENN, JOHN H.
Kennedy, J. F.
Presenting the Distinguished

Service Medal to John Glenn
(outline of speech). CUB:64

GLICK, DAVID
Freehof, S. B.
David Glick. WALE:210

GOALS See Success

Gobat, Charles Albert
The development of the Hague
Conventions of July 29, 1899
(Nobel Lecture for 1902, Oslo,
July 18, 1906). NOLP 1:30

GOBAT, CHARLES ALBERT
Løvland, J. G.
Toast to C. A. Gobat [present-
ing the Nobel Prize for Peace
for 1902, Oslo, July 18, 1906].
NOLP 1:29

GOD
Drummond, H.
Greatest thing in the world.
BREWE 5:1941
Lubbers, A. D.
God and Joe College.
SCHW:69
Read, D. H. C.
Is God over thirty? Religion
and the youth revolt.
BA 1966-67:129
Religious science. BURT:180
Robespierre, M.
Festival of the Supreme Being.
BREWE 9:3340
"If God did not exist, it would
be necessary to invent him."
BREWE 9:3330
Moral ideas and Republican
principles. BREWE 9:3334
Whitefield, G.
Kingdom of God.
BREWE 10:3885
Zellner, L. R.
What can we prove about God?
ARN:337; ARS:187

---- See also Death of God theology

Godfrey, James L.
Presents Frank Borden Hanes.
LYI:38

Godley, Robert
The demand for responsible government. (Wellington, Nov. 15,
1850). MACS:66 sel.

Goedhart, G. J. van Heuven
  Refugee problems and their
    solutions (Nobel Lecture,
    Dec. 12, 1955). NOLP 3:97

GOETHALS, GEORGE W.
  Willcox, W. R.
    Introducing G. W. Goethals
    to the Economic Club of
    New York, March 5, 1914.
    LYI:183

Goh Keng Swee
  Elite combat party (Communist
    Party). MONS:394
  How Singapore's monetary sys-
    tem now works (Singapore,
    Sept. 20, 1969).
    MONSA:282
  A remarkable phenomenon:
    why Singapore is different
    ... (March 29, 1968).
    MONSA:277
  Some delusions of the decade
    of development. MONS:385

Goheen, Robert F.
  Sorting it out. (Princeton
    Univ., June 4, 1972).
    HOR:21

Goldberg, Arthur J.
  Human rights and détente (Bel-
    grade, Oct. 6, 1977).
    BA 1977-78:71

Golden, James L.
  Moments to remember (com-
    mencement address--John
    Glenn High School).
    BRP:236
  Political speaking since the
    1920's. LINR:167

Goldfarb, Solomon D.
  Art of reconstruction.
    WALE:61
  Embers and cinders.
    WALE:67
  My cup runneth over. WALE:70

Goldhaber, Gerald M.
  Organizational communication
    (Monterrey, Mexico, Oct.
    29, 1975). LINRST:44

Goldman, Emma
  Anarchy vs. patriotism.

(New York, 1910). HURH:166
    "Patriotism--a menace to liberty."
    Same as her Anarchy vs.
    patriotism

---- and others (Sarah and Angelina
    Grimké)
  Statement [before the] Subcommittee
    on Constitutional Amendments
    of the Committee on the Judi-
    ciary of the U.S. Senate.
    BOST:215

Goldman, Israel M.
  Biography of an angel. WALE:72
  Book of life. WALE:73
  Let thy garments be always white.
    WALE:75
  Man who walked with God.
    WALE:77

Goldwater, Barry M.
  Acceptance speech, San Francisco,
    California, July 17, 1964.
    Same as his Extremism in de-
    fense of liberty (accepting
    nomination for presidency)
  Campaign speech, Washington,
    D.C., October 21, 1964.
    SIN:345
  Extremism in defense of liberty
    (accepting nomination for
    presidency, July 17, 1964).
    MAC:251; MACR:292; MDV:115;
    SIN:337
  I accept your nomination. Same
    as his Extremism in defense
    of liberty (accepting nomination
    for Presidency)
  Nomination acceptance speech.
    Same as his Extremism in de-
    fense of liberty (accepting
    nomination for Presidency)
  Total victory in the Cold War.
    ANN 18:42
  Why we must be stronger militar-
    ily. BAS:92 (outline only);
    LAA:8
  Will to be strong. Same as his
    Why we must be stronger
    militarily

Golgi, Camilio
  The neuron doctrine--theory and
    facts (Nobel Lecture, Dec. 11,
    1906). NOLM 1:189

GOLGI, CAMILIO
  Mörner, K. A. H.

Presentation [of the Nobel
Prize for Physiology or
Medicine to Camilio Golgi
and Santiago Ramon y Cajal,
Dec. 12, 1906]. NOLM 1:185

GOOD AND EVIL
Graham, W. F.
Confusing evil with good.
LINR:179

GOOD WILL SPEECHES
Nixon, R. M.
Radio-television address from
Moscow. ARS:242
Theater begins with wonder
(outline of speech). CUB:70

Goodall, Clifford H.
Energy statement. TAC:219

GOODFELLOWS See Brotherliness

Goodloe, Joseph W.
A Black-operated firm. (Afro-
American Student Union,
Harvard Univ. School of
Business Administration,
May 12, 1971). VER:253

Goodman, Julian B.
Broadcast journalism: serving
the democratic process.
(Ithaca, N.Y., Oct. 22,
1976). BA 1976-77:52
Community and communications.
MOP:381

Goodman, Stanley J.
Raising the fallen image of
business. (New York,
January 7, 1974).
BA 1973-74:160

GOODY, HENRY
Greenberg, S.
Henry Goody. WALE:214

Gordis, Robert
Latter-Day Joseph. WALE:81

Gordon, David W.
Fruitful tears. WALE:83

Gordon, John Brown
It was purely a peace police
organization. CUR:98

Gossage, Howard Luck
Our fictitious freedom of the
press. MDV:285

Gossett, William T.
Presents Harry Emerson Fosdick.
LYI:157

GOSSIP
Barrow, I.
Slander. BREWE 1:224
Butler, J.
Government of the tongue.
BREWE 3:842
Massillon, J. B.
Curse of a malignant tongue.
BREWE 8:2980

Gottheil, Richard
Jews as a race and as a nation.
BREWE 6:2294

Gould, Jeffrey C.
My responsibility as an agricultural citizen. BREWW:147

GOVERNMENT See Democracy;
Industry and state; Municipal
government; Political science;
State, The; State rights; Suffrage. Also Name of country
or state with subdivision Politics and government, e.g.
Great Britain - Politics and
government; United States -
Politics and government

GOVERNMENT, RESISTANCE TO
Boucher, J.
Civil liberty and nonresistance.
ANN 2:343; POC:552
Griswold, E. N.
Dissent, protest, and disobedi-
ence. ANN 18:670;
BA 1967-68:141; JEF:196
Hubbard, W.
Happiness of a people in the
wisdom of their rulers directing
and in obedience of their
brethren attending unto what
Israel ought to do. ANN 1:248
King, M. L., Jr.
Love, law, and civil disobedi-
ence. FON:943; LINR:63;
LINRS:70; LINRST:75; STOT:321
Nonviolence and social change.
OE:157
Nonviolence: moral challenge

for peace and justice.
NOLP 3:333; THOMS:99
Sacks, M.
The value of disobedience.
LINRS:148; LINRST:152
Thoreau, H. D.
Civil disobedience.
BOORA 1:318

GOVERNMENT BANKING   See
Banks and banking; Inde-
pendent treasury

GOVERNMENT REGULATION OF
INDUSTRY   See   Industry
and state

GOVERNMENT SPENDING POLICY
Brown, E. G., Jr.
Proposals for change: an
inaugural address.
BA 1978-79:103

GOVERNORS   See   Public officials

Grady, Henry W.
New South (speech to the New
England Society).
ANN 11:240; BAS:121 (out-
line only); BOORA 1:465;
LINS:254
New South and the race prob-
lem. Same as his Race
problem
Race problem (speech to the
Boston Merchants' Associa-
tion). BREWE 6:2299

GRAFT (IN POLITICS)   See
Elections - Corrupt practices

Graham, D. A.
Some facts about Southern
lynchings. (Indianapolis,
June 4, 1899). FON:613

Graham, Frank Porter
Presents Robert M. Hutchins.
LYI:96

Graham, William F. (Billy
Graham)
Confusing evil with good.
LINR:179
"Learn the lesson of the worm."
Same as his National humil-
ity
National humility. (New York,

1957). HURH:339
Our bicentennial (Dec. 31, 1975).
BA 1975-76:34

GRAHAM, WILLIAM F. (BILLY
GRAHAM)
DuVall, W. O.
Presents Billy Graham.
LYI:160

Granit, Ragnar
The development of retinal neuro-
physiology (Nobel Lecture, Dec.
12, 1967). NOLM 4:255
Presentation [of the Nobel Prize
for Physiology or Medicine to
John Carew Eccles, Alan Lloyd
Hodgkin, and Andrew Fielding
Huxley, Dec. 11, 1963].
NOLM 4:3

GRANIT, RAGNAR
Bernhard, C. G.
Presentation [of the Nobel Prize
for Physiology or Medicine to
Ragnar Granit, Haldan Keffer
Hartline, and George Wald,
Dec. 12, 1967]. NOLM 4:251

Granqvist, G.
Presentation [of the Nobel Prize
for Physics for 1914 to Max
Von Laue, Nov. 12, 1915].
NOLPH 1:343

Grant, Ulysses Simpson
Eighth annual message.
STAT 2:1318
Fifth annual message.
STAT 2:1254
First annual message.
STAT 2:1188
First inaugural address.
USINAU:129; USINAUG:129
For annexation (of the Dominican
Republic). ANN 10:231
Fourth annual message.
STAT 2:1233
Second annual message.
STAT 2:1203
Second inaugural address.
USINAU:132; USINAUG:132
Separation of church and school.
ANN 10:365
Seventh annual message.
STAT 2:1294
Sixth annual message.
STAT 2:1275

Third annual message.
STAT 2:1220

GRANT, ULYSSES SIMPSON
Conkling, R.
Nomination of U. S. Grant for
a third term. BREWE 4:1366
Farrar, F. W.
Funeral oration on General
Grant. BREWE 6:2128
McKinley, W.
Grant (at dedication of
Grant monument in New
York City). BREWE 8:2905

Grappe, Allen
The age of food. BREWW:112

Grass, Fonda
The sky's the limit.
BREWW:115

Grattan, Henry
Against English imperialism.
Same as his Declaration of
Irish rights, April 19, 1780
Declaration of Irish rights,
April 19, 1780.
BREWE 6:2314; CLAYP:120
Free people. Same as his
Making his second motion
for a Declaration of Irish
rights, April 16, 1782
Invective against Corry.
BREWE 6:2330
Making his second motion for
a Declaration of Irish
rights, April 16, 1782.
BRYH:244
Unsurrendering fidelity to coun-
try. BREWE 6:2333

Gray, William H.
Justice should recognize no
color. (Arkansas Constitutional Convention, 1868).
FON:353

GREAT BRITAIN
Abdul Rahman, T.
What the Commonwealth
means (response to welcome
address by British Prime
Minister). MONS:22
Beloff, M.
Americanisation of British
intellectual life. MYDG:114
Bristol, G. D.

Grievances and oppressions un-
der Charles I. BREWE 5:1861
Canning, G.
England in repose.
BREWE 3:941
Chamberlain, J.
Empire and home rule.
MCB:60; STRM:387
Cromwell, O.
Debating whether or not to be-
come King of England.
BREWE 4:1485
Curran, J. P.
England and English liberties--
in the case of Rowan.
BREWE 4:1546
Ethelbert
Coming of Christianity.
BRYH:3
Gladstone, W. E.
Fundamental error of English
colonial aggrandizement.
BREWE 6:2266
On domestic and foreign affairs.
MCB:39; STRM:316
Hyde, E.
"Discretion" as despotism.
BREWE 7:2562
Laurier, W.
Canada, England and the United
States in 1899. BREWE 7:2737
Lloyd George, D.
The budget. BRYH:461;
JAE:170; MCB:233; STRM:407

---- ARMY
Bristol, G. D.
Army in domestic politics.
BREWE 5:1865
Fox, C. J.
Address on the King's speech
(protesting the call-up of the
militia). STRM:121
William I
Speech to his troops before the
battle of Hastings. BRYH:27

---- COLONIES
Bell, F. H. D.
The defence of the Empire in
the Great War. MACS:273 sel.
Berkeley, W.
Speech to the Virginia House
of Burgesses. POC:169
Bernard, F.
Speech to the Council and
House of Representatives.
POC:227

---- PARLIAMENT
Bacon, F.
Upon the motion of subsidy
(November 15, 1598 speech).
BRYH:90
Bradlaugh, C.
Appeal for justice.   JAE:142
Churchill, W. L. S.
Parliament in the air raids
(September 17, 1940
speech). STRM:481
Cromwell, O.
Address to Parliament,
September 4, 1654.   BRYH:144
On the dissolution of Parlia-
ment (First Protectorate
Parliament).   CLAYP:14
Dering, E.
Religious controversy in
Parliament.   BREWE 5:1808
Elizabeth I
Speech at the dissolution of
Parliament.   BRYH:75
Speech at the proroguing of
Parliament.   BRYH:77
Fox, C. J.
In favor of Mr. Grey's
motion for Parliamentary
reform.   BRYH:254
Grimstone, H.
Projecting canker worms
and caterpillars.
BREWE 6:2341
Lenthall, W.
Opening the long Parliament
under Charles I.
BREWE 7:2767
Mansfield, W. M.
Reply to the Earl of Chatham
against Parliamentary ex-
emption from arrest for
debt.   BREWE 8:2947
Oxford and Asquith, H. H.
Parliament Bill, 1911.
MCB:162
Wellesley, A.
Against Parliamentary re-
form.   STRM:171
Wentworth, P.
Liberty of the Commons.
BRYH:79; CLAYP:1
Wilkes, J.
Denies the right of the
House of Commons to re-
ject duly elected members.
STRM:39
Wyndham, W.
Royal prerogative delegated

from the people (Army Bill,
1734).   BREWE 10:3927

---- POLITICS AND GOVERNMENT
Attlee, C. R.
The Labour programme.
MCB:471
Beaconsfield, B. D.
Against democracy for England.
BREWE 1:296
Meaning of conservatism.
BREWE 1:309; BRYF:534;
MCB:431
Tory democracy.   JAE:139
Bristol, G. D.
Army in domestic politics.
BREWE 5:1865
Burke, E.
Principle in politics: speech
at Bristol, previous to the
election, 1780 (defends his
Parliamentary conduct).
BREWE 2:812; BRYH:211
Churchill, R. H. S.
Administration of Chips.
STRM:355
Age of action.   BREWE 3:1144
Trust the people speech.
MCB:441
Churchill, W. L. S.
The Conservative programme.
MCB:464
Curran, J. P.
On government by attachment.
BREWE 4:1557
Curzon of Kedleston, G.
Debate on the Parliament
Bill.   MCB:169
Depew, C. M.
Poetry and politics in Britain.
BREWE 5:1796
Hardie, J. K.
Socialist Commonwealth.
MCB:451
Keynes, J. M.
Am I a Liberal?   MCB:456
Lowe, R.
Coming of democracy.
MCB:138
Macaulay, T. B.
Consent or force in govern-
ment.   BREWE 8:2888
Reform Bill.   CLAYP:295;
MCB:110
Mill, J. S.
Representation of the people.
MCB:154
Russell, J. R.

Reform of the franchise.
MCB:87
Sidney, A.
Governments for the people
and not the people for gov-
ernments (scaffold speech).
BREWE 9:3454
Smith, S.
"Wounds, shrieks, and tears"
in government.
BREWE 9:3490

GREAT SOCIETY See United
States - Social policy

GREATNESS See Fame

Grede, William J.
America, a frontier.
ANN 17:154

GREECE, ANCIENT
Demosthenes
First Olynthiac oration.
SAG:199
First Philippic. COG:40;
SAG:188
On the Chersoneus.
SAG:235
On the crown.
BREWE 5:1688; COG:151
Oration on the peace.
BREWE 5:1759; SAG:223
Second Olynthiac.
BREWE 5:1754; COG:56;
SAG:205
Second Philippic.
BREWE 5:1763; SAG:228
Third Olynthiac. SAG:212
Third Philippic. COG:91;
SAG:249
Hypereides
Funeral oration. COG:210
Isocrates
Address to Philip.
COG:67; SAG:137
Areopagiticus--"A few wise
laws wisely administered."
BREWE 7:2589
Lysias
Against Eratosthenes for
murder (on the execution
without trial of Pole-
marchus). BREWE 8:2851;
SAG:39
Funeral oration. COG:9

GREECE, MODERN
Clay, H.

Greek Revolution.
BREWE 4:1268
Menzies, R. G.
Greece and the Anzac spirit.
MCA:138
Palmerston, H. J. T.
Affairs in Greece. MCB:5
Truman, H. S.
Aid to Greece and Turkey.
ANN 16:434; GRG:76; LAA:49
Webster, D. and others
Debate on the Greek Revolution.
ANN 5:108

GREEK LITERATURE
Seferis, G.
Some notes on modern Greek
tradition. NOL:484

Green, Alfred M.
Let us take up the sword.
(Philadelphia, April 20, 1861).
FON:249

Green, Edith
Representative Edith Green speaks
in support of the Equal Rights
Amendment. BOST:237

Green, John P.
These evils call loudly for redress. (Pittsburgh, May,
1884). FON:499

Green, William
Modern trade unionism. (Cambridge, Mass., 1925).
HURH:205
"... Trade unionism is not a discovery or a formula. It grew
and evolved slowly out of the
needs of human experience."
Same as his Modern trade
unionism

Greenberg, Simon
Henry Goody. WALE:214
We weep today. WALE:84

Greener, Richard T.
Emigration of colored citizens
from the southern states.
(Saratoga, N.Y., Sept. 12,
1879). FON:466

Greenidge, Terence See Sykes,
C., jt. auth.

GREETINGS <u>See</u> Welcoming
  addresses

Gregory, Dick
  Let your son fight for free-
    dom. (Selma, Ala., Sept.
    1963). FON:981

Gregory of Nazianzus, Saint
  Eulogy on Basil of Caesarea.
  BREWE 6:2336

Greve, Donald
  The American Indian. (St.
    Louis, Mo., Dec. 9, 1969).
  LINRS:100

Grey, Sir George
  A radical programme, 1877
    (New Zealand House of
    Representatives, Aug. 17,
    1877). MACS:181 sel.

---- and others (John Ballance)
  A Liberal Party (New Zea-
    land House of Representa-
    tives, Oct. 29, 1877).
    MACS:182 sel.

---- <u>See</u> Atkinson, H., jt. auth.

Griffin, Clare E.
  Presents James Palmer.
  LYI:67

Griffin, Robert P.
  Responds to an introduction.
    PRS:144
  When freedom dies in its
    sleep (Kalamazoo, Mich.,
    Aug. 18, 1978).
    BA 1978-79:60

Griffiths, Martha W. and others
  (Emanuel Celler)
  House debates the Equal
    Rights Amendment (Aug.
    10, 1970). BOST:230

Grignard, Victor
  The use of organomagnesium
    compounds in preparative
    organic chemistry (Nobel
    Lecture, Dec. 11, 1912).
    NOLC 1:234

GRIGNARD, VICTOR
Söderbaum, H. G.

Presentation [of the Nobel Prize
  for Chemistry to Victor Grignard and Paul Sabatier, Dec.
  11, 1912]. NOLC 1:217

Grimes, James <u>See</u> Sumner, C.,
  jt. auth.

Grimké, Angelina <u>See</u> Goldman,
  Emma

Grimke, Francis J.
  Equality of rights for all citizens,
    Black and white, alike.
    (Washington, Nov. 20, 1898).
    FON:668

Grimké, Sarah <u>See</u> Goldman,
  Emma

Grimstone, Sir Harbottle, Bart.
  Projecting canker worms and
    caterpillars. BREWE 6:2341

Grisham, G. N.
  The functions of the Negro
    scholar. (Kansas City, Mo.,
    Dec. 28, 1897). FON:599

GRISSOM, VIRGIL
Sevareid, E.
  Eulogy for the astronauts.
  MOP:189

Griswold, A. Whitney
  On conversation--chiefly aca-
    demic. CROCK:75
  This tongue-tied democracy.
    Same as his On conversation--
    chiefly academic

Griswold, Erwin N.
  Dissent--1968 style. Same as
    his Dissent, protest, and dis-
    obedience
  Dissent, protest, and disobedi-
    ence (Tulane University School
    of Law, April 16, 1968).
    ANN 18:670; BA 1967-68:141;
    JEF:196
  Organization techniques in a
    speech on the moral and legal
    implications of dissent. Same
    as his Dissent, protest, and
    disobedience

Grollman, Earl A.
  If we love, we must lose.
    WALE:87

Gronlund, Laurence See Jones,
    A., jt. auth.

Gronouski, John A.
    Mail service. BRP:223

Gruening, Ernest
    United States policy and actions
    in Vietnam. BA 1965-66:23

Gruenther, Alfred M.
    "The competition is very
    tough, and in this contest,
    there is no prize for second
    best." Same as his NATO
    NATO. (New York, Dec. 7,
    1956). HURH:334

Grundy, Felix and others (R. M.
    Johnson and J. Randolph)
    Debate over war with England.
    ANN 4:291

Guadet, Marguerite Elie
    Reply to Robespierre.
    BREWE 6:2244

GUATEMALA
    Dulles, J. F.
        Why the Arbenz government
        was overthrown in Guate-
        mala. LAA:117

GUIDED MISSILES - DEFENSES
    Nixon, R. M.
        Questions of survival; the
        antiballistic missile sys-
        tem. BA 1968-69:9
    Wiesner, J. B.
        Argument against the ABM.
        BA 1968-69:19

Guillaume, Charles-Edouard
    Invar and clinvar (Nobel
    Lecture, Dec. 11, 1920).
    NOLPH 1:444

GUILLAUME, CHARLES-EDOUARD
    Ekstrand, A. G.
        Presentation [of the Nobel
        Prize for Physics to
        Charles-Edouard Guil-
        laume, Dec. 11, 1920].
        NOLPH 1:441

Guizot, Francois Pierre Guillaume
    Civilization and the individual
    man. BREWE 6:2344

Gullberg, Hjalmar
    Presentation [of the Nobel Prize
    for Literature to Gabriela
    Mistral, 1945]. NOB 14:167;
    NOL:405
    Presentation [of the Nobel Prize
    for Literature to Juan Ramón
    Jiménez, 1956]. NOB 10:3;
    NOL:513

Gullstrand, Allvar
    How I found the mechanism of
    intracapsular accommodation
    (Nobel Lecture, Dec. 11, 1911).
    NOLM 1:414
    Presentation [of the Nobel Prize
    for Physics for 1924 to Karl
    Manne Georg Siegbahn, Dec.
    11, 1925]. NOLPH 2:73
    Presentation [of the Nobel Prize
    for Physics for 1923 to Robert
    Andrews Millikan, May 23,
    1924]. NOLPH 2:51

GULLSTRAND, ALLVAR
    Mörner, K. A. H.
        Presentation [of the Nobel Prize
        for Physiology or Medicine to
        Allvar Gullstrand, Dec. 11,
        1911]. NOLM 1:411

Gunsaulus, Frank W.
    Healthy heresies. BREWE 6:2353

Gustafsson, T.
    Presentation [of the Nobel Prize
    for Physics to Hannes Alfvén
    and Louis Néel, Dec. 11,
    1970]. NOLPH 4:303

Gwinn, Joseph M.
    Presents Charles Lindbergh.
    LYI:188

- H -

Haak, Jan F. W.
    Responds to an introduction.
    PRS:140

HAAS, FRANCIS B.
    Hill, H.
        Presents Francis B. Haas.
        LYI:93

HABEAS CORPUS
    Stephens, A. H.

Civil rights in the Con-
federacy. ANN 9:493

HABEAS CORPUS SUSPENSION
BILL, 1817
Romilly, Sir S.
Habeas Corpus Suspension
Bill. STRM:143

Haber, Fritz
The synthesis of ammonia from
its elements (Nobel Prize
for 1918, June 2, 1920).
NOLC 1:326

HABER, FRITZ
Ekstrand, A. G.
Presentation [of the Nobel
Prize for Chemistry to Fritz
Haber, 1918, June 2, 1920].
NOLC 1:321

HADFIELD, JAMES
Erskine, T.
Homicidal insanity (J. Had-
field). BREWE 6:2058;
BRYH:294

HAEMIN
Fischer, H.
On haemin and the relationships between haemin and
chlorophyll. NOLC 2:165

HAEMOGLOBIN See Hemoglobin

Hageman, Marianne
Wisdom of the heart.
SCHW:177

Hagerup, Georg Francis
The work of the Institute of
International Law (Nobel
Lecture for 1904, Aug.
24, 1912).
NOLP 1:64

Hagg, G.
Presentation [of the Nobel
Prize for Chemistry to
Dorothy Crowfoot Hodgkin,
Dec. 11, 1964].
NOLC 4:67
Presentation [of the Nobel
Prize for Chemistry to
Linus Carl Pauling, Dec.
11, 1954].
NOLC 3:425

Presentation [of the Nobel Prize
for Chemistry to Max Ferdinand
Perutz and John Cowdery Kendrew, Dec. 11, 1962].
NOLC 3:649

Häggquist, G.
Presentation [of the Nobel Prize
for Physiology or Medicine to
Hans Spemann, Dec. 12, 1935].
NOLM 2:377

HAGUE CONVENTIONS
Gobat, C. A.
The development of the Hague
Conventions of July 29, 1899
(Nobel Lecture for 1902, Oslo,
July 18, 1906).
NOLP 1:30
Renault, L.
The work at the Hague in 1899
and in 1907 (Nobel Lecture for
1907, May 18, 1908).
NOLP 1:143

Hahn, Otto
From the natural transmutations
of uranium to its artificial fis-
sion (Nobel Lecture for 1944,
Dec. 13, 1946).
NOLC 3:51

HAHN, OTTO
Westgren, A.
Presentation [of the Nobel Prize
for Chemistry for 1944 to Otto
Hahn, Dec. 13, 1946].
NOLC 3:47

Haiman, Franklyn S.
Rhetoric of 1968: a farewell to
rational discourse (Univ. of
Kansas, June 28, 1968).
LINR:153; LINRS:133;
LINRST:156

Hains, John
Lamp of freedom. SCHW:6
New day dawns. SCHW:140

HAIR
Burton, S.
You (male) should wear long
hair. BAS:200 (outline only)

HAITI
Butler, B. F. and others
Congressional debate on Haiti

and Santo Domingo, January
13, 1869. ANN 10:143
Holly, J. T.
The Negro race, self-government and the Haitian revolution. FON:169
Russwurm, J. B.
The condition and prospects
of Haiti. FON:33

Hale, Edward Everett
Boston's place in history.
BREWE 6:2355

HALIFAX, EDWARD FREDERICK
LINDLEY WOOD, 3rd
VISCOUNT
Douglas, L. W.
Presents Lord Halifax.
LYI:222

Hall, Carl
A heap of trouble. EHN:316

Hall, Prince
Pray God give us the strength
to bear up under all our
troubles. (Menotomy,
Mass., June 24, 1797).
FON:13

Hall, Ronald O.
Fear and faith. VI:98

Hallett, Benjamin
Sovereignty of the people
(Luther v. Borden case).
ANN 7:410

Hallström, Per
Broadcast lecture [on Johannes
Vilhelm Jensen, 1944].
NOL:393
Presentation [of the Nobel
Prize for Literature to
Eugene Gladstone O'Neill,
1936]. NOB 19:125;
NOL:330
Presentation [of the Nobel
Prize for Literature to
Frans Eemil Sillanpää,
1939]. NOB 16:223;
NOL:386
Presentation [of the Nobel
Prize for Literature to
George Bernard Shaw,
1925]. NOB 16:77; NOL:224
Presentation [of the Nobel

Prize for Literature to Henri
Bergson, 1927]. NOB 2:267;
NOL:242
Presentation [of the Nobel Prize
for Literature to Ivan Aleksee-
vich Bunin, 1933]. NOB 3:285;
NOL:309
Presentation [of the Nobel Prize
for Literature to Jacinto Bena-
vente, 1922]. NOB 2:179;
NOL:186
Presentation [of the Nobel Prize
for Literature to Luigi Piran-
dello, 1934]. NOB 20:71;
NOL:320
Presentation [of the Nobel Prize
for Literature to Pearl Buck,
1938]. NOB 3:149; NOL:354
Presentation [of the Nobel Prize
for Literature to Roger Martin
DuGard, 1937]. NOB 14:3;
NOL:342
Presentation [of the Nobel Prize
for Literature to Sigrid Undset,
1928]. NOB 18:163; NOL:251
Presentation [of the Nobel Prize
for Literature to William
Butler Yeats, 1923].
NOB 18:275; NOL:194

Halsbury, Hardinge Stanley Giffard,
1st Earl of See Curzon of
Kedleston, George, jt. auth.

Hambro, Carl Joachim
Presentation [of the Nobel Prize
for Peace to George Catlett
Marshall, Dec. 10, 1953].
NOLP 3:65
Presentation [of the Nobel Prize
for Peace to the International
Committee of the Red Cross
and the League of the Red
Cross Societies, Dec. 10,
1963]. NOLP 3:295

Hamdan bin Sheikh Tahir, Haji
Education for service--to soci-
ety, the nation and our creator
(June 17, 1967). MONSA:149
Problems of national education
(Univ. of Malaya, April 11,
1969). MONSA:155 selections

Hamilton, Adam and others
(Michael Savage)
The economy under the Labour
government (New Zealand

House of Representatives,
July 21, 1938). MACS:334
sel.
The Social Security Bill, 1938
(New Zealand House of
Representatives, Aug. 16,
1938). MACS:337 sel.

Hamilton, Alexander
Coercion of delinquent states.
BREWE 6:2361
On an act granting to Con-
gress certain imposts and
duties. ALS:133
On the Federal Constitution,
June 24, 1788. HURH:35
Report on manufactures.
BOORA 1:178
"The states can never lose
their powers until the whole
people of the United States
are robbed of their liber-
ties." Same as his On the
Federal Constitution, June
24, 1788

HAMILTON, ALEXANDER
Morris, G.
Oration over Hamilton.
BREWE 8:3075; HURH:54
Otis, H. G.
Hamilton's influence on
American institutions.
BREWE 8:3111

Hamilton, Andrew
In the case of Zenger--for
free speech in America.
BREWE 6:2373

Hamilton, William
A defense of the Negro.
(New York, January 2,
1809). FON:26
Why a Negro convention is
necessary. (New York--
4th Convention of the
Colored People, June 2 to
June 13, 1834). FON:56

Hammarskjöld, Dag
Values of nationalism and
internationalism (Stanford
University commencement
address). HURS:206

HAMMARSKJÖLD, DAG
Edberg, R.

Acceptance [of the Nobel Prize
for Peace for Dag Hammar-
skjöld, Dec. 10, 1961].
NOLP 3:248
Jahn, G.
Presentation [of the Nobel Prize
for Peace to Dag Hammar-
skjöld, Dec. 10, 1961].
NOLP 3:239

Hammarsten, E.
Presentation [of the Nobel Prize
for Physiology or Medicine
to Albert Szent-Györgyi Von
Nagyrapolt, Dec. 11, 1937].
NOLM 2:435
Presentation [of the Nobel Prize
for Physiology or Medicine
to Axel Hugo Theodor Theorell,
Dec. 12, 1955]. NOLM 3:477
Presentation [of the Nobel Prize
for Physiology or Medicine to
Hans Adolf Krebs and Fritz
Albert Lipmann, Dec. 11,
1953]. NOLM 3:395
Presentation [of the Nobel Prize
for Physiology or Medicine
to Otto Heinrich Warburg,
Dec. 10, 1931]. NOLM 2:251

Hammarsten, O.
Presentation [of the Nobel Prize
for Chemistry to Fritz Pregl,
Dec. 11, 1923]. NOLC 2:25

Hammer, Robert A.
Disciple of Aaron. WALE:89

Hampden, John
Patriot's duty defined: against
own impeachment.
BREWE 6:2385

HAMPDEN, JOHN
Holborne, J.
In defense of John Hampden.
BREWE 7:2524
Hyde, E.
In John Hampden's case.
BREWE 7:2564

Hampton, Wade
Present hour in South Carolina
(inaugural address of would-be
governor). CUR:159

Hamsun, Knut Pedersen
Acceptance [of the Nobel Prize

for Literature, 1920].
NOB 9:123; NOL:170

HAMSUN, KNUT PEDERSEN
Hjärne, H.
Presentation [of the Nobel
Prize for Literature to
Knut Pedersen Hamsun,
1920]. NOB 9:119; NOL:167

Hamzah bin Dato Abu Samah
Challenging opportunity for
the press in Malaysia
(Kuala Lumpur, Sept. 6,
1969). MONSA:110
The most powerful instrument
for social cohesion (Kuala
Lumpur, Oct. 18, 1969).
MONSA:115

Hamzah bin Sendut See Hamzah
Sendut

Hamzah Sendut
Joint efforts urged for uniting
various ethnic groups
(Penang Hill, Dec. 16,
1969). MONSA:172
Some new approaches to uni-
versity education (Kuala
Lumpur). MONSA:168
Trends and problems of gov-
ernment (Malaysia).
MONS:253

Hancher, Virgil Melvin
Art of contemplation.
CROCK:132
Presents Eleanor Roosevelt.
LYI:244
Presents Franklyn Bliss Sny-
der. LYI:99

Hancock, John
Boston Massacre. (Boston,
Mass., March 5, 1774).
BRN:26; HURH:24
Boston Massacre oration
(third anniversary).
BREWE 6:2393; POC:262
Fight and even die. Same
as his Boston Massacre
Moving the adoption of the
Federal Constitution.
BREWE 6:2389
"We fear not death." Same
as his Boston Massacre

HANCOCK, WINFIELD SCOTT
Dougherty, D.
"Hancock the superb."
BREWE 5:1904

HAND, AUGUSTUS N.
Buchanan, J. B.
Presents Augustus N. Hand.
LYI:133

Hand, Learned
Judge's freedom before the law.
ANN 15:233
Meaning of liberty. BRR:46

Handy, Arthur W.
Nat Turner. (New York City
College, 1889). FON:538

HANES, FRANK BORDEN
Godfrey, J. L.
Presents Frank Borden Hanes.
LYI:38

Hanley, John W.
The day innovation died (Houston,
Tex., Sept. 26, 1978).
BA 1978-79:122

Hannah, John A.
Civil rights and the public univer-
sities. BA 1965-66:93
Meeting world food news (Hono-
lulu, Jan. 10, 1977).
BA 1976-77:103

HANOI
Reeves, R. A.
Journey to Hanoi. VI:83

Hansberger, Robert V.
Responds to an introduction.
PRS:146

Hansberry, Lorraine
A challenge to artists. (New
York, Oct. 27, 1962). FON:954

Hanson, C. W. D.
Introduces Benson Ford, vice
president, Ford Motor Com-
pany. PRS:22
Introduces Gene Lockhart.
PRS:51

Hansson, Michael
The Nansen International Office

for Refugees (Nobel Lecture,
Dec. 10, 1938). NOLP 2:268

Harden, Arthur
The function of phosphate in
alcoholic fermentation
(Nobel Lecture, Dec. 12,
1929). NOLC 2:131

HARDEN, ARTHUR
Söderbaum, H. G.
Presentation [of the Nobel
Prize for Chemistry to
Arthur Harden and Hans
Karl August Simon von
Euler-Chelpin, Dec. 12,
1929]. NOLC 2:127

Hardie, J. Keir
Socialist Commonwealth. (H.
of Commons, April 23,
1901). MCB:451

Hardin, Ben, 1784-1852
The Wilkinson and Murdaugh
case. (Harrodsburg, Ky.,
March 15, 1839). BLY:48

Harding, Harold F.
Matter of doubt and grave
concern. BA 1968-69:121

Harding, Warren G.
First annual message.
STAT 3:2616
Inaugural address.
USINAU:207; USINAUG:207
"It is our purpose to prosper
America first." ANN 14:292
Presents Marie S. Curie.
LYI:179
Return to normalcy. Same as
his "It is our purpose to
prosper America first"
Second annual message.
STAT 3:2628

HARDY, THOMAS
Erskine, T.
In defense of Thomas Hardy.
BREWE 6:2066

Hare, Julius Charles
Children of light.
BREWE 6:2402

Harlan, John M. and others
(O. W. Holmes, Jr.)
Northern Securities Company

v. United States, 1904: opinion
for the court and dissenting
opinion. ANN 12:576

---- See also following jt. auths.
Bradley, J. P.; Brown, H. B.;
Fuller, M. W.; White, E. D.

Harmann, Z.
UNICEF: achievement and challenge (Nobel Lecture, Dec. 11,
1965). NOLP 3:365

Harnwell, Gaylord P.
Responds to an introduction.
PRS:142

Harper, Frances Ellen Watkins
Address at the centennial anniversary of the Pennsylvania Society
for Promoting the Abolition of
Slavery. (Philadelphia, April
14, 1875). FON:430
The great problem to be solved.
Same as her Address at the
centennial anniversary of the
Pennsylvania Society for Promoting the Abolition of Slavery

Harper, Paul C.
What's happening, baby? (Off-
the-Street Club, Chicago, June
21, 1966). JEF:232; JEFF:202;
KEO:252

Harper, Robert Goodloe
Defending Judge Chase.
BREWE 6:2425

Harriman, W. Averell
Challenges to peace and freedom.
ANN 18:328

Harris, James G.
The prayer amendment. (Fort
Worth, Tex., Oct. 3, 1971).
BA 1971-72:143

Harris, LaDonna
American Indian education and
pluralism. MAES:96

Harrison, Benjamin
Controversy over Hawaii (for
annexation). ANN 11:479
First annual message.
STAT 2:1628
Fourth annual message.
STAT 2:1708

Inaugural address.
BREWE 6:2408; USINAU:153;
USINAUG:153
Second annual message.
STAT 2:1653
Third annual message.
STAT 2:1676

Harrison, Hubert H.
What socialism means to us.
(1912). FON:698

Harrison, Richard
Leadership--a goal for us all.
BREWW:150

Harrison, Thomas
Speech on the scaffold.
BREWE 6:2421

HARRISON, THOMAS
Nottingham, H. F.
Opening the prosecution for
regicide under Charles II
(trial of T. Harrison).
BREWE 6:2159

Harrison, William Henry
Inaugural address. (March 4,
1841). HOW:67;
USINAU:71; USINAUG:71

Hart, Gary
Big government: real or
imaginary? (Western
Electronic Manufacturers'
Association, April 20, 1976).
LINRST:100

Hartline, Haldan Keffer
Visual receptors and retinal
interaction (Nobel Lecture,
Dec. 12, 1967).
NOLM 4:269

HARTLINE, HALDAN KEFFER
Bernhard, C. G.
Presentation [of the Nobel
Prize for Physiology or
Medicine to Ragnar Granit,
Haldan Keffer Hartline, and
George Wald, Dec. 12,
1967]. NOLM 4:251

Hartzog, George B., Jr.
Finding America. (Tucson,
1973). BA 1972-73:194

HARVARD LAW REVIEW
Frankfurter, F.
The Zeitgeist and the Judiciary.
FRIP:340

HARVARD UNIVERSITY
Capp, A.
Is this your university?
STOT:297
Eliot, C. W.
Harvard and Yale. HURH:130
Inaugural address as president
of Harvard. ANN 10:201
Everett, E.
State funds for Harvard.
ANN 7:502
Washington, B. T.
Address delivered at the Har-
vard alumni dinner in 1896.
HURH:144

Hassel, Odd
Structural aspects of interatomic
charge-transfer bonding (Nobel
Lecture, June 9, 1970).
NOLC 4:314

HASSEL, ODD
Fredga, A.
Presentation [of the Nobel Prize
for Chemistry to Derek H. R.
Barton and Odd Hassel, Dec.
11, 1969]. NOLC 4:295

Hasselberg, K. B.
Presentation [of the Nobel Prize
for Chemistry to Ernest Ruther-
ford, Dec. 11, 1908].
NOLC 1:125
Presentation [of the Nobel Prize
for Physics to Albert Abraham
Michelson, Dec. 12, 1907].
NOLPH 1:159
Presentation [of the Nobel Prize
for Physics to Gabriel Lipp-
mann, Dec. 14, 1908].
NOLPH 1:183

HASTINGS, WARREN
Fox, C. J.
Against Warren Hastings.
BREWE 6:2192
Sheridan, R. B.
Against Warren Hastings.
BREWE 9:3422

Hatch, Orrin G. See Hayakawa,
S. I., jt. auth.

Hatcher, Richard Gordon
Which is the path of change?
(N.A.A.C.P. Legal De-
fense Fund, May, 1968).
FON:1110

HATE
Korf, J.
And old hate walked on
through time. SCHW:189

Hatfield, Mark O.
The energy crisis. (Oregon,
March 2, 1974).
BA 1973-74:105
Global interdependence: "Life,
Liberty, and the Pursuit of
Happiness" in today's world.
(Washington, Sept. 11,
1974). BA 1974-75:89
If we fall down in the land of
peace (San Antonio, Tex.,
Sept. 30, 1979).
BA 1979-80:67
Noise. (Noise Abatement
Council of America, Oct.
8, 1969). LINRS:211
Reconciliation and peace.
(Washington, Feb. 1, 1973).
BA 1972-73:91
Response to introduction.
PRS:92

Hauptmann, Gerhart Johann
Robert
Acceptance [of the Nobel Prize
for Literature, 1912].
NOB 8:7; NOL:122

HAUPTMANN, GERHART JOHANN
ROBERT
Hildebrand, H.
Presentation [of the Nobel
Prize for Literature to
Gerhart Johann Robert
Hauptmann, 1912].
NOB 8:3; NOL:118

Hausman, Louis
Older Americans: a natural
resource (Syracuse, N.Y.,
Nov. 18, 1976).
LINRST:36

HAWAIIAN ISLANDS
Cleveland, G.
Controversy over Hawaii
(against annexation).

ANN 11:480
Harrison, B.
Controversy over Hawaii (for
annexation). ANN 11:479
Kalakaua, D.
His Majesty's address to the
people of Lahaina. ALA:57
Malone, G. W. and others
Statehood for Hawaii.
ANN 17:522
Scarborough, W. S.
The ethics of the Hawaiian
question. FON:570

HAWLEY, JOSEPH B.
Clemens, S. L.
Presents Joseph B. Hawley.
LYI:148

Haworth, Walter Norman
The structure of carbohydrates
and of vitamin C (Nobel Lecture, Dec. 11, 1937).
NOLC 2:414

HAWORTH, WALTER NORMAN
Palmaer, W.
Presentation [of the Nobel Prize
for Chemistry to Walter Nor-
man Haworth and Paul Karrer,
Dec. 11, 1937]. NOLC 2:407

Hay, William See Walpole, R.
jt. auth.

Hayakawa, Samuel I. and others
(Orrin G. Hatch and Daniel
P. Moynihan)
Senate debate over ratification of
treaties concerning the Panama
Canal. BA 1977-78:17

Hayden, Lewis
Deliver us from such a Moses.
(Boston, Dec. 27, 1865).
FON:334

Haydon, Harold
The testimony of sculpture (Chi-
cago). EHN:375; MOP:384;
MOPR:380

Hayes, A. J.
Responds to an introduction.
PRS:153

Hayes, Alfred
Presents Indira Gandhi. LYI:199

Hayes, John W. See Jones, A.,
jt. auth.

Hayes, Kimble
Crossbreeding beef cattle:
progress or regression?
BREWW:214

Hayes, Patricia Ann
Madame Butterfly and the
collegian (Indiana University, 1967). LINR:262;
LINRS:265

Hayes, Rutherford B.
First annual message.
STAT 2:1334
Fourth annual message.
STAT 2:1395
Inaugural address.
BREWE 7:2434; USINAU:135;
USINAUG:135
Second annual message.
STAT 2:1355
Third annual message.
STAT 2:1371
Veto of the Army Appropriation Act. ANN 10:449

HAYES, RUTHERFORD B.
Lawson, J.
I protest against Hayes's
Southern policy. FON:457

HAYMARKET SQUARE RIOTS
See Chicago Haymarket
Square Riots

Hayne, Robert Young
On Foot's Resolution (January
21, 1830). BREWE 7:2441

Haynes, Roy A.
Success of prohibition.
ANN 14:523

HAYS, WILL H.
Landis, F.
Witty after-dinner speech
on Will Hays. LYI:224

Hazlitt, William
On wit and humor.
BREWE 7:2449

HEALTH
Freedom from hunger (outline
of speech to persuade that
continued good health of Amer-

ican people requires easy access to pharmaceutical vitamins and food supplements).
CUB:48

---- See also Mental health; National
Health Association; Proteins;
Sick. Also Names of illnesses
i.e. Backaches; Blood-diseases;
Insanity

HEALTH, DRINKING OF See Toasts

HEART
Einthoven, W.
The string galvanometer and
the measurement of the action
currents of the heart.
NOLM 2:94

Hecker, Frederick Karl Franz
Liberty in the New Atlantis.
BREWE 7:2457

Hedges, Job Elmer
Presents Edward D. Duffield.
LYI:69

Hedrén, G.
Presentation [of the Nobel Prize
for Physiology or Medicine to
Karl Landsteiner, Dec. 11,
1930]. NOLM 2:229

Heisenberg, Werner
The development of quantum mechanics (Nobel Lecture for
1932, Dec. 11, 1933).
NOLPH 2:290

HEISENBERG, WERNER
Pleijel, H.
Presentation [of the Nobel
Prize for Physics for 1932
to Werner Heisenberg and for
1933 to Erwin Schrodinger and
Paul Adrien Maurice Dirac,
Dec. 11, 1933]. NOLPH 2:283

HEISER, VICTOR
Sumner, G. L.
Presents Victor Heiser.
LYI:174

HELIUM
Onnes, H. K.
Investigations into the properties of substances at low
temperatures, which have

led, amongst other things, to
the preparation of liquid helium.
NOLPH 1:306

HELL
  Bede
    Torments of hell. BREWE 1:344
  Edwards, J.
    Eternity of Hell torments.
    BREWE 5:1977

Hellström, Gustaf
  Presentation [of the Nobel
  Prize for Literature to
  William Faulkner, 1949].
  NOB 19:3; NOL:440

Helman, Leonard A.
  Risks of life. WALE:90

Helmholtz, Hermann Ludwig
  Ferdinand von
  Mystery of creation.
  BREWE 7:2465

Hemin See Haemin

Hemingway, Ernest
  Acceptance [of the Nobel Prize
  for Literature, 1954].
  NOB 9:7; NOL:501

HEMINGWAY, ERNEST
  Österling, A.
    Presentation [of the Nobel
    Prize for Literature to
    Ernest Miller Hemingway,
    1954]. NOB 9:3; NOL:497

HEMOGLOBIN
  Perutz, M. F.
    X-ray analysis of haemo-
    globin. NOLC 3:653
  Whipple, G. H.
    Hemoglobin regeneration as
    influenced by diet and other
    factors. NOLM 2:346

HEMOPHILIA See Blood-diseases

Hench, Philip Showalter
  The reversibility of certain rheumatic and non-rheumatic conditions by the use of cortisone
  or of the pituitary adrenocorticotropic hormone (Nobel
  Lecture, Dec. 11, 1950).
  NOLM 3:311

HENCH, PHILIP SHOWALTER
  Liljestrand, G.
    Presentation [of the Nobel
    Prize for Physiology or Medi-
    cine to Edward Calvin Kendall,
    Tadeus Reichstein, and Philip
    Showalter Hench, Dec. 11,
    1950]. NOLM 3:263

Henderson, Arthur
  Essential elements of a universal
  and enduring peace (Nobel Lecture, Dec. 11, 1934).
  NOLP 2:185

HENDERSON, ARTHUR
  Mowinckel, J. L.
    Presentation [of the Nobel
    Prize for Peace to Arthur
    Henderson, Dec. 10, 1934].
    NOLP 2:179

Hennings, Thomas C. See Jenner,
  W. E., jt. auth.

Henry, David D.
  Perceptions of the university
  (Univ. of Utah, June 6, 1969).
  HOR:70

Henry, Jacob
  On religion and elective office.
  ANN 4:239; BOORA 1:220
  Private belief and public office.
  Same as his On religion and
  elective office

Henry, Patrick
  Against ratification. Same as
  his June 4th 1788 speech in
  the Virginia Ratifying Conven-
  tion
  Against the Federal Constitution,
  June 5, 1788. BREWE 7:2488
  "... as for me, give me liberty,
  or give me death." Same as
  his Liberty or death
  Bill of Rights, June 14, 1788.
  BREWE 7:2484
  Call to arms. Same as his
  Liberty or death
  "Give me liberty or give me
  death." Same as his Liberty
  or death
  June 4th, 1788 speech in the
  Virginia Ratifying Convention.
  BREWE 7:2478; LINS:136
  Liberty or death (Richmond, Va.,

March 23, 1775). ANN 2:321;
BAS:39 (outline only);
BEN:13; BREWE 7:2473;
HURH:27; HURS:209;
OLIS:22; POC:305

Liberty or empire? Same
as his Against the Federal
Constitution, June 5, 1788

Nation--not a Federation, June
14, 1788 (on eighth section
of Federal Constitution).
BREWE 7:2480

"We, the people" or "We, the
states. " Same as his June
4th, 1788 speech in the
Virginia Ratifying Convention

---- See also Mason, G., jt. auth.

Henschen, F.
Presentation [of the Nobel Prize
for Physiology or Medicine
for 1928 to Charles Jules
Henri Nicolle]. NOLM 2:175
Presentation [of the Nobel Prize
for Physiology or Medicine
for 1933 to Thomas Hunt
Morgan, June 4, 1934].
NOLM 2:307

Hepburn, William P.
Regulation of railroad rates.
ANN 13:40

Herder, Johann Gottfried von
Meaning of inspiration.
BREWE 7:2497

Herink, Russel
A succession of goals.
BREWW:141

Herndon, Angelo
Give the people bread. (Atlanta, Ga., 1932). FON:779

HEROES AND HEROISM
Carlyle, T.
Heroic in history.
BREWE 3:962
Choate, R.
Puritan and Spartan hero-
ism. BREWE 3:1135
Chrysostom, J.
Heroes of faith.
BREWE 3:1139

Herron, George Davis
Christianity and the use of

Private property.
ANN 12:226

Hershey, Alfred D.
Idiosyncrasies of DNA structure
(Nobel Lecture, Dec. 12, 1969).
NOLM 4:417

HERSHEY, ALFRED D.
Gard, S.
Presentation [of the Nobel Prize
for Physiology or Medicine to
Max Delbrück, Alfred D.
Hershey, and Salvador E. Luria,
Dec. 10, 1969]. NOLM 4:401

Hertz, Gustav
The results of electron-impact
tests in the light of Bohr's
theory of atoms (Nobel Lecture
for 1925, Dec. 11, 1926).
NOLPH 2:112

HERTZ, GUSTAV
Oseen, C. W.
Presentation [of the Nobel Prize
for Physics for 1925 to James
Franck and Gustav Hertz, Dec.
11, 1926]. NOLPH 2:95

Hesburgh, Theodore M.
Higher education begins the seven-
ties. (Univ. of Notre Dame,
Oct. 5, 1970). BA 1970-71:85;
BAAE:277
The problems and opportunities on
a very interdependent planet
(Bryn Mawr College, May 11,
1975). HOR:142
Service to others (Salt Lake City,
June 9, 1979).
BA 1979-80:180

Hess, Victor Franz
Unsolved problems in physics:
tasks for the immediate future
in cosmic ray studies (Nobel
Lecture, Dec. 12, 1936).
NOLPH 2:360

Hess, Walter Rudolf
The central control of the activity
of internal organs (Nobel Lecture, Dec. 12, 1949).
NOLM 3:247

HESS, WALTER RUDOLF
Olivecrona, H.
Presentation [of the Nobel Prize

for Physiology or Medicine
to Walter Rudolf Hess and
Antonio Caetano De Abreu
Freire Egas Moniz, Dec.
12, 1949]. NOLM 3:243

HESSE, HERMANN
Österling, A.
Presentation [of the Nobel
Prize for Literature to
Hermann Hesse, 1946].
NOB 9:233; NOL:412
Vallotton, H.
Acceptance [of the Nobel
Prize for Literature for
Hermann Hesse, 1946].
NOB 9:237; NOL:416

Heuss, John
Introduction to baccalaureate
sermon. PRS:55

Hevesy, George De
Some applications of isotopic
indicators (Nobel Lecture
for 1943, Dec. 12, 1944).
NOLC 3:9

HEVESY, GEORGE DE
Westgren, A.
Presentation [of the Nobel
Prize for Chemistry for
1943 to George De Hevesy,
Dec. 12, 1944].
NOLC 3:5

Heymans, Corneille Jean Francois
The part played by vascular
presso- and chemo-receptors
in respiratory control (Nobel
Lecture for 1938, Dec. 12,
1945). NOLM 2:460

Heyrovsky, Jaroslav
The trends of polarography
(Nobel Lecture, Dec. 11,
1959). NOLC 3:564

HEYROVSKY, JAROSLAV
Olander, A.
Presentation of the Nobel
Prize for Chemistry to
Jaroslav Heyrovsky, Dec.
11, 1959. NOLC 3:561

HEYSE, PAUL JOHANN LUDWIG
Wirsén, C. D. af
Presentation [of the Nobel

Prize for Literature to Paul
Johann Ludwig Heyse, 1910].
NOB 7:279; NOL:100

Hiatt, Howard H.
Prevention of the last epidemic
(Cambridge, Mass., Feb. 9,
1980). BA 1979-80:56

Hibben, Joseph W.
Introduces Bishop James A. Pike.
PRS:69
Introduces Braj K. Nehru, Am-
bassador from India. PRS:26
Introduces Dr. Howard B.
Sprague. PRS:61
Introduces Hobart Rowen of News-
week Magazine. PRS:95
Introduces the Honorable Otto
Kerner, governor of Illinois.
PRS:29
Introduces Willy Brandt, mayor
of West Bertlin. PRS:37

Higgins, Marguerite
Responds to introduction.
PRS:107

HIGGINS, MARGUERITE
Coulter, T. H.
Introducing Marguerite (Maggie)
Higgins to the Executives' Club
of Chicago. LYI:113

HIGH PRESSURE (SCIENCE)
Bergius, F.
Chemical reactions under high
pressure. NOLC 2:244

HIGHER EDUCATION See Education, Higher

Higinbotham, George
Against assisted immigration.
MCA:52
For the annexation of New Guinea.
MCA:43

Hildebert of Lavardin, Abp. of Tours
Rebecca at the well.
BREWE 7:2502

Hildebrand, Hans
Presentation [of the Nobel Prize
for Chemistry to Wilhelm
Ostwald, Dec. 12, 1909].
NOLC 1:147
Presentation [of the Nobel Prize

duction (Nobel Lecture, Dec.
11, 1963). NOLM 4:32

HODGKIN, ALAN LLOYD
Granit, R.
Presentation [of the Nobel
Prize for Physiology or
Medicine to John Carew
Eccles, Alan Lloyd Hodgkin,
and Andrew Fielding Huxley,
Dec. 11, 1963]. NOLM 4:3

Hodgkin, Dorothy Crowfoot
The x-ray analysis of compli-
cated molecules (Nobel
Lecture, Dec. 11, 1964).
NOLC 4:71

HODGKIN, DOROTHY CROWFOOT
Hagg, G.
Presentation [of the Nobel
Prize for Chemistry to
Dorothy Crowfoot Hodgkin,
Dec. 11, 1964]. NOLC 4:67

Hoff, Jacobus Henricus Van't
Osmotic pressure and chemical
equilibrium. (Nobel Lec-
ture, Dec. 13, 1901).
NOLC 1:5

HOFF, JACOBUS HENRICUS
VAN'T
Odhner, C. T.
Presentation [of the Nobel
Prize for Chemistry to
Jacobus Henricus Van't
Hoff, Dec. 13, 1901].
NOLC 1:3

HOFFA, JAMES
James Hoffa (satiric speech).
BURT:47

HOFFMAN, PAUL G.
Lamont, T. S.
Presents Paul G. Hoffman.
LYI:71

Hofstadter, Robert
The electron-scattering method
and its application to the
structure of nuclei and
nucleons (Nobel Lecture,
Dec. 11, 1961).
NOLPH 3:560

HOFSTADTER, ROBERT
Waller, I.

Presentation [of the Nobel Prize
for Physics to Robert Hofstadter
and Rudolf Ludwig Mossbauer,
Dec. 11, 1961]. NOLPH 3:555

Holborne, Sir Robert
In defense of John Hampden.
BREWE 7:2524

Holden, W. Sprague
Newspapers of the U.S.A.--an
appraisal. ARS:107

Holland, H. E. See Massey, W.
F., jt. auth.

Holland, Harry
The socialist objective of the
labour movement (New Zealand
House of Representatives, Oct.
30, 1918). MACS:232 sel.

---- and others (Sir Robert Stout)
The 1913 Waterside Strike (Welling-
ton, April 29, 1914).
MACS:230 sel.

Holland, Jerome H.
Options along the pathway of com-
munity involvement. (Hampton
Institute, May 26, 1974).
HOR:8

Holland, Sidney
Forward defence--from the Middle
East to Malaya, 1955 (New
Zealand House of Representa-
tives, March 24, 1955).
MACS:392 sel.
The Suez Crisis, 1956 (New Zea-
land House of Representatives,
Aug. 7, 1956). MACS:397 sel.

Holley, Alexander Lyman
Theory and practice in industrial
engineering. ANN 10:366

Holley, Robert W.
Alanine transfer RNA (Nobel Lec-
ture, Dec. 12, 1968).
NOLM 4:324

HOLLEY, ROBERT W.
Reichard, P.
Presentation [of the Nobel Prize
for Physiology or Medicine to
Robert W. Holley, Har Gobind
Khorana, and Marshall W. Niren-

Hollis, Christopher   156

berg, Dec. 12, 1968].
NOLM 4:321

Hollis, Christopher See Sykes,
C., jt. auth.

Holly, James T.
The Negro race, self-government and the Haitian revolution. (1855). FON:169

Holman, William Arthur
Against sending troops to
South Africa. MCA:109

Holmes, Oliver Wendell
Dorothy Q. (Boston, May 23,
1884). HURH:139
Introduces Matthew Arnold.
LYI:44
"There were tones in the voice
that whispered then you may
hear today in a hundred
men." Same as his Dorothy
Q.

Holmes, Oliver Wendell, Jr.
Dissenting opinion on Abrams
vs. United States.
ANN 14:244; BOORA 2:666
John Marshall. (Mass.
Supreme Judicial Court,
Feb. 4, 1901). FRIP:257
Law and the court. (Harvard
Law School Association of
New York, Feb. 15, 1913).
FRIP:260
Lechner v. New York, 1905;
dissenting opinion for the
Supreme Court.
BOORA 2:662
"Live--I am coming" response
to birthday greeting (Wash-
ington, March 7, 1931).
GRG:48; HURH:215
Nixon v. Herndon: opinion
for the court. ANN 14:534
On his ninetieth birthday.
Same as his "Live--I am
coming:" response to birth-
day greeting
Path of the law. BOORA 2:593

---- See also following jt. auths.
Harlan, J. M.; Sanford,
E. T.; Sutherland, G.

Holmgren, I.
Presentation [of the Nobel

Prize for Physiology or Medicine to George Hoyt Whipple,
George Richards Minot, and
William Parry Murphy, Dec.
12, 1934]. NOLM 2:335

Holt, Roger
The second dust bowl.
BREWW:137

Holtzman, Elizabeth
In celebration of the inauguration
of the Susan B. Anthony coin
(Rochester, N.Y., July 2,
1979). BA 1979-80:174
Women and equality under the law
(Madison, Wisc., March 26,
1977). BA 1976-77:80

Holyoake, Keith J.
A military contribution in Vietnam,
1965 (New Zealand House of
Representatives, May 28, 1965).
MACS:398 sel.
The National Development Confer-
ence, 1968 (Wellington, Aug.
27-29, 1968). MACS:455 sel.

HOME
Brunsting, L.
Kid dreams. SCHW:49
Dedication services of a Christian
home. BNH:59

HOME RULE BILLS See Ireland

HOMESTEAD BILL, 1852
Sutherland, J.
Free land and the supply of
labor. ANN 8:180

HONESTY
Be honest. BURT:122

HONG KONG
Lee Kuan Yew
Hong Kong and Singapore: a
tale of two cities. MONSA:264

Hood, William R.
Uncle Tom is dead! (Cincinnati,
Ohio, Oct. 27, 1951).
FON:843

Hooker, Thomas
The soul's exaltation. JON:104
The soul's vocation, doctrine 3
(1637-8). JON:82
The soul's vocation, doctrine 7.

JON:93
Unbelievers preparing for
    Christ. POC:331

Hoover, Herbert C.
    Acceptance speech, Constitution
        Hall, Washington, D.C.,
        August 11, 1932. SIN:88
    Acceptance speech, Stanford
        University Stadium, Palo
        Alto, California, August
        11, 1928. Same as his
        Accepting the nomination
        for presidency
    Accepting the nomination for
        presidency (Palo Alto,
        Aug. 11, 1928). SIN:4
    Against the proposed New Deal
        (October 31, 1932).
        ANN 15:188
    Bill of Rights. (San Diego,
        Calif., Sept. 15, 1935).
        HURH:229
    Campaign speech, Madison
        Square Garden, New York
        City, October 31, 1932.
        SIN:103
    Campaign speech, New York.
        Same as his Speech at New
        York City, October 22, 1928
    First annual message.
        STAT 3:2746
    Fourth annual message.
        STAT 3:2795
    Holy crusade for liberty.
        BAD:53
    "I suggest that the United Na-
        tions be reorganized without
        the Communist nations in
        it." Same as his United
        Nations
    In defense of tradition (Detroit,
        1932). ROD:39
    Inaugural address.
        USINAU:225; USINAUG:225
    Military policy for the Cold
        War. Same as his Our
        national policies in this
        crisis
    Moral standards in an indus-
        trial era. ANN 14:428
    New Deal and European col-
        lectivism. Same as his
        Road to freedom
    On American individualism.
        Same as his Speech at New
        York City, October 22,
        1928

Our national policies in this crisis.
    ANN 17:46
Reassuring touch: President
    Hoover speaks, 1931. ROD:15
Road to freedom. ANN 15:384
Rugged individualism. Same as
    his Speech at New York City,
    October 22, 1928
Second annual message.
    STAT 3:2772
Speech at New York City, October
    22, 1928. ANN 14:595;
    BOORA 2:803; SIN:21
Third annual message.
    STAT 3:2783
United Nations. (April 27, 1950).
    HURH:287
Veto of the Muscle Shoals Bill.
    ANN 15:79
War comes to Europe. GRG:61

Hoover, J. Edgar
    Menace of the Communist Party.
        ANN 16:451
    Responds to an introduction.
        PRS:140

Hope, John
    We are struggling for equality.
        (Nashville, 1896). FON:594

HOPE
    Dow, L., Jr.
        Hope and despair.
        BREWE 5:1934

Hopkins, Sir Frederick Gowland
    The earlier history of vitamin re-
        search (Nobel Lecture, Dec.
        11, 1929). NOLM 2:211

HOPKINS, SIR FREDERICK GOW-
        LAND
    Liljestrand, G.
        Presentation [of the Nobel Prize
        for Physiology or Medicine to
        Christiaan Eijkman and Sir
        Frederick Gowland Hopkins,
        Dec. 11, 1929]. NOLM 2:193

Hopkins, Harry L.
    18,000,000 on relief. ANN 15:261
    "... they are just like the rest
        of us." ROD:127

HORMONES
    Reichstein, T.
        Chemistry of the adrenal cortex

hormones. NOLM 3:291
Ruzicka, L. S.
  Multimembered rings, higher
  terpene compounds, and
  male sex hormones.
  NOLC 2:468

Horn, Francis H.
  The student revolt, a defense
  of the older generation
  (1968). HOR:49

Horner, Matina Souretis
  Opportunity for educational in-
  novation. (Cambridge,
  Mass., Nov. 16, 1972).
  BA 1972-73:184

HORSE-RACING
  Thuraisingham, E. E. S. C.
  The prince of sportsmen.
  MONSA:187

HOTELS
  Lavenson, J.
  Think strawberries.
  VERD:259

Houphouet-Boigny, Felix
  French Africa and the French
  Union. EMP:73

HOURS OF LABOR
  Black, H. L.
  Need to share what we have.
  ROD:75
  Holmes, O. W., Jr.
  Lochner v. New York, 1905;
  dissenting opinion for the
  Supreme Court.
  BOORA 2:662
  Parkes, H.
  Eight-hours movement.
  MCA:33
  Peckham, R. W. and others
  Lochner v. New York, 1905;
  opinion for the court and
  dissenting opinion.
  ANN 13:8

HOUSE COMMITTEE ON UN-
  AMERICAN ACTIVITIES
  See United States - Con-
  gress - House of Repre-
  sentatives - Committee on
  UnAmerican Activities

HOUSING
  Karos, P. A.

Haven of the defeated.
  ARS:148
Savage, J.
  Slums as a common nuisance
  (Meeker v. Van Renssalaer
  case). ANN 6:279
Zwerling, J. C.
  Federal Government should con-
  tinue its present housing pro-
  gram for low-income groups
  rather than change to the
  proposed rent subsidy plan.
  BAS:196 (outline only)

Houssay, Bernardo Alberto
  The role of the hypophysis in
  carbohydrate metabolism and
  in diabetes (Nobel Lecture,
  Dec. 12, 1947). NOLM 3:210

HOUSSAY, BERNARDO ALBERTO
  Theorell, H.
  Presentation [of the Nobel Prize
  for Physiology or Medicine to
  Carl Ferdinand Cori, Gerty
  Theresa Cori-Radnitz, and
  Bernardo Alberto Houssay,
  Dec. 11, 1947]. NOLM 3:179

Houston, Samuel
  His defense at the Bar of the
  House. BREWE 7:2532
  On his defeat as a Union candidate.
  BREWE 7:2530
  Sam Houston's speech, at Inde-
  pendence, Texas, May 10.
  ECH:174

Houtman, Mary
  Dangers of security. SCHW:54

Howard, John A.
  The innovation mirage. (Rock-
  ford, Ill., Sept. 9, 1970).
  BA 1970-71:94
  The new furies: skepticism,
  criticism, and coercion
  (Racine, Wisc., June 6, 1974).
  LINRST:146
  "... our sacred honor" (Rockford
  College, Illinois, Sept. 10,
  1975). BA 1975-76:9

HOWARD UNIVERSITY
  Powell, A. C.
  Can any good thing come out
  of Nazareth? FON:1027;
  SMHR:154

Howarth, Don
2S Draft deferment should be
retained. REIR:130

Howe, Harold, II
The Brown decision, pluralism,
and the schools in the 1980s
(Jeffersonville, Vermont,
Aug. 1, 1979).
BA 1979-80:101
Changing the pecking order.
BA 1967-68:111
Public education for a humane
society. (New York,
Nov. 20, 1972).
BA 1972-73:161

Howell, Wes
A new century in agriculture.
BREWW:211

Hubbard, William
Happiness of a people in the
wisdom of their rulers
directing and in obedience
of their brethren attending
unto what Israel ought to do.
ANN 1:248

Huber, Max
Acceptance [of the Nobel Prize
for Peace for the International Committee of the
Red Cross, 1944, Dec. 10,
1945]. NOLP 2:293

Huffman, John A.
Retrospect '73--Biblical les-
sons we can learn from
Watergate (Pittsburgh,
Dec. 30, 1973). TAC:221

Huggins, Charles Brenton
Endocrine-induced regression
of cancers (Nobel Lecture,
Dec. 13, 1966).
NOLM 4:235

HUGGINS, CHARLES BRENTON
Klein, G.
Presentation [of the Nobel
Prize for Physiology or
Medicine to Peyton Rous
and Charles Brenton Hug-
gins, Dec. 13, 1966].
NOLM 4:215

Hughes, Charles Evans
"In the great enterprise of

making democracy workable we
are all partners." Same as
his 150th anniversary of the
First Congress
National Labor Relations Board
v. Jones and Laughlin Steel
Corporation, 1937: opinion
for the Supreme Court.
ROD:207
New power of government ac-
cepted. Same as his National
Labor Relations Board v. Jones
and Laughlin Steel Corporation,
1937; opinion for the Supreme
Court
150th anniversary of the First
Congress. (Washington, March
4, 1939). HURH:237
Schechter Poultry Corporation v.
United States, 1935: opinion
for the Supreme Court.
ANN 15:301; ROD:186
Small step toward racial equality:
opinion for the Supreme Court
on Mitchell case, 1941.
ROD:224

HUGHES, CHARLES EVANS
Pepper, G. W.
Presents Charles Evans
Hughes. LYI:127

Hughes, Langston
Negro writers have been on the
blacklist all their lives. (Na-
tional Assembly of the Authors'
League of America, May, 1957).
FON:916
Negroes speak of war. (Paris,
July, 1934). FON:787

Hughes, Ted
Capturing animals. MDYG: 191

Hughes, Thomas
Highest manhood. BREWE 7:2539

Hughes, William Morris
Australian Judas. MCA:125

Hugo, Victor Marie, Comte de
Liberty tree in Paris.
BREWE 7:2548
Moral force in world politics.
BREWE 7:2553
On the centennial of Voltaire's
death. BREWE 7:2550
Oration on Honoré de Balzac.
BREWE 7:2546

Huitfeldt, Jennifer
The service of sex. (Madison,
Wisc., 1971). LINRS:114

Hulett, John
We've decided to stop begging.
(Los Angeles, May 22,
1966). FON:1019

HULL, CORDELL
Jahn, G.
Presentation [of the Nobel
Prize for Peace to Cordell
Hull, Dec. 10. 1945].
NOLP 2:311
Osborne, L.
Acceptance [of the Nobel
Prize for Peace for Cordell
Hull, Dec. 10, 1945].
NOLP 2:318

Hulthén, E.
Presentation [of the Nobel
Prize for Physics to
Emilio Gino Segrè and Owen
Chamberlain, Dec. 11,
1959]. NOLPH 3:487
Presentation [of the Nobel Prize
for Physics to Felix Bloch
and Edward Mills Purcell,
Dec. 11, 1952].
NOLPH 3:199
Presentation [of the Nobel Prize
for Physics to Frits
Zernike, Dec. 11, 1953].
NOLPH 3:237
Presentation [of the Nobel Prize
for Physics to Sir Edward
Victor Appleton, Dec. 12,
1947]. NOLPH 3:75

HUMAN NATURE
Bushnell, H.
Dignity of human nature.
BREWE 3:825

HUMAN RIGHTS See Civil rights

HUMANITIES
Coles, R.
A "larger vision" of the
humanities. BA 1977-78:163
Duffey, J. D.
General education: the
rule of the humanities.
BA 1977-78:146

HUMBOLDT, WILHELM FREIHERR
VON
Challemel-Lacour, P. A.
Humboldt and the Teutonic in-
tellect. BREWE 3:1018

HUMILITY
Graham, W. F.
National humility. HURH:339

HUMOR
Rice, G. P.
The comic spirit and the public
speaker. EHN:283

HUMOROUS SPEECHES See After-
dinner speeches

Humphrey, Hubert H., Jr.
Acceptance speech, Chicago, Illi-
nois, August 29, 1968.
SIN:372
American system. CAPG:21
Anniversary of war on poverty.
CAPG:174
Campaign speech, Salt Lake City,
Utah, September 30, 1968.
SIN:380
Guns and butter are tied together.
LAA:207
I am optimistic about America
(Washington, Oct. 22, 1977).
BA 1977-78:192
Impromptu audience; adaptation in
a speech to a university audi-
ence. (April 9, 1965, Louisi-
ana State University).
JEF:192; JEFF:185
Open door (21st anniversary of
Churchill's "Iron curtain"
speech). LINR:236
Problem-solution division: a
speech on the open-door policy.
(Fulton, Missouri, March 5,
1967). JEF:238; JEFF:207

HUMPHREY, HUBERT H., JR.
Califano, J. A.
A tribute to the man of the
people. BA 1977-78:197
Carter, J.
My good friend Hubert
Humphrey. BA 1977-78:200
Mondale, W. F.
A time to celebrate life.
BA 1977-78:205
Nomination of Hubert Horatio

Humphrey, Jr. (outline of
speech). CUB:100

Humphreys, Benjamin G.
Justice but not equality for
the Negro. ANN 9:626

HUNGARY
Downing, G. T.
May Hungary be free.
FON:102

Hunt, Everett Lee
Lincoln's rhetorical triumph at
Cooper Union (centennial
speech). BA 1969-70:189

Hunter, Robert Mercer
A Northern party is seeking to
convert the government into
an instrument of warfare
upon slavery (1850).
(Washington, March 25,
1850). DAVF:144

HUNTLEY, CHESTER ROBERT
Cragg, R. T.
Presents Chet Huntley.
LYI:109

Hurst, Charles G.
Immorality, racism, and sur-
vival. (Chicago-Annual
Summer Conf. - Speech
Communication Association,
July 11, 1970). STOT:343

Hurwitz, Jacob
Crown of our head has fallen.
WALE:93

HUSAIN, ZAKIR
Wang, G. W.
Tribute to Dr. Azkir Husain
(presenting him with Doctor
of Laws degree). MONS:277

Hutchins, Robert Maynard
All our institutions are in dis-
array. (Long Beach,
Calif., May 20, 1974).
BA 1974-75:117
America and the war. Same
as his Drifting into suicide
Drifting into suicide.
ANN 16:66
The institutional illusion.
(Chicago, April 3, 1971).

BA 1971-72:161
Message to the younger generation.
MDV:198
Where do we go from here in edu-
cation? CROCK:110

HUTCHINS, ROBERT MAYNARD
Graham, F. P.
Presents Robert M. Hutchins.
LYI:96

Hutchinson, Thomas
Speech to both Houses. POC:280

Huxley, Andrew Fielding
The quantitative analysis of excita-
tion and conduction in nerve
(Nobel Lecture, Dec. 11, 1963).
NOLM 4:52

HUXLEY, ANDREW FIELDING
Granit, R.
Presentation [of the Nobel Prize
for Physiology or Medicine to
John Carew Eccles, Alan Lloyd
Hodgkin, and Andrew Fielding
Huxley, Dec. 11, 1963].
NOLM 4:3

Huxley, Thomas Henry
Method of scientific investigation.
ARS:264; BRYF:521
Science and culture. (Mason Col-
lege, Birmingham, Oct. 1,
1880). MCB:376
Threefold unity of life.
BREWE 7:2557

Hyde, Edward
"Discretion" as a despotism.
BREWE 7:2562
In John Hampden's case.
BREWE 7:2564

HYDROGEN
Lamb, W. E.
Fine structure of the hydrogen
bomb. NOLPH 3:286
Urey, H. C.
Some thermodynamic properties
of hydrogen and deuterium.
NOLC 2:339

HYDROGENATION
Sabatier, P.
The method of direct hydro-
genation by catalysis.
NOLC 1:221

Hypereides
  Funeral oration.   COG:210

HYPOCHONDRIA See Sick

- I -

Ibrahim, Ahmad M.
  Muslims must face modern
  challenges. MONS:441

ICE
  Miller, J.
  Why ice floats. MOP:20;
  MOPR:59

Ickes, Harold L.
  "Americans fight joyously in a
  just cause." Same as his
  What constitutes an Ameri-
  can?
  What constitutes an American?
  (New York, May 18, 1941).
  HURH:260

IDEALISM
  Dickey, J. S.
  Betrayal of idealism (con-
  vocation address).
  BA 1967-68:136
  Eucken, R.
  Naturalism or idealism?
  NOL:74
  Parson, M. J.
  Idealism: what's wrong with
  it? BA 1975-76:166

IDEAS
  Ascoli, M.
  Scarcity of ideas. ARS:201
  Chapin, E. H.
  Sovereignty of ideas.
  BREWE 3:1036

IDEOLOGY
  Eliezer, C. J.
  Ideology and education.
  MONSA:231

ILLNESS See Medicine

ILLUMINATI
  Morse, J.
  The present dangers and
  consequent duties of the
  citizens. DAVF:45

Tappan, D.
  A warning to Harvard seniors
  against world revolution (1798).
  DAVF:49
Welch, R.
  More stately mansions (1964).
  DAVF:327

IMAGINATION
  Ingersoll, R. G.
  Imagination. BREWE 7:2585

IMMIGRATION AND EMIGRATION
  Addams, J.
  Foreign-born children in the
  primary grades. ANN 12:130
  Gardner, H. J.
  New England nativism.
  ANN 8:484
  Levin, L. C.
  Native Americans and the for-
  eign-born. ANN 7:313
  Lodge, H. C.
  For immigration restrictions.
  ANN 12:88
  McWhirter, A. J.
  Appeal to European immigrants
  to come to the South.
  ANN 10:587
  Meade, E. R.
  Chinese immigration to the
  United States. ANN 10:386
  Roosevelt, T.
  Sixth annual message.
  STAT 3:2194
  Truman, H. S.
  Veto of the McCarran-Walter
  Immigration Act. ANN 17:131
  Turner, H. M.
  Justice or emigration should be
  our watchword. FON:561
  Webster, D.
  For reform of the naturalization
  laws. ANN 7:168

---- See also Migration, Internal

---- AUSTRALIA
  Deakin, A.
  For a white Australia. MCA:88
  Higinbotham, G.
  Against assisted immigration.
  MCA:52

IMMORTALITY
  Carson, A.
  Glories of immortality.
  BREWE 3:981

Castelar, E.
  In the Campo Santo of Pisa.
  BREWE 3:1003
Donne, J.
  Man immortal, body and
  soul. BREWE 5:1888
Leighton, R.
  Immortality. BREWE 7:2761

IMMUNITY
  Metchnikoff, E.
    On the present state of the
    question of immunity in
    infectious diseases.
    NOLM 1:281

IMMUNOLOGY
  Burnet, Sir F. M.
    Immunological recognition of
    self. NOLM 3:689
  Medawar, P. B.
    Immunological tolerance.
    NOLM 3:704

IMPEACHMENTS
  Jordan, B. C. (and others)
    Hearings on articles of im-
    peachment by the Committee
    of the Judiciary of the
    House of Representatives.
    BA 1974-75:15

---- See Names of individuals,
  e.g. Crawley, F.; Hamp-
  den, J.; Johnson, A.;
  Nixon, R. M.

IMPERIALISM
  Beveridge, A. J.
    March of the flag.
    ANN 12:198; BOORA 2:622;
    GRG:14; LINS:276
    Philippine question.
    ANN 12:336; BRR:29
  Bryan, W. J.
    Imperialism (accepting Demo-
    cratic nomination for Presi-
    dency, 1900). ANN 12:345
    Naboth's Vineyard. GRG:11
  Butler, B. F. and others
    Congressional debate on
    Haiti and Santo Domingo,
    January 13, 1869.
    ANN 10:143
  Carnot, L. N. M.
    Against imperialism in
    France. BREWE 3:967

Hoar, G. F.
  Lust of empire. ANN 12:248

IMPROMPTU SPEECHES See
  After-dinner speeches

INAUGURAL ADDRESSES
  Adams, J.
    Inaugural address. BREWE 1:39;
    USINAU:7; USINAUG:7
  Adams, J. Q.
    Inaugural address. ANN 5:138;
    USINAU:47; USINAUG:47
  Andrus, C. D.
    The inaugural address (Gov-
    ernor of Idaho).
    BA 1970-71:137
  Arthur, C. A.
    Inaugural address.
    BREWE 1:180
  Bigelow, J.
    Future of arts and sciences.
    ANN 4:449
  Birenbaum, W. M.
    Time for reconstruction.
    BA 1969-70:154
  Brown, E. G., Jr.
    Proposals for change: an in-
    augural address.
    BA 1978-79:103
  Buchanan, J.
    Inaugural address.
    BREWE 2:707; USINAU:111;
    USINAUG:111
  Carlyle, T.
    Inaugural address at Edinburgh.
    BREWE 3:951
  Carter, J.
    The inaugural address.
    BA 1976-77:18; JAM:38
    Inauguration address.
    BA 1970-71:142
  Chamberlain, D. H.
    Present hour in South Carolina
    (inaugural address of would-be
    governor). CUR:158
  Cleveland, G.
    First inaugural address.
    BREWE 4:1301; USINAU:149;
    USINAUG:149
    Second inaugural address.
    USINAU:163; USINAUG:163
  Coolidge, C.
    Inaugural address.
    USINAU:215; USINAUG:215
  Davis, J.
    Inaugural address in 1861.

ANN 9:238; BREWE 5:1656;
ECH:137
Dunn, O. J.
We ask an equal chance in
the race of life. FON:355
Eisenhower, D. D.
First inaugural address.
HURH:304; USINAU:257;
USINAUG:257
Price of peace: second in-
augural address.
USINAU:263; USINAUG:263
Eliot, C. W.
Inaugural address as presi-
dent of Harvard.
ANN 10:201
Gardner, H. J.
New England nativism.
ANN 8:484
Garfield, J. A.
Inaugural address.
USINAU:141; USINAUG:141
Grant, U. S.
First inaugural address.
USINAU:129; USINAUG:129
Second inaugural address.
USINAU:132; USINAUG:132
Hampton, W.
Present hour in South Caro-
lina (inaugural address of
would-be governor).
CUR:159
Harding, W. G.
Inaugural address.
USINAU:207; USINAUG:207
Harrison, B.
Inaugural address.
BREWE 6:2408; USINAU:153;
USINAUG:153
Harrison, W. H.
Inaugural address.
HOW:67; USINAU:71;
USINAUG:71
Hayes, R. B.
Inaugural address.
BREWE 7:2434; USINAU:135;
USINAUG:135
Hoover, H.
Inaugural address.
USINAU:225; USINAUG:225
Jackson, A.
First inaugural address.
USINAU:55; USINAUG:55
Second inaugural address--
"State rights and Federal
sovereignty." BREWE 7:2597;
HURH:71; USINAU:58;
USINAUG:58

Jefferson, T.
First inaugural address, democ-
racy defined. AND:166;
ANN 4:143; BOORA 1:212;
BREWE 7:2612; HURH:48;
LINS:150; OLIS:28; USINAU:13;
USINAUG:13
Second inaugural address.
USINAU:17; USINAUG:17
Johnson, A.
Inaugural address (1st speech
after Lincoln's death).
BREWE 7:2626
Johnson, L. B.
Inaugural address.
USINAU:271; USINAUG:271
Kennedy, J. F.
Inaugural address. ALS:265;
ANN 18:5; ARN:312; ARS:226;
BAS:145 (outline only);
BEN:143; BOORA 2:913;
BRR:82; BRYF:437; BRYO:232;
GRG:113; HURH:358; LINR:297;
LINRS:296; LINRST:366;
LINS:375; MAC:244; MACR:284;
MDV:127; OLIS:282; THOMS:17;
USINAU:267; USINAUG:267
Lincoln, A.
First inaugural address.
ANN 9:250; BOSR:1; HOW:239;
LINS:218; USINAU:119;
USINAUG:119
Second inaugural address.
AND:48; ANN 9:555; BEN:49;
BOORA 1:423; BREWE 7:2795;
BRR:80; CUB:86 (outline);
HURH:114; LINS:226;
USINAU:127; USINAUG:127
Lindsley, P.
Education of every child in the
Republic. ANN 5:157
MacDonald, P.
Inaugural address, Window
Rock, Navajo Nation, January
7, 1975. MAES:213
McKinley, W.
First inaugural address.
USINAU:169; USINAUG:169
Second inaugural address.
USINAU:178; USINAUG:178
Madison, J.
First inaugural address.
USINAU:23; USINAUG:23
Second inaugural address.
USINAU:26; USINAUG:26
Monroe, J.
First inaugural address.
USINAU:29; USINAUG:29

Second inaugural address.
USINAU:37; USINAUG:37
Nixon, R. M.
Inaugural address.
BA 1968-1969:113; ERP:93;
HURH:393; USINAU:275;
USINAUG:275
Second inaugural address.
BA 1972-73:15; USINAUG:280
Pierce, F.
Inaugural address.
USINAU:103; USINAUG:103
Polk, J. K.
Inaugural address.
ANN 7:286; USINAU:89;
USINAUG:89
Quezon, M. L.
Inaugural address.
CURM:16
Roosevelt, F. D.
First inaugural address.
ALS:207; AND:67; ANN 15:205;
BEN:74; BOORA 2:839;
GRG:50; HURH:219;
LINS:321; ROD:63;
USINAU:235; USINAUG:235
Fourth inaugural address.
USINAU:248; USINAUG:248
Second inaugural address.
USINAU:240; USINAUG:240
Third inaugural address.
USINAU:244; USINAUG:244
Roosevelt, T.
Inaugural address.
USINAU:183; USINAUG:183
Taft, W. H.
Inaugural address.
USINAU:187; USINAUG:187
Taylor, Z.
Inaugural address.
USINAU:99; USINAUG:99
Truman, H. S.
Inaugural address.
ANN 16:561; BOORA 2:891;
USINAU:251; USINAUG:251
Van Buren, M.
Inaugural address.
USINAU:61; USINAUG:61
Walker, R. J.
Address to the people of
Kansas. ANN 8:452
Washington, G.
First inaugural address.
ANN 3:344; BOORA 1:172;
BREWE 10:3737;
USINAU:1; USINAUG:1
Second inaugural address.
USINAU:5; USINAUG:5

Wilson, J.
Study of law in the United
States. ANN 3:380
Wilson, W.
First inaugural address.
ANN 13:412; USINAU:199;
USINAUG:199
Second inaugural address.
USINAU:203; USINAUG:203

---- See also Installation speeches;
Offices - Acceptance

Inche Ahmad bin Mohamad Ibrahim
See Ibrahim, Ahmad M.

Inche Senu bin Abdul Rahman See
Abdul Rahman, Tunku

Inche Yusof bin Ishak
Lest we forget (Singapore, Jan.
18, 1970). MONSA:348 selections

INCOME TAX See Taxation

INDEPENDENCE DAY See Fourth
of July

INDEPENDENT TREASURY
Calhoun, J. C.
Replying to Henry Clay (from
"Independent treasury debate").
BREWE 3:921
Clay, C. C., Sr.
Subtreasury Bill of 1837.
BREWE 3:1216
Van Buren, M.
Fourth annual message.
STAT 1:543
Third annual message.
STAT 1:517

INDIA
Gandhi, M. K.
Speech in London (1931).
BRN:109

INDIAN EDUCATION ACT
Barlow, E.
Education on Indian terms.
MAES:90

INDIAN EDUCATION RESOURCES
CENTER, ALBUQUERQUE,
N.M.
Benham, W. J.
An Indian education resources
center. MAES:114

INDIAN HEALTH SERVICE
Blue Spruce, G.
Needed: Indian health pro-
fessionals. MAES:171

INDIAN SELF-DETERMINATION
AND EDUCATION AS-
SISTANCE ACT
MacDonald, P.
Statement of the implementa-
tion of P.L. 93-638 Indian
Self-Determination and Edu-
cation Assistance Act,
Window Rock, Navajo Na-
tion, April 3, 1975.
MAES:189

INDIAN WIT AND HUMOR
Maestas, J. R.
The subtle use of humor by
the great Indian chief Osceola. MAES:307

INDIANA
Webster, D.
Reception at Madison, Indi-
ana. OLIS:36

---- SUPREME COURT
Dowling, A.
Constitutionality of a compulsory school law: opinion
for the court. ANN 12:417

INDIANS, TREATMENT OF
Trimble, A.
Keynote address NCAI Con-
vention, October 18, 1976.
MAES:233

INDIANS IN SINGAPORE
Lee Kuan Yew
Tribute to India and Indians.
MONSA:244

INDIANS OF NORTH AMERICA
Blue, B.
Thinking out loud.
MAES:419
Bruce, B. K.
A call for a change in our
Indian policy. FON:471
Chino, W.
Indian affairs--what has
been done and what needs
to be done. BA 1969-70:179
Cushing, C.
Extermination of the Indians.

BREWE 4:1584
Dohrer, J.
Our forgotten man. LINRS:269
Frelinghuysen, T.
The Cherokee lands. HOW:189
Greve, D.
The American Indian.
LINRS:100
Jackson, A.
Seventh annual message.
ANN 6:164; STAT 1:415
Joseph, Chief
From where the sun now stands.
ALA:63
Keeler, W. W.
Inaugural address of the chief
of the Cherokees.
BA 1971-72:74
Kidwell, C. S.
American Indian attitudes
toward nature. MAES:277
Lee, G. P.
Effective "Indian leadership"
color-blind, but not naive.
MAES:183
Red Eagle
Indian rights. ANN 10:242
Red Jacket
Missionary effort. ANN 4:194;
BREWE 7:2571; HURH:57
Spotted tail
We are young no longer.
ALA:37
Ybarra, B.
The wheel of poverty.
BAPR:356; BAPRR:266

---- See also Cherokee Indians;
Navaho Indians; see also Names
of Indians, e.g. Logan, J.;
Old Tassel; Red Eagle; Red
Jacket; Tecumseh; Weatherford,
W. Also this subject with sub-
head - Government relations

---- AGED
Peaches, D.
Statement on the problems of
the elderly American Indians
at the Conference on Indian
Elders, Albuquerque, New
Mexico, July 17, 1975.
MAES:179

---- CIVIL RIGHTS
Savilla, E. M.
Address to the Assembly of the
National Congress of American

Indians at San Diego, California, October 1974. MAES:225

---- CIVILIZATION
Sawyer, T. E.
Assimilation versus self-identity. MAES:197
West, D.
Cultural differences: a base. MAES:120
Yazzie, E.
Navajo wisdom. MAES:261

---- CULTURAL ASSIMILATION
George, D.
Brotherhood and understanding. MAES:393
My people, the Indians. MAES:397
Trimble, C.
Harmony--from where the sun now stands. MAES:388

---- ECONOMIC CONDITIONS
MacDonald, P.
Statement of Chairman of Navajo Tribal Council, April 14, 1975. MAES:243

---- EDUCATION
Barlow, E. J.
Education on Indian terms. MAES:90
If a man loses something. MAES:343
Multicultural education: its effective management. MAES:110
Benham, W. J.
An Indian education resources center. MAES:114
Demmert, W. G.
Tribal chartered education. MAES:156
Harris, L.
American Indian education and pluralism. MAES:96
MacDonald, P.
Statement before the Conference on Financing of Public Schools on Indian Reservations, April 3, 1975. MAES:105
McKeag, J.
Testimony of Jana McKeag, Education Director, National Congress of American In-

dians, July 19, 1975. MAES:249
Maestas, J. R.
With a touch of the master's hand. MAES:130
Platero, D.
Discussions of critical issues affecting Navajo education programs and policies. MAES:149
Rainer, J. C.
Institute of American Indian Arts Commencement exercises, Friday, May 21, 1976. MAES:219
Testimony: hearings before the Senate Appropriations Subcommittee on the Interior and Related Agencies, May 13, 1975. MAES:255
Sockey, C. E.
Excellence in Indian education. MAES:141
West, D.
Cultural differences: a base. MAES:120

---- GOVERNMENT RELATIONS
Arthur, C. A.
First annual message. STAT 2:1424
Atcitty, W. R.
Remarks. MAES:38
Barlow, E. J.
If a man loses something. MAES:343
Bennett, R.
The fall and rise of Indian sovereignty. MAES:11
Cleveland, G.
First annual message (first term). STAT 2:1514
Harrison, B.
Third annual message. STAT 2:1676
Jackson, A.
First annual message. ANN 5:330; BOORA 1:264; STAT 1:294
Second annual address. ANN 5:418; STAT 1:314
MacDonald, P.
Statement before the Indian sovereignty Conference of American Indians, Harvard, February 22, 1975. MAES:22
Statement of the implementation of P.L. 93-638 Indian Self-Determination and Education Assistance Act, Window Rock,

Navajo Nation, April 3,
1975. MAES:189
Peaches, D.
Statement on the problems
of the elderly American In-
dians at the Conference on
Indian Elders, Albuquerque,
New Mexico, July 17, 1975.
MAES:179
Seneca, M.
Address delivered at Brigham
Young University February,
1975. MAES:26
Thompson, M.
The BIA at work. MAES:57
Trimble, C.
Harmony--from where the
sun now stands. MAES:388
Trudell, J.
Commitment. MAES:83
Van Buren, M.
First annual message.
STAT 1:472
Second annual message.
STAT 1:494
Washington, G.
Fourth annual address.
STAT 1:12
Seventh annual address.
STAT 1:27
Third annual address.
STAT 1:7

---- HISTORY - STUDY &
TEACHING
Barlow, E. J.
If a man loses something.
MAES:343
Costo, R.
Indian history--fact or fic-
tion. MAES:321

---- LAND TENURE
Wah-shee, J.
A land settlement--what does
it mean? MAES:45

---- LANGUAGES - STUDY AND
TEACHING
Beaudin, J. A.
Testimony to the Senate Edu-
cation Committee May 6,
1975 at the State Capitol
concerning Senate Bill 145.
MAES:245

---- ORATORY
Momaday, N. S.

Oral tradition of the American
Indian. MAES:294

---- RACE IDENTITY
Sawyer, T. E.
Assimilation versus self-identity.
MAES:197

---- RELIGION AND MYTHOLOGY
Whitemen, H. V.
Spiritual roots of Indian suc-
cess. MAES:377

---- RESERVATIONS
MacDonald, P.
Statement before the Conference
on Financing of Public Schools
on Indian Reservations, April 3,
1975. MAES:105

---- SCHOLARSHIPS, FELLOWSHIPS,
ETC.
Rainer, J. C.
Testimony: hearings before the
Senate Appropriations Subcom-
mittee on the Interior and Re-
lated Agencies, May 13, 1975.
MAES:255

---- SOCIAL CONDITIONS
Mills, B.
New Indian, new commitment,
February, 1974. MAES:402

---- SOCIAL LIFE AND CUSTOMS
Mills, B.
New Indian, new commitment,
February, 1974. MAES:402

---- TRIBAL GOVERNMENT
Demmert, W. G.
Tribal chartered education.
MAES:156
Wilson, D.
Real Indian leaders condemn
A.I.M. MAES:63

---- URBAN RESIDENCE
Bellecourt, V.
American Indian Movement.
MAES:66

---- WISCONSIN
Beaudin, J. A.
Testimony to the Senate Educa-
tion Committee May 6, 1975 at
the State Capitol concerning
Senate Bill 145. MAES:245

---- WOMEN
Wittstock, L. W.
  Native American women in
  the feminist milieu.
  MAES:373
Yazzie, E.
  Special problems of Indian
  women in education.
  MAES:360

---- WARS See Seminole War,
1st, Florida, 1817-1818

INDIVIDUALISM
Eisenhower, D. D.
  Faith in the individual.
  CAPG:31
Kerr, C.
  The independent spirit.
  HOR:114
Schell, G.
  Shackled by stereotypes.
  CAPB:381

INDONESIA
May, D.
  Djakarta style. MDYG:168

---- FOREIGN RELATIONS
Razak, T. A.
  And then came peace (Peace
  Agreement between Malaysia
  and Indonesia). MONS:94

INDUCTION See Inaugural addresses; Installation
speeches

INDUSTRIAL ARTS
Webster, D.
  Progress of the mechanic
  arts. BREWE 10:3856

INDUSTRIAL RELATIONS
Brandeis, L. D.
  Curse of bigness.
  BOORA 2:759
Fisk, T.
  War of capital against labor.
  ANN 6:118
Fortune, T. T.
  The present relations of
  labor and capital. FON:506
Lincoln, A.
  First annual message.
  STAT 2:1054
Roosevelt, T.
  Eighth annual message.

STAT 3:2296
  Sixth annual message.
  STAT 3:2194
Truman, H. S.
  Second annual message.
  STAT 3:2939
Webster, D.
  Technical progress and prosper-
  ity. ANN 6:266
White, W. A.
  Speaking for the consumer.
  HURH:234

---- See also Industry; Labor unions

---- MALAYSIA
Suffian bin Hashim
  Warning to the white-collar
  worker. MONSA:138

INDUSTRIAL WORKERS OF THE
WORLD
De Leon, D.
  Political power of labor.
  ANN 13:19

INDUSTRY
Baldwin, S. B.
  Good will in industry.
  MCB:243
Carty, J. J.
  Pure science and industrial re-
  search. ANN 14:9
Chapin, E. H.
  Peaceful industry.
  BREWE 3:1037
Clay, H.
  American industry, 1824.
  ANN 5:114
Hoover, H. C.
  Moral standard in an industrial
  era. ANN 14:428

---- See also Business; Industrial
relations; Laissez-faire

INDUSTRY AND SOCIETY
Eisenhower, D. D.
  Faith in the individual.
  CAPG:31
Grede, W. J.
  America, a frontier.
  ANN 17:154

INDUSTRY AND STATE
Carpenter, C. U.
  Justification of big business.
  ANN 13:327

Champion, G.
Consensus complex vs. the
free market. BA 1965-66:187
Drumm, S. L.
War on prosperity.
CAPG:185
Friedman, M.
The future of capitalism.
LINRST:243
Hanley, J. W.
The day innovation died.
BA 1978-79:122
Hart, G.
Big government: real or
imaginary? LINRST:100
Hoover, H. C.
Campaign speech, Madison
Square Garden, New York
City, October 31, 1932.
SIN:103
Speech at New York City,
October 22, 1928.
ANN 14:595; BOORA 2:803
Veto of the Muscle Shoals
Bill. ANN 15:79
Johari, M. K.
A national chamber needed.
MONSA:103
Richey, H. S.
The real cause of inflation:
government services.
LINRST:108
Romney, G.
Our unique economic prin-
ciples: the market place
should determine price.
CAPG:40
Roosevelt, F. D.
Fifth annual message.
STAT 3:2883
Stanton, F.
Remarks on government
regulation of broadcasting
(accepting Printers' Ink
gold medal). MDV:277
Sutherland, G. and others
New State Ice Company v.
Liebmann: opinion for the
court and dissenting opinion.
ANN 15:140
Taft, R. A.
New problems of government.
ANN 15:571
Should the government
guarantee employment?
ANN 16:263
Van Buren, M.
Against government aid

for business losses. ANN 6:314
Waite, M. R. and others
Munn v. Illinois, 1876: opinion
for the court and dissenting
opinion. ANN 10:377
Willkie, W. L.
Private enterprise--we have
gone far enough down the road
to federal control. BAD:69

INFLATION (FINANCE)
Muskie, E. S.
Too many questions ... not
enough answers.
BA 1978-79:112
Richey, H. S.
The real cause of inflation:
government services.
LINRST:108

INFORMATIVE SPEECHES
Bragg, L.
Art of talking about science.
MOP:358
Burton, S.
You (male) should wear long
hair. BAS:200 (outline only)
King, M. L., Jr.
Love, law, and civil disobedi-
ence. FON:943; LINR:63;
LINRS:70; LINRST:75; STOT:321
Klein, P. A.
Big things happen in small
places (outline of speech ex-
plaining protein synthesis).
CUR:34
Koblish, C. F.
Diamonds, their mining, sell-
ing, perfecting, and the deter-
mining of their quality.
BAS:206 (outline only)
Menninger, K.
Healthier than healthy.
LINR:54
Miller, J.
Why ice floats. MOP:20;
MOPR:59
Peters, L.
What is totalitarianism?
LINR:50
Ragan, D. O.
Backaches. MOP:366
Sonberg, H. A.
Unidentified flying objects;
their history and various ex-
planations which have been
given concerning their nature.
BAS:203 (outline only)

Suggestions for preparation of
the informative speech.
With examples of.
BRP:46, 169

---- See also Reports

Ingalls, John James
Undiscovered country.
BREWE 7:2574

Ingebretsen, Herman Smitt
Presentation [of the Nobel
Prize for Peace to John
Raleigh Mott, Dec. 10,
1946]. NOLP 2:354

Ingersoll, Charles Jared
Influence of America on the
mind. ANN 5:95

Ingersoll, Robert Green
Absurdity of religion.
ANN 11:267
At his brother's grave.
ALA:69; BREWE 7:2580;
HURH:156
Blaine, the plumed knight.
Same as his Nominating
Blaine
Grave of Napoleon. Same as
his Liberty of man, wom-
an, and child
Imagination. BREWE 7:2585
Liberty of man, woman, and
child. BREWE 7:2583
Life. BREWE 7:2587
"Life is a narrow vale between
the cold and barren peaks
of two eternities. " Same
as his Nominating Blaine
Nominating Blaine.
BREWE 7:2578: HURH:154

INHIBITION
Eccles, J. C.
The ionic mechanism of
postsynaptic inhibition.
NOLM 4:6
Sherrington, Sir C. S.
Inhibition as a coordinative
factor. NOLM 2:278

INQUIRY, SPEECHES OF See
Informative speeches

INSANE - CARE AND TREATMENT
Seward, W. H.

Providing for the indigent insane. ANN 8:283

INSANITY
Erskine, T.
Homicidal insanity (J. Had-
field). BREWE 6:2058;
BRYH:294

INSECTICIDES
Müller, P. H.
Dichloro-diphenyl-trichloroe-
thane and newer insecticides.
NOLM 3:227

INSECTS, INJURIOUS AND BENE-
FICIAL - CONTROL
Klayton, R. J.
Bureau of Forests and Waters
should control pests by biological means rather than pesticides. BAS:188 (outline only)

INSPIRATIONAL TALKS
Bunche, R. J.
Barriers of race can be sur-
mounted. CAPG:66
Eisenhower, D. D.
Price of peace: second in-
augural address.
USINAU:263; USINAUG:263
Suggestions for preparation of
inspirational talks. PAE:189

INSTALLATION SPEECHES
Abdul Rahman, T.
Our university: pledge to na-
tion (installation speech as
Chancellor of University of
Malaya). MONS:28
Installation services for general
officers. BNH:53; BOS:53
Installation services for men's
organizations. BNH:56;
BOS:56
Peel, R.
Plea for higher education (in-
stallation speech as Lord
Rector of University of Glas-
gow). BREWE 8:3153
Suggestions for preparing installa-
tion speeches. PAE:186

---- See also Inaugural addresses

INSTITUTE OF INTERNATIONAL
LAW
Hagerup, G. F.

INSTITUTIONS, SIZE OF

The work of the Institute of
International Law (Nobel
Lecture for 1904, Aug. 24,
1912). NOLP 1:64
Irgens, J.
Welcome [presenting the
Nobel Prize for Peace to
the Institute of International
Law for 1904, Aug. 24,
1912]. NOLP 1:61

INSTITUTIONS, SIZE OF
Babbidge, H. D.
On thinking big. HOR:121

INSTRUCTION, SPEECHES OF
See Informative speeches

INSULIN
Banting, F. G.
Diabetes and insulin.
NOLM 2:50
Macleod, J. J. R.
The physiology of insulin and
its source in the animal
body. NOLM 2:71

INSURANCE - ACCIDENT
Clemens, S. L.
Accident insurance--etc.
MUS:291

INSURANCE - LIFE
Eisenhower, D. D.
Faith in the individual.
CAPG:31

INSURANCE - PROPERTY
Title insurance racket.
BURT:136

INTEGRATION
Browne, R. S.
A case for separation.
FON:1121
---- and others
Separation or integration:
which way for America?
BA 1968-69:143
Galamison, M. A.
Integration must work--
nothing else can. FON:959
James, D.
"Given time we'll get it to-
gether." BA 1974-75:135

---- See also Segregation

INTELLECT
Beloff, M.
Americanisation of British in-
tellectual life. MDYG:114
Campbell, A.
Mind the master force.
BREWE 3:935
Everett, E.
Circumstances favorable to the
progress of literature in Amer-
ica. ANN 5:118
Huxley, T. H.
Method of scientific investiga-
tion. ARS:264
Ingersoll, C. J.
Influence of America on the
mind. ANN 5:95
Living or the dead. BURT:127

INTERNAL SECURITY - MALAYSIA
Rahman, D. I. B. A.
Commendable features of public-
spiritedness and co-operation.
MONSA:76
Government is determined to
take drastic measures if....
MONSA:72
Security situation in Malaysia:
a warning and pledge.
MONSA:69

INTERNAL SECURITY ACT, 1950
Truman, H. S.
Veto of the Internal Security
Act. ANN 17:35

INTERNATIONAL COOPERATION
Balch, E. G.
Toward human unity or beyond
nationalism (Nobel Lecture for
1946, April 7, 1948).
NOLP 2:333
Branting, K. H.
Fraternity among nations
(Nobel Lecture for 1921, June
19, 1922). NOLP 1:324
Cremer, W. R.
The progress and advantages of
international arbitration (Nobel
Lecture for 1903, Jan. 15,
1905). NOLP 1:46
Fried, P.
Price of peace. SCHW:35
Hammarskjöld, D.
Values of nationalism and inter-
nationalism (Stanford University
commencement address).
HURS:206

Lange, C. L.
Internationalism (Nobel Lec-
ture, Dec. 13, 1921).
NOLP 1:336
McKeever, P.
The United States and the
United Nations. BRYF:479
Roosevelt, T.
International peace (Nobel
Lecture for 1906, May 5,
1910). NOLP 1:102
Stevenson, A. E.
Strengthening international
developing institutions.
ALS:281

INTERNATIONAL ECONOMIC
RELATIONS
Stevenson, A., III
Economic interdependence:
the world at a crossroads.
BA 1978-79:178

INTERNATIONAL LABOR OR-
GANIZATION
Lionaes, A.
Presentation [of the Nobel
Prize for Peace to the
International Labor Organi-
zation, Dec. 10, 1969].
NOLP 3:415
Manickavasagam, V.
ILO represents the social
conscience of the world.
MONSA:106 selections
Morse, D. A.
ILO and the social infra-
structure of peace (Nobel
Lecture, Dec. 11, 1969).
NOLP 3:424

INTERNATIONAL LAW See Law
and lawyers

INTERNATIONAL RELATIONS
Acheson, D. G.
Ethics of international rela-
tions today. ARS:229
Chateaubriand, F. A. R.
Has one government the right
to intervene in the internal
affairs of another?
BREWE 3:1060
Eisenhower, M. S.
A new historical perspective,
interdependence. HOR:157
Hesburgh, T. M.
The problems and opportun-

ities on a very interdependent
planet. HOR:142
Hugo, V. M.
Moral forces in world politics.
BREWE 7:2553
Lee Kuan Yew
Changes in values and concepts.
MONS:348
Lubbers, A. D.
Road to right. SCHW:159
Worden, G. J.
Person to person. SCHW:174

INTERNATIONALISM See International cooperation; Nationalism

INTERSTATE COMMERCE
Roosevelt, T.
Seventh annual message.
STAT 3:2240

---- See also Railroads and state

INTERVIEWING
Scott, R.
A job-seeking interview: a
transcript. MOPR:381

INTOLERANCE See Religious
liberty

INTRODUCTIONS
Ace of aces (outline of speech).
CUB:62
Ashmore, H. S.
Presents J. William Fulbright.
LYI:205
Bard, G. M.
Introduces Alexander Rorke,
Jr. PRS:69
Introduces Arthur Godfrey.
PRS:45
Introduces Dr. Deane W.
Malott, president of Cornell
University. PRS:115
Introduces Dr. Henry A. Kis-
singer. PRS:124
Introduces George Ratterman.
PRS:62
Introduces Gilbert W. Fitz-
hugh. PRS:17
Introduces Walter W. Heller,
chairman of the President's
Council on Economic Advisers.
PRS:33
Introduces William F. Buckley,
Jr., columnist. PRS:57
Blakely, R. J.

Presents Stephen Hayes
Bush. LYI:77
Blumenschein, C. M.
Introduces Smith Hempstone.
PRS:23
Borsch, R. A.
Introduces Irish Prime Min-
ister William Norton.
PRS:41
Introduces Selwyn Lloyd,
former British Secretary of
State for Foreign Affairs.
PRS:39
Brorby, M.
Introduces Arnold J. Toyn-
bee, professor, author and
historian of Great Britain.
LYI:86
Buchanan, J. G.
Presents Augustus N. Hand.
LYI:133
Bullock, H.
Presents Lester B. Pearson.
LYI:207
Burgess, W. R.
Presents Paul H. Douglas.
LYI:231
Butler, N. M.
Presents Wilbur L. Cross.
LYI:97
Cavanagh, J. P.
Presents George Alfred
Brown. LYI:203
Caveny, C. C.
Greets Joey Bishop, sub-
stituting for Sir Cedric
Hardwicke. PRS:118
Introduces David E. Bell,
director of the Bureau of
the Budget. PRS:92
Introduces Dr. George W.
Beadle, chancellor of the
University of Chicago.
PRS:50
Introduces Dr. Jonas E.
Salk. PRS:88
Introduces Henry J. Taylor,
former United States Am-
bassador to Switzerland.
PRS:25
Introduces Leonard E.
Read. PRS:98
Introduces Ogden Nash.
PRS:106
Introduces Robert E. Brook-
er, president of Whirlpool
Corporation. PRS:9
Introduces Senator John G.

Tower of Texas. PRS:111
Introduces Senator Kenneth B.
Keating. PRS:27
Chandler, M.
Introduces Roscoe Drummond.
PRS:122
Choate, J. H.
Presents James Bryce.
LYI:237
Clemens, S. L.
Presents Henry M. Stanley.
LYI:117
Presents Joseph B. Hawley.
LYI:148
Presents Winston Churchill.
LYI:198
Coulter, T. H.
Introducing Marguerite (Maggie)
Higgins to the Executives'
Club of Chicago. LYI:113
Cragg, R. T.
Introduces Judge Lester H.
Loble of Juvenile Court of
Helena, Montana. PRS:38
Presents Cyril Northcote.
LYI:45
Croarkin, W.
Presents Frank F. Rosenthal.
LYI:165
Presents William David O'Brien.
LYI:163
Cullman, H. S.
Presents Roger L. Stevens.
LYI:29
Daniels, J.
Presents Sir Norman Birkett.
LYI:135
Davis, C. R.
Presents Will Durant. LYI:56
Davis, J. W.
Presents Lester B. Pearson.
LYI:220
Day, J. E.
Introduces G. Keith Funston,
president New York Stock Ex-
change. PRS:10
Introduces John L. Lewis,
American labor leader.
LYI:61
Depew, C. M.
Presents William Jennings
Bryan. LYI:227
Dirksen, E.
Presents Robert A. Taft.
LYI:210
Donovan, H.
Presents Henry R. Luce.
LYI:103

Douglas, L. W.
  Presents Lord Halifax.
  LYI:222
Dreier, A.
  Introduces James T. Quirk.
  PRS:18
  Introduces the Honorable
  William Proxmire, United
  States Senator from Wiscon-
  sin. PRS:34
DuVall, W. O.
  Presents Billy Graham.
  LYI:160
Erickson, D. J.
  Presents W. E. Whitehead.
  LYI:63
Fawcett, N. G.
  Introduces E. W. Ingram,
  president, White Castle,
  Inc. PRS:6
Fisher, C. T., Jr.
  Presents George C. Kenney.
  LYI:150
Ford, G. S.
  Presents Christopher Morley.
  LYI:55
Ford, H. II
  Presents Elmo Roper.
  LYI:73
Fraser, L.
  Presents James F. Byrnes.
  LYI:218
Godfrey, J. L.
  Presents Frank Borden
  Hanes. LYI:38
Gossett, W. T.
  Presents Harry Emerson
  Fosdick. LYI:157
Graham, F. P.
  Presents Robert M.
  Hutchins. LYI:96
Griffin, C. E.
  Presents James Palmer.
  LYI:67
Gwinn, J. M.
  Presents Charles Lindbergh.
  LYI:188
Hancher, V. M.
  Presents Eleanor Roosevelt.
  LYI:244
  Presents Franklyn Bliss
  Snyder. LYI:99
Hanson, C. W. D.
  Introduces Benson Ford,
  vice-president, Ford Motor
  Company. PRS:22
  Introduces Gene Lockhart.
  PRS:51

Harding, W. G.
  Presents Marie S. Curie.
  LYI:179
Hayes, A.
  Presents Indira Gandhi.
  LYI:199
Hedges, J. E.
  Presents Edward D. Duffield.
  LYI:69
Hibben, J. W.
  Introduces Bishop James A.
  Pike. PRS:69
  Introduces Braj K. Nehru, Am-
  bassador from India. PRS:26
  Introduces Dr. Howard B.
  Sprague. PRS:61
  Introduces Hobart Rowen of
  Newsweek Magazine. PRS:95
  Introduces the Honorable Otto
  Kerner, governor of Illinois.
  PRS:29
  Introduces Willy Brandt, mayor
  of West Berlin. PRS:37
Hill, H.
  Presents Francis B. Haas.
  LYI:93
Hills, L.
  Presents Fred Sparks. LYI:115
Holmes, O. W.
  Introduces Matthew Arnold.
  LYI:44
Introduction of speakers (12 exam-
  ples). HNWSN:59
Introduction of the head of the
  Executive Committee of the
  Chicago Central Area Commit-
  tee. PRS:21
Introductions for doctors.
  BOS:25; (6 examples) BNH:25
Introductions for evangelists (19
  examples). BNH:13; BON:26;
  BOS:13
Introductions for housewives (5
  examples). BNH:33; BOS:33
Introductions for literary persons
  (2 examples). BNH:18; BOS:18
Introductions for medical doctors.
  BON:29
Introductions for men in general
  (10 examples). BNH:19;
  BON:15; BOS:19
Introductions for ministers (16
  examples). BNH:9; BOS:9
Introductions for mission society
  leaders (4 examples). BNH:35;
  BOS:35
Introductions for missionaries.
  BON:34

Introductions for mothers-in-
law (4 examples). BNH:32;
BOS:34
Introductions for nurses (4
examples). BNH:32;
BOS:32
Introductions for politicians
(3 examples). BNH:31;
BOS:31
Introductions for prize winners.
BON:32
Introductions for public offi-
cials. BON:23; BOS:27;
(3 examples) BNH:27
Introductions for singers and
musicians (12 examples).
BNH:22; BOS:22
Introductions for teachers (10
examples). BNH:28;
BON:20; BOS:28
Introductions for women.
BON:38
Jessel, G.
Presents Groucho Marx.
LYI:32
Presents Jack Benny.
LYI:30
Kipke, H. G.
Introduces John K. Herbert,
president of the Magazine
Publishers Association.
PRS:21
Knight, J. R.
Introduces Lieutenant
Thomas A. Dooley, United
States Navy. PRS:67
Knoch, W. G.
Introduces Robert Taft, Jr.,
Congressman-at-large from
Ohio. PRS:32
Lamont, T. S.
Presents Paul G. Hoffman.
LYI:71
Presents Eleanor Robson
Belmont. LYI:23
Presents W. L. Mackenzie
King. LYI:233
Landis, F.
Witty after-dinner speech on
Will Hays. LYI:224
Langlie, A. B.
Presents Norman S. Mar-
shall. LYI:155
Lewe, J. C.
Presents Thomas C. Clark
(Attorney General of the
United States). LYI:137
Lewis, J. H.

Introduction of Jacob M. Dick-
inson. LYI:217
Lowe, J. A.
Presents E. J. Pratt. LYI:49
Lusty, R.
Presents Sir Norman Birkett.
LYI:54
McCloud, B. G.
Presents C. D. Jackson.
PRS:23
McLain, H. O.
Presents David Seabury. LYI:98
Martin, C.
Presents McGeorge Bundy.
LYI:88
Martin, J. W.
Introducing Speaker Sam Ray-
burn. LYI:195
Martin, T. W.
Presents Charles F. Kettering.
LYI:181
Mason, W. C.
Presents George Wharton Pep-
per. LYI:129
Meloney, Mrs. W. B.
Introducing Dorothy Thompson.
LYI:112
Merriam, J. C.
Presents Ray Lyman Wilbur.
LYI:82
Milburn, J. G.
Presents James R. Day.
LYI:90
Mulroy, T. R.
Presents Ilka Chase. LYI:17
Murphy, H. D.
Introduces Dr. Norman Vincent
Peale. PRS:103
Introduces Dr. Ralph W. Sock-
man. PRS:117
Introduces Lee Wulff. PRS:67
Introduces Senator Hubert
Humphrey from Minnesota.
PRS:40
Nix, L.
Presents Edmon Low. LYI:40
Nizer, L.
Presents Albert Einstein.
LYI:176
Presents George Gershwin.
LYI:15
Presents Grover A. Whalen.
LYI:65
Presents Harry Woodburn
Chase. LYI:91
Presents Heywood Broun.
LYI:105
Noonan, T. C.

Introduces Robert C. Tyson, chairman of the finance committee, United States Steel Corporation. PRS:15

Willcox, W. R.
Introducing G. W. Goethals to the Economic Club of New York, March 5, 1914. LYI:183

Wilson, E. F.
Introduces Wilbur M. Brucker, then Secretary of the Army. PRS:41

Youle, C.
Introduces Charles B. Thornton. PRS:100
Introduces Don Whitehead, chief of the Washington bureau of the New York Herald Tribune. PRS:65
Introduces Percy Brundage, the director of the Federal Budget. PRS:31
Introduces Stanley C. Hope, president, National Association of Manufacturers. PRS:15
Introduces W. Randolph Burgess, United States permanent representative on the North Atlantic Council. PRS:30
Presents S. Clarke Beise, president of the Bank of America. PRS:15

Zumwalt, E.
Introduction to Edmund G. Brown, Jr. JAM:33

---- See also Responses to introductions; Welcoming addresses

INVENTIONS AND INVENTORS
DuPont, H. B.
Greatest invention of them all. ANN 17:530
Durfee, J.
Influence of scientific discovery and invention on social and political progress. ANN 7:128
Ziegler, K.
Consequences and development of an invention. NOLC 4:6

INVESTIGATION See Research

INVESTMENTS
Investors. BURT:133

IONOSPHERE
Appleton, Sir E. V.
The ionosphere. NOLPH 3:79

IONS
Onsager, L.
The motion of ions: principles and concepts. NOLC 4:272
Wilson, C. T. R.
On the cloud method of making visible ions and the tracks of ionizing particles. NOLPH 2:194

IRAN
Demosthenes
Oration on the liberty of the Rhodians. SAG:180

IRELAND
Canning, G.
Hate in politics. BREWE 3:946
Curran, J. P.
Liberties of the indolent. BREWE 4:1550
On government by attachment. BREWE 4:1557
Davitt, M.
Ireland a nation, self-chartered and self-ruled. BREWE 5:1666
Gladstone, W. E.
Home Rule, June 7, 1886. MCB:301
Home rule and autonomy. BREWE 6:2278
Grattan, H.
Declaration of Irish rights, April 19, 1780. BREWE 6:2314; CLAYP:120
Making his second motion for a Declaration of Irish rights, April 16, 1782. BRYH:244
Unsurrendering fidelity to country. BREWE 6:2333
Meagher, T. F.
Withering influence of provincial subjection. BREWE 8:2999
O'Connell, D.
Demand for justice to Ireland. BREWE 8:3107
On repeal of the Union. BREWE 8:3099; BRYH:358; MCB:288; STRM:198
Oxford and Asquith, H. H. A.

Debate on the Government
of Ireland Bill.   MCB:321
Palmerston, H. J. T.
Against war on Ireland.
BREWE 8:3134
Parnell, C. S.
Against nonresident landlords.
BREWE 8:3145
At Ennis (boycotting defined
and defended).   BRYF:544;
MCB:296; STRM:346
Sheil, R. L.
Ireland's part in English
achievement.
BREWE 9:3413
Smith, S.
"Wounds, shrieks, and tears"
in government.
BREWE 9:3490

Irgens, Johannes
Welcome [presenting the Nobel
Prize for Peace to the In-
stitute of International Law
for 1904, Aug. 24, 1912].
NOLP 1:61

IRRIGATION - SOUTH DAKOTA
Gage, P.
The Oahe Project--yes or
no? BREWW:191

Irwin, Henry
The true aim of education.
CURM:167

Ising, G.
Presentation [of the Nobel
Prize for Physics to Pat-
rick Maynard Stuart
Blackett, Dec. 13, 1948].
NOLPH 3:93

Ismail bin Mohammed Ali
The central Bank--the "financial conscience" of the
government (Kuala Lam-
pur, Sept. 1970).
MONSA:189

ISOLATIONISM See United
States - Neutrality

ISOTOPES
Aston, F. W.
Mass spectra and isotopes.
NOLC 2:7
Soddy, F.

The origins of the conceptions
of isotopes. NOLC 1:371

ISOTOPIC INDICATORS See Radioactive tracers

ISRAEL
Ghali, W.
Egyptian in Israel. MDYG:152

---- FOREIGN RELATIONS - EGYPT
Carter, J.
Announcing the Camp David ac-
cords. BA 1978-79:142

ITALY
Cavour, C. B.
Rome and Italy. BREWE 3:1012
Mazzini, G.
To the young men of Italy.
BREWE 8:2992
Roosevelt, F. D.
Italy enters this war.
ANN 16:8

Ivens, Mike
I still believe in the future of
farming. BREWW:195

IVY ORATIONS See Commencement
addresses

- J -

Jackson, Andrew
Autonomy of the executive.
ANN 6:58
Eighth annual message.
STAT 1:445
Farewell address, 1837.
ANN 6:298
Fifth annual message.
STAT 1:373
First annual message.
ANN 5:330; BOORA 1:264;
STAT 1:294
First inaugural address.
USINAU:55; USINAUG:55
Fourth annual message.
STAT 1:358
Independence of Texas.
ANN 6:293
On the Indian removal. Same as
his Second annual message
Permanent habitation for the
American Indians. Same as

his Seventh annual mes-
sage
Second annual address.
ANN 5:418; STAT 1:314
Second inaugural address--
"State rights and Fed-
eral sovereignty. " (Wash-
ington, March 4,
1833). BREWE 7:2597;
HURH:71; USINAU:58;
USINAUG:58
Seventh annual message.
ANN 6:164; STAT 1:415
Sixth annual message.
STAT 1:389
Third annual message.
STAT 1:344
Veto message of July 10, 1832.
ANN 5:524
Veto of Maysville Road Bill.
ANN 5:374
"Without union, our independence
and liberty would never have
been achieved; without union
they never can be maintained. "
Same as his Second in-
augural address--"State
rights and federal sover-
eignty. "

JACKSON, ANDREW
Benton, T. H.
Political career of Andrew
Jackson. BREWE 2:411
Calhoun, J. C.
Denouncing Andrew Jackson.
BREWE 3:919
Clay, H.
Dictators in American
politics. BLY:33;
BREWE 4:1124
Crockett, D.
Fourth of July oration, 1834.
HAW:136
Robbins, A.
Fourth of July oration,
July 4, 1834. HAW:160

Jackson, Esther M.
American theatre and the
speech profession.
BA 1965-66:200

JACKSON, GEORGE
Davis, A.
The legacy of George Jack-
son. FON:1191

Jackson, Robert H.
The Communist Party is a secret
conclave. American Com-
munications Association, C.I.O.
et al v. Charles T. Douds;
United Steel Workers of America et al v. National Labor
Relations Board. (1949).
DAVF:292
Court broadens the rights of citizens: the Second Flag Salute
Case, 1943. ROD:214
To secure the existing order
against revolutionary radicalism (1950). (Eugene Dennis
et al v. U.S.A.). DAVF:294

---- and others (H. L. Black; W.
O. Douglas; F. Frankfurter)
West Virginia Board of Education
et al v. Barnette et al:
opinion for the court and dissenting opinion. ANN 16:148

---- See also Black, H. L., jt.
auth.

Jacob, François
Genetics of the bacterial cell
(Nobel Prize, Dec. 11, 1965).
NOLM 4:148

JACOB, FRANÇOIS
Gard, S.
Presentation [of the Nobel Prize
for Physiology or Medicine to
François Jacob, André Lwoff,
and Jacques Monod, Dec. 11,
1965]. NOLM 4:143

Jacobusse, K. Don
Big man. SCHW:204
Peace through patriotism.
SCHW:168
Uncommon thought. SCHW:79

Jahn, Gunnar
Presentation [of the Nobel Prize
for Peace to Albert John
Luthuli for 1960, Dec. 10,
1961]. NOLP 3:209
Presentation [of the Nobel Prize
for Peace for 1952 to Albert
Schweitzer, Dec. 10, 1953].
NOLP 3:37
Presentation [of the Nobel Prize
for Peace to Cordell Hull,
Dec. 10, 1945]. NOLP 2:311

Presentation [of the Nobel
Prize for Peace to Dag
Hammarskjöld, Dec. 10,
1961]. NOLP 3:239
Presentation [of the Nobel
Prize for Peace to Emily
Greene Balch, Dec. 10,
1946]. NOLP 2:325
Presentation [of the Nobel
Prize for Peace to the
Friends Service Council and
the American Friends Serv-
ice Committee, Dec. 10,
1947]. NOLP 2:373
Presentation [of the Nobel
Prize for Peace to
Georges Pire, Dec. 10,
1958]. NOLP 3:151
Presentation [of the Nobel
Prize for Peace to the
International Committee of
the Red Cross, 1944, Dec.
10, 1945]. NOLP 2:289
Presentation [of the Nobel
Prize for Peace to Léon
Jouhaux, Dec. 10, 1951].
NOLP 3:3
Presentation [of the Nobel
Prize for Peace to Lester
Bowles Pearson, Dec. 10,
1957]. NOLP 3:119
Presentation [of the Nobel
Prize for Peace, 1962, to
Linus Carl Pauling, Dec.
10, 1963]. NOLP 3:259
Presentation [of the Nobel
Prize for Peace to Lord
Boyd Orr of Brechin, Dec.
10, 1949]. NOLP 2:407
Presentation [of the Nobel
Prize for Peace to Martin
Luther King, Jr., Dec. 10,
1964]. NOLP 3:325
Presentation [of the Nobel
Prize for Peace to the
Office of the United Nations
High Commissioner for
Refugees, Dec. 10, 1955].
NOLP 3:89
Presentation [of the Nobel
Prize for Peace to Philip
John Noel-Baker, Dec. 10,
1959]. NOLP 3:175
Presentation [of the Nobel
Prize for Peace to Ralph
Johnson Bunche, Dec. 10,
1950]. NOLP 2:435

James, Daniel
"Given time we'll get it together."
(Pensacola, Fla., Feb. 14,
1975). BA 1974-75:135

JAMES, WILLIAM
Santayana, G.
Genteel tradition in American
philosophy. ANN 13:277

JAPAN
Tuohy, F.
Three windows on Japan.
MDYG:161

JAPANESE IN THE UNITED STATES
Black, H. L. and others
Korematsu v. United States:
opinion for the court and dis-
senting opinion. ANN 16:234
Mink, P. T.
Seeking a link with the past.
BA 1971-72:59
Stone, H. F.
Fear and hysteria: the Japanese
relocation, "Hirabayashi v.
United States," 1943: opinion
for the Supreme Court.
ROD:316
Tardiff, V.
Americans with Japanese faces.
SCHW:20

Jarrow, Charles
Case for the non-voter. KEO:229

Jay, John, 1745-1829
Protest against colonial government. BREWE 7:2601

Jay, Peter See Sanford, N., jt.
auth.

JAY TREATY See Treaties

JAZZ MUSIC
Bernstein, L.
World of jazz. ARN:320;
ARS:67

Jefferson, Thomas
Eighth annual message.
STAT 1:94
Fifth annual message.
STAT 1:77
First annual message.
STAT 1:48
First inaugural: democracy

defined (Washington, March
4, 1801). AND:116;
ANN 1:143; BOORA 1:212;
BREWE 7:2612; HURH:48;
LINS:140; OLIS:28;
USINAU:13; USINAUG:13
Fourth annual message.
STAT 1:73
Jeffersonian democracy defines.
Same as his First inaugural:
democracy defined
Lewis and Clark expedition.
ANN 4:158
Second annual message.
STAT 1:64
Second inaugural address.
USINAU:17; USINAUG:17
Seventh annual message.
STAT 1:89
Sixth annual message.
STAT 1:83
Third annual message.
STAT 1:68
"We are all Republicans; we
are all Federalists."
Same as his First in-
augural: democracy defined

JEFFERSON, THOMAS
Aly, B.
Remarks on Jefferson Day.
BAP:273
Chase, S. P.
Thomas Jefferson and the
colonial view of manhood
rights. BREWE 3:1044
Everett, E.
Adams and Jefferson.
HURH:64
Peden, W.
Is Thomas Jefferson rele-
vant? BA 1972-73:94
Roosevelt, F. D.
Undelivered Jefferson Day
address. MDV:32
Smith, J. M.
On the fourteenth query of
Thomas Jefferson's Notes
on Virginia. FON:215
Webster, D.
Eulogy on Adams and Jef-
ferson. BREWE 10:3848
Wirt, W.
Death of Jefferson and
Adams. BREWE 10:3905

Jeffrey, Robert C.
Ethics in public discourse.

(New York, Nov. 11, 1973).
BA 1973-74:119

JEHOVAH WITNESSES
Jackson, R. H. and others
West Virginia Board of Education et al v. Barnette et al:
opinion for the court and dissenting opinion. ANN 16:148

Jekyll, Sir Joseph
Resistance to unlawful authority
(impeachment of H. Sache-
verell). BREWE 7:2617

Jenner, William E. and others
(T. C. Hennings, Jr.)
Proposal to limit the power of the
Supreme Court. ANN 17:491

Jensen, J. Hans D.
Glimpses at the history of the
nuclear structure theory
(Nobel Lecture, Dec. 12, 1963).
NOLPH 4:40

JENSEN, J. HANS D.
Waller, I.
Presentation [of the Nobel Prize
for Physics to Eugene P.
Wigner, Maria Goeppert Mayer
and J. Hans D. Jensen, Dec.
12, 1963]. NOLPH 4:3

Jensen, Johannes Vilhelm
Acceptance [of the Nobel Prize
for Literature, 1944].
NOB 8:263; NOL:400

JENSEN, JOHANNES VILHELM
Hallström, P.
Broadcast lecture [on Johannes
Vilhelm Jensen, 1944].
NOL:393
Österling, A.
Presentation [of the Nobel
Prize for Literature to
Johannes Vilhelm Jensen,
1944]. NOB 8:259; NOL:397

Jervois, Sir William
New Zealand's defence and Royal
Navy supremacy (New Zealand
Institute, Oct. 4, 1884).
MACS:245 sel.

Jessel, George
Presents Groucho Marx. LYI:32

Presents Jack Benny.
LYI:30

JESUS CHRIST
Aelred, Saint
On manliness.   BREWE 1:113
Athanasius, Saint
Divinity of Christ.
BREWE 1:182
Bourdaloue, L.
Passion of Christ.
BREWE 2:590
Didon, H.
Christ and higher criticism.
BREWE 5:1856
Great Disturber (outline of
speech to celebrate ac-
ceptance of Christ's offer
of salvation through obedi-
ence to His Word).   CUB:95

---- See also Crucifixion

JESUS FREAKS
Elson, E. L. R.
The Black and Jewish com-
munities.   VERD:273

JEWS
Gottheil, R.
Jews as a race and as a
nation.   BREWE 6:2294
Kamin, L.
Defense of the Jew.
CAPB:366
Macaulay, T. B.
Tribute to the Jews.
BREWE 8:2886
Rylaarsdam, J.
Undesirable one.   SCHW:1
What makes Sammy laugh?
BURT:60

JEWS IN THE UNITED STATES
Brackenridge, H. M.
Vindication of civil rights
for Jews.   ANN 4:552
Henry, J.
On religion and elective
office.   ANN 4:239;
BOORA 1:220

JIMENEZ, JUAN RAMON
Benitez, J.
Acceptance [of the Nobel
Prize for Literature for
Juan Ramón Jiménez, 1956].
NOB 10:7; NOL:517

Gullberg, H.
Presentation [of the Nobel Prize
for Literature to Juan Ramón
Jiménez, 1956].   NOB 10:3;
NOL:513

JOBS   See   Business

Johansson, J. E.
Presentation [of the Nobel Prize
for Physiology or Medicine for
1922 to Archibald Vivian Hill
and Otto Fritz Meyerhof, Dec.
12, 1923].   NOLM 2:3
Presentation [of the Nobel Prize
for Physiology or Medicine to
August Krogh, Dec. 11, 1920].
NOLM 1:529

Johari, Mohammed Khir
All schools are the same.
MONS:145
Key to open the doors to all
hearts and minds.   MONS:141
Malaysian Brothers (diamond
jubilee of Y.M.C.A. of Kuala
Lumpur).   MONS:150
Nation building and the four-way
test (Kuala Lumpur, July 1-3,
1970).   MONSA:100
A national chamber needed (Kuala
Lumpur, March 26, 1970).
MONSA:103
Successful teacher.   MONS:146

JOHN BIRCH SOCIETY
Welch, R.
More stately mansions (1964).
DAVF:327

JOHN PAUL II (POPE)
Sevareid, E.
Pope John Paul's message.
BA 1979-80:155

Johnsen, Anders
Remarks [presenting the Nobel
Prize for Peace to Thomas
Woodrow Wilson, 1919, Dec.
10, 1920].   NOLP 1:293

Johnson, Andrew
Against the radical Republicans.
ANN 10:8
Annual message to Congress,
December 3, 1866.   ANN 10:81;
STAT 2:1129
At Cleveland in 1866.

BREWE 7:2640
At St. Louis. BREWE 7:2628
End itself is evil (third annual
message, 1867). CUR:61;
STAT 2:1144
First annual message. Same
as his Presidential plan
of Reconstruction
First reconstruction veto.
Same as his Veto of the
first Reconstruction Act,
1867
Fourth annual message.
STAT 2:1167
Inaugural address (1st speech
after Lincoln's death).
BREWE 7:2626
Presidential plan of Recon-
struction. CUR:8;
STAT 2:1112
Representation for all Southern
states. Same as his An-
nual message to Congress,
December 3, 1866
St. Louis speech for which
he was impeached. Same
as his At St. Louis
Second annual message.
Same as his Annual mes-
sage to Congress, Decem-
ber 3, 1866
Second reconstruction veto.
ANN 10:98
Spirit of mutual conciliation.
Same as his Presidential
plan of Reconstruction
Third annual message. Same
as his End itself is evil
Veto of Freedmen's Bureau
Bill. ANN 10:3
Veto of Tenure of Office Act.
ANN 10:90
Veto of the first Reconstruc-
tion Act, 1867. ANN 10:93

---- and others (L. Trumbull)
Debate on civil and states'
rights. ANN 10:11

JOHNSON, ANDREW
Boutwell, G. S.
President Johnson's "High
crimes and misdemeanors."
BREWE 2:604
Butler, B. F.
"Article Ten"; (Impeaching
A. Johnson). BREWE 3:832
Curtis, B. R.

Defense of President Johnson.
BREWE 4:1563
Evarts, W. M.
Weakest spot in the American
system (defense at impeach-
ment of A. Johnson).
BREWE 6:2082
Hayden, L.
Deliver us from such a Moses.
FON:334
Sumner, C. and others
Impeachment of Andrew John-
son. ANN 10:126

Johnson, James Weldon
Africa at the Peace Table and
the descendants of Africans
in our American democracy.
(N.A.A.C.P., Jan. 6, 1919).
FON:730
Our democracy and the ballot.
(New York, March 10,
1923). FON:757

Johnson, Lyndon Baines
Acceptance speech, Atlantic City,
New Jersey, August 27, 1964.
SIN:329
Address on voting rights. Same
as his Address to a Joint Ses-
sion of Congress, March 15,
1965
Address to a Joint Session of
Congress, March 15, 1965.
AND:81; BOORA 2:919;
CROCK:164; MDV:144; REIR:143
As the days dwindle down.
(Temple, Texas, Sept. 16,
1972). BA 1972-73:138
Campaign speech, Washington,
D.C., October 7, 1964.
SIN:334
Education opportunity message.
CAPG:112
First annual message. Same as
his State of the Union Mes-
sage, January 8, 1964
Great Society (commencement ad-
dress at University of Michi-
gan). ANN 18:216; CAPG:15;
MDV:108; MUS:135
Inaugural address.
USINAU:271; USINAUG:271
Johnson doctrine; why the United
States intervened in the
Dominican Republic. LAA:160
Let us continue. Same as his
Remarks to a Joint Session

of the Congress, November
27, 1963
Obligation of power.
ANN 18:368
Our foreign policy must always
be an extension of this na-
tion's domestic policy.
LAA:3
A president defends his policies
by argument from author-
ities. (San Antonio, Tex.,
National Legislative Confer-
ence, Sept. 29, 1967).
JEF:331; JEFF:316
Remarks to a Joint Session of
the Congress, November 27,
1963. ANN 18:203
Remarks to the nation (de-
clining nomination to Presi-
dency). ANN 18:613;
BA 1967-68:63
Right to vote. Same as his
Address to a Joint Session
of Congress, March 15,
1965
Second annual message.
STAT 3:3161
Speech at a Joint Session of
the Tennessee State Legis-
lature. BA 1966-67:11
Speech before the National
Legislative Conference.
BA 1967-68:11
State of the Union Message,
January 8, 1964.
STAT 3:3156
Third annual message.
STAT 3:3171
University of Michigan com-
mencement address. Same
as his Great Society
Vietnam: the struggle to be
free (On accepting Na-
tional Freedom Award).
BA 1965-66:11
Voting Rights Law of 1965--
a victory for freedom.
CAPG:97
War on poverty. ANN 18:212
We shall overcome. Same
as his Address to a Joint
Session of Congress,
March 15, 1965
Why must we take this painful
road? LAA:185
Withdrawal speech. Same as
his Remarks to the nation
(declining nomination to
Presidency)

JOHNSON, LYNDON BAINES
Rusk, D.
Eulogy of Lyndon Baines John-
son. BA 1972-73:132
Stevenson, A. E.
Presents Lyndon B. Johnson.
LYI:197

Johnson, Mordecai W.
Faith of the American Negro (at
Harvard commencement,
June 22, 1922). FON:742

Johnson, Richard M. See Grundy,
F., jt. auth.

Johnstone, Abraham
Address to the people of color.
(July 8, 1797). FON:16

Joliot, Jean Frédéric
Chemical evidence of the trans-
mutation of elements (Nobel
Lecture, Dec. 12, 1935).
NOLC 2:369

JOLIOT, JEAN FREDERIC
Palmaer, W.
Presentation [of the Nobel Prize
for Chemistry to Jean Frédéric
Joliot and Irène Joliot-Curie,
Dec. 12, 1935]. NOLC 2:359

Joliot-Curie, Irène
Artificial production of radioactive
elements (Nobel Lecture, Dec.
12, 1935). NOLC 2:366

JOLIOT-CURIE, IRENE
Palmaer, W.
Presentation [of the Nobel Prize
for Chemistry to Jean Frédéric
Joliot and Irène Joliot-Curie,
Dec. 12, 1935]. NOLC 2:359

JOLSON, AL
Nussbaum, M.
Al Jolson. WALE:225

Jones, A. L.
A question of ecology: the cries
of wolf (Cleveland, Dec. 14,
1971). LINRST:115

Jones, Aaron and others (B. R.
Tucker; J. W. Hayes; L.
Gronlund; C. Studebaker)
Trusts in America.
ANN 12:279

JONES, FREDERICK S.
Streeter, F. S.
Introducing an educator
(Frederick S. Jones).
LYI:85

Jones, Howard Mumford
Farewell to the English Department.   REIR:232

Jones, James C. See Cass,
L., jt. auth.

Jones, Jenkin Lloyd
"Let's bring back Dad": a
solid value system (Ohio
Chamber of Commerce,
March 14, 1973).
LINRST:254
Who is tampering with the soul
of America? (American
Society of Newspaper
Editors, Oct. 16, 1961).
LINR:211; LINRS:220

Jones, William N.
Why Negroes should support
the Communists. (Harlem,
Oct. 2, 1932). FON:785

Jordan, Barbara C.
Keynote address to the Demo-
cratic National Convention
(New York, July 12, 1976).
BA 1976-77:11; JAM:7;
LINRST:334

---- (and others) Joshua Eilberg,
Walter Flowers
Hearings on articles of im-
peachment by the Commit-
tee of the Judiciary of the
House of Representatives.
(Washington, July 24-30,
1974). BA 1974-75:15

Jordan, David Starr
Moral aspect of the protective
tariff. ANN 13:147

Jordan, Len
Opportunities in H.S.A.
(Harvard Student Agencies).
REIR:101 (outline)

Jordan, Vernon E., Jr.
The Black agenda for the
1980s (Chicago, July 22,

1979). BA 1979-80:87
The Black and Jewish communi-
ties. (American Jewish Com-
mittee, Atlanta Chapter, June
2, 1974). VERD:273
Blacks and the Nixon administra-
tion: the next four years.
(Washington, D.C., March 16,
1973). BA 1972-73:39
Survival. (Cleveland, January 28,
1972). BA 1971-72:49
Under the hammer: freedom,
justice, and dignity. (Wash-
ington, May 4, 1974).
LINRST:215
Unfinished business (Columbia,
S.C., March 10, 1976).
BA 1975-76:88

Jordan, William Joseph
The League and the Spanish Civil
War (League of Nations Coun-
cil, May 28, 1937).
MACS:361 sel.

Joseph, Chief, The Nez Perce
From where the sun now stands.
ALA:63
Surrender speech. Same as his
From where the sun now stands

Jouhaux, Léon
Fifty years of trade-union activity
in behalf of peace (Nobel Lecture, Dec. 11, 1951).
NOLP 3:10

JOUHAUX, LEON
Jahn, G.
Presentation of the Nobel Prize
for Peace to Léon Jouhaux,
Dec. 10, 1951. NOLP 3:3

JOURNALISM AND JOURNALISTS
Gallagher, W.
Upon acceptance of the 1967
William Allen White Foundation
Award for Journalists Merit.
BA 1966-67:148; JEF:327;
JEFF:311
Goodman, J. B.
Broadcast journalism.
BA 1976-77:52
Holden, W. S.
Newspapers of the U.S.A.
ARS:107
Lippmann, W.
On understanding society.

BAAGB:412
Sevareid, E.
Parting thoughts.
BA 1977-78:143
Welcome to newspaper editor
as speaker at a civic club.
HNWM:44

---- See also Newspapers; Press

---- MALAYSIA
Hamzah bin Dato Abu Samah
Challenging opportunity for
the press in Malaysia.
MONSA:110

JOYCE, JAMES
Woolsey, J. M.
Opinion December 6, 1933
(Ulysses case--freedom of
reading). ANN 15:236

JUBILEE CELEBRATIONS See
Anniversaries

Judd, Walter H.
Responds to introduction.
PRS:126

JUDGES See Law and lawyers;
United States - Supreme
Court

JUDICIAL REVIEW
Gibson, J. B.
Against judicial review:
dissenting opinion on Eakin
v. Raub. ANN 5:174

Julian, George W.
The strength and weakness of
the slave power
Cincinnati, 1852. DAVF:122

Jung, Leo
Mother's immortality.
WALE:96

JURIES
Marshall, D. S.
Why abolish the jury trial?
MONSA:324

JURISPRUDENCE See Law and
lawyers

JURY
Drayton, W. H.

Charge to the Grand Juries,
November 5 & 15, 1774.
POC:297

---- See also Trial by jury

JUSTICE
Bede
Meeting of mercy and justice.
BREWE 1:340
Bradlaugh, C.
Appeal for justice. JAE:142
Cicero, M. T.
Supernatural justice.
BREWE 3:1178
Clayton, J. M.
Justice the supreme law of na-
tions. BREWE 4:1290
King, M. L., Jr.
Nonviolence: moral challenge
for peace and justice.
NOLP 3:333; THOMS:99
Muhammad, E.
We must have justice.
FON:969
Osias, C.
Justice and separation of
powers. CURM:190
Roosevelt, F. D.
Philosophy of social justice
through social action (campaign
speech in Detroit October 2,
1932). ARS:135
Taft, R. A.
Equal justice under law.
BEN:100

JUVENILE DELINQUENCY See
Crime and criminals

- K -

Kahn, Arthur D.
John F. Kennedy. WALE:218

Kahn, I.
Like water spilled on the ground.
WALE:98
Vote against prayer and for God.
KEO:300

Kalakaua, David, King of Hawaii
His Majesty's address to the
people of Lahaina. ALA:57

Kaler, Irving
The Ku Klux Klan as a subversive

conspiratorial organization.
(Washington, 1966). DAVF:355

Kamin, Lester
Defense of the Jew. (Baylor
University, 1941). CAPB:366

Kanapathy, V.
Technological change and management policies (Hydera-
bad, June, 1970).
MONSA:202

Kane, Anthony
Glory of notoriety. REIR:223

KANSAS
Buchanan, J.
First annual message.
STAT 1:942
Second annual message.
STAT 1:969
Douglas, S. A.
Kansas and "Squatter sov-
ereignty." BREWE 5:1924
Sumner, C.
Crime against Kansas.
ANN 8:267; BREWE 9:3557;
HURH:85
Walker, R. J.
Address to the people of
Kansas. ANN 8:452

KANSAS-NEBRASKA BILL
Buchanan, J.
First annual message.
STAT 1:942
Chase, S. P. and others
Opposition to the Kansas-
Nebraska Bill (January,
1854). ANN 8:251
Douglas, S. A.
Defense of the Kansas-
Nebraska Bill (January 30,
1854). ANN 8:254
Pierce, F.
Third annual message.
STAT 1:895

Kaplan, Louis
Three basic questions.
WALE:99

Kaplan, Solomon M.
Man's true measurements.
WALE:102

Karenga, Maulana Ron
The Black community and the uni-

versity: a community organizer's
perspective. (Yale University,
1968). LINRS:255

Karlfeldt, Erik Axel
Presentation [of the Nobel Prize
for Literature to Anatole
France, 1921]. NOB 6:85;
NOL:174
Presentation [of the Nobel Prize
for Literature to Sinclair
Lewis, 1930]. NOB 11:237;
NOL:271

KARLFELDT, ERIK AXEL
Österling, A.
Presentation [of the Nobel Prize
for Literature to Erik Axel
Karlfeldt, 1931]. NOB 10:101;
NOL:295

Karos, Peter A.
Haven of the defeated. ARS:148

Karrer, Paul
Carotenoids, flavins and vitamin
A and B_2 (Nobel Lecture, Dec.
11, 1937). NOLC 2:433

KARRER, PAUL
Palmaer, W.
Presentation [of the Nobel Prize
for Chemistry to Walter Nor-
man Haworth and Paul Karrer,
Dec. 11, 1937]. NOLC 2:407

Kastler, Alfred
Optical methods for studying
Hertzian resonances (Nobel
Lecture, Dec. 12, 1966).
NOLPH 4:186

KASTLER, ALFRED
Waller, I.
Presentation [of the Nobel Prize
for Physics to Alfred Kastler,
Dec. 12, 1966].
NOLPH 4:183

Katz, Bernhard
On the quantal mechanism of
neural transmitter release
(Nobel Lecture, Dec. 12,
1970). NOLM 4:485

KATZ, BERNHARD
Uvnäs, B.

Presentation [of the Nobel
Prize for Physiology or
Medicine to Julius Axelrod,
Ulf Von Euler, and Bernhard
Katz, Dec. 12, 1970].
NOLM 4:441

Katz, Reuben M.
Psalm of life. WALE:103

Katzenbach, Nicholas de Belle-
ville
Civil Rights Act of 1964:
respect for law. CAPB:88

Kaunda, Kenneth
Toast to President Ford (April
9, 1975). JAM:23

Kawabata, Yasunari
Acceptance speech [for the
Nobel Prize for Literature,
1968]. NOB 11:7

KAWABATA, YASUNARI
Österling, A.
Presentation address [of
the Nobel Prize for Literature to Yasunari Kawa-
bata, 1968]. NOB 11:3

Keating, Kenneth B.
Responds to an introduction.
PRS:132

KEATS, JOHN
Gittings, R.
Exploring the known.
MDYG:207

Kee, Robert See Ayer, A. J.,
jt. auth.

Keeler, William Wayne
Inaugural address of the chief
of the Cherokees.
(Tahlequah, Okl., Sept.
4, 1971). BA 1971-72:74

Keeney, Barnaby C.
Afterword: how to make a
commencement speech
(Brown Univ., May 28,
1964). HOR:165

KEFAUVER, ESTES
Waller, H. H.
Presents Estes Kefauver.
LYI:230

Kelley, Clarence M.
Terrorism, the ultimate evil
(Washington, Jan. 13, 1976).
BA 1975-76:117

Kellogg, Frank Billings
Acceptance and banquet speech
[for the Nobel Prize for
Peace, 1929, Dec. 10, 1930].
NOLP 2:79

KELLOGG, FRANK BILLINGS
Mowinckel, J. L.
Presentation [of the Nobel Prize
for Peace to Frank Billings
Kellogg, 1929, Dec. 10, 1930].
NOLP 2:73

KELLY, EDWARD
Barry, R.
Sentencing of "Ned" Kelly.
MCA:74

Kelly, William F.
Responds to an introduction.
PRS:129

Kemeny, John G.
An optimist looks at America's
future (Boston College, June
4, 1973). HOR:128
Valedictory to the graduates
(Dartmouth, June 10, 1973).
HOR:2

Kendall, Edward Calvin
The development of cortisone as
a therapeutic agent (Nobel
Lecture, Dec. 11, 1950).
NOLM 3:270

KENDALL, EDWARD CALVIN
Liljestrand, G.
Presentation [of the Nobel
Prize for Physiology or Medi-
cine to Edward Calvin Ken-
dall, Tadeus Reichstein, and
Philip Shawalter Hench, Dec.
11, 1950]. NOLM 3:263

Kendrew, John Cowdery
Myoglobin and the structure of
proteins (Nobel Lecture, Dec.
11, 1962). NOLC 3:676

KENDREW, JOHN COWDERY
Hagg, G.
Presentation of the Nobel Prize
for Chemistry to Max Ferdi-

nand Perutz and John Cow-
dery Kendrew, Dec. 11,
1962. NOLC 3:649

Kennan, George Frost
Responds to an introduction.
PRS:148
Statement on Vietnam.
BA 1965-66:56

Kennedy, Edward M.
China policy for the seventies.
BA 1968-69:73
Eulogy to Robert F. Kennedy.
Same as his Tribute to
Senator Robert F. Kennedy
La Raza and the law. (Wash-
ington, D.C., March 3,
1972). BA 1971-72:68
Statement to the people of
Massachusetts. MACR:318
Tribute to Senator Robert F.
Kennedy. BA 1967-68:174;
LINRS:303

Kennedy, John Fitzgerald
Acceptance address, 1960.
Same as his New frontier
Acceptance speech, Los Ange-
les, California, July 15,
1960. Same as his New
frontier
Address to the Ministers of
Houston. Same as his
Religion in government
Address to the nation October
22, 1962. ANN 18:140;
LAA:147; MUS:340
"Ask not what your country
can do for you--ask what
you can do for your country."
Same as his Inaugural ad-
dress
Berlin crisis. (July 25, 1961).
THOMS:22
Campaign speech, Houston,
Texas, September 12, 1960.
Same as his Religion in
government (to Greater
Houston Ministerial Asso-
ciation)
Cuban missile crisis. Same
as his Address to the
nation October 22, 1962
Federal aid to education.
ANN 18:8
First annual message.
STAT 3:3122

History will be our judge.
LINS:371
Ich bin ein Berliner (Berlin, June
26, 1963). ALA:129; AND:79;
LINR:294; LINRS:293
Inaugural address (Washington,
Jan. 20, 1961). ALS:265;
ANN 18:5; ARN:312; ARS:226;
BAS:145 (outline only); BEN:143;
BOORA 2:913; BRR:82;
BRYF:437; BRYO:232; GRG:113;
HURH:358; LINR:297; LINRS:296;
LINRST:366; LINS:375;
MAC:244; MACR:284; MDV:127;
OLIS:282; THOMS:17;
USINAU:267; USINAUG:267
Intellectual and the politician.
BAP:285; LINR:267
Long twilight struggle.
ANN 18:54
Negro and the American promise.
ANN 18:152
New frontier (Los Angeles, July
15, 1960). CAPG:8;
HURH:353; SIN:298
Nuclear Test-Ban Treaty. Same
as his Step toward peace
Presenting the Distinguished
Service Medal to John Glenn
(outline of speech). CUB:64
President Kennedy's televised re-
port to the Nation on the Berlin
crisis. Same as his Berlin
crisis
Religion in government (to Greater
Houston Ministerial Associa-
tion). ANN 17:589; SIN:303
Second annual message.
STAT 3:3132
Soviet missiles in Cuba. Same
as his Address to the nation
October 22, 1962
Soviets are building nuclear mis-
sile sites in Cuba. Same as
his Address to the nation,
October 22, 1962
Special message to the Congress
on Civil Rights. (Feb. 28,
1963). THOMS:50
Special message to the Congress
on the nation's youth.
(Feb. 14, 1963). THOMS:34
Step toward peace. ANN 18:192
Strategy of peace. Same as his
Toward a strategy of peace
Tax cut. STAT 3:3144
Third annual message. Same as
his Tax cut

Toward a strategy of peace.
KEO:312; MDV:2
Undelivered Dallas speech.
ANN 18:197
"We stand today on the edge
of a New Frontier."
Same as his New frontier

---- See also Nixon, R. M., jt.
auth.

KENNEDY, JOHN FITZGERALD
Johnson, L. B.
Remarks to a Joint Session
of the Congress, November
27, 1963. ANN 18:203
Kahn, A. D.
John F. Kennedy.
WALE:218
Levine, E. B.
John F. Kennedy.
WALE:221
Macmillan, (M.) H.
Tribute to President Ken-
nedy. ALA:135
Mansfield, M. J.
Eulogy for John F. Ken-
nedy. ANN 18:202
Stevenson, A. E.
Tribute to John F. Kennedy
at the General Assembly
of the United Nations.
GRG:122; HURH:371

Kennedy, Robert F.
Address to the Free University
of Berlin. MDV:95
Civil rights. Same as his
Law Day address, Univer-
sity of Georgia
Counterinsurgency. ANN 18:323
Fruitful tension. BA 1966-67:138
Kennedy's decision to seek
Presidential nomination.
THOMS:131
Law Day address--University
of Georgia (Athens, Ga.,
May 6, 1961). CAPG:73;
THOMS:120
Responds to introductions.
PRS:135; 136
Vietnam--illusion and reality.
ANN 18:599

KENNEDY, ROBERT F.
Brademas, J.
Eulogy for Robert Kennedy.
JAM:43

Kennedy, E. M.
Tribute to Senator Robert F.
Kennedy. BA 1967-68:174;
LINRS:303
Percy, C. H.
Eulogy for Robert Kennedy.
JAM:42

KENNEY, GEORGE C.
Fisher, C. T., Jr.
Presents George C. Kenney.
LYI:150

Kenny, Anthony
Self out of season. MDYG:199

Kenrick, Francis Patrick
Episcopal rights and parish
autonomy. ANN 5:437

KENTUCKY - ECONOMIC CONDI-
TIONS
Chandler, A. B.
Address to the General As-
sembly, Frankfort, Kentucky,
April 20, 1936. BLY:258

KENYON COLLEGE
Everett, E.
Plea for support of an Ohio
college. ANN 6:26

Kermicle, John
Bridging the gap. BREWW:94

KERNER REPORT
Abernathy, R. D.
The Kerner report, promises
and realities. FON:1145

Kerr, Clark
The independent spirit (Swarth-
more College, June, 1952).
HOR:114
Perspectives on the prophets of
doom (Univ. of California,
June 12, 1965). HOR:34
Urban-grant university (centennial
meeting of City College).
BA 1967-68:86

Kerr, Deborah See Murrow, E.
R., jt. auth.

Kerry, John F.
John Kerry's speech before the
Senate Foreign Relations
Committee. Same as his

Vietnam veterans against
the war
Vietnam veterans against the
war (Washington, April 22,
1971). JAM:9; LINRS:244;
LINRST:288

Kestenbaum, Jerome
Live each day. WALE:106
Prescription for humanity.
WALE:107
Standard of life. WALE:109

KETTERING, CHARLES F.
Martin, T. W.
Presents Charles F. Ket-
tering. LYI:181

Keynes, John Maynard
Am I a Liberal? (Liberal
Summer School, Cam-
bridge, Aug. 1, 1925).
MCB:456

KEYNOTE SPEECHES See
Campaign speeches

Khorana, Har Gobind
Nucleic acid synthesis in the
study of the genetic code
(Nobel Lecture, Dec. 12,
1968). NOLM 4:341

KHORANA, HAR GOBIND
Reichard, P.
Presentation [of the Nobel
Prize for Physiology or
Medicine to Robert W.
Holley, Har Gobind Khor-
ana, and Marshall W.
Nirenberg, Dec. 12, 1968].
NOLM 4:321

Kidwell, Clara Sue
American Indian attitudes
toward nature, a bicen-
tennial perspective.
MAES:277

Killens, John O.
White liberals and the Black
revolution. (New York,
June 15, 1964). FON:1001

King, Martin Luther, Jr.
The American dream. (Lin-
coln University, June 6,
1961). FON:933

Declaration of independence from
the war in Vietnam. VI:115
Give us the ballot--we will trans-
form the South. (Washington,
D.C., May 17, 1957).
FON:919
Honoring Dr. DuBois.
SMHR:204
"I have a dream." (Washington,
Aug. 28, 1963). AND:50;
ANN 18:156; ARS:154; BRR:78;
CAPG:83; FON:971; GRG:117;
HURH:366; LINR:290; LINRS:289;
LINRST:362; LINS:379;
MAC:247; MACR:288; MDV:156;
MUS:336; OE:152; OLIS:289;
SMHV:182; THOMS:94
I see the promised land. (April
3, 1968, Memphis). FON:1108
A long way to go. SMHV:188
Love, law, and civil disobedi-
ence (Fellowship of the Con-
cerned, Nov. 16, 1961).
FON:943; LINR:63; LINRS:70;
LINRST:75; STOT:321
Nonviolence and social change.
(Nov., 1967). OE:157
Nonviolence: moral challenge for
peace and justice (Nobel Lec-
ture, Dec. 11, 1964).
NOLP 3:333; THOMS:99
The philosophy of the student non-
violent movement. Same as
his Love, law, and civil dis-
obedience
The quest for peace and justice.
Same as his Nonviolence:
moral challenge for peace and
justice
A time to break silence. (New
York, April 4, 1967).
FON:1048
Where do we go from here?
(Atlanta, Ga., August 16,
1967--Tenth Anniversary Con-
vention of the Southern Chris-
tian Leadership Conference).
FON:1068

KING, MARTIN LUTHER, JR.
Carter, J.
Speech at the Martin Luther
King, Jr. Hospital. JAM:25
Cleaver, E.
Meditation on the assassination
of Martin Luther King, Jr.
OE:229
Franklin, J. H.

Martin Luther King and
American traditions.
BA 1968-69:45
Gallagher, B. G.
Memorial convocation ad-
dress (on Martin Luther
King, Jr.). BA 1967-68:169
Jahn, G.
Presentation [of the Nobel
Prize for Peace to Martin
Luther King, Jr., Dec. 10,
1964]. NOLP 3:325
Mays, B. E.
Eulogy on Dr. Martin
Luther King, Jr.
BA 1967-68:161; BAAGB:399;
SMHV:296

King, Mrs. Martin Luther, Jr.
We need to be united. (At-
lantic City-Automobile
Workers' Const. Conv.,
April 22, 1970). FON:1169

KING, RICHARD COREY
Go on and prosper (outline of
eulogistic speech). CUB:76

King, Rufus
Against the extension of slavery
to the new states. Same
as his On the Missouri
Bill
For federal government by the
people. BREWE 7:2642
On the Missouri Bill.
ANN 4:579

King, Thomas Starr
Fourth of July oration, 1860
(San Francisco). HAW:231
The two declarations of in-
dependence: 1776 and 1861.
(Sacramento, July 4, 1861).
HAW:260

KING, W. L. MACKENZIE
Lamont, T. W.
Presents W. L. Mackenzie
King. LYI:233

Kingsbury, F. J.
In defense of the city.
ANN 12:61

Kingsley, Charles
Human soot; address at Liverpool in behalf of the

Kirkdale Ragged Schools.
BREWE 7:2645
Massacre of the innocents.
BRYH:392

Kinross, Lord See Sykes, C., jt.
auth.

Kipke, Harry G.
Introduces John K. Herbert,
president of the Magazine
Publishers Association.
PRS:21

KIPLING, RUDYARD
Wirsén, C. D. af
Presentation [of the Nobel Prize
for Literature to Rudyard Kip-
ling, 1907]. NOB 11:89;
NOL:58

Kirk, Grayson
Responsibilities of the educated
man (at centennial of University
of Denver). LINR:143

Kirkpatrick, Lyman B.
Responds to an introduction.
PRS:141

Kissinger, Henry Alfred
Address before the World Food
Conference. (Rome, Nov. 5,
1974). BA 1974-75:62
America's permanent interests
(Boston, March 11, 1976).
BA 1975-76:48
Responds to introduction.
PRS:124
A review of the foreign policy
(Washington, April 19, 1980).
BA 1979-80:9
Statement to the Senate Foreign
Relations Committee. (Wash-
ington, Sept. 7, 1973).
BA 1973-74:87

Kitslaar, John L.
Is busing the answer? (Madison,
Wisc., 1976). LINRST:294

Klaaren, Mary Ann
Divine command. SCHW:96

Klason, P.
Presentation [of the Nobel Prize
for Chemistry to Henri Moissan, 1906]. NOLC 1:91

Presentation [of the Nobel
Prize for Physics to Joseph
John Thomson, Dec. 11,
1906]. NOLPH 1:141

Klayton, Ronald J.
Bureau of Forests and Waters
should control pests by
biological means rather
than pesticides. BAS:188
(outline only)

Klein, G.
Presentation [of the Nobel
Prize for Physiology or
Medicine to Peyton Rous
and Charles Brenton Hug-
gins, Dec. 13, 1966].
NOLM 4:215

Klein, Isaac
Before her time. WALE:110

Klein, Joel T.
Question most frequently
asked. WALE:112

Klein, O. B.
Presentation [of the Nobel
Prize for Physics to Chen
Ning Yang and Tsung Dao
Lee, Dec. 11, 1957].
NOLPH 3:389
Presentation [of the Nobel
Prize for Physics to Hans
Albrecht Bethe, Dec. 11,
1967]. NOLPH 4:211

Klein, Paul A.
Big things happen in small
places (outline of speech
explaining process of protein synthesis). CUB:94

Klemme, Diane
The age of Gerontion. (West
Yellowstone, Montana,
May, 1970). LINRS:152

Knight, Joseph R.
Introduces Lieutenant Thomas
A. Dooley, United States
Navy. PRS:67

KNIGHTS OF LABOR
Gibbons, J.
Defense of the Knights of
Labor. ANN 11:131

Knoch, Win G.
Introduces Robert Taft, Jr.,
Congressman-at-large from
Ohio. PRS:32

Knopwood, Robert
On the everpresent God. MCA:11

Knott, James Proctor
Glories of Duluth (Jan. 27, 1871).
BLY:135; BREWE 7:2653

KNOWLEDGE, THEORY OF
Chapin, E. H.
Sovereignty of ideas.
BREWE 3:1036
Drummond, H.
Preparation for learning.
BREWE 5:1959
Young, O. D.
How we meet ourselves (semi-
centennial of Hendrix College).
HURH:227

---- See also Learning and scholarship

Knox, Frank
Lend-lease and national defense.
ANN 16:48

Knox, John
Against tyrants. BREWE 7:2665

Knudsen, G.
Presentation [of the Nobel Prize
for Peace to Theodore Roosevelt, Dec. 10, 1906].
NOLP 1:97

Koblish, Cameron F.
Diamonds, their mining, selling,
perfecting, and the determining of their quality. BAS:206
(outline only)

Koch, Robert
The current state of the struggle
against tuberculosis (Nobel
Lecture, Dec. 12, 1905).
NOLM 1:169

KOCH, ROBERT
Mörner, K. A. H.
Presentation [of the Nobel
Prize for Physiology or Medi-
cine to Robert Koch, Dec. 12,
1905]. NOLM 1:163

Kocher, Emil Theodor
  Concerning pathological mani-
    festations in low-grade
    thyroid diseases (Nobel
    Lecture, Dec. 11, 1909).
    NOLM 1:330

KOCHER, EMIL THEODOR
  Mörner, K. A. H.
    Presentation [of the Nobel
    Prize for Physiology or
    Medicine to Emil Theodor
    Kocher, Dec. 11, 1909].
    NOLM 1:327

Koht, Halvdan
  Presentation [of the Nobel
    Prize for Peace to Jane
    Addams and Nicholas
    Murray Butler, Dec. 10,
    1931]. NOLP 2:125

KOPECHNE, MARY JO
  Kennedy, E. M.
    Statement to the people of
    Massachusetts. MACR:318

KOREAN WAR, 1950-1953
  Cornish, D. T.
    A warrior against fate.
    BA 1975-76:207
  Eisenhower, D. D.
    Crusade for peace.
    ANN 17:199
  MacArthur, D.
    Defends his conduct of the
    war in Korea. ALS:243;
    ANN 17:79; ARS:279;
    BAS:82 (outline only);
    BEN:113; BOSR:22; GRG:88;
    HURH:293; HURS:214;
    LINS:337
  McCarthy, J. R.
    Annual Kansas Day Republi-
    can banquet speech.
    BOSR:53
  Stevenson, A. E.
    Campaign speech, Academy
    of Music, Brooklyn, New
    York, October 31, 1952.
    SIN:255
  Truman, H. S.
    Preventing a new world war.
    ANN 17:75; BAP:291
    Sixth annual message.
    STAT 3:2976
    State of the Union (1952).
    STAT 3:2984

Korf, James
  And old hate walked on through
    time. SCHW:189

Kornberg, Arthur
  The biologic synthesis of de-
    oxyribonucleic acid (Nobel
    Lecture, Dec. 11, 1959).
    NOLM 3:665

KORNBERG, ARTHUR
  Theorell, H.
    Presentation [of the Nobel Prize
    for Physiology or Medicine to
    Severo Ochoa and Arthur Korn-
    berg, Dec. 11, 1959].
    NOLM 3:641

Korteling, Marian
  Renascence. SCHW:39

Kosman, Morris
  Eulogy for Irving Wolberg (July
    29, 1976). JAM:44

Kossel, Albrecht
  The chemical composition of the
    cell nucleus (Nobel Lecture,
    Dec. 12, 1910). NOLM 1:394

KOSSEL, ALBRECHT
  Mörner, K. A. H.
    Presentation [of the Nobel
    Prize for Physiology or Medi-
    cine to Albrecht Kossel, Dec.
    12, 1910]. NOLM 1:389

Kossuth, Louis
  Local self-government.
    BREWE 7:2672

KOSSUTH, LOUIS
  Downing, G. T.
    May Hungary be free.
    FON:102

Krebs, Hans Adolf
  The citric acid cycle (Nobel Lec-
    ture, Dec. 11, 1953).
    NOLM 3:399

KREBS, HANS ADOLF
  Hammarsten, E.
    Presentation [of the Nobel
    Prize for Physiology or Medi-
    cine to Hans Adolf Krebs and
    Fritz Albert Lipmann, Dec.
    11, 1953]. NOLM 3:395

KREBS CYCLE
Krebs, H. A.
    The citric acid cycle.
    NOLM 3:399
Lipmann, F. A.
    Development of the acetyla-
    tion problem: a personal
    account. NOLM 3:413

Krogh, August
    A contribution to the physiology
    of the capillaries (Nobel
    Lecture, Dec. 11, 1920).
    NOLM 1:536
KROGH, AUGUST
Johansson, J. E.
    Presentation [of the Nobel
    Prize for Physiology or
    Medicine to August Krogh,
    Dec. 11, 1920].
    NOLM 1:529

Krug, Judith F.
    In defense of liberty: ex-
    tremism and other vices
    (Baton Rouge, April 17,
    1975). BA 1975-76:193

Kubicek, Kathryn
    Global crisis. BREWW:128

Kuiper, Della Rae
    "You're an American,
    aren't you?" SCHW:186

KU KLUX KLAN
Gordon, J. B.
    It was purely a peace
    police organization.
    CUR:98
    Grand dragon of the Ku Klux
    Klan. BURT:65
Kaler, I.
    The Ku Klux Klan as a
    subversive, conspiratorial
    organization (1966).
    DAVF:355
Sherman, J.
    It is essentially a Rebel
    organization. CUR:102

Kusch, Polykarp
    The magnetic moment of the
    electron (Nobel Lecture,
    Dec. 12, 1955).
    NOLPH 3:298

KUSCH, POLYKARP
Waller, I.
    Presentation [of the Nobel Prize
    for Physics to Willis Eugene
    Lamb and Polykarp Kusch,
    Dec. 12, 1955]. NOLPH 3:283

- L -

LABOR AND LABORING CLASSES
Berle, A. A., Jr.
    Emerging common law of free
    enterprise. ANN 16:573
Brandeis, L. D.
    Law and the laboring classes.
    ANN 13:23
De Leon, D.
    Political power of labor.
    ANN 13:19
Everett, E.
    Universal and uncoerced co-
    operation. BREWE 6:2115
Fisk, T.
    War of capital against labor.
    ANN 6:118
Furuseth, A.
    Work is worship. ANN 14:561
Olson, C. L.
    Migratory labor and civil lib-
    erties. ANN 15:587
Roosevelt, T.
    Annual message, December 6,
    1904. STAT 2:2105
    Fifth annual message.
    ANN 13:1; STAT 3:2144
Wheeler, A.
    Product of labor. ANN 11:113

---- See also Capitalism; Child
    labor; Industrial relations;
    Labor unions; Strikes and
    lockouts; Work

---- AUSTRALIA
Parkes, H.
    Eight-hours movement.
    MCA:33

LABOR DAY
Altgeld, J. P.
    Children of toil. ANN 11:445
Furuseth, A.
    Work is worship. ANN 14:561

LABOR LAWS AND LEGISLATION
Hughes, C. E.

National Labor Relations
Board v. Jones and Laughlin
Steel Corporation, 1937;
opinion for the Supreme
Court. ROD:207

---- TAFT HARTLEY LAW
Taft, R. A.
   Analysis of the Taft-Hartley
   Act. ANN 16:414

LABOR PARTY - AUSTRALIA
Chifley, J. B.
   Things worth fighting for.
   MCA:166

---- GREAT BRITAIN
Attlee, C. R.
   The Labour programme.
   MCB:471
Gaitskell, H.
   Labour politics and demo-
   cratic socialism. MCB:250

---- See also Great Britain -
   Politics and government

---- NEW ZEALAND
Holland, H.
   The socialist objective of
   the labour movement.
   MACS:232 sel.

LABOR UNIONS
Abdul Rahman, T.
   Warming to trade unions.
   MONS:45
Baldwin, S. B.
   Goodwill in industry.
   MCB:243; STRM:433
Bevin, E.
   Testimony at the "Docker's
   Inquiry." STRM:423
Billings
   United States v. Working-
   men's Amalgamated Council
   of New Orleans, 1893.
   ANN 11:435
Crosswaith, F. R.
   The Negro labor committee.
   FON:857
Gibbons, J.
   Defense of the Knights of
   Labor. ANN 11:131
Green, W.
   Modern trade unionism.
   HURH:205
Jouhaux, L.

Fifty years of trade-union activ-
   ity in behalf of peace (Nobel
   Lecture, Dec. 11, 1951).
   NOLP 3:10
King, Mrs. M. L., Jr.
   We need to be unified.
   FON:1169
Lee Kuan Yew
   Unionism: rethinking is vital
   (opening National Trade Union
   Conference). MONS:366
Lewis, J. L.
   Industrial unions. ANN 15:511
   Labor and the nation.
   HURH:232
Moore, E.
   Trade unions and the "me-
   chanic" arts. ANN 6:17
Murray, P.
   Collective bargaining and in-
   dustrial democracy.
   ANN 16:15
Myers, I.
   Finish the good work of uniting
   colored and white workingmen.
   FON:367
Nair, C. D.
   The role of trade union re-
   search and documentation serv-
   ices. MONSA:334
Narayanan, P. P.
   Role of trade unions in South-
   East Asia. MONS:295
Parry, D.
   Organized labor as the "Great
   Muscle Trust." ANN 12:513
Robinson, F.
   Labor as the source of reform.
   ANN 6:69
Savage, J.
   People v. Fisher: opinion for
   the court. ANN 6:172
Shaw, L.
   Commonwealth of Massachusetts
   v. Hunt: opinion for the court.
   ANN 6:172

---- See also Labor Day; Labor
   Laws and legislation; Strikes
   and lockouts

---- AGRICULTURE
Wright, T.
   "Viva la Huelga." BREWW:174

---- MALAYSIA
Alatas, S. H.
   Sheep and lions in trade unions.
   MONSA:179 selections

---- SINGAPORE
Lee Kuan Yew
Self respect is what our
trade unions have and....
MONSA:255

Labori, Fernand
Conspiracy against Dreyfus.
BREWE 7:2684

Labouisse, Henry R.
Acceptance [of the Nobel Prize
for Peace, Dec. 10, 1965].
NOLP 3:362

Lacordaire, Jean Baptiste Henri
Rationalism and miracles.
BREWE 7:2695
Sacred cause of the human
race (Panegyric of Daniel
O'Connell). BREWE 7:2692

LAFAYETTE, MARIE JOSEPH
PAUL ROCH YVES GIL-
BERT DE MOTIER,
MARQUIS DE
Adams, J. Q.
Life and character of Lafay-
ette. BREWE 1:79

LaFollette, Philip F.
Party of our time. BAD:120

La Follette, Robert Marion, Sr.
Against war with Germany.
ANN 14:104
Free speech in wartime.
CUB:53 (outline only)
Opposition to Wilson's War
Message. Same as his
Against war with Germany
"The right to cast the ballot
is regarded as sacred.
The right to make the bal-
lot is equally sacred."
Same as his Which shall
rule, manhood or money?
A small group of men hold
in their hands the business
of this country. (Wash-
ington, March 17, 1908).
DAVF:200
Soldier's pay. GRG:36
Which shall rule, manhood or
money? (Milwaukee,
1902). HURH:158

LA FONTAINE, HENRI MARIE
Moe, R.
Presentation [of the Nobel
Prize for Peace to Henri
Marie La Fontaine, Dec. 10,
1913]. NOLP 1:269

Lagerkvist, Pär Fabian
Acceptance [of the Nobel Prize
for Literature, 1951].
NOB 10:205; NOL:469

LAGERKVIST, PAR FABIAN
Österling, A.
Presentation [of the Nobel
Prize for Literature to Pär
Fabian Lagerkvist, 1951].
NOB 10:201; NOL:466

Lagerlöf, Selma Ottiliana Lovisa
Acceptance [of the Nobel Prize
for Literature, 1909].
NOB 10:283; NOL:94

LAGERLÖF, SELMA OTTILIANA
LOVISA
Annerstedt, C.
Presentation [of the Nobel
Prize for Literature to Selma
Ottiliana Lovisa Lagerlöf,
1909]. NOB 10:279; NOL:90

LAISSEZ-FAIRE
Crawford, F. C.
Jobs, freedom, and opportun-
ity. ANN 16:132
Grede, W. J.
America, a frontier.
ANN 17:154
Marcus, S.
Can free enterprise survive
success? BA 1975-76:152
Morelli, L.
Vocational agriculture, the
FFA, and our free enterprise
system. BREWW:78
Romney, G.
Our unique economic prin-
ciples: the market place
should determine price.
CAPG:40
Willkie, W. L.
Private enterprise--we have
gone far enough down the road
to federal control. BAD:69

LAKE OAHE
Gage, P.

The Oahe Project--yes or
no? BREWW:191

Lamartine, Alphonse Marie
Louis de
Revolution of 1848.
BREWE 7:2702

Lamas, Carlos Saavedra See
Saavedra Lamas, C.

Lamb, Willis Eugene
Fine structure of the hydrogen
bomb (Nobel Lecture, Dec.
12, 1955). NOLPH 3:286

LAMB, WILLIS EUGENE
Waller, I.
Presentation [of the Nobel
Prize for Physics to Willis
Eugene Lamb and Polykarp
Kusch, Dec. 12, 1955].
NOLPH 3:283

Lamont, Thomas S.
Presents Paul G. Hoffman.
LYI:71

Lamont, Thomas William
Presents Eleanor Robson Bel-
mont. LYI:23
Presents W. L. Mackenzie
King. LYI:233

LAND SETTLEMENT - NEW
ZEALAND
McKenzie, J.
Land for Settlements Bill,
1894. MACS:205 sel.
Massey, W. F.
Freehold tenure.
MACS:216 sel.
Taylor, T. E.
Leasehold defended.
MACS:219 sel.
Ward, J. G.
Advances to settlers, 1894.
MACS:207 sel.

---- UNITED STATES
Wah-shee, J.
A land settlement--what
does it mean? MAES:45

LAND TENURE - NEW ZEALAND
Taylor, T. E.
Leasehold defended.
MACS:219 sel.

LAND USE, RURAL
Lipton, J.
Land preservation in the North-
east. BREWW:75

LAND USE, URBAN
Lucas, M.
The waste of our precious
farmland. BREWW:102

LANDAU, LEV DAVIDOVIC
Waller, I.
Presentation [of the Nobel
Prize for Physics to Lev
Davidovic Landau, 1962].
NOLPH 3:607

Landis, Frederick
Presents Will H. Hays. Same
as his Witty after-dinner
speech on Will Hays
Witty after-dinner speech on
Will Hays. LYI:224

Landon, Alfred M.
Acceptance speech, Topeka,
Kansas, July 23, 1936.
SIN:136
Action challenged. ROD:162
Campaign speech, New York
City, October 29, 1936.
SIN:145
Federal and family finances.
BAD:62

Landsteiner, Karl
On individual differences in hu-
man blood (Nobel Lecture,
Dec. 11, 1930). NOLM 2:234

LANDSTEINER, KARL
Hedrén, G.
Presentation [of the Nobel
Prize for Physiology or Medi-
cine to Karl Landsteiner, Dec.
11, 1930]. NOLM 2:229

Lang, John Dunmore
"Little While" of the Saviour's
absence and the prospect of
his speedy return. MCA:64

Lange, Christian Louis
Internationalism (Nobel Lecture,
Dec. 13, 1921). NOLP 1:336
Presentation [of the Nobel Prize
for Peace to Carlos Saavedra
Lamas, Dec. 10, 1936].

NOLP 2:217
Presentation [of the Nobel
Prize for Peace, 1933, to
Norman Angell, Dec. 10,
1934]. NOLP 2:147
Presentation [of the Nobel
Prize for Peace to Viscount
Cecil of Chelwood, Dec.
10, 1937]. NOLP 2:235

Langer, Elizabeth
Instrument of revelation (Ripon,
Wisc., 1957). LINR:301;
LINRS:300; LINRST:370

Langlie, Arthur B.
Presents Norman S. Marshall.
LYI:155

Langmuir, Irving
Surface chemistry (Nobel Lec-
ture, Dec. 14, 1932).
NOLC 2:287

LANGMUIR, IRVING
Söderbaum, H. G.
Presentation [of the Nobel
Prize for Chemistry to
Irving Langmuir, Dec. 14,
1932]. NOLC 2:283

Langston, Charles H.
Should colored men be subject
to the pains and penalties
of the Fugitive Slave
Law? (1858). FON:208

Langston, John Mercer
Equality before the law
(anniversary of adoption
of Fifteenth Amendment).
(Oberlin College, May 17,
1874). FON:409
The other phase of reconstruction (Jersey City, N.J.,
April 17, 1877). SMHV:46

LANGUAGE AND LANGUAGES
Aziz, U.
Languages: anguish and
confusion. MONSA:167
Bacon, W. A.
Language and the lived world.
BA 1976-77:174
Toh Chin Chye
The role of the university
in a multi-racial society.
MONSA:291

Lansdowne, Henry Charles Keith
Petty Fitzmaurice, 5th Mar-
quis See Curzon of Kedleston,
G., jt. auth.

Lansing, John
Answering Alexander Hamilton.
BREWE 7:2710

Lardner, Dionysius
Plurality of worlds.
BREWE 7:2716

Latimer, Hugh
Duties and respect of judges.
BREWE 7:2721
On the pickings of officeholders.
BREWE 7:2729
Sermon on the ploughers. Same
as his Sermon on the plow
Sermon on the plow.
BREWE 7:2724; BRYH:47

LATTIMORE, OWEN J.
Youngdahl, L.
United States v. Lattimore.
ANN 17:300

Laue, Max von
Concerning the detection of x-ray
interferences (Nobel Lecture
for 1914, Nov. 12, 1915).
NOLPH 1:347

LAUE, MAX VON
Granqvist, G.
Presentation [of the Nobel
Prize for Physics for 1914
to Max Von Laue, Nov. 12,
1915]. NOLPH 1:343

Laughlin, James Laurence
Against free coinage of silver.
ANN 12:75

Laurance, John and others (J.
Madison)
General welfare and the limits
of government authority.
ANN 3:491

Laurier, Sir Wilfrid
Canada, England and the United
States in 1899. BREWE 7:2737
Character and work of Gladstone.
BREWE 7:2732

Lavenson, James
Think strawberries. (American

Medical Association, Feb.
7, 1974). VERD:259

Laveran, Charles Louis Alphonse
Protozoa as causes of disease
(Nobel Lecture, Dec. 11,
1907). NOLM 1:264

LAVERAN, CHARLES LOUIS
ALPHONSE
Sundberg, C.
Presentation [of the Nobel
Prize for Physiology or
Medicine to Charles Louis
Alphonse Laveran].
NOLM 1:259

LAW AND LAWYERS
Azmi, B. H. M.
Duty of a lawyer. MONS:97
Bayard, J. A.
Federal judiciary.
BREWE 1:249
Brandeis, L. D.
Law and the laboring classes.
ANN 13:23
Brewer, D. J.
Independent judiciary as the
salvation of the nation.
ANN 11:423
Brougham and Vaux, H. P. B.
Present state of the law,
(1828). STRM:153
Burger, W. E.
State of the Judiciary.
BA 1970-71:13
Choate, J. H.
Bench and the bar.
HURH:133
Cousin, V.
Foundations of law.
BREWE 4:1428
Cox, A.
Creativity in law and gov-
ernment. BA 1973-74:49
Crockett, G. W.
Racism in the law.
FON:1131
Curtis, G. W.
Liberty under the law.
BAS:141 (outline only);
LINS:249
Davis, D.
Ex parte Milligan, 1866:
opinion for the court.
ANN 10:31
Dawson, M.
My profession. CAPB:363

Dixon, O.
Law and the scientific expert.
MCA:176
Field, D. D.
In re Milligan--martial law
as lawlessness.
BREWE 6:2147
Frankfurter, F.
John Marshall and the judicial
function, September 22, 1955.
FRIP:353
The Zeitgeist and the Judiciary.
FRIP:340
Griswold, E. N.
Dissent, protest, and disobedi-
ence. ANN 18:670;
BA 1967-68:141; JEF:196
Hand, L.
Judge's freedom before the
law. ANN 15:233
Holmes, O. W., Jr.
Path of the law.
BOORA 2:593
Isocrates
Areopagiticus. "A few wise
laws wisely administered."
BREWE 7:2589
Katzenbach, N. de B.
Civil Rights Act of 1964: re-
spect for law. CAPG:88
Kennedy, R. F.
Law Day address--University
of Georgia. CAPG:73;
THOMS:120
Latimer, H.
Duties and respect of judges.
BREWE 7:2721
Lee Kuan Yew
Law and its disciples.
MONS:374
McGill, W. J.
Science and the law.
BA 1977-78:83
Mansfield, W. M.
In the case of John Wilkes.
BREWE 8:2943
In the case of the Dean of St.
Asaph. BREWE 8:2945
Marbury, W. L.
Of movers and immobilists.
BA 1965-66:77
Marshall, J.
Speech in Virginia Convention
on Ratification of the Consti-
tution, June 20, 1788.
FRIP:90
Moneta, E. T.
Peace and law in the Italian

tradition (Nobel Lecture,
1907, Aug. 25, 1909).
NOLP 1:114
Pym, J.
Laws as the safeguard of
liberty. BREWE 8:3253
Rantoul, R., Jr.
On the barbarity of the
common law. ANN 6:262
Royer-Collard, P. P.
"Sacrilege" in law.
BREWE 9:3345
Shaw, L.
Law as a restraint on power.
ANN 5:217
Thurman, A. G.
Vested rights and the ob-
ligations of contracts.
BREWE 9:3626
Welcome to a State Attorney
General as speaker at a
civic club. HNWM:42
Wilson, J.
Study of law in the United
States. ANN 3:380
Yamzon, V.
The lawyer shall never re-
treat. CURM:323
Young, J.
Property under the common
law (Coster v. Lorillard
case). ANN 6:181

---- See also Courts; Defense,
Speeches of; Judicial re-
view; Jury; Justice; Law
enforcement; United States
- Supreme Court

LAW DAY
Kennedy, R. F.
Law Day address--Univer-
sity of Georgia. CAPG:73;
THOMS:120

LAW ENFORCEMENT
Wallace, G. C.
Address on law enforce-
ment. MAC:271;
MACR:312

---- NEW ZEALAND
Forbes, G. W.
The Public Safety Conser-
vation Bill, 1932.
MACS:314 sel.

Lawrence, David L.
Speaker of the year award (1962).
TAC:227

Lawrence, Ernest Orlando
The evolution of the cyclotron
(Nobel Lecture for 1939, Dec.
11, 1951). NOLPH 2:430

LAWRENCE, GERTRUDE
Sumner, G. L.
Presents Gertrude Lawrence.
LYI:22

Lawson, Jesse
I protest against Hayes's Southern
policy. (Princeton, N.Y.,
August, 1877). FON:457
The remedy for anarchy.
(Bethel Literary and Historical
Association, Washington,
D.C., Feb. 5, 1902).
FON:639

LAWYERS See Law and lawyers

Laxness, Halldór Kiljan
Acceptance [of the Nobel Prize
for Literature, 1955].
NOB 12:7; NOL:508

LAXNESS, HALLDOR KILJAN
Wessén, E.
Presentation [of the Nobel
Prize for Literature to Halldór
Kiljan Laxness, 1955].
NOB 12:3; NOL:505

LEACOCK, STEPHEN
Seaman, Sir O.
Presents Stephen Leacock.
LYI:47

LEADERSHIP
Clark, C.
Courage of leadership.
BREWE 3:1207
Harrison, R.
Leadership--a goal for us all.
BREWW:150
Lee, G. P.
Effective "Indian leadership"
color-blind, but not naive.
MAES:183
Lee Kuan Yew
Problems of leadership.
MONS:371

Meyer, S.
   What leadership means to
   me. BREWW:171
Mott, J. R.
   The leadership demanded
   in this momentous time
   (Nobel Lecture, Dec. 13,
   1946). NOLP 2:362
Muskie, E. S.
   The astronauts on the moon.
   BAAGB:409

LEAGUE OF NATIONS
Borah, W. E.
   League of Nations.
   HURH:190
Cecil, R.
   The future of civilization
   (Nobel Lecture for 1937,
   June 1, 1938). NOLP 2:246
Jordan, W. J.
   The League and the Spanish
   Civil War. MACS:361 sel.
Lodge, H. C.
   In opposition to the Pro-
   posed League of Nations.
   BOORA 2:783
---- and others
   Senate and the League of
   Nations, November 19, 1919
   debate. ANN 14:196
Nash, W.
   Collective security and the
   League of Nations.
   MACS:356 sel.
Wilson, W.
   Appeal for support of the
   League of Nations (Omaha,
   Nebraska speech).
   ANN 14:187
   For the League of Nations
   (Des Moines, Iowa speech).
   LINS:300

---- See also Peace Conference,
   1919

LEARNING AND SCHOLARSHIP
Barzun, J.
   Place and price of excel-
   lence. ARS:28
Bowdoin, J.
   Encouragement of knowl-
   edge. ANN 2:540
Bowen, W. G.
   Commitment to scholarship
   and research.
   BA 1978-79:41

Curtis, G. W.
   Duty of the American scholar.
   ANN 8:411
Emerson, R. W.
   American scholar. ANN 6:367;
   ARS:39; BAS:156 (outline only);
   BOORA 1:283; BREWE 5:2003;
   LINS:162; OLIS:47
Everett, E.
   Circumstances favorable to the
   progress of literature in
   America. ANN 5:118
Kennedy, J. F.
   Intellectual and the politician.
   BAP:285; LINR:267
Kirk, G.
   Responsibilities of the educated
   man (at centennial of University
   of Denver). LINR:143
Morgan, E. S.
   What every Yale freshman
   should know. ARS:35
Phillips, W.
   Scholar in a Republic.
   ANN 10:488
Thani Nayagam, X.
   Age and learning. MONS:187

---- See also Education, Higher; Intellect; Knowledge, Theory of;
   Research

Lederberg, Joshua
   A view of genetics (Nobel Lecture
   for 1958, May 29, 1959).
   NOLM 3:615

LEDERBERG, JOSHUA
Caspersson, T.
   Presentation [of the Nobel
   Prize for Physiology or Medi-
   cine to George Wells Beadle,
   Edward Lawrie Tatum, and
   Joshua Lederberg, Dec. 11,
   1958]. NOLM 3:583

Lee, George P.
   Effective "Indian leadership"
   color-blind, but not naive.
   MAES:183

Lee, Henry
   Funeral oration on Washington.
   BREWE 7:2744

Lee, Sir Henry Hau Shik
   Great institution (Central Bank of
   Malaya). MONS:164

Lee, Irving G.
Four ways of looking at a
  speech. ARS:12

Lee, John A.
The Auckland Riot, 1932
  (New Zealand House of
  Representatives, April 19,
  1932). MACS:312 sel.

Lee, Richard Henry
Address to the people of England. BREWE 7:2752

Lee, Robert E.
Gen. R. E. Lee's address to
  his troops. Same as his
  To the Army of Northern
  Virginia
To the Army of Northern Virginia. (Headquarters Army
  of Northern Virginia, Oct.
  2d, 1862). ECH:188

LEE, ROBERT E.
Stanley, A. O.
  Address in honor of Robert
  E. Lee. BLY:216

Lee, Tsung Dao
Weak interactions and noncon-
  servation of parity (Nobel
  Lecture, Dec. 11, 1957).
  NOLPH 3:406

LEE, TSUNG DAO
Klein, O. B.
  Presentation [of the Nobel
  Prize for Physics to Chen
  Ning Yang and Tsung Dao
  Lee, Dec. 11, 1957].
  NOLPH 3:389

Lee, W. Leonard
Through the looking glass.
  SCHW:106

Lee Kuan Yew
Aim: a more equal society.
  MONS:369
Brighter future for all peoples
  of Singapore if ... (Singa-
  pore, Feb. 6, 1969).
  MONSA:239
Changes in values and con-
  cepts. MONS:348
Democratic socialism under
  stress in Asia.

MONS:345
First step in nation building (Singa-
  pore). MONS:358
Hong Kong and Singapore: a tale
  of two cities (Univ. of Hong
  Kong, Feb. 18, 1970).
  MONSA:264
Law and its disciples. MONS:374
Leaders' responsibility in sus-
  taining a democratic system
  (Singapore, March 21, 1970).
  MONSA:269
Lesson we have to learn (opening
  new Science Tower at the
  University of Singapore).
  MONS:361
The moral for Commonwealth
  members and Britain (London,
  Jan. 9, 1969). MONSA:259
A new relevance and a fresh valid-
  ity for Commonwealth (Singa-
  pore, Jan. 14, 1971).
  MONSA:272
Our future is at stake--crucial
  years ahead (Singapore, May
  6, 1968). MONSA:247
Problems of leadership.
  MONS:371
The Rhodesian problem and the
  change of mood in Britain
  (London, Jan. 10, 1969).
  MONSA:251
Self respect is what our trade
  unions have and ... (Singa-
  pore, Nov. 16, 1969).
  MONSA:255
Tribute to India and Indians
  (Singapore, May 19, 1968).
  MONSA:244
Unionism: rethinking is vital
  (opening National Trade Union
  Conference). MONS:366

Leenhouts, Thelma
Men of conscience. SCHW:119

LEGISLATORS See Law and
  lawyers; Public officials;
  United States - Congress

Legum, Colin
Pan-Africanism, the Communists,
  and the West. ARS:255

Lehman, Herbert H.
Freedom and individual security.
  ANN 17:21

Leighton, Robert
Immortality. BREWE 7:2761

Leloir, Luis F.
Two decades of research on
the biosynthesis of sac-
charides (Nobel Lecture,
Dec. 11, 1970).
NOLC 4:338

LELOIR, LUIS F.
Myrbäck, K.
Presentation [of the Nobel
Prize for Chemistry to Luis
F. Leloir, Dec. 11, 1970].
NOLC 4:335

Lemke, William
Introduction of the aims of the
Union Party of the United
States. BAD:117

Lenard, Philipp Eduard Anton von
On cathode rays (Nobel Lecture for 1905, May 28,
1906). NOLPH 1:105

LENARD, PHILIPP EDUARD
ANTON VON
Lindstedt, A.
Presentation [of the Nobel
Prize for Physics for 1905
to Philipp Eduard Anton von
Lenard, May 28, 1906].
NOLPH 1:101

LEND LEASE LAW
Knox, F.
Lend-lease and national de-
fense. ANN 16:48
Roosevelt, F. D.
Proposal for Lend-Lease.
ANN 16:40
Wheeler, B. K.
Menace of Lend-Lease.
ANN 16:46

Lenin, Nikolai
Advance or retreat. Same as
his War, peace, and revolu-
tionary democracy
War, peace and revolutionary
democracy. (The First All-
Russian Congress of Soviets,
Tauride Palace, Leningrad,
June 17, 1917). BRN:81

Lenoir, William
Interest of the few and the liberties of the people. ANN 3:300

Lenthall, William
Opening the long Parliament under
Charles I. BREWE 7:2767

LEOPOLD, NATHAN
Darrow, C.
Defense of Richard Loeb and
Nathan Leopold. HURH:196

Lerner, Daniel
Comfort and fun: morality in a
nice society. ARS:168

Levai, Blase
Broken sword. SCHW:144

Levenson, Joseph
Live hopefully! WALE:116
Servant of the Lord has died.
WALE:118

Levin, Lewis C.
Native Americans and the foreign-
born. ANN 7:313

Levine, Etan B.
John F. Kennedy. WALE:221

Lew Sip Hon
Our stake in natural rubber.
MONS:302

Lewe, John C.
Presents Thomas C. Clark (Attor-
ney General of the United
States). LYI:137

Lewis, C. S.
Social morality. ARS:177
Three parts of morality. ARS:175

Lewis, David
His speech on the scaffold.
BREWE 7:2772

Lewis, Ellis
Mott v. Pennsylvania Railroad
Company: opinion for the court.
ANN 9:61

Lewis, James Hamilton
Introduction of Jacob M. Dickinson.
LYI:217

Lewis, John
    We are in a serious revolution.
    (Washington, D.C., August
    28, 1963). FON:975

Lewis, John L.
    Industrial unions. ANN 15:511
    Labor and the nation. (Wash-
    ington, Sept. 3, 1937).
    HURH:232
    "Labor, like Israel, has many
    sorrows." Same as his
    Labor and the nation

LEWIS, JOHN L.
    Day, J. E.
    Introduces John L. Lewis,
    American labor leader.
    LYI:61

LEWIS, LLOYD
    Stevenson, A. E.
    Farewell to a friend (Lloyd
    Lewis). ALA:119

Lewis, Sinclair
    The American fear of litera-
    ture (Nobel Lecture, Dec.
    12, 1930). ANN 15:62;
    BEN:208; BOORA 2:824;
    NOL:278

LEWIS, SINCLAIR
    Karlfeldt, E. A.
    Presentation [of the Nobel
    Prize for Literature to
    Sinclair Lewis, 1930].
    NOB 11:237; NOL:271

Lewis, W. Deming
    Founder's Day remarks.
    BAS:164 (outline only)

LEWIS AND CLARK EXPEDITION
    Jefferson, T.
    Lewis and Clark expedition.
    ANN 4:158

LIABILITIES See Success

LIARS See Truthfulness and
    falsehood

Libby, Willard Frank
    Radiocarbon dating (Nobel Lec-
    ture, Dec. 12, 1960).
    NOLC 3:593

LIBBY, WILLARD FRANK
    Westgren, A.
    Presentation [of the Nobel Prize
    for Chemistry to Willard Frank
    Libby, Dec. 12, 1960].
    NOLC 3:589

LIBERAL ARTS See Education,
    Higher

LIBERAL PARTY - GREAT BRITAIN
    Keynes, J. M.
    Am I a Liberal? MCB:456

---- See also Great Britain - Politics
    and government

---- NEW ZEALAND
    Grey, Sir G.
    A Liberal Party. MACS:182
    sel.

LIBERALISM
    Ascoli, M.
    Scarcity of ideas. ARS:201
    Hatcher, R. G.
    Which is the path of change?
    FON:1110
    Oglesby, C.
    How can we continue to sack the
    ports of Asia and still dream
    of Jesus. LAA:15
    Schlesinger, A. M., Jr.
    Challenge of abundance.
    ARS:196

LIBERTY
    Aly, B.
    Remarks on Jefferson Day.
    BAP:273
    Ball, J.
    Bondmen and freemen: address
    to the rebels at Blackheath.
    BRYH:42
    Boucher, J.
    Civil liberty and nonresistance.
    ANN 2:343; POC:552
    Calhoun, J. C.
    Individual liberty. BREWE 3:925
    Carson, H. L.
    American liberty. BREWE 3:995
    Cotton, J.
    A treatise of the covenant of
    grace. JON:48
    Cousin, V.
    Liberty an inalienable right.
    BREWE 4:1426

Curran, J. P.
England and English liber-
ties--in the case of Rowan.
BREWE 4:1546
In the case of Justice
Johnson--civil liberty and
arbitrary arrests.
BREWE 4:1499

Curtis, G. W.
Liberty under the law.
BAS:141 (outline only);
LINS:249

Depew, C. M.
Unveiling the Statue of
Liberty. BREWE 5:1782

Dickinson, J.
Before the Pennsylvania
Assembly, March 24,
1760. POC:182

Douglass, F.
If there is no struggle there
is no progress. FON:197

Drayton, W. H.
Charge to the Grand Juries,
November 5 & 15, 1774.
POC:297

Everett, E.
History of liberty.
BREWE 6:2092

Fuller, Z.
Tree of liberty (George
Washington birthday ad-
dress). ANN 5:355

Goldwater, B. M.
Extremism in defense of
liberty (accepting nomination
for presidency, July 17,
1964). MAC:251; MACR:292;
MDV:115; SIN:337

Hand, L.
Meaning of liberty.
BRR:46

Henry, P.
Liberty or death.
ANN 2:231; BAS:39 (outline
only); BEN:13; BREWE 7:2473;
HURH:27; HURS:209;
OLIS:22; POC:305

Howard, J. A.
"... our sacred honor."
BA 1975-76:9

Hugo, V. M.
Liberty tree in Paris.
BREWE 7:2548

Ingersoll, R. G.
Liberty of man, woman,
and child. BREWE 7:2583

Jacobusse, K. D.

Uncommon thought. SCHW:79

Johnson, L. B.
Vietnam: the struggle to be
free (on accepting National
Freedom Award).
BA 1965-66:11

Kennedy, J. F.
Ich bin ein Berliner.
ALA:129; AND:79; LINR:294;
LINRS:293

Kennedy, R. F.
Address to the Free University
of Berlin. MDV:95

Lehman, H. H.
Freedom and individual security.
ANN 17:21

Lubbers, A. D.
Road to right. SCHW:159

Montalembert, C. F. T.
Devotion to freedom.
BREWE 8:3048

Ngwa, J.
Our common tradition in peril.
SCHW:123

Pym, J.
Law as the safeguard of liberty.
BREWE 8:3253

Romulo, C. P.
Bandung address. CROCK:141

Roosevelt, F. D.
Four human freedoms.
ANN 16:42; ROD:278;
STAT 3:2855

Rowan, C. T.
Commencement address (at
Howard University, June 5,
1964). HURS:216

Sargent, F. W.
The computer and civil liberties. BA 1973-74:141

Schurz, C.
True Americanism. ANN 9:97

Smith, W.
Eulogium. POC:3

Wentworth, P.
Liberty of the Commons.
BRYH:79; CLAYP:1

West, S.
Election sermon. POC:578

Winthrop, J.
Little speech on liberty.
HURH:17; POC:135

Zubly, J. J.
Law of liberty. POC:611

---- See also Civil rights; Democracy; Fourth of July; Free
speech; Liberty of the press;

Religious liberty; Teaching,
Freedom of; United States -
Constitution; United States -
Economic policy

LIBERTY OF THE PRESS
Brennan, W. J., Jr.
Conciliation between the
press and the law.
BA 1979-80:119
Gossage, H. L.
Our fictitious freedom of
the press. MDV:285
Mathias, C. M.
The First Amendment:
freedom and responsibility.
BA 1977-78:134
Royster, V. C.
What the people grant, they
can take away.
BA 1978-79:191
Schorr, D.
In defense of privilege.
BA 1978-79:202
Shaw, R. M.
Danger of getting used to
lies. LINR:191

LIBERTY PARTY
Smith, G.
On the character, scope
and duties of the Liberty
Party. MDT:93

LIBRARIES AND LIBRARIANS
Choate, R.
Books and civilization in
America. BREWE 3:1120
Phelps, W. L.
Owning books. HURH:225

---- See also Dedication addresses - Libraries

LIBRARY OF CONGRESS See
United States - Library of
Congress

LIES See Truthfulness and
Falsehood

LIFE
Arnold, T.
Realities of life and death.
BREWE 1:173
Chalmers, T.
Use of the living.
BREWE 3:1025

Dwight, T.
Pursuit of excellence.
BREWE 5:1968
Fisher, J.
Jeopardy of daily life.
BREWE 6:2164
Gladstone, W. E.
Destiny and individual aspiration.
BREWE 6:2288
Huxley, T. H.
Threefold unity of life.
BREWE 7:2557
Ingersoll, R. G.
Life. BREWE 7:2587
Live today. BURT:131
Our changing world. BURT:129
Tyndall, J.
Origin of life. BREWE 9:3664

---- See also Behavior

LIFE INSURANCE See Insurance -
Life

LIGHT
Frank, I. M.
Optics of light sources moving
in refractive media.
NOLPH 3:442
Lorentz, H. A.
The theory of electrons and the
propagation of light.
NOLPH 1:14
Raman, Sir C. V.
The molecular scattering of
light. NOLPH 2:267
Zeeman, P.
Light radiation in a magnetic
field. NOLPH 1:33

Lilienthal, David E.
Democratic faith. Same as his
My faith in democracy
My faith in democracy. ALA:111

Liljestrand, G.
Presentation [of the Nobel Prize
for Physiology or Medicine to
André Frederic Cournand,
Werner Theodor Otto Forssmann,
and Dickinson Woodruff Rich-
ards Jr., Dec. 11, 1956].
NOLM 3:501
Presentation [of the Nobel Prize
for Physiology or Medicine to
Christiaan Eijkman and Sir
Frederick Gowland Hopkins,
Dec. 11, 1929].

NOLM 2:193
Presentation [of the Nobel Prize
for Physiology or Medicine
to Edward Calvin Kendall,
Tadeus Reichstein, and
Philip Showalter Hench,
Dec. 11, 1950].
NOLM 3:263
Presentation [of the Nobel Prize
for Physiology or Medicine
to Sir Alexander Fleming,
Ernst Boris Chain, and Sir
Howard Walter Florey, Dec.
11, 1945]. NOLM 3:77
Presentation [of the Nobel Prize
for Physiology or Medicine
to Sir Charles Scott Sherrington and Edgar Douglas
Adrian, Dec. 12, 1932].
NOLM 2:273
Presentation [of the Nobel Prize
for Physiology or Medicine
to Sir Henry Hallett Dale
and Otto Loewi, Dec. 12,
1936]. NOLM 2:397

Lillehei, C. Walton See
Sevareid, E., jt. auth.

Lim, P. G. (Miss)
Women's role in national development. MONS:339

Lim Chong Eu
The message of Rukunegara
(Penang, Nov. 1, 1970).
MONSA:147

Lim Chong Yah
Teaching profession and nation
building (Malaysia).
MONS:317

Lim Kim San
Massive exercise for survival.
MONS:408
Three major problems of de-
veloping countries.
MONS:412
Youth leadership (May 25,
1968). MONSA:310

Lim Swee Aun
Doubting Thomases were wrong
(opening of Chemical Com-
pany of Malaysian factory).
MONS:153

Lincoln, Abraham
Against the extension of slavery.
Same as his Speech at Peoria
Campaign speech for United States
Senate--Chicago, July 10, 1858.
Same as his Reply to Douglas
at Chicago
Cooper Institute address (New
York, Feb. 27, 1860).
ANN 9:158; BREWE 7:2791;
FRIP:204; LINS:201
Danger to our liberty. Same as
his Perpetuation of our political
institutions
Dred Scott Decision. ANN 8:459
Farewell to Springfield (outline of
speech). CUB:78
First annual message.
STAT 2:1054
First inaugural address.
ANN 9:250; BOSR:1; HOW:239;
LINS:281; USINAU:119;
USINAUG:119
First joint debate at Ottawa, Au-
gust 21, 1858. ANN 9:11
Fourth annual message.
STAT 2:1097
Gettysburg address (Nov. 19,
1863). ALA:29; ANN 9:462;
BAS:131 (outline only); BEN:47;
BOORA 1:418; BREWE 7:2794;
CUB:79; HURH:112
"A house divided against itself
cannot stand." (Springfield,
Ill., June 16, 1858).
ANN 9:1; BAS:100 (outline only);
BREWE 7:2777; FRIP:197;
HURH:88
"I believe this government cannot
endure permanently, half slave
and half free." Same as his
"A house divided against itself
cannot stand"
Interrogating Douglas. Same as
his Second joint debate at Free-
port, August 27, 1858
Labor, education, and the Amer-
ican farmer. ANN 9:121
Last public address, April 11,
1865. Same as his Speech
before death
Lincoln-Douglas joint debate at
Alton, October 15, 1858.
ANN 9:26
Message to Congress, July 5,
1861. ANN 9:268
On John Brown. Same as his
Cooper Institute Address

Perpetuation of our political in-
stitutions (1837).
ANN 6:424; MOP:368
Plea for compensated eman-
cipation. ANN 9:328
Program for reconstruction.
Same as his Third annual
message
Reply to Douglas at Chicago.
OLIS:150
Righteous and speedy peace.
Same as his Speech before
death, April 11, 1865
Second annual message to
Congress. BOORA 1:396;
STAT 2:1068
Second inaugural address
(Washington, March 4,
1869). AND:48; ANN 9:555;
BEN:49; BOORA 1:423;
BREWE 7:2795; BRR:80;
CUB:86 (outline); HURH:114;
LINS:226; USINAU:127;
USINAUG:127
Second joint debate at Free-
port, August 27, 1858.
ANN 9:15; BREWE 7:2785
Speech at Charleston, Sep-
tember 18, 1858.
ANN 9:21
Speech at Galesburg, October
7, 1858. ANN 9:23
Speech at Jonesboro, Septem-
ber 15, 1858. ANN 9:19
Speech at Peoria, October
16, 1854. ANN 8:491;
FRIP:165
Speech before death, April
11, 1865. ANN 9:573;
BREWE 7:2796; CUR:4
Speech on repeal of the Mis-
souri Compromise, October
16, 1854. Same as his
Speech at Peoria, October
16, 1854
Third annual message.
ANN 9:473; STAT 2:1084
War to preserve the Union.
Same as his Message to
Congress, July 5, 1861
"... we here highly resolve
that these dead shall not
have died in vain." Same
as his Gettysburg address
"With malice toward none,
with charity for all, with
firmness in the right...."
Same as his Second in-

augural address
With malice toward none. Same
as his Second inaugural address

LINCOLN, ABRAHAM
Beaconsfield, B. D.
Assassination of Lincoln.
BREWE 1:295
Beecher, H. W.
Effect of the death of Lincoln.
BREWE 1:365
Bingham, J. A.
Against the assassins of Presi-
dent Lincoln. BREWE 2:445
Brooks, P.
Character of Abraham Lincoln.
BREWE 2:644
Douglass, F.
Oration in memory of Abraham
Lincoln (at unveiling of Freed-
men's Monument, Washington,
D. C.). FRIP:242
Douglass, H. F.
I do not believe in the antislavery
of Abraham Lincoln. FON:232
Emerson, R. W.
Greatness of a plain American.
BREWE 5:1999
Hunt, E. L.
Lincoln's rhetorical triumph at
Cooper Union (centennial
speech). BA 1969-70:189
Jacobusse, K. D.
Big man. SCHW:204
McGill, R. E.
Meaning of Lincoln today (cen-
tennial of Lincoln's speech at
Cooper Institute). LINS:360
Runkel, H. W.
Making Lincoln live.
BAPR:351; BAPRR:259
Sandburg, C.
On Lincoln (at 150th anniversary
of Lincoln's birth). GRG:101;
HURH:347
Wise, S. S.
Abraham Lincoln, man and
American. HURH:169

Lindbergh, Charles Augustus
America first. Same as his In-
dependent policy
Dissident view: Charles Lindbergh
argues against intervention.
Same as his Independent policy
Independent policy. ANN 16:72;
HURH:254; ROD:290
"Those of us who believe in an

independent America must
band together and organize
for strength." Same as his
Independent policy

LINDBERGH, CHARLES
AUGUSTUS
Gwinn, J. M.
Presents Charles Lindbergh.
LYI:188

Lindh, A. E.
Presentation [of the Nobel Prize
for Physics to Cecil Frank
Powell, Dec. 11, 1950].
NOLPH 3:139
Presentation [of the Nobel Prize
for Physics to Percy Wil-
liams Bridgman, Dec. 11,
1946]. NOLPH 3:53

Lindsay, John V.
A politician adapts his introduction and conclusion to an
audience of students. (Harvard Republican Club, April
20, 1968). JEF:194
Reality and rhetoric.
BA 1967-68:79
Vietnam moratorium address.
(New York, Oct. 15,
1969). AND:153

Lindsley, Philip
Dangers of a sectarian college.
ANN 5:310
Education for every child of
the Republic. ANN 5:157

Lindstedt, A.
Presentation [of the Nobel Prize
for Physics for 1905 to
Philipp Eduard Anton von
Lenard, May 28, 1906].
NOLPH 1:101

Lingg, Louis
Address at trial, Chicago,
October 7-9, 1886.
ACC:39; PAF:34

Linowitz, Sol M.
Let candles be brought (New
York, March 8, 1977).
BA 1976-77:149

Lionaes, Aase
Presentation [of the Nobel Prize

for Peace to the International
Labor Organization, Dec. 10,
1969]. NOLP 3:415
Presentation [of the Nobel Prize
for Peace to Norman Ernest
Borlaug, Dec. 10, 1970].
NOLP 3:445
Presentation [of the Nobel Prize
for Peace to René-Samuel Cas-
sin, Dec. 10, 1968].
NOLP 3:385
Presentation [of the Nobel Prize
for Peace to the United Nations
Children's Fund, Dec. 10,
1965]. NOLP 3:353

Lipis, Philip L.
Darkness at noon. WALE:120
Dreams fulfilled. WALE:122
Four good signs. WALE:124
Look beyond the shadows.
WALE:128

Lipmann, Fritz Albert
Development of the acetylation
problem: a personal account
(Nobel Lecture, Dec. 11, 1953).
NOLM 3:413

LIPMANN, FRITZ ALBERT
Hammarsten, E.
Presentation [of the Nobel
Prize for Physiology or Medi-
cine to Hans Adolf Krebs and
Fritz Albert Lipmann, Dec.
11, 1953]. NOLM 3:395

Lipnick, Bernard
Family's tribute. WALE:130

Lippmann, Gabriel
Colour photography (Nobel Lec-
ture, Dec. 14, 1908).
NOLPH 1:186

LIPPMANN, GABRIEL
Hasselberg, K. B.
Presentation [of the Nobel Prize
for Physics to Gabriel Lipp-
mann, Dec. 14, 1908].
NOLPH 1:183
Lippman, Walter
On understanding society.
(Columbia University, 1969).
BAAGB:412
Our world today. MDV:26
Rise of personal government in
the United States. BAD:97

Lipton, Jeffrey
  Land preservation in the
    Northeast. BREWW:75

LIQUIDS
  Waals, J. D. V. D.
    The equation of state for
    gases and liquids.
    NOLPH 1:254

LIQUOR PROBLEM See Al-
  coholism; Prohibition

LITERARY PRIZES See Literature

LITERATURE
  Andrić, I.
    Acceptance [of the Nobel
    Prize for Literature, 1961].
    NOB 1:121; NOL:565
  Arnold, M.
    Literature and science.
    MCB:388
  Ashley, L. R. N.
    A guided tour of gobbledy-
    gook. REID:408
  Avebury, J. L.
    Hundred best books.
    BREWE 7:2820
  Bacon, W. A.
    The seacoast of Bohemia:
    truth in literature.
    BA 1977-78:170
  Buchan, J.
    Novel and the fairy tale.
    ARS:54
  Camus, A.
    Acceptance [of the Nobel
    Prize for Literature, 1957].
    NOB 4:7; NOL:524
  Depew, C. M.
    Poetry and politics in
    Britain. BREWE 5:1796
  Drummond, H.
    Talk on books.
    BREWE 5:1964
  Elliott, J.
    There's always a mongoose.
    MDYG:223
  Everett, E.
    Circumstances favorable to
    the progress of literature
    in America. ANN 5:118
  Faulkner, W.
    On accepting the Nobel
    Prize, exhorts the young
    writers of the world.

    ALA:125; ANN 17:33; ARS:52;
    BOORA 2:988; GRG:86;
    HURH:291; MOPR:379;
    NOB 19:7; NOL:444
  Gittings, R.
    Exploring the known.
    MDYG:207
  Gladstone, W. E.
    Use of books. BREWE 6:2289
  Hemingway, E.
    Acceptance [of the Nobel Prize
    for Literature, 1954].
    NOB 9:7; NOL:501
  Introductions for literary persons
    (2 examples). BNH:18
  Lewis, S.
    The American fear of litera-
    ture. ANN 15:62; BEN:208;
    BOORA 2:824; NOL:278
  Macaulay, T. B.
    Literature of England.
    BREWE 8:2876
  Marshall, A.
    I first saw the light of day.
    MDYG:231
  Montgomery, J.
    Modern English literature.
    BREWE 8:3052
  Russell, J. R.
    Science and literature as modes
    of progress. BREWE 9:3359
  Smith, G.
    Lamps of fiction (at centenary
    of Sir Walter Scott).
    BREWE 9:3465
  Steinbeck, J.
    Acceptance [of the Nobel Prize
    for Literature, 1962].
    NOB 19:205; NOL:575
  Thackeray, W. M.
    Authors and their patrons.
    BREWE 9:3604
    Novelist's future labors.
    BREWE 9:3606
    Reality of the novelist's crea-
    tion. BREWE 9:3602
  Whitehead, A. N.
    Technical education and its re-
    lation to science and literature.
    MCB:403
  Woolsey, J. M.
    Opinion December 6, 1933
    (Ulysses case--freedom of
    reading). ANN 15:236

---- See also Acceptance speeches -
    Rewards (Prizes); Black au-
    thors; Book reviews; Books and
    reading; Poetry and poets

Little, Malcolm
  The ballot or the bullet (Cleve-
    land, April 3, 1964).
    AND:135; FON:985;
    REIR:47; SMHV:214
  Black revolution (April 8,
    1964). SMHV:235
  Prospects for freedom (New
    York, January 7, 1965).
    SMHV:250
  To young people. (New York,
    Dec. 31, 1964). FON:1004

---- See also Farmer, J., jt.
  auth.

LITTLE, MALCOLM
  Breitman, G.
    Myths about Malcolm X:
    another view. LINR:120
  Cleage, A.
    Myths about Malcolm X.
    LINR:108
  Davis, O.
    Malcolm was our manhood,
    our living Black manhood.
    FON:1010

LIVESTOCK See AGRICULTURE

Livingston, Edward
  Against the Alien Act. Same
    as his On the Alien Bill
  On the Alien Bill. ANN 4:49

Livingston, Homer J.
  Responds to an introduction
    and speaks briefly at the
    dedication of a new manu-
    facturing plant. PRS:130

Livingston, P. R. See Sanford,
  N., jt. auth.

Livingston, Robert R.
  Wealth and poverty, aristoc-
    racy and Republicanism.
    BREWE 7:2801

LLEWELLYN, SIR WILLIAM
  Phelps, W. L.
    Presents Sir William
    Llewellyn. LYI:26

Lloyd George, David
  Appeal to the nation (London,
    Sept. 19, 1914).
    MCB:483

The Budget (Limehouse, London,
  July 30, 1909). BRYH:461;
  JAE:170; MCB:233; STRM:407
The Budget and the people. Same
  as his The budget
Speech at Limehouse, July 30,
  1909. Same as his The budget

LOANS See Lend Lease Law

LOCAL GOVERNMENT - CITIZEN
  PARTICIPATION
  Gardner, J. W.
    People power. BA 1974-75:158

Lodge, Henry Cabot
  For immigration restrictions.
    ANN 12:88
  For intervention in Cuba.
    ANN 12:85
  "If a man is going to be an
    American at all let him be so
    without any qualifying adjec-
    tives." Same as his Our fore-
    fathers
  In opposition to the Proposed
    League of Nations.
    BOORA 2:783
  Our forefathers. (Brooklyn, Dec.
    21, 1888). HURH:141
  Speech on the League of Nations.
    Same as his In opposition to
    the Proposed League of Nations

---- and others (J. T. Robinson)
  Senate and the League of Nations,
    November 19, 1919 debate.
    ANN 14:196

Lodge, Henry Cabot, Jr.
  For abolishing the Electoral Col-
    lege. ANN 17:2
  "Man can improve his material
    and physical lot without sacri-
    ficing his civil rights." Same
    as his United Nations
  United Nations. (Chicago, Ill.,
    Sept. 2, 1958). HURH:344

LODGE SPEECHES See Club
  speeches

LOEB, RICHARD
  Darrow, C.
    Defense of Richard Loeb and
    Nathan Leopold. HURH:196

Loewi, Otto
  The chemical transmission of

nerve action (Nobel Lecture,
Dec. 12, 1936).
NOLM 2:416

LOEWI, OTTO
Liljestrand, G.
Presentation [of the Nobel
Prize for Physiology or
Medicine to Sir Henry Hal-
lett Dale and Otto Loewi,
Dec. 12, 1936].
NOLM 2:397

Logan, John, Chief of the
Mingoes
On the murder of his family.
ALA:9; BOORA 1:62;
BREWE 7:2569
Speech to Lord Dunmore.
Same as his On the murder
of his family

Loguen, J. W.
I won't obey the Fugitive Slave
Law. (Syracuse, N.Y.,
Oct. 4, 1850). FON:97

LONDON - ARCHITECTURE
Banham, R.
Fourth monument.
MDYG:216

Long, Huey P.
Every man a king. BEN:80
Sharing our wealth (January,
1935 radio speech).
ANN 15:318; BAD:109

Lonnquist, Ken
Ghosts (Madison, Wisc.,
1977). LINRST:176

LORD'S SUPPER See Communion

Lorentz, Hendrik Antoon
The theory of electrons and the
propagation of light (Nobel
Lecture, Dec. 11, 1902).
NOLPH 1:14

LORENTZ, HENDRIK ANTOON
Theel, Hj.
Presentation [of the Nobel
Prize for Physics to Hen-
drik Antoon Lorentz and
Pieter Zeeman, 1902].
NOLPH 1:11

Lorge, Barry
Great auto rally (outline).
REIR:93

LOTTERIES See Gambling

LOUIS VI, KING OF FRANCE
Deseze, R.
Defending Louis VI.
BREWE 5:1811

LOUISIANA
Lincoln, A.
Speech before death, April 11,
1865. ANN 9:573;
BREWE 7:2796; CUR:4
Quincy, J., 1772-1864
On the admission of Louisiana.
ANN 4:283

LOUISIANA PURCHASE
Jefferson, T.
Third annual message.
STAT 1:68
White, S.
Opposition to the Louisiana
Purchase. ANN 4:175

Loula, Louise A.
Drunken orgy. SCHW:149

LOVE
Drummond, H.
Greatest thing in the world.
BREWE 5:1941
Elliott, J.
There's always a mongoose.
MDYG:223
Klaaren, M. A.
Divine command. SCHW:96
Power of love. BURT:149

Lovell, Sir Bernard
Our present knowledge of the universe. MDYG:239

Lovell, James
Boston Massacre oration.
POC:231

Lovell, John
Funeral oration. POC:138

Løvland, Jørgen Gunnarsson
Banquet speech [presenting the
Nobel Prize for Peace to
Bertha von Suttner, 1905, April
18, 1906]. NOLP 1:82

Presentation [of the Nobel Prize for Peace to Alfred Hermann Fried, Dec. 10, 1911]. NOLP 1:238

Presentation [of the Nobel Prize for Peace to Auguste Marie François Beernaert, Dec. 10, 1909]. NOLP 1:211

Presentation [of the Nobel Prize for Peace to Baron d'Estournelles de Constant, Dec. 10, 1909]. NOLP 1:216

Presentation [of the Nobel Prize for Peace to Ernesto Teodoro Moneta, Dec. 10, 1907]. NOLP 1:113

Presentation [of the Nobel Prize for Peace to Fredrik Bajer, Dec. 10, 1908]. NOLP 1:188

Presentation [of the Nobel Prize for Peace to Klas Pontus Arnoldson, Dec. 10, 1908]. NOLP 1:173

Presentation [of the Nobel Prize for Peace to Louis Renault, Dec. 10, 1907]. NOLP 1:141

Presentation [of the Nobel Prize for Peace to the Permanent International Peace Bureau, Dec. 10, 1910]. NOLP 1:223

Presentation [of the Nobel Prize for Peace to Tobias Michael Carel Asser, Dec. 10, 1911]. NOLP 1:233

Toast to C. A. Gobat [presenting the Nobel Prize for Peace for 1902, Oslo, July 18, 1906]. NOLP 1:29

Toast to E. Ducommun [presenting the Nobel Prize for Peace for 1902, Oslo, May 16, 1904]. NOLP 1:15

Welcome [presenting the Nobel Prize for Peace, 1903, to William Randal Cremer, Jan. 15, 1905]. NOLP 1:45

LOW, EDMON
Nix, L.
  Presents Edmon Low.
  LYI:40

Lowe, John Adams
Presents E. J. Pratt. LYI:49

Lowe, Robert, 1st Viscount Sherbrooke
Against the extension of democracy. Same as his Coming of democracy
Coming of democracy. (H. of Commons, March 13, 1866). MCB:138

Lowell, James Russell
Poetical and the practical in America. BREWE 7:2808
Pope and his times. BREWE 7:2815

LOYALTY See Patriotism

Lubbers, Arend D.
God and Joe College. SCHW:69
Road to right. SCHW:159

Lubbock, Sir John See Avebury, J. L.

Lucas, Marty
The waste of our precious farmland. BREWW:102

Luce, Claire Boothe
Optimism about the future (Washington, Oct. 10, 1979). BA 1979-80:168

LUCE, HENRY R.
Donovan, H.
  Presents Henry R. Luce. LYI:103

Lundy, Robert F.
World divided by three (politics, science, and religion). MONS:489

Luria, Salvador E.
Phage, colicins and macroregulatory phenomena (Nobel Lecture, Dec. 10, 1969). NOLM 4:426

LURIA, SALVADOR E.
Gard, S.
  Presentation [of the Nobel Prize for Physiology or Medicine to Max Delbrück, Alfred D. Hershey, and Salvador E. Luria, Dec. 10, 1969]. NOLM 4:401

Lusty, Robert
    Presents Sir Norman Birkett.
    LYI:54

Luther, Martin
    Before the Diet of Worms.
    BREWE 7:2829
    Pith of Paul's chief doctrine.
    BREWE 7:2833

Luthuli, Albert John
    Africa and freedom (Nobel
        Lecture for 1960, Dec.
        11, 1961). MDV:79;
        NOLP 3:217

LUTHULI, ALBERT JOHN
    Jahn, G.
        Presentation [of the Nobel
        Prize for Peace to Albert
        John Luthuli for 1960,
        Dec. 10, 1961].
        NOLP 3:209

Lwoff, André
    Interaction among virus, cell,
        and organism (Nobel Lec-
        ture, Dec. 11, 1965).
        NOLM 4:186

LWOFF, ANDRE
    Gard, S.
        Presentation [of the Nobel
        Prize for Physiology or
        Medicine to François Jacob,
        André Lwoff, and Jacques
        Monod, Dec. 11, 1965].
        NOLM 4:143

Lygon, Lady Mary See Sykes,
    C., jt. auth.

Lynch, James
    Colored men standing in the
        way of their own race.
        (Philadelphia, May, 1865).
        FON:316

LYNCHING
    Chapman, J. R.
        Coatesville. ARS:163
    Graham, D. A.
        Some facts about Southern
        lynchings. FON:613
    Wells-Barnett, I. M.
        Lynching, our national
        crime. FON:687
    White, G. H.

I raise my voice against one
    of the most dangerous evils in
    our country. FON:624

Lyndhurst, John Singleton Copley,
    1st Baron
    Russia and the Crimean War.
    BREWE 7:2842

Lynen, Feodor
    The pathway from "activated acetic
        acid" to the terpenes and fatty
        acids (Nobel Lecture, Dec. 11,
        1964). NOLM 4:103

LYNEN, FEODOR
    Bergstrom, S.
        Presentation [of the Nobel Prize
        for Physiology or Medicine to
        Konrad Bloch and Feodor Ly-
        nen, Dec. 11, 1964].
        NOLM 4:75

Lysias
    Against Eratosthenes for murder
        (on the execution without trial
        of Polemarchus).
        BREWE 3:2851; SAG:39
    Funeral oration. COG:9

Lyttleton, George See Walpole, R.,
    jt. auth.

Lytton, Edward George Earle Lytton
    Bulwer-Lytton, 1st Baron
    Demosthenes and the nobility of
        the classics. BREWE 8:2869

- M -

MacArthur, Douglas
    Address to the joint session of
        Congress. Same as his De-
        fends his conduct of the war
        in Korea
    Defends his conduct of the war in
        Korea (Washington, April 19,
        1951). ALS:243; ANN 17:79;
        ARS:279; BAS:82 (outline only);
        BEN:113; BOSR:22; GRG:88;
        HURH:293; HURS:214;
        LINS:337
    Duty, honor, country. Same as
        his Farewell to the cadets
        (accepting Sylvanus Thayer
        award for service to his nation)

Farewell address to Congress.
Same as his Defends his
conduct of the war in Korea
Farewell to the cadets (accept-
ing Sylvanus Thayer award
for service to his nation,
West Point, May 12, 1962).
LINR:264; LINRS:283;
LINRST:357; MDV:20;
MUS:332
Hope of all mankind. ALA:105
"Old soldiers never die; they
just fade away." Same as
his Defends his conduct of
the war in Korea
Remarks and final speech at
Japanese surrender.
ANN 16:339
Today the guns are silent.
Same as his Remarks and
final speech at Japanese
surrender

MACARTHUR, DOUGLAS
Truman, H. S.
Preventing a new world war.
ANN 17:75; BAP:291

MacAulay, John A.
The Red Cross in a changing
world (Nobel Lecture,
Dec. 11, 1963).
NOLP 3:311

Macaulay, Thomas B.
Consent or force in govern-
ment. BREWE 8:2888
Literature of England.
BREWE 8:2876
Parliamentary reform. Same
as his Reform Bill
Popular education.
BREWE 8:2883
Reform Bill. (H. of Com-
mons, March 2, 1831).
CLAYP:295; MCB:110
Reform Bill. JAE:52
Speech on Parliamentary re-
form, House of Commons,
March 2, 1831. Same
as his Reform Bill
Tribute to the Jews.
BREWE 8:2886

McBath, James Harvey
The vital university. (Los
Angeles, June 5, 1975).
BA 1974-75:127

McCARRAN-WALTER IMMIGRATION
ACT, 1952
Truman, H. S.
Veto of the McCarran-Walter
Immigration Act. ANN 17:131

McCarthy, Eugene J.
Address on Viet Nam (February
1, 1967). REIR:117

McCarthy, Joseph Raymond
Annual Kansas Day Republican
banquet speech. BOSR:53
Communists in the State Department. ANN 17:16
A conspiracy of blackest infamy
(1951). (Washington, June 14,
1951). DAVF:304

McCARTHY, JOSEPH RAYMOND
Benton, W.
For the expulsion of Senator
McCarthy. ANN 17:108
Ferguson, J.
Witch trials. CAPB:377
McGowan, E. D.
Stop the foes of Negro free-
dom. FON:860

McClafferty, John J. See Murrow,
E. R., jt. auth.

McClellan, John L.
Responds to an introduction.
PRS:161

McCloud, Bentley G.
Introduces C. J. Jackson.
PRS:23

MacColl, Rene
Borrowed plumage. MDYG:174

McCorkle, Samuel
A sermon for the anniversary of
American independence, July
24th, 1786. (Salisbury, N.C.).
HAW:292

McCORMICK, ANNE O'HARE
Spencer, H. R.
Introducing Anne O'Hare Mc-
Cormick. LYI:107

Macdonald, Sir John Alexander
On the treaty of Washington.
BREWE 8:2891
Prerogative and public right.
BREWE 8:2895

MacDonald, Peter
  Exploring new energy frontiers
    (Albuquerque, New Mexico,
    February 20, 1975).
    MAES:165
  Inaugural address, Window
    Rock, Navajo Nation, Janu-
    ary 7, 1975. MAES:213
  Statement before the Confer-
    ence on Financing of Public
    Schools on Indian Reserva-
    tions, April 3, 1975.
    MAES:105
  Statement before the Indian
    sovereignty Conference of
    American Indians, Harvard,
    February 22, 1975.
    MAES:22
  Statement of Chairman of Navajo
    Tribal Council, April 14,
    1975. MAES:243
  Statement of the implementation
    of P.L. 93-638 Indian Self-
    Determination and Education
    Assistance Act, Window
    Rock, Navajo Nation, April
    3, 1975. MAES:189

McDuffie, George
  Natural slavery of the Negro.
    ANN 6:191

McElwee, Robert
  A plea for universal education
    in the South. (Nashville,
    Tenn., Jan. 23, 1883).
    FON:477

McGechan, R. O.
  Legal arguments for adopting
    the Statute of Westminster,
    1944 (Victoria Univ.).
    MACS:284 sel.

McGill, Ralph E.
  Meaning of Lincoln today
    (centennial of Lincoln's
    speech at Cooper Institute).
    LINS:360

McGill, William J.
  The public challenge and the
    campus response.
    (Berkeley, July 15, 1971).
    BA 1971-72:182
  Requiem for Joe College.
    BA 1969-70:139
  Requiem for the countercul-
      ture: problems of a new stu-
      dent generation (Columbia
      Univ., May 14, 1975).
      HOR:66
  Science and the law (New York,
      Sept. 20, 1977). BA 1977-78:83
  Simple justice and existential vic-
      tims (Reno, Nev., Oct. 6,
      1978). BA 1978-79:23

McGovern, George
  Acceptance speech, Miami Beach,
      Florida, July 14, 1972.
      SIN:408
  American politics: a personal
      view. BA 1972-73:22
  Campaign speech, Washington,
      D.C., August 5, 1972.
      SIN:413
  Ignorance curtain vs. the open
      door. BA 1966-67:48

McGowan, Carl
  Eulogy on Adlai E. Stevenson.
      BA 1965-66:227

McGowan, Edward D.
  Stop the foes of Negro freedom.
      (Detroit, April 30, 1953).
      FON:860

McGraw, Harold W.
  Business's responsibility in an
      information society (Washing-
      ton, Oct. 17, 1977).
      BA 1977-78:121

MACHINE AGE See Machinery

MACHINERY
  Webster, D.
      Technical progress and prosper-
      ity. ANN 6:266

McIntyre, Thomas J.
  Keeping the Senate independent
      (Washington, March 1, 1978).
      BA 1977-78:44

Macios, Miguel Angel
  Model studies of structural design
      and construction should be con-
      ducted prior to the building of
      structure rather than on the
      site studies made after the
      completion of the project.
      BAS:193 (outline only)

Mack, Enoch
Fourth of July oration, 1838
(Dover, New Hampshire).
HAW:164

McKeag, Jana
Testimony of Jana McKeag,
Education Director, Na-
tional Congress of American
Indians, July 19, 1975.
MAES:249

McKeever, Porter
The United States and the
United Nations (Los Ange-
les, May 19, 1972).
BRYF:479

McKenna, J. and others (R. R.
Day)
United States v. United States
Steel Corporation et al:
opinion for the court and
dissenting opinion.
ANN 14:258

McKenzie, John
Land for Settlements Bill,
1894 (New Zealand House
of Representatives, July
20, 1894). MACS:205 sel.

McKinley, William
Alternatives in Cuba. Same
as his First annual mes-
sage
American patriotism (at dedi-
cation of Cuyahoga County
Soldiers' and Sailors'
monument in Cleveland).
BREWE 8:2899
At the Pan-American Exposi-
tion. ANN 12:428
First annual message.
ANN 12:161; STAT 2:1858
First inaugural address.
USINAU:169; USINAUG:169
Fourth annual message.
STAT 2:1971
Grant (at dedication of Grant
monument in New York
City). BREWE 8:2905
Last speech. Same as his
At the Pan-American Ex-
position
Reciprocal trade agreements.
Same as his At the Pan-
American Exposition

Second annual message.
STAT 2:1881
Second inaugural address.
USINAU:178; USINAUG:178
Third annual message.
STAT 2:1922
War message, April 11, 1898.
ANN 12:173

McKINLEY, WILLIAM
Lawson, J.
The remedy for anarchy.
FON:639
Roosevelt, T.
First annual message.
ANN 12:433; STAT 2:2014

McKinney, Stanley M.
Soils--our basic natural resources
--the key to man's survival.
BREWW:187

Mackintosh, Sir James
Canada and the autonomy of Brit-
ish colonies. BREWE 8:2909
In behalf of free speech: on the
trial of Jean Peltier accused
of libeling Napoleon Bonaparte.
BREWE 8:2919
Peltier and the French Revolution.
Same as his In behalf of free
speech: on the trial of Jean
Peltier accused of libeling
Napoleon Bonaparte

McKissick, Floyd B.
Speech at the National Conference
on Black Power, July 21,
1967. BOSC:127; FON:1065
The student and the ghetto. (Coe
College, Cedar Rapids, Iowa,
May, 1969). OE:216
Why the Negro must rebel. Same
as his Speech at the National
Conference on Black Power,
July 21, 1967

McLain, Harold O.
Presents David Seabury. LYI:98

McLaren, Moray See Sykes, C.,
jt. auth.

Macleod, John James Richard
The physiology of insulin and its
source in the animal body
(Nobel Lecture for 1923, May
26, 1925). NOLM 2:71

MACLEOD, JOHN JAMES
    RICHARD
  Sjöquist, J.
    Presentation [of the Nobel
    Prize for Physiology or
    Medicine for 1923 to Fred-
    erick Grant Banting and John
    James Richard Macleod,
    1925]. NOLM 2:45

McMillan, Edwin Mattison
  The transuranium elements:
    early history (Nobel Lec-
    ture, Dec. 12, 1951).
    NOLC 3:314

McMILLAN, EDWIN MATTISON
  Westgren, A.
    Presentation [of the Nobel
    Prize for Chemistry to Ed-
    win Mattison McMillan and
    Glenn Theodore Seaborg,
    Dec. 12, 1951].
    NOLC 3:309

Macmillan, Harold
  Tribute to President Kennedy.
    ALA:135
  "The wind of change." (Cape
    Town, Feb. 3, 1960).
    MCB:75

McNally, Joseph
  "Terrible beauty is born"
    (golden jubilee of St.
    Joseph's Novitiate and silver
    jubilee of Rev. Brother
    Michael in Penang).
    MONS:334

McNAMARA, JOHN JOSEPH
  Darrow, C.
    To the jury; self-defense.
    GRG:31

McNamara, Robert S.
  Address before the American
    Society of Newspaper
    Editors. BA 1966-67:160
  Military hardware, economic
    assistance, and civic ac-
    tion. ANN 18:356
  Nuclear strategy. ANN 18:527
  Searching for new solutions to
    poverty (Boston, Jan. 14,
    1977). BA 1976-77:91

McNARY-HAUGEN BILL
  Coolidge, C.

Vetoing the farmer: nonplanning
  as a way of life. ANN 14:568

MACROMOLECULES
  Natta, G.
    From the stereospecific poly-
    merization to the asymmetric
    autocatalytic synthesis of macro-
    molecules. NOLC 4:27
  Staudinger, H.
    Macromolecular chemistry.
    NOLC 3:397

McWhirter, A. J.
  Appeal to European immigrants to
    come to the South.
    ANN 10:587

Madison, James
  Agriculture and conservation.
    ANN 4:503
  Bill of Rights proposed.
    ANN 3:354
  Civil and religious functions of
    government. ANN 4:287
  Eighth annual message.
    STAT 1:140
  Fifth annual message.
    STAT 1:122
  First annual message.
    STAT 1:102
  First inaugural address.
    USINAU:23; USINAUG:23
  Fourth annual message.
    STAT 1:115
  On the commerce clause.
    ANN 4:462
  Second annual message.
    STAT 1:105
  Second inaugural address.
    USINAU:26; USINAUG:26
  Seventh annual message.
    STAT 1:133
  Sixth annual message.
    STAT 1:129
  State sovereignty and federal
    supremacy (Richmond, Va.,
    June 6, 1788).
    BREWE 8:2926; HURH:40
  Third annual message.
    STAT 1:111
  War message. ANN 4:314
  "Would it be possible for govern-
    ment to have credit, without
    having the power of raising
    money?" Same as His State
    sovereignty and federal suprem-
    acy

---- See also Laurance, J., jt.
   auth.

Madrid, Steve
   I am proud to be a part of it.
   BREWW:153

Maestas, John R.
   The subtle use of humor by
   the great Indian chief Osceola. MAES:307
   With a touch of the master's
   hand. MAES:130

MAETERLINCK, MAURICE
   Wauters, C. C. M. A.
      Acceptance [of the Nobel
      Prize for Literature for
      Maurice Maeterlinck, 1911].
      NOL:114
   Wirsén, C. D. af
      Presentation [of the Nobel
      Prize for Literature to
      Maurice Polydore Marie
      Bernhard Maeterlinck,
      1911]. NOB 12:139;
      NOL:107

MAGNESIUM
   Grignard, V.
      The use of organomagnesium
      compounds in preparative
      organic chemistry.
      NOLC 1:234

MAGNETISM
   Néel, L.
      Magnetism and the local
      molecular field.
      NOLPH 4:318

MALACAÑAN
   Quirino, E.
      Commemorating a national
      event. CURM:239

MALARIA
   Ross, Sir R.
      Researches on malaria.
      NOLM 1:25

MALAYA
   Muhammad Ghazali bin Shafie
      Loyalty to the nation
      (Malaya). MONS:218
   Sambanthan, V. T.
      Basic objectives of M.I.C.
      (Malayan Indian Congress).
      MONS:135

MALAYA, FEDERATION OF
   Muhammad Ghazali bin Shafie
      Independent Malaya--our rights
      and obligations. MONS:211

MALAYAN LANGUAGE
   Abdul Rahman, T.
      Basis of our unity. MONS:41
      English language must continue.
      MONS:7

MALAYSIA
   Abdul Rahman, T.
      Big challenges ahead.
      MONS:25
      Concept of Malaysia becomes a
      reality. MONS:12
      Fight for Merdeka. MONS:1
      Soul of our nation. MONS:36
   Goh Keng Swee
      Some delusions of the decade
      of development. MONS:385
   Johari, M. K.
      A national chamber needed.
      MONSA:103
   Lee, H. H. S.
      Great institution (Central Bank
      of Malaya). MONS:164
   Lim, P. G.
      Women's role in national de-
      velopment. MONS:339
   Manickavasagam, V.
      Era of opportunity. MONS:162
   Muhammad Ghazali bin Shafie
      Malaysia and the Asian per-
      spective. MONS:222
      Power politics and nation build-
      ing (Malaysia). MONS:232
   Rahman, Dr. I. bin A.
      Unexpected ally after inde-
      pendence. MONS:99
   Razak, T. A.
      Alliance policy for unity.
      MONS:47
      Democracy and development in
      Malaysia. MONS:80
      Putting life into development
      plans. MONS:86
      UMNO's twentieth milestone
      (20th anniversary of United
      Malay National Organization).
      MONS:53
      Vital issues must be resolved
      if we are to survive.
      MONSA:1
   Senu bin Abdul Rahman
      Let our voice be heard (New
      Year message). MONS:160

A call to UMNO leaders:
time for slogan chanting is
over. MONSA:20
The significance of Five-
Power Defence Agreement.
MONSA:29
We will uphold concepts of
parliamentary democracy.
MONSA:41 selections
Tan Chee Khoon
Monstrous piece of legislation
(Internal Security Act--
Malaysia). MONS:190

---- RELIGION
Tuan Haji Ali bin Munawar
Religion in Malay society.
MONS:308

MALAYSIAN CHINESE ASSOCIA-
TION
Tan Siew Sin
Malays and Chinese must
co-exist. MONSA:85
The role of M.C.A. and the
loyalty of Malaysian Chinese.
MONSA:78

MALCOLM X See Little, Malcolm

Malcolm, George A.
Judge Andres Borromeo did
his duty! CURM:183

Malone, George W. and others
(F. A. Seaton)
Statehood for Hawaii.
ANN 17:522

Malott, Deane W.
Responds to introduction.
PRS:117

MAN
Aelred, Saint
On manliness. BREWE 1:113
Burton, S.
You (male) should wear long
hair. BAS:200 (outline only)
Channing, W. E.
Man above the state.
BREWE 5:1032
Hughes, T.
Highest manhood.
BREWE 7:2539
Welcome to husbands at Ladies
Civic Club. HNWM:45

MANAGEMENT See Business

MANCHESTER, WILLIAM
Crooks, J.
Defense of "The death of a
President." REIR:182

Mandela, Nelson Rolihlahla
Indictment of South Africa.
EMP:94

Manickavasagam, V.
Era of opportunity. MONS:162
ILO represents the social con-
science of the world (Geneva,
June, 1970). MONSA:106
selections

Manley, Albert E.
Charge to the graduates (Spelman
College, May 18, 1975).
HOR:6

Mann, Horace
The necessity of education in a
Republican government. (ca.
1838). HOW:148
Slavery in the territories.
ANN 8:7

Mann, Thomas
Acceptance [of the Nobel Prize
for Literature, 1929].
NOB 12:225; NOL:263

MANN, THOMAS
Böök, F.
Presentation [of the Nobel Prize
for Literature to Thomas
Mann, 1929]. NOB 12:221;
NOL:260

Manning, Henry Edward, Cardinal
Rome the eternal.
BREWE 8:2934

Mannix, Daniel
Case against conscription.
MCA:134

Mansfield, Michael J.
Assessment in Vietnam.
BA 1967-68:49
Eulogy for John F. Kennedy.
ANN 18:202
Pacific perspective.
BA 1968-69:98

Mansfield, William Murray, 1st
Earl of
In the case of John Wilkes.
BREWE 8:2943
In the case of the Dean of
St. Asaph. BREWE 8:2945
Reply to the Earl of Chatham
against Parliamentary ex-
emption from arrest for
debt. BREWE 8:2947

MANUFACTURERS AND MANU-
FACTURING
Clay, H.
Manufacturing and a protec-
tive tariff. ANN 4:612
Coxe, T.
Prospects for American
manufacturing. ANN 3:196
Hamilton, A.
Report on manufactures.
BOORA 1:178

MAORIS
Tirikatene, E.
Maiden speech in Parliament.
MACS:179

MARA INSTITUTE OF TECHNOL-
OGY
Suffian bin Hashim
Only Malays can initiate
the institutional changes.
MONSA:140

Marbury, William L.
Of movers and immobilists.
BA 1965-66:77

MARCH ON WASHINGTON
MOVEMENT
Randolph, A. P.
A call for mass action.
FON:822

Marconi, Guglielmo
Wireless telegraphic com-
munication (Nobel Lecture,
Dec. 11, 1909).
NOLPH 1:196

MARCONI, GUGLIELMO
Hildebrand, H.
Presentation [of the Nobel
Prize for Physics to Gug-
lielmo Marconi and Carl
Ferdinand Braun, Dec. 11,
1909]. NOLPH 1:193

Marcus, Stanley
Can free enterprise survive suc-
cess? (Omaha, Nov. 18, 1975).
BA 1975-76:152

MARIE ANTOINETTE, CONSORT OF
LOUIS XVI, KING OF FRANCE
Burke, E.
Age of chivalry.
BREWE 2:817

MARRIAGE
Coleridge, J. D. C.
Sacredness of matrimony.
BREWE 4:1355
Marriage ceremony. BNH:69

Marshall, Arthur
I first saw the light of day.
MDYG:231

Marshall, David Saul
Duty of citizens. MONS:448
Fundamental and minority rights.
MONS:450
History of Singapore's struggle for
nationhood, 1945-1959 (Singa-
pore, July 12, 1969).
MONSA:313
What is academic freedom?
MONS:453
Why abolish the jury trial?
Warnings of danger ahead
(Singapore, Dec. 16, 1969).
MONSA:324

Marshall, George C.
Address at Harvard University
(June 5, 1947). ANN 16:438;
BOORA 2:884; GRG:82;
HURH:283
Essentials of peace (Nobel Lec-
ture, Dec. 11, 1953).
NOLP 3:76
Marshall Plan. Same as his Ad-
dress at Harvard University
"Our policy is directed not
against any country or doctrine
but against hunger, poverty,
desperation and chaos." Same
as his Address at Harvard
University

MARSHALL, GEORGE C.
Hambro, C. J.
Presentation of the Nobel Prize
for Peace to George Catlett
Marshall, Dec. 10, 1953.

NOLP 3:65
Truman, H. S.
Presents George C. Marshall.
LYI:41

Marshall, J. R.
NAFTA, 1965 (New Zealand
House of Representatives,
Aug. 17, 1965). MACS:448
sel.

Marshall, John
Address on constitutionality of
Alien and Sedition Laws.
(Dec., 1798). FRIP:99
Cherokee Nation v. State of
Georgia: opinion for the
Supreme Court. ANN 5:427
Cohens v. Virginia, 1821:
opinion for the Supreme
Court. ANN 5:1
Dartmouth College v. Wood-
ward. Same as his Trustees
of Dartmouth College v.
Woodward: opinion for the
Supreme Court
Gibbons v. Ogden, 1824:
opinion for the Supreme
Court. ANN 5:128
Justice and the Federal Con-
stitution (Virginia Convention
on Ratification of the Consti-
tution, June 10, 1788).
BREWE 8:2950; FRIP:76
McCulloch v. Maryland: opinion
for the Supreme Court.
ANN 4:530; BOORA 1:241
Marbury v. Madison: opinion
for the Supreme Court.
ANN 4:165
Opposing Patrick Henry. Same
as his Justice and the Federal Constitution
Speech in Virginia Convention
on Ratification of the Consti-
tution, June 10, 1788.
Same as his Justice and
the Federal Constitution
Speech in Virginia Convention
on Ratification of the Constitution, June 20, 1788.
FRIP:90
Trustees of Dartmouth College
v. Woodward: opinion for
the Supreme Court.
ANN 4:522

MARSHALL, JOHN
Frankfurter, F.

John Marshall and the judicial
function, September 22, 1955.
FRIP:353
Holmes, O. W., Jr.
John Marshall. FRIP:257
Vander Jagt, G.
John Marshall. SCHW:201

MARSHALL, NORMAN S.
Langlie, A. B.
Presents Norman S. Marshall.
LYI:155

Marshall, Thomas R.
National power and the American
peace policy (on public land
sales, 1841). BREWE 8:2964

Marshall, Thurgood
In praise of the sit-in strikes.
(Charlotte, N.C., March 20,
1960). FON:930
The legal attack to secure civil
rights. (NAACP Wartime Conf.,
July 13, 1944). OE:123
Segregation and desegregation.
(New Orleans-Dillard Univ.,
Spring, 1954). FON:866

MARSHALL ISLANDS
Anjain, J.
Speech before the Senate Com-
mittee on Energy and Natural
Resources, June 16, 1977.
JAM:12

MARSHALL PLAN See Reconstruction, 1939-1951

Martin, Alfonso
Responds to an introduction.
PRS:139

Martin, Archer John Porter
The development of partition
chromatography (Nobel Lecture, Dec. 12, 1952).
NOLC 3:359

MARTIN, ARCHER JOHN PORTER
Tiselius, A. W. K.
Presentation [of the Nobel Prize
for Chemistry to Archer John
Porter Martin and Richard
Laurence Millington Synge,
Dec. 12, 1952]. NOLC 3:355

Martin, Charles
Presents McGeorge Bundy. LYI:88

Martin, David
  Trouble in the university.
    MDYG:121

Martin, Douglas
  A case for optimism. EHN:124;
    MOP:154; MOPR:130

Martin, Joseph W.
  Introducing Speaker Sam Ray-
    burn. LYI:195

Martin, Luther
  Is the government federal or
    national? BREWE 8:2970
  People versus the states.
    Same as his Portion of the
    report of the proceedings of
    the General Convention held
    at Philadelphia in 1787
  Portion of the report of the
    proceedings of the General
    Convention held at Philadel-
    phia in 1787. ANN 3:166

Martin, Thomas W.
  Presents Charles F. Kettering.
    LYI:181

Marvin, Richard
  Man's other society. MOP:377

MARX, GROUCHO
  Jessel, G.
    Presents Groucho Marx.
    LYI:32

Mason, George
  Natural propensity of rulers to
    oppress. BREWE 8:2976

---- and others (P. Henry and
    E. Pendelton)
  Debates in the Virginia Ratify-
    ing Convention. ANN 3:278

Mason, J. M.
  Speech of J. M. Mason, at
    Richmond, Va., June 8,
    1861. ECH:166

Mason, John, Jr.
  Oration delivered on the 4th
    of July, 1818 at Williams-
    burg, Virginia. HAW:300

Mason, William Clarke
  Presents George Wharton
    Pepper. LYI:129

MASS MEDIA
  Gallup, G.
    Mass information or mass en-
      tertainment. ANN 17:215
  Goodman, J. B.
    Community and communications.
      MOP:381
  Hausman, L.
    Older Americans: a natural re-
      source. LINRST:36

---- See also Communication

MASS SPECTROMETRY
  Aston, F. W.
    Mass spectra and isotopes.
      NOLC 2:7

MASSACHUSETTS
  Hoar, G. F.
    Great men of Massachusetts.
      BREWE 7:2516
  Kennedy, J. F.
    History will be our judge.
      LINS:371

---- SUPREME COURT
  Sumner, C.
    Segregation and the common
      school (Sarah C. Roberts v.
      City of Boston case, 1849).
      ANN 7:507

Massey, William Ferguson
  Freehold tenure (New Zealand
    House of Representatives, Nov.
    16, 1909). MACS:216 sel.
  The Meat Board, 1922 (Wellington,
    Jan. 10, 1922). MACS:301

---- and others (H. E. Holland)
  Repeal of income tax on farmers,
    1923 (New Zealand House of
    Representatives, Aug. 14, 1923).
    MACS:304

Massillon, Jean Baptiste
  Curse of a malignant tongue.
    BREWE 8:2980

MATHEMATICS
  Eliezer, C. J.
    Mathematics the queen of the
      arts. MONS:265

Mather, Cotton
  At the sound of the trumpet.
    BREWE 8:2986

"Bostonian Evenezer."
POC:395

Mather, Increase
Discourse concerning the un-
certainty of the times of
men. POC:377
Speech at the Boston Town
Meeting. POC:172

Mathias, Charles M.
The First Amendment: free-
dom and responsibility
(Bloomington, Minn., Oct.
26, 1977). BA 1977-78:134
Privacy on the ropes (Univ. of
Minnesota, Oct. 20, 1978).
BA 1978-79:70
Truth in government. (Wash-
ington, D.C., April 17,
1973). BA 1972-73:60

Mathias, Tim
Is agriculture on its way out?
BREWW:64

MATTER
Perrin, J. B.
Discontinuous structure of
matter. NOLPH 2:138

MATTER, KINETIC THEORY OF
Hinshelwood, Sir C. N.
Chemical kinetics in the
past few decades.
NOLC 3:474

Mauriac, François
Acceptance [of the Nobel Prize
for Literature, 1952].
NOB 13:7; NOL:481

MAURIAC, FRANÇOIS
Österling, A.
Presentation [of the Nobel
Prize for Literature to
François Mauriac, 1952].
NOB 13:3; NOL:477

Maxton, James See Baldwin,
S. B., jt. auth.

May, Catherine
The American farmer.
(American Agricultural
Editors Association, June
23, 1970). LINRS:117

May, Derwent
Djakarta style. MDYG:168

May, Samuel J.
Enfranchisement of women.
ANN 7:342

Mayer, Maria Goeppert
The shell model (Nobel Lecture,
Dec. 12, 1963).
NOLPH 4:18

MAYER, MARIA GOEPPERT
Waller, I.
Presentation [of the Nobel Prize
for Physics to Eugene P. Wigner, Maria Goeppert Mayer and
J. Hans D. Jensen, Dec. 12,
1963]. NOLPH 4:3

Mayhew, Jonathan
Discourse on the anniversary of
the death of Charles I.
ANN 1:481; POC:508
On unlimited submission to rulers.
Same as his Discourse on the
anniversary of the death of
Charles I
Unlimited submission and non-re-
sistance to the Higher Powers.
Same as his Discourse on the
Anniversary of the death of
Charles I

Maynard, Horace See Butler, B.
F., jt. auth.

Mays, Benjamin E.
Eulogy on Dr. Martin Luther
King, Jr. (Morehouse College,
Atlanta, April 9, 1968).
BA 1967-68:161; BAAGB:399;
SMHV:296

MAYSVILLE ROAD BILL, 1830
Jackson, A.
Veto of Maysville Road Bill.
ANN 5:374

Mazzini, Giuseppe
To the young men of Italy.
BREWE 8:2992

Mead, Margaret
The planetary crisis and the chal-
lenge to scientists. (New
York, Dec. 6, 1973).
BA 1973-74:97

Meade, Edwin R.
  Chinese immigration to the
  United States. ANN 10:386

Meagher, Thomas Francis
  Withering influence of provincial
  subjection. BREWE 8:2999

Meany, George
  Responds to an introduction.
  PRS:156

MEAT INDUSTRY AND TRADE -
NEW ZEALAND
  Massey, W. F.
  The Meat Board, 1922.
  MACS:301 sel.

MEDALS See Presentation
  speeches - Medals

Medawar, Peter Brian
  Immunological tolerance (Nobel
  Lecture, Dec. 12, 1960).
  NOLM 3:704

MEDAWAR, PETER BRIAN
  Gard, S.
  Presentation [of the Nobel
  Prize for Physiology or
  Medicine to Sir Frank
  Macfarlane Burnet and Peter
  Brian Medawar, Dec. 12,
  1960]. NOLM 3:685

MEDICAL CARE
  Blue Spruce, G.
  Needed: Indian health pro-
  fessionals. MAES:171

MEDICINE
  Farber, S. M.
  Why national concern for
  bio-medical communication?
  BA 1966-67:118
  Watson, T. J., Jr.
  Medical care.
  BA 1970-71:115; BAPR:359;
  BAPRR:266

---- See also Mental health;
  Physicians

Meek, Alexander Beaufort
  Oration (Tuscaloosa, July 4,
  1833). HAW:307

Melanchthon, Philip
  Safety of the virtuous.
  BREWE 8:3007

Meloney, Mrs. William Brown
  Introducing Dorothy Thompson.
  LYI:112
  Presents Dorothy Thompson.
  Same as her Introducing Dorothy
  Thompson

MEMBERSHIP DRIVES See Club
  speeches

MEMORIAL DAY
  Coolidge, C.
  Destiny of America. ANN 14:409

MEMORIAL SPEECHES
  Franklin, J. H.
  Martin Luther King and Ameri-
  can traditions. BA 1968-69:45
  Gallagher, B. G.
  Memorial convocation address
  (On Martin Luther King, Jr.).
  BA 1967-68:169
  Hugo, V. M.
  On the centennial of Voltaire's
  death. BREWE 7:2550
  Mather, I.
  Discourse concerning the uncer-
  tainty of the times of men.
  POC:377
  Palmerston, H. J. T.
  On the death of Cobden.
  BREWE 8:3131
  Stevenson, A. E.
  Address at the memorial service
  for Sir Winston Churchill.
  LINR:305; LINRS:307;
  LINRST:373
  Thatcher, P.
  Boston Massacre oration, March
  5, 1776. POC:272

---- See also Commemorative addresses; Eulogies; Tributes

Menefee, Richard Hickman, 1809-1841
  Speech (House of Representatives,
  Jan. 8, 1838). BLY:84

Menninger, Karl
  Healthier than healthy. LINR:54

Menninger, William C.
  Responds to an introduction.
  PRS:135

MENTAL DEFICIENCY
Weisensel, K.
David: and a whole lot of
other neat people.
LINRST:71

MENTAL HEALTH
Menninger, K.
Healthier than healthy.
LINR:54

Menzies, Robert Gordon
Eulogy of Churchill.   MCA:151
Greece and the Anzac spirit.
MCA:138
On the nationalisation of the
Suez Canal.   MCA:144

MERCY
Bede
Meeting of mercy and justice.
BREWE 1:340
Wycliffe, J.
Mercy to damned men in
Hell.   BREWE 10:3922

Merriam, John Campbell
Presents Ray Lyman Wilbur.
LYI:82

MESONS
Yukawa, H.
Meson theory in its develop-
ments.   NOLPH 3:128

Metchnikoff, Elie
On the present state of the
question of immunity in
infectious diseases (Nobel
Lecture, Dec. 11, 1908).
NOLM 1:281

METCHNIKOFF, ELIE
Mörner, K. A. H.
Presentation [of the Nobel
Prize for Physiology or
Medicine to Elie Metchnikoff
and Paul Ehrlich, Dec. 11,
1908].   NOLM 1:277

MEXICANS IN THE UNITED
STATES
Ponce, F. V.
La causa.   LINRS:66;
LINRST:68
Rodriguez, A. M.
This is our quest: to fight
for the right.
BA 1968-69:129

MEXICO
Diaz, P.
Mexican progress.
BREWE 5:1832

Meyer, Steve
What leadership means to me.
BREWW:171

Meyerhof, Otto Fritz
Energy conversions in muscle
(Nobel Lecture for 1922, Dec.
12, 1923).   NOLM 2:27

MEYERHOF, OTTO FRITZ
Johansson, J. E.
Presentation [of the Nobel Prize
for Physiology or Medicine for
1922 to Archibald Vivian Hill
and Otto Fritz Meyerhof, Dec.
12, 1923].   NOLM 2:3

Meyerson, Martin
The ivory tower of Babel (Annapo-
lis, October 16, 1971).
HOR:99

Michelson, Albert Abraham
Recent advances in spectroscopy
(Nobel Lecture, Dec. 12, 1907).
NOLPH 1:166

MICHELSON, ALBERT ABRAHAM
Hasselberg, K. B.
Presentation [of the Nobel Prize
for Physics to Albert Abraham
Michelson, Dec. 12, 1907].
NOLPH 1:159

Middendorf, J. William
World sea power: United States
vs. USSR. (San Francisco,
Dec. 3, 1974).   LINRST:234

MIGRATION, INTERNAL
DuBois, W. E. B.
The great migration north.
FON:721
Greener, R. T.
Emigration of colored citizens
from the southern states.
FON:466

Milburn, John G.
Presents James R. Day.   LYI:90

MILES, NELSON A.
Depew, C. M.

Military spirit in America.
BREWE 5:1785

Milgrom, Jacob
He cannot be replaced.
WALE:132

MILITARY ACADEMY
Washington, G.
Eighth annual message.
ANN 3:604; STAT 1:31

---- See also West Point

MILITARY COMMISSIONS, AC-
CEPTANCE OF See
Acceptance speeches -
Military commissions

MILITARY SERVICE, COMPUL-
SORY See Conscription

MILITARY TRAINING See
United States - Army

Mill, John Stuart
Representation of the people.
(H. of Commons, April 13,
1866). MCB:154
A tribute to William Lloyd
Garrison. REID:395
selections

Miller, George F.
They are all heroes. (Brook-
lyn, May 14, 1918).
FON:719

Miller, Hugh
Pledge science gives to hope.
BREWE 8:3013

Miller, Joyce
Why ice floats. MOP:20;
MOPR:59

Miller, Kelly
The Brownsville affair. (Amer-
ican Negro Academy, 1907).
FON:654

Miller, Samuel F. and others
(S. J. Field)
Slaughter house cases, 1875:
opinion for the court and
dissenting opinion.
ANN 10:302

Miller, Thomas E.
A plea against the disfranchisement
of the Negro. (South Carolina,
Oct. 26, 1895). FON:582

Millikan, Robert Andrews
The electron and the light-quant
from the experimental point of
view (Nobel Lecture for 1923,
May 23, 1924). NOLPH 2:54

MILLIKAN, ROBERT ANDREWS
Gullstrand, A.
Presentation [of the Nobel Prize
for Physics for 1923 to Robert
Andrews Millikan, May 23,
1924]. NOLPH 2:51

Mills, Billy
New Indian, new commitment,
February, 1974. MAES:402

Milton, John
For the liberty of unlicensed printing. BREWE 8:3017

MIND See Intellect; Thought and
thinking

Minda, Albert G.
He died climbing. WALE:134
Vision that looks beyond.
WALE:137

MINDANAO
Alunan, R. R.
Mindanao, the land of promise.
CURM:108

MINES AND MINERAL RESOURCES -
PHILIPPINE ISLANDS
Uewaki, T.
Discovery of hidden mineral
veins with the aid of plants and
animals, etc. CURM:292

MINISTERIAL RESPONSIBILITY -
NEW ZEALAND
Wakefield, E. G.
The demand for responsible
government. MACS:86 sel.

MINISTERS See Religion

Mink, Patsy Takemoto
Seeking a link with the past.
(Los Angeles, Nov. 6, 1971).
BA 1971-72:59

Minot, George Richards
  The development of liver therapy
    in pernicious anemia (Nobel
    Lecture, Dec. 12, 1934).
    NOLM 2:357

MINOT, GEORGE RICHARDS
  Holmgren, I.
    Presentation [of the Nobel
    Prize for Physiology or
    Medicine to George Hoyt
    Whipple, George Richards
    Minot, and William Parry
    Murphy, Dec. 12, 1934].
    NOLM 2:335

Minow, Newton N.
  Television: the vast wasteland.
    Same as his Television and
    the public interest
  Television and the public in-
    terest. ANN 18:12;
    MDV:248
  Vast wasteland. Same as his
    Television and the public
    interest

Mirabeau, Honoré Gabriel Riqueti,
    Comte de
  Against the charge of treason.
    BREWE 8:3039
  Against the establishment of
    religion. BREWE 8:3034
  Announcing the death of Frank-
    lin. BREWE 8:3035
  Defying the French aristocracy.
    BREWE 8:3033
  His defense of himself. Same
    as his Against the charge
    of treason
  Justifying revolution.
    BREWE 8:3038
  On Necker's project--"And yet
    you deliberate."
    BREWE 8:3024
  Reason immutable and sovereign.
    BREWE 8:3036

MIRACLES
  Lacordaire, J. B. H.
    Rationalism and miracles.
    BREWE 7:2695

MISSIONS AND MISSIONARIES
  Girls' auxiliary (or similar
    girls' missionary group).
    HNWN:24
  Introductions for mission

society leaders (4 examples).
    BNH:35
McNally, J.
  "Terrible beauty is born" (golden
    jubilee of St. Joseph's Novitiate
    and silver jubilee of Rev.
    Brother Michael in Penang).
    MONS:334
Red Jacket
  Missionary effort. ANN 4:194;
    BREWE 7:2571; HURH:57
Welcome to missionary appointees
    (3 examples). HNWM:57
Welcome to parents and ladies of
    the Woman's Missionary Society
    on Education Day. HNWM:21
Welcome to returning missionary
    (3 examples). HNWM:55
Welcome to Royal Ambassadors
    (or similar Boys' Missionary
    group). HNWM:23

MISSOURI COMPROMISE See
  Slavery in the United States

MISTRAL, FREDERIC
  Wirsén, C. D. af
    Presentation [of the Nobel Prize
    for Literature to Frédéric Mis-
    tral and José de Echegaray
    y Eizaguirre, 1904]. HOL:23;
    NOB 13:119

Mistral, Gabriela
  Acceptance [of the Nobel Prize
    for Literature, 1945].
    NOB 14:170; NOL:408

MISTRAL, GABRIELA
  Gullberg, H.
    Presentation [of the Nobel Prize
    for Literature to Gabriela Mis-
    tral, 1945]. NOB 14:167;
    NOL:405

Mitchell, Don G.
  Responds to an introduction.
    PRS:148

Mitchell, James P.
  Responds to an introduction.
    PRS:143

Mitford, Nancy See Sykes, C., jt.
    auth.

Moe, Ragnvald
  Presentation [of the Nobel Prize

for Peace to Elihu Root,
1912, Dec. 10, 1913].
NOLP 1:245
Presentation [of the Nobel Prize
for Peace to Henri Marie
La Fontaine, Dec. 10,
1913]. NOLP 1:269
Presentation [of the Nobel Prize
for Peace to the International
Committee of the Red
Cross, Dec. 10, 1917].
NOLP 1:281

Mohamed Khir Johari See
Johari, Mohammed Khir

MOISSAN, HENRI
Klason, P.
Presentation [of the Nobel
Prize for Chemistry to Henri
Moissan, 1906]. NOLC 1:91

MOLECULAR BEAMS
Stern, O.
The method of molecular
rays. NOLPH 3:8

MOLECULES
Debye, P. J. W.
Methods to determine the
electrical and geometrical
structure of molecules.
NOLC 2:383
Hodgkin, D. C.
The x-ray analysis of com-
plicated molecules.
NOLC 4:71

Momaday, N. Scott
Oral tradition of the American
Indian (Brigham Young Uni-
versity, 1975). MAES:294

MOMMSEN, CHRISTIAN MATTHIAS
THEODOR
Wirsén, C. D. af
Presentation [of the Nobel
Prize for Literature to
Christian Matthias Theodor
Mommsen, 1902]. NOL:7;
NOB 13:235

MONARCHY
Elizabeth I
Queen and the royal suc-
cession. BRYH:69
Sheridan, R. B.
Example of kings.
BREWE 9:3440

Mondale, Walter F.
Strengthening Sino-American relations (Peking University, August
27, 1979). BA 1979-80:28
A time to celebrate life (Washington, Jan. 15, 1978).
BA 1977-78:205

Moneta, Ernesto Teodoro
Peace and law in the Italian tradi-
tion (Nobel Lecture, 1907,
Aug. 25, 1909). NOLP 1:114

MONETA, ERNESTO TEODORO
Løvland, J. G.
Presentation [of the Nobel Prize
for Peace to Ernesto Teodoro
Moneta, Dec. 10, 1907].
NOLP 1:113

MONETARY POLICY - SINGAPORE
Goh Keng Swee
How Singapore's monetary sys-
tem now works. MONSA:282

MONEY
Church, F.
The yen to make a mark with
the dollar. BA 1978-79:168
Crawford, W. H.
Issue and control of money un-
der the Constitution.
BREWE 4:1462
Morgenthau, H., Jr.
Roosevelt monetary program.
BAD:23
Peel, R.
Bank charter--the currency.
STRM:213
Ruskin, J.
Iscariot in modern England.
BREWE 9:3354
Wesley, J.
Use of money. BRYH:191

---- See also Banks and banking;
Credit; Silver; Wealth

MONIZ, EGAS
Olivecrona, H.
Presentation [of the Nobel Prize
for Physiology or Medicine to
Walter Rudolf Hess and Antonio
Caetano De Abreu Freire Egas
Moniz, Dec. 12, 1949].
NOLM 3:243

MONKEYS
Reynolds, V.

Chimpanzee worlds.
MDYG:259

Monod, Jacques
From enzymatic adaptation to
allosteric transitions
(Nobel Lecture, Dec. 11,
1965). NOLM 4:188

MONOD, JACQUES
Gard, S.
Presentation [of the Nobel
Prize for Physiology or
Medicine to François Jacob,
André Lwoff, and Jacques
Monod, Dec. 11, 1965].
NOLM 4:143

MONOPOLIES
Colepeper, J.
Against monopolies.
BREWE 4:1494
Fuller, M. W. and others
United States v. E. C.
Knight Company, 1895;
opinion for the Supreme
Court and dissenting opinion.
ANN 12:23
Marshall, J.
Gibbons v. Ogden, 1824:
opinion for the Supreme
Court. ANN 5:128
Wilson, W.
Fear of monopoly.
ANN 13:356

Monroe, James
Eighth annual message.
STAT 1:214
Federal experiments in history.
BREWE 8:3041
Fifth annual message.
STAT 1:181
First annual message.
STAT 1:148
First inaugural address.
USINAU:29; USINAUG:29
Fourth annual message.
STAT 1:174
Monroe doctrine (Washington,
Dec. 2, 1823). ANN 5:73;
BOORA 1:256; HURH:59;
STAT 1:202
Second annual message.
STAT 1:156
Second inaugural address.
USINAU:37; USINAUG:37
Seventh annual message.
Same as his Monroe Doctrine

Sixth annual message.
STAT 1:192
Third annual message.
STAT 1:165
"... we should consider any attempt
on their part to extend their
system to any portion of this
hemisphere, as dangerous to
our peace and safety." Same
as his Monroe Doctrine

MONROE DOCTRINE
Monroe, J.
Monroe doctrine. ANN 5:73;
BOORA 1:256; HURH:59;
STAT 1:202
Polk, J. K.
First annual message.
ANN 7:301; STAT 1:634
Roosevelt, T.
Annual message, December 6,
1904. STAT 2:2105
Fifth annual message.
ANN 13:1; STAT 3:2144
Smith, G.
Liberty destroyed by national
pride (Mexican Treaty and
Monroe Doctrine).
BREWE 9:3459

Montalembert, Charles Forbes Rene
de Tryon, Comte de
Deo et Caesari fidelis.
BREWE 8:3050
Devotion to freedom.
BREWE 8:3048
For freedom of education.
BREWE 8:3046

Montelius, O.
Presentation [of the Nobel Prize
for Chemistry to Otto Wallach,
Dec. 12, 1910]. NOLC 1:175
Presentation [of the Nobel Prize
for Physics to Johannes Diderik
Van der Waals, Dec. 12, 1910].
NOLPH 1:251

Montgomery, James
Modern English literature.
BREWE 8:3052

MONTGOMERY DECLARATION OF
1861
King, T. S.
The two declarations of inde-
pendence: 1776 and 1861.
HAW:260

MONUMENTS See Dedication
   addresses - Monuments

Moody, Dwight Lyman
   On Daniel and the value of
      character. BREWE 8:3057

Moore, Ely
   Trade unions and the "me-
      chanic" arts. ANN 6:17

MOORE, HENRY
   Haydon, H.
      Testimony of sculpture.
      MOP:384; MOPR:380

Moore, Paul
   A biblical faith for a president
      (New York, Nov. 21, 1976).
      BA 1976-77:24

Moore, Sydenham
   A Southern response to John
      Brown and black republican-
      ism (1859). (Washington,
      Dec. 8, 1859). DAVF:146

Moorehead, J. R.
   Plight of small business.
      ANN 13:322

Moos, Malcolm
   Darkness over the Ivory Tower.
      BA 1968-69:55
   Restoring the tidemarks of
      trust. (South Bend, Ind.,
      May 20, 1973).
      BA 1973-74:148

MORAL RE-ARMAMENT
   Abdul Rahman, T.
      These truths to remember.
      MONSA:68

MORALS See Behavior; Ethics;
   Vietnamese War, 1957--
   Moral and religious aspects;
   War and morals

More, Sir Thomas
   Speech when on trial for life.
      BREWE 8:3062

MORE, SIR THOMAS
   Kenny, A.
      Self out of season.
      MDYG:199

Morelli, Laurie
   Vocational agriculture, the FFA,
      and our free enterprise system.
      BREWW:78

Morgan, Charles, Jr.
   Time to speak. KEO:308
   Who's to blame in Birmingham?
      Same as his Time to speak

Morgan, Edmund S.
   What every Yale freshman should
      know. ARS:35

Morgan, Mike
   Building a better rural community
      today for a better agriculture
      tomorrow. BREWW:198

Morgan, Thomas Hunt
   The relation of genetics to physiol-
      ogy and medicine (Nobel Lec-
      ture for 1933, June 4, 1934).
      NOLM 2:313

MORGAN, THOMAS HUNT
   Henschen, F.
      Presentation [of the Nobel Prize
      for Physiology or Medicine for
      1933 to Thomas Hunt Morgan,
      June 4, 1934]. NOLM 2:307

Morgenthau, Henry, Jr.
   Roosevelt monetary program.
      BAD:23

MORLEY, CHRISTOPHER
   Ford, G. S.
      Presents Christopher Morley.
      LYI:55

Morley of Blackburn, John Morley,
      1st Viscount
   Golden art of truth-telling.
      BREWE 8:3068

---- See also Curzon of Kedleston,
      George, jt. auth.

Mörner, K. A. H.
   Presentation [of the Nobel Prize
      for Chemistry to Eduard Buch-
      ner, Dec. 11, 1907].
      NOLC 1:99
   Presentation [of the Nobel Prize
      for Physiology or Medicine to
      Albrecht Kossel, Dec. 12,
      1910]. NOLM 1:389

Presentation [of the Nobel Prize
for Physiology or Medicine
to Allvar Gullstrand, Dec.
11, 1911]. NOLM 1:411
Presentation [of the Nobel Prize
for Physiology or Medicine
to Camilio Golgi and Santiago
Rámon Y Cajal, Dec. 12,
1906]. NOLM 1:185
Presentation [of the Nobel Prize
for Physiology or Medicine
to Elie Metchnikoff and Paul
Ehrlich, Dec. 11, 1908].
NOLM 1:277
Presentation [of the Nobel Prize
for Physiology or Medicine
to Emil Adolf Von Behring,
Dec. 12, 1901]. NOLM 1:3
Presentation [of the Nobel Prize
for Physiology or Medicine
to Emil Theodor Kocher,
Dec. 11, 1909]. NOLM 1:327
Presentation [of the Nobel Prize
for Physiology or Medicine
to Ivan Petrovich Pavlov,
Dec. 12, 1904]. NOLM 1:135
Presentation [of the Nobel Prize
for Physiology or Medicine
to Niels Ryberg Finsen,
1903]. NOLM 1:123
Presentation [of the Nobel Prize
for Physiology or Medicine
to Robert Koch, Dec. 12,
1905]. NOLM 1:163
Presentation [of the Nobel Prize
for Physiology or Medicine
to Sir Ronald Ross, Dec.
12, 1902]. NOLM 1:21

Morris, Charles S.
The Wilmington massacre.
(Boston, Jan., 1899).
FON:604

Morris, Gouverneur
"I charge you to protect his
fame. It is all that he has
left." Same as his Oration
over Hamilton
Oration at the funeral of Alexander Hamilton. Same as
his Oration over Hamilton
Oration over Hamilton (New
York, July 14, 1804).
BREWE 8:3075; HURH:54

Morris, William
Art, wealth, and riches.
BRYH:422

Morrison, Howard C.
In the pursuit of excellence.
BREWW:61

Morse, David A.
ILO and the social infrastructure
of peace (Nobel Lecture, Dec.
11, 1969). NOLP 3:424

Morse, Doug
Lab farms in vocational agriculture. BREWW:144

Morse, Jedidiah
The present dangers and consequent duties of the citizens
(1799). (Charlestown, Mass.,
April 25, 1799). DAVF:45

Morse, Wayne L.
Need for a bipartisan foreign
policy. ANN 17:11
Rejoiner to Joseph Alsop's attack.
BRR:72
Verbiage of defense and attack.
BRR:71

Morton, Oliver Perry
Reasons for Negro suffrage.
BREWE 8:3079

Morton, Perez
Oration at the reinterment of
Warren. POC:320

Morton, Thurston B.
Responds to introduction.
PRS:98

Mosley, Lady See Sykes, C., jt.
auth.

Mossbauer, Rudolf Ludwig
Recoilless nuclear resonance ab-
sorption of gamma radiation
(Nobel Lecture, Dec. 11, 1961).
NOLPH 3:584

MOSSBAUER, RUDOLF LUDWIG
Waller, I.
Presentation [of the Nobel Prize
for Physics to Robert Hofstadter
and Rudolf Ludwig Mossbauer,
Dec. 11, 1961]. NOLPH 3:555

Mote, Carl H.
The ruling oligarchy wants to
engage in a foreign war (1941).
(Washington, 1941). DAVF:255

MOTHERS
  Introductions for mothers-in-
    law (4 examples). BNH:34
  Jung, L.
    Mother's immortality.
    WALE:96
  Welcome to mothers on Chil-
    dren's Day. HNWM:7

MOTHERS AND DAUGHTERS
  Welcome to daughters at
    Mother-Daughter banquet.
    HNWM:36
  Welcome to mothers at Mother-
    Daughter banquet.
    HNWM:35

MOTHER'S DAY
  Holy motherhood (welcome ad-
    dress on Mother's Day).
    HNWM:8
  Love in search of a word
    (welcome address on
    Mother's Day). HNWM:6
  Pictures of mother (welcome
    address on Mother's Day).
    HNWM:7
  Welcome to mothers: Mother's
    Day, a day of remembrance.
    HNWM:5

MOTHER-IN-LAW See Mothers

Moton, Robert Russa
  Some elements necessary to
    race development. (Tuske-
    gee, May, 1912). FON:692

Mott, John Raleigh
  The leadership demanded in
    this momentous time (Nobel
    Lecture, Dec. 13, 1946).
    NOLP 2:362

MOTT, JOHN RALEIGH
  Ingebretsen, H. S.
    Presentation [of the Nobel
    Prize for Peace to John
    Raleigh Mott, Dec. 10,
    1946]. NOLP 2:354

Mount, Anson
  The Playboy philosophy--pro.
    (Atlanta, March 16-18,
    1970). LINRS:157;
    LINRST:181

MOVING PICTURES - CENSORSHIP
  Murrow, E. R. and others.

Movies and censorship.
  ARS:127

Mowinckel, Johan Ludwig
  Presentation [of the Nobel Prize
    for Peace to Arthur Henderson,
    Dec. 10, 1934]. NOLP 2:179
  Presentation [of the Nobel Prize
    for Peace to Frank Billings
    Kellogg, 1929, Dec. 10, 1930].
    NOPL 2:73
  Presentation [of the Nobel Prize
    for Peace to Nathan Söderblom,
    Dec. 11, 1930]. NOLP 2:73

Moynihan, Daniel
  The middle of the journey. (White
    House, Dec. 21, 1970).
    BA 1970-71:29
  World wide amnesty for political
    prisoners (New York, Nov.
    12, 1975). BA 1975-76:65

---- See also Hayakawa, S. I., jt.
  auth.

Muench, Alosius
  Rural families and welfare.
    ANN 15:462

Muhammad, Elijah
  We must have justice. (June 21,
    1963). FON:969

Muhammad Ghazali bin Shafie
  Elements of Malaysian foreign
    policy (March 23, 1969).
    MONSA:119
  Guide-lines and strategies for
    achieving national unity (July
    17, 1969). MONSA:124 selec-
    tions
  Independent Malaya--our rights
    and obligations. MONS:211
  Let us not mimic the democracy
    of Westminster 1957 (March 5,
    1971). MONSA:131 selections
  Loyalty to the nation (Malaya).
    MONS:218
  Malaysia and the Asian perspec-
    tive. MONS:222
  The most dramatic fact of interna-
    tional life (April 28, 1970).
    MONSA:130
  Power politics and nation-building
    (Malaysia). MONS:232
  Strategy for the future: role of
    youths in national development

(Kuala Lumpur, July 31,
1970). MONSA:129

Mulford, Samuel
Speech to the Assembly at
New York. POC:174

Müller, Friedrich Max
Impassable barrier between
brutes and man.
BREWE 8:3086

Muller, Hermann Joseph
The production of mutations
(Nobel Lecture, Dec. 12,
1946). NOLM 3:154

MULLER, HERMANN JOSEPH
Caspersson, T.
Presentation [of the Nobel
Prize for Physiology or
Medicine to Hermann Joseph
Muller, Dec. 12, 1946].
NOLM 3:149

Müller, Paul Hermann
Dichloro-diphenyl-trichloroethane and newer insecti-
cides (Nobel Lecture, Dec.
11, 1948). NOLM 3:227

MÜLLER, PAUL HERMANN
Fischer, G.
Presentation [of the Nobel
Prize for Physiology or
Medicine to Paul Hermann
Müller, Dec. 11, 1948].
NOLM 3:227

Mulliken, Robert S.
Spectroscopy, molecular orbitals, and chemical bonding
(Nobel Lecture, Dec. 12,
1966). NOLC 4:131

MULLIKEN, ROBERT S.
Fischer-Hjalmars, I.
Presentation [of the Nobel
Prize for Chemistry to
Robert S. Mulliken, Dec.
12, 1966]. NOLC 4:127

Mullins, James See Butler,
B. J., jt. auth.

Mulroy, Thomas R.
Presents Ilka Chase. LYI:17

Mumford, Lewis
Human way out. MDV:13

Mundt, Karl E.
Responds to an introduction.
PRS:109

MUNICH FOUR POWER AGREE-
MENT, 1938
Churchill, W. L. S.
On the Munich Agreement (Oc-
tober 5, 1938). BRYH:521

MUNICIPAL GOVERNMENT
Wilson, W.
Commission city government.
ANN 13:269

MUNITIONS
Bismarck, O.
Plea for imperial armament.
BREWE 2:456

Munoz-Marin, Luis
Future of Puerto Rico.
ANN 16:312

MURDER
Hardin, B.
The Wilkinson and Murdaugh
case. BLY:48

Murphy, Frank See Black, H. L.,
jt. auth.

Murphy, Howard D.
Introduces Dr. Norman Vincent
Peale. PRS:103
Introduces Dr. Ralph W. Sockman.
PRS:117
Introduces Lee Wulff. PRS:67
Introduces Senator Hubert H.
Humphrey from Minnesota.
PRS:40

Murphy, Patrick V.
What the police expect of the citi-
zenry. (Washington, Dec. 7,
1970). BA 1970-71:122

Murphy, William Parry
Pernicious anemia (Nobel Lecture,
Dec. 12, 1934). NOLM 2:369

MURPHY, WILLIAM PARRY
Holmgren, I.
Presentation [of the Nobel Prize

for Physiology or Medicine
to George Hoyt Whipple,
George Richards Minot,
and William Parry Murphy,
Dec. 12, 1934].
NOLM 2:335

Murray, Philip
Collective bargaining and in-
dustrial democracy.
ANN 16:15

Murrow, Edward R.
Broadcaster talks to his col-
leagues. MDV:263

---- and others (D. Kerr, P.
Preminger and J. J. Mc-
Clafferty)
Movies and censorship.
ARS:127

MUSCLE SHOALS BILL
Hoover, H. C.
Veto of the Muscle Shoals
Bill. ANN 15:79

MUSCLES
Hill, A. V.
The mechanism of muscular
contraction. NOLM 2:10
Meyerhof, O. F.
Energy conversions in
muscle. NOLM 2:27

MUSCULAR DYSTROPHY
Bunting, J. E.
The pay is good. BAPR:364

MUSIC AND MUSICIANS
Bernstein, L.
American musical comedy.
KEO:274
Dedication of a musical in-
strument. BNH:65
Introductions for singers and
musicians (12 examples).
BNH:22
Welcome to adult choir mem-
bers. HNWM:31
Welcome to children's choir
members. HNWM:31
Welcome to youth choir mem-
bers. HNWM:32

---- See also Art and artists;
Jazz music

Muskie, Edmund S.
The astronauts on the moon.
(Jeffersonville, Indiana, July
25, 1969). BAAGB:409
Election eve address. (Television,
Nov. 2, 1970). STOT:262
Environment: can man prosper and
survive? BA 1969-70:98
Too many questions ... not enough
answers (Washington, Feb. 13,
1979). BA 1978-79:112

MUSLIMS
Ibrahim, A. M.
Muslims must face modern chal-
lenges. MONS:441

MUTATION (BIOLOGY)
Muller, H. J.
The production of mutations.
NOLM 3:154

Myers, Isaac
Finish the good work of uniting
colored and white workingmen.
(Philadelphia, August 18, 1869,
National Labor Union-3rd Na-
tional Convention). FON:367

Myers, Nancy Jeanne
Moppet manipulation. ARS:123

MYOGLOBIN
Kendrew, J. C.
Myoglobin and the structure of
proteins. NOLC 3:676

Myrbäck, K.
Presentation [of the Nobel Prize
for Chemistry to Luis F.
Leloir, Dec. 11, 1970].
NOLC 4:335
Presentation [of the Nobel Prize
for Chemistry to Melvin Calvin,
Dec. 11, 1961]. NOLC 3:615

- N -

NAACP See National Association
for the Advancement of Colored
People

Nader, Ralph
Meet the press. (Washington,
D.C., May 30, 1971).
BA 1971-72:79

Nail, William A.
  What did you say? (7th Indiana
    University Broadcasting In-
    stitute, Bloomington, Indi-
    ana, July 17, 1971).
    VER:272

Nair, C. Devan
  Nation building and the jealous
    gods of the past (Singapore,
    Sept. 18, 1969).
    MONSA:342
  Reflections on Rabindranath
    Tagore. MONS:190
  The role of trade union re-
    search and documentation
    services. MONSA:334

Nansen, Fridtjof
  The suffering people of Europe
    (Nobel Lecture, Dec. 19,
    1922). NOLP 1:361
  Speech at Award Ceremony
    [presenting the Nobel Prize
    for Peace to Joseph Austen
    Chamberlain and Charles
    Gates Dawes for 1925, Dec.
    10, 1926]. NOLP 1:383
  Speech at Award Ceremony
    [presenting Nobel Prize
    for Peace to Aristide Bri-
    and and Gustav Stresemann,
    Dec. 10, 1926]. NOLP 2:3

NANSEN, FRIDTJOF
  Stang, F.
    Presentation [of the Nobel
    Prize for Peace to Fridtjof
    Nansen, Dec. 10, 1922].
    NOLP 1:353

NANSEN INTERNATIONAL OF-
    FICE FOR REFUGEES
  Hansson, M.
    The Nansen International
    Office for Refugees (Nobel
    Lecture, Dec. 10, 1938).
    NOLP 2:268
  Stang, F.
    Presentation [of the Nobel
    Prize for Peace to the
    Nansen International Office
    for Refugees, Dec. 10,
    1938]. NOLP 2:265

Narayanan, Palayil Pathazapulrayil
  Role of trade unions in
    South-East Asia. MONS:295

Nash, Ogden
  Responds to introduction.
    PRS:106

Nash, Walter
  Collective security and the League
    of Nations (King's Theatre,
    Sept. 16, 1935). MACS:356 sel.

Nation, Carry A.
  Spiritual authority for my Chris-
    tian work. BLY:183 selections

NATIONAL ADVISORY COMMISSION
    ON CIVIL DISORDERS
  Abernathy, R. D.
    The Kerner report, promises
    and realities. FON:1145

NATIONAL AFRO-AMERICAN
    LEAGUE
  Fortune, T. T.
    It is time to call a halt.
    FON:556

NATIONAL ASSOCIATION FOR THE
    ADVANCEMENT OF COLORED
    PEOPLE
  DuBois, W. E. B.
    Address to the National Negro
    Convention. OE:88
  Marshall, T.
    The legal attack to secure civil
    rights. OE:123
  Wilkins, R.
    Keynote address to the NAACP
    annual convention, Los Angeles,
    July 5, 1966. AND:101;
    BOSC:89; OE:166

NATIONAL CHARACTERISTICS -
    AMERICAN
  Depew, C. M.
    Military spirit in America.
    BREWE 5:1785
  Everett, E.
    Moral forces which make Amer-
    ican progress. BREWE 6:2112
  Garfield, J. S.
    Conflict of ideas in America.
    BREWE 6:2231
  Ickes, H. L.
    What constitutes an American?
    HURH:260
  Lodge, H. C.
    Our forefathers. HURH:141
  Lowell, J. R.
    Poetical and the practical in

America.   BREWE 7:2808
Sinclair, G.
    The Americans.   REID:396
    selections
Story, J.
    Intellectual achievement in
    America.   BREWE 9:3531

---- GERMAN
Challemel-Lacour, P. A.
    Humboldt and the Teutonic
    intellect.   BREWE 3:1018

NATIONAL COMMITTEE TO DE-
    FEND NEGRO LEADERSHIP
McGowan, E. D.
    Stop the foes of Negro free-
    dom.   FON:860

NATIONAL DEFENSES See
    North Atlantic Treaty Or-
    ganization; World War,
    1939-1945 - Civilian activ-
    ities. See also Names of
    countries or hemispheres
    with subdivision Defenses,
    e.g. United States - Defenses

NATIONAL HEALTH SERVICE
    BILL
Bevan, A.
    National Health Service Bill.
    STRM:445

NATIONAL LABOR RELATIONS
    BOARD See Labor laws
    and legislation

NATIONAL LABOR UNION
Myers, I.
    Finish the good work of
    uniting colored and white
    workingmen.   FON:367

NATIONAL LIBERTY PARTY
Taylor, G. E.
    Revolution by the ballot.
    FON:647

NATIONAL NEGRO CONGRESS
Randolph, A. P.
    The crisis of the Negro
    and the Constitution.
    FON:816
    The task of the Negro peo-
    ple.   FON:807

NATIONAL NEGRO LABOR COUNCIL
Hood, W. R.
    Uncle Tom is dead! FON:843

NATIONAL PROGRESSIVES OF
    AMERICA
LaFollette, P. F.
    Party of our time. BAD:120

NATIONAL RECOVERY ADMINISTRA-
    TION
Hughes, C. E.
    Schechter Poultry Corporation
    v. United States, 1935; opinion
    for the Supreme Court.
    ANN 15:301; ROD:186
Roosevelt, F. D.
    Fireside chat: AAA and NRA,
    July 24, 1933. ANN 15:210

NATIONAL STATE
Nair, C. D.
    Nation building and the jealous
    gods of the past. MONSA:342

NATIONALISM
Hammarskjöld, D.
    Values of nationalism and inter-
    nationalism (Stanford University
    commencement address).
    HURS:206

---- See also Citizenship

---- ASIA
Rajaratnam, S.
    Asia needs the spirit of Sisyphus
    to succeed. MONSA:303

---- UNITED STATES
Gardner, H. J.
    New England nativism.
    ANN 8:484
Levin, L. C.
    Native Americans and foreign-
    born. ANN 7:313
Schurz, C.
    True Americanism. ANN 9:97

---- ---- See also National charac-
    teristics - American

NATO See North Atlantic Treaty
    Organization

Natta, Giulio
    From the stereospecific polymeri-
    zation to the asymmetric auto-

catalytic synthesis of macromolecules (Nobel Lecture,
Dec. 12, 1963). NOLC 4:27

NATTA, GIULIO
  Fredga, A.
    Presentation [of the Nobel
    Prize for Chemistry to Karl
    Ziegler and Giulio Natta,
    Dec. 12, 1963].
    NOLC 4:3

NATURAL GAS BILL
  Eisenhower, D. D.
    Veto of Natural Gas Bill.
    ANN 17:370

NATURAL PRODUCTS
  Robinson, Sir R.
    Some polycyclic natural
    products. NOLC 3:166
  Woodward, R. B.
    Recent advances in the
    chemistry of natural prod-
    ucts. NOLC 4:100

NATURAL RESOURCES See
  Conservation of natural
  resources

NATURALISM
  Eucken, R.
    Naturalism or idealism?
    NOL:74

NATURALIZATION See Immigration and emigration

NATURE
  Cyril, Saint
    Infinite artifices of nature.
    BREWE 4:1594
  Fénelon, F.
    Nature as a revelation.
    BREWE 6:2142
  Kidwell, C. S.
    American Indian attitudes
    toward nature. MAES:277
  Wigner, E. P.
    Events, laws of nature, and
    invariance principles.
    NOLPH 4:6

NAVAHO INDIANS
  MacDonald, P.
    Inaugural address, Window
    Rock, Navajo Nation, Janu-
    ary 7, 1975. MAES:213

Yazzie, E.
  Navajo wisdom. MAES:261

---- EDUCATION
  Atcitty, T. E.
    The future is at hand.
    MAES:160
  Platero, D.
    Discussions of critical issues
    affecting Navajo education pro-
    gram and policies. MAES:149

---- OIL LEASES
  MacDonald, P.
    Exploring new energy frontiers.
    MAES:165

---- RELIGION AND MYTHOLOGY
  Yazzie, E.
    Navajo wisdom as found in
    Navajo oral history. MAES:263

NAVAJO COMMUNITY COLLEGE
  Atcitty, T. E.
    The future is at hand.
    MAES:160

Neal, Joanne
  DDT: friend or foe?
  BREWW:183

NEAR EAST - 20TH CENTURY
  Eagleton, T. F.
    1977: year of opportunity in the
    Middle East? LINRST:124

Neebe, Oscar
  Address at trial, Chicago, October
  7-9, 1886. ACC:29; PAF:28

Néel, Louis
  Magnetism and the local molecular
  field (Nobel Lecture, Dec. 11,
  1970). NOLPH 4:318

NEEL, LOUIS
  Gustafsson, T.
    Presentation [of the Nobel Prize
    for Physics to Hannes Alfvén
    and Louis Néel, Dec. 11, 1970].
    NOLPH 4:303

NEGRO LABOR COMMITTEE
  Crosswaith, F. R.
    The Negro labor committee.
    FON:857

NEGROES See Blacks

NEHRU, JAWAHARLAL
  Stevenson, A. E.
    Presents Pandit Jawaharlal
    Nehru. LYI:242

Neil, William C.
  The triumph of equal school
    rights in Boston. (Boston,
    Dec. 17, 1855). FON:164

Nelson, Gaylord A.
  Against the nomination of
    Gerald R. Ford. (Wash-
    ington, D.C., Nov. 27,
    1973). BA 1973-74:188

Nernst, Walther Hermann
  Studies in chemical thermo-
    dynamics (Nobel Lecture
    for 1920, Dec. 12, 1921).
    NOLC 1:353

NERNST, WALTHER HERMANN
  DeGeer, G.
    Presentation [of the Nobel
    Prize for Chemistry to
    Walther Hermann Nernst,
    1920, Dec. 12, 1921].
    NOLC 1:349

NERVES
  Dale, Sir H. H.
    Some recent extensions of
    the chemical transmission
    of the effects of nerve im-
    pulses. NOLM 2:402
  Hodgkin, A. L.
    The ionic basis of nervous
    conduction. NOLM 4:32
  Loewi, O.
    The chemical transmission
    of nerve action.
    NOLM 2:416

Ness, Frederic W.
  Freedom and the labyrinth
    (Millikin Univ., May 21,
    1972). HOR:87

NEURAL TRANSMISSION
  Katz, B.
    On the quantal mechanism
    of neural transmitter re-
    lease. NOLM 4:485
  Von Euler, U.
    Adrenergic neurotransmitter
    functions. NOLM 4:470

NEUROFIBRILS
  Adrian, E. D.
    The activity of the nerve fibres.
    NOLM 2:293
  Erlanger, J.
    Some observations on the re-
    sponses of single nerve fibers.
    NOLM 3:50
  Gasser, H. S.
    Mammalian nerve fibers.
    NOLM 3:34

NEURONS
  Golgi, C.
    The neuron doctrine--theory and
    facts. NOLM 1:189
  Ramon y Cajal, S.
    The structure and connexions of
    neurons. NOLM 1:220

NEUROSPORA
  Beadle, G. W.
    Genes and chemical reactions
    in Neurospora. NOLM 3:587

NEUTRALITY See United States -
    Neutrality

NEUTRONS
  Chadwick, J.
    The neutron and its properties.
    NOLPH 2:339

NEW DEAL See Democratic Party;
    United States - Economic condi-
    tions

NEW ENGLAND
  Clemens, S. L.
    New England weather.
    HURH:128
  Curtis, G. W.
    Liberty under law. BAS:141
    (outline only); LINS:249

NEW GUINEA
  Higinbotham, G.
    For the annexation of New
    Guinea. MCA:43

NEW LEFT See Right and Left
    (political science)

NEW YEAR
  New Year prayer. BNH:74
  Senu bin Abdul Rahman
    Let our voice be heard (New
    Year message). MONS:160

NEW YORK (CITY)
  Wood, F.
    Proposal for the secession
    of New York City.
    ANN 9:233

---- CITY COLLEGE
  Kerr, C.
    Urban-grant university (cen-
    tennial meeting of City Col-
    lege). BA 1967-68:86

NEW YORK (STATE)
  Smith, A. E.
    The cooing dove. BRYO:249

---- SUPREME COURT
  Roesch, G. F.
    Constitutionality of a New
    York child labor law:
    opinion for the court.
    ANN 13:571

NEW ZEALAND - CONSTITUTION
  Atkinson, H.
    The abolition of the prov-
    inces, 1876. MACS:111 sel.
  Featherston, I.
    The demand for responsible
    government. MACS:84 sel.
    "Provincialism" 1856.
    MACS:96 sel.
  Sewell, H.
    "Centralist" interpretation
    of the Constitution.
    MACS:93 sel.
    The 'compact of 1856.'
    MACS:99 sel.

---- DEFENSES
  Allen, J.
    The Naval Defence Bill,
    1908. MACS:270 sel.
  Holland, S.
    Forward defence--from the
    Middle East to Malaya,
    1955. MACS:392 sel.
  Jervois, Sir W.
    New Zealand's defence and
    Royal Navy supremacy.
    MACS:245 sel.
  Ward, Sir J.
    New Zealand support for
    the Royal Navy, 1891-1908.
    MACS:254 sel.

---- ECONOMIC POLICY
  Holyoake, K. J.

The National Development Conference, 1968. MACS:455 sel.

---- HISTORY
  Coates, D.
    Missionary opposition to the
    New Zealand Company.
    MACS:4 sel.
  Vogel, J.
    Colonization by public works
    and immigration. MACS:42 sel.
  Wakefield, E. G.
    Extending the 'frontier' of New
    South Wales. MACS:3 sel.

---- POLITICS AND GOVERNMENT
  Atkinson, H.
    The abolition of the provinces,
    1876. MACS:111 sel.
  Ballance, J.
    The 1890 election: the opposi-
    tion case. MACS:201 sel.
  Coates, J. G.
    The 1925 election: the Coates
    campaign. MACS:307 sel.
  Featherston, I.
    The demand for responsible
    government. MACS:84 sel.
    "Provincialism" 1856.
    MACS:96 sel.
  Godley, R.
    The demand for responsible
    government. MACS:66 sel.
  McGechan, R. O.
    Legal arguments for adopting
    the Statute of Westminster,
    1944. MACS:284 sel.
  Sewell, H.
    "Centralist" interpretation of
    the Constitution. MACS:93 sel.
    The 'compact' of 1856.
    MACS:99 sel.
  Wakefield, E. G.
    The demand for responsible
    government. MACS:86 sel.

NEW ZEALAND COMPANY
  Coates, D.
    Missionary opposition to the
    New England Company.
    MACS:4 sel.

Newman, John Henry, Cardinal
  Christianity and scientific investi-
    gation. (Catholic University of
    Ireland, Dublin, 1855).
    MCB:361
  Property as a disadvantage.
    BREWE 8:3093

NEWSPAPERS
  Holden, W. S.
    Newspapers of the U.S.A.
    ARS:107

---- See also Free speech; Jour-
    nalism and Journalists;
    Liberty of the Press

Newton, Huey P.
  The transformation of the Black
    Panther Party. (Univ. of
    California, Berkeley, May
    19, 1971). FON:1182

NEWTON, HUEY P.
  Garry, C. R.
    In defense of Huey Newton.
    ERP:161
  Seale, B.
    Free Huey. SMHR:175

Ngwa, Jacob
  Africa and the United States--
    partners for peace.
    SCHW:192
  Our common tradition in peril.
    SCHW:123

NIAGARA MOVEMENT
  DuBois, W. E. B.
    The value of agitation.
    FON:663

NICARAGUA
  Coolidge, C.
    Intervention in Nicaragua.
    ANN 14:519

NICARAGUA CANAL
  McKinley, W.
    Second annual message.
    STAT 2:1881
    Third annual message.
    STAT 2:1922

NICKEL STEEL
  Guillaume, C. E.
    Invar and clinvar.
    NOLPH 1:444

Nicolle, Charles Jules Henri
  Investigations on typhus
    (Nobel Lecture for 1928).
    NOLM 2:180

NICOLLE, CHARLES JULES HENRI
  Henschen, F.

    Presentation [of the Nobel Prize
    for Physiology or Medicine for
    1928 to Charles Jules Henri
    Nicolle]. NOLM 2:175

Nielson, Arthur C., Sr.
  Responds to an introduction.
  PRS:155

Nies, Nola
  Warrior and the woman.
  SCHW:10

NIGERIA
  Akintola, S. L. and others
    Nigeria debates self-government.
    EMP:65
  Gardiner, R. K.
    Citizenship and political liberal-
    ism. EMP:106
  Okpara, M. I.
    Progress without tears: ad-
    dress at convocation, University
    of Nigeria. EMP:138

Niles, John and others (J. C. Cal-
    houn)
  Debate on the Yucatan Bill.
  ANN 7:426

Ningkan, Stephen Kalong
  Three problems of Sarawak.
  MONS:326

Nirenberg, Marshall W.
  The genetic code (Nobel Lecture,
  Dec. 12, 1968). NOLM 4:370

NIRENBERG, MARSHALL W.
  Reichard, P.
    Presentation [of the Nobel Prize
    for Physiology or Medicine to
    Robert W. Holley, Har Gobind
    Khorana, and Marshall W.
    Nirenberg, Dec. 12, 1968].
    NOLM 4:321

NITROGEN - FIXATION
  Virtanen, A. I.
    The biological fixation of nitro-
    gen and the preservation of
    fodder in agriculture, and their
    importance to human nutrition.
    NOLC 3:74

Nix, Lucile
  Presents Edmon Low. LYI:40

Montelius, O.
Presentation [of the Nobel
Prize for Chemistry to Otto
Wallach, Dec. 12, 1910].
NOLC 1:175

Mörner, K.A.H.
Presentation [of the Nobel
Prize for Chemistry to Edu-
ard Buchner, Dec. 11, 1907].
NOLC 1:99

Mulliken, R. S.
Spectroscopy, molecular
orbitals, and chemical bonding. NOLC 4:131

Myrbäck, K.
Presentation [of the Nobel
Prize for Chemistry to
Luis F. Leloir, Dec. 11,
1970]. NOLC 4:335
Presentation [of the Nobel
Prize for Chemistry to Mel-
vin Calvin, Dec. 11, 1961].
NOLC 3:615

Natta, G.
From the stereospecific
polymerization to the
asymmetric autocatalytic
synthesis of macromolecules.
NOLC 4:27

Nernst, W. H.
Studies in chemical thermodynamics. NOLC 1:353

Nordström, T.
Presentation [of the Nobel
Prize for Chemistry to
Alfred Werner, Dec. 11,
1913]. NOLC 1:253

Norrish, R. G. W.
Some fast reactions in gases
studied by flash photolysis
and kinetic spectroscopy.
NOLC 4:206

Northrop, J. H.
The preparation of pure
enzymes and virus pro-
teins. NOLC 3:124

Odhner, C. T.
Presentation [of the Nobel
Prize for Chemistry to
Jacobus Henricus Van't
Hoff, Dec. 13, 1901].
NOLC 1:3

Olander, A.
Presentation [of the Nobel
Prize for Chemistry to
Jaroslav Heyrovsky, Dec.
11, 1959]. NOLC 3:561
Presentation [of the Nobel

Prize for Chemistry to Manfred
Eigen, R. G. W. Norrish and
George Porter, Dec. 11, 1967].
NOLC 4:165
Presentation [of the Nobel Prize
for Chemistry to Sir Cyril Nor-
man Hinshelwood and Nikolai
Nikolaevic Semenov, Dec. 11,
1956]. NOLC 3:471

Onsager, L.
The motion of ions: principles
and concepts. NOLC 4:272

Ostwald, W.
On catalysis. NOLC 1:150

Palmaer, W.
Presentation [of the Nobel
Prize for Chemistry for 1931
to Carl Bosch and Friedrich
Bergius, May 21, 1932].
NOLC 2:189
Presentation [of the Nobel Prize
for Chemistry for 1934 to
Harold Clayton Urey, Feb. 14,
1935]. NOLC 2:333
Presentation [of the Nobel Prize
for Chemistry to Jean Frédéric
Joliot and Irène Joliot-Curie,
Dec. 12, 1935]. NOLC 2:359
Presentation [of the Nobel Prize
for Chemistry to Walter Norman
Haworth and Paul Karrer, Dec.
11, 1937]. NOLC 2:407

Pauling, L. C.
Modern structural chemistry.
NOLC 3:429

Perutz, M. F.
X-ray analysis of haemoglobin.
NOLC 3:653

Porter, G.
Flash photolysis and some of
its applications. NOLC 4:241

Pregl, F.
Quantitative micro-analysis of
organic substances.
NOLC 2:28

Ramsay, Sir W.
The rare gases of the atmos-
phere. NOLC 1:68

Richards, T. W.
Atomic weights. NOLC 1:280

Robinson, Sir R.
Some polycyclic natural products. NOLC 3:166

Rutherford, E.
The chemical nature of the
alpha particles from radioactive
substances. NOLC 1:129

Ruzicka, L. S.

Arrhenius, Dec. 11, 1903].
NOLC 1:43
Urey, H. C.
Some thermodynamic proper-
ties of hydrogen and deut-
erium. NOLC 2:339
Vigneaud, V. D.
A trail of sulfur research:
from insulin to oxytocin.
NOLC 3:446
Virtanen, A. I.
The biological fixation of
nitrogen and the preservation
of fodder in agriculture,
and their importance to
human nutrition. NOLC 3:74
Wallach, O.
Alicyclic compounds.
NOLC 1:178
Werner, A.
On the constitution and con-
figuration of higher-order
compounds. NOLC 1:256
Westgren, A.
Presentation [of the Nobel
Prize for Chemistry to
Arne Wilhelm Kaurin Tise-
lius, Dec. 13, 1948].
NOLC 3:191
Presentation [of the Nobel
Prize for Chemistry to
Artturi Ilmari Virtanen,
Dec. 12, 1945]. NOLC 3:71
Presentation [of the Nobel
Prize for Chemistry to
Edwin Mattison McMillan
and Glenn Theodore Sea-
borg, Dec. 12, 1951].
NOLC 3:309
Presentation [of the Nobel
Prize for Chemistry for
1943 to George De Hevesy,
Dec. 12, 1944]. NOLC 3:5
Presentation [of the Nobel
Prize for Chemistry for
1944 to Otto Hahn, Dec.
13, 1946]. NOLC 3:47
Presentation [of the Nobel
Prize for Chemistry to
Petrus Josephus Wilhelmus
Debye, Dec. 12, 1936].
NOLC 2:379
Presentation [of the Nobel
Prize for Chemistry to
Willard Frank Libby, Dec.
12, 1960]. NOLC 3:589
Wieland, H. O.
The chemistry of the bile

acids. NOLC 2:94
Willstätter, R. M.
On plant pigments. NOLC 1:301
Windaus, A. O. R.
Constitution of sterols and their
connection with other substances
occurring in nature.
NOLC 2:105
Woodward, R. B.
Recent advances in the chemis-
try of natural products.
NOLC 4:100
Ziegler, K.
Consequences and development
of an invention. NOLC 4:6
Zsigmondy, R. A.
Properties of colloids.
NOLC 2:45

NOBEL PRIZE FOR LITERATURE
Agnon, S. Y.
Acceptance [of the Nobel Prize
for Literature, 1966].
NOB 1:5; NOL:614
Andrić, I.
Acceptance [of the Nobel Prize
for Literature, 1961].
NOB 1:121; NOL:565
Annerstedt, C.
Presentation [of the Nobel Prize
for Literature to Selma Ottiliana
Lovisa Lagerlöf, 1909].
NOB 10:279; NOL:90
Asturias, M. A.
Acceptance [of the Nobel Prize
for Literature, 1967].
NOB 2:7; NOL:626
Benitez, J.
Acceptance [of the Nobel Prize
for Literature for Juan Ramón
Jiménez, 1956]. NOB 10:7;
NOL:517
Bergson, H.
Acceptance [of the Nobel Prize
for Literature, 1927].
NOB 2:273; NOL:246
Bjørnson, B. M.
Acceptance [of the Nobel Prize
for Literature, 1903].
NOL:16; NOB 3:81
Böök, F.
Presentation [of the Nobel Prize
for Literature to Thomas
Mann, 1929]. NOB 12:221;
NOL:260
Buck, P.
Acceptance [of the Nobel Prize
for Literature, 1938].

Presentation [of the Nobel Prize for Literature to Frédéric Mistral and José de Echegaray y Eizaguirre, 1904]. NOL:23; NOB 13:119
Presentation [of the Nobel Prize for Literature to Giosue Carducci, 1906]. NOB 5:3; NOL:48
Presentation [of the Nobel Prize for Literature to Halldor Kiljan Laxness, 1955]. NOB 12:3; NOL:505
Presentation [of the Nobel Prize for Literature to Henryk Sienkiewicz, 1905]. NOL:36; NOB 17:173
Presentation [of the Nobel Prize for Literature to Maurice Polydore Marie Bernhard Maeterlinck, 1911]. NOB 12:139; NOL:107
Presentation [of the Nobel Prize for Literature to Paul Johann Ludwig Heyse, 1910]. NOB 7:279; NOL:100
Presentation [of the Nobel Prize for Literature to Rudyard Kipling, 1907]. NOB 11:89; NOL:58
Presentation [of the Nobel Prize for Literature to Sully Prudhomme, 1901]. NOL:2; NOB 16:303
Yeats, W. B.
Acceptance [of the Nobel Prize for Literature, 1923]. NOB 18:263; NOL:199
The Irish dramatic movement. NOL:201

NOBEL PRIZE FOR PEACE
Arnoldson, K. P.
World referendum (Nobel Lecture, Dec. 10, 1908). NOLP 1:175
Angell, N.
Peace and the public mind (Nobel Lecture for 1934, June 12, 1935). NOLP 2:153
Backhouse, M. A.
The international service of the Society of Friends (Nobel Lecture, Dec. 12, 1947). NOLP 2:380
Bajer, F.
The organization of the

Peace Movement (Nobel Lecture, 1908, May 18, 1909). NOLP 1:190
Balch, E. G.
Toward human unity or beyond nationalism (Nobel Lecture for 1946, April 7, 1948). NOLP 2:333
Bjørnson, B.
Introduction [presenting the Nobel Prize for Peace to Bertha von Suttner, 1905, April 18, 1906]. NOLP 1:81
Boissier, L. L.
Some aspects of the mission of the International Committee of the Red Cross (Nobel Lecture, Dec. 11, 1963). NOLP 3:301
Borlaugh, N. E.
The green revolution, peace, and humanity (Nobel Lecture, Dec. 11, 1970). NOLP 3:454
Boyd Orr, J.
Science and peace (Nobel Lecture, Dec. 12, 1949). NOLP 2:415
Branting, K. H.
Fraternity among nations (Nobel Lecture for 1921, June 19, 1922). NOLP 1:324
Briand, A.
Acceptance of the Nobel Prize for Peace, Dec. 10, 1926. NOLP 2:3
Buen, A. J.
Remarks [presenting the Nobel Prize for Peace to Leon Victor Auguste Bourgeois, Dec. 10, 1920]. NOLP 1:304
Buisson, F. E.
Changes in concepts of war and peace (Nobel Lecture, 1927, May 31, 1928). NOLP 2:35
Bunche, R. J.
Some reflections on peace in our time (Nobel Lecture, Dec. 11, 1950). NOLP 2:443
Butler, N. M.
Radio address (Nobel Lecture, Dec. 12, 1931). NOLP 2:136
Cadbury, H. J.
Quakers and peace (Nobel Lecture, Dec. 12, 1947). NOLP 2:391
Cassin, R. S.
The charter of human rights (Nobel Lectures, Dec. 11, 1968). NOLP 3:394

Cecil, R.
The future of civilization
(Nobel Lecture for 1937,
June 1, 1938). NOLP 2:246

Chamberlain, J.
Acceptance [of the Nobel
Prize for Peace for 1925,
Dec. 10, 1926].
NOLP 1:394

Chapuisat, E.
The activity of the International Committee of the
Red Cross during the war,
1939-1945 (Nobel Lecture
for 1944, Dec. 11, 1945).
NOLP 2:295

Cremer, W. R.
The progress and advantages
of international arbitration
(Nobel Lecture for 1903,
Jan. 15, 1905).
NOLP 1:46

Dawes, C. G.
Acceptance [of the Nobel
Prize for Peace for 1925,
Dec. 10, 1926].
NOLP 1:399

Ducommun, E.
The futility of war demon-
strated by history (Nobel
Lecture for 1902).
NOLP 1:17

Edberg, R.
Acceptance of the Nobel
Prize for Peace for Dag
Hammarskjöld, Dec. 10,
1961. NOLP 3:248

Gobat, C. A.
The development of the
Hague Conventions of July
22, 1899 (Nobel Lecture
for 1902, Oslo, July 18,
1906). NOLP 1:30

Goedhart, G. J. v. H.
Refugee problems and their
solutions (Nobel Lecture,
Dec. 12, 1955). NOLP 3:97

Hagerup, G. F.
The work of the Institute
of International Law (Nobel
Lecture for 1904, Aug. 24,
1912). NOLP 1:64

Hambro, C. J.
Presentation [of the Nobel
Prize for Peace to George
Catlett Marshall, Dec. 10,
1953]. NOLP 3:65
Presentation [of the Nobel

Prize for Peace to the International Committee of the Red
Cross and the League of the
Red Cross Societies, Dec. 10,
1963]. NOLP 3:295

Hansson, M.
The Nansen International Office
for Refugees (Nobel Lecture,
Dec, 10, 1938). NOLP 2:268

Harmann, Z.
UNICEF: achievement and challenge (Nobel Lecture, Dec.
11, 1965). NOLP 3:365

Henderson, A.
Essential elements of a univer-
sal and enduring peace (Nobel
Lecture, Dec. 11, 1934).
NOLP 2:185

Huber, M.
Acceptance [of the Nobel Prize
for Peace, 1944, for the Inter-
national Committee of the Red
Cross, Dec. 10, 1945].
NOLP 2:293

Hull, C.
Acceptance [of the Nobel Prize
for Peace to Cordell Hull, Dec.
10, 1945]. NOLP 2:318

Ingebretsen, H. S.
Presentation [of the Nobel Prize
for Peace to John Raleigh Mott,
Dec. 10, 1946]. NOLP 2:354

Irgens, J.
Welcome [presenting the Nobel
Prize for Peace to the Institute
of International Law for 1904,
Aug. 24, 1912]. NOLP 1:61

Jahn, G.
Presentation [of the Nobel Prize
for Peace to Albert John
Luthuli for 1960, Dec. 10,
1961]. NOLP 3:209
Presentation [of the Nobel Prize
for Peace for 1952 to Albert
Schweitzer, Dec. 10, 1953].
NOLP 3:37
Presentation [of the Nobel Prize
for Peace to Cordell Hull, Dec.
10, 1945]. NOLP 2:311
Presentation [of the Nobel Prize
for Peace to Dag Hammar-
skjöld, Dec. 10, 1961].
NOLP 3:239
Presentation [of the Nobel Prize
for Peace to Emily Greene
Balch, Dec. 10, 1946].
NOLP 2:325
Presentation [of the Nobel Prize

for Peace to the Friends
Service Council and the
American Friends Service
Committee, Dec. 10, 1947].
NOLP 2:373
Presentation [of the Nobel
Prize for Peace to Georges
Pire, Dec. 10, 1958].
NOLP 3:151
Presentation [of the Nobel
Prize for Peace to the Inter-
national Committee of the
Red Cross, 1944, Dec. 10,
1945]. NOLP 2:289
Presentation [of the Nobel
Prize for Peace to Léon
Jouhaux, Dec. 10, 1951].
NOLP 3:3
Presentation [of the Nobel
Prize for Peace to Lester
Bowles Pearson, Dec. 10,
1957]. NOLP 3:119
Presentation [of the Nobel
Prize for Peace for 1962
to Linus Carl Pauling, Dec.
10, 1963]. NOLP 3:259
Presentation [of the Nobel
Prize for Peace to Lord
Boyd Orr of Brechin, Dec.
10, 1949]. NOLP 2:407
Presentation [of the Nobel
Prize for Peace to Martin
Luther King, Jr., Dec. 10,
1964]. NOLP 3:325
Presentation [of the Nobel
Prize for Peace to the Of-
fice of the United Nations
High Commissioner for
Refugees, Dec. 10, 1955].
NOLP 3:89
Presentation [of the Nobel
Prize for Peace to Philip
John Noel-Baker, Dec. 10,
1959]. NOLP 3:175
Presentation [of the Nobel
Prize for Peace to Ralph
Johnson Bunche, Dec. 10,
1950]. NOLP 2:435
Johnsen, A.
Remarks [presenting the
Nobel Prize for Peace to
Thomas Woodrow Wilson,
1919, Dec. 10, 1920].
NOLP 1:293
Jouhaux, L.
Fifty years of trade-union
activity in behalf of peace
(Nobel Lecture, Dec. 11,

1951). NOLP 3:10
Kellogg, F. B.
Acceptance and banquet speech
[for the Nobel Prize for Peace,
1929 (Dec. 10, 1930)].
NOLP 2:79
King, M. L., Jr.
Nonviolence: moral challenge
for peace and justice.
NOLP 3:333; THOMS:99
Knudsen, G.
Presentation [of the Nobel Prize
for Peace to Theodore Roose-
velt, Dec. 10, 1906].
NOLP 1:97
Koht, H.
Presentation [of the Nobel Prize
for Peace to Jane Addams and
Nicholas Murray Butler, Dec.
10, 1931]. NOLP 2:125
Labouisse, H. R.
Acceptance [of the Nobel Prize
for Peace, Dec. 10, 1965].
NOLP 3:362
Lange, C. L.
Internationalism (Nobel Lecture,
Dec. 13, 1921). NOLP 1:336
Presentation [of the Nobel Prize
for Peace to Carlos Saavedra
Lamas, Dec. 10, 1936].
NOLP 2:217
Presentation [of the Nobel Prize
for Peace, 1933, to Norman
Angell, Dec. 10, 1934].
NOLP 2:147
Presentation [of the Nobel Prize
for Peace to Viscount Cecil of
Chelwood, Dec. 10, 1937].
NOLP 2:235
Lionaes, A.
Presentation [of the Nobel Prize
for Peace to the International
Labor Organization, Dec. 10,
1969]. NOLP 3:415
Presentation [of the Nobel Prize
for Peace to Norman Ernest Bor-
laug, Dec. 10, 1970].
NOLP 3:445
Presentation [of the Nobel Prize
for Peace to René-Samuel Cas-
sin, Dec. 10, 1968].
NOLP 3:385
Presentation [of the Nobel Prize
for Peace to the United Nations
Children's Fund, Dec. 10,
1965]. NOLP 3:353
Løvland, J. G.
Banquet speech [presenting the

Nobel Prize for Peace to
Bertha von Suttner, 1905,
April 18, 1906]. NOLP 1:82
Presentation [of the Nobel
Prize for Peace to Alfred
Hermann Fried, Dec. 10,
1911]. NOLP 1:238
Presentation [of the Nobel
Prize for Peace to Auguste
Marie François Beernaert,
Dec. 10, 1909].
NOLP 1:211
Presentation [of the Nobel
Prize for Peace to Baron
d'Estournelles de Constant,
Dec. 10, 1909].
NOLP 1:216
Presentation [of the Nobel
Prize for Peace to Ernesto
Teodoro Moneta, Dec. 10,
1907]. NOLP 1:113
Presentation [of the Nobel
Prize for Peace to Fredrik
Bajer, Dec. 10, 1908].
NOLP 1:188
Presentation [of the Nobel
Prize for Peace to Klas
Pontus Arnoldson, Dec. 10,
1908]. NOLP 1:173
Presentation [of the Nobel
Prize for Peace to Louis
Renault, Dec. 10, 1907].
NOLP 1:141
Presentation [of the Nobel
Prize for Peace to the
Permanent International
Peace Bureau, Dec. 10,
1910]. NOLP 1:223
Presentation [of the Nobel
Prize for Peace to Tobias
Michael Carel Asser, Dec.
10, 1911]. NOLP 1:233
Toast to E. Ducommun
[presenting the Nobel Prize
for Peace, 1902].
NOLP 1:15
Toast to C. A. Gobat [pre-
senting the Nobel Prize for
Peace for 1902, Oslo, July
18, 1906]. NOLP 1:29
Welcome [presenting the
Nobel Prize for Peace, 1903
to William Randal Cremer,
Jan. 15, 1905].
NOLP 1:45
Luthuli, A. J.
Africa and freedom.
MDV:79; NOLP 3:209

MacAulay, J. A.
The Red Cross in a changing
world (Nobel Lecture, Dec. 11,
1963). NOLP 3:311
Marshall, G. C.
Essentials of peace (Nobel Lec-
ture, Dec. 11, 1953).
NOLP 3:76
Moe, R.
Presentation [of the Nobel Prize
for Peace to Elihu Root, 1912,
Dec. 10, 1913]. NOLP 1:245
Presentation [of the Nobel Prize
for Peace to Henri Marie La
Fontaine, Dec. 10, 1913].
NOLP 1:269
Presentation [of the Nobel Prize
for Peace to the International
Committee of the Red Cross,
Dec. 10, 1917]. NOLP 1:281
Moneta, E. T.
Peace and law in the Italian
tradition (Nobel Lecture, 1907,
Aug. 25, 1909). NOLP 1:114
Morse, D. A.
ILO and the social infrastructure
of peace (Nobel Lecture, Dec.
11, 1969). NOLP 3:424
Mott, J. R.
The leadership demanded in
this momentous time (Nobel
Lecture, Dec. 13, 1946).
NOLP 2:362
Mowinckel, J. L.
Presentation [of the Nobel Prize
for Peace to Arthur Henderson,
Dec. 10, 1934]. NOLP 2:179
Presentation [of the Nobel Prize
for Peace to Frank Billings
Kellogg, 1929, Dec. 10, 1930].
NOLP 2:73
Presentation [of the Nobel Prize
for Peace to Nathan Söderblom,
Dec. 11, 1930]. NOLP 2:73
Nansen, F.
Speech at Award Ceremony
[presenting Nobel Prize for
Peace to Aristide Briand and
Gustav Stresemann, Dec. 10,
1926]. NOLP 2:3
Speech at Award Ceremony
[presenting the Nobel Prize
for Peace to Joseph Austen
Chamberlain and Charles Gates
Dawes for 1925, Dec. 10,
1926]. NOLP 1:383
The suffering people of Europe
(Nobel Lecture, Dec. 19, 1922).

NOLP 1:361

Noel-Baker, P. J.
    Peace and the arms race
    (Nobel Lecture, Dec. 11,
    1959). NOLP 3:186

Pauling, L. C.
    Science and peace (Nobel Lec-
    ture for 1962, Dec. 11,
    1963). NOLP 3:271

Pearson, L. B.
    The four faces of peace
    (Nobel Lecture, Dec. 11,
    1957). NOLP 3:129

Peirce, H. H. D.
    Acceptance [of the Nobel
    Prize for Peace for Theo-
    dore Roosevelt, Dec. 10,
    1906]. NOLP 1:99

Pire, G.
    Brotherly love: foundation
    of peace (Nobel Lecture,
    Dec. 11, 1958). NOLP 3:157

Quidde, L.
    Security and disarmament
    (Nobel Lecture, Dec. 10,
    1927). NOLP 2:47

Renault, L.
    The work at the Hague in
    1899 and in 1907 (Nobel Lec-
    ture for 1907, May 18,
    1908). NOLP 1:143

Roosevelt, T.
    International peace (Nobel
    Lecture for 1906, May 5,
    1910). NOLP 1:102

Root, E.
    Towards making peace per-
    manent (Nobel Lecture for
    1912). NOLP 1:247

Saavedra Lamas, C.
    Radio address (Nobel Lec-
    ture, Nov. 29, 1936).
    NOLP 2:225

Schmedeman, A. G.
    Acceptance [of the Nobel
    Prize for Peace for Wood-
    row Wilson, 1919, Dec. 10,
    1920]. NOLP 1:294

Schweitzer, A.
    The problem of peace
    (Nobel Lecture for 1952,
    Nov. 4, 1954). NOLP 3:46

Söderblom, N.
    The role of the church in
    promoting peace (Nobel Lec-
    ture, Dec. 11, 1930).
    NOLP 2:93

Stang, F.

Presentation [of the Nobel Prize
for Peace, 1935, to Carl Von
Ossietzky, Dec. 10, 1936].
NOLP 2:207

Presentation [of the Nobel Prize
for Peace to Ferdinand Edouard
Buisson and Ludwig Quidde,
Dec. 10, 1927]. NOLP 2:29

Presentation [of the Nobel Prize
for Peace to Fridtjof Nansen,
Dec. 10, 1922]. NOLP 1:353

Presentation [of the Nobel Prize
for Peace to the Nansen International Office for Refugees,
Dec. 10, 1938]. NOLP 2:265

Stresemann, G.
    The new Germany (Nobel Lec-
    ture for 1926, June 29, 1927).
    NOLP 2:8

Suttner, B. V.
    The evolution of the Peace Move-
    ment (Nobel Lecture for 1905,
    April 18, 1906). NOLP 1:84

NOBEL PRIZE FOR PHYSICS

Alfvén, H.
    Plasma physics, space research
    and the origin of the solar sys-
    tem. NOLPH 4:306

Alvarez, L. W.
    Recent developments in particle
    physics. NOLPH 4:241

Anderson, C. D.
    The production and properties
    of positrons. NOLPH 2:365

Appleton, Sir E. V.
    The ionosphere. NOLPH 3:79

Arrhenius, S. A.
    Presentation [of the Nobel Prize
    for Physics for 1921 to Albert
    Einstein, July 11, 1923].
    NOLPH 1:482
    Presentation [of the Nobel Prize
    for Physics to Niels Bohr, Dec.
    11, 1922]. NOLPH 2:3

Bardeen, J.
    Semiconductor research leading
    to the point contact transistor.
    NOLPH 3:318

Barkla, C. G.
    Characteristic Röntgen radiation.
    NOLPH 1:392

Basov, N. G.
    Semiconductor lasers.
    NOLPH 4:89

Becquerel, A. H.
    On radioactivity, a new property
    of matter. NOLPH 1:52

Bekesy, G. V.
Concerning the pleasures of observing, and the mechanisms of the inner ear. NOLM 3:722

Bergstrand, H.
Presentation [of the Nobel Prize for Physiology or Medicine to Max Theiler, Dec. 11, 1951]. NOLM 3:347

Bergstrom, S.
Presentation [of the Nobel Prize for Physiology or Medicine to Konrad Bloch and Feodor Lynen, Dec. 11, 1964]. NOLM 4:75

Bernhard, C. G.
Presentation [of the Nobel Prize for Physiology or Medicine to Georg Von Bekesy, Dec. 11, 1961]. NOLM 3:719
Presentation [of the Nobel Prize for Physiology or Medicine to Ragnar Granit, Haldan Keffer Hartline, and George Wald, Dec. 12, 1967]. NOLM 4:251

Bloch, K.
The biological synthesis of cholesterol. NOLM 4:78

Bovet, D.
The relationships between isosterism and competitive phenomena in the field of drug therapy of the autonomic nervous system and that of the neuromuscular transmission. NOLM 3:552

Burnet, Sir F. M.
Immunological recognition of self. NOLM 3:689

Carrel, A.
Suture of blood-vessels and transplantation of organs. NOLM 1:442

Caspersson, T.
Presentation [of the Nobel Prize for Physiology or Medicine to George Wells Beadle, Edward Lawrie Tatum, and Joshua Lederberg, Dec. 11, 1958]. NOLM 3:583
Presentation [of the Nobel Prize for Physiology or Medicine to Hermann Joseph

Muller, Dec. 12, 1946]. NOLM 3:149

Chain, E. B.
The chemical structure of the penicillins. NOLM 3:110

Cori, C.
Polysaccharide phosphorylase. NOLM 3:186

Cournand, A. F.
Control of the pulmonary circulation in man with some remarks on methodology. NOLM 3:529

Crick, F. H. C.
On the genetic code. NOLM 3:811

Dale, Sir H. H.
Some recent extensions of the chemical transmission of the effects of nerve impulses. NOLM 2:402

Dam, H.
The discovery of vitamin K, its biological functions and therapeutical application. NOLM 3:8

Delbrück, M.
A physicist's renewed look at biology--twenty years later. NOLM 4:404

Domack, G. J. P.
Further progress in chemotherapy of bacterial infections. NOLM 2:490

Eccles, J. C.
The ionic mechanism of postsynaptic inhibition. NOLM 4:6

Ehrlich, P.
Partial cell functions. NOLM 1:304

Eijkman, C.
Antineuritic vitamin and beriberi. NOLM 2:199

Einthoven, W.
The string galvanometer and the measurement of the action currents of the heart. NOLM 2:94

Enders, J. F.
The cultivation of the poliomyelitis viruses in tissue culture. NOLM 3:448

Engström, A.
Presentation [of the Nobel Prize for Physiology or Medicine to Francis Harry Compton Crick, James Dewey

Watson, and Maurice Hugh
Frederick Wilkins, Dec.
11, 1962]. NOLM 3:751

Erlanger, J.
Some observations on the re-
sponses of single nerve fibers.
NOLM 3:50

Fibiger, J. A. G.
Investigations on Spiroptera
carcinoma and the experi-
mental induction of cancer.
NOLM 2:122

Fischer, G.
Presentation [of the Nobel
Prize for Physiology or
Medicine to Paul Hermann
Müller, Dec. 11, 1948].
NOLM 3:227

Fleming, Sir A.
Penicillin. NOLM 3:83

Florey, Sir H. W.
Penicillin. NOLM 3:96

Forssmann, W. T. O.
The role of heart catheterization and angiocardiography
in the development of modern
medicine. NOLM 3:506

Gard, S.
Presentation [of the Nobel
Prize for Physiology or
Medicine to François Jacob,
André Lwoff, and Jacques
Monod, Dec. 11, 1965].
NOLM 4:143
Presentation [of the Nobel
Prize for Physiology or
Medicine to John Franklin
Enders, Thomas Huckle
Weller, and Frederick
Chapman Robbins, Dec. 11,
1954]. NOLM 3:443
Presentation [of the Nobel
Prize for Physiology or
Medicine to Max Delbrück,
Alfred D. Hershey, and
Salvador E. Luria, Dec. 10,
1969]. NOLM 4:401
Presentation [of the Nobel
Prize for Physiology or
Medicine to Sir Frank Mac-
farlane Burnet and Peter
Brian Medawar, Dec. 12,
1960]. NOLM 3:685

Gasser, H. S.
Mammalian nerve fibers.
NOLM 3:34

Golgi, C.
The neuron doctrine--theory

and facts. NOLM 1:189

Granit, R.
The development of retinal
neurophysiology.
NOLM 4:255
Presentation [of the Nobel Prize
for Physiology or Medicine to
John Carew Eccles, Alan Lloyd
Hodgkin, and Andrew Fielding
Huxley, Dec. 11, 1963].
NOLM 4:3

Gullstrand, A.
How I found the mechanism of
intracapsular accommodation.
NOLM 1:414

Häggquist, G.
Presentation [of the Nobel Prize
for Physiology or Medicine to
Hans Spemann, Dec. 12, 1935].
NOLM 2:377

Hammarsten, E.
Presentation [of the Nobel Prize
for Physiology or Medicine to
Albert Szent-Györgyi Von Nagy-
rapolt, Dec. 11, 1937].
NOLM 2:435
Presentation [of the Nobel Prize
for Physiology or Medicine to
Axel Hugo Theodor Theorell,
Dec. 12, 1955].
NOLM 3:477
Presentation [of the Nobel Prize
for Physiology or Medicine to
Hans Adolf Krebs and Fritz
Albert Lipmann, Dec. 11,
1953]. NOLM 3:395
Presentation [of the Nobel Prize
for Physiology or Medicine to
Otto Heinrich Warburg, Dec.
10, 1931]. NOLM 2:251

Hartline, H. K.
Visual receptors and retinal
interaction. NOLM 4:269

Hedrén, G.
Presentation [of the Nobel Prize
for Physiology or Medicine to
Karl Landsteiner, Dec. 11,
1930]. NOLM 2:229

Hench, P. S.
The reversibility of certain
rheumatic and nonrheumatic
conditions by the use of cortisone or of the pituitary
adrenocorticotropic hormone.
NOLM 3:311

Henschen, F.
Presentation [of the Nobel Prize
for Physiology or Medicine for

1928 to Charles Jules Henri Nicolle]. NOLM 2:175
Presentation [of the Nobel Prize for Physiology or Medicine for 1933 to Thomas Hunt Morgan, June 4, 1934]. NOLM 2:307

Hershey, A. D.
Idiosyncrasies of DNA structure. NOLM 4:417

Hess, W. R.
The central control of the activity of internal organs. NOLM 3:247

Heymans, C. J. F.
The part played by vascular presso- and chemoreceptors in respiratory control. NOLM 2:460

Hill, A. V.
The mechanism of muscular contraction. NOLM 2:10

Hodgkin, A. L.
The ionic basis of nervous conduction. NOLM 4:32

Holley, R. W.
Alanine transfer RNA. NOLM 4:324

Holmgren, I.
Presentation [of the Nobel Prize for Physiology or Medicine to George Hoyt Whipple, George Richards Minot, and William Parry Murphy, Dec. 12, 1934]. NOLM 2:335

Hopkins, Sir F. G.
The earlier history of vitamin research. NOLM 2:211

Houssay, B. A.
The role of the Hypophysis in carbohydrate metabolism and in diabetes. NOLM 3:210

Huggins, C. B.
Endocrine-induced regression of cancers. NOLM 4:235

Huxley, A. F.
The quantitative analysis of excitation and conduction in nerve. NOLM 4:52

Jacob, F.
Genetics of the bacterial cell. NOLM 4:148

Johansson, J. E.
Presentation [of the Nobel

Prize for Physiology or Medicine for 1922 to Archibald Vivian Hill and Otto Fritz Meyerhof, Dec. 12, 1923]. NOLM 2:3
Presentation [of the Nobel Prize for Physiology or Medicine to August Krogh, Dec. 11, 1920]. NOLM 1:529

Katz, B.
On the quantal mechanism of neural transmitter release. NOLM 4:485

Kendall, E. C.
The development of cortisone as a therapeutic agent. NOLM 3:270

Khorana, H. G.
Nucleic acid synthesis in the study of the genetic code. NOLM 4:341

Klein, G.
Presentation [of the Nobel Prize for Physiology or Medicine to Peyton Rous and Charles Brenton Huggins, Dec. 13, 1966]. NOLM 4:215

Koch, R.
The current state of the struggle against tuberculosis. NOLM 1:169

Kocher, E. T.
Concerning pathological manifestations in low-grade thyroid diseases. NOLM 1:330

Kornberg, A.
The biologic synthesis of deoxyribonucleic acid. NOLM 3:665

Kossel, A.
The chemical composition of the cell nucleus. NOLM 1:394

Krebs, H. A.
The citric acid cycle. NOLM 3:399

Krogh, A.
A contribution to the physiology of the capillaries. NOLM 1:536

Landsteiner, K.
On individual differences in human blood. NOLM 2:234

Laveran, C. L. A.
Protozoa as causes of disease. NOLM 1:264

Lederberg, J.
A view of genetics. NOLM 3:615

cine to Ivan Petrovich Pavlov, Dec. 12, 1904].
NOLM 1:135
Presentation [of the Nobel Prize for Physiology or Medicine to Niels Ryberg Finsen, 1903]. NOLM 1:123
Presentation [of the Nobel Prize for Physiology or Medicine to Robert Koch, Dec. 12, 1905].
NOLM 1:163
Presentation [of the Nobel Prize for Physiology or Medicine to Sir Ronald Ross, Dec. 12, 1902]. NOLM 1:21

Muller, H. J.
The production of mutations. NOLM 3:154

Müller, P. H.
Dichloro-diphenyl-trichloroethane and newer insecticides. NOLM 3:227

Murphy, W. P.
Pernicious anemia. NOLM 2:369

Nicolle, C. J. H.
Investigations on typhus. NOLM 2:180

Nirenberg, M. W.
The genetic code. NOLM 4:370

Ochoa, S.
Enzymatic synthesis of ribonucleic acid. NOLM 3:645

Olivecrona, H.
Presentation [of the Nobel Prize for Physiology or Medicine to Walter Rudolf Hess and Antonio Caetano De Abreu Freire Egas Moniz, Dec. 12, 1949]. NOLM 3:243

Pavlov, I. P.
Physiology of digestion. NOLM 1:141

Petterson, A.
Presentation [of the Nobel Prize for Physiology or Medicine to Jules Bordet, 1919]. NOLM 1:519

Ramon y Cajal, S.
The structure and connexions of neurons. NOLM 1:220

Reichard, P.
Presentation [of the Nobel

Prize for Physiology or Medicine to Robert W. Holley, Har Gobind Khorana, and Marshall W. Nirenberg, Dec. 12, 1968]. NOLM 4:321

Reichstein, T.
Chemistry of the adrenal cortex hormones. NOLM 3:291

Richards, D. W.
The contributions of right heart catheterization to physiology and medicine, with some observations on the physiopathology of pulmonary heart disease. NOLM 3:513

Richet, C. R.
Anaphylaxis. NOLM 1:473

Ross, Sir R.
Researches on malaria. NOLM 1:25

Rous, P.
The challenge to man of the neoplastic cell. NOLM 4:220

Sherrington, Sir C. S.
Inhibition as a coordinative factor. NOLM 2:278

Sjöquist, J.
Presentation [of the Nobel Prize for Physiology or Medicine for 1923 to Frederick Grant Banting and John James Richard Macleod, 1925]. NOLM 2:45

Spemann, H.
The organizer-effect in embryonic development. NOLM 2:381

Sundberg, C.
Presentation [of the Nobel Prize for Physiology or Medicine to Charles Louis Alphonse Laveran, Dec. 11, 1907]. NOLM 1:259
Presentation [of the Nobel Prize for Physiology or Medicine to Charles Robert Richet, Dec. 11, 1913]. NOLM 1:469

Szent-Györgyi, A.
Oxidation, energy transfer, and vitamins. NOLM 2:440

Tatum, E. L.
A case history in biological research. NOLM 3:602

Theiler, M.
The development of vaccines against yellow fever. NOLM 3:351

Theorell, A. H. T.
The nature and mode of action of oxidation enzymes.
NOLM 3:480
Presentation [of the Nobel Prize for Physiology or Medicine to Carl Ferdinand Cori, Gerty Theresa Cori-Radnitz, and Bernardo Alberto Houssay, Dec. 11, 1947]. NOLM 3:179
Presentation [of the Nobel Prize for Physiology or Medicine to Severo Ochoa and Arthur Kornberg, Dec. 11, 1959]. NOLM 3:641
Uvnäs, B.
Presentation [of the Nobel Prize for Physiology or Medicine to Daniel Bovet, Dec. 11, 1957].
NOLM 3:549
Presentation [of the Nobel Prize for Physiology or Medicine to Julius Axelrod, Ulf Von Euler, and Bernhard Katz, Dec. 12, 1970]. NOLM 4:441
Von Euler, U.
Adrenergic neurotransmitter functions. NOLM 4:470
Wagner-Jauregg, J.
The treatment of dementia paralytica by malaria inoculation. NOLM 2:159
Waksman, S. A.
Streptomycin: background, isolation, properties, and utilization. NOLM 3:370
Wald, G.
The molecular basis of visual excitation.
NOLM 4:292
Wallgren, A.
Presentation [of the Nobel Prize for Physiology or Medicine to Selman Abraham Waksman, Dec. 12, 1952]. NOLM 3:365
Warburg, O. H.
The oxygen-transferring ferment of respiration.
NOLM 2:254
Watson, J. D.
The involvement of RNA in the synthesis of proteins.
NOLM 3:785
Wernstedt, W.

Presentation [of the Nobel Prize for Physiology or Medicine for 1926 to Johannes Andreas Grib Fibiger, Dec. 12, 1927]. NOLM 2:119
Presentation [of the Nobel Prize for Physiology or Medicine to Julius Wagner-Jauregg, Dec. 12, 1927]. NOLM 2:155
Whipple, G. H.
Hemoglobin regeneration as influenced by diet and other factors. NOLM 2:346
Wilkins, M. H. F.
The molecular configuration of nucleic acids. NOLM 3:754
Yalow, R. S.
"Let us join hands, hearts and minds." BA 1977-78:181

Noel-Baker, Philip John
Peace and the arms race (Nobel Lecture, Dec. 11, 1959). NOLP 3:186

NOEL-BAKER, PHILIP JOHN
Jahn, G.
Presentation [of the Nobel Prize for Peace to Philip John Noel-Baker, Dec. 10, 1959]. NOLP 3:175

NOISE
Hatfield, M. O.
Noise. LINRS:211

NOMINATIONS
Conkling, R.
Nomination of U.S. Grant for a third term. BREWE 4:1366
Dougherty, D.
"Hancock the superb."
BREWE 5:1904
Ingersoll, R. G.
Nominating Blaine.
BREWE 7:2578; HURH:154
Johnson, L. B.
Remarks to the nation (declining nomination to Presidency).
ANN 18:613; BA 1967-68:63
Lincoln, A.
"A house divided against itself cannot stand." ANN 9:1;
BAS:100 (outline only);
BREWE 7:2777; FRIP:197;
HURH:88
Nomination of Hubert Horatio Humphrey, Jr. (outline of

speech). CUB:100
Nomination of someone for an
office (3 examples).
BNH:94
Rogers, W.
Nominating Calvin Coolidge.
BAP:298; BAPR: 366
Suggestions for nomination or
speech of praise. With
examples of. PAE:185

---- See also Acceptance speeches
- Nominations; Candidates

NONVIOLENCE
King, M. L., Jr.
Nonviolence: moral challenge
for peace and justice.
NOLP 3:333; THOMS:99

Noonan, T. Clifford
Introduces the Very Reverend
Theodore M. Hesburgh,
president of Notre Dame
University. PRS:48

NORADRENALIN METABOLISM
Axelrod, J.
Noradrenaline: fate and con-
trol of its biosynthesis.
NOLM 4:444

Nordmeyer, Arnold
The 'Black budget' 1958 (June
26, 1958). MACS:434 sel.

Nordström, T.
Presentation [of the Nobel Prize
for Chemistry to Alfred
Werner, Dec. 11, 1913].
NOLC 1:253
Presentation [of the Nobel Prize
for Physics to Heike Kamerlingh Onnes, Dec. 11,
1913]. NOLPH 1:303

Norris, George W.
Opposition to Wilson's War
Message. ANN 14:101

Norrish, R. G. W.
Some fast reactions in gases
studied by flash photolysis
and kinetic spectroscopy
(Nobel Lecture, Dec. 11,
1967). NOLC 4:206

NORRISH, R. G. W.
Olander, H. A.

Presentation [of the Nobel
Prize for Chemistry to Manfred Eigen, R. G. W. Norrish
and George Porter, Dec. 11,
1967]. NOLC 4:165

NORTH ATLANTIC PACT See
North Atlantic Treaty Organization

NORTH ATLANTIC TREATY OR-
GANIZATION
Acheson, D. G.
North Atlantic Pact.
ANN 16:587
Gruenther, A. M.
NATO. HURH:334
Taft, R. A.
Against the treaty (North At-
lantic Pact). ANN 16:591

Northcote, Cyril See Parkinson,
Cyril Northcote

Northrop, John Howard
The preparation of pure enzymes
and virus proteins (Nobel Lecture, Dec. 12, 1946).
NOLC 3:124

NORTHROP, JOHN HOWARD
Tiselius, A. W. K.
Presentation [of the Nobel
Prize for Chemistry to James
Batcheller Sumner, John
Howard Northrop, and Wendell
Meredith Stanley, Dec. 12,
1946]. NOLC 3:109

Norton, Eleanor Holmes
In pursuit of equality in academe:
new themes and dissonant
chords (Chicago, March 7,
1976). BA 1976-77:65

Nottingham, Heneage Finch, 1st
Earl of
Opening the prosecution for regi-
cide under Charles II (trial of
T. Harrison). BREWE 6:2159

NRA See National Recovery Administration

NUCLEAR INDUCTION
Bloch, F.
The principle of nuclear in-
duction. NOLPH 3:203

NUCLEAR MAGNETISM
   Purcell, E. M.
      Research in nuclear magnet-
      ism. NOLPH 3:219

NUCLEAR PHYSICS
   Jensen, J. H. D.
      Glimpses at the history of
      the nuclear structure theory.
      NOLPH 4:40

NUCLEAR SHELL THEORY
   Mayer, M. G.
      The shell model.
      NOLPH 4:18

NUCLEAR WARFARE See Atomic
   warfare

NUCLEIC ACIDS
   Khorana, H. G.
      Nucleic acid synthesis on the
      study of the genetic code.
      NOLM 4:341
   Wilkins, M. H. F.
      The molecular configuration
      of nucleic acids.
      NOLM 3:754

NUCLEOTIDES
   Todd, Sir A. R.
      Synthesis in the study of
      nucleotides. NOLC 3:522

NURENBURG TRIALS See World
   War, 1939-1945 - War
   criminals

NURSES AND NURSING
   Introductions for nurses (4
      examples). BNH:32

Nussbaum, Max
   Al Jolson. WALE:225

NUTRITION
   Pyke, M.
      Man eats dog. MDYG:280

NUTRITION POLICY
   Hannah, J. A.
      Meeting world food news.
      BA 1976-77:103

NYE, GERALD P., JR.
   Connally, T. T. and others
      Censure of Senator Nye.
      BRR:69

- O -

OATHS
   Cox, S. S.
      Against the ironclad oath.
      BREWE 4:1436

O'BRIEN, WILLIAM DAVID
   Croarkin, W.
      Presents William David
      O'Brien. LYI:163

OBSCENITY
   Brennan, W. J., Jr. and others
      Ginzburg et al v. United
      States: opinion for the court
      and dissenting opinion.
      ANN 18:350

OCCUPATIONS
   Scott, R.
      A job-seeking interview: a
      transcript. MOPR:381

Ochoa, Severo
   Enzymatic synthesis of ribonu-
      cleic acid (Nobel Lecture,
      Dec. 11, 1959). NOLM 3:645

OCHOA, SEVERO
   Theorell, H.
      Presentation [of the Nobel
      Prize for Physiology or Medi-
      cine to Severo Ochoa and
      Arthur Kornberg, Dec. 11,
      1959]. NOLM 3:641

Ockenga, Harold J.
   Evangelical Christianity.
      ANN 16:115

O'Connell, Daniel
   Catholic rights in Ireland (Dublin,
      Feb. 23, 1814). CLAYP:281
   Demand for justice to Ireland.
      BREWE 8:3107
   Ireland worth dying for. Same
      as his On repeal of the Union
   On repeal of the Union (Tara
      Hill, Ireland, Aug. 15, 1843).
      BREWE 8:3099; BRYH:358;
      MCB:288; STRM:198
   Speech at Tara. Same as his On
      repeal of the Union
   Speech at a meeting to recover
      Catholic rights. Same as his
      Catholic rights in Ireland

Speech at Tara. Same as his
On repeal of the Union

O'CONNELL, DANIEL
Lacordaire, J. B. H.
Sacred cause of the human
race (panegyric of Daniel
O'Connell). BREWE 7:2692

O'Connell, James T.
Responds to an introduction.
PRS:138

Odegaard, Charles E.
Bridging the generation gap, the
march downtown (Univ. of
Washington, June 13, 1970).
HOR:42
Responds to an introduction.
PRS:155

Odhner, C. T.
Presentation [of the Nobel Prize
for Chemistry to Jacobus
Henricus Van't Hoff, Dec.
13, 1901]. NOLC 1:3
Presentation [of the Nobel Prize
for Physics to Wilhelm Conrad Röntgen, 1901].
NOLPH 1:3

OFFICE - ACCEPTANCE
Accepting an office (2 examples).
BNH:87
Coolidge, C.
Have faith in Massachusetts
(on being elected President
of Massachusetts Senate).
BOORA 2:752

OFFICERS See Acceptance
speeches - Nominations;
Candidates; Educators; Executives; Inaugural addresses;
Installation speeches; Nominations; Offices - Acceptance;
Public officials; Presidents -
United States. Also subheads
under this subject

OFFICERS, PRESIDING
Suggestions for a presiding officer. PAE:195

OFFICERS, RETIRING
Suggestions for preparation of
a speech for a retiring
officer. PAE:187

Oglesby, Carl
How can we continue to sack the
ports of Asia and still dream
of Jesus. LAA:15

OHIO CANAL
Clinton, D.
Address at the Licking Summit
near Newark, Ohio. HAW:119

Okpara, Michael Iheonukara
Progress without tears; address
at convocation, University of
Nigeria. EMP:138

Olander, A.
Presentation [of the Nobel Prize
for Chemistry to Jaroslav
Heyrovsky, Dec. 11, 1959].
NOLC 3:561
Presentation [of the Nobel Prize
for Chemistry to Manfred
Eigen, R. G. W. Norrish and
George Porter, Dec. 11,
1967]. NOLC 4:165
Presentation [of the Nobel Prize
for Chemistry to Sir Cyril
Norman Hinshelwood and
Nikolai Nikolaovic Semenov,
Dec. 11, 1956]. NOLC 3:471

OLD AGE
Hausman, L.
Older Americans: a natural
resource. LINRST:36
Klemme, D.
The age of Gerontion.
LINSR:152
Spotted Tail
We are young no longer.
ALA:37
Thani Nayagam, X.
Age and learning. MONS:187

Old Tassel, Indian chief
Plea for his home.
BREWE 7:2569

Olivecrona, H.
Presentation [of the Nobel Prize
for Physiology or Medicine to
Walter Rudolf Hess and An-
tonio Caetano De Abreu Freire
Egas Moniz, Dec. 12, 1949].
NOLM 3:243

Oliver, Robert T.
Culture and communication.

ARS:19
Responds to an introduction.
PRS:152

Olmsted, Frederick Law
Unplanned growth of cities.
ANN 10:224

Olney, Richard
Presents Woodrow Wilson.
LYI:215

Olson, Culbert L.
Migratory labor and civil liberties.   ANN 15:587

Olson, Harvey S.
Introduces Admiral John S.
McCain.   PRS:56
Introduces Charles O. Finley,
owner, Kansas City Ath-
letics.   BRS:114
Introduces Dr. Glenn T. Sea-
borg, chairman of the
Atomic Energy Commission.
PRS:47
Introduces Dr. Luther L.
Terry, United States Surgeon
General.   PRS:42
Introduces Dr. Max Rafferty,
State Superintendent of
Public Instruction (California).
PRS:53
Introduces Dr. Walter H. Judd.
PRS:125
Introduces Earl B. Hathaway,
president of Firestone Tire
and Rubber Company.   PRS:13
Introduces Harry Schwartz of
the New York Times.
PRS:60
Introduces Marguerite Higgins.
PRS:107
Introduces Ronald Reagan.
PRS:49
Introduces Senator Everett M.
Dirksen.   PRS:121
Introduces Senator Karl E.
Mundt.   PRS:108
Introduces the Honorable Hervé
Alphand, French Ambas-
sador to the United States.
PRS:35
Introduces William McChesney
Martin, Jr., chairman,
board of governors, Federal
Reserve System.   PRS:63

O'NEILL, EUGENE GLADSTONE
Brown, J. E.
Acceptance [of the Nobel Prize
for Literature for Eugene
Gladstone O'Neill, 1936].
NOB 19:131; NOL:336
Hallström, P.
Presentation [of the Nobel
Prize for Literature to Eugene
Gladstone O'Neill, 1936].
NOB 19:125; NOL:330

Ong Pang Boon
Educational pyramid.   MONS:436

ONN BIN JAFFIR
Abdul Rahman, T.
Dato Onn--a great leader.
MONS:33

Onnes, Heike Kamerlingh
Investigations into the properties
of substances at low temperatures, which have led, amongst
other things, to the preparation
of liquid helium (Nobel Lecture, Dec. 11, 1913).
NOLPH 1:306

ONNES, HEIKE KAMERLINGH
Nordstrom, T.
Presentation [of the Nobel
Prize for Physics to Heike
Kamerlingh Onnes, Dec. 11,
1913].   NOLPH 1:303

Onsager, Lars
The motion of ions: principles
and concepts (Nobel Lecture,
Dec. 11, 1968).   NOLC 4:272

ONSAGER, LARS
Claesson, S.
Presentation [of the Nobel
Prize for Chemistry to Lars
Onsager, Dec. 11, 1968].
NOLC 4:269

OPENING ADDRESSES
Boorstin, D. J.
Beginnings.   BA 1976-77:138
Douglass, F.
The abilities and possibilities
of our race.   FON:326
Lee Kuan Yew
Unionism: rethinking is vital
(opening National Trade Union

Conference).   MONS:366
Lim See Aun
   Doubting Thomases were
   wrong (opening of Chemical
   Company of Malaysian fac-
   tory).   MONS:153
Thomson, T. J. B.
   Spirit of humanity (opening
   of Federal Court of Malaysia).
   MONS:285
Trimble, A.
   Keynote address NCAI Con-
   vention, October 18, 1976.
   MAES:233
Webster, D.
   Railroad in New Hampshire
   (opening Northern Railroad).
   ANN 7:388

---- See also Club speeches; Dedication addresses; Welcoming
   addresses

Oppenheimer, J. Robert
   Prospect in the arts and sciences (at Columbia University
   bicentennial anniversary
   celebration).   New York,
   Dec. 26, 1954.   HURH:319;
   HURS:211
   "We know too much for one
   man to know much."   Same
   as his Prospect in the arts
   and sciences

OPPORTUNITY
   Manickavasagam, V.
   Era of opportunity.
   MONS:162

OPTIMISM
   Martin, D.
   A case for optimism.
   EHN:124; MOP:154; MOPR:130

OREGON
   Calhoun, J. C.
   On territorial expansion.
   ANN 7:87
   Cobb, H.
   "Fifty-four forty or right."
   BREWE 4:1317
   Winthrop, R. C.
   Oregon question.   ANN 7:317

ORGANIC COMPOUNDS
   Pregl, F.
   Quantitative micro-analysis

of organic substances.
   NOLC 2:28

ORGANIZATION
   Goldhaber, G. M.
   Organizational communication.
   LINRST:44

ORGANIZED LABOR   See   Labor
   Unions

ORGANS (ANATOMY)
   Hess, W. R.
   The central control of the
   activity of internal organs.
   NOLM 3:247

ORIENT
   Dean, V. M.
   Minds of the non-western
   world.   ARS:234

Orr, John Boyd   See   Boyd Orr,
   John

Osborne, Lithgow
   Acceptance [of the Nobel Prize
   for Peace for Cordell Hull,
   Dec. 10, 1945].   NOLP 2:318

Osborne, Peter
   It is time for us to be up and
   doing.   (New Haven African
   Church, July 5, 1832).
   FON:47

Osceola   See   Maestas, J. R.

Oseen, C. W.
   Presentation [of the Nobel Prize
   for Physics for 1925 to James
   Franck and Gustav Hertz, Dec.
   11, 1926].   NOLPH 2:95
   Presentation [of the Nobel Prize
   for Physics to Jean Baptiste
   Perrin, Dec. 11, 1926].
   NOLPH 2:135
   Presentation [of the Nobel Prize
   for Physics to Louis-Victor
   De Broglie, Dec. 12, 1929].
   NOLPH 2:241
   Presentation [of the Nobel Prize
   for Physics for 1928 to Owen
   Willans Richardson, Dec. 12,
   1929].   NOLPH 2:221

Osgood, David
   An American Thanksgiving for

divine favor. (Medford,
Mass., Feb. 19, 1795).
DAVF:42

Osias, Camilo
Justice and separation of powers
(National Assembly, May 23,
1938). CURM:190

Osmeña, Sergio
The National Assembly, its
aims and accomplishments
(Bulacan, May 7, 1910).
CURM:50

OSSIETZKY, CARL VON
Stang, F.
Presentation [of the Nobel
Prize for Peace, 1935, to
Carl Von Ossietzky, Dec.
10, 1936]. NOLP 2:207

Österling, Anders
Presentation [of the Nobel Prize
for Literature to Albert
Camus, 1957]. NOB 4:3;
NOL:522
Presentation [of the Nobel Prize
for Literature to André
Gide, 1947]. NOB 7:3;
NOL:422
Presentation [of the Nobel Prize
for Literature to Bertrand
Arthur William Russell,
1950]. NOB 15:255; NOL:449
Presentation [of the Nobel Prize
for Literature to Erik Axel
Karlfeldt, 1931]. NOB 10:101;
NOL:295
Presentation [of the Nobel Prize
for Literature to Ernest
Miller Hemingway, 1954].
NOB 9:3; NOL:497
Presentation [of the Nobel Prize
for Literature to François
Mauriac, 1952]. NOB 13:3;
NOL:477
Presentation [of the Nobel Prize
for Literature to Giorgos
Seferis, 1963]. NOB 17:3;
NOL:580
Presentation [of the Nobel Prize
for Literature to Hermann
Hesse, 1946]. NOB 9:233;
NOL:412
Presentation [of the Nobel Prize
for Literature to Ivo Andrić,
1961]. NOB 1:117; NOL:562

Presentation [of the Nobel Prize
for Literature to Johannes Vil-
helm Jensen, 1944].
NOB 8:259; NOL:397
Presentation [of the Nobel Prize
for Literature to John Gals-
worthy, 1932]. NOB 6:227;
NOL:302
Presentation [of the Nobel Prize
for Literature to John Stein-
beck, 1962]. NOB 19:201;
NOL:572
Presentation [of the Nobel Prize
for Literature to Miguel Angel
Asturias, 1967]. NOB 2:3;
NOL:624
Presentation [of the Nobel Prize
for Literature to Mikhail Alek-
sandrovich Sholokhov, 1965].
NOB 17:37; NOL:603
Presentation [of the Nobel Prize
for Literature to Pär Fabian
Lagerkvist, 1951].
NOB 10:201; NOL:466
Presentation [of the Nobel Prize
for Literature to Saint-John
Perse, 1960]. NOB 20:3;
NOL:553
Presentation [of the Nobel Prize
for Literature to Salvatore
Quasimodo, 1959]. NOB 20:281;
NOL:534
Presentation [of the Nobel Prize
for Literature to Shmuel Yosef
Agnon and Leonie Nelly Sachs,
1966]. NOB 1:3; NOB 16:3;
NOL:611
Presentation [of the Nobel Prize
for Literature to Thomas
Stearns Eliot, 1948].
NOB 5:261; NOL:431
Presentation address [of the Nobel
Prize for Literature to Yasun-
ari Kawabata, 1968].
NOB 11:3

Ostwald, Wilhelm
On catalysis (Nobel Lecture, Dec.
12, 1909). NOLC 1:150

OSTWALD, WILHELM
Hildebrand, H.
Presentation [of the Nobel
Prize for Chemistry to Wil-
helm Ostwald, Dec. 12, 1909].
NOLC 1:147

Otis, Harrison Gray
Abolitionism is equivalent to

revolution (1835) (Faneuil
Hall, Boston, Aug. 22,
1835). DAVF:138
Hamilton's influence on Ameri-
can institutions.
BREWE 8:3111

Otis, James
Against Writs of Assistance.
Same as his Writs of As-
sistance, February, 1761
For individual sovereignty and
against "Writs of Assistance."
Same as his Writs of As-
sistance, February, 1761
Speech against the Writs of
Assistance. Same as his
Writs of Assistance, Febru-
ary, 1761
Writs of Assistance, February,
1761. ANN 2:74;
BREWE 8:3125; POC:90

OUTLINES (SPEECH) See
Speeches - Outlines of

Overhill, Jack
Regular snob. MDYG:75

Oxford and Asquith, Herbert
Henry, 1st Earl of
'The Commons and constitu-
tional change. Same as
his Parliament Bill, 1911
Parliament Bill, 1911. (H.
of Commons, July 24, 1911).
MCB:162

---- and others (Sir Edward Car-
son and John E. Redmond)
Debate on the Government of
Ireland Bill. (H. of Com-
mons, April 11, 1912).
MCB:321

OXFORD UNIVERSITY
Eliezer, C. J.
Toast to Oxford. MONS:271

- P -

PACIFIC See Orient

PACIFISM
Walker, A.
Why I am a Christian
pacifist. MCA:204

PAINE, THOMAS
Erskine, T.
Against Thomas Williams for
the publication of Paine's Age
of Reason. BREWE 6:2038
Free speech and fundamental
rights: defense of Tom Paine.
BREWE 6:2069; CLAYP:166

PAINTERS See Art and artists

PAINTING See Art and artists

Palewski, Gaston See Sykes, C.,
jt. auth.

Palmaer, W.
Presentation [of the Nobel Prize
for Chemistry, 1931 to Carl
Bosch and Friedrich Bergius,
May 21, 1932]. NOLC 2:189
Presentation [of the Nobel Prize
for Chemistry for 1934 to
Harold Clayton Urey, Feb. 14,
1935]. NOLC 2:333
Presentation [of the Nobel Prize
for Chemistry to Jean Frédéric
Joliot and Irène Joliot-Curie,
Dec. 12, 1935]. NOLC 2:359
Presentation [of the Nobel Prize
for Chemistry to Walter Nor-
man Haworth and Paul Karrer,
Dec. 11, 1937]. NOLC 2:407

PALMER, JAMES
Griffin, C. E.
Presents James Palmer.
LYI:67

Palmer, Joseph
Africa: continent of change.
(Chicago Council on Foreign
Relations, Dec. 5, 1968.
Speech in 2nd ed. given at
Brandeis Univ. in 1966).
LINRS:33
New Africa: continent of change.
LINR:32

Palmerston, Henry John Temple,
3d Viscount
Against war on Ireland.
BREWE 8:3134
"Civis Romanus sum speech."
Same as his On affairs in
Greece
On affairs in Greece (H. of
Commons, June 25, 1850).
MCB:5

PALMERSTON, HENRY JOHN TEMPLE
On the death of Cobden.
BREWE 8:3131

PALMERSTON, HENRY JOHN
TEMPLE, 3d VISCOUNT
Stanley, A. P.
Palmerston and the duty of
England (funeral oration).
BREWE 9:3506

Palovesik, Susan
Ripples of hope.   BREWW:179

PANAMA CANAL
Hayakawa, S. I.
Senate debate over ratification
of treaties concerning the
Panama Canal.
BA 1977-78:17
Roosevelt, T.
"I took the Canal Zone."
STAT 2:2073
Rusk, D.
For ratification of treaties
with Panama.   BA 1977-78:9

PANAMA CANAL TREATIES, 1977
Hayakawa, S. I.
Senate debate over ratifica-
tion of treaties concerning
the Panama Canal.
BA 1977-78:17
McIntyre, T. J.
Keeping the Senate independent.
BA 1977-78:44
Rusk, D.
For ratification of treaties
with Panama.   BA 1977-78:9

PANAMA CONGRESS, 1826
Adams, J. Q.
On participating in a con-
gress of American nations.
ANN 5:188

Pandora, Gary See Andino, Judy

Pankhurst, Mrs. Emmeline
(Goulden)
Importance of the vote.
BRYH:442
Speech at the Bow Street Police
Court (Oct. 24, 1908).
BRYF:499; BRYH:455

Paredes, Quintin
A brief sketch of the Philip-
pines--past, present and

future (Baltimore, April 4,
1938).   CURM:214

PARENT AND CHILD
Welcome to parents and ladies of
the Woman's Missionary Society on Education Day.
HNWM:21

PARIS
Buckley, F. R.
La Folle epoque.   MDYG:181

PARITY NONCONSERVATION
Lee, T. D.
Weak interactions and noncon-
servation of parity.
NOLPH 3:406
Yang, C. N.
The law of parity conservation
and other symmetry laws of
physics.   NOLPH 3:393

Parker, Theodore
Critique of American churches.
ANN 7:486
Discourse on the death of Daniel
Webster.   BREWE 8:3137
On Daniel Webster after the
Compromise of 1850.   Same
as his Discourse on the death
of Daniel Webster
Present crisis in American af-
fairs.   ANN 8:372
State of the nation (1850).
ANN 8:114
Transient and permanent in
Christianity.   LINS:178

Parkes, Henry
Eight-hour movement.   MCA:33
New constellation.   MCA:37

PARKINSON, CYRIL NORTHCOTE
Cragg, R. T.
Presents Cyril Northcote.
LYI:45

PARKS See Dedication addresses
- Parks

PARLIAMENT ACT, 1911
Curzon of Kedleston, G. and
others
Debate on the Parliament Bill.
MCB:169
Oxford and Asquith, H. H.
Parliament Bill, 1911.
MCB:162

PARLIAMENTARY FORM OF
    GOVERNMENT See Great
    Britain - Parliament

Parnell, Charles Stewart
    Against nonresident landlords.
        BREWE 8:3145
    At Ennis (boycotting defined
        and defended) (Ennis, Ire-
        land, Sept. 19, 1880).
        BRYF:544; MCB:296;
        STRM:346
    His first speech in America.
        BREWE 8:3143
    The Irish land question. Same
        as his At Ennis (boycotting
        defined and defended)

Parry, David
    Organized labor as the "Great
        Muscle Trust." ANN 12:513

Parry, William Edward
    New Zealand citizenship, 1948
        (New Zealand House of
        Representatives, Aug. 17,
        1948). MACS:294 sel.

Parson, Mary Jean
    Idealism: what's wrong with
        it? (New York, July 14,
        1975). BA 1975-76:166

Parsons, Albert R.
    Address at trial, Chicago, Oc-
        tober 7-9, 1886. ACC:90;
        PAF:65

Parsons, Theodore and others
    (E. Pearson)
    Disputation on "The Legality
        of Enslaving the Africans."
        POC:27

PARTICLES
    Alvarez, L. W.
        Recent developments in
        particle physics.
        NOLPH 4:241
    Gell-Mann, M.
        Symmetry and currents in
        particle physics.
        NOLPH 4:299

PARTICLES (NUCLEAR PHYSICS)
    Cerenkov, P. A.
        Radiation of particles moving
        at a velocity exceeding that

of light, and some of the pos-
        sibilities for their use in ex-
        perimental physics.
        NOLPH 3:423
    Cockcroft, Sir J. D.
        Experiments on the interaction
        of high-speed nucleons with
        atomic nuclei. NOLPH 3:167
    Glaser, D. A.
        Elementary particles and bub-
        ble chambers. NOLPH 3:529
    Hofstadter, R.
        The electron-scattering method
        and its application to the struc-
        ture of nuclei and nucleons.
        NOLPH 3:560
    Walton, E. T. S.
        The artificial production of
        fast particles. NOLPH 3:187

PASSION
    Saurin, J.
        Effect of passion.
        BREWE 9:3371

PATIENCE
    Tertullian, Q. S. F.
        Beauty of patience.
        BREWE 9:3597

PATRIOTISM
    Abdul Rahman, T.
        Soul of our nation. MONS:36
    Bocobo, J. C.
        Love of country. CURM:149
    Bolingbroke, H. S.-J.
        Patriotism. BREWE 2:550
    Clay, H.
        Noblest public virtue.
        BREWE 4:1271
    Goldman, E.
        Anarchy vs. patriotism.
        HURH:166
    Grattan, H.
        Unsurrendering fidelity to
        country. BREWE 6:2333
    Hampden, J.
        Patriot's duty defined: against
        own impeachment.
        BREWE 6:2385
    Jacobusse, K. D.
        Peace through patriotism.
        SCHW:168
    King, T. S.
        Fourth of July oration, 1860.
        HAW:231
    McKinley, W.
        American patriotism (at dedi-

cation of Cuyahoga County
Soldiers' and Sailors' Monu-
ment in Cleveland).
BREWE 8:2899
Muhammad Ghazali bin Shafie
Loyalty to the nation (Malaya).
MONS:218
Sheridan, R. B.
Patriotism and perquisites.
BREWE 9:3439
Walpole, R.
On patriots (at motion to
dismiss him from Council).
BREWE 10:3724

Patterson, Morehead
Responds to an introduction.
PRS:160

Patterson, William L.
"Free by '63." (Civil Rights
Congress, 1960). FON:924

Patton, George S.
"Flanks are something for the
enemy to worry about."
(France, July 31, 1944).
HURH:274

Paul VI (Giovanni Battista Montini
- Pope)
Address before United Nations.
BA 1965-66:67; OLIS:297
Key to peace. BAS:150 (outline
only)

Paul, Nathaniel
The abolition of slavery.
(Albany, N.Y., July 5, 1827).
FON:37

Pauli, Wolfgang
Exclusion principle and quantum
mechanics (Nobel Lecture
for 1945, Dec. 13, 1946).
NOLPH 3:27

PAULI, WOLFGANG
Waller, I.
Presentation [of the Nobel
Prize for Physics for 1945
to Wolfgang Pauli, Dec. 13,
1946]. NOLPH 3:25

Pauling, Linus Carl
Modern structural chemistry
(Nobel Lecture, Dec. 11,
1954). NOLC 3:429

Science and peace (Nobel Lecture
for 1962, Dec. 11, 1963).
NOLP 3:271

PAULING, LINUS CARL
Hagg, G.
Presentation [of the Nobel
Prize for Chemistry to Linus
Carl Pauling, Dec. 11, 1954].
NOLC 3:425
Jahn, G.
Presentation [of the Nobel
Prize for Peace for 1962 to
Linus Carl Pauling, Dec. 10,
1963]. NOLP 3:259

Pavlov, Ivan Petrovich
Physiology of digestion (Nobel
Lecture, Dec. 12, 1904).
NOLM 1:141

PAVLOV, IVAN PETROVICH
Mörner, K. A. H.
Presentation [of the Nobel
Prize for Physiology or Medi-
cine to Ivan Petrovich Pavlov,
Dec. 12, 1904]. NOLM 1:135

Payne, Daniel A.
Slavery brutalizes man. (Fords-
boro, N.Y., June, 1839).
FON:66

Payne, James R.
Australia and the Vietnam War.
VI:75

PEACE
Angell, N.
Peace and the public mind
(Nobel Lecture for 1934,
June 12, 1935). NOLP 2:153
Arnoldson, K. P.
World referendum (Nobel Lec-
ture, Dec. 10, 1908).
NOLP 1:175
Aubert, J.
Vietnam and world peace.
VI:104
Bennett, J. C.
Issue of peace: the voice of
religion. BA 1965-66:142
Blake, E. C.
Ecumenism and peace.
VI:132
Borlaug, N. E.
The green revolution, peace,
humanity (Nobel Lecture, Dec.

11, 1970). NOLP 3:454
Buisson, F. E.
  Changes in concepts of war
  and peace (Nobel Lecture,
  1927, May 31, 1928).
  NOLP 2:35
Bunche, R. J.
  Some reflections on peace in
  our time (Nobel Lecture,
  Dec. 11, 1950).
  NOLP 2:443
Butler, N. M.
  Radio address (Nobel Lec-
  ture, Dec. 12, 1931).
  NOLP 2:136
Cadbury, H. J.
  Quakers and peace (Nobel
  Lecture, Dec. 12, 1947).
  NOLP 2:391
Chandler, R.
  Quest for peace. SCHW:180
Churchill, W. L. S.
  Sinews of peace (speech at
  Fulton, Missouri).
  ANN 16:365; MCB:541
Cremer, W. R.
  The progress and advantages
  of international arbitration
  (Nobel Lecture for 1903,
  Jan. 15, 1905). NOLP 1:46
Demosthenes
  Oration on the peace.
  BREWE 5:1759; SAG:223
Dulles, J. F.
  Peace through law.
  ANN 17:528
Eisenhower, D. D.
  Crusade for peace.
  ANN 17:199
  Price of peace: second in-
  augural address.
  USINAU:263; USINAUG:263
Field, D. D.
  Cost of "Blood and Iron."
  BREWE 6:2157
Fosdick, H. E.
  Unknown soldier.
  LINS:312
Garfield, J. A.
  Revolution and the logic of
  coercion. BREWE 6:2226
Gobat, C. A.
  The development of the
  Hague Conventions of July
  29, 1899 (Nobel Lecture
  for 1902, Oslo, July 18,
  1906). NOLP 1:30
Henderson, A.

Essential elements of a uni-
  versal and enduring peace
  (Nobel Lecture, Dec. 11,
  1934). NOLP 2:185
Hildebrandt, T.
  Christian way. SCHW:198
Inozemstev, N. N.
  Alternative to war. MDV:69
Jacobusse, K. D.
  Peace through patriotism.
  SCHW:168
Jouhaux, L.
  Fifty years of trade-union
  activity in behalf of peace
  (Nobel Lecture, Dec. 11,
  1951). NOLP 3:10
Kellogg, F. B.
  Acceptance and banquet speech
  [for the Nobel Prize for
  Peace, 1929 (Dec. 10, 1930)].
  NOLP 2:79
Kennedy, J. F.
  Step toward peace.
  ANN 18:192
  Toward a strategy of peace.
  KEO:312; MDV:2
Korf, J.
  And old hate walked on through
  time. SCHW:189
Loula, L. A.
  Drunken orgy. SCHW:149
Marshall, G. C.
  Essentials of peace (Nobel
  Lecture, Dec. 11, 1953).
  NOLP 3:76
Moneta, E. T.
  Peace and law in the Italian
  tradition (Nobel Lecture, 1907,
  Aug. 25, 1909). NOLP 1:114
Nixon, R. M.
  Pursuit of peace.
  BA 1969-70:9; ERP:145
Noel-Baker, P. J.
  Peace and the arms race
  (Nobel Lecture, Dec. 11,
  1959). NOLP 3:186
Paul VI
  Key to peace. BAS:150 (out-
  line only)
Pearson, L. B.
  The four faces of peace (Nobel
  Lecture, Dec. 11, 1957).
  NOLP 3:129
Pire, G.
  Brotherly love: foundation of
  peace (Nobel Lecture, Dec.
  11, 1958). NOLP 3:157
Razak, T. A.

And then came peace (Peace
Agreement between Malaysia
and Indonesia). MONS:94

Roosevelt, F. D.
Quarantining the aggressors.
ANN 15:502; BEN:93;
BOORA 2:847; BRYF:474;
ROD:263

Root, E.
Towards making peace per-
manent (Nobel Lecture for
1912). NOLP 1:247

Saavedra Lamas, C.
Radio address (Nobel Lec-
ture, Nov. 29, 1936).
NOLP 2:225

Schweitzer, A.
The problem of peace (Nobel
Lecture for 1952, Nov. 4,
1954). NOLP 3:46

Söderblom, N.
The role of the church in
promoting peace (Nobel Lecture, Dec. 11, 1930).
NOLP 2:93

Swets, P.
Bootstraps and moonshots.
SCHW:183

Vander Jagt, G.
Price of the best. SCHW:59

Van Engen, B.
Casual approach to war.
SCHW:195

Wallace, H. A.
Is American foreign policy
leading to war?
ANN 16:370

Wilson, W.
Peace without victory.
ANN 14:65; FRIP:286;
HURH:173

---- See also League of Nations;
United Nations

PEACE CONFERENCE, 1919
Trotter, W. M.
How I managed to reach the
Peace Conference. FON:470

---- SESSION JANUARY 25
Wilson, W.
Peace Conference at Paris:
Session, January 25, 1919.
HURH:185

---- SESSION, FEBRUARY 15
Wilson, W.

Speech at Peace Conference at
Paris (Session February 15,
1919). ANN 14:180

PEACE MOVEMENT
Bajer, F.
The organization of the Peace
Movement (Nobel Lecture,
1908, May 18, 1909).
NOLP 1:190

Suttner, B. V.
The evolution of the Peace
Movement (Nobel Lecture for
1905, April 18, 1906).
NOLP 1:84

Peaches, Daniel
Statement on the problems of the
elderly American Indians at
the Conference on Indian Elders, Albuquerque, New Mexico, July 17, 1975. MAES:179

Peale, Norman Vincent
Responds to introductions.
PRS:104; 113

Pearl, Chaim
Seal of truth. WALE:140

PEARL HARBOR See World War,
1939-1945 - United States

Pearson, Eliphalet See Parsons,
T., jt. auth.

Pearson, Lester B.
The four faces of peace (Nobel
Lecture, Dec. 11, 1957).
NOLP 3:129

PEARSON, LESTER B.
Bullock, H.
Presents Lester B. Pearson.
LYI:207

Davis, J. W.
Presents Lester B. Pearson.
LYI:220

Jahn, G.
Presentation [of the Nobel
Prize for Peace to Lester
Bowles Pearson, Dec. 10,
1957]. NOLP 3:119

Peckham, Rufus William and others
(J. M. Harlan and O. W.
Holmes, Jr.)
Lochner v. New York, 1905:

opinion for the court and
dissenting opinion. ANN 13:8

Peden, William
Is Thomas Jefferson relevant?
(Columbia, Mo., April 13,
1972). BA 1972-73:94

Peel, Sir Robert, Bart.
Bank charter--the currency.
STRM:213
On the repeal of the Corn Laws.
BREWE 8:3148; JAE:102
Plea for higher education (in-
stallation speech as Lord
Rector of University of
Glasgow). BREWE 8:3153

Peirce, Herbert H. D.
Acceptance [of the Nobel Prize
for Peace for Theodore
Roosevelt, Dec. 10, 1906].
NOLP 1:99

Pelham, Henry See Walpole,
R., jt. auth.

PELTIER, JEAN
Mackintosh, J.
In behalf of free speech: on
the trial of Jean Peltier
accused of libelling Napoleon
Bonaparte. BREWE 8:2919

PENAL COLONIES
Higinbotham, G.
For the annexation of New
Guinea. MCA:43

PENANG UNIVERSITY See University of Penang

Pendleton, Edmund
Liberty and government in
America. BREWE 8:3156

---- See also Mason, G., jt. auth.

PENICILLIN
Chain, E. B.
The chemical structure of the
penicillins. NOLM 3:110
Fleming, Sir A.
Penicillin. NOLM 3:83
Florey, Sir H. W.
Penicillin. NOLM 3:96

Penn, William
Golden rule against tyranny.
BREWE 8:3162

Pennings, Burrell
New men for a new world.
SCHW:153

Pennington, J. W. C.
The position and duties of the
colored people. (Poughkeepsie,
N.Y., August 24, 1863).
FON:271

PENNSYLVANIA - SUPREME COURT
Gibson, J. B.
Against judicial review: dis-
senting opinion on Eakin v.
Raub. ANN 5:174

PENSIONS
Curran, J. P.
Against pensions.
BREWE 4:1543

---- MILITARY
Cleveland, G.
Skeptical view of pension
legislation. ANN 11:90

Pepper, George Wharton
Introducing Ferdinand Foch.
LYI:145
Presents Charles Evans Hughes.
LYI:127
Presents Earl Warren.
LYI:121

PEPPER, GEORGE WHARTON
Mason, W. C.
Presents George Wharton
Pepper. LYI:129

Percy, Charles H.
Chicagoan goes South.
BA 1965-66:106
Eulogy for Robert Kennedy (July
30, 1968). JAM:42
For the nomination of Gerald R.
Ford. (Washington, D.C.,
Nov. 27, 1973).
BA 1973-74:189
Responds to an introduction.
PRS:147

Pericles
Funeral oration. Same as his
On those who died in the war

On those who died in the war.
ARS:191; BAS:133 (outline
only); BREWE 8:3169;
SAG:33
On the cause of Athenian greatness. Same as his On those
who died in the war
Pericles' funeral speech. Same
as his On those who died in
the war

Perkins, James A.
Bridging the generation gap,
how the New Deal became
today's establishment (Univ.
of Notre Dame, June 2,
1968). HOR:56

PERMANENT COURT OF INTER-
NATIONAL JUSTICE
Coughlin, C. E.
The menace of the World
Court (1935). DAVF:249

PERMANENT INTERNATIONAL
PEACE BUREAU
Løvland, J. G.
Presentation [of the Nobel
Prize for Peace to the Per-
manent International Peace
Bureau, Dec. 10, 1910].
NOLP 1:223

PERNICIOUS ANEMIA
Minot, G. R.
The development of liver
therapy in pernicious anemia.
NOLM 2:357
Murphy, W. P.
Pernicious anemia.
NOLM 2:369

Perrin, Jean Baptiste
Discontinuous structure of matter (Nobel Lecture, Dec.
11, 1926). NOLPH 2:138

PERRIN, JEAN BAPTISTE
Oseen, C. W.
Presentation [of the Nobel
Prize for Physics to Jean
Baptiste Perrin, Dec. 11,
1926]. NOLPH 2:135

Perrott, Russell See Forten,
J., jt. auth.

Perry, Micajah See Walpole,
R., jt. auth.

Perse, Saint-John
Acceptance [of the Nobel Prize
for Literature, 1960].
NOB 20:7; NOL:556

PERSE, SAINT-JOHN
Österling, A.
Presentation [of the Nobel
Prize for Literature to Saint-
John Perse, 1960].
NOB 20:3; NOL:553

PERSIA See Iran

PERSUASIVE SPEECHES
Beecher, L.
A plea for the West. HOW:133
Crary, D. R.
Plague of people. LINR:220
Crittenden, T. T.
Trade and commerce for the
southwestern states.
ANN 11:16
Davies, S.
Curse of cowardice.
ANN 2:23; POC:534
Demosthenes
First Olynthiac oration.
SAG:199
First Philippic. COG:40;
SAG:188
On the Chersoneus. SAG:235
Oration on the peace.
BREWE 5:1759; SAG:223
Second Olynthiac.
BREWE 5:1754; COG:56;
SAG:205
Second Philippic.
BREWE 5:1763; SAG:228
Third Olynthiac. SAG:212
Third Philippic. COG:91;
SAG:249
Freedom from hunger (outline of
speech to persuade that con-
tinued good health of American
people requires easy access
to pharmaceutical vitamins and
food supplements). CUB:48
Geiman, C. K.
Are they really "unteachable"?
LINR:94
Hall, C.
A heap of trouble. EHN:316
Hardin, B.
The Wilkinson and Murdaugh
case. BLY:48
Isocrates
Panogyric. COG:27; SAG:99

Perutz, Max Ferdinand
X-ray analysis of haemoglobin
(Nobel Lecture, Dec. 11,
1962). NOLC 3:653

PERUTZ, MAX FERDINAND
Hagg, G.
Presentation [of the Nobel
Prize for Chemistry to Max
Ferdinand Perutz and John
Cowdery Kendrew, Dec. 11,
1962]. NOLC 3:649

PESTS See Insects, Injurious
and beneficial - Control

Peters, A. D. See Sykes, C.,
jt. auth.

Peters, Lauralee
What is totalitarianism?
LINR:50

Peterson, Martha
In these present crises. (Univ.
of Nebraska, June 17, 1970).
BA 1970-71:73

PETITION OF RIGHT, 1628
Eliot, J.
On the Petition of Right.
BREWE 5:1986; BRYH:123

PETROV, VLADIMIR
Ward, E. J.
Petrov case. MCA:196

Petterson, A.
Presentation [of the Nobel Prize
for Physiology or Medicine
to Jules Bordet, 1919].
NOLM 1:519

PHAGE
Luria, S. E.
Phage, colicins and macro-
regulatory phenomena.
NOLM 4:426

PHASE TRANSFORMATIONS
Zernike, F.
How I discovered phase
contrast. NOLPH 3:239

Phelps, William Lyon
Owning books. (New Haven,
Conn., April 6, 1933).
HURH:225

Presents André Chevrillon.
LYI:52
Presents Sir William Llewellyn.
LYI:26
"You should own no book that you
are afraid to mark up."
Same as his Owning books

PHILANTHROPY See Charities

PHILIP II, KING OF MACEDONIA,
382-336 B.C.
Demosthenes
First Olynthiac oration.
SAG:199
First Philippic. COG:40;
SAG:188
On the crown. BREWE 5:1688;
COG:151
Oration on the peace.
BREWE 5:1759; SAG:223
Second Olynthiac.
BREWE 5:1754; COG:56;
SAG:205
Second Philippic.
BREWE 5:1763; SAG:228
Third Olynthiac. SAG:212
Third Philippic. COG:91;
SAG:249
Isocrates
Address to Philip. COG:67;
SAG:137
On the Chersoneus. SAG:235

PHILIPPINE ISLANDS
Beveridge, A. J.
Philippine question.
ANN 12:336; BRR:29
Bocobo, J. C.
Love of country. CURM:149
Evangelista, T.
The needs of a nation.
CURM:160
McKinley, W.
Fourth annual message.
STAT 2:1971
Quezon, M. L.
On Spain's contribution to the
Philippines. CURM:24
Romulo, C. P.
Bandung address. CROCK:141
Roosevelt, T.
First annual message.
ANN 12:433; STAT 2:2014

---- ARMY
Vargas, J. B.
The role of the army.
CURM:98

---- CONSTITUTION
Recto, C. M.
 The preparation of the Con-
 stitution. CURM:250
Vinzone, W. Q.
 Defects in the draft of the
 Constitution. CURM:304

---- FOREIGN RELATIONS -
 UNITED STATES
Paredes, Q.
 A brief sketch of the Philip-
 pines--past, present and
 future. CURM:214

---- HISTORY
Paredes, Q.
 A brief sketch of the Philip-
 pines--past, present and
 future. CURM:214

---- NATIONAL ASSEMBLY
Osmeña, S.
 The National Assembly, its
 aims and accomplishments.
 CURM:50

---- POLITICS AND GOVERNMENT
Osmeña, S.
 The National Assembly, its
 aims and accomplishments.
 CURM:50
Quezon, M. L.
 Filipinos of today and
 Filipinos of yesterday.
 CURM:29
 Inaugural address. CURM:16
Quirino, E.
 Commemorating a national
 event. CURM:239
Romulo, C. P.
 The mind of a new common-
 wealth. CURM:267
Roxas, M.
 A farewell to the Assembly.
 CURM:282

Phillips, Charles
Dinas Island speech on Washington. BREWE 8:3176

Phillips, Wendell
John Brown and the spirit of
 "59". BREWE 8:3181
Fourth of July oration (Boston,
 July 4, 1854). HAW:23
Murder of Lovejoy (Boston,
 Dec. 8, 1837). ALS:161;

HURH:74
On the philosophy of the Abolition
 Movement. (January 27, 1853).
 MDT:35
The proclamation, how to make
 it efficient. (Music Hall, Bos-
 ton, Jan. 4, 1863). MDT:148
Scholar in a Republic.
 ANN 10:488
Toussaint L'Ouverture. OLIS:170
Under the flag. Boston's Music
 Hall, April 21, 1861).
 MDT:119
"When he fell, civil authority was
 trampled under foot." Same
 as his Murder of Lovejoy

PHILLIPS, WENDELL
Curtis, G. W.
 Eulogy on Wendell Phillips.
 BREWE 4:1571

PHILOSOPHY
Ayers, A. J. and others
 What are philosophers for?
 MDYG:101
Santayana, G.
 Genteel tradition in American
 philosophy. ANN 13:277

PHOTOCHEMISTRY
Porter, G.
 Flash photolysis and some of
 its applications. NOLC 4:241

PHOTOSYNTHESIS
Calvin, M.
 The path of carbon in photo-
 synthesis. NOLC 3:618

PHYSICIANS
Introductions for doctors (6 ex-
 amples). BNH:25
Raskas, B. S.
 Physician's prayer. WALE:149
Skinner, C. O.
 "Bottoms up" (toast to gyne-
 cologists). HURH:311

PHYSICS
Bothe, W.
 The coincidence method.
 NOLPH 3:271
Bridgman, P. W.
 General survey of certain re-
 sults in the field of high-
 pressure physics.
 NOLPH 3:53

PICASSO, PABLO
Carlat, J.
Green parrot.   LINR:46;
LINRS:59

Pickens, William
Kind of democracy the Negro
race expects. (WWI, 1917).
FON:601

Pierce, Franklin
First annual message.
STAT 1:856
Fourth annual message.
STAT 1:918
Inaugural address.
USINAU:103; USINAUG:103
Military academy. ANN 6:273
Second annual message.
STAT 1:875
Third annual message.
STAT 1:895

PILGRIM FATHERS
Adams, J. Q.
Oration at Plymouth (com-
memoration of the landing
of the Pilgrims).
BREWE 1:65
Webster, D.
Plymouth oration.
BREWE 10:3846

Pinchback, Pinkney Benton Stewart
The whole race must protest.
(1897).   FON:596

Pinkney, William
Missouri question.
BREWE 8:3195
On the first issues of Civil
War. Same as his Mis-
souri question

Pinson, William M., Jr.
The Playboy philosophy--con.
(Atlanta, 1970).   LINRS:170;
LINRST:193

PIONEER GIRLS
Welcome to Girl Scouts (or
Pioneer Girls, etc.).
HNWM:50

Pirandello, Luigi
Acceptance [of the Nobel Prize
for Literature, 1934].
NOB 20:77; NOL:324

PIRANDELLO, LUIGI
Hallström, P.
Presentation [of the Nobel
Prize for Literature to Luigi
Pirandello, 1934].
NOB 20:71; NOL:320

Pire, Georges
Brotherly love: foundation of
peace (Nobel Lecture, Dec.
11, 1958). NOLP 3:157

PIRE, GEORGES
Jahn, G.
Presentation [of the Nobel
Prize for Peace to Georges
Pire, Dec. 10, 1958].
NOLP 3:151

Pitt, William, 1st Earl of Chatham,
1708-1778
Address to the throne concerning
affairs in America, November
18, 1777. ALS:105;
BREWE 3:1067; BRYH:201
Attempt to subjugate America.
Same as his Address to the
throne concerning affairs in
America, November 18, 1777
Chatham's last speech.
BREWE 3:1086
Debate in 1741 on wages of
sailors. See Walpole, R.,
jt. auth.
English Constitution.
BREWE 3:1077
On American policy. (January
20, 1775). (House of Lords,
Jan. 20, 1775). CLAYP:40
On an address to the throne.
Same as his Address to the
throne concerning affairs in
America, November 18, 1777
On restoring peace with America
(speech on his Amendment to
the Address of Thanks). Same
as his Address to the throne
concerning affairs in America,
November 18, 1777
On the right to tax America.
STRM:11
Speech on the government policy
in America. Same as his On
American policy, January 20,
1775

Pitt, William, 1759-1806
Abolition of the slave-trade.

Same as his Indicts the
slave trade and foresees
a liberated Africa
Against French Republicanism.
BREWE 8:3202
England's share in the slave
trade. Same as his Indicts
the slave trade and foresees
a liberated Africa
Indicts the slave trade and
foresees a liberated Africa
(House of Commons, April
2, 1792). BREWE 8:3208;
CLAYP:138; JAE:12;
STRM:91
Iniquity of slavery. Same as
his Indicts the slave trade
and foresees a liberated
Africa
Speech on the slave trade.
Same as his Indicts the
slave trade and foresees
a liberated Africa

---- and others (G. Tierney)
Deliverance of Europe (con-
tains his Against French
Republicanism speech).
BRYH:281

Planck, Max
The genesis and present state
of development of the quantum theory (Nobel Lecture
for 1918, June 2, 1920).
NOLPH 1:407

PLANCK, MAX
Ekstrand, A. G.
Presentation [of the Nobel
Prize for Physics for 1918
to Max Planck, June 2,
1920]. NOLPH 1:405

PLANNED ECONOMY See United
States - Economic policy

PLANNING, ECONOMIC See
Economic policy

PLANT PIGMENTS
Willstätter, R. M.
On plant pigments.
NOLC 1:301

PLANTATIONS
Cardozo, F. L.
Break up the plantation
system. FON:350

PLASMA PHYSICS
Alfvén, H.
Plasma physics, space re-
search and the origin of the
solar system. NOLPH 4:306
Tamm, I. E.
General characteristics of
radiations emitted by systems
moving with super-light velocities with some applications to
plasma physics. NOLPH 3:470

Platero, Dillon
Discussions of critical issues affecting Navajo education program and policies presented at
the Seminar for Navajo Re-
servation School Administra-
tors, July 26, 1976. MAES:149

PLAYBOY
Mount, A.
The Playboy philosophy--pro.
LINRS:157
Pinson, W. M., Jr.
The Playboy philosophy--con.
LINRS:170; LINRST:193

Pleijel, H.
Presentation [of the Nobel Prize
for Physics to Clinton Joseph
Davisson and George Paget
Thomson, Dec. 13, 1937].
NOLPH 2:387
Presentation [of the Nobel Prize
for Physics to Enrico Fermi,
Dec. 12, 1938].
NOLPH 2:409
Presentation [of the Nobel Prize
for Physics to James Chad-
wick, Dec. 12, 1935].
NOLPH 2:333
Presentation [of the Nobel Prize
for Physics for 1932 to Werner
Heisenberg and for 1933 to
Erwin Schrodinger and Paul
Adrien Maurice Dirac, Dec.
11, 1933]. NOLPH 2:283
Presentation [of the Nobel Prize
for Physics to Sir Chandrasek-
hara Venkata Raman, Dec.
11, 1930]. NOLPH 2:263

Plumer, William
State control of Dartmouth College. ANN 4:420

Plunket, William Conyngham,
1st Baron
Prosecuting Robert Emmet.
BREWE 8:3213

PLURALISM (SOCIAL SCIENCE)
Harris, L.
American Indian education
and pluralism.   MAES:96
Howe, H., II
The Brown decision, plural-
ism, and the schools in the
1980s.   BA 1979-80:101

Poe, Edgar Allan
Love for the beautiful in speech.
BREWE 8:3222

POETRY AND POETS
Eliot, T. S.
Acceptance [of the Nobel
Prize for Literature, 1948].
NOB 5:267; NOL:435
Lowell, J. R.
Poetical and the practical
in America.   BREWE 7:2808
Perse, S.
Acceptance [of the Nobel
Prize for Literature, 1960].
NOB 20:7; NOL:556
Poe, E. A.
Love for the beautiful in
speech.   BREWE 8:3222
Quasimodo, S.
The poet and the politician.
NOL:540
Robertson, F. W.
Highest form of expression.
BREWE 9:3319

Pogrebin, Letty Cottin
Commencement address (Rutgers
Univ.)   TAC:242

POLAROGRAPH AND POLAROG-
RAPHY
Heyrovsky, J.
The trends of polarography.
NOLC 3:564

POLICE
Police.   BURT:32
Warren, E. and others
Miranda v. Arizona: opinion
for the court and dissenting
opinion.   ANN 18:427
Welcome to Chief of Police as
speaker at a civic club.

HNWM:41
Wilson, O. W.
Police arrest privileges in a
free society.   ANN 18:36

POLIOMYELITIS
Enders, J. F.
The cultivation of the poliomyelitis viruses in tissue culture.   NOLM 3:448

POLITICAL CONVENTIONS
Gale, J.
Great American institution.
REIR:161

---- See also Acceptance speeches
- Nominations; Candidates;
Congresses and conventions;
Democratic Party; Republican
Party.   Also Subheads under
this subject

---- DEMOCRATIC
Bryan, W. J.
Cross of gold.   ANN 12:100;
BAS:50 (outline only); BEN:52;
BOORA 2:575; BREWE 2:694;
HURH:147; LINS:268; OLIS:207
Voorhees, D. W.
Speech in the Tilden conven-
tion.   BREWE 10:3697

---- REPUBLICAN
Curtis, G. W.
His sovereignty under his hat.
BREWE 4:1570

POLITICAL PARTIES
Brooke, E. W.
Crisis in the two-party sys-
tem.   BA 1965-66:170

---- See also Names of parties,
e.g. Conservative Party -
Great Britain; Democratic Party; Labor Party - Great
Britain; Liberal Party - Great
Britain; Liberty Party; Republican Party; Union Party

---- NEW ZEALAND
Stout, R.
A call for liberal and con-
servative parties, 1876.
MACS:180 sel.

POLITICAL PRISONERS
Borah, W. E.

Release of political prisoners.
ANN 14:405
Moynihan, D. P.
World wide amnesty for poli-
tical prisoners.
BA 1975-76:65

POLITICAL SCIENCE
Cousin, V.
True politics. BREWE 4:1431
Dix, J. A.
Christianity and politics.
BREWE 5:1883
Kennedy, J. F.
Intellectual and the politician.
BAP:285; LINR:267
Religion in government.
ANN 17:589; SIN:303
Kossuth, L.
Local self-government.
BREWE 7:2672
LaFollette, R. M., Sr.
Which shall rule, manhood
or money? HURH:158
Marshall, D. S.
Fundamental and minority
rights. MONS:450
Monroe, J.
Federal experiments in his-
tory. BREWE 8:3041
Root, E.
Invisible government: Short
Ballot Amendment.
ANN 13:528
Russell, B. A. W.
What desires are politically
important? NOL:452
Schurz, C.
Public offices as private
perquisites. BREWE 9:3384
Smith, A. E.
Religion and politics.
HURH:209
Weicker, L. P.
Televised debates.
BA 1976-77:61
Willkie, W. L.
Loyal opposition. GRG:63;
HURH:243

---- See also Communism; Right
and left (political science);
Socialism; United States -
Politics and government

POLITICIANS
Introductions for politicians (3
examples). BNH:31

POLITICS See Campaign speeches;
Candidates; Civil service;
Political Science; World poli-
tics, 1945- . Also names of
countries with subdivision
Politics and government, e.g.
Great Britain - Politics and
government

POLITICS, PRACTICAL
Fulbright, J. W.
Press and politicians.
ERP:159

Polk, James K.
Annexation of Texas and Oregon.
Same as his Inaugural address
California and Mexico. Same as
his Third annual message
First annual message.
ANN 7:301; STAT 1:634
Fourth annual message.
STAT 1:731
Inaugural address. ANN 7:286;
USINAU:89; USINAUG:89
Reaffirmation of the Monroe Doc-
trine. Same as his First an-
nual message
Second annual message.
STAT 1:664
Third annual message.
ANN 7:374; STAT 1:699

POLK, JAMES K.
Dayton, W. L.
Arraigning President Polk.
BREWE 5:1676

Pollak, George
Light from sorrow. WALE:143

POLLUTION
Jones, A. L.
A question of ecology: the
cries of wolf. LINRST:115

POLYSACCHARIDES
Cori, C.
Polysaccharide phosphorylase.
NOLM 3:186

Ponce, Felipe V.
La causa (Indiana University,
1971). LINRS:66; LINRST:68

Pontier, Glenn
Plea for understanding.
SCHW:136

POPE, ALEXANDER
  Lowell, J. R.
    Pope and his time.
    BREWE 7:2815

Poplack, Alvin M.
  Preparation for eternity.
    WALE:146

POPULATION
  Crary, D. R.
    Plague of people.   LINR:220
  Stratton, R. D.
    Food: a world crisis.
    BREWW:81

POPULATION POLICY -
    MALAYSIA
  Razak, T. A.
    Devastating consequences of
    excessive population growth.
    MONSA:9

Porter, George
  Flash photolysis and some of
    its applications (Nobel Lec-
    ture, Dec. 11, 1967).
    NOLC 4:241

PORTER, GEORGE
  Olander, H. A.
    Presentation [of the Nobel
    Prize for Chemistry to
    Manfred Eigen, R. G. W.
    Norrish and George Porter,
    Dec. 11, 1967]. NOLC 4:165

POSITRONS
  Anderson, C. D.
    The production and proper-
    ties of positrons.
    NOLPH 2:365

POST WAR PLANNING See
    Reconstruction, 1939-1951

POSTAL SERVICE
  Gronouski, J. A.
    Mail service. BRP:223

Potter, Henry Codman
  Washington and American
    aristocracy (100th anniver-
    sary of Washington's first
    inauguration).
    BREWE 8:3225

POVERTY
  Drumm, S. L.

War on prosperity. CAPG:185
Humphrey, H. H., Jr.
  Anniversary of war on pover-
  ty. CAPG:174
Johnson, L. B.
  War on poverty. ANN 18:212
McNamara, R. S.
  Searching for new solutions to
  poverty. BA 1976-77:91
Shriver, S.
  Address at the Chicago Anti-
  poverty Conference. CAPG:180
Wirtz, W. W.
  Economic Opportunity Act of
  1964. CAPG:165
Ybarra, B.
  The wheel of poverty.
  BAPR:356; BAPRR:266
Young, W. M.
  Crisis of the cities: the
  danger of the ghetto.
  BA 1966-67:82; OE:177;
  SMHV:160

---- MALAYSIA
Suffian bin Hashim
  Only Malays can initiate the
  institutional changes.
  MONSA:140

Powell, Adam Clayton
  Can any good thing come out of
  Nazareth? (Howard Univer-
  sity, May 29, 1966).
  FON:1027; SMHR:154

Powell, Cecil Frank
  The cosmic radiation (Nobel Lec-
  ture, Dec. 11, 1950).
  NOLPH 3:144

POWELL, CECIL FRANK
  Lindh, A. E.
    Presentation [of the Nobel
    Prize for Physics to Cecil
    Frank Powell, Dec. 11, 1950].
    NOLPH 3:139

Powell, Lewis Franklin, Jr.
  The eroding authority. (San
  Francisco, August 13, 1972).
  BA 1972-73:101

Power, Donald C.
  Responds to an introduction.
  PRS:147

POWER
  Russell, B. A. W.

What desires are politically
important? NOL:452

POWER RESOURCES
  Carter, J.
    Energy and the national goals.
    BA 1979-80:76
    Energy problems.
    BA 1976-77:117
  Hatfield, M. O.
    The energy crisis.
    BA 1973-74:105
  MacDonald, P.
    Exploring new energy frontiers.
    MAES:165
  Mead, M.
    The planetary crisis and the
    challenge to scientists.
    BA 1973-74:97

---- RESEARCH
  Root, T. C.
    The failure of scientists to
    communicate.
    BA 1977-78:110

PRAISE, SPEECHES OF See
  Eulogies; Tributes

PRATT, E. J.
  Lowe, J. A.
    Presents E. J. Pratt.
    LYI:49

Pray, Francis C.
  Public relations in education
    (Pittsburgh, Oct. 27, 1955).
    TAC:209

PRAYERS
  Augustine, Saint
    On our Lord's prayer.
    BREWE 1:188
  Christmas prayer. BNH:75
  New Year prayer. BNH:74
  Prayer at a time of doubt or
    sorrow. BNH:73
  Prayer for commitment day.
    BNH:74
  Prayer for Easter. BNH:76
  Prayer for Thanksgiving.
    BNH:76

PREACHERS See Clergy

Pregl, Fritz
  Quantitative micro-analysis of
    organic substances (Nobel

Lecture, Dec. 11, 1923).
    NOLC 2:28

PREGL, FRITZ
  Hammarsten, O.
    Presentation [of the Nobel
    Prize for Chemistry to Fritz
    Pregl, Dec. 11, 1923].
    NOLC 2:25

PREJUDICE See Discrimination

Preminger, Otto See Murrow,
  E. R., jt. auth.

Prentiss, Seargent Smith
  On New England's Forefathers'
    Day. BREWE 8:3233

PREPAREDNESS, MILITARY See
  Names of countries or hemis-
  pheres with subdivision Defenses, e.g. United States -
  Defenses

PRESENTATION SPEECHES
  Suggestions for preparation of
    speeches of presentation.
    With examples of. PAE:181

---- DEGREES, ACADEMIC
  Eliezer, C. J.
    Educated man with a sense of
    urgency (presenting Doctor of
    Laws degree). MONS:275
  Wang, G. W.
    Tribute to Dr. Azkir Husain
    (presenting him with Doctor
    of Laws degree). MONS:277

---- GIFTS
  Presenting a gift (5 examples).
    BNH:86
  Suggestions for the preparation
    of a speech presenting a gift
    or award. MILS:10

---- MEDALS
  Kennedy, J. F.
    Presenting the Distinguished
    Service Medal to John Glenn
    (outline of speech). CUB:64
  Lamont, T. W.
    Presents Eleanor Robson Bel-
    mont. LYI:23
  Smith, W.
    Eulogium. POC:3
  Truman, H. S.

Dec. 11, 1963]. NOLM 4:3

Grandqvist, G.
Presentation [of the Nobel
Prize for Physics for 1914
to Max Von Laue, Nov. 12,
1915]. NOLPH 1:343

Gullberg, H.
Presentation [of the Nobel
Prize for Literature to
Gabriela Mistral, 1945].
NOB 14:167; NOL:405
Presentation [of the Nobel
Prize for Literature to Juan
Ramón Jiménez, 1956].
NOB 10:3; NOL:513

Gullstrand, A.
Presentation [of the Nobel
Prize for Physics for 1924
to Karl Manne Georg Sieg-
bahn, Dec. 11, 1925].
NOLPH 2:73
Presentation [of the Nobel
Prize for Physics for 1923
to Robert Andrews Millikan,
May 23, 1924].
NOLPH 2:51

Gustafsson, T.
Presentation [of the Nobel
Prize for Physics to Hannes
Alfvén and Louis Néel,
Dec. 11, 1970].
NOLPH 4:303

Hagg, G.
Presentation [of the Nobel
Prize for Chemistry to
Dorothy Crowfoot Hodgkin,
Dec. 11, 1964].
NOLC 4:67
Presentation [of the Nobel
Prize for Chemistry to
Linus Carl Pauling, Dec.
11, 1954]. NOLC 3:425
Presentation [of the Nobel
Prize for Chemistry to
Max Ferdinand Perutz and
John Cowdery Kendrew,
Dec. 11, 1962].
NOLC 3:649

Häggquist, G.
Presentation [of the Nobel
Prize for Physiology or
Medicine to Hans Spemann,
Dec. 12, 1935]. NOLM 2:377

Hallström, P.
Broadcast lecture [on
Johannes Vilhelm Jensen,
1944]. NOL:393
Presentation [of the Nobel

Prize for Literature to Eugene
Gladstone O'Neill, 1936].
NOB 19:125; NOL:330
Presentation [of the Nobel
Prize for Literature to Frans
Eemil Sillanpää, 1939].
NOB 16:223; NOL:386
Presentation [of the Nobel
Prize for Literature to George
Bernard Shaw, 1925].
NOB 16:77; NOL:224
Presentation [of the Nobel
Prize for Literature to Henri
Bergson, 1927]. NOB 2:267;
NOL:242
Presentation [of the Nobel
Prize for Literature to Ivan
Alekseevich Bunin, 1933].
NOB 3:285; NOL:309
Presentation [of the Nobel
Prize for Literature to Jacinto
Benavente, 1922].
NOB 2:179; NOL:186
Presentation [of the Nobel
Prize for Literature to Luigi
Pirandello, 1934].
NOB 20:71; NOL:320
Presentation [of the Nobel
Prize for Literature to Pearl
Buck, 1938]. NOB 3:149;
NOL:354
Presentation [of the Nobel
Prize for Literature to Roger
Martin DuGard, 1937].
NOB 14:3; NOL:342
Presentation [of the Nobel
Prize for Literature to Sigrid
Undset, 1928]. NOB 18:163;
NOL:251
Presentation [of the Nobel
Prize for Literature to Wil-
liam Butler Yeats, 1923].
NOB 18:275; NOL:194
Presentation [of the Nobel
Prize for Literature to Wil-
liam Faulkner, 1949].
NOB 19:3; NOL:440

Hambro, C. J.
Presentation [of the Nobel
Prize for Peace to George
Catlett Marshall, Dec. 10,
1953]. NOLP 3:65
Presentation [of the Nobel
Prize for Peace to the Inter-
national Committee of the
Red Cross and the League of
the Red Cross Societies,
Dec. 10, 1963]. NOLP 3:295

Hammersten, O.
Presentation [of the Nobel
Prize for Chemistry to Fritz
Pregl, Dec. 11, 1923].
NOLC 2:25
Presentation [of the Nobel
Prize for Physiology or
Medicine to Albert Szent-
Györgyi Von Nagyrapolt,
Dec. 11, 1937].
NOLM 2:435
Presentation [of the Nobel
Prize for Physiology or
Medicine to Axel Hugo Theo-
dor Theorell, Dec. 12,
1955]. NOLM 3:477
Presentation [of the Nobel
Prize for Physiology or
Medicine to Hans Adolf
Krebs and Fritz Albert Lip-
mann, Dec. 11, 1953].
NOLM 3:395
Presentation [of the Nobel
Prize for Physiology or
Medicine to Otto Heinrich
Warburg, Dec. 10, 1931].
NOLM 2:251
Hasselberg, K. B.
Presentation [of the Nobel
Prize for Chemistry to
Ernest Rutherford, Dec. 11,
1908]. NOLC 1:125
Presentation [of the Nobel
Prize for Physics to Albert
Abraham Michelson, Dec.
12, 1907]. NOLPH 1:159
Presentation [of the Nobel
Prize for Physics to Gabriel
Lippmann, Dec. 14, 1908].
NOLPH 1:183
Hedrén, G.
Presentation [of the Nobel
Prize for Physiology or
Medicine to Karl Landsteiner,
Dec. 11, 1930].
NOLM 2:229
Henschen, F.
Presentation [of the Nobel
Prize for Physiology or
Medicine for 1928 to Charles
Jules Henri Nicolle].
NOLM 2:175
Presentation [of the Nobel
Prize for Physiology or
Medicine for 1933 to Thomas
Hunt Morgan, June 4, 1934].
NOLM 2:307
Hildebrand, H.

Presentation [of the Nobel
Prize for Chemistry to Wil-
helm Ostwald, Dec. 12, 1909].
NOLC 1:147
Presentation [of the Nobel
Prize for Literature to Gerhart
Johann Robert Hauptmann,
1912]. NOB 8:3; NOL:118
Presentation [of the Nobel
Prize for Physics to Guglielmo
Marconi and Carl Ferdinand
Braun, Dec. 11, 1909].
NOLPH 1:193
Hjärne, H.
Presentation [of the Nobel
Prize for Literature to Carl
Friedrich Spitteler, 1919].
NOB 17:267; NOL:161
Presentation [of the Nobel
Prize for Literature to Knut
Pedersen Hamsun, 1920].
NOB 9:119; NOL:167
Presentation [of the Nobel
Prize for Literature to
Rabindranath Tagore, 1913].
NOB 18:10; NOL:127
Presentation [of the Nobel
Prize for Literature to Rudolf
Christoph Eucken, 1908].
NOB 6:3; NOL:67
Holmgren, I.
Presentation [of the Nobel
Prize for Physiology or Medi-
cine to George Hoyt Whipple,
George Richards Minot, and
William Parry Murphy, Dec.
12, 1934]. NOLM 2:335
Hulthén, E.
Presentation [of the Nobel
Prize for Physics to Emilio
Gino Segrè and Owen Chamber-
lain, Dec. 11, 1959].
NOLPH 3:487
Presentation [of the Nobel
Prize for Physics to Felix
Bloch and Edward Mills Pur-
cell, Dec. 11, 1952].
NOLPH 3:199
Presentation [of the Nobel
Prize for Physics to Frits
Zernike, Dec. 11, 1953].
NOLPH 3:237
Presentation [of the Nobel
Prize for Physics to Sir Ed-
ward Victor Appleton, Dec.
12, 1947]. NOLPH 3:75
Ingebretsen, H. S.
Presentation [of the Nobel

Prize for Peace to John
Raleigh Mott, Dec. 10,
1946]. NOLP 2:354

Irgens, J.
Welcome [presenting the Nobel
Prize for Peace to the In-
stitute of International Law
for 1904, Aug. 24, 1912].
NOLP 1:61

Ising, G.
Presentation [of the Nobel
Prize for Physics to Patrick
Maynard Stuart Blackett,
Dec. 13, 1948].
NOLPH 3:93

Jahn, G.
Presentation [of the Nobel
Prize for Peace to Albert
John Luthuli for 1960, Dec.
10, 1961]. NOLP 3:209
Presentation [of the Nobel
Prize for Peace for 1952
to Albert Schweitzer, Dec.
10, 1953]. NOLP 3:37
Presentation [of the Nobel
Prize for Peace to Cordell
Hull, Dec. 10, 1945].
NOLP 2:311
Presentation [of the Nobel
Prize for Peace to Dag
Hammarskjöld, Dec. 10,
1961]. NOLP 3:239
Presentation [of the Nobel
Prize for Peace to Emily
Greene Balch, Dec. 10,
1946]. NOLP 2:325
Presentation [of the Nobel
Prize for Peace to the
Friends Service Council
and the American Friends
Service Committee, Dec.
10, 1947]. NOLP 2:373
Presentation [of the Nobel
Prize for Peace to Georges
Pire, Dec. 10, 1958].
NOLP 3:151
Presentation [of the Nobel
Prize for Peace to the
International Committee of
the Red Cross, 1944, Dec.
10, 1945]. NOLP 2:289
Presentation [of the Nobel
Prize for Peace to Léon
Jouhaux, Dec. 10, 1951].
NOLP 3:3
Presentation [of the Nobel
Prize for Peace to Lester
Bowles Pearson, Dec. 10,

1957]. NOLP 3:119
Presentation [of the Nobel
Prize for Peace for 1962 to
Linus Carl Pauling, Dec. 10,
1963]. NOLP 3:259
Presentation [of the Nobel
Prize for Peace to Lord Boyd
Orr of Brechin, Dec. 10,
1949]. NOLP 2:407
Presentation [of the Nobel
Prize for Peace to Martin
Luther King, Jr., Dec. 10,
1964]. NOLP 3:325
Presentation [of the Nobel
Prize for Peace to the Office
of the United Nations High
Commissioner for Refugees,
Dec. 10, 1955]. NOLP 3:89
Presentation [of the Nobel
Prize for Peace to Philip
John Noel-Baker, Dec. 10,
1959]. NOLP 3:175
Presentation [of the Nobel
Prize for Peace to Ralph
Johnson Bunche, Dec. 10,
1950]. NOLP 2:435

Johansson, J. E.
Presentation [of the Nobel
Prize for Physiology or Medi-
cine for 1922 to Archibald
Vivian Hill and Otto Fritz
Meyerhof, Dec. 12, 1923].
NOLM 2:3
Presentation [of the Nobel
Prize for Physiology or Medi-
cine to August Krogh, Dec.
11, 1920]. NOLM 1:529

Johnsen, A.
Remarks [presenting the Nobel
Prize for Peace to Thomas
Woodrow Wilson, 1919, Dec.
10, 1920]. NOLP 1:293

Karlfeldt, E. A.
Presentation [of the Nobel
Prize for Literature to Anatole
France, 1921]. NOB 6:85;
NOL:174
Presentation [of the Nobel
Prize for Literature to Sin-
clair Lewis, 1930].
NOB 11:237; NOL:271

Klason, P.
Presentation [of the Nobel
Prize for Chemistry to Henri
Moissan, 1906]. NOLC 1:91
Presentation [of the Nobel
Prize for Physics to Joseph
John Thomson, Dec. 11,

11, 1951]. NOLPH 3:163
Presentation [of the Nobel
Prize for Physics to Willis
Eugene Lamb and Polykarp
Kusch, Dec. 12, 1955].
NOLPH 3:283
Presentation [of the Nobel
Prize for Physics for 1945
to Wolfgang Pauli, Dec. 13,
1946]. NOLPH 3:25
Wallgren, A.
Presentation [of the Nobel
Prize for Physiology or
Medicine to Selman Abraham
Waksman, Dec. 12, 1952].
NOLM 3:365
Wernstedt, W.
Presentation [of the Nobel
Prize for Physiology or
Medicine for 1926 to Johan-
nes Andreas Grib Fibiger,
Dec. 12, 1927].
NOLM 2:119
Presentation [of the Nobel
Prize for Physiology or
Medicine to Julius Wagner-
Jauregg, Dec. 12, 1927].
NOLM 2:155
Wessén, E.
Presentation [of the Nobel
Prize for Literature to
Halldor Kiljan Laxness,
1955]. NOB 12:3; NOL:505
Westgren, A.
Presentation [of the Nobel
Prize for Chemistry to
Arne Wilhelm Kaurin Tise-
lius, Dec. 13, 1948].
NOLC 3:191
Presentation [of the Nobel
Prize for Chemistry to
Artturi Ilmari Virtanen,
Dec. 12, 1945].
NOLC 3:71
Presentation [of the Nobel
Prize for Chemistry to
Edwin Mattison McMillan
and Glenn Theodore Sea-
borg, Dec. 12, 1951].
NOLC 3:309
Presentation [of the Nobel
Prize for Chemistry for
1943 to George De Hevesy,
Dec. 12, 1944].
NOLC 3:5
Presentation [of the Nobel
Prize for Chemistry for
1944 to Otto Hahn, Dec.

13, 1946]. NOLC 3:47
Presentation [of the Nobel
Prize for Chemistry to Petrus
Josephus Wilhelmus Debye,
Dec. 12, 1936].
NOLC 2:379
Presentation [of the Nobel
Prize for Chemistry to Wil-
lard Frank Libby, Dec. 12,
1960]. NOLC 3:589
Wirsen, C. D. af
Presentation [of the Nobel
Prize for Literature to
Bjørnstjerne Martinus Bjørn-
son, 1903]. NOL:14;
NOB 3:77
Presentation [of the Nobel
Prize for Literature to
Christian Matthias Theodor
Mommsen, 1902]. NOL:7;
NOB 13:235
Presentation [of the Nobel
Prize for Literature to
Frédéric Mistral and José
de Echegaray y Eizaguirre,
1904]. NOL:23; NOB 13:119
Presentation [of the Nobel
Prize for Literature to
Giosué Carducci, 1906].
NOB 5:3; NOL:48
Presentation [of the Nobel
Prize for Literature to
Henryk Sienkiewicz, 1905].
NOL:36; NOB 17:173
Presentation [of the Nobel
Prize for Literature to
Maurice Polydore Marie
Bernhard Maeterlinck, 1911].
NOB 12:139; NOL:107
Presentation [of the Nobel
Prize for Literature to Paul
Johann Ludwig Heyse, 1910].
NOB 7:279; NOL:100
Presentation [of the Nobel
Prize for Literature to Rud-
yard Kipling, 1907].
NOB 11:89; NOL:58
Presentation [of the Nobel
Prize for Literature to Sully
Prudhomme, 1901].
NOL:2; NOB 16:303

PRESIDENTIAL PRIMARIES See
    Primaries

PRESIDENTS See Educators;
    Executives; Inaugural ad-
    dresses; Installation speeches;

Nominations; Officers; Offices - Acceptance; Presidents - United States; Public
officials

---- UNITED STATES
Bayard, T. F.
Plea for conciliation in
1876. BREWE 1:265
Clay, H.
Against the growing power
of the executive.
ANN 6:565
Bank and the power of the
executive. ANN 6:46
Ford, G. R.
The third presidential debate.
BA 1976-77:30
Fulbright, J. W.
Arrogance of power.
ANN 18:362
Jackson, A.
Autonomy of the executive.
ANN 6:58
Johnson, A.
Veto of Tenure of Office
Act. ANN 10:90
Johnson, L. B.
Obligation of power.
ANN 18:368
Kennedy, R. F.
Kennedy's decision to seek
Presidential nomination.
THOMS:131
Moore, P.
A biblical faith for a presi-
dent. BA 1976-77:24
Nixon, R. M.
Campaign speech, radio
broadcast, September 19,
1968. SIN:366
Randolph, J., 1773-1833
"Blifil and Black George--
Puritan and blackleg" (from
debate on Executive patron-
age). BREWE 9:3292
Taft, W. H.
Limited presidential power.
ANN 14:41
Thurman, A. G.
Tilden-Hayes election.
BREWE 9:3621
Truckman, B.
Presidential eligibility.
REIR:107 (outline)
Truman, H. S.
Powers of the President.
HURH:316

---- See also Inaugural addresses

---- ELECTION
Lawson, J.
I protest against Hayes's
Southern policy. FON:457

---- ---- See Electoral College

PRESIDING OFFICERS See
Officers, Presiding

PRESS
Agnew, S.
Address before the Midwest
Regional Republican Commit-
tee. BA 1969-70:59
Berryer, P. A.
Censorship of the press.
BREWE 2:443
Clark, T. C.
Sheppard v. Maxwell, warden:
opinion for the court.
ANN 18:402
Fulbright, J. W.
"The neglect of the song."
BA 1974-75:109
Press and the politicians.
ERP:159
Kennedy, R. F.
Fruitful tension.
BA 1966-67:138
Royer-Collard, P. P.
Against press censorship.
BREWE 9:3347
Senu bin Abdul Rahman
Pledge to newsmen.
MONS:156
Shaw, R. M.
Danger of getting used to lies.
LINR:191
Stanton, F.
Address before the Interna-
tional Radio and Television
Society. BA 1969-70:71
Stewart, P.
Or of the press.
BA 1974-75:97
Sulzberger, A. O.
Business and the press: is
the press anti-business?
EHN:387

Price, Joseph C.
The race problem stated.
SMHV:78

Price, Steven
Agriculture--the real answer to
starvation. BREWW:161

PRIMARIES
Roosevelt, F. D.
Fireside chat on party
primaries, June 24, 1938.
FRIP:324

PRIMROSE LEAGUE
Salisbury, R. A. T. G.
Speech to the Primrose
League. STRM:375

PRIVACY, RIGHT OF
Mathias, C. M.
Privacy on the ropes.
BA 1978-79:70

PRIZES See Acceptance speeches
- Rewards (Prizes); Pre-
sentation speeches - Re-
wards (Prizes)

Prochnow, Herbert V.
Introduces Clarence B. Randall
as moderator of panel.
PRS:12
Introduces Dr. David Horowitz,
governor of the Bank of
Israel. PRS:31
Introduces Peter G. Peterson,
president of Bell and Howell
Company. PRS:8
Presents James C. Downs,
Jr., chairman of the board
of the Real Estate Research
Corporation. PRS:14
Presents Richard J. Daley,
mayor of Chicago. PRS:28
Toast to the mayor of Copen-
hagen. PRS:56

Prochorov, Alexander M.
Quantum electronics (Nobel
Lecture, Dec. 11, 1964).
NOLPH 4:110

PROCHOROV, ALEXANDER M.
Edlén, B.
Presentation [of the Nobel
Prize for Physics to
Charles H. Townes, Nikolai
G. Basov, and Alexander
M. Prochorov, Dec. 11,
1964]. NOLPH 4:55

PRODIGAL SON (PARABLE)
Ditzen, L. R.
The right ticket but the wrong
train. REID:404

PROFESSIONS
Dawson, M.
My profession. CAPB:363

PROGRESS
Brown, H. A.
One century's achievement
(Valley Forge centennial).
BREWE 2:683
Cass, L.
American progress and foreign
oppression. BREWE 3:989
Chapin, E. H.
Source of modern progress.
BREWE 3:1038
Dewey, J.
School and social progress.
ANN 12:255
Durfee, J.
Influence of scientific discov-
ery and invention on social
and political progress.
ANN 7:128
Russell, J.
Science and literature as
modes of progress.
BREWE 9:3359
Smith, G.
Origin and causes of progress.
BREWE 9:3471
Webb, J. E.
From Runnymede to Ganymede.
BA 1967-68:194
Wilson, Woodrow
What is progress? BEN:62

PROHIBITION
Haynes, R. A.
Success of prohibition.
ANN 14:523

PROLETARIAT See Labor and
laboring classes

PROMOTION See Sales talks and
salesmanship

PROPAGANDA, ANTI-AMERICAN
Bray, C. W.
De-mystifying anti-American-
ism. BA 1979-80:38

PROPERTY
  Sanford, N. and others
    Debate on property and
    suffrage.   ANN 5:4
  Sutherland, J.
    Free land and the supply of
    labor.   ANN 8:180

---- See also Real estate

PROPHECIES
  Brown, B. G.
    Prophecy.   BREWE 2:675

PROSECUTION
  Aeschines
    Against Ctesiphon.
    BREWE 1:114; COG:120
  Bingham, J. A.
    Against the assassins of
    President Lincoln.
    BREWE 2:445
  Cicero, M. T.
    First oration against Cati-
    line.   BREWE 3:1159
    First oration against Verres.
    BREWE 3:1174
    Fourth Philippic.
    BREWE 3:1201
    Second oration against Cati-
    line.   BREWE 3:1171
  Coke, E.
    Prosecuting Sir Walter
    Raleigh.   BREWE 4:1348
  Connally, T. T. and others
    Censure of Senator Nye.
    BRR:69
  Dorset, E. S.
    In favor of slitting Prynne's
    nose.   BREWE 5:1899
  Erskine, T.
    Against Thomas Williams
    for the publication of Paine's
    Age of Reason.
    BREWE 6:2038
  Lysias
    Against Eratosthenes for
    murder (on the execution
    without trial of Polemarchus).
    BREWE 8:2851; SAG:39
  Nottingham, H. F.
    Opening the prosecution for
    regicide under Charles II
    (trial of T. Harrison).
    BREWE 6:2159
  Plunket, W. C.
    Prosecuting Robert Emmet.
    BREWE 8:3213

Sheridan, R. B.
  Against Warren Hastings.
  BREWE 9:3422
Webster, D.
  Knapp White murder case.
  BREWE 10:3865

PROSTITUTION
  Huitfeldt, J.
    The service of sex.
    LINRS:114

PROTECTION See Free trade and
  protection

PROTEINS
  Kendrew, J. C.
    Myoglobin and the structure of
    proteins.   NOLC 3:676
  Klein, P. A.
    Big things happen in small
    places (outline of speech ex-
    plaining protein synthesis).
    CUB:34

PROTESTANT DISSENTERS See
  Church

PROTON AND ANTIPROTON
  ANNIHILATION
  Chamberlain, O.
    The early antiproton work.
    NOLPH 3:489
  Segrè, E. G.
    Properties of antinucleons.
    NOLPH 3:508

PROTOZOA
  Laveran, C. L. A.
    Protozoa as causes of disease.
    NOLM 1:264

PRUDHOMME, SULLY
  Wirsén, C. D. af
    Presentation [of the Nobel
    Prize for Literature to Sully
    Prudhomme, 1901].   NOL:2;
    NOB 16:303

PRUSSIA See Germany

PRYNNE, WILLIAM
  Dorset, E. S.
    In favor of slitting Prynne's
    nose.   BREWE 5:1899

PUBLIC FINANCE See Finance -
  United States

PUBLIC LANDS See United
States - Public lands

PUBLIC OFFICIALS
Dewey, T. E.
Public service. ANN 16:471
Introductions for public officials
(3 examples). BNH:27
Lewe, J. C.
Presents Thomas C. Clark
(Attorney General of the
United States). LYI:137
Welcome to public official
speaker at a civic club.
HNWM:41

---- See also Law and lawyers

---- INTRODUCTION OF See
Introductions

PUBLIC OPINION
Buchanan, C.
Planning and public opinion.
MDYG:130
Lippmann, W.
On understanding society.
BAAGB:412
Lodge, H. C., Jr.
United Nations. HURH:344

PUBLIC RELATIONS
Barton, B.
Which knew not Joseph.
BRYF:554; BRYO:228
Wagner, R. B.
Public relations. ANN 16:285

---- AGRICULTURE
Kermicle, J.
Bridging the gap.
BREWW:94
Spray, C.
Consumer education: the
farmer's responsibility.
BREWW:67

---- SCHOOLS
Pray, F. C.
Public relations in education.
TAC:209

PUBLIC RELATIONS AND POLI-
TICS - MALAYSIA
Hamzah bin Dato Abu Samah
The most powerful instru-
ment for social cohesion.
MONSA:115

PUBLIC SERVICE See Citizenship;
Public officials

PUBLIC SPEAKING
Arnold, C. C.
Speech as a liberal study.
ARS:2
Braden, W. W.
Has TV made the public
speaker obsolete? EHN:309;
MOPR:360
Caird, J.
Art of eloquence.
BREWE 3:855
Carleton, W. G.
Effective speech in a democ-
racy. ARS:5
Cousin, V.
Eloquence and the fine arts.
BREWE 4:1419
Golden, J. L.
Political speaking since the
1920's. LINR:167
Haiman, F. S.
Rhetoric of 1968: a farewell
to rational discourse.
LINR:153
Hunt, E. L.
Lincoln's rhetorical triumph
at Cooper Union (centennial
speech). BA 1969-70:189
Jackson, E. M.
American theatre and the
speech profession.
BA 1965-66:200
Lawrence, D. L.
Speaker of the year award.
TAC:227
Lee, I. G.
Four ways of looking at a
speech. ARS:12
Schrier, W.
Address at Hope College
Alumni banquet, May 31,
1958. SCHW:236
Address to the 60th Anniver-
sary Oratorial Banquet,
March 1, 1957. SCHW:226
Behind the scenes in oratory.
SCHW:231
Coaching oratory. SCHW:239
Wigglesworth, M.
Prayse of eloquence. POC:8
Witherspoon, J.
On eloquence. POC:44

---- See also Debates and debating;
Speeches - Outlines of. Also

types of speeches; e.g. After-
dinner speeches; Introductions; Responses

PUBLIC WELFARE
tenBroek, J.
Today's challenge in public
welfare. MDV:233

PUERTO RICO
Munoz-Marin, L.
Future of Puerto Rico.
ANN 16:312

PUERTO RICANS IN THE UNITED
STATES
Zimbardo, P.
Puerto Ricans and the neigh-
borhood: a persuasive inter-
view. STOT:305

PULMONARY CIRCULATION
Cournand, A. F.
Control of the pulmonary
circulation in man with
some remarks on methodol-
ogy. NOLM 3:529

Pulteney, William
Against standing armies.
BREWE 8:3244

Purcell, Edward Mills
Research in nuclear magnetism
(Nobel Lecture, Dec. 11,
1952). NOLPH 3:219

PURCELL, EDWARD MILLS
Hulthén, E.
Presentation [of the Nobel
Prize for Physics to Felix
Bloch and Edward Mills
Purcell, Dec. 11, 1952].
NOLPH 3:199

PURITANS
Bulkeley, P.
City set upon a hill.
ANN 1:211
Curtis, G. W.
Liberty under the law.
BAS:141 (outline only);
LINS:249

Pursley, Jerry See Andino, Judy

Purvis, Robert
The American government and

the Negro. (New York, May
8, 1860). FON:227
The good time is at hand. (New
York, May 12, 1863).
FON:266

Pusey, Nathan M.
Thanksgiving and entreaty, a
President's valedictory.
(Harvard, June 15, 1971).
HOR:26

PUSEY, NATHAN M.
Stipp, J. E.
Introduces Nathan M. Pusey,
President, Harvard University.
LYI:83

Putnam, Frank
The Negro's part in new national
problems. (1900). FON:629

Pyke, Magnus
Man eats dog. MDYG:280

Pym, John
Law as the safeguard of liberty.
BREWE 8:3253
On grievances in the reign of
Charles I. BREWE 8:3252

- Q -

QUAKERS See Friends, Society of

QUALITY OF LIFE
Kemeny, J. G.
An optimist looks at America's
future. HOR:128

QUANTUM ELECTRODYNAMICS
Feynman, R. P.
The development of the space-
time view of quantum electro-
dynamics. NOLPH 4:155
Tomonaga, S. I.
Development of quantum elec-
trodynamics. NOLPH 4:126

QUANTUM ELECTRONICS
Prochorov, A. M.
Quantum electronics.
NOLPH 4:110

QUANTUM FIELD THEORY
Schwinger, J.

Relativistic quantum field
theory. NOLPH 4:140

QUANTUM THEORY
Born, M.
The statistical interpretation
of quantum mechanics.
NOLPH 3:256
Heisenberg, W.
The development of quantum
mechanics. NOLPH 2:290
Pauli, W.
Exclusion principle and
quantum mechanics.
NOLPH 3:27
Planck, M.
The genesis and present state
of development of the quantum
theory. NOLPH 1:407

Quasimodo, Salvatore
Acceptance [of the Nobel Prize
for Literature, 1959].
NOB 20:285; NOL:537
The poet and the politician
(Nobel lecture, Dec. 11,
1959). NOL:540

QUASIMODO, SALVATORE
Österling, A.
Presentation [of the Nobel
Prize for Literature to Sal-
vatore Quasimodo, 1959].
NOB 20:281; NOL:534

Quezon, Manuel L.
Filipinos of today and Filipinos
of yesterday (Aug. 19,
1938). CURM:29
Inaugural address (Manila,
Nov. 15, 1935). CURM:16
On Spain's contribution to the
Philippines (Manila, Jan.
11, 1936). CURM:24

Quidde, Ludwig
Security and disarmament
(Nobel Lecture, Dec. 10,
1927). NOLP 2:47

QUIDDE, LUDWIG
Stang, F.
Presentation [of the Nobel
Prize for Peace to Ferdinand
Edouard Buisson and Ludwig
Quidde, Dec. 10, 1927].
NOLP 2:29

Quincy, Josiah, 1744-1775
Defence of British soldiers,
1770. BREWE 9:3269; POC:95
Lenity of the law to human in-
firmity (Weem et al): British
soldiers arraigned for the
Boston Massacre. Same as
his Defence of the British
soldiers, 1770
"Let us look to the end."
POC:295
Speech in defence of the soldier.
Same as his Defence of Brit-
ish soldiers, 1770

Quincy, Josiah, 1772-1864
Against the admission of new
states. Same as his On the
admission of Louisiana
Against the conquest of Canada.
BREWE 9:3274
At the second centennial of Bos-
ton. BREWE 9:3272
On the admission of Louisiana.
ANN 4:283

Quinn, William F.
Responds to an introduction.
PRS:157

Quirino, Elpidio
Commemorating a national event
(Malacañan Palace, Nov. 15,
1936). CURM:239

- R -

RACE PREJUDICE See Discrimination; Racism; Segregation

RACE PROBLEMS
Barnett, F. L.
Race unity. FON:461
Bruce, J. E.
Negro plea for organized re-
sistance to white men.
ANN 11:214
Bulkley, W. L.
Race prejudice as viewed from
an economic standpoint.
FON:680
Bunche, R. J.
Barriers of race can be sur-
mounted. CAPG:66
Farmer, J. and others

Debate at Cornell University, March 7, 1961. OE:248

Franklin, J. H.
American's window to the world: her race problem. FON:907

Grady, H. W.
Race problem (speech to the Boston Merchants' Association). BREWE 6:2299

McKissick, F. B.
The student and the ghetto. OE:216

Morgan, C., Jr.
Time to speak. KEO:308

Moton, R. R.
Some elements necessary to race development. FON:692

Price, J. D.
The race problem stated. SMHV:78

Romulo, C. P.
Bandung address. CROCK:141

Roosevelt, T.
Sixth annual message. STAT 3:2194

Rowan, C. T.
New frontiers in racial relations. OE:201

Seale, B.
Free Huey. MACR:322

Simmons, B.
As time runs out. LINRS:251

RACE RELATIONS - MALAYSIA

Abdul Rahman, T.
What Abraham Lincoln said: Tunku's pledge to people of Malaysia. MONSA:65

Hamzah Sendut
Joint efforts urged for uniting various ethnic groups. MONSA:172

Johari, M. K.
Nation building and the four-way test. MONSA:100

Razak, T. A.
A new strategy to provide more jobs. MONSA:36
A rightful place for everyone in Malaysia. MONSA:12

Sambanthan, V. T.
Be a harmonising factor. MONSA:95

Rachovsky, Isaiah
Loom of time. WALE:147

RACISM

Carmichael, S.
Power and racism. BOSC:101

Crockett, G. W.
Racism in the law. FON:1131

DuBois, W. E. B.
Shall the Negro be encouraged to seek cultural equality? FON:772

Forman, J.
Black manifesto. FON:1156; OE:235

Harrison, H. H.
What socialism means to us. FON:698

Hurst, C. G.
Immorality, racism, and survival. STOT:343

Wells-Barnett, I. M.
Lynching, our national crime. FON:687

RADIATION

Barkla, C. G.
Characteristic Röntgen radiation. NOLPH 1:392

Mossbauer, R. L.
Recoilless nuclear resonance absorption of gamma radiation. NOLPH 3:584

Townes, C. H.
Production of coherent radiation by atoms and molecules. NOLPH 4:58

Wien, W.
On the laws of thermal radiation. NOLPH 1:275

RADIO

Braun, C. F.
Electrical oscillations and wireless telegraphy. NOLPH 1:226

Marconi, G.
Wireless telegraphic communication. NOLPH 1:196

RADIO BROADCASTING

Shaw, G. B.
Truth by radio. JEF:396; JEFF:378

---- See also Television broadcasting

RADIOACTIVE POLLUTION

Pauling, L. C.
Science and peace (Nobel Lec-

ture for 1962, Dec. 11, 1963).
NOLP 3:271

RADIOACTIVE SUBSTANCES
Curie, P.
Radioactive substances, espe-
cially radium. NOLPH 1:73
Joliot-Curie, I.
Artificial production of radio-
active elements.
NOLC 2:366
Rutherford, E.
The chemical nature of the
alpha particles from radio-
active substances.
NOLC 1:129

RADIOACTIVE TRACERS
Hevesy, G. D.
Some applications of isotopic
indicators. NOLC 3:9

RADIOACTIVITY
Becquerel, A. H.
On radioactivity, a new
property of matter.
NOLPH 1:52
Fermi, E.
Artificial radioactivity pro-
duced by neutron bombard-
ment. NOLPH 2:414

RADIOCARBON DATING
Libby, W. F.
Radiocarbon dating.
NOLC 3:593

RADIUM
Curie, M.
Radium and the new concepts
in chemistry. NOLC 1:202

Ragan, Dennis Owen
Backaches. MOP:366;
MOPR:358

RAHMAN, (PARAMOUNT RULER)
ABDUL d. 1960
Thomson, T. J. B.
Brightness is darkened (eulogy
on Tuanku Abdul Rahman
Ibni Al-Marhum Tuanku
Mohammed, first King of
Malaysia). MONS:281

Rahman, Dr. Ismail bin Abdul
Commendable features of public-
spiritedness and co-opera-

tion (July 7, 1969).
MONSA:76
Government is determined to take
drastic measures if ... (July
4, 1969). MONSA:72
New era of regional cooperation.
MONS:103
Security situation in Malaysia: a
warning and pledge by Tun
Ismail (July 5, 1969).
MONSA:69
Unexpected ally after independ-
ence. MONS:99

RAILROADS
Bell, J.
Trans-continental railroads.
BREWE 1:390
Buchanan, J.
Second annual message.
STAT 1:969
Hepburn, W. P.
Regulation of railroad rates.
ANN 13:40
Roosevelt, T.
Fifth annual message.
ANN 13:1; STAT 3:2144
Webster, D.
Railroad in New Hampshire
(opening Northern Railroad).
ANN 7:388
Whitney, A.
Railroad to the Pacific.
ANN 7:272

RAILROADS AND STATE
Roosevelt, T.
Sixth annual message.
STAT 3:2194

Rainer, John C.
Institute of American Indian Arts
Commencement exercises,
Friday, May 21, 1976.
MAES:219
Testimony: hearings before the
Senate Appropriations Subcom-
mittee on the Interior and
Related Agencies, May 13,
1975. MAES:255

Rainey, Joseph H.
Eulogy on Charles Sumner.
(Washington, April 27, 1874).
FON:403

Rajaratnam, S.
Asia needs the spirit of Sisyphus

to succeed (Manila, April 12,
1970).   MONSA:303
Asia's unfinished revolution.
MONS:425
Faith in United Nations charter
(on admission of Singapore).
MONS:421
Parliament of Religion.
MONS:417
Urgency of real problems facing
the less developed nations
(New York, Oct. 7, 1969).
MONSA:295

Raleigh, Sir Walter
Speech on the scaffold.
BREWE 9:3280; BRYH:104

RALEIGH, SIR WALTER
Coke, E.
Prosecuting Sir Walter
Raleigh.   BREWE 4:1348

Raman, Sir Chandrasekhara Venkata
The molecular scattering of
light (Nobel Lecture, Dec.
11, 1930).   NOLPH 2:267

RAMAN, SIR CHANDRASEKHARA
VENKATA
Pleijel, H.
Presentation [of the Nobel
Prize for Physics to Sir
Chandrasekhara Venkata
Raman, Dec. 11, 1930].
NOLPH 2:263

Ramani, Radhakrishna
Malaysia's stand in Kashmir
dispute.   MONS:240
Man of clear vision (tribute to
Adlai E. Stevenson).
MONS:250
Twenty four days in May (ex-
pression of thanks as Presi-
dent of Security Council of
United Nations).   MONS:248

Ramon y Cajal, Santiago
The structure and connexions
of neurons (Nobel Lecture,
Dec. 12, 1906).
NOLM 1:220

RAMON Y CAJAL, SANTIAGO
Mörner, K. A. H.
Presentation [of the Nobel
Prize for Physiology or

Medicine to Camilio Golgi and
Santiago Ramon y Cajal, Dec.
12, 1906].   NOLM 1:185

Ramsay, Sir William
The rare gases of the atmos-
phere (Nobel Lecture, Dec.
12, 1904).   NOLC 1:68

RAMSAY, SIR WILLIAM
Cederblom, J. E.
Presentation [of the Nobel
Prize for Chemistry to Sir
William Ramsay, Dec. 12,
1904].   NOLC 1:65

Ramsey, R. Paul
Counting the costs.   VI:24

Randolph, A. Philip
A call for mass action (Detroit,
Sept. 26-27, 1942).   FON:822
The crisis of the Negro and the
Constitution.   (2nd National
Negro Congress, 1937).
FON:816
Liberty, justice and democracy
(Detroit, Sept. 27, 1942).
SMHV:110
March on Washington address.
(1941).   OE:113
The task of the Negro people.
(Chicago, 1936).   FON:807

Randolph, Edmund
In defence of Aaron Burr, 1807.
BREWE 9:3284

Randolph, John
Japanese "Lunchbox" universities.   REIR:15

Randolph, John, 1773-1833
Against a protective tariff (1816).
ANN 4:427
Against protective tariffs.   Same
as his On the tariff (1824)
Against trade restrictions.
ANN 4:248
"Blifil and black George--Puritan
and blackleg" (from debate on
Executive patronage).
BREWE 9:3292
On the tariff (1824).
BREWE 9:3305

---- See also following jt. auths.
Grundy, F.; Webster, D.

Ransley, Marie
  The life and death of our lakes.
  (Univ. of Wisconsin, 1971).
  LINRS:63

Ransom, Reverdy C.
  William Lloyd Garrison: a
  centennial oration (Boston,
  Dec. 10, 1905). SMHV:66

Rantoul, Robert, Jr.
  On the barbarity of the common
  law. ANN 6:262

Rapier, James T.
  Civil Rights Bill. (Washington,
  Feb. 4, 1875). FON:418

Raskas, Bernard S.
  Physician's prayer. WALE:149

Rawson, Edward
  Thanksgiving. (Charlestown,
  Mass., June 20, 1676).
  HURH:20
  "... that the Lord may behold
  us as a people, offering
  praise and thereby glorifying
  Him...." Same as his
  Thanksgiving

Rayburn, Samuel
  Impressive accomplishments
  (75th Congress). BAD:83

RAYBURN, SAMUEL
  Martin, J. W.
    Introducing Speaker Sam Ray-
    burn. LYI:195

Rayleigh, John William Strutt,
  Baron
  The density of gases in the air
  and the discovery of argon
  (Nobel Lecture, Dec. 12,
  1904). NOLPH 1:90

RAYLEIGH, JOHN WILLIAM
  STRUTT, BARON, 1842-1919
  Cederblom, J. E.
    Presentation [of the Nobel
    Prize for Physics to Lord
    Rayleigh, Dec. 12, 1904].
    NOLPH 1:87

Razak, Tun Abdul
  Alliance policy for unity.
  MONS:47

And then came peace (Peace
  agreement between Malaysia
  and Indonesia). MONS:94
The beginning of a new realism in
  Malaysia: the period ahead is
  challenging (June 13, 1969).
  MONSA:24
Bridge of communication (on de-
  parture to America). MONS:59
A call to UMNO leaders: time
  for slogan chanting is over....
  (Sept. 22, 1970). MONSA:20
Correct words for a toast!
  MONS:91
Crucial cross-roads of history.
  MONS:64
Democracy and development in
  Malaysia. MONS:80
The development strategy for
  success of second Malaysian
  plan (Kuala Lumpur, Feb. 3,
  1970). MONSA:4
Devastating consequences of ex-
  cessive population growth
  (Kuala Lumpur, March 18,
  1970). MONSA:9
Hopes and anxieties of the coun-
  tries of Southeast Asia
  (Singapore, Jan. 15, 1971).
  MONSA:47
Most unfortunate of conflicts.
  MONS:69
A new strategy to provide more
  jobs. MONSA:36
Problems of war and peace
  (Lusaka, Sept. 10, 1970).
  MONSA:15
Putting life into development
  plans. MONS:86
A rightful place for everyone in
  Malaysia (Hotel Merlin, Aug.
  20, 1970). MONSA:12
The significance of Five-Power
  Defence Agreement (Canberra,
  June 19-20, 1969). MONSA:29
UMNO's twentieth milestone (20th
  anniversary of United Malay
  National Organization).
  MONS:53
Vital issues must be resolved if
  we are to survive (National
  Consultative Council, Jan. 27,
  1970). MONSA:1
We will uphold concepts of par-
  liamentary democracy (Jan.
  23, 1971). MONSA:41 selec-
  tions

Read, David H. C.
  Is God over thirty? Religion
  and the youth revolt.
  BA 1966-67:129

Read, Leonard E.
  Responds to introduction.
  PRS:98

READING See Books and reading;
  Literature

Reagan, Ronald
  Responds to an introduction.
  PRS:157
  Time for choosing. CAPG:48

REAL ESTATE
  Investor. BURT:175

REAL PROPERTY See Real
  Estate

REASON
  Clevenger, T.
    To have lived without reason.
    CAPB:373
  Wesley, J.
    Poverty of reason.
    BREWE 10:3874

RECOMBINANT DNA
  McGill, W. J.
    Science and the law.
    BA 1977-78:83

RECONSTRUCTION
  Adams, E. J.
    These are revolutionary
    times. FON:342
  Blair, A.
    Military government.
    BREWE 2:504
  Brockett, J. A.
    Reply to Grady. ANN 11:250
  Cardozo, F. L.
    Break up the plantation sys-
    tem. FON:350
  Chamberlain, D. H.
    Present hour in South Caro-
    lina (inaugural address of
    would-be governor).
    CUR:158
  Conkling, R.
    Stalwart standpoint.
    BREWE 4:1369
  Davis, D.
    Ex parte Milligan, 1866;

opinion for the court.
    ANN 10:31
Davis, H. W.
  Constitutional difficulties of re-
  construction. BREWE 5:1647
DeBow, J. D. B.
  That feeling of hostility.
  CUR:52
Dunn, O. J.
  We ask an equal chance in the
  race of life. FON:355
Gordon, J. B.
  It was purely a peace police
  organization. CUR:98
Grant, U. S.
  First annual message.
  STAT 2:1188
Gray, W. H.
  Justice should recognize no
  color. FON:353
Hampton, W.
  Present hour in South Carolina
  (inaugural address of would-be
  governor). CUR:159
Hayden, L.
  Deliver us from such a
  Moses. FON:334
Johnson, A.
  Against the radical Republi-
  cans. ANN 10:8
  Annual message to Congress,
  December 3, 1868.
  ANN 10:81; STAT 2:1129
  At Cleveland in 1866.
  BREWE 7:2640
  At St. Louis. BREWE 7:2628
  End itself is evil (third annual
  message, 1867). CUR:61;
  STAT 2:1144
  Fourth annual message.
  STAT 2:1167
  Presidential plan of Recon-
  struction. CUR:8;
  STAT 2:1112
  Second reconstruction veto.
  ANN 10:98
  Veto of Freedmen's Bureau
  Bill. ANN 10:3
  Veto of the first Reconstruc-
  tion Act, 1867. ANN 10:93
---- and others
  Debate on civil and states'
  rights. ANN 10:11
Langston, J. M.
  The other phase of reconstruc-
  tion. SMHV:46
Lincoln, A.
  Speech before death, April 11,

1865. ANN 9:573;
BREWE 7:2796; CUR:4
Third annual message.
ANN 9:473; STAT 2:1084
Seward, W. H.
Reconciliation in 1865.
BREWE 9:3408
Sherman, J.
It is essentially a Rebel organization. CUR:102
Stevens, T.
On reconstruction. CUR:13
Radical view of reconstruction. BREWE 9:3529;
CUR:58
Rights of the conqueror.
ANN 9:608
Sumner, C.
Proper guaranties for security. CUR:12
Turner, H. M.
I claim the rights of a man.
FON:357

RECONSTRUCTION, 1939-1951
Acheson, D.
Marshall Plan; relief and reconstruction are chiefly
matters of American self-interest. LAA:55
Marshall, G. C.
Address at Harvard University. ANN 16:438;
BOORA 2:884; GRG:82;
HURH:283

Recto, Claro M.
The preparation of the Constitution (House of Representatives, Feb. 8, 1935).
CURM:250

RECYCLING (WASTE, ETC.)
Hirschler, P.
How to beautify your farm.
BREWW:124
Howell, W.
A new century in agriculture.
BREWW:211

RED CROSS
Boissier, L. L.
Some aspects of the mission
of the International Committee of the Red Cross (Nobel
Lecture, Dec. 11, 1963).
NOLP 3:301
Chapuisat, E.

The activity of the International
Committee of the Red Cross
during the War, 1939-1945
(Nobel Lecture for 1944, Dec.
11, 1945). NOLP 2:295
Hambro, C. J.
Presentation [of the Nobel
Prize for Peace to the International Committee of the Red
Cross and the League of the
Red Cross Societies, Dec. 10,
1963]. NOLP 3:295
Huber, M.
Acceptance [of the Nobel Prize
for Peace for the International
Committee of the Red Cross,
1944, Dec. 10, 1945].
NOLP 2:293
Jahn, G.
Presentation [of the Nobel
Prize for Peace to the International Committee of the Red
Cross, 1944, Dec. 10, 1945].
NOLP 2:289
MacAulay, J. A.
The Red Cross in a changing
world (Nobel Lecture, Dec.
11, 1963). NOLP 3:311
Moe, R.
Presentation [of the Nobel
Prize for Peace to the International Committee of the Red
Cross, Dec. 10, 1917].
NOLP 1:281

Red Eagle, Chief of the Teton Sioux
Nation
Indian rights. ANN 10:242

Red Jacket, Seneca chief
Against white missions among
the Indians. Same as his
Missionary effort
Missionary effort (Seneca, N.Y.,
1805). ANN 4:194;
BREWE 7:2571; HURH:57
"You have got our country ...
you want to force your religion upon us." Same as his
Missionary effort

Redmond, John E. See Oxford and
Asquith, Herbert Henry Asquith, 1st Earl of, jt. auth.

Reed, Thomas Brackett
Immortality and good deeds
(semi-centennial of Girard
College). BREWE 9:3307

Reeves, Richard Ambrose
Journey to Hanoi. VI:83

REFORM
Emerson, R. W.
Man the reformer.
BREWE 5:2008
Wright, F.
Of existing evils and their
remedy. ANN 5:290

---- See also Great Britain -
Politics and government;
Reform Act (1867); Reform
Bills (1831, 1832); Social
problems

REFORM ACT (1867)
Beaconsfield, B. D.
Reform Bill of 1867 (Edin-
burgh speech, October 29,
1867). STRM:296
Lowe, R.
Coming of democracy.
MCB:138
Mill, J. S.
Representation of the people.
MCB:154

REFORM BILLS (1831, 1832)
Brougham and Vaux, H. P. B.
Supports the Reform Bill.
BRYH:322
Macaulay, T. B.
Reform Bill. CLAYP:295;
JAE:52; MCB:110
Russell, J. R.
Reform the franchise.
MCB:87
Smith, S.
Mrs. Partington in politics.
BREWE 9:3479
Reform and stomach troubles.
BREWE 9:3484

REFUGEES
Goedhart, G. J. v. H.
Refugee problems and their
solutions (Nobel Lecture,
Dec. 12, 1955). NOLP 3:97
Hansson, M.
The Nansen International Of-
fice for Refugees (Nobel
Lecture, Dec. 10, 1938).
NOLP 2:268

REFUSE AND REFUSE DISPOSAL
Hall, C.
A heap of trouble. EHN:316

Reichard, P.
Presentation [of the Nobel Prize
for Physiology or Medicine to
Robert W. Holley, Har Gobind
Khorana, and Marshall W.
Nirenberg, Dec. 12, 1968].
NOLM 4:321

Reichstein, Tadeus
Chemistry of the adrenal cortex
hormones (Nobel Lecture,
Dec. 11, 1950). NOLM 3:291

REICHSTEIN, TADEUS
Liljestrand, G.
Presentation [of the Nobel
Prize for Physiology of Medi-
cine to Edward Calvin Kendall,
Tadeus Reichstein, and Philip
Showalter Hench, Dec. 11,
1950]. NOLM 3:263

Reid, Charlotte T.
Tribute to Dwight D. Eisenhower.
BA 1968-69:165

Reinert, Paul C.
America, America, how does
your garden grow? (Loyola
Univ., Chicago, June 10,
1972). HOR:82

Reischauer, Edwin O.
Statement before the Senate For-
eign Relations Committee.
BA 1966-67:70

RELATIVITY
Einstein, A.
Fundamental ideas and problems of the theory of relativity. NOLPH 1:482

RELIEF   See Unemployed

RELIGION
Bede
On the nativity of St. Peter
and St. Paul.   BRYH:9
Beecher, H. W.
On fellowship.   HURH:118
Buteyn, D. P.
Invisible abutments.   SCHW:44
Chrysostom, J.
Heroes of faith.
BREWE 3:1139
Cotton, J.
God's promise to his planta-
tions.   ANN 1:107

Cox, S. S.
  Sermon on the mount.
  BREWE 4:1446
Dering, E.
  For the encouragement of
  learning. BREWE 5:1805
  Religious controversy in
  Parliament. BREWE 5:1808
Edwards, J.
  Sinners in the hands of an
  angry God. ANN 1:423;
  BREWE 5:1982; HURH:21;
  LINS:121
Fosdick, H. E.
  Shall the Fundamentalists
  win? ANN 14:325
Gibbons, J.
  To the Parliament of Reli-
  gions. BREWE 6:2248
Graham, W. F.
  National humility.
  HURH:339
Ingersoll, R. G.
  Absurdity of religion.
  ANN 11:267
Kennedy, J. F.
  Religion in government.
  ANN 17:589; SIN:303
Korteling, M.
  Renascence. SCHW:39
Latimer, H.
  On the pickings of office-
  holders. BREWE 7:2729
  Sermon on the plow.
  BREWE 7:2724; BRYH:47
Luther, M.
  Pith of Paul's chief doc-
  trine. BREWE 7:2833
Mather, C.
  At the sound of the trumpet.
  BREWE 8:2986
  "Boston Ebenezer." POC:395
Melanchthon, P.
  Safety of the virtuous.
  BREWE 8:3007
Mirabeau, H. G. R.
  Against the establishment
  of religion. BREWE 8:3034
Our changing world. BURT:129
Rajaratnam, S.
  Parliament of Religion.
  MONS:417
Sheen, F. J.
  Change of hearts. HURH:264
Smith, A. E.
  Religion and politics.
  HURH:209
Sunday, W. A.

Evangelism. HURH:170
Thio Chan Bee
  Christian laymen and the world
  of politics. MONS:465
Tillich, P. J.
  "What is truth?" ARS:180
Wycliffe, J.
  Concerning a grain of corn.
  BREWE 10:3924

---- See also Church; Church and
      State; Clergy; Faith; God;
      Prayers; Sermons; Sin

RELIGION AND SCIENCE
  Conant, J. B.
    Science and spiritual values.
    ARS:88
  Newman, J. H.
    Christianity and scientific in-
    vestigation. MCB:361
  Sevareid, E. and others
    Science and religion: who will
    play God? MOP:391

RELIGION AND STATE See
  Church and state

RELIGIOUS EDUCATION
  Welcome to parents at vacation
    Bible school commencement.
    HNWM:19

RELIGIOUS LIBERTY
  Binney, B.
    Valedictory oration. POC:51
  Bradlaugh, C.
    Appeal for justice. JAE:142
  Chew, S.
    Speech, &c. POC:77
  Danton, G. J.
    Freedom of worship.
    BREWE 5:1631
  Henry, J.
    On religion and elective office.
    ANN 4:239; BOORA 1:220
  Jackson, R. H. and others
    West Virginia Board of Educa-
    tion et al v. Barnette et al:
    opinion for the court and dis-
    senting opinion. ANN 16:148
  Sheil, R. L.
    Religious toleration.
    MCB:269
  Smith, A. E.
    Campaign speech, Oklahoma
    City, Sept. 20, 1928.
    SIN:52

Remond, Charles Lenox
Rights of colored citizens in
traveling. (Mass. H. of
Rep., February, 1842).
ANN 7:74; FON:72
Slavery and the Irish.
SMHR:110
Slavery as it concerns the
British (London, June 24,
1840). SMHV:16

Renault, Louis
The work at the Hague in 1899
and in 1907 (Nobel Lecture
for 1907, May 18, 1908).
NOLP 1:143

RENAULT, LOUIS
Løvland, J. G.
Presentation [of the Nobel
Prize for Peace to Louis
Renault, Dec. 10, 1907].
NOLP 1:141

REPARTEE See Responses

REPORTS
Benchley, R. C.
Treasurer's report.
HURH:211
Suggestions for preparation or
reports on conventions.
PAE:188
You get what you ask for (out-
line of speech). CUB:31

---- See also Club speeches; Congresses and conventions

REPUBLICAN PARTY
Brooke, E. W.
Crisis in the two-party
system. BA 1965-66:170
Hoover, H. C.
Road to freedom.
ANN 15:384
Lincoln, A.
Lincoln-Douglas joint debate
at Alton, October 15, 1858.
ANN 9:26
Roosevelt, F. D.
Republican leadership and
national defense. ANN 16:36
Taft, R. A.
Declaration of Republican
principles--the New Deal is
rapidly receding. BAD:74
Tilden, S. J.

Negro suffrage.
ANN 10:122

REPUBLICS See Democracy

RESEARCH
Bowen, W. G.
Commitment to scholarship
and research. BA 1978-79:41
Carty, J. J.
Pure science and industrial
research. ANN 14:9
Huxley, T. H.
Method of scientific investiga-
tion. ARS:264
Rowland, H. A.
Appeal for pure scientific re-
search in America.
ANN 12:262

RESIGNATIONS
Nixon, R. M.
Our long national nightmare is
over--speech of resignation.
BA 1974-75:43

---- See Officers, Retiring

RESPIRATION
Heymans, C. J. F.
The part played by vascular
presso- and chemo-receptors
in respiratory control.
NOLM 2:460
Warburg, O. H.
The oxygen-transferring fer-
ment of respiration.
NOLM 2:254

RESPONSES TO INTRODUCTION
Alphand, H.
Responds to introductions.
PRS:159; 198
Alsop, J.
Responds to an introduction.
PRS:154
Anspach, C. L.
Responds to an introduction.
PRS:138
Appling, H., Jr.
Responds to an introduction.
PRS:144
Bell, D. E.
Responds to introduction.
PRS:94
Bishop, J.
Responds to introduction (when
substituting for Sir Cedric

Responds to introduction.
PRS:128
Weaver, A. T.
Responds to an introduction.
PRS:137

---- See also Responses to welcome

RESPONSES TO PRESENTATION
See   Acceptance Speeches

RESPONSES TO SPEECHES OF
BLAME See Defense,
Speeches of

RESPONSES TO TOASTS
Carpenter, M. H.
Replying to the Grand Duke
Alexis (response to Duke's
toast "To the President of
the United States").
BREWE 3:974

RESPONSES TO TRIBUTES
Holmes, O. W., Jr.
"Live-I am coming:" re-
sponse to birthday greeting.
GRG:48; HURH:215

RESPONSES TO WELCOME
Abdul Rahman, T.
What the Commonwealth
means (response to welcome
address by British Prime
Minister). MONS:22
Parnell, C. S.
His first speech in America.
BREWE 8:3143
Phillips, C.
Dinas Island speech on Wash-
ington. BREWE 8:3176
Suggestions for preparation of
a response to a speech of
welcome. MILS:12

RESPONSIBILITY, MINISTERIAL
See Ministerial responsibility

Reston, James
Remarks at the Centennial
Charter Day Convocation,
the Ohio State University,
March 22, 1970. BAAE:285

RETAIL TRADE See Business

RETIREMENT See Officers,
Retiring

REUNIONS, CLASS
Schrier, W.
Address at Hope College
Alumni banquet, May 31, 1958.
SCHW:236
Washington, B. T.
Address delivered at the Har-
vard Alumni dinner in 1896.
HURH:144

Revels, Hiram R.
A plea for desegregated schools.
(Washington, Feb. 8, 1871).
FON:371

REVOLUTION, AMERICAN See
United States - History -
Revolution

REVOLUTION, FRENCH See
France - History - Revolution,
1789-1799; France - History -
Revolution, 1848

REVOLUTIONISTS
Pusey, N. M.
Thanksgiving and entreaty, a
President's valedictory.
HOR:26

REVOLUTIONS
Brown, H. R.
The Third World and the
ghetto. FON:1088
Kennedy, R. F.
Counterinsurgency. ANN 18:323
Rustin, B.
A way out of the exploding
ghetto. FON:1078
Tappan, D.
A warning to Harvard seniors
against world revolution (1798).
DAVF:49

REWARDS (PRIZES) See Accept-
ance speeches - Rewards
(Prizes); Presentation speeches
- Rewards (Prizes)

Reynolds, Sir Joshua
Genius and imitation.
BREWE 9:3313

Reynolds, Vernon
Chimpanzee worlds. MDYG:259

RHETORIC
Haiman, F. S.

The rhetoric of 1968: a
farewell to rational discourse.
LINRS:133

RHODE ISLAND - CONSTITUTION
Dorr, T.
People's right to remake
their constitution. ANN 7:56
Hallett, B.
Sovereignty of the people
(Luther v. Borden case).
ANN 7:410

RHODES
Demosthenes
Oration on the liberty of the
Rhodians. SAG:180

RHODESIA
Lee Kuan Yew
The Rhodesian problem and
the change of mood in
Britain. MONSA:251

RIBONUCLEIC ACID
Holley, R. W.
Alanine transfer RNA.
NOLM 4:324
Ochoa, S.
Enzymatic synthesis of ribo-
nucleic acid. NOLM 3:645
Watson, J. D.
The involvement of RNA in
the synthesis of proteins.
NOLM 3:785

Rice, George P.
The comic spirit and the public
speaker. (Indianapolis,
Oct. 9, 1974). EHN:283

Richards, Dickinson Woodruff
The contributions of right
heart catheterization to
physiology and medicine,
with some observations on
the physiopathology of pulmonary heart disease
(Nobel Lecture, Dec. 11,
1956). NOLM 3:513

RICHARDS, DICKINSON WOOD-
RUFF
Liljestrand, G.
Presentation [of the Nobel
Prize for Physiology or
Medicine to André Frederic
Cournand, Werner Theodor

Otto Forssmann, and Dickinson
Woodruff Richards Jr., Dec.
11, 1956]. NOLM 3:501

Richards, Theodore William
Atomic weights (Nobel Lecture
for 1914, Dec. 6, 1919).
NOLC 1:280

Richardson, Elliot L.
Vulnerability and vigilance.
(New York, Dec. 11, 1973).
BA 1973-74:13

Richardson, Owen Willans
Thermionic phenomena and the
laws which govern them (Nobel
Lecture for 1928, Dec. 12,
1929). NOLPH 2:224

RICHARDSON, OWEN WILLANS
Oseen, C. W.
Presentation [of the Nobel
Prize for Physics for 1928
to Owen Willans Richardson,
Dec. 12, 1929]. NOLPH 2:221

Richet, Charles Robert
Anaphylaxis (Nobel Lecture, Dec.
11, 1913). NOLM 1:473

RICHET, CHARLES ROBERT
Sundberg, C.
Presentation [of the Nobel
Prize for Physiology or Medi-
cine to Charles Robert Richet,
Dec. 11, 1913]. NOLM 1:469

Richey, Herbert S.
The real cause of inflation:
government services. (Columbus, Ohio, March 16, 1977).
LINRST:108

RIGHT AND LEFT (POLITICAL
SCIENCE)
McIntyre, T. J.
Keeping the Senate independent.
BA 1977-78:44
Oglesby, C.
How can we continue to sack
the ports of Asia and still
dream of Jesus. LAA:15
Rockefeller, N. A.
Extremism. KEO:320;
MAC:268; MACR:309

RIGHTS See Civil rights; Petition of Right, 1628; United States - Constitution

Rindo, John P.
Life, librium, and the pursuit of happiness (Gatlinburg, Tex., 1976). LINRST:230

RISK-TAKING (PSYCHOLOGY)
Wriston, W. B.
Risk and other four-letter words. BA 1979-80:191

Rittenhouse, David
Oration, &c. POC:142

ROADS
Crockett, D.
Raccoon in a bag.
BREWE 4:1482

Robbins, Asher
Fourth of July oration, July 4, 1834 (Philadelphia).
HAW:160

Robbins, Frederick Chapman
See also Enders, J. F.

ROBBINS, FREDERICK CHAPMAN
Gard, S.
Presentation [of the Nobel Prize for Physiology or Medicine to John Franklin Enders, Thomas Huckle Weller, and Frederick Chapman Robbins, Dec. 11, 1954]. NOLM 3:443

Roberts, James
Art of seduction. REIR:84

Robertson, Frederick W.
Highest form of expression.
BREWE 9:3319

Robeson, Paul
Anti-imperialists must defend Africa. (New York, June 6, 1946). FON:833
The Negro artist looks ahead. (Conference for Equal Rights for Negroes in the Arts, Sciences and Professions, New York, Dec. 1951).
FON:849

Robespierre, Maximilien
Against capital punishment.
BREWE 9:3326
Defense from the charge of tyranny. BREWE 9:3341
Demanding the King's death.
BREWE 9:3338
Festival of the Supreme Being.
BREWE 9:3340
His defense of terrorism.
BREWE 9:3331
"If God did not exist, it would be necessary to invent him."
BREWE 9:3330
Last words. Same as his Defense from the charge of tyranny
Moral ideas and Republican principles. BREWE 9:3334

Robinson, Frederick
A Jacksonian attack on monopoly (1834) (Boston Trades Union, July 4, 1834). DAVF:69
Labor as the source of reform.
ANN 6:69

Robinson, Sir Robert
Some polycyclic natural products (Nobel Lecture, Dec. 12, 1947). NOLC 3:166

ROBINSON, SIR ROBERT
Fredga, A.
Presentation [of the Nobel Prize for Chemistry to Sir Robert Robinson, Dec. 12, 1947]. NOLC 3:166

Robinson, William E. See Butler, B. F., jt. auth.

Rock, John S.
I will sink or swim with my race. (Boston, March 5, 1858). FON:203
Negro hopes for emancipation.
ANN 9:318
We ask for our rights. (Abington, Mass., August 1, 1862).
FON:257
What if the slaves are emancipated? (Massachusetts Anti-Slavery Society, Jan. 23, 1862). FON:250

Rockefeller, David
Responds to an introduction.
PRS:149

Rockefeller, Nelson A.
Extremism. KEO:320;
MAC:268; MACR:309

---- See also Burger, W. E., jt.
auth.

Rodriguez, Armando M.
This is our quest: to fight for
the right. BA 1968-69:129

Roesch, George F.
Constitutionality of a New York
child labor law: opinion
for the court. ANN 12:571

Rogers, Jack
Day before Christmas (Univ.
of Nebraska, 1953).
KEO:232; STOT:269

Rogers, Will
Education and wealth. (New
York, Dec. 4, 1924).
HURH:200
"I am here tonight representing
poverty." Same as his Edu-
cation and Wealth
Morgenthau's plan. GRG:55
Nominating Calvin Coolidge
(1924). BAP:298; BAPR:366
Presents Franklin Delano Roose-
velt. LYI:213

Rogers, William P.
Responds to an introduction.
PRS:142

Rogers, William Pierce
A brief assessment of where
we stand today. (Judicial
Conf. of the 2nd Judicial
Circuit of the U.S. Court
of Appeals, Buck Hill Falls,
Pa.). BA 1974-75:54

Rokeach, Milton
Images of the consumer's
changing mind on and off
Madison Avenue. ARS:115

ROMAN CATHOLIC CHURCH
Beecher, L.
A plea for the West.
HOW:133
Gibbons, J.
Progress of the Catholic
Church in America.

ANN 11:148
Kenrick, F. P.
Episcopal rights and parish
autonomy. ANN 5:437
Smith, S.
Results of oppression.
BREWE 9:3482; JAE:40

ROMAN CATHOLICS IN IRELAND
O'Connell, D.
Catholic rights in Ireland.
CLAYP:281
Sheil, R. L.
In defense of Irish Catholics.
BREWE 9:3419

ROME
Cavour, C. B.
Rome and Italy.
BREWE 3:1012
Manning, H. E.
Rome the eternal.
BREWE 8:2934

Romilly, Sir Samuel
Habeas Corpus Suspension Bill.
STRM:143

Romney, George
From the bottom to the top.
CAPG:140
Our unique economic principles:
the market place should deter-
mine price. CAPG:40

Romulo, Carlos P.
Bandung address. CROCK:141
The mind of a new common-
wealth (Notre Dame Univ.,
Dec. 9, 1935). CURM:267
Responds to an introduction.
PRS:161

RÖNTGEN, WILHELM CONRAD
Odhner, C. T.
Presentation [of the Nobel
Prize for Physics to Wilhelm
Conrad Röntgen, 1901].
NOLPH 1:3

Roosevelt, Eleanor Anna
Defense of American territorial
policies. ANN 17:128
United Nations. (Chicago, July
2, 1952). HURH:297
"Without the United Nations our
country would walk alone,
ruled by fear, instead of

confidence and hope. " Same
as her United Nations

ROOSEVELT, ELEANOR ANNA
Hancher, V. M.
Presents Eleanor Roosevelt.
LYI:244
Stevenson, A. E.
Eulogy on Eleanor Roosevelt.
BRP:230

Roosevelt, Franklin Delano
Acceptance of renomination for
the presidency, June 27,
1936. SIN:125
Acceptance speech, Chicago,
Illinois, July 2, 1932.
SIN:68
Acceptance speech, Philadelphia,
Pennsylvania, June 27, 1932.
Same as his Acceptance of
renomination for the presi-
dency, June 27, 1936
Acceptance speech via radio to
convention, Washington,
D.C., July 19, 1940.
SIN:156
Acceptance speech on renomina-
tion for president, July 20,
1944. SIN:194
Acceptance speech, Radio broad-
cast, San Diego, California,
July 20, 1944. Same as his
Acceptance speech on re-
nomination for president,
July 20, 1944
Action defended (campaign
speech, October 31, 1936).
ROD:168
Address at the annual gathering
of the White House Corre-
spondents' Association, Feb-
ruary 12, 1943. ANN 16:130
Address at University of Penn-
sylvania, September 20, 1940.
FRIP:331
Address on Constitution Day,
September 17, 1937.
FRIP:317
Address to the Commonwealth
Club, September 23, 1932.
ANN 15:158; ROD:31; SIN:77
Address to the people. Same
as his Broadcast address,
March 9, 1937
Address to White House Cor-
respondents' Association
dinner, March 15, 1941.

CROCK:11
Address to Young Democratic
Clubs of America, August 24,
1935. FRIP:304
Aid to the Democracies; our
country is going to play its
part. Same as his Address
to White House Correspondents'
Association dinner, March 15,
1941
American business is moving
ahead. BAD:1
Arsenal of democracy. Same as
his Preservation of American
independence
Battle with the Court. Same as
his Broadcast address, March
9, 1937 (proposal for the re-
form of the Federal Judiciary)
Broadcast address, March 9,
1937 (proposal for the reform
of the Federal Judiciary).
ANN 15:431; FRIP:309; ROD:192
Call for federal responsibility
(October 13, 1932).
ANN 15:185
Campaign speech, Chicago, Illi-
nois, October 14, 1936.
SIN:129
Campaign speech, Cleveland,
Ohio, November 2, 1940.
SIN:164
Campaign speech, San Francisco,
California, September 23,
1932. Same as his Address
to the Commonwealth Club,
September 23, 1932
Campaign speech, Washington,
D.C., September 23, 1944.
Same as his Opening campaign
speech at dinner of Interna-
tional Brotherhood of Team-
sters
Casablanca Conference. Same
as his Address at the annual
gathering of the White House
Correspondents' Association,
February 12, 1943
Casting the die: FDR requests
a Declaration of War against
Japan, 1941. Same as his
War address (December 8,
1941)
Challenge and hope. Same as
his Address to the Common-
wealth Club, September 23,
1932
Challenge and promise. Same

Progress of the recovery pro-
gram. Same as his Fireside
chat: AAA and NRA, July
24, 1933
Proposal for Lend-Lease.
ANN 16:40
The "Quarantine" speech. Same
as his Quarantining the ag-
gressors
Quarantining the aggressors
(Chicago, Oct. 5, 1937).
ANN 15:502; BEN:93;
BOORA 2:847; BRYF:474;
ROD:263
Relief, recovery, and reform.
Same as his Fireside chat on
the accomplishments of the
New Deal
Republican leadership and na-
tional defense. ANN 16:36
Request for a Declaration of
War. Same as his War ad-
dress (December 8, 1941)
Restating American Foreign
Policy: FDR's Chautauqua
speech, 1936. ROD:252
Right to security. ANN 15:315
Second annual message.
ANN 15:309; ROD:106;
STAT 3:2811
Second inaugural address.
USINAU:240; USINAUG:240
Second New Deal. Same as his
Second annual message
Seventh annual message.
STAT 3:2849
Sixth annual message. Same
as his Message to Con-
gress, January 4, 1939
Teamsters' Union speech.
Same as his Opening cam-
paign speech at dinner of
International Brotherhood
of Teamsters
Tentative trial balloon: the
"Quarantine speech." Same
as his Quarantining the
aggressors
Tenth annual message. Same
as his Message to Con-
gress, January 7, 1943
Third annual message.
STAT 3:2819
Third inaugural address.
USINAU:244; USINAUG:244
This nation will remain neutral.
ROD:274
Total national defense. Same

as his Navy Day address on
the attack on the destroyer
Kearney
Turning point. Same as his
Second annual message
Twelfth annual message. Same
as his Message to Congress
on the state of the nation,
January 6, 1945
Undelivered Jefferson Day ad-
dress. MDV:32
Undelivered last speech. Same
as his Undelivered Jefferson
Day address
War address (Washington, Dec.
8, 1941). ANN 16:103;
CUB:88 (outline); GRG:71;
HURH:265; LINS:327;
MAC:242; MACR:282;
MOPR:377; ROD:306
War in Europe: the President
addresses the people, 1939.
Same as his This nation will
remain neutral
"We are going to win the war
and we are going to win the
peace that follows." Same
as his War address (December
8, 1941)
What the New Deal has done for
business (campaign speech in
Chicago, October 14, 1936).
ANN 15:379
"With absolute faith that our
common cause will greatly
succeed." Same as his
Preservation of American in-
dependence

ROOSEVELT, FRANKLIN DELANO
Roger, W.
Presents Franklin Delano
Roosevelt. LYI:213
Schlesinger, A., Jr.
Roosevelt's place in history.
BA 1971-72:133

Roosevelt, Theodore
Annual message, December 6,
1905. STAT 2:2105
Conservation of public lands.
Same as his Public domain:
the people's heritage
Controlling the trusts. Same
as his First annual message
Corollary to the Monroe Doctrine. Same as his Fifth
annual message

Eighth annual message.
STAT 3:2296
Fifth annual message.
ANN 13:1; STAT 3:2144
First annual message.
ANN 12:433; STAT 2:2014
Fourth annual message.
Same as his Annual message
"I took the Canal Zone."
STAT 2:2073
"I wish to preach not the doctrine of ignoble ease but the doctrine of the strenuous life." Same as his Strenuous life
Inaugural address. USINAU:183
International peace (Nobel Lecture for 1906, May 5, 1910). NOLP 1:102
Issues of the coming election.
ANN 11:170
Man with the muck-rake (at dedication of Office Building of the House of Representatives, April 14, 1906).
ARS:102; GRG:24; HURH:291; LINS:283; OLIS:217
Message to Congress, December 5, 1905. Same as his Fifth annual message
New nationalism (at dedication of John Brown Memorial Park, Osawatomic, Kansas).
ANN 13:250; BOORA 2:711
Public domain: the people's heritage. ANN 13:161
Second annual message.
STAT 2:2053
Seventh annual message.
STAT 3:2240
Sixth annual message.
STAT 3:2194
Strenuous life (Chicago, April 10, 1899). BEN:189; HURH:150
Third annual message. Same as his "I took the Canal Zone"

ROOSEVELT, THEODORE
Knudsen, G.
Presentation [of the Nobel Prize for Peace to Theodore Roosevelt, Dec. 10, 1906].
NOLP 1:97
Miller, K.
The Brownsville affair.

FON:654
Peirce, H. D. D.
Acceptance [of the Nobel Prize for Peace for Theodore Roosevelt, Dec. 10, 1906].
NOLP 1:99

Root, Elihu
European War and the preservation of America's ideals.
ANN 14:70
Introducing H. Watterson to New England Society of New York.
LYI:111
Invisible government: Short Ballot Amendment.
ANN 13:528
Proper pace of political change.
ANN 13:436
Towards making peace permanent (Nobel Lecture for 1912).
NOLP 1:247

ROOT, ELIHU
Moe, R.
Presentation [of the Nobel Prize for Peace to Elihu Root, 1912, Dec. 10, 1913].
NOLP 1:245

Root, Trent C.
The failure of scientists to communicate (Tucson, Ariz., Oct. 25, 1977). BA 1977-78:110

Roper, Bruce
A fable come true. BREWW:201

ROPER, ELMO
Ford, H. II
Presents Elmo Roper.
LYI:73

Rosebery, Archibald Philip Primrose, 5th Earl of See Curzon of Kedleston, George, jt. auth.

ROSENTHAL, FRANK F.
Croarkin, W.
Presents Frank F. Rosenthal.
LYI:165

Rosenthal, Norbert L.
My son, my son. WALE:152

Ross, John See Sanford, N., jt. auth.

Ross, Sir Ronald
  Researches on malaria (Nobel
  Lecture, Dec. 12, 1902).
  NOLM 1:25

ROSS, SIR RONALD
  Mörner, K. A. H.
    Presentation [of the Nobel
    Prize for Physiology or
    Medicine to Sir Ronald Ross,
    Dec. 12, 1902]. NOLM 1:21

Rosten, Leo
  Myths by which we live.
  KEO:240

Rostow, Eugene V.
  Choice in foreign policy.
  ANN 18:605

ROTARIANS
  Sandosham, A. A.
    He stood up and drank the
    toast and joined in the ap-
    plause! MONSA:224

ROTARY CLUB
  Yeang, C. H.
    The building of peaceful
    bridge the rotary way.
    MONSA:218

ROTARY CLUB OF KUALA
  LUMPUR
  Johari, M. K.
    Nation building and the four-
    way test. MONSA:100

Rous, Peyton
  The challenge to man of the
  neoplastic cell (Nobel Lecture, Dec. 13, 1966).
  NOLM 4:220

ROUS, PEYTON
  Klein, G.
    Presentation [of the Nobel
    Prize for Physiology or
    Medicine to Peyton Rous
    and Charles Brenton Hug-
    gins, Dec. 13, 1966].
    NOLM 4:215

Routtenberg, Max J.
  Crown of a good name.
  WALE:154

ROWAN, ARCHIBALD HAMILTON
  Curran, J. P.

England and English liberties--
  in the case of Rowan.
  BREWE 4:1546

Rowan, Carl T.
  New frontiers in racial relations.
  (Youngstown, State University,
  Oct. 24, 1968). OE:201

Rowe, James N.
  An American prisoner of war in
  South Vietnam. (Leavenworth,
  Kansas). LINRS:45;
  LINRST:56

Rowen, Hobart
  Responds to introduction.
  PRS:96

Rowland, Henry A.
  Appeal for pure scientific re-
  search in America.
  ANN 12:262

Roxas, Manuel
  A farewell to the Assembly (National Assembly, Aug. 15,
  1938). CURM:282

Royer-Collard, Pierre Paul
  Against press censorship.
  BREWE 9:3347
  "Sacrilege" in law.
  BREWE 9:3345

Royster, Vermont C.
  What the people grant, they can
  take away (Washington, Dec.
  5, 1978). BA 1978-79:191

RUBBER
  Lew Sip Hon
    Our stake in natural rubber.
    MONS:302

Rubel, Charles M.
  Beauties of Japheth and the glory
  of Shem. WALE:157

Ruckelshaus, Jill See Steinem,
  G., jt. auth.

Ruckelshaus, William D.
  The environment revolution.
  (Williamsburg, Va., Jan. 29,
  1972). BA 1971-72:125

Rudberg, E. G.
  Presentation [of the Nobel Prize

Rudin, Jacob P.
for Physics to William Shockley, John Bardeen and Walter
Houser Brattain, Dec. 11,
1956]. NOLPH 3:315

Rudin, Jacob P.
Shadows in the sun. WALE:160

RUKUNEGARA
Lim Chong Eu
The message of Rukunegara.
MONSA:147

Rumbold, Richard
Against booted and spurred
privilege. BREWE 9:3352

Runkel, Howard W.
Making Lincoln live. (Oregon
State Legislature, Feb. 12,
1957). BAPR:351;
BAPRR:259

RURAL DEVELOPMENT See
Land use, Rural

RURAL LIFE
Morgan, M.
Building a better rural com-
munity today for a better
agriculture tomorrow.
BREWW:198
Wilson, W. H.
Interaction of country and
city. ANN 14:4

Rush, Benjamin
Thoughts on female education.
ANN 3:207

Rush, Richard
Fourth of July oration, 1812
(Washington, July 4, 1812).
HAW:16

Rush, Wayne
Feeding the hungry world.
BREWW:91

Rusk, Dean
Eulogy of Lyndon Baines John-
son. (Washington, D.C.,
Jan. 24, 1973).
BA 1972-73:132
For ratification of treaties
with Panama. (Washington,
Oct. 14, 1977).
BA 1977-78:9

Formulating foreign policy.
ANN 18:20

Ruskin, John
Iscariot in modern England.
BREWE 9:3354

Russell, Bertrand Arthur William
What desires are politically
important? (Nobel lecture,
Dec. 11, 1950). NOL:452

RUSSELL, BERTRAND ARTHUR
WILLIAM
Österling, A.
Presentation [of the Nobel
Prize for Literature to Bert-
rand Arthur William Russell,
1950]. NOB 15:255; NOL:449
Waller, H. H.
Presents Bertrand Russell.
LYI:94

Russell, John Russell, 1st Earl of
Reform of Parliament. Same as
his Reform of the franchise
Reform of the franchise. (Com-
mons, March 1, 1831).
MCB:87
Science and literature as modes
of progress. BREWE 9:3359

Russell, Richard and others (P. H.
Douglas)
Pro's and con's of civil rights.
BRR:73

RUSSIA
Lenin, N.
War, peace and revolutionary
democracy. BRN:81
Lyndhurst, J. S. C.
Russia and the Crimean War.
BREWE 7:2842

---- FOREIGN RELATIONS
Churchill, W. L. S.
Sinews of peace (speech at
Fulton, Missouri).
ANN 16:365; MCB:541
Inozemstev, N. N.
Alternative to war. MDV:69

---- See also United States - Foreign relations - Russia

Russwurm, John Browne
The condition and prospects of

Haiti. (Brunswick, Maine, Sept. 6, 1826). FON:33

Rustin, Bayard
A way out of the exploding ghetto. (Detroit, 1967). FON:1078

---- See also Brown, R. S., jt. auth.

Rutherford, Ernest
The chemical nature of the alpha particles from radioactive substances (Nobel Lecture, Dec. 11, 1908). NOLC 1:129

RUTHERFORD, ERNEST
Hasselberg, K. B.
Presentation [of the Nobel Prize for Chemistry to Ernest Rutherford, Dec. 11, 1908]. NOLC 1:125

Rutledge, John
Speech in time of Revolution. BREWE 9:3368; POC:325
Speech to both Houses. Same as his Speech in time of Revolution

Ružička, Leopold Stephen
Multimembered rings, higher terpene compounds, and male sex hormones (Nobel Lecture for 1939, Dec. 12, 1945). NOLC 2:468

Ryder, Sir Dudley See Walpole, R., jt. auth.

Rylaarsdam, Jeannette
Undesirable one. SCHW:1

- S -

Saavedra Lamas, Carlos
Radio address (Nobel Lecture, Nov. 29, 1936). NOLP 2:225

SAAVEDRA LAMAS, CARLOS
Lange, C. L.
Presentation [of the Nobel Prize for Peace to Carlos

Saavedra Lamas, Dec. 10, 1936]. NOLP 2:217

Sabatier, Paul
The method of direct hydrogenation by catalysis (Nobel Lecture, Dec. 11, 1912). NOLC 1:221

SABATIER, PAUL
Söderbaum, H. G.
Presentation [of the Nobel Prize for Chemistry to Victor Grignard and Paul Sabatier, Dec. 11, 1912]. NOLC 1:217

Sacco, Nicola
I am never guilty See Sacco, Nicola and Vanzetti, Bartolomeo Proclaim their innocence

---- and Vanzetti, Bartolomeo
Proclaim their innocence. ALA:85; ANN 14:527

SACHEVERELL, HENRY
Jekyll, J.
Resistance to unlawful authority (impeachment of H. Sacheverell). BREWE 7:2617

Sachs, Leonie Nelly
Acceptance [of the Nobel Prize for Literature, 1966]. NOB 16:5; NOL:619

SACHS, LEONIE NELLY
Österling, A.
Presentation [of the Nobel Prize for literature to Shmuel Yosef Agnon and Leonie Nelly Sachs, 1966]. NOB 1:3; NOB 16:3; NOL:611

Sacks, Marvin
The value of disobedience (Indiana University, 1971). LINRS:148; LINRST:152

SAFETY REGULATIONS
Franklin, B. H.
Consumer safety and health. BA 1978-79:133

SALES TALKS AND SALESMANSHIP
Domiano, P.
Break down at United (Swim-

ming Pool Company).
REIR:38
You, too, can be a millionaire.
BURT:118

Salisbury, Robert Arthur Talbot
Gascoyne-Cecil, 3d Marquis
of
Speech to the Primrose League.
STRM:375

Salk, Jonas E.
Responds to introduction.
PRS:89

Salkowitz, Selig
King's answer. WALE:163

Salm, Nell
Matter of time. SCHW:83

SALVATION
Hooker, T.
The soul's vocation, doctrine
3. JON:82
The soul's vocation, doctrine
7. JON:93

SALVATION ARMY
Karos, P. A.
Haven of the defeated.
ARS:148

Sambanthan, V. T.
Basic objectives of M.I.C.
(Malayan Indian Congress).
MONS:135
Be a harmonising factor (Kuala
Lumpur, Nov. 8, 1970).
MONSA:95

Sampson, B. K.
To my white fellow citizens.
(Fairfield, Ohio, Thanks-
giving Day, 1867).
FON:347

Sampson, Edith S.
Choose one of five (North
Central College, Ill., May
30, 1965). MOP:386;
REID:398

Sandburg, Carl
Abraham Lincoln. Same as
his On Lincoln (at 150th
anniversary of Lincoln's
birth)

On Lincoln (at 150th anniversary
of Lincoln's birth). (Washington, Feb. 12, 1959).
GRG:101; HURH:347
"On occasions he was seen to
weep in a way that made weep-
ing decent, appropriate and
majestic." Same as his On
Lincoln (at 150th anniversary
of Lincoln's birth)

Sanders, Clinton S.
Responds to introduction.
PRS:90

Sandosham, A. A.
He stood up and drank the toast
and joined in the applause.
MONSA:224

Sanford, E. T. and others (O. W.
Holmes, Jr.)
Gitlow v. New York: opinion for
the court and dissenting opinion. ANN 14:476

Sanford, Nathan and others (M. Van
Buren; J. Kent; P. R. Liv-
ingston; J. Cramer; D. Buel,
Jr.; J. Ross; P. Jay)
Debate on property and suffrage.
ANN 5:4

Sanford, Terry
After Vietnam, a new United
States foreign policy (Southwestern, Memphis, May 31,
1971). HOR:132

Sanger, Frederick
The chemistry of insulin (Nobel
Lecture, Dec. 11, 1958).
NOLC 3:544

SANGER, FREDERICK
Tiselius, A. W. K.
Presentation [of the Nobel
Prize for Chemistry to
Frederick Sanger, Dec. 11,
1958]. NOLC 3:541

SANITATION
Kingsley, C.
Massacre of the innocents.
BRYH:392

Santayana, George
Genteel tradition in American
philosophy. ANN 13:277

SANTO DOMINGO
  Butler, B. F. and others
    Congressional debate on
    Haiti and Santo Domingo,
    January 13, 1869.
    ANN 10:143

Sara, Martha J.
  Do not refuse us.
    BA 1969-70:148

SARAWAK
  Ningkan, S. K.
    Three problems of Sarawak.
    MONS:326

Sargent, Francis W.
  The computer and civil liber-
    ties. (Boston University,
    Oct. 4, 1973).
    BA 1973-74:141

SATELLITES See Communica-
  tions satellites

SATIRIC SPEECHES
  Bolton, T.
    Oration (burlesque of War-
      ren's second Boston Massa-
      cre oration). POC:301
  Buchwald, A.
    Parody of political speeches.
    JAM:27
    Grand dragon of the Ku Klux
      Klan. BURT:65
    James Hoffa (satiric speech).
    BURT:47
  Rogers, W.
    Morgenthau's plan. GRG:55
    Nominating Calvin Coolidge.
    BAP:298; BAPR:366

Saurin, Jacques
  Effect of passion.
    BREWE 9:3371

Savage, John
  People v. Fisher: opinion for
    the court. ANN 6:172
  Slums as a common nuisance
    (Meeker v. Van Rensselaer
    case). ANN 6:279

Savage, Michael Joseph
  New Zealand's war aims, 1939
    (Sept. 5, 1939).
    MACS:365 sel.

---- See also Hamilton, A., jt.
  auth.

Savilla, Elmer M.
  Address to the Assembly of the
    National Congress of American
    Indians at San Diego, Califor-
    nia, October 1974. MAES:225

Sawhill, John C.
  Energy and the job market
    (Champion, Pa., Sept. 29,
    1975). BA 1975-76:102

Sawyer, Thomas E.
  Assimilation versus self-identity:
    a modern native American per-
    spective, an address to the
    Western Social Science Asso-
    ciation Conference, Arizona
    State Univ., Tempe, Ariz.,
    May 1, 1976. MAES:197

Sayre, Francis B.
  The tall ships (Newport, R.I.,
    June 27, 1976).
    BA 1976-77:181

SCAFFOLD SPEECHES See De-
  fense, Speeches of

Scarborough, William Sanders
  The ethics of the Hawaiian ques-
    tion. (Wilberforce Univ.,
    March, 1894). FON:570

Schalliol, Charles
  The strangler (Indiana Univ.,
    March, 1967). LINR:246;
    LINRS:260; LINRST:298

Schell, George
  Shackled by stereotypes. (Baylor
    University, 1962). CAPB:381

Schlegel, Karl Wilhelm F. Von
  Philosophy of history.
    BREWE 9:3377

Schlesinger, Arthur M., Jr.
  Challenge of abundance.
    ARS:196
  Roosevelt's place in history.
    (New York, Jan. 30, 1972).
    BA 1971-72:133

Schmedeman, Albert G.
  Acceptance [of the Nobel Prize

for Peace for Woodrow Wilson, 1919, Dec. 10, 1920].
NOLP 1:294

Schmitt, Harrison
New policy options through technology (Baltimore, March 19, 1980).
BA 1979-80:133

Schnadig, Edgar L.
Presents Gerald Wendt.
LYI:186

SCHOLARS See Learning and scholarship

SCHOOL INTEGRATION
Howe, H., II
The Brown decision, pluralism, and the schools in the 1980s. BA 1979-80:101
Kitslaar, J. L.
Is busing the answer?
LINRST:294

Schorr, Daniel
In defense of privilege (San Francisco, Dec. 14, 1978).
BA 1978-79:202

Schrier, William
Address at Hope College Alumni banquet, May 31, 1958.
SCHW:236
Address to the 60th Anniversary Oratorical Banquet, March 1, 1957. SCHW:226
Behind the scenes in oratory.
SCHW:231
Coaching oratory. SCHW:239

Schrodinger, Erwin
The fundamental idea of wave mechanics (Nobel Lecture, Dec. 12, 1933).
NOLPH 2:305

SCHRODINGER, ERWIN
Pleijel, H.
Presentation [of the Nobel Prize for Physics for 1932 to Werner Heisenberg and for 1933 to Erwin Schrodinger and Paul Adrien Maurice Dirac, Dec. 11, 1933]. NOLPH 2:283

Schroeder, Patricia
You can do it. (Houston, Feb. 9, 1973). BA 1972-73:86

Schück, Henrik
Presentation [of the Nobel Prize for Literature to Grazia Deledda, 1926]. NOB 5:117;
NOL:232

Schurz, Carl
Civil service reform. Same as his Necessity and progress of Civil Service reform
The irrepressible conflict (1860).
DAVF:130
Necessity and progress of Civil Service reform. ANN 11:493
Need for a rational forest policy.
ANN 11:200
Old world and the new. (New York, Nov. 5, 1881).
HURH:135
Public offices as private perquisites. BREWE 9:3384
True Americanism. ANN 9:97

Schwab, Michael
Address at trial, Chicago, October 7-9, 1886. ACC:24;
PAF:25

Schweitzer, Albert
The problem of peace (Nobel Lecture for 1952, Nov. 4, 1954). NOLP 3:46

SCHWEITZER, ALBERT
Hageman, M.
Wisdom of the heart.
SCHW:177
Jahn, G.
Presentation [of the Nobel Prize for Peace for 1952 to Albert Schweitzer, Dec. 10, 1953]. NOLP 3:37

Schwellenbach, Lewis B.
First seven years of the New Deal: let's view the record.
BAD:47

Schwinger, Julian
Relativistic quantum field theory (Nobel Lecture, Dec. 11, 1965). NOLPH 4:140

SCHWINGER, JULIAN
  Waller, I.
    Presentation [of the Nobel
    Prize for Physics to Sin-
    Itiro Tomonaga, Julian
    Schwinger, and Richard P.
    Feynman, Dec. 11, 1965].
    NOLPH 4:123

SCIENCE AND CIVILIZATION
  Tan Siew Sin
    The big question before us.
    MONSA:93

SCIENCE AND RELIGION See
  Religion and science

SCIENCE AND SCIENTISTS
  Arnold, M.
    Literature and science.
    MCB:388
  Bigelow, J.
    Future of arts and sciences.
    ANN 4:449
  Boyd Orr, J.
    Science and peace (Nobel
    Lecture, Dec. 12, 1949).
    NOLP 2:415
  Bragg, L.
    Art of talking about science.
    MOP:358
  Brown, H. S.
    Science, technology, and
    world development.
    ARS:83
    Social responsibility of sci-
    ence. BAP:280
  Dixon, O.
    Law and the scientific ex-
    pert. MCA:176
  Durfee, J.
    Influence of scientific dis-
    covery and invention on
    social and political progress.
    ANN 7:128
  Huxley, T. H.
    Method of scientific investi-
    gation. ARS:264; BRYF:521
    Science and culture.
    MCB:376
  Lee Kuan Yew
    Lesson we have to learn
    (opening new Science Tower
    at University of Singapore).
    MONS:361
  Miller, H.
    Pledge science gives to
    hope. BREWE 8:3013

Oppenheimer, J. R.
  Prospect in the arts and sci-
  ences (at Colombia University
  bicentennial anniversary cele-
  bration). HURH:319;
  HURS:211
Russell, J. R.
  Science and literature as
  modes of progress.
  BREWE 9:3359
Seaborg, G. T.
  Positive power of science.
  BA 1969-70:108
Smith, G.
  Secret beyond science.
  BREWE 9:3476
Urey, H. C.
  Science and society (at 100th
  anniversary Academic Convo-
  cation of Cooper Union for
  the Advancement of Science and
  Art). ARS:78
Whitehead, A. N.
  Technical education and its
  relation to science and litera-
  ture. MCB:403
Wiesner, J. B.
  Science in the affluent society
  (centennial celebration of Na-
  tional Academy of Sciences).
  ANN 18:186
Wydler, J. W.
  Science and the public trust.
  BA 1979-80:139

---- See also Atomic energy

SCIENCE AND THE HUMANITIES
  Snow, Sir C. P.
    The two cultures. MCB:417

SCIENCE NEWS
  Farber, S. M.
    Why national concern for bio-
    medical communication?
    BA 1966-67:118

SCOTLAND
  Belhaven, J. H.
    Plea for the national life of
    Scotland. BREWE 1:371

Scott, Richard and others (Jane
    Farwell)
  A job-seeking interview: a
  transcript. MOPR:381

SCOTT, SIR WALTER
  Smith, G.

Scranton, William W.
Lamps of fiction (at centenary of Sir Walter Scott).
BREWE 9:3465

Scranton, William W.
Responds to introduction.
PRS:110

SCRANTON, WILLIAM W.
Watson, A. K.
Presents William W. Scranton. LYI:201

Seaborg, Glenn Theodore
Positive power of science.
BA 1969-70:108
The transuranium elements: present status (Nobel Lecture, Dec. 12, 1951).
NOLC 3:325

SEABORG, GLENN THEODORE
Westgren, A.
Presentation [of the Nobel Prize for Chemistry to Edwin Mattison McMillan and Glenn Theodore Seaborg, Dec. 12, 1951].
NOLC 3:309

SEABURY, DAVID
McLain, H. O.
Presents David Seabury.
LYI:98

Seale, Bobby
Free Huey. (March 16, 1968).
MACR:322; SMHR:175

Seaman, Sir Owen
Presents Stephen Leacock.
LYI:47

Seaton, Fred A. See Malone, G. W., jt. auth.

SECESSION See Confederate States of America; State rights; United States - History - Civil War - Causes

SECRET SOCIETIES
Morse, Jedidiah
The present dangers and consequent duties of the citizens (1799).
DAVF:45

Smith, G.
A voice from the past (1870). (Syracuse, N.Y., Nov. 1870).
DAVF:154

SECTIONALISM (UNITED STATES)
Lincoln, A.
Second annual message to Congress. BOORA 1:396; STAT 2:1068
Pierce, F.
Fourth annual message.
STAT 1:918
Turner, F. J.
Sectionalism and national unity. ANN 14:493

SECURITY See Internal Security Act, 1950; Social security

SECURITY, INTERNATIONAL - EUROPE
Goldberg, A. J.
Human rights and détente.
BA 1977-78:71

Seddon, Richard John and others
The South African War contingent, 1899 (New Zealand House of Representatives, Sept. 28, 1899).
MACS:260 sel.

SEDUCTION
Roberts, J.
Art of seduction. REIR:84

Seeley, John R.
Tendency in English history. (Cambridge University, 1882).
MCB:50

Seenivasagam, Dharma Raja
Frankenstein in the making.
MONS:199

Seferis, Giorgos
Acceptance [of the Nobel Prize for Literature, 1963].
NOB 17:5; NOL:582
Some notes on modern Greek tradition (Nobel lecture, Dec. 11, 1963). NOL:484

SEFERIS, GIORGOS
Österling, A.
Presentation [of the Nobel Prize for Literature to

Giorgos Seferis, 1963].
NOB 17:3; NOL:580

Segrè, Emilio Gino
Properties of antinucleons
(Nobel Lecture, Dec. 11,
1959). NOLPH 3:508

SEGRE, EMILIO GINO
Hulthèn, E.
Presentation [of the Nobel
Prize for Physics to Emilio
Gino Segrè and Owen
Chamberlain, Dec. 11,
1959]. NOLPH 3:487

SEGREGATION
Brown, H. B. and others
Plessy v. Ferguson: opinion
for the court and dissenting
opinion. ANN 12:92
Davis, B. J.
The Negro people on the
march. FON:902
Farmer, J.
The "Movement" now.
FON:1040
Feldmann, M. H.
Eyes of the whole world.
SCHW:156
Green, J. P.
These evils call loudly for
redress. FON:499
Hope, J.
We are struggling for equal-
ity. FON:594
Hughes, C. E.
Small step toward racial
equality: opinion for the
Supreme Court on Mitchell
case, 1941. ROD:224
King, M. L., Jr.
The American dream.
FON:933
Give us the ballot--we will
transform the South.
FON:919
Marshall, T.
Segregation and desegrega-
tion. FON:866
Pinchback, P. B. S.
The whole race must pro-
test. FON:596
Randolph, A. P.
A call for mass action.
FON:822
Trotter, W. M.
Segregation destroys fellow-
ship and citizenship. FON:702

---- See also Civil rights; Discrimination; Negroes; Race
problems; Segregation in education

---- RESISTANCE TO
King, M. L., Jr.
Love, law, and civil disobedi-
ence. FON:943; LINR:63;
LINRS:70; LINRST:75;
STOT:321
Nonviolence and social change.
OE:157
Revels, H. R.
A plea for desegregated
schools. FON:371

SEGREGATION IN EDUCATION
Nell, W. C.
The triumph of equal school
rights in Boston. FON:164
Revels, H. R.
A plea for desegregated
schools. FON:371
Sumner, C.
Segregation and the common
school (Sarah C. Roberts v.
City of Boston case, 1849).
ANN 7:507
Warren, E.
Brown et al v. Board of Edu-
cation of Topeka et al: opinion
for the court. ANN 17:253;
BOORA 2:904
Wilkins, R.
The conspiracy to deny equal-
ity. FON:892

---- See also Blacks, Civil rights

SELF DEFENSE See Defense,
Speeches of

SELF GOVERNMENT
Akintola, S. L. and others
Nigeria debates self-govern-
ment. EMP:65
Eddy, E. D., Jr.
Student involvement in educa-
tional policy.
BA 1965-66:221; LINR:251
Gardiner, R. K.
Citizenship and political
liberalism. EMP:106
Holly, J. T.
The Negro race, self-govern-
ment and the Haitian revolu-
tion. FON:169

SELF-RESPECT
  Manley, A. E.
    Charge to the graduates.
    HOR:6

Sellers, Rose Z.
  Presents Harry D. Gideonse.
  LYI:80

SELLING See Sales talks and
  salesmanship

Semenov, Nikolai Nikolaevic
  Some problems relating to
    chain reactions and to the
    theory of combustion (Nobel
    Lecture, Dec. 11, 1956).
    NOLC 3:487

SEMENOV, NIKOLAI NIKOLAEVIC
  Olander, A.
    Presentation [of the Nobel
    Prize for Chemistry to Sir
    Cyril Norman Hinshelwood
    and Nikolai Nikolaevic
    Semenov, Dec. 11, 1956].
    NOLC 3:471

SEMICENTENNIAL CELEBRA-
  TIONS See Anniversaries

SEMICONDUCTOR LASERS
  Basov, N. G.
    Semiconductor lasers.
    NOLPH 4:89

SEMICONDUCTORS
  Bardeen, J.
    Semiconductor research lead-
    ing to the point contact
    transistor. NOLPH 3:318
  Brattain, W. H.
    Surface properties of semi-
    conductors. NOLPH 3:377

SEMINOLE WAR, 1st, FLORIDA,
  1817-1818
  Clay, H.
    On the Seminole War.
    BREWE 4:1236
  Monroe, J.
    Second annual message.
    STAT 1:156

Sendut, Hamzah See Hamzah
  Sendut

Seneca, Lucius Annaeus
  Address to Nero.
  BREWE 9:3390

Seneca, Martin
  Address delivered at Brigham
    Young University February,
    1975. MAES:26

Senu bin Abdul Rahman
  Let our voice be heard. (New
    Year message). MONS:160
  Pledge to newsmen. MONS:156

SEPARATION OF POWERS
  Osias, C.
    Justice and separation of
    powers. CURM:190

SERMONS
  Aelfric
    Sermon on the sacrifice on
    Easter-Day. BRYH:14
  Aelred, Saint
    Sermon after absence.
    BREWE 1:111
  Anonymous
    Sermon for the third Sunday
    after Trinity (by an unknown
    Medieval preacher). BRYH:31
  Arnold, T.
    Realities of life and death.
    BREWE 1:173
  Bacon, L.
    Sermon from Mark XII, 34.
    HAW:57
  Ball, J.
    We have the pain and travail.
    BRYH:42
  Baxter, R.
    Unwilllingness to improve.
    BREWE 1:242
  Bede
    Sermon for any day.
    BREWE 1:343
  Beecher, H. W.
    Success of American democ-
    racy (anniversary of attack
    on Fort Sumter). OLIS:191
  Bonaventura, Saint
    Life of service.
    BREWE 2:552
  Boucher, J.
    Civil liberty and nonresistance.
    ANN 2:343; POC:552
  Bulkeley, P.
    City set upon a hill.

ANN 1:211
The gospel-covenant.
JON:30
Bunyan, J.
Heavenly footman.
BREWE 2:716
Burrows, J. L.
Opposition to the theater in
time of war. ANN 9:402
Cahill, D. W.
Last judgment. BREWE 3:851
Chauncy, C.
Caveat against enthusiasm.
POC:488
Chiu Ban It
Be strong and of good
courage (enthronement ser-
mon). MONS:456
Colman, B.
Piety and duty of rulers to
comfort and encourage the
ministry of Christ.
POC:412
Cotton, J.
God's promise to his planta-
tions. ANN 1:107
A treatise of the covenant
of grace. JON:48
Viall I: the powring out of
the seven vials or An ex-
position, with an application
of the 16th Chapter of Reve-
lation. POC:363
The way of life. JON:121
Cyprian, Saint
Unshackled living.
BREWE 4:1588
Davenport, J.
The saint's anchor-hold.
JON:147
Davies, S.
Curse of cowardice.
ANN 2:23; POC:534
Ditzen, L. R.
The right ticket but the
wrong train. REID:404
Donne, J.
Sermon preached at St.
Paul's (Easter Day, 1625).
BRYH:109
Dumper, A. C.
Church in a secular state.
MONS:485
Dwight, T.
On the duty of Americans
at the present crisis.
ANN 4:33
Pursuit of excellence.

BREWE 5:1968
Edwards, J.
Farewell-sermon. POC:443
Fisher, J.
Jeopardy of daily life.
BREWE 6:2164
Frelinghuysen, T.
Revivalist sermon. ANN 1:344
Graham, W. F.
Confusing evil with good.
LINR:179
Great Disturber (outline of speech
to celebrate acceptance of
Christ's offer of salvation
through obedience to His
Word). CUB:95
Gunsaulus, F. W.
Healthy heresies.
BREWE 6:2353
Hare, J. C.
Children of light.
BREWE 6:2402
Hatfield, M. O.
If we fall down in the land of
peace. BA 1979-80:67
Herder, J. G.
Meaning of inspiration.
BREWE 7:2497
Hooker, T.
The soul's exaltation.
JON:104
The soul's vocation, doctrine
3. JON:82
The soul's vocation, doctrine
7. JON:93
Unbelievers preparing for
Christ. POC:331
Hubbard, W.
Happiness of a people in the
wisdom of their rulers direct-
ing and in obedience of their
brethren attending unto what
Israel ought to do.
ANN 1:248
Huffman, J. A.
Retrospect '73--Biblical les-
sons we can learn from Water-
gate. TAC:221
Knopwood, R.
On the everpresent God.
MCA:11
Knox, J.
Against tyrants.
BREWE 7:2665
Lang, J. D.
"Little While" of the Saviour's
absence and the prospect of
his speedy return. MCA:64

McCorkle, S.
    A sermon for the anniversary
    of American independence,
    July 24th, 1786. HAW:292
Mather, I.
    Discourse concerning the
    uncertainty of the times of
    men. POC:377
Mayhew, J.
    Discourse on the anniversary
    of the death of Charles I.
    ANN 1:481; POC:508
Parker, T.
    Transient and permanent in
    Christianity. LINS:178
Saurin, J.
    Effect of passion.
    BREWE 9:3371
Sayre, F. B.
    The tall ships.
    BA 1976-77:181
Shepard, T.
    Election sermon. POC:355
    The parable of the ten vir-
    gins. JON:133
    The sound believer. JON:63
Spurgeon, C. H.
    Everlasting oxydization.
    BREWE 9:3500
Stoddard, S.
    Defects of preachers im-
    proved. POC:430
Stone, B. W.
    "And I will gladly spend and
    be spent for you though the
    more abundantly I love you,
    the less I be loved." BLY:19
Symonds, W.
    Britain's claim to a New
    World empire justified.
    ANN 1:32
Taylor, J.
    Foolish exchange.
    BREWE 9:3590
Tennent, G.
    Danger of an unconverted
    ministry. POC:469
Tillotson, J.
    Sermon against evil speaking.
    BRYH:156
Tyndale, W.
    Use and abuse of images and
    relics. BREWE 9:3660
Wesley, J.
    Sacri fames auri.
    BREWE 10:3877
    Use of money. BRYH:191
West, S.

Election sermon. POC:578
Whitefield, G.
    Abraham's offering up his son
    Isaac. OLIS:6
Winthrop, J.
    Modell of Christian charity.
    BOORA 1:10
Woodmason, C.
    You are to take these free
    booters and desperadoes.
    POC:548
Wulfstan
    Sermon of the Wolf to the
    English when the Danes perse-
    cuted them most, which was
    in the year 1014 from the in-
    carnation of our Lord Jesus
    Christ. BRYH:21
Wycliffe, J.
    Good lore for simple folk.
    BREWE 10:3920
Zubly, J. J.
    Law of liberty. POC:611

---- See also Baccalaureate ad-
    dresses; Church; Funeral ser-
    mons; Religion; also subject
    of sermons, e.g. Faith

SERUM THERAPY
    Behring, E. A. V.
    Serum therapy in therapeutics
    and medical science.
    NOLM 1:6

SERVICE See Citizenship

SERVICE MEN See Army; Pen-
    sions, Military; Soldiers;
    United States - Army -
    Veterans

SESQUICENTENNIAL CELEBRA-
    TIONS See Anniversaries

Sevareid, Eric
    Eulogy for the astronauts.
    MOP:189; MOPR:165
    Eulogy for Wernher Von Braun.
    (June 17, 1977). EHN:373
    Parting thoughts (Washington,
    Nov. 30, 1977).
    BA 1977-78:143
    Pope John Paul's message (CBS,
    Oct. 3, 1979).
    BA 1979-80:155

---- and others (C. W. Lillehei,
    J. Bonner, W. Sullivan, J. J.

Wright, H. Cox, F. C. Fry)
Science and religion: who will
play God? MOP:391

Sevier, Randolph
Responds to an introduction.
PRS:158

Seward, William Henry
Fourth of July oration, 1840
(Cherry Valley, N.Y.).
HAW:183
Freedom in the new territories.
(Senate, March 11, 1850).
HOW:226
Higher law than the Constitution.
Same as his On the admission
of California to the Union
Irrepressible conflict (Roches-
ter, N.Y., Oct. 25, 1858).
ANN 9:32; BREWE 9:3394;
HURH:99
On the admission of California
to the Union. ANN 8:29
Promise of Alaska. ANN 10:193
Prosperity and education.
ANN 6:140
Providing for the indigent in-
sane. ANN 8:283
Reconciliation in 1865.
BREWE 9:3408

Sewell, Henry
"Centralist" interpretation of
the Constitution. (New Zealand House of Representa-
tives, April 25, 1856).
MACS:93

---- and others (Edward William
Stafford)
The 'compact of 1856' (New
Zealand House of Repre-
sentatives, June 10, 1856).
MACS:99

Shaftesbury, Anthony Ashley
Cooper, 7th Earl of
Employment of Children.
JAE:81

SHAME See Ethics

Shaw, George Bernard
Presents Major Barbara.
LYI:50
Truth by radio. (BBC, 1939).
JEF:396; JEFF:378

Universities and education.
KEO:237

---- and others (G. K. Chesterton;
H. Belloc)
Do we agree? BRYH:474

SHAW, GEORGE BERNARD
Dale, J.
Rehearsing with George Ber-
nard Shaw. MDYG:44
Hallström, P.
Presentation [of the Nobel
Prize for Literature to George
Bernard Shaw, 1925].
NOB 16:77; NOL:224

Shaw, Lemuel
Commonwealth of Massachusetts
v. Hunt: opinion for the
court. ANN 7:61;
BOORA 1:303
Law as a restraint on power.
ANN 5:217

Shaw, Robert M.
Danger of getting used to lies.
LINR:191

SHAWCROSS, HARTLEY
Tweed, H.
Presents Hartley Shawcross.
LYI:123

Sheen, Fulton J., Bp.
Change of hearts. (Washing-
ton, March 23, 1941).
HURH:264
"A revolution that will change
your hearts." Same as his
Change of hearts

Sheil, Richard Lalor
In defense of Irish Catholics.
BREWE 9:3419
Ireland's part in English achieve-
ment. BREWE 9:3413
Religious toleration. (Penenden
Heath, Kent, Oct. 24, 1828).
MCB:269

Shellabarger, Samuel See Butler,
B. F., jt. auth.

SHELLEY, PERCY BYSSHE
Talfourd, T. N.
Queen against Moxon-Shelley
as a blasphemer.
BREWE 9:3565

Shepard, Thomas
  Election sermon. POC:355
  The parable of the ten virgins
    (1636-1640). JON:133
  The sound believer (1645).
    JON:63

SHEPPARD, SAMUEL
  Clark, T. C.
    Sheppard v. Maxwell, war-
    den: opinion for the court.
    ANN 18:402

Sheridan, Richard Brinsley
  Against Warren Hastings.
    BREWE 9:3422
  Closing speech against Hast-
    ings--the Hoard of the
    Begums of Oude. Same
    as his Against Warren
    Hastings
  Example of kings.
    BREWE 9:3440
  On the French Revolution.
    BREWE 9:3438
  Patriotism and perquisites.
    BREWE 9:3439

Sherman, John
  General financial policy of the
    government. BREWE 9:3442
  It is essentially a Rebel or-
    ganization. CUR:102

Sherrington, Sir Charles Scott
  Inhibition as a coordinative
    factor (Nobel Lecture,
    Dec. 12, 1932).
    NOLM 2:278

SHERRINGTON, SIR CHARLES
    SCOTT
  Liljestrand, G.
    Presentation [of the Nobel
    Prize for Physiology or
    Medicine to Sir Charles
    Scott Sherrington and Edgar
    Douglas Adrian, Dec. 12,
    1932]. NOLM 2:273

Shockley, William
  Transistor technology evokes
    new physics (Nobel Lecture,
    Dec. 11, 1956).
    NOLPH 3:344

SHOCKLEY, WILLIAM
  Rudberg, E. G.

  Presentation [of the Nobel
    Prize for Physics to William
    Shockley, John Bardeen and
    Walter Houser Brattain, Dec.
    11, 1956]. NOLPH 3:315

SHOLOKHOV, MIKHAIL ALEK-
    SANDROVICH
  Österling, A.
    Presentation [of the Nobel
    Prize for Literature to Mik-
    hail Aleksandrovich Sholokhov,
    1965]. NOB 17:37; NOL:603

Shriver, Sargent
  Address at the Chicago Antipover-
    ty Conference. CAPG:180

Shtull, Jacob
  Man of deed. WALE:164

Shull, Martha A.
  Presents Bruce Catton. LYI:42

Shulman, Charles E.
  Alfred S. Alschuler. WALE:229

SICK
  Hypochondriac. BURT:106
  Sickness. BURT:7

Sidney, Algernon
  Governments for the people and
    not the people for govern-
    ments (scaffold speech).
    BREWE 9:3454

Siegbahn, Karl Manne Georg
  Presentation [of the Nobel Prize
    for Physics to Arthur Holly
    Compton and Charles Thomson
    Rees Wilson, Dec. 12, 1927].
    NOLPH 2:169
  Presentation [of the Nobel Prize
    for Physics to Donald Arthur
    Glaser, Dec. 12, 1960].
    NOLPH 3:525
  Presentation [of the Nobel Prize
    for Physics to Pavel Alekse-
    jevič Cerenkov, Il'ja Michaj-
    lovič Frank and Igor'
    Evgen'evič Tamm, Dec. 11,
    1958]. NOLPH 3:423
  The x-ray spectra and the struc-
    ture of the atoms (Nobel Lec-
    ture for 1924, Dec. 11, 1925).
    NOLPH 2:81

SIEGBAHN, KARL MANNE GEORG
Gullstrand, A.
Presentation [of the Nobel
Prize for Physics for 1924
to Karl Manne Georg Sieg-
bahn, Dec. 11, 1925].
NOLPH 2:73

Sienkiewicz, Henryk
Acceptance [of the Nobel Prize
for Literature, 1905].
NOL:45; NOB 17:183

SIENKIEWICZ, HENRYK
Wirsén, C. D. af
Presentation [of the Nobel
Prize for Literature to
Henryk Sienkiewicz, 1905].
NOL:36; NOB 17:173

SILANPÄÄ, FRANS EEMIL
Hallström, P.
Presentation [of the Nobel
Prize for Literature to
Frans Eemil Sillanpää,
1939]. NOB 16:223; NOL:386

Silver, Samuel M.
Come back. WALE:166

SILVER
Bland, R. P.
Parting of the ways.
BREWE 2:530
Bryan, W. J.
Cross of gold. ANN 12:100;
BAS:50 (outline only);
BEN:52; BOORA 2:575;
BREWE 2:694; HURH:147;
LINS:268; OLIS:207
Fitch, T.
A fervent appeal for free
silver (1889). DAVF:190
Laughlin, J. L.
Against free coinage of
silver. ANN 12:75
Warner, A. J. and others
The British plot to enslave
the world (1892). DAVF:192

Simmons, Brent
As time runs out (1969).
LINRS:251

Simmons, David A.
Presents Walter S. Fenton.
LYI:131

Simon, E. Yechiel
Heavenly glow. WALE:169
Two arks. WALE:172

Simon, Sir John See Baldwin,
S. B., jt. auth.

Simon, Ralph
This was a man! WALE:174
Upward climb. WALE:175

SIMPLICITY
Fénelon, F.
True and false simplicity.
BREWE 6:2137

SIN
Edwards, J.
Sinners in the hands of an
angry God. ANN 1:423;
BREWE 5:1982; HURH:21;
LINS:121
Shepard, T.
The sound believer. JON:63
Tillotson, J.
Sermon against evil speaking.
BRYH:156

Sinclair, Sir Archibald See
Baldwin, S. B., jt. auth.

Sinclair, Gordon
The Americans (Toronto, June,
1973). REID:396

SINGAPORE
Goh Keng Swee
A remarkable phenomenon:
why Singapore is different.
MONSA:277
Some delusions of the decade
of development. MONS:385
Inche Yusof bin Ishak
Lest we forget. MONSA:348
Lee Kuan Yew
Aim: a more equal society.
MONS:369
Brighter future for all peoples
of Singapore if....
MONSA:239
First step in nation building
(Singapore). MONS:358
Hong Kong and Singapore: a
tale of two cities.
MONSA:264
Marshall, D. S.
Fundamental and minority
rights. MONS:450

Rajaratnam, S.
  Faith in United Nations
  charter (on admission of
  Singapore). MONS:421
Toh Chin Chye
  The beginnings of the city
  state and its achievement.
  MONSA:288
  Lesson of the Three King-
  doms. MONS:375
  Singapore in the eye of the
  storm. MONS:377

---- ECONOMIC CONDITIONS
Lim Kim San
  Massive exercise for sur-
  vival. MONS:408
  Three major problems of
  developing countries.
  MONS:412

---- EDUCATION See Education
- Singapore

---- FOREIGN RELATIONS
Abdul Rahman, T.
  Break with Singapore.
  MONS:19

---- HISTORY
Lee Kuan Yew
  Tribute to India and Indians.
  MONSA:244
Marshall, D. S.
  History of Singapore's strug-
  gle for nationhood, 1945-
  1959. MONSA:313

---- PARLIAMENT
Lee Kuan Yew
  The future is at stake--
  crucial years ahead.
  MONSA:247

---- RELIGION
Dumper, A. C.
  Church in a secular state.
  MONS:485

SINGAPORE NAVAL BASE
Coates, J. G.
  Support for the Singapore
  Naval Base, 1927.
  MACS:278 selections

SIOUX INDIANS See Dakota
Indians

Siwertz, S.
  Presentation [of the Nobel Prize
  for Literature to Sir Winston
  Leonard Spencer Churchill,
  1953]. NOB 4:177; NOL:488

SIZE OF INSTITUTIONS See Institutions, Size of

Sjöquist, J.
  Presentation [of the Nobel Prize
  for Physiology or Medicine
  for 1923 to Frederick Grant
  Banting and John James
  Richard Macleod, 1925].
  NOLM 2:45

SKEPTICISM
Howard, J. A.
  The new furies: skepticism,
  criticism, and coercion.
  LINRST:146

Skidelsky, Robert
  Grand alternatives. MDYG:142

Skinner, Cornelia Otis
  "Bottoms up" (toast to gyne-
  cologists). (Lake Placid,
  N.Y., June, 1953). HURH:311
  "A toast from the ladies of
  America ... Bottoms up!"
  Same as her "Bottoms up"
  (toast to gynecologists)

Slabach, David
  Five hundred miles south.
  BREWW:208

SLANDER See Gossip

SLAUGHTER AND SLAUGHTERING
  HOUSES
Miller, S. F. and others
  Slaughter house cases, 1875:
  opinion for the court and dis-
  senting opinion. ANN 10:302

SLAVERY
Bacon, L.
  Plea for Africa. HAW:60
Chapman, J. R.
  Coatesville. ARS:163
Derby, E. G. V. S.
  Emancipation of British Ne-
  groes. BREWE 5:1800
Garnet, H. H.
  A plea in behalf of the Cuban

revolution. FON:380
Pitt, W., 1759-1806
   Indicts the slave trade and
   foresees a liberated Africa.
   BREWE 8:3208; CLAYP:136;
   JAE:12; STRM:91
Price, J. C.
   The race problem stated.
   SMHV:78
Remond, C. L.
   Slavery and the Irish.
   SMHR:110
   Slavery as it concerns the
   British. SMHV:16
Walker, D.
   We must have unity.
   SMHV:11
Wilberforce, W.
   Horrors of the British slave
   trade in the eighteenth cen-
   tury. BREWE 10:3891

SLAVERY IN THE UNITED
   STATES
Benjamin, J. P.
   Slavery as established by
   law. BREWE 1:406
Brown, W. W.
   Slavery as it is, and its in-
   fluence upon the American
   people. FON:90
Buchanan, J.
   Fourth annual message.
   ANN 9:209; STAT 1:1025
   Third annual message.
   STAT 1:1001
Calhoun, J. C.
   Danger of abolitionist peti-
   tions (February, 1837).
   ANN 6:346
   On the slavery question.
   ANN 8:16; HURH:77; OLIS:93
Chase, S. P.
   Thomas Jefferson and the
   colonial view of manhood
   rights. BREWE 3:1044
   Three great eras.
   BREWE 3:1056
---- and others
   Opposition to the Kansas-
   Nebraska Bill (January,
   1854). ANN 8:251
Clay, H.
   Compromise of 1850 (Febru-
   ary 5 & 6, 1850 speech).
   ANN 8:1; BREWE 4:1273;
   HURH:83; OLIS:66
   Slavery and expansion, May

13 and May 21, 1850.
   ANN 8:36
Davis, S. H.
   We must assert our rightful
   claims and plead our own
   cause. FON:77
Dayton, W. L.
   Issues against slavery forced
   by the Mexican War.
   BREWE 5:1679
Douglas, S. A.
   Defense of the Kansas-Nebraska
   Bill (January 30, 1854).
   ANN 8:254
   Fifth joint debate at Galesburg,
   October 7, 1858. ANN 9:22
   Lincoln-Douglas joint debate
   at Alton, October 15, 1858.
   ANN 9:30
   Opening speech of Lincoln-
   Douglas debate, Ottawa, Au-
   gust 21, 1858. ANN 9:8
   Reply to Lincoln, Freeport,
   August 27, 1858. ANN 9:17;
   BREWE 5:1912; HURH:94
   Reply to the Jonesboro speech.
   ANN 9:20
Douglass, F.
   If there is no struggle there
   is no progress. FON:197
   The mission of the war.
   FON:283
   Nature of slavery (speech at
   Rochester, New York, Decem-
   ber 1, 1850). BOSR:113;
   FRIP:222
   Reception speech--at Finsbury
   Chapel, Moorsfield, England,
   May 12, 1846. OE:30
   Slavery: speech at Rochester,
   July 5, 1852. FON:104;
   SMHR:125
   What is my duty as an anti-
   slavery voter. FRIP:229
   What to the slave is the
   Fourth of July? JAM:19;
   OE:41
Douglass, H. F.
   I do not believe in the anti-
   slavery of Abraham Lincoln.
   FON:232
Emerson, R. W.
   On the Fugitive Slave Law.
   ANN 8:261
Fillmore, M.
   Second annual message.
   STAT 8:808
Forten, J. and others

Abolition movement. MDT:35
The proclamation, how to
make it efficient. MDT:148

Pinkney, W.
Missouri question.
BREWE 8:3195

Purvis, R.
The American government
and the Negro. FON:227
The good time is at hand.
FON:266

Rock, J. S.
I will sink or swim with my
race. FON:203
Negro hopes for emancipation.
ANN 9:318
We ask for our rights.
FON:257
What if the slaves are eman-
cipated? FON:250

Schurz, C.
The irrepressible conflict
(1860). DAVF:130

Seward, W. H.
Freedom in the new terri-
tories. HOW:226
On the admission of California to the Union. ANN 8:29

Smith, G.
On the character, scope and
duties of the Liberty Party.
MDT:93

Stevens, T.
Against Webster and northern
compromisers.
BREWE 9:3522

Sumner, C.
Antislavery duties of the
Whig Party. HOW:218
A Republican appeal for unity
(1855). DAVF:132
Resolutions on secession and
reconstruction. ANN 9:323

Thoreau, H. D.
Fourth of July oration,
1854. HAW:200
Slavery in Massachusetts.
OLIS:118

Tyler, J.
From the sinks of Europe
a plotter has come (1835).
DAVF:140

Walker, R. J.
Address to the people of
Kansas. ANN 8:452

Ward, S. R.
Speech on the Fugitive Slave
Bill. FON:93

Wears, I. C.
Lincoln's colonization proposal
is anti-Christian. FON:259

Webster, D.
On the Clay Compromise.
ANN 8:24
Supporting the Compromise of
1850. BREWE 10:3868

Whipper, W.
Eulogy on William Wilberforce.
FON:49

Williams, F.
Duty of colored men in the
present national crisis.
FON:281

Williams, P.
Oration on the abolition of the
slave trade. FON:20
Slavery and colonization.
FON:43

---- See also Blacks, Dred Scott
Decision; Emancipation Proclamation; United States - History - Civil War

SLUMS See Housing

Smith, Alfred Emanuel
Acceptance speech, Albany, New
York, August 22, 1928.
SIN:34
Campaign speech, Oklahoma
City, Sept. 20, 1928.
SIN:52
The cooing dove (Albany, Oct.
23, 1926). BRYF:548;
BRYO:249
"I do not want any Catholic in
the United States to vote for
me because I am a Catholic."
Same as his Religion and
politics
Religion and politics. (Oklahoma
City, Sept. 20, 1928).
HURH:209

Smith, Charles Stewart
The fallacy of industrial education as the solution of the
race problem (Nashville,
Jan. 28, 1899). FON:607

Smith, Eric R.
United we stand, divided we fall.
BREWW:134

Smith, Gerrit
Liberty destroyed by national

pride (Mexican Treaty and
Monroe Doctrine).
BREWE 9:3459
On the character, scope and
duties of the Liberty Party.
(1847).   MDT:93
A voice from the past (1870).
(Syracuse, N.Y., Nov.
1870).   DAVF:154

Smith, Goldwin
Lamps of fiction (at centenary
of Sir Walter Scott).
BREWE 9:3465
Origin and causes of progress.
BREWE 9:3471
Secret beyond science.
BREWE 9:3476

Smith, James McCune
On the fourteenth query of
Thomas Jefferson's Notes
on Virginia. (1859).
FON:215

Smith, Jonathan
On the Federal Constitution.
(Massachusetts Convention,
Jan. 24 or 25, 1788).
ARN:385; ARS:272

Smith, Margaret Chase
Declaration of conscience--
twenty years later.
BA 1969-70:133

Smith, Sydney
Mrs. Partington in politics.
BREWE 9:3479
Plea for Catholic emancipation.
Same as his Results of
oppression
Reform and stomach troubles.
BREWE 9:3484
Results of oppression.
BREWE 9:3482; JAE:40
"Wounds, shrieks, and tears"
in government.
BREWE 9:3490

Smith, William
Eulogium. POC:3

Snell, Bertrand
Bankruptcy and moral disin-
tegration. BAD:90

Snow, Sir Charles Percy
The two cultures. (Cam-

bridge Univ., May 7, 1959).
MCB:417

SNOW, SIR CHARLES PERCY
Weaver, W.
Presents Sir Charles Percy
Snow. LYI:171

SNYDER, FRANKLIN BLISS
Hancher, V. M.
Presents Franklyn Bliss Sny-
der. LYI:99

SOCIAL AND ECONOMIC SECURITY
See Insurance, Social

SOCIAL CHANGE
Howard, J. A.
The new furies: skepticism,
criticism, and coercion.
LINRST:146

SOCIAL CLASSES
Conant, J. B.
Education for a classless so-
ciety. ANN 16:22

SOCIAL PROBLEMS
Dinwoodie, S. D.
Inner city--our shame.
ARS:216
Gardner, J. W.
In behalf of a troubled nation.
BA 1967-68:102
Roosevelt, F. D.
Philosophy of social justice
through social action (cam-
paign speech in Detroit Octo-
ber 2, 1932). ARS:135

---- See also Alcoholism; Child
labor; Crime and criminals;
Immigration and emigration;
Poverty; Race problems;
Unemployed

SOCIAL SECURITY
Eisenhower, D. D.
State of the Union (January 9,
1958). STAT 3:3076
Houtman, M.
Dangers of security. SCHW:54
Roosevelt, F. D.
Presidential remarks on the
occasion of the signing of the
Social Security Act. BAD:13
Right to security.
ANN 15:315

---- NEW ZEALAND
Atkinson, H.
Proposal for a National In-
surance scheme, 1882.
MACS:186
Hamilton, A.
The Social Security Bill,
1938. MACS:337

SOCIAL SERVICE See Citizenship

SOCIAL VALUES
Jones, J. L.
"Let's bring back Dad": a
solid value system.
LINRST:254

SOCIALISM
Clark, P. H.
Socialism: the remedy for
the evils of society.
FON:451
Crispi, F.
Socialism and discontent.
BREWE 4:1469
De Leon, D.
Aims of socialism.
ANN 12:106
Engel, G.
Address at trial, Chicago,
October 7-9, 1886.
ACC:43; PAF:37
Fielden, S.
Address at trial, Chicago,
October 7-9, 1886.
ACC:49; PAF:41
Gaitskell, H.
Labour, politics and demo-
cratic socialism. MCB:250
Hardie, J. K.
Socialist Commonwealth.
MCB:451
Harrison, H. H.
What socialism means to us.
FON:698
Lee Kuan Yew
Democratic socialism under
stress in Asia. MONS:345
Lehman, H. H.
Freedom and individual secur-
ity. ANN 17:21
Randolph, A. P.
The task of the Negro people.
FON:87
Spies, A.
Address at trial, Chicago,
October 7-9, 1886. ACC:1;
ANN 11:117; PAF:11

---- See also Industry and state;
Labor and laboring classes;
Labor unions; Socialist Party

---- NEW ZEALAND
Hamilton, A.
The economy under the Labour
government. MACS:334
Holland, H.
The socialist objective of the
labour movement. MACS:232

SOCIALIST PARTY
Debs, E. V.
The issue. ANN 13:137
Thomas, N.
Townsend Plan and cough
drops. BOSR:92

Sockey, Clennon E.
Excellence in Indian education
(Scottsdale, Ariz., Dec. 11-
13, 1974). MAES:141

Sockman, Ralph W.
Responds to introduction.
PRS:118

Socrates
Address to his judges after they
had condemned him. Same as
his On being declared guilty
On being declared guilty.
BAS:67 (outline only);
BREWE 9:3493
On his condemnation to death.
Same as his On being declared
guilty

Soddy, Frederick
The origins of the conceptions of
isotopes (Nobel Lecture for
1921, Dec. 12, 1922).
NOLC 1:371

SODDY, FREDERICK
Söderbaum, H. G.
Presentation [of the Nobel
Prize for Chemistry to Fred-
erick Soddy, 1921, Dec. 12,
1922]. NOLC 1:367

Söderbaum, H. G.
Presentation [of the Nobel Prize
for Chemistry to Arthur
Harden and Hans Karl August
Simon von Euler-Chelpin,
Dec. 12, 1929]. NOLC 2:127
Presentation [of the Nobel Prize

for Chemistry to Francis
William Aston, Dec. 12,
1922]. NOLC 2:3
Presentation [of the Nobel
Prize for Chemistry to
Frederick Soddy, 1921, Dec.
12, 1922]. NOLC 1:367
Presentation [of the Nobel
Prize for Chemistry to
Hans Fischer, Dec. 11,
1930]. NOLC 2:161
Presentation [of the Nobel
Prize for Chemistry to
Heinrich Otto Wieland, 1927
and Adolf Otto Reinhold
Windaus, 1828, Dec. 12,
1928]. NOLC 2:89
Presentation [of the Nobel
Prize for Chemistry to
Irving Langmuir, Dec. 14,
1932]. NOLC 2:283
Presentation [of the Nobel
Prize for Physics to Nils
Gustaf Dalen, 1912].
NOLPH 1:293
Presentation [of the Nobel
Prize for Chemistry to
Richard Adolf Zsigmondy,
1925, Dec. 11, 1926].
NOLC 2:41
Presentation [of the Nobel
Prize for Chemistry to
Theodor Svedberg, 1926,
May 19, 1927]. NOLC 2:63
Presentation [of the Nobel
Prize for Chemistry to
Victor Grignard and Paul
Sabatier, Dec. 11, 1912].
NOLC 1:217
The role of the church in pro-
moting peace (Nobel Lec-
ture, Dec. 11, 1930).
NOLP 2:93

SÖDERBLOM, NATHAN
Mowinckel, J. L.
Presentation [of the Nobel
Prize for Peace to Nathan
Söderblom, Dec. 11, 1930].
NOLP 2:73

SOIL - EXHAUSTION
Bozeman, M.
Soil--America's lifeblood.
BREWW:85

SOIL CONSERVATION
Bozeman, M.

Soil--America's lifeblood.
BREWW:85
McKinney, S. M.
Soils--our basic natural re-
sources--the key to man's
survival. BREWW:187

SOIL EROSION
Holt, R.
The second dust bowl.
BREWW:137

SOILS, SALTS IN
Holt, R.
The second dust bowl.
BREWW:137

SOLDIERS
Brandli, W.
Taps and reveille. SCHW:30
Welcome to military personnel.
HNWM:25

---- See also Army; United States -
Army; Veterans

SOLDIERS' BONUS See Pensions,
Military

SOLZHENITSYN, ALEKSANDR
Gierow, K. R.
Presentation address [of the
Nobel Prize for Literature to
Aleksandr Solzhenitsyn, 1970].
NOB 18:3

Sonberg, H. Alexander
Unidentified flying objects; their
history, and various explanations which have been given
concerning their nature.
BAS:203 (outline only)

SONGS See Music and musicians

SONS See Fathers and sons;
Parent and child

SOUL
Hooker, T.
The soul's exaltation.
JON:104

SOUTH AFRICA
Mandela, N. R.
Indictment of South Africa.
EMP:94
Ngwa, J.

Our common tradition in
peril. SCHW:123

SOUTH AFRICAN WAR, 1899-1902
Holman, W. A.
   Against sending troops to
   South Africa. MCA:109
Seddon, R. J.
   The South African War con-
   tingent, 1899. MACS:260
   sel.

SOUTH AMERICA
Adams, J. Q.
   On participating in a con-
   gress of American nations.
   ANN 5:188
Clay, H.
   Emancipation of South Amer-
   ican Republics. ANN 4:488;
   BREWE 4:1240

SOUTH CAROLINA
Chamberlain, D. H.
   Present hour in South Caro-
   lina (inaugural address of
   would-be governor).
   CUR:158
Hampton, W.
   Present hour in South Caro-
   lina (inaugural address of
   would-be governor).
   CUR:159

SOUTHERN STATES
Crittenden, T. T.
   Trade and commerce for the
   southwestern states.
   ANN 11:16
Grady, H. W.
   New South (speech to the
   New England Society).
   ANN 11:240; BAS:121 (outline
   only); BOORA 1:465;
   LINS:254
   Race problem (speech to the
   Boston Merchants' Associa-
   tion). ANN 11:240;
   BREWE 6:2299
Stephens, A. H.
   South and the public domain.
   BREWE 9:3513

SOVEREIGNTY
MacDonald, P.
   Statement before the Indian
   sovereignty Conference of
   American Indians, Harvard,

February 22, 1975.
MAES:22

SPACE FLIGHT
Armstrong, N.
   Moon rendezvous.
   BAAGB:404
Glenn, J. H.
   Address before the Joint Meet-
   ing of Congress. HURH:362
Muskie, E. S.
   The astronauts on the moon.
   BAAGB:409
Von Braun, W.
   Earth benefits from space and
   space technology.
   BA 1971-72:111
Webb, J. E.
   From Runnymede to Gany-
   mede. BA 1967-68:194

Spain, Jayne Baker
   A woman could be President.
   (U.S.A.F. Academy Public
   Affairs Forum, Feb. 25,
   1971). VER:249

SPAIN - HISTORY - CIVIL WAR,
   1936-1939
Jordan, W. J.
   The League and the Spanish
   Civil War. MACS:361

---- POLITICS AND GOVERNMENT
Castelar, E.
   Plea for Republican institu-
   tions. BREWE 3:998

Spalding, Rufus Paine See
   Butler, B. F., jt. auth.

SPANISH AMERICAN WAR See
   United States - History -
   War of 1898

SPANISH IN THE PHILIPPINE
   ISLANDS
Quezon, M. L.
   On Spain's contribution to the
   Philippines. CURM:24

SPANISH IN THE UNITED STATES
Kennedy, E. M.
   La Raza and the law.
   BA 1971-72:68

SPARKS, FRED
Hills, L.

Presents Fred Sparks.
LYI:115

SPEAKER, THANKING See
Thanks

SPEAKING See Debates and
debating; Public speaking

SPECTROSCOPY
Michelson, A. A.
Recent advances in spectro-
scopy. NOLPH 1:166

SPEECH, FREEDOM OF See
Free speech; Liberty of
the press

SPEECHES - OUTLINES OF
Ace of aces (outline of speech).
CUB:62
Bernard, Saint
Why another crusade?
BAS:43 (outline only)
Bryan, W. J.
Cross of gold. BAS:50
(outline only)
Burton, S.
You (male) should wear long
hair. BAS:200 (outline only)
Cataline
To his soldiers. BAS:37
(outline only)
Constitution, right or wrong
(outline of speech celebrat-
ing Constitution Day).
CUB:80
Curtis, G. W.
Liberty under law.
BAS:141 (outline only)
Davis, J.
On withdrawing from the
Union. BAS:71 (outline only)
Douglas, S. A.
Reply to Lincoln at Chicago,
July 9, 1858. BAS:45
(outline only)
Emerson, R. W.
American scholar.
BAS:156 (outline only)
Freedom from hunger (outline
of speech to persuade that
continued good health of
American people requires
easy access to pharmaceuti-
cal vitamins and food sup-
plements). CUB:48
Glenn, J. H.

Accepting the Distinguished
Service Medal (outline of
speech). CUB:65
Go on and prosper (outline of
eulogistic speech). CUB:76
Goldwater, B. M.
Why we must be stronger
militarily. BAS:92 (outline
only)
Grady, H. W.
New South. BAS:121 (outline
only)
Great Disturber (outline of speech
to celebrate acceptance of
Christ's offer of salvation
through obedience to His
word). CUB:95
Henry, P.
Liberty or death. BAS:39
(outline only)
Howdy, pardner (outline of speech
to welcome Dr. Gifford Win-
gate as new Chairman of the
Drama and Speech Department
at Texas Western College).
CUB:66
Jordan, L.
Opportunities in H.S.A. (Har-
vard Student Agencies).
REIR:101 (outline)
Kennedy, J. F.
Inaugural address. BAS:146
(outline only)
Presenting the Distinguished
Service Medal to John Glenn
(outline of speech). CUB:64
Klayton, R. J.
Bureau of Forests and Waters
should control pests by bio-
logical means rather than
pesticides. BAS:188 (outline
only)
Kobish, C. F.
Diamonds, their mining,
selling, perfecting, and the
determining of their quality.
BAS:206 (outline only)
LaFollette, R. M., Sr.
Free speech in wartime.
CUB:53 (outline only)
Lewis, W. D.
Founder's Day remarks.
BAS:164 (outline only)
Lincoln, A.
Farewell to Springfield (out-
line of speech). CUB:78
"A house divided against itself
cannot stand." BAS:100

(outline only)
Lorge, B.
  Great auto rally (outline).
  REIR:93
MacArthur, D.
  Defends his conduct of the
  war in Korea. BAS:82
  (outline only)
Macios, M. A.
  Model studies of structural
  design and construction
  should be conducted prior
  to the building of structure
  rather than on the site
  studies made after the
  completion of the project.
  BAS:193 (outline only)
Miner by choice (outline of
  speech in response to wel-
  come). CUB:68
Nomination of Hubert Horatio
  Humphrey, Jr. (outline of
  speech). CUB:100
Paradox (outline of commencement speech). CUB:91
Paul VI
  Key to peace. BAS:150
  (outline only)
Pericles
  On those who died in the
  war. BAS:133 (outline only)
Socrates
  On being declared guilty.
  BAS:67 (outline only)
Sonberg, H. A.
  Unidentified flying objects:
  their history and various
  explanations which have
  been given concerning their
  nature. BAS:203 (outline
  only)
Suggestions for organization
  and outlining a speech.
  BRP:54, 57
Textbooks and all that: an
  inquiry into the operation
  of the college bookstore
  (outline). CUB:28
Theater begins with wonder
  (Outline of speech). CUB:70
Truckman, B.
  Presidential eligibility.
  REIR:107 (outline)
Washington, B. T.
  Address at the opening of
  the Atlanta Exposition.
  BAS:77 (outline only)
Westmoreland, W. C.

Vietnam--the situation today
  (1967). BAS:59 (outline only)
Why go second class? (outline
  of speech to persuade City of
  Del Norte it should establish
  a Juvenile Court). CUB:42
You get what you ask for (outline
  of speech). CUB:31
Zola, E.
  Appeal for Dreyfus. BAS:110
  (outline only)
Zwerling, J. C.
  Federal Government should
  continue its present housing
  program for low-income
  groups rather than change to
  the proposed rent subsidy
  plan. BAS:196 (outline only)

Spellman, Francis J.
  Presents Maxwell D. Taylor.
  LYI:143

Spemann, Hans
  The organizer-effect in embryonic
  development (Nobel Lecture,
  Dec. 12, 1935). NOLM 2:381

SPEMANN, HANS
  Häggquist, G.
    Presentation [of the Nobel
    Prize for Physiology or Medi-
    cine to Hans Spemann, Dec.
    12, 1935]. NOLM 2:377

Spencer, Henry R.
  Introducing Anne O'Hare McCormick. LYI:107

Spencer, Samuel Reid, Jr.
  A call for new missionaries.
  (Due West, S.C., May 23,
  1971). BA 1971-72:172

Speth, Gus
  Environmental regulation and the
  immobilization of truth (Washington, Feb. 28, 1980).
  BA 1979-80:145

Spies, August
  Address at trial, Chicago, Octo-
  ber 7-9, 1886. ACC:1;
  ANN 11:117; PAF:11

SPITTELER, CARL FRIEDRICH
  Hjärne, H.
    Presentation [of the Nobel

Prize for Literature to
Carl Friedrich Spitteler,
1919]. NOB 17:267; NOL:161

SPORTS
Welcome to All-sports church
banquet. HNWM:33

Spotted Tail, Brule Chief
We are young no longer.
ALA:37

Spottswood, Stephen G.
The Nixon administration's anti-
negro policy. (Buck Hill
Falls, Pa., 1970).
LINRS:109

Spray, Charlie
Consumer education: the
farmer's responsibility.
BREWW:67
A new crisis in agriculture.
BREWW:71

Springen, Phyllis Jones
The dimensions of the oppres-
sion of women (Buck Hill
Falls, Pa., Dec., 1970).
LINRS:109; LINRST:130

Spurgeon, Charles Haddon
Everlasting oxydization.
BREWE 9:3500

Stafford, Edward William See
Sewell, Henry, jt. auth.

STAGE See Theater

STAMP ACT, 1765
Chauncy, C.
Good news from a far coun-
try (repeal of Stamp Act).
BREWE 3:1090

Stang, Fredrik
Presentation [of the Nobel Prize
for Peace, 1935, to Carl
Von Ossietzky, Dec. 10,
1936]. NOLP 2:207
Presentation [of the Nobel Prize
for Peace to Ferdinand
Edouard Buisson and Ludwig
Quidde, Dec. 10, 1927].
NOLP 2:29
Presentation [of the Nobel Prize
for Peace to Fridtjof Nansen,

Dec. 10, 1922].
NOLP 1:353
Presentation [of the Nobel Prize
for Peace to the Nansen Inter-
national Office for Refugees,
Dec. 10, 1938]. NOLP 2:265

Stanley, Arthur Penrhyn
Palmerston and the duty of Eng-
land (funeral oration).
BREWE 9:3506

Stanley, Augustus Owsley
Address in honor of Robert E.
Lee. (Chicago, April 9,
1907). BLY:216

STANLEY, HENRY M.
Presents Henry M. Stanley.
LYI:117

Stanley, J.
Tribute to a fallen Black soldier.
(Chicago, Sept. 8, 1963).
FON:268

Stanley, Wendell Meredith
The isolation and properties of
crystalline tobacco mosaic
(Nobel Lecture, Dec. 12,
1946). NOLC 3:137

STANLEY, WENDELL MEREDITH
Tiselius, A. W. K.
Presentation [of the Nobel
Prize for Chemistry to James
Batcheller Sumner, John
Howard Northrop, and Wendell
Meredith Stanley, Dec. 12,
1946]. NOLC 3:109

Stanmeyer, William A.
Urban crime: its causes and
control. (Hillsdale, Mich.,
Oct. 26, 1972). LINRST:303

Stanton, Elizabeth Cady
Address on the Divorce Bill,
1861. BOORA 1:367
Natural rights of civilized wom-
en. ANN 9:151

Stanton, Frank
Address before the International
Radio and Television Society.
BA 1969-70:71
Remarks on government regula-
tion of broadcasting (accept-

ing Printers' Ink gold medal).
MDV:277
Reply to the Vice President.
(New York--International
Radio and Television Society,
Nov. 25, 1969). STOT:282

Stark, Johannes
Structural and spectral changes
of chemical atoms (Nobel
Lecture for 1919, June 3,
1920). NOLPH 1:427

STARK, JOHANNES
Ekstrand, A. G.
Presentation [of the Nobel
Prize for Physics for 1919
to Johannes Stark, June 3,
1920]. NOLPH 1:423

STARS
Bethe, H. A.
Energy production in stars.
NOLPH 4:215

STARVATION
Wivell, C. A.
World hunger: a question
of rights. BREWW:119

Stasheff, Edward
What will the satellites say?
KEO:262

STATE, THE
Channing, W. E.
Man above the state.
BREWE 3:1032

---- See also Church and state;
Education and state; Industry
and state

STATE GOVERNMENTS
Smith, A. E.
The cooing dove. BRYF:548;
BRYO:249

STATE RIGHTS
Calhoun, J. C.
Force Bill. BREWE 3:866
Douglas, S. A.
Fifth joint debate at Gales-
burg, October 7, 1858.
ANN 9:22
Opening speech of Lincoln-
Douglas debate, Ottawa,
August 21, 1858. ANN 9:8

Reply to Lincoln at Chicago,
July 9, 1858. ANN 9:4;
BAS:45 (outline only); OLIS:133
Hayne, R. Y.
On Foot's Resolution (January
21, 1830). BREWE 7:2441
Henry, P.
Against the Federal Constitu-
tion, June 5, 1788.
BREWE 7:2488
Jackson, A.
Second inaugural address--
"State rights and Federal
sovereignty." BREWE 7:2597;
HURH:71; USINAU:58;
USINAUG:58
Johnson, A. and others
Debate on civil and state
rights. ANN 10:11
Madison, J.
State sovereignty and federal
supremacy. BREWE 8:2926;
HURH:40
Martin, L.
Portion of the report of the
proceedings of the General
Convention held at Philadelphia
in 1787. ANN 3:166

---- See also Foot's Resolution;
United States - History - Civil
War - Causes

STATUES See Dedication addresses - Statues

STATUTE OF WESTMINSTER
Fraser, P.
The adoption of the Statute
of Westminster. MACS:286
McGechan, R. O.
Legal arguments for adopting
the Statute of Westminster,
1944. MACS:284

Staudinger, Hermann
Macromolecular chemistry (Nobel
Lecture, Dec. 11, 1953).
NOLC 3:397

STAUDINGER, HERMANN
Fredga, A.
Presentation [of the Nobel
Prize for Chemistry to Her-
mann Staudinger, Dec. 11,
1953]. NOLC 3:393

Steele, Harland
   House that Sam built. SCHW:25

Steffens, Gretchen
   Law of the land. SCHW:132

Steinbeck, John
   Acceptance [of the Nobel Prize
      for Literature, 1962].
      NOB 19:205; NOL:575

STEINBECK, JOHN
   Österling, A.
      Presentation [of the Nobel
        Prize for Literature to
        John Steinbeck, 1962].
        NOB 19:201; NOL:572

Steinem, Gloria
   Speech at the U.S. Naval
      Academy (May 12, 1972).
      JAM:46

---- and others (J. Ruckelshaus)
   Meet the press.
      BA 1972-73:65

Stendahl, Krister
   Faith that enlivens the mind
      (Hickory, N.C., Jan. 8,
      1977). BA 1976-77:168

Stephen, Campbell See Baldwin,
   S. B., jt. auth.

Stephens, Alexander Hamilton
   African slavery, the corner-
      stone of the Southern con-
      federacy. Same as his On
      the Confederate Constitution
   Against secession. Same as
      his Sanctity of the Union
   Civil rights in the Confederacy.
      ANN 9:493
   On the Confederate Constitution
      (Savannah, March 22, 1861).
      BREWE 9:3517; ECH:77
   Sanctity of the Union.
      ANN 9:199
   South and the public domain.
      BREWE 9:3513
   Speech of Hon. A. H. Stephens,
      delivered in the hall of the
      House of Representatives
      of Georgia, Nov. 14, 1860.
      ECH:7
   Speech of Hon. A. H. Stephens
      at Atlanta Ga., April 30,

1861. ECH:157
   Speech of Hon. A. H. Stephens at
      Richmond, Va., April 22,
      1861. ECH:191

Stephens, Donald A.
   Spirit of Merdeka. MONS:322

Stern, Harry J.
   Work of art. WALE:178

Stern, Otto
   The method of molecular rays
      (Nobel Lecture for 1943, Dec.
      12, 1946). NOLPH 3:8

STEROIDS
   Diels, O. P. H.
      Description and importance of
      the aromatic basic skeleton of
      the steroids. NOLC 3:259

STEROLS
   Windaus, A. O. R.
      Constitution of sterols and
      their connection with other
      substances occurring in nature.
      NOLC 2:105

STEVENS, ROGER L.
   Cullman, H. S.
      Presents Roger L. Stevens.
      LYI:29

Stevens, Thaddeus
   Against Webster and northern
      compromisers.
      BREWE 9:3522
   Ascendency of the Union Party.
      Same as his Radical view of
      reconstruction
   Concerning wartime taxes in the
      North. ANN 9:335
   Education as a public duty.
      ANN 6:136
   Fruit of foul rebellion. Same as
      his On reconstruction
   Issue against Andrew Johnson.
      Same as his Radical view of
      reconstruction
   On reconstruction. CUR:13
   Radical view of reconstruction.
      BREWE 9:3529; CUR:58
   Rights of the conqueror.
      ANN 9:608

Stevenson, Adlai, III
   Economic interdependence: the

world at a crossroads (New
York, Dec. 13, 1978).
BA 1978-79:178
Acceptance of nomination. Same
as his Agrees to run for
President
Acceptance speech, Chicago,
Illinois, August 17, 1956.
SIN:282
Acceptance speech, Chicago,
Illinois, July 26, 1952.
Same as his Agrees to run
for President
Address at the memorial serv-
ice for Sir Winston Churchill
(Jan. 28, 1965).
LINR:305; LINRS:307;
LINRST:373
Agrees to run for President
(Chicago, Ill., July 26,
1952). ANN 17:196; BEN:123;
GRG:96; HURH:302; LINS:345;
SIN:251
Bay of Pigs. ANN 18:25
Campaign speech, Academy of
Music, Brooklyn, New
York, October 31, 1952.
SIN:255
Campaign speech, Minneapolis,
Minnesota, September 29,
1956. SIN:288
City--a cause for statesmanship.
ARS:219
Eulogy: John Fitzgerald Ken-
nedy. Same as his Tribute
to John F. Kennedy at the
General Assembly of the
United Nations
Eulogy on Eleanor Roosevelt.
BRP:230
Farewell to a friend (Lloyd
Lewis). ALA:119
Foreign policy: the shades of
gray. MDV:56
Meaning of the United Nations.
ANN 18:317
Nature of patriotism. Same as
his Speech to the American
Legion, August 27, 1952
"The ordeal of the twentieth
century ... is far from
over." Same as his Agrees
to run for President
Premeditated attempt: the
building of the sites (United
Nations, 1962). LINR:87;
LINRS:93
Presents Lyndon B. Johnson.

LYI:197
Presents Pandit Jawaharlal
Nehru. LYI:242
Prospects for democracy around
the world. LINS:350
Sir Winston Churchill. Same as
his Address at the memorial
service for Sir Winston
Churchill
The speaker seeks a favorable
hearing. (Yale University,
1955). JEF:189; JEFF:182
Speech to the American Legion,
August 27, 1952. BEN:129
Strengthening international de-
veloping institutions. ALS:281
Today's most fateful fact (ac-
cepting honorary degree of
Doctor of Laws). OLIS:272
Trained intelligence: education
and womanpower (Radcliffe
College commencement ad-
dress). MDV:205
Tribute to John F. Kennedy at
the General Assembly of the
United Nations (New York,
Nov. 26, 1963). GRG:122;
HURH:371
"We shall honor him in the best
way that lies open to us--by
getting on with the everlasting
search for peace and justice
for which all mankind is
praying." Same as his Tribute
to John F. Kennedy at the
General Assembly of the United
Nations

STEVENSON, ADLAI E.
McGowan, C.
Eulogy on Adlai E. Stevenson.
BA 1965-66:227
Ramani, R.
Man of clear vision (tribute to
Adlai E. Stevenson).
MONS:250

Stewart, Potter
Or of the press. (New Haven,
Conn., Nov. 2, 1974).
BA 1974-75:97

Still, William
A defense of independent voting.
(Philadelphia, March 10, 1874).
FON:398

Stimson, Henry L.
    United States and the Caribbean.
    ANN 15:72

Stipp, John E.
    Introduces Nathan M. Pusey,
    President, Harvard Univer-
    sity. LYI:83

Stirling, William See Sykes,
    C., jt. auth.

Stiskin, Maurice N.
    Man is a soul. WALE:179

STOCK AND STOCK BREEDING
    See Agriculture

STOCKDALE, JOHN
    Erskine, T.
        Speech in behalf of John
        Stockdale. BREWE 6:2050

Stoddard, Solomon
    Defects of preachers reproved.
    POC:430

Stone, Barton W., 1772-1844
    "And I will gladly spend and
    be spent for you though the
    more abundantly I love you,
    the less I be loved."
    BLY:19

Stone, Harlan Fiske
    Fear and hysteria: the Japan-
    ese relocation, "Hirabayashi
    v. United States," 1943:
    opinion for the Supreme
    Court. ROD:316

Story, Joseph
    Intellectual achievement in
    America. BREWE 9:3531

---- See also Taney, R. B., jt.
    auth.

Stout, Robert
    A call for liberal and con-
    servative parties, 1876
    (New Zealand House of
    Representatives, Aug. 18,
    1876). MACS:180

---- See also Holland, H., jt. auth.

Stowe, Leland
    Children, peanuts--and you.
    MOP:263

Strafford, Thomas Wentworth, 1st
    Earl of
    Defense before the House of
    Lords. BREWE 9:3540;
    BRYH:131
    His defense when impeached for
    treason. Same as his De-
    fense before the House of
    Lords
    Speech at his trial for treason.
    Same as his Defense before
    the House of Lords

Stratton, Richard D.
    Food: a world crisis.
    BREWW:81

Stratton, Thomas
    Agriculture--America's greatest
    tool. BREWW:109

Street, William S.
    Introduces Dr. Charles E. Ode-
    gaard, president of the Uni-
    versity of Washington.
    PRS:46

Streeter, Frank S.
    Introducing an educator (Fred-
    erick S. Jones). LYI:85

STREPTOMYCIN
    Waksman, S. A.
        Streptomycin: background,
        isolation, properties, and
        utilization. NOLM 3:370

Stresemann, Gustav
    The new Germany (Nobel Lec-
    ture, 1926, June 29, 1927).
    NOLP 2:8

STRESEMANN, GUSTAV
    Nansen, F.
        Speech at Award Ceremony
        [presenting Nobel Prize for
        Peace to Aristide Briand and
        Gustav Stresemann, Dec. 10,
        1926]. NOLP 2:3

STRIKES AND LOCKOUTS
    Tan Chee Khoon
        Intellectual elite and the
        worker. MONS:197

---- NEW ZEALAND
Holland, H.
    The 1913 Waterside Strike.
    MACS:230 sel.
Lee, J. A.
    The Auckland Riot, 1932.
    MACS:312 sel.

Strutt, John William See Ray-
    leigh, John William Strutt,
    Baron, 1842-1919

Stuart, Julia Davis
What can I do that matters?
    (Detroit, Sept. 19, 1967).
    BRYF:512

Studebaker, Clement See Jones,
    A., jt. auth.

STUDENT DEMONSTRATIONS
Moos, M.
    Darkness over the Ivory
    Tower. BA 1968-69:55

STUDENT MOVEMENTS
Horn, F. H.
    The student revolt, a de-
    fense of the older generation.
    HOR:49
McGill, W. J.
    Requiem for the countercul-
    ture: problems of a new
    student generation. HOR:66
Odegaard, C. E.
    Bridging the generation gap,
    the march downtown.
    HOR:42
Perkins, J. A.
    Bridging the generation gap,
    how the New Deal became
    today's establishment.
    HOR:56

STUDENTS
Bittner, J. R.
    The news media and campus
    unrest. STOT:290
Brewster, K., Jr.
    Due process radicalism.
    HOR:37
Bronowski, J.
    Protest--past and present.
    BA 1969-70:1119
Bunting, M. I.
    Their questions. HOR:93
Capp, A.
    Is this your university?

STOT:297
Cry on the campus. BURT:102
Damrin, D. E.
    The James Scholars and the
    university. BRYF:528;
    BRYO:243
Eddy, E. D., Jr.
    Student involvement in educa-
    tional policy. BA 1965-66:221;
    LINR:251
Hayes, P. A.
    Madame Butterfly and the col-
    legian. LINR:262
Jordan, L.
    Opportunities in H.S.A. (Har-
    vard Student Agencies).
    REIR:101 (outline)
Kane, A.
    Glory of notoriety. REIR:223
Kerr, C.
    Perspectives on the prophets
    of doom. HOR:34
Lindsay, J. V.
    A politician adapts his intro-
    duction and conclusion to an
    audience of students. JEF:194
Lubbers, A. D.
    God and Joe College.
    SCHW:69
McGill, W. J.
    Requiem for Joe College.
    BA 1969-70:139
McKissick, F. B.
    The student and the ghetto.
    OE:216
Martin, D.
    Trouble in the university.
    MDYG:121
Moos, M.
    Darkness over the Ivory Tower.
    BA 1968-69:55
Nixon, R. M.
    Campus revolutionaries.
    BAAGB:386
Pusey, N. M.
    Thanksgiving and entreaty, a
    President's valedictory.
    HOR:26
Thani Nayagam, X.
    Town versus gown. MONS:183
Wald, G.
    Generation in search of a fu-
    ture. BA 1968-1969:33
Welcome to a delegation of for-
    eign students. HNWM:48
Welcome to a freshman class.
    HNWM:50

---- See also Black students; Colleges and universities; Commencement addresses; Edu-
cation, Higher; Learning and
scholarship; Youth

STUDENTS, PARTICIPATION IN
SCHOOL GOVERNMENT See
Self government in education

SUBSIDY See Taxation

SUBSTITUTE SPEAKERS
Bishop, J.
Responds to introduction (when
substituting for Sir Cedric
Hardwicke). PRS:119
Caveny, C. C.
Greets Joey Bishop, sub-
stituting for Sir Cedric
Hardwicke, PRS:118

SUBTREASURY BILL See Independent treasury

SUCCESS
Art of success. BURT:112
Fosdick, H. E.
Power to see it through.
CROCK:58
You, too, can be a millionaire.
BURT:118

---- See also Behavior; Fame;
Inspiration talks

SUEZ CANAL
Eisenhower, D. D.
Crisis in the Middle East.
ANN 17:411
Holland, S.
The Suez crisis, 1956.
MACS:397 sel.
Menzies, R. G.
On the nationalisation of the
Suez Canal. MCA:144

Suffian bin Hashim
The danger of living our lives
in isolation (April 4, 1970).
MONSA:137
Important factors for ensuring
efficient, loyal public service (Oct. 4, 1969).
MONSA:132
Only Malays can initiate the
institutional changes (Petal-
ing Jaya, Oct. 11, 1969).

MONSA:140
University should slow down:
call to education planners
(Univ. of Malaya, June 20,
1970). MONSA:144
Warning to the white-collar worker (Kuala Lumpur, Jan. 25,
1970). MONSA:138

SUFFRAGE
Carpenter, M. H.
In favor of universal suffrage.
BREWE 3:978
Chamberlain, J.
Megaphone and manhood suf-
frage. BREWE 3:1026
Frelinghuysen, F. T.
In favor of universal suffrage.
BREWE 6:2203
Sanford, N. and others
Debate on property and suf-
frage. ANN 5:4
Still, W.
A defense of independent vot-
ing. FON:398

---- See also Blacks - Politics and
suffrage; Elections; Woman -
Suffrage

SUGARS
Fischer, H. E.
Syntheses in the purine and
sugar group. NOLC 1:21
Leloir, L. F.
Two decades of research on
the biosynthesis of saccharides.
NOLC 4:338

SUICIDE
Hayes, P. A.
Madame Butterfly and the
collegian. LINR:262;
LINRS:265

SULFUR
Vigneaud, V. D.
A trail of sulfur research:
from insulin to oxytocin.
NOLC 3:446

Sullivan, John H.
The United States and the com-
ing world food crisis (River
Falls, Wisc., April 26, 1979).
BA 1979-80:46

Sullivan, Louis
Characteristics and tendencies of

American architecture.
ANN 11:40
Young architect.   ANN 12:385

Sullivan, Walter See Sevareid,
E., jt. auth.

Sulzberger, Arthur Ochs
Business and the press: is the
press anti-business? (Detroit, March 14, 1977).
EHN:387

Sumner, Charles
Against annexation (of the
Dominican Republic).
ANN 10:233
Antislavery duties of the Whig
Party. (Boston-Whig State
Convention, Sept. 23, 1846).
HOW:218
Crime against Kansas (Wash-
ington, May, 1856).
ANN 8:267; BREWE 9:3557;
HURH:85
Denouncing Douglas and Butler.
Same as his Crime against
Kansas
"An essential wickedness that
makes other public crimes
seem like public virtues."
Same as his Crime against
Kansas
Naboth's vineyard.   Same as
his Against annexation (of
the Dominican Republic)
Proper guaranties for security.
CUR:12
A Republican appeal for unity
(1855). (Nov. 2, 1855,
Faneuil Hall). DAVF:132
Resolutions on secession and
reconstruction. ANN 9:323
Segregation and the common
school (Sarah C. Roberts v.
City of Boston case, 1849).
ANN 7:507
True grandeur of nations.
BREWE 9:3548
War and the common law of
Nations. Same as his War
system of the Commonwealth
of Nations
War system of the Common-
wealth of Nations. ANN 7:548

---- and others (J. Grimes)
Impeachment of Andrew Johnson.
ANN 10:126

SUMNER, CHARLES
Brooks, P. S.
Assault on Sumner.
BREWE 2:654
Burlingame, A.
Massachusetts and the Sumner
assault. BREWE 2:820
Conkling, R.
Against Senator Sumner.
BREWE 4:1374
Rainey, J. H.
Eulogy on Charles Sumner.
FON:403

Sumner, G. Lynn
Presents Gertrude Lawrence.
LYI:22
Presents Victor Heiser. LYI:174

Sumner, James Batcheller
The chemical nature of enzymes
(Nobel Lecture, Dec. 12,
1946). NOLC 3:114

SUMNER, JAMES BATCHELLER
Tiselius, A. W. K.
Presentation [of the Nobel
Prize for Chemistry to James
Batcheller Sumner, John
Howard Northrop, and Wendell
Meredith Stanley, Dec. 12,
1946]. NOLC 3:109

Sunday, William A. (Billy Sunday)
Evangelism. (New York, 1914).
HURH:170
"I like to have a man have a
definite experience in reli-
gion." Same as his Evangelism

SUNDAY LEGISLATION
Terry, D. S. and others
On Sunday closing laws:
opinion for the court and
dissenting opinion (Ex parte
Newman case). ANN 9:85

SUNDAY SCHOOLS
Welcome to Sunday school offi-
cers. HNWM:28
Welcome to visitors in Sunday
school (3 examples).
HNWM:52

Sundberg, O.
Presentation [of the Nobel Prize
for Physiology or Medicine to
Charles Louis Alphonse Laveran, Dec. 11, 1907].

NOLM 1:259
Presentation [of the Nobel Prize
for Physiology or Medicine
to Charles Robert Richet,
Dec. 11, 1913].   NOLM 1:469

SUPREME COURT OF THE
    UNITED STATES See United
    States - Supreme Court

SURFACE CHEMISTRY
    Langmuir, I.
       Surface chemistry.
       NOLC 2:287

SURRATT, MARY E.
    Aiken, F. A.
       Defense of Mrs. Mary E.
       Surratt. BREWE 1:120

Sutherland, George and others
    (W. H. Taft and O. W.
    Holmes, Jr.)
    Adkins v. Children's Hospital:
       opinion for the court and
       dissenting opinion.
       ANN 14:391
    ---- (L. D. Brandeis)
       (New State Ice Company v.
       Liebmann: opinion for
       the court and dissenting
       opinion. ANN 15:140

Sutherland, Josiah
    Free land and the supply of
       labor. ANN 8:180

Sutro, John See Sykes, C., jt.
    auth.

Suttner, Bertha Von
    The evolution of the Peace
       Movement (Nobel Lecture
       for 1905, April 18, 1906).
       NOLP 1:84

SUTTNER, BERTHA VON
    Bjørnson, G.
       Introduction [presenting the
       Nobel Prize for Peace to
       Bertha von Suttner, 1905,
       April 18, 1906]. NOLP 1:81
    Løvland, J. G.
       Banquet speech [presenting
       the Nobel Prize for Peace
       to Bertha von Suttner, 1905,
       April 18, 1906]. NOLP 1:82

Sutton, Preston M.
    Liberal arts in an agricultural
       college. ANN 11:18

Svedberg, Theodor
    The ultracentrifuge (Nobel Lec-
       ture for 1926, May 19, 1927).
       NOLC 2:67

SVEDBERG, THEODOR
    Söderbaum, H. G.
       Presentation [of the Nobel
       Prize for Chemistry to Theo-
       dor Svedberg, 1926, May 19,
       1927].   NOLC 2:63

Swarensky, Manfred E.
    Bridge of love. WALE:181
    Spiritual portrait. WALE:183

Swearingen, John E.
    Environmental pollution: a na-
       tional problem. (Indiana
       State Chamber of Commerce,
       Indianapolis, Nov. 6, 1969).
       BAAGB:392

Swets, Paul
    Bootstraps and moonshots.
       SCHW:183

Swimmer, Ross O.
    Cherokee history. MAES:314

Syed Hussein Alatas
    Malaysia and its intellectual
       revolution. MONS:469
    Primary aim of a university.
       MONS:475

Sykes, Christopher and others
    Evelyn Waugh--the man.
       MDYG:11

Symonds, William
    Britain's claim to a New World
       empire justified. ANN 1:32

Synge, Richard Laurence Millington
    Applications of partition chroma-
       tography (Nobel Lecture, Dec.
       12, 1952). NOLC 3:374

SYNGE, RICHARD LAURENCE
    MILLINGTON
    Tiselius, A. W. K.
       Presentation [of the Nobel

Prize for Chemistry to
Archer John Porter Martin
and Richard Laurence
Millington Synge, Dec. 12,
1952]. NOLC 3:355

Szent-Györgyi, Albert
Oxidation, energy transfer, and
vitamins (Nobel Lecture,
Dec. 11, 1937). NOLM 2:440

SZENT-GYÖRGYI, ALBERT
Hammarsten, E.
Presentation [of the Nobel
Prize for Physiology or
Medicine to Albert Szent-
Györgyi Von Nagyrapolt,
Dec. 11, 1937]. NOLM 2:435

- T -

Taft, Robert A.
Against the treaty (North Atlantic
Pact). ANN 16:591
Analysis of the Taft-Hartley
Act. ANN 16:414
Declaration of Republican prin-
ciples--the New Deal is
rapidly receding. BAD:74
Equal justice under law.
BEN:100
New problems of government.
ANN 15:571
Opposition to the Roosevelt
war policies. ANN 16:94
Should the government guarantee
employment? ANN 16:263

TAFT, ROBERT A.
Dirksen, E.
Presents Robert A. Taft.
LYI:210

Taft, William Howard
Antitrust: "Mere size is no
sin." Same as his Third
annual message; part I,
December 5, 1911
Cabinet and the Congress.
Same as his Fourth annual
message; part III, Decem-
ber 19, 1912
Defense of a high tariff. Same
as his Tariff fiasco: the
Winona address
Dollar diplomacy. Same as

his Fourth annual message:
part I, December 3, 1912
First annual message.
STAT 3:2338
Fourth annual message: part I,
December 3, 1912.
ANN 13:369; STAT 3:2486
Fourth annual message: part II,
December 6, 1912.
STAT 3:2511
Fourth annual message: part III,
December 19, 1912.
ANN 13:366; STAT 3:2531
Inaugural address. USINAU:187
Limited presidential power.
ANN 14:41
Second annual message.
STAT 3:2369
Tariff fiasco: the Winona ad-
dress. ANN 13:176
Third annual message: part I,
December 5, 1911.
STAT 3:2432
Third annual message: part II,
December 7, 1911.
STAT 3:2444
Third annual message: part III,
December 20, 1911.
STAT 3:2464
Third annual message: part IV,
December 21, 1911.
STAT 3:2469
Veto of Arizona Enabling Act.
ANN 13:272

---- See also Sutherland, G., jt.
auth.

TAFT-HARTLEY BILL See
Labor law and legislation -
Taft-Hartley Law

TAGORE, RABINDRANATH
Hjärne, H.
Presentation [of the Nobel
Prize for Literature to Rabin-
dranath Tagore, 1913].
NOB 18:10; NOL:127
Nair, C. V. D.
Reflections on Rabindranath
Tagore. MONS:190

Talfourd, Thomas Noon
Queen against Moxon-Shelley
as a blasphemer.
BREWE 9:3565

Talmage, Thomas Dewitt
On Admiral Dewey and the

American Navy.
BREWE 9:3584

TAMIL LANGUAGE
Abdul Rahman, T.
"All the earth is my home-
land. " MONS:31

Tamm, Igor' Evgen'evič
General characteristics of radiations emitted by systems
moving with super-light
velocities with some applications to plasma physics
(Nobel Lecture, Dec. 11,
1958). NOLPH 3:470

TAMM, IGOR' EVGEN'EVIC
Siegbahn, K.
Presentation [of the Nobel
Prize for Physics to Pavel
Aleksejevič Cerenkov, Il'ja
Michajlovič Frank and Igor'
Evgen'evič Tamm, Dec. 11,
1958]. NOLPH 3:423

Tan Chee Khoon
Intellectual elite and the worker.
MONS:197
Monstrous piece of legislation
(Internal Security Act--
Malaysia). MONS:190
The teachers' dilemma: the
government gets the blame
(Univ. of Malaya, Jan. 4-5,
1968). MONSA:180

Tan Siew Sin
The big question before us.
(Kuala Lumpur, March 28,
1968). MONSA:93
Commonwealth trade: an ex-
plosive situation. MONS:127
Malays and Chinese must co-
exist (July 24, 1969).
MONSA:85
Meeting place of cultures.
MONS:115
Mission of the M.C.A.
MONS:117
The need for dedicated service
by civil servants (Kuala
Lumpur, Feb. 4, 1968).
MONSA:89
Our constitution: a fair com-
promise. MONS:109
The role of M.C.A. and the
loyalty of Malaysian Chinese

(Kuala Lumpur, March 7,
1969). MONSA:78

Tan Sri Muhammed Ghazali See
Muhammed Ghazali bin Shafie

Tan Sri V. T. Sambanthan See
Sambanthan, V. T.

Taney, Roger Brooke
Dred Scott Case: opinion for the
Supreme Court. ANN 8:440
Dred Scott V. Sandford. Same
as his Dred Scott case

---- and others (J. Story)
Charles River bridge v. Warren
bridge: opinion for the court
and dissenting opinion.
ANN 6:326

Tanner, B. T.
The Sioux's revenge. (Philadel-
phia, July 13, 1876).
FON:443

Tappan, David
A warning to Harvard seniors
against world revolution.
(June 19, 1798). DAVF:49

Tappan, Henry P.
Call for a secularized university.
ANN 9:79

Tardiff, Vivian
Americans with Japanese faces.
SCHW:20

TARIFF
Borah, W. E.
Western farming and the
tariff. ANN 15:28
Clay, H.
American industry, 1824.
ANN 5:114
American system.
BREWE 4:1249; HOW:32
Manufacturing and a protective
tariff. ANN 4:612
System of real reciprocity.
ANN 5:392
Cleveland, G.
Fourth annual message (first
term). STAT 2:1598
On tariff revision.
ANN 11:154; STAT 2:1587
Dallas, G. M.

Pennsylvania idea.
BREWE 4:1599
Dawes, H. L.
Tariff Commission of 1880.
BREWE 5:1671
Harrison, B.
Second annual message.
STAT 2:1653
Jordan, D. S.
Moral aspects of the pro-
tective tariff. ANN 13:147
McKinley, W.
At the Pan-American Ex-
position. ANN 12:428
Randolph, J., 1773-1833
Against a protective tariff.
ANN 4:427
On the tariff (1824).
BREWE 9:3305
Taft, W. H.
Tariff fiasco: the Winona
address. ANN 13:176
Third annual message: part
III, December 20, 1911.
STAT 3:2464

---- See also Commerce; Corn
Laws; Free trade and pro-
tection

Tatum, Edward Lawrie
A case history in biological
research (Nobel Lecture,
Dec. 11, 1958).
NOLM 3:602

TATUM, EDWARD LAWRIE
Caspersson, T.
Presentation [of the Nobel
Prize for Physiology or
Medicine to George Wells
Beadle, Edward Lawrie
Tatum, and Joshua Leder-
berg, Dec. 11, 1958].
NOLM 3:583

TAXATION
Bacon, F.
Upon the motion of subsidy
(November 15, 1598
speech). BRYH:90
Chesterfield, P. D. S.
Against revenues from
drunkenness and vice.
BREWE 3:1095
Danton, G. J.
Squeezing the sponge.
BREWE 5:1631

Hamilton, A.
On an act granting to Con-
gress certain imposts and
duties. ALS:133
Income tax--legalized larceny.
BURT:50
Kennedy, J. F.
Tax cut. STAT 3:3144
Lewis, E.
Mott v. Pennsylvania Railroad
Company: opinion for the
court. ANN 9:61
Lloyd George, D.
The budget. BRYH:461;
JA E:170; MCB:233;
STRM:407
Mulford, S.
Speech to the Assembly at
New-York. POC:174
Pitt, W., 1708-1778
On the right to tax America.
STRM:11
Roosevelt, F. D.
The President asks Congress
for tax revision. BAD:8
Roosevelt, T.
Seventh annual message.
STAT 3:2240
Sherman, J.
General financial policy of the
government. BREWE 9:3442
Stevens, T.
Concerning wartime taxes in
the North. ANN 9:335

---- NEW ZEALAND
Ballance, J.
A land tax of a halfpenny in
the pound on land exceeding
£500 in value, 1878.
MACS:184 sel.
Grey, Sir G.
A radical programme, 1877.
MACS:181 sel.
Massey, W. F.
Repeal of income tax on
farmers, 1923. MACS:304 sel.
Nordmeyer, A.
The "Black budget" 1958.
MACS:434 sel.

Taylor, Deems
Presents Grace George.
LYI:19

Taylor, Frederick W.
On scientific management.
BOORA 2:740

Taylor, George Edwin
Revolution by the ballot.
(St. Louis, July 5, 1904).
FON:647

Taylor, Jeremy
Foolish exchange.
BREWE 9:3590

TAYLOR, MAXWELL D.
Spellman, F.J.
Presents Maxwell D. Taylor.
LYI:143

Taylor, Orlando L.
African origins of Black Eng-
lish. (Univ. of Texas,
Oct. 23, 1969). JEF:443

Taylor, Thomas E.
Leasehold defended (New Zealand House of Representa-
tives Nov. 16, 1909).
MACS:219 sel.

Taylor, Zachary
First annual message.
STAT 1:774
Inaugural address.
USINAU:99

TEACHER APPRECIATION DAY
Welcome to teachers on
Teacher Appreciation Day.
HNWM:17

TEACHERS
Introductions for teachers (10
examples). BNH:28
Johari, M. K.
Successful teacher.
MONS:146
Welcome to teachers on Educa-
tion Day. HNWM:18

---- See also Education; Educators

TEACHING, FREEDOM OF
Marshall, D. S.
What is academic freedom?
MONS:453
Nixon, R. M.
Academic freedom: a force
in human history. CAPG:148
Toh Chin Chye
Essentials of academic free-
dom. MONS:379

TECHNICAL EDUCATION
Whitehead, A. N.
Technical education and its
relation to science and literature. MCB:403

TECHNOLOGY
Brown, H. S.
Science, technology, and
world development. ARS:83
Kanapathy, V.
Technological change and
management policies.
MONSA:202

TECHNOLOGY AND CIVILIZATION
Dubos, R.
Social attitudes and techno-
logical civilization.
BA 1978-79:11
Linowitz, S. M.
Let candles be brought.
BA 1976-77:149

TECHNOLOGY AND STATE
Schmitt, H.
New policy options through
technology. BA 1979-80:133

Tecumseh, Shawnee chief
To General Proctor.
BREWE 7:2567

TELEVISION BROADCASTING
Agnew, Spiro
Television news coverage;
network censorship.
ARN:367; BRYF:467; ERP:153;
LINRS:191; LINRST:221;
MACR:331; STAT:274
Braden, W. W.
Has TV made the public
speaker obsolete? EHN:309;
MOPR:360
Gallup, G.
Mass information or mass
entertainment. ANN 17:215
Goodman, J. B.
Broadcast journalism: serving
the democratic process.
BA 1976-77:52
Minow, N. N.
Television and the public in-
terest. ANN 18:12; MDV:248
Murrow, E. R.
Broadcaster talks to his col-
leagues. MDV:263

Myers, N. J.
Moppet manipulation.
ARS:123
Stanton, F.
Address before the International Radio and Television Society. BA 1969-70:71
Remarks on government regulation of broadcasting (accepting Printers' Ink gold medal). MDV:277
Reply to the Vice President. STOT:282

Teller, Morris
What the Lord requires.
WALE:185

tenBroek, Jacobus
Today's challenge in public welfare. MDV:233

Tennent, Gilbert
Danger of an unconverted ministry. POC:469

TENNESSEE VALLEY AUTHORITY See Dams

TENURE OF OFFICE ACT, 1867
Johnson, A.
Veto of Tenure of Office Act. ANN 10:90

Terrell, Mary Church
The progress of colored women. (1904). FON:643

TERRITORIAL EXPANSION See United States - Territorial expansion

TERRORISM
Kelley, C. M.
Terrorism, the ultimate evil. BA 1975-76:117

Terry, David Smith and others (S. J. Field)
On Sunday closing laws: opinion for the court and dissenting opinion (Ex parte Newman case).
ANN 9:85

Tertullian, Quintus Septimius Florens
Beauty of patience.
BREWE 9:3597

TEXAS
Giddings, J. R.
Texas and slavery.
ANN 7:201
Jackson, A.
Independence of Texas.
ANN 6:293
Tyler, J.
Fourth annual message.
STAT 1:613

Thackeray, William Makepeace
Authors and their patrons.
BREWE 9:3604
Novelist's future labors.
BREWE 9:3606
Reality of the novelist's creation.
BREWE 9:3602

Thani Nayagam, Xavier S.
Age and learning. MONS:187
Town versus gown. MONS:183

THANKS
Appreciation on a day of dedication. BOS:68
Nine examples of brief thanks to special committees.
BNH:46
Nineteen examples of short speeches of public appreciation. BNH:43
Public appreciation. BOS:43
Ramani, R.
Twenty four days in May (expression of thanks as President of Security Council of United Nations). MONS:248
Thanks to special committees.
BOS:46
Words of appreciation.
BON:61

---- See also Acceptance speeches;
Responses to tributes

THANKSGIVING DAY
Osgood, D.
An American Thanksgiving for divine favor (1795). DAVF:42
Parker, T.
State of the nation (1850).
ANN 8:114
Prayer for Thanksgiving.
BNH:76
Rawson, E.
Thanksgiving. HURH:20
Sampson, B. K.

To my white fellow citizens.
FON:347

Thant, U.
Future of the United Nations.
MDV:45

Thatcher, Peter
Boston Massacre oration, March
5, 1776.   POC:272

Thayer, Robert H.
America's cultural relations
abroad.   ANN 17:545

THEATER
Burrows, J. L.
Opposition to the theater in
time of war.   ANN 9:402
Jackson, E. M.
American theatre and the
speech profession.
BA 1965-66:200
Theater begins with wonder
(outline of speech).   CUB:70

---- See also Music and musicians

Théel, Hj.
Presentation [of the Nobel
Prize for Physics to Hendrik
Antoon Lorentz and Pieter
Zeeman, 1902].
NOLPH 1:11
Presentation [of the Nobel Prize
for Chemistry to Hermann
Emil Fischer, Dec. 12,
1902].   NOLC 1:17

Theiler, Max
The development of vaccines
against yellow fever (Nobel
Lecture, Dec. 11, 1951).
NOLM 3:351

THEILER, MAX
Bergstrand, H.
Presentation [of the Nobel
Prize for Physiology or
Medicine to Max Theiler,
Dec. 11, 1951].
NOLM 3:347

Theorell, Axel Hugo Theodor
The nature and mode of action
of oxidation enzymes (Nobel
Lecture, Dec. 12, 1955).
NOLM 3:480

THEORELL, AXEL HUGO THEODOR
Hammarsten, E.
Presentation [of the Nobel
Prize for Physiology or Medi-
cine to Axel Hugo Theodor
Theorell, Dec. 12, 1955].
NOLM 3:477

Theorell, H.
Presentation [of the Nobel Prize
for Physiology or Medicine
to Carl Ferdinand Cori, Gerty
Theresa Cori-Radnitz, and
Bernardo Alberto Houssay,
Dec. 11, 1947].   NOLM 3:179
Presentation [of the Nobel Prize
for Physiology or Medicine to
Severo Ochoa and Arthur Korn-
berg, Dec. 11, 1959].
NOLM 3:641

THERMIONIC EMISSION
Richardson, O. W.
Thermionic phenomena and the
laws which govern them.
NOLPH 2:224

THERMODYNAMICS
Giauque, W. F.
Some consequences of low-
temperature research in
chemical thermodynamics.
NOLC 3:227

Thibeault, Mary Lou
The hazards of equity.   (Commencement Address, Hartford
Colleges for Women, June 1,
1974).   VERD:265

Thiers, Louis Adolphe
Mexico and Louis Napoleon's
policies.   BREWE 9:3610

Thio Chan Bee
Christian laymen and the world
of politics.   MONS:465
Inspired education through inspired educators.   MONS:463

Thomas, Dylan
Life among the culture vultures.
ANN 17:239

Thomas, James B.
"Light of the world."   SCHW:110

Thomas, Norman
America and the war.   (New

York, June 29, 1941).
HURH:261
Townsend Plan and cough drops.
BOSR:92
"We have better work for our
sons to do than to have
them die." Same as his
America and the war

Thompson, Dorothy
"Democracy and freedom face
the bitterest of tests."
Same as her Hitler's plans
for Canada and the United
States
Hitler's plans for Canada and
the United States (Toronto,
May 2, 1941). HURH:257

THOMPSON, DOROTHY
Meloney, Mrs. W. B.
Introducing Dorothy Thomp-
son. LYI:112

Thompson, Morris
The BIA at work. MAES:57

Thomson, George Paget
Electronic waves (Nobel Lecture for 1937, June 7,
1938). NOLPH 2:397

THOMSON, GEORGE PAGET
Pleijel, H.
Presentation [of the Nobel
Prize for Physics to Clinton
Joseph Davisson and George
Paget Thomson, Dec. 13,
1937]. NOLPH 2:387

Thomson, Joseph John
Carriers of negative electricity
(Nobel Lecture, Dec. 11,
1906). NOLPH 1:145

THOMSON, JOSEPH JOHN
Klason, J. P.
Presentation [of the Nobel
Prize for Physics to Joseph
John Thomson, Dec. 11,
1906]. NOLPH 1:141

Thomson, Tun Sir James
Beveridge
Brightness is darkened (eulogy
on Tuanku Abdul Rahman
Ibni Al-Marhum Tuanku
Mohammed, first King of

Malaysia). MONS:281
Let these be his epitaph (eulogy
on Sultan Hissamuddin Alam
Shah Ibni Al-Marhum Sultan
Ala'Iddin Sulaiman Shah).
MONS:283
Spirit of humanity (opening of
Federal Court of Malaysia).
MONS:285

Thoreau, Henry David
Civil disobedience. BOORA 1:318
Fourth of July oration, 1854
(Boston). HAW:200
Plea for Captain John Brown.
ANN 9:136
Slavery in Massachusetts.
OLIS:118
Walking westward. ANN 8:125

Thorne, Will See Baldwin, S. B.,
jt. auth.

Thornton, Charles B.
Responds to introduction.
PRS:101

THOUGHT AND THINKING
Don't limit yourself. BURT:115
Hancher, V. M.
Art of contemplation.
CROCK:132

Thuraisingham, Ernest Emmanual
Sir Clough
Call to Ceylonese to have one
and only loyalty to rulers of
Malaysia
MONSA:185
Lotteries: Hell, Hitler and Ber-
nard Shaw. MONS:167
Milestones in Malayan education.
MONS:173
The prince of sportsmen (Kuala
Lumpur, Sept. 18, 1970).
MONSA:187
Spirit of teaching. MONS:169

Thurman, Allen G.
Tilden-Hayes election.
BREWE 9:3621
Vested rights and the obligations
of contracts. BREWE 9:3626

THYROID GLAND - DISEASES
Kocher, E. T.
Concerning pathological manifestations in low-grade thyroid
diseases. NOLM 1:330

Tierney, George See Pitt, W.,
1759-1806

Tilden, Samuel Jones
Arraignment of the Republican
Party. Same as his Negro
suffrage
Negro suffrage. ANN 10:122

Tillich, Paul J.
"What is truth?" ARS:180

Tillotson, John
Sermon against evil speaking.
BRYH:156

Tilton, Theodore
The Negro; a speech. (1863).
MDT:161

TIME
Salm, N.
Matter of time. SCHW:83

Tirikatene, Eruera
Maiden speech in Parliament
(Sept. 29, 1932).
MACS:179 sel.

Tiselius, Arne Wilhelm Kaurin
Electrophoresis and adsorption
analysis as aids in investi-
gations of large-molecular
weight substances and their
breakdown (Nobel Lecture,
Dec. 13, 1948). NOLC 3:195
Presentation [of the Nobel Prize
for Chemistry to Archer
John Porter Martin and
Richard Laurence Millington
Synge, Dec. 12, 1952].
NOLC 3:355
Presentation [of the Nobel Prize
for Chemistry to Frederick
Sanger, Dec. 11, 1958].
NOLC 3:541
Presentation [of the Nobel Prize
for Chemistry to James
Batcheller Sumner, John
Howard Northrop, and
Wendell Meredith Stanley,
Dec. 12, 1946]. NOLC 3:109
Presentation [of the Nobel Prize
for Chemistry to William
Francis Giauque, Dec. 12,
1949]. NOLC 3:221

TISELIUS, ARNE WILHELM
KAURIN
Westgren, A.
Presentation [of the Nobel
Prize for Chemistry to Arne
Wilhelm Kaurin Tiselius, Dec.
13, 1948]. NOLC 3:191

TOASTMASTERS
Frustrated toastmaster.
BURT:160
Suggestions for the toastmaster.
BURT:56, 151
Toastmaster's responsibilities.
PRS:1

TOASTS
Eliezer, C. J.
Toast to Oxford. MONS:271
Elizabeth II, Queen of England
Toast to President Ford and
to the American people.
JAM:22
Ford, G. R.
Toast to Queen Elizabeth.
JAM:21
Kaunda, K.
Toast to President Ford.
JAM:23
Løvland, J. G.
Toast to C. A. Gobat [pre-
senting the Nobel Prize for
Peace for 1902, Oslo, July
18, 1906]. NOLP 1:29
Toast to E. Ducommun [pre-
senting the Nobel Prize for
Peace, 1902]. NOLP 1:15
Prochnow, H. V.
Toast to the mayor of Copen-
hagen. PRS:56
Razak, T. A.
Correct words for a toast!
MONS:91
Skinner, C. O.
"Bottoms up" (toast to gyne-
cologists). HURH:311

Todd, Sir Alexander Robertus
Synthesis in the study of nucleotides (Nobel Lecture, Dec.
11, 1957). NOLC 3:522

TODD, SIR ALEXANDER ROBERTUS
Fredga, A.
Presentation [of the Nobel
Prize for Chemistry to Sir
Alexander Robertus Todd,

Dec. 11, 1957].
NOLC 3:519

Todd, Oliver See Ayer, A. J.,
jt. auth.

Toh Chin Chye
The beginnings of the city state
and its achievement (Singa-
pore, Aug. 29, 1969).
MONSA:288
Essentials of academic freedom.
MONS:379
Lesson of the Three Kingdoms.
MONS:375
The role of the university in
a multi-racial society
(Singapore, Nov. 28, 1968).
MONSA:291
Singapore in the eye of the
storm.   MONS:377

Tomonaga, Sin-Itiro
Development of quantum electrodynamics (Nobel Lecture for
1965, May 6, 1966).
NOLPH 4:126

TOMONAGA, SIN-ITIRO
Waller, I.
Presentation [of the Nobel
Prize for Physics to Sin-
Itiro Tomonaga, Julian
Schwinger, and Richard P.
Feynman, Dec. 11, 1965].
NOLPH 4:123

Tomsky, Mervin B.
Bitter and the sweet.
WALE:187
Righteous shall flourish like
the palm-tree.   WALE:188
Symphony of life.   WALE:190

Tooke, John Horne
On the "Murders at Lexington
and Concord" (at his trial
for libel).   BREWE 9:3633

Toombs, Robert
For secession.   Same as his
"Let us depart in peace"
"Let us depart in peace. "
ANN 9:192; BREWE 9:3646
Robert Toombs' address to
the people of Georgia.
(Washington, Dec. 23, 1860).
ECH:103

Territorial acquisition and Civil
War.   BREWE 9:3641

Torata, Count de
Acceptance [of the Nobel Prize
for Literature for Jacinto
Benavente, 1922].   NOL:191

TORIES - ENGLAND
Beaconsfield, B. D.
Tory democracy.   JAE:139

Törnebladh, H. R.
Presentation [of the Nobel Prize
for Chemistry to Svante Au-
gust Arrhenius, Dec. 11, 1903].
NOLC 1:43
Presentation [of the Nobel Prize
for Physics to Antoine Henri
Becquerel, Pierre Curie and
Marie Sklodowska-Curie,
Dec. 11, 1903].
NOLPH 1:47

TORY PARTY (GREAT BRITAIN)
See Conservative Party (Great
Britain)

TOSCANINI, ARTURO
Langer, E.
Instrument of revelation.
LINR:301; LINRS:300;
LINRST:370

TOTALITARIANISM
Peters, L.
What is totalitarianism?
LINR:50

TOUSSAINT L'OUVERTURE,
PIERRE DOMINIQUE
Phillips, W.
Toussaint L'Ouverture.
OLIS:170

Tower, John G.
Responds to introduction.
PRS:112

Townes, Charles R.
Production of coherent radiation
by atoms and molecules (Nobel
Lecture, Dec. 11, 1964).
NOLPH 4:58

TOWNES, CHARLES H.
Edlén, B.
Presentation [of the Nobel

Prize for Physics to Charles
H. Townes, Nikolai G. Basov,
and Alexander M. Prochorov,
Dec. 11, 1964]. NOLPH 4:55

TOWNSEND PLAN
Thomas, N.
Townsend Plan and cough
drops. BOSR:92

TOYNBEE, ARNOLD J.
Brorby, M.
Introduces Arnold J. Toyn-
bee, professor, author and
historian of Great Britain.
LYI:86

TRADE See Business; Commerce

TRADE REGULATION
Marcus, S.
Can free enterprise survive
success? BA 1975-76:152
Speth, G.
Environmental regulation
and the immobilization of
truth. BA 1979-80:145

TRADE UNION (POLITICAL FUND)
BILL
Baldwin, S. B., 1st Earl of
Bewdley
Good will in industry.
MCB:243; STRM:433

TRADE UNIONS See Labor
Unions

Trafton, Cathy
The moral dimensions of the
world food problem.
BREWW:206

TRAITORS See Treason

TRANQUILIZING DRUGS
Rindo, J. P.
Life, librium, and the pur-
suit of happiness.
LINRST:230

TRANSISTORS
Bardeen, J.
Semiconductor research
leading to the point contact
transistor. NOLPH 3:318
Shockley, W.
Transistor technology evokes
new physics. NOLPH 3:344

TRANSMUTATION
Joliot, J. F.
Chemical evidence of the
transmutation of elements.
NOLC 2:369

TRANSPLANTATION OF ORGANS,
TISSUES, ETC.
Carrel, A.
Suture of blood-vessels and
transplantation of organs.
NOLM 1:442

TRANSPORTATION See Railroads;
Roads

TRANSURANIUM ELEMENTS
McMillan, E. M.
The transuranium elements:
early history. NOLC 3:314
Seaborg, G. T.
The transuranium elements:
present status. NOLC 3:325

TRAVEL
Benton, T. H.
"There is East; there is India."
BREWE 2:429

---- See also Railroads

TREASON
Erskine, T.
In defense of Thomas Hardy.
BREWE 6:2066

TREATIES
Ames, F.
Jay Treaty. BREWE 1:156
Barbour, J.
Treaties as supreme laws.
BREWE 1:209
Clayton, J. M.
Clayton-Bulwer treaty and ex-
pansion. BREWE 4:1283
Macdonald, J. A.
On the treaty of Washington.
BREWE 8:2891

TRIAL BY JURY
Black, H. L.
United States v. Lovett, Watson, and Dodd: opinion for
the court. ANN 16:404

TRIBUTES
Abdul Rahman, T.
Dato Onn--a great leader.
MONS:33

Adams, J. Q.
Life and character of Lafay-
ette. BREWE 1:79
Brooks, P.
Character of Abraham Lin-
coln. BREWE 2:644
Cox, S. S.
Stephen A. Douglas and his
place in history.
BREWE 4:1449
Dewey, O.
Genius of Demosthenes.
BREWE 5:1822
Emerson, R. W.
Memory of Burns.
HURH:106
Fox, C. J.
Character of the Duke of
Bedford. BREWE 6:2182
Hageman, M.
Wisdom of the heart.
SCHW:177
Holmes, O. W.
Dorothy Q. HURH:139
Holmes, O. W., Jr.
John Marshall. FRIP:257
Ingersoll, R. G.
At his brother's grave.
ALA:69; BREWE 7:2580;
HURH:156
Jacobusse, K. D.
Big man. SCHW:204
Johnson, L. B.
Remarks to a Joint Session
of the Congress, November
27, 1963. ANN 18:203
Kennedy, E. M.
Tribute to Senator Robert F.
Kennedy. BA 1967-68:174;
LINRS:303
Laurier, W.
Character and work of Glad-
stone. BREWE 7:2732
Macmillan, H.
Tribute to President Kennedy.
ALA:135
Mill, J. S.
A tribute to William Lloyd
Garrison. REID:395
Nair, C. V. D.
Reflections on Rabindranath
Tagore. MONS:190
Ramani, R.
Man of clear vision (tribute
to Adlai E. Stevenson).
MONS:250
Reid, C. T.
Tribute to Dwight D. Eisen-

hower. BA 1968-1969:165
Roosevelt, F. D.
Undelivered Jefferson Day ad-
dress. MDV:32
Stanley, A. P.
Palmerston and the duty of
England (funeral oration).
BREWE 9:3506
Stevenson, A. E.
Tribute to John F. Kennedy
at the General Assembly of
the United Nations. GRG:122;
HURH:371
Tribute to a pastor's wife (2
examples). BNH:77
Vander Jagt, G.
John Marshall. SCHW:201
Vest, G. G.
Man's best friend--his dog.
ALA:45; HURH:161
Wang, G. W.
Tribute to Dr. Azkir Husain
(presenting him with Doctor
of Laws degree). MONS:277
Wise, S. S.
Abraham Lincoln, man and
American. HURH:169

---- See also Commemorative addresses; Eulogies; Memorial
speeches; Responses to tributes

Trilling, Lionel
Presents T. S. Eliot. LYI:35

Trimble, Al
Keynote address NCAI Conven-
tion, October 18, 1976.
MAES:233

Trimble, Chuck
Harmony--from where the sun
now stands (1974). MAES:388

Trippe, Juan T.
Presents Vannevar Bush.
LYI:177

Trotter, Virginia Karp
A shift in the balance. (Kansas
State University, Feb. 15,
1975). BA 1974-75:148

Trotter, William Monroe
How I managed to reach the
Peace Conference. (Boston,
July, 1919). FON:740
Segregation destroys fellowship

and citizenship. (Washington, 1914). FON:702

Truckman, Bill
Presidential eligibility.
REIR:107 (outline)

Trudell, John
Commitment. MAES:83

Truman, Harry S.
Acceptance speech, Democratic
Party National Convention
(Philadelphia, July 15,
1948). OLIS:262; SIN:220
Aid to Greece and Turkey.
ANN 16:434; GRG:76;
LAA:49
Announcement of the dropping
of an atomic bomb on
Hiroshima. Same as his
Announcement of the first
use of the atomic bomb
Announcement of the first use
of the atomic bomb.
ANN 16:334
Campaign speech, Harlem,
New York, October 29,
1948. SIN:226
Civil Rights (February 2, 1948).
ANN 16:510
Eighth annual message. Same
as his Fair Deal in retro-
spect, January 7, 1953
Fair Deal in retrospect, Janu-
ary 7, 1953. STAT 3:2993
Fifth annual message. Same
as his State of the Union
(1950)
First annual message.
STAT 3:2900
Fourth annual message.
STAT 3:2961
Inaugural address. ANN 16:561;
BOORA 2:891; USINAU:251
Korea and the policy of con-
tainment. Same as his
Preventing a new world war
Korean crisis. Same as his
Preventing a new world war
Navy Day speech on foreign
policy. ANN 16:393
"Our government cannot func-
tion properly unless the
President is master in his
own house." Same as his
Power so the President
Point Four Program.

ANN 16:595
Postwar foreign policy. Same
as his Navy Day speech on
foreign policy
Powers of the President. (New
York, May 8, 1954).
HURH:316
Presents George C. Marshall.
LYI:141
Presents Winston Churchill.
LYI:211
Preventing a new world war.
ANN 17:75; BAP:291
Second annual message.
STAT 3:2939
Seventh annual message. Same
as his State of the Union
(1952)
Sixth annual message.
STAT 3:2976
State of the Union (1950).
STAT 3:2967
State of the Union (1952).
STAT 3:2984
Third annual message.
STAT 3:2951
Truman doctrine. Same as his
Aid to Greece and Turkey
Veto of the Internal Security Act.
ANN 17:35
Veto of the McCarran-Walter
Immigration Act. ANN 17:131

TRUMAN, HARRY S.
Clifford, C. M.
We must renew our confidence.
BA 1972-73:109
Webb, W. P.
Presents Harry S. Truman.
LYI:193

TRUMAN DOCTRINE See Reconstruction, 1939-1951

Trumbull, Lyman
Announcing the death of Douglas.
BREWE 9:3654

---- See also Johnson, A., jt. auth.

TRUSTS, INDUSTRIAL
Brooks, T. J.
Antitrust laws as applied to
farmers. ANN 13:331
Harlan, J. M. and others
Northern Securities Company
v. United States, 1904:
opinion for the court and

dissenting opinion.
ANN 12:576
Jones, A. and others
Trusts in America.
ANN 12:279
McKenna, J. and others
United States v. United States
Steel Corporation et al:
opinion for the court and
dissenting opinion.
ANN 14:258
Roosevelt, T.
Eighth annual message.
STAT 3:2296
Fifth annual message.
ANN 13:1; STAT 3:2144
First annual message.
ANN 12:433; STAT 2:2014
"I took the Canal Zone."
STAT 2:2073
Second annual message.
STAT 2:2053
Seventh annual message.
STAT 3:2240
Taft, W. H.
Third annual message: part
I, December 5, 1911.
STAT 3:2432
White, E. D. and others
Standard Oil Company of
New Jersey v. United
States, 1911; opinion for
the court and dissenting
opinion. ANN 13:310

---- See also Capitalism; Corporations; Monopolies

Truth, Sojourner
When woman gets her rights
man will be right. (New
York, May 9 and 10, 1867).
FON:345
Woman's rights. (Akron, Ohio,
1851. Woman's Rights Con-
vention). FON:100

TRUTHFULNESS AND FALSE-
HOOD
Dod, A. B.
Value of truth.
BREWE 5:1885
Mathias, C. M.
Truth in government.
BA 1972-73:60
Morley of Blackburn, J. M.
Golden art of truth-telling.
BREWE 8:3068

Shaw, G. B.
Truth by radio.   JEF:396;
JEFF:378
Tillich, P. J.
"What is truth?" ARS:180

Tuan Haji Ali bin Munawar
Religion in Malay society.
MONS:308

Tuanku Abdul Rahman Ibni Al-
Marhum Tuanku Mohammed
See Rhaman, (Paramount
Ruler) Abdul d. 1960

TUBERCULOSIS
Koch, R.
The current state of the strug-
gle against tuberculosis.
NOLM 1:169

Tucker, Benjamin R. See Jones,
A., jt. auth.

Tun Abdul Razak See Razak,
Tun Abdul

Tun Dr. Ismail See Rahman, Dr.
Ismail bin Abdul

Tun Sir Henry H. S. Lee See
Lee, Sir Henry Hau Shik

Tunku Abdul Rahman See Abdul
Rahman, Tunku

Tuohy, Frank
Three windows on Japan.
MDYG:161

TURENNE, HENRI
Flechier, E.
Death of Turenne.
BREWE 6:2174

Turitz, Leo E.
Measure of greatness. WALE:192

TURKEY
Hird, P.
Suffer suffer Yeddy.
MDYG:66
Truman, H. S.
Aid to Greece and Turkey.
ANN 16:434; GRG:76; LAA:49

Turner, Frederick Jackson
Sectionalism and national unity.
ANN 14:493

Turner, Henry McNeal
  How long? How long, O
    Heaven? (Philadelphia,
    August 5, 1876). FON:445
  I claim the rights of a man.
    (Georgia, Sept. 3, 1868).
    FON:357
  Justice or emigration should
    be our watchword. (Cin-
    cinnati, Nov. 1893).
    FON:561
  Reasons for a new political
    party. (Atlanta, Ga., Feb.
    12, 1886). FON:504

Turner, Jonathan Baldwin
  Industrial university for Illinois.
    ANN 8:157

TURNER, NAT
  Handy, A. W.
    Nat Turner. FON:538

Tweed, Harrison
  Presents Dillon Anderson.
    LYI:125
  Presents Hartley Shawcross.
    LYI:123

Tyler, John
  First annual message.
    STAT 1:566
  Fourth annual message.
    STAT 1:613
  From the sinks of Europe a
    plotter has come. (Glou-
    cester Courthouse, Va.,
    1835). DAVF:140
  Second annual message.
    STAT 1:581
  Third annual message.
    STAT 1:598

TYLER, JOHN
  Clay, H.
    Noblest public virtue.
    BREWE 4:1271

Tyndall, John
  Democracy and higher in-
    tellect. BREWE 9:3668
  Origin of life.
    BREWE 9:3664

Tyndale, William
  Use and abuse of images and
    relics. BREWE 9:3660

TYPHUS FEVER
  Nicolle, C. J. H.
    Investigations on typhus.
    NOLM 2:180

TYRANNY
  Fox, C. J.
    On the East India Bill.
    BREWE 6:2189
  Knox, J.
    Against tyrants.
    BREWE 7:2665
  Penn, W.
    Golden rule against tyranny.
    BREWE 8:3162

- U -

Udall, Morris K.
  United States and Vietnam--what
    lies ahead.
    BA 1967-68:21

Uewaki, T.
  Discovery of hidden mineral
    veins with the aid of plants
    and animals, etc. (Los Baños,
    Laguna, March 1, 1935).
    CURM:292

UNAMERICAN ACTIVITIES See
    United States - Congress -
    House of Representatives -
    Committee on UnAmerican
    Activities

UNDERDEVELOPED AREAS
  Muhammad Ghazali bin Shafie
    The most dramatic fact of
    international life. MONSA:130
  Rajaratnam, S.
    Urgency of real problems fac-
    ing the less developed nations.
    MONSA:295

---- FOREIGN RELATIONS
  Razak, T. A.
    Problems of war and peace.
    MONSA:15

Undset, Sigrid
  Acceptance [of the Nobel Prize
    for Literature, 1928].
    NOB 18:167; NOL:255

UNDSET, SIGRID
  Hallström, P.
    Presentation [of the Nobel
    Prize for Literature to
    Sigrid Undset, 1928].
    NOB 18:163; NOL:251

UNEMPLOYED
  Coffman, L. D.
    Adult education for the un-
    employed.   ANN 15:98
  Herndon, A.
    Give the people bread.
    FON:770
  Hopkins, H.
    "... they are just like the
    rest of us." ROD:127
  Nixon, R. M.
    A new economic policy.
    BAAE:263
  Wagner, R. F.
    To feed the hungry.   ROD:77

---- BLACKS
  Jordan, V. E.
    Unfinished business.
    BA 1975-76:88

Ungku Omar Ahmad
  Two countries in one.
  MONS:331

UNION PARTY
  Coughlin, C. E.
    Money changers in the temple.
    ANN 15:388
  Lemke, W.
    Introduction of the aims of
    the Union Party of the
    United States.   BAD:117

UNIONS, TRADE See Labor
  unions

UNITED FARM WORKERS OR-
  GANIZATION COMMITTEE
  Wright, T.
    "Viva la Huelga."
    BREWW:174

UNITED MALAY NATIONAL
  ORGANISATION
  Razak, T. A.
    We will uphold concepts of
    parliamentary democracy.
    MONSA:41 selections

UNITED NATIONAL ORGANIZATION
  Razak, T. A.

UMNO's twentieth milestone
  (20th anniversary of United
  Malay National Organization).
  MONS:53

UNITED NATIONS
  Attlee, C. R.
    Speech in Commons on the
    United Nations Charter.
    MCB:536
  Churchill, W. L. S.
    Sinews of peace (speech at
    Fulton, Missouri).
    ANN 16:365; MCB:541
  De Tuncq, D.
    UN: symbol or reality?
    SCHW:165
  Evatt, H. V.
    Australia and the United Na-
    tions charter.   MC:161
  Fraser, P.
    Universal collective security--
    amendments to the United Na-
    tions Charter, 1945.
    MACS:378 sel.
  Hoover, H. C.
    United Nations.   HURH:287
  Lodge, H. C., Jr.
    United Nations.   HURH:344
  McKeever, P.
    The United States and the
    United Nations.   BRYF:479
  Moynihan, D. P.
    World wide amnesty for poli-
    tical prisoners.
    BA 1975-76:65
  Paul VI
    Address before United Nations.
    BA 1965-66:67; OLIS:297
  Rajaratnam, S.
    Faith in United Nations charter
    (on admission of Singapore).
    MONS:421
    Urgency of real problems fac-
    ing the less developed nations.
    MONSA:295
  Ramani, R.
    Twenty four days in May (ex-
    pression of thanks as President
    of Security Council of United
    Nations).   MONS:248
  Roosevelt, E. A.
    United Nations.   HURH:297
  Stevenson, A. E.
    Meaning of the United Nations.
    ANN 18:317
  Thant, U.
    Future of the United Nations.
    MDV:45

Vandenberg, A. H.
Sovereignty and the United
Nations. ANN 16:331

---- HIGH COMMISSIONER FOR
REFUGEES
Jahn, G.
Presentation of the Nobel
Prize for Peace to the Of-
fice of the United Nations
High Commissioner for
Refugees, Dec. 10, 1955.
NOLP 3:89

UNITED NATIONS CHILDREN'S
FUND
Harmann, Z.
UNICEF: achievement and
challenge (Nobel Lecture,
Dec. 11, 1965).
NOLP 3:365
Lionaes, A.
Presentation of the Nobel
Prize for Peace to the
United Nations Children's
Fund, Dec. 10, 1965.
NOLP 3:353

UNITED PARTY - NEW ZEALAND
Ward, Sir J.
The 1928 election.
MACS:311 sel.

UNITED STATES
Berrien, J. M.
Effect of the Mexican con-
quest. BREWE 2:439
Brownlow, W. G.
Value of the American
Union. BREWE 2:690
Buteyn, D. P.
Invisible abutments.
SCHW:44
Calhoun, J. C.
On the internal improve-
ment, 1817. ANN 4:457
Carter, J.
Fireside chat: unity on
U. S. goals. LINRST:340
The inaugural address.
BA 1976-77:18; JAM:38
Choate, R.
On American nationality
(82nd anniversary of Amer-
ican independence).
ANN 9:54
Clay, C. M.
America as a moral force.

BREWE 3:1213
Aspirations for the Union.
BREWE 3:1212
Clay, H.
In favor of a paternal policy
of internal improvements.
BREWE 4:1260
Internal improvements and the
powers of Congress.
ANN 4:482
Clayton, J. M.
Clayton-Bulwer treaty and ex-
pansion. BREWE 4:1283
Clifford, C. M.
We must renew our confidence.
BA 1972-73:109
Cobden, R.
Small states and great achieve-
ments. BREWE 4:1336
Coolidge, C.
Destiny of America.
ANN 14:409
Cox, A.
Can the dream survive?
BA 1979-80:157
Dilke, C. W.
America. BREWE 5:1873
Dow, L., Jr.
Improvement in America.
BREWE 5:1933
Emerson, R. W.
Young American. ANN 7:182
Hains, J.
Lamp of freedom. SCHW:6
Harding, W. G.
"It is our purpose to prosper
America first." ANN 14:292
Houtman, M.
Dangers of security.
SCHW:54
Humphrey, H. H., Jr.
I am optimistic about America.
BA 1977-78:192
Ingersoll, C. J.
Influence of America on the
mind. ANN 5:95
Johnson, L. B.
State of the Union Message,
January 8, 1964.
STAT 3:3156
Jones, J. L.
Who is tampering with the
soul of America?
LINR:211; LINRS:220
Lee, W. L.
Through the looking glass.
SCHW:106
Lippmann, W.

Our world today. MDV:26
McGill, R. E.
  Meaning of Lincoln today
  (centennial of Lincoln's
  speech at Cooper Institute).
  LINS:360
Marshall, T. R.
  National power and the
  American peace policy (on
  public land sales, 1841).
  BREWE 8:2964
Nixon, R. M.
  State of the Union message,
  1972. BA 1971-72:13
Parker, T.
  State of the nation (1850).
  ANN 8:114
Pennings, B.
  New men for a new world.
  SCHW:153
Roosevelt, F. D.
  Immigrants and revolution-
  ists. ALA:93
Schura, C.
  True Americanism.
  ANN 9:97
Truman, H. S.
  State of the Union (1950).
  STAT 3:2967
  State of the Union (1952).
  STAT 3:2984
Van Voorst, B.
  Clock. SCHW:74
Worden, G.
  Publican. SCHW:92

---- See also New England; Sectionalism (United States);
  Southern States; West, The.
  Also Annual messages under
  name of each President i.e.
  Jackson, A. First annual
  message

---- ARMY
Depew, C. M.
  Military spirit in America.
  BREWE 5:1785
LaFollette, R. M., Sr.
  Soldier's pay. GRG:36
Nies, N.
  Warrior and the woman.
  SCHW:10
Roosevelt, T.
  Seventh annual message.
  STAT 3:2240
Washington, G.
  Address to the officers of
  the army. ANN 2:598

---- See also Army Appropriation
  Act; Conscription; Veterans -
  Education

---- BUDGET
Muskie, E. S.
  Too many questions ... not
  enough answers.
  BA 1978-79:112

---- BUREAU OF INDIAN AFFAIRS
Sockey, C. E.
  Excellence in Indian education.
  MAES:141
Thompson, M.
  The BIA at work. MAES:57

---- CONGRESS
Clay, H.
  Internal improvements and the
  powers of Congress.
  ANN 4:482
Hughes, C. E.
  150th anniversary of the First
  Congress. HURH:237
Marshall, J.
  Marbury v. Madison: opinion
  for the Supreme Court.
  ANN 4:165
Rayburn, S.
  Impressive accomplishments
  (75th Congress). BAD:83
Roosevelt, F. D.
  Message to Congress, January
  4, 1939. STAT 3:2842
  Message to Congress on the
  state of the nation, January 6,
  1945. STAT 3:2882
Taft, W. H.
  Fourth annual message; part
  III, December 19, 1912.
  ANN 13:366; STAT 3:2531
Wilson, W.
  Appeal to the voters to return
  a Democratic Congress.
  ANN 14:166

---- For Annual addresses of various Presidents to Congress
  See Names of Presidents
  e.g. Roosevelt, F. D. First
  annual message

---- ---- HOUSE OF REPRE-
  SENTATIVES - COMMITTEE
  ON UNAMERICAN ACTIVITIES
Bosman, R. A.
  Witch hunt. SCHW:128

the Constitution, June 20,
1788. FRIP:90
McCulloch v. Maryland:
opinion for the Supreme
Court. ANN 4:530;
BOORA 1:241
Martin, L.
Is the government federal
or national? BREWE 8:2970
Portion of the report of
the proceedings of the Gen-
eral Convention held at
Philadelphia in 1787.
ANN 3:166
Mason, G.
Natural propensity of rulers
to oppress. BREWE 8:2976
---- and others
Debates in the Virginia
Ratifying Convention.
ANN 3:278
Monroe, J.
Federal experiments in
history. BREWE 8:3041
Pendleton, E.
Liberty and government in
America. BREWE 8:3156
Randolph, A. P.
The crisis of the Negro and
the Constitution. FON:816
Roosevelt, F. D.
Address on Constitution
Day, September 17, 1937.
FRIP:317
Message to Congress, Janu-
ary 11, 1944. ANN 16:211;
ROD:337; STAT 3:2875
Root, E.
Invisible government: Short
Ballot Amendment.
ANN 13:528
Smith, J.
On the Federal Constitution.
ARN:385; ARS:272

---- ---- See also State rights.
Also names of Bills and
Resolution e.g. Foot's
Resolution

---- DECLARATION OF INDE-
PENDENCE
Burger, W. E.
Bicentennial of American
independence. BA 1976-77:185
Everheart, W. E.
We hold these truths.
BA 1975-76:27

---- ---- See also Fourth of July

---- DEFENSES
Dulles, J. F.
Strategy of massive retalia-
tion. ANN 17:250
Eisenhower, D. D.
State of the Union (January 9,
1958). STAT 3:3076
Goldwater, B. M.
Why we must be stronger
militarily. BAS:92 (outline
only); LAA:8
Kennedy, J. F.
Address to the nation, October
22, 1962. ANN 18:140;
LAA:147; MUS:340
Undelivered Dallas speech.
ANN 18:197
McNamara, R. S.
Military hardware, economic
assistance and civic action.
ANN 18:356
Nuclear strategy. ANN 18:527
Nixon, R. M.
Question of survival; the anti-
ballistic missile system.
BA 1968-69:9
Roosevelt, F. D.
Republican leadership and na-
tional defense. ANN 16:36
Wiesner, J. B.
Argument against the ABM.
BA 1968-1969:19

---- ECONOMIC CONDITIONS
Ameringer, O.
Overproduction and undercon-
sumption. ANN 15:129
Brandeis, L. D.
Danger of inaction: dissenting
opinion for the Supreme Court
on New State Ice Co. v.
Liebmann, 1931. ROD:73
Church, F.
The yen to make a mark with
the dollar. BA 1978-79:168
Cleveland, G.
Third annual message (second
term). STAT 2:1794
Connor, J. T.
Impact on the American econ-
omy of the Vietnamese pro-
gram. BA 1969-70:47
Cram, R. A.
What is a free man?
ANN 15:498
Eisenhower, D. D.

Third annual message.
STAT 3:3038
Ford, G. R.
State of the Union ad-
dress. JAM:31
Friedman, M.
The future of capitalism.
LINRST:243
Herndon, A.
Give the people bread.
FON:779
Hoover, H. C.
Fourth annual message.
STAT 3:3038
Holy crusade for liberty.
BAD:53
In defense of tradition.
(Detroit, 1932). ROD:39
Reassuring touch: Presi-
dent Hoover speaks, 1931.
ROD:15
Road to freedom.
ANN 15:384
Second annual message.
STAT 3:2772
Third annual message.
STAT 3:2783
Hopkins, H. L.
18,000,000 on relief.
ANN 15:261
Humphrey, H. H., Jr.
Anniversary of war on
poverty. CAPG:174
Johnson, L. B.
War on poverty.
ANN 18:212
LaFollette, P. F.
Party of our time.
BAD:120
Long, H. P.
Sharing our wealth (January,
1935 radio speech).
ANN 15:318; BAD:109
Muench, A.
Rural families and welfare.
ANN 15:462
Roosevelt, F. D.
Address to the Common-
wealth Club, September 23,
1932. ANN 15:158;
ROD:31; SIN:77
American business is mov-
ing ahead. BAD:1
Fifth annual message.
STAT 3:2833
Fireside chat on the ac-
complishments of the New
Deal. ANN 15:263

First annual message.
STAT 3:2806
Fourth annual message.
STAT 3:2827
Second annual message.
ANN 15:309; ROD:106;
STAT 3:2811
What the New Deal has done
for business (campaign speech
in Chicago, October 14, 1936).
ANN 15:379
Schwellenbach, L. B.
First seven years of the New
Deal: let's view the record.
BAD:47
Shriver, S.
Address at the Chicago Anti-
poverty Conference.
CAPG:180
Snell, B.
Bankruptcy and moral disinte-
gration. BAD:90
Taft, R. A.
Declaration of Republican
principles--the New Deal is
rapidly receding. BAD:74
New problems of government.
ANN 15:571
Truman, H. S.
Fair Deal in retrospect, Janu-
ary 7, 1953. STAT 3:2993
Van Buren, M.
Against government aid for
business losses. ANN 6:314
Wagner, R. F.
To feed the hungry. ROD:77
Wallace, H. A.
Pigs and pig iron. ANN 15:336
Webster, D.
Reception at Madison, Indiana.
OLIS:36
Wirtz, W. W.
Economic Opportunity Act of
1964. CAPG:165

---- ---- See also Business cycles;
National Recovery Administration; Also Annual messages
under name of each President
i.e. Arthur, C. A. Third
annual address

---- ECONOMIC POLICY
Chisholm, S.
Economic injustice in America
today. BA 1971-72:27
Eccles, M. S.
Government spending is sound.

BAD:29
Landon, A. M.
Action challenged.   ROD:162
Nixon, R. M.
A new economic policy.
BAAE:263
Romney, G.
Our unique economic prin-
ciples: the market place
should determine price.
CAPG:40
Roosevelt, F. D.
Action defended (campaign
speech, October 31, 1936).
ROD:168
Wagner, R. F.
Pump-priming--it is neces-
sary for business recovery.
BAD:44
Wallace, H. A.
Economic bill of rights.
ANN 16:268

---- ---- See also Laissez-faire;
United States - Foreign
Relations

---- FEDERAL TRADE COM-
MISSION
Engman, L. A.
Federal Trade Commission.
TAC:214

---- FOREIGN POLICY
Goldwater, B. M.
Campaign speech, Washington,
D.C., October 21, 1964.
SIN:345

---- ---- See United States -
Foreign Relations

---- FOREIGN RELATIONS
Acheson, D.
Marshall Plan; relief and
reconstruction are chiefly
matters of American self-
interest. LAA:55
Strategy of freedom.
ANN 17:42
Baldwin, R. S.
Executive prerogative in
foreign policy.   ANN 7:423
Bray, C. W.
De-mystifying anti-Ameri-
canism.   BA 1979-80:38
Bush, G.
Views of US foreign policy

in the future.   BA 1978-79:159
Calhoun, J. C.
Against general resolutions
on foreign affairs.   ANN 7:336
Cass, L. and others
Suitability of moral declarations
in foreign policy.   ANN 8:167
Dulles, J. F.
Containment or liberation?
ANN 17:204
Modern foreign policy.
HURH:324
Eisenhower, D. D.
Price of peace: second in-
augural address.
USINAU:263; USINAUG:263
Fillmore, M.
First annual message.
ANN 8:109; STAT 1:792
Fulbright, J. W.
Arrogance of power.
ANN 18:362
Foreign policy--old myths and
new realities.   ANN 18:225;
HURH:374
Two Americas.
BA 1965-66:115
Goldwater, B. M.
Total victory in the Cold War.
ANN 18:42
Hoover, H. C.
Our national policies in this
crisis.   ANN 17:46
Humphrey, H. H.
Problem-solution division: a
speech on the open-door policy.
JEF:238; JEFF:207
Johnson, L. B.
Obligation of power.
ANN 18:368
Our foreign policy must al-
ways be an extension of this
nation's domestic policy.
LAA:3
Second annual message.
STAT 3:3161
Kennedy, J. F.
Long twilight struggle.
ANN 18:54
Kissinger, H. A.
America's permanent interests.
BA 1975-76:48
A review of the foreign policy.
BA 1979-80:9
Statement to the Senate For-
eign Relations Committee.
BA 1973-74:87
Lodge, H. C., Jr.

United Nations. HURH:344
MacArthur, D.
Defends his conduct of the
war in Korea. ALS:243;
ANN 17:79; ARS:279;
BAS:82 (outline only);
BEN:113; BOSR:22; GRG:88;
HURH:293; HURS:214;
LINS:337
McNamara, R. S.
Address before the American
Society of Newspaper Editors.
BA 1966-67:160
Military hardware, economic
assistance, and civic action.
ANN 18:356
Nuclear strategy. ANN 18:527
Morse, W. L.
Need for a bipartisan for-
eign policy. ANN 17:11
Mumford, L.
Human way out. MDV:13
Nixon, R. M. and others
Opening statements: the
fourth debate. GRG:106
Roosevelt, A. E.
Defense of American terri-
torial policies. ANN 17:128
Roosevelt, F. D.
First war address before
Congress. HURH:269;
STAT 3:2861
Four human freedoms.
ANN 16:42; ROD:278;
STAT 3:2855
Message to Congress,
January 4, 1939.
STAT 3:2842
Restating American foreign
policy: FDR's Chautauqua
speech, 1936. ROD:252
Seventh annual message.
STAT 3:2849
Third annual message.
STAT 3:2819
Root, E.
European War and the
preservation of America's
ideals. ANN 14:70
Rusk, D.
Formulating foreign policy.
ANN 18:20
Sanford, T.
After Vietnam, a new
United States foreign policy.
HOR:132
Steele, H.
House that Sam built.

SCHW:25
Stevenson, A. E.
Foreign policy: the shades of
gray. MDV:56
Taft, W. H.
Fourth annual message: part
I, December 3, 1912.
ANN 13:369
Third annual message: part
II, December 7, 1911.
STAT 3:2444
Truman, H. S.
Fair Deal in retrospect,
January 7, 1953. STAT 3:2993
First annual message.
STAT 3:2900
Navy Day speech on foreign
policy. ANN 16:393
State of the Union (1952).
STAT 3:2984
Vance, C. R.
Human rights and the foreign
policy. BA 1976-77:127
Wallace, H. A.
Is American foreign policy
leading to war? ANN 16:370
Wilson, W.
Second annual message.
STAT 3:2551

---- ---- See also Economic as-
sistance, American; Monroe
Doctrine; United States -
Neutrality; World War, 1939-
1945 - United States - Aid to
Great Britain; See also Annual
messages under name of each
President, i.e. Jackson, A.
Second annual message

---- ---- AFRICA
Fabunmi, L.
Black and white keys.
SCHW:206
Kaunda, K.
Toast to President Ford.
JAM:23
Ngwa, J.
Africa and the United States--
partners for peace.
SCHW:192

---- ---- BARBARY STATES
Jefferson, T.
First annual message.
STAT 1:58

---- ---- CANADA
Bright, J.

Will the United States sub-
jugate Canada?
BREWE 2:620
Laurier, W.
Canada, England and the
United States in 1899.
BREWE 7:2737
Stevenson, A. E.
Today's most fateful fact
(accepting honorary degree
of Doctor of Laws). OLIS:272

---- ---- CHINA
Brzezinski, Z.
Our China policy in a wider
context. BA 1978-79:150
Fulbright, J. W.
Two Americas.
BA 1965-66:115
Kennedy, E. M.
China policy for the seventies.
BA 1968-1969:73
McGovern, G.
Ignorance curtain vs. the
open door. BA 1966-67:48
Mondale, W. F.
Strengthening Sino-American
relations. BA 1979-80:28

---- ---- CUBA
Castro, F.
Cuba is no longer an Amer-
ican colony. LAA:127
Kennedy, J. F.
Address to the nation, Octo-
ber 22, 1962. ANN 18:140;
LAA:147; MUS:340
Stevenson, A. E.
Bay of Pigs. ANN 18:25
Premeditated attempt: the
building of the sites.
LINR:87; LINRS:93

---- ---- DOMINICAN REPUBLIC
Fulbright, J. W.
Intervention in Santo Domingo:
we are much closer to being
the most unrevolutionary
nation on earth. LAA:165
Johnson, L. B.
Johnson doctrine; why the
United States intervened in
the Dominican Republic.
LAA:160

---- ---- EAST (FAR EAST)
Brooke, E. W.
Report on Vietnam and

East Asia. BA 1966-67:23
Harriman, W. A.
Challenges to peace and free-
dom. ANN 18:328
McGovern, G.
Ignorance curtain vs. the open
door. BA 1966-67:48
Mansfield, M. J.
Pacific perspective.
BA 1968-69:98
Reischauer, E. O.
Statement before the Senate
Foreign Relations Committee.
BA 1966-67:70

---- ---- EUROPE
Humphrey, H. H., Jr.
Open door (21st anniversary
of Churchill's "Iron Curtain"
speech). LINR:236

---- ---- FRANCE
Adams, J.
Third annual address.
STAT 1:49
Jackson, A.
Seventh annual message.
ANN 6:164; STAT 1:415
Sixth annual message.
STAT 1:389

---- ---- GREAT BRITAIN
Depew, C. M.
England and America since the
Spanish War. BREWE 5:1790
Douglas, S. A.
"Expansion" and co-operation
with England. BREWE 5:1918
Laurier, W.
Canada, England, and the
United States in 1899.
BREWE 7:2737
Madison, J.
Third annual message.
STAT 1:111
See also World War, 1939-1945 -
United States - Aid to Great
Britain

---- ---- GREECE
Truman, H. S.
Aid to Greece and Turkey.
ANN 16:434; GRG:76; LAA:49
Webster, D. and others
Debate on the Greek Revolu-
tion. ANN 5:108

---- ---- LATIN AMERICA
Fulbright, J. W.

Boucher, J.
  Civil liberty and nonre-
  sistance. ANN 2:343;
  POC:552
Burke, E.
  Conciliation with America.
  ALS:29 (with analysis);
  ANN 2:312; BREWE 2:806;
  CLAYP:50; STRM:39
Dickinson, J.
  Before the Pennsylvania As-
  sembly, March 24, 1760.
  POC:182
  Declaration of the Colonies
  on taking up arms.
  BREWE 5:1849
  Speech against independence.
  ANN 2:438
Galloway, J.
  Speech for the petition to
  change the form of govern-
  ment. POC:200
Henry, P.
  Liberty or death. ANN 2:321;
  BAS:39 (outline only);
  BEN:13; BREWE 7:2473;
  HURH:27; HURS:209;
  OLIS:22; POC:305
Howard, J. A.
  "... our sacred honor."
  BA 1975-76:9
Hutchinson, T.
  Speech to both Houses.
  POC:280
Jay, J.
  Protest against colonial
  government.
  BREWE 7:2601
Lee, R. H.
  Address to the people of
  England. BREWE 7:2752
Morton, P.
  Oration at the reinterment
  of Warren. POC:320
Pitt, W., 1708-1778
  Address to the throne con-
  cerning affairs in America,
  November 18, 1777.
  ALS:105; BREWE 3:1067;
  BRYH:201
  On American policy, Janu-
  ary 20, 1775. CLAYP:40
  On the right to tax America.
  STRM:11
Quincy, J., 1744-1775
  "Let us look to the end."
  POC:295
Rutledge, J.

Speech in time of revolution.
  BREWE 9:3368; POC:325
Tooke, J. H.
  On the "Murders at Lexington
  and Concord" (at his trial for
  libel). BREWE 9:3633
Varnum, J. M. and others
  Disputation on "Whether Brit-
  ish America can under present
  circumstances consistent with
  good policy, affect to become
  an independent state."
  POC:14
Warren, J.
  Constitutional liberty and ar-
  bitrary power.
  BREWE 10:3727
Washington, G.
  Address to the officers of the
  army. ANN 2:598
West, S.
  Election sermon. POC:578
Wilkes, J.
  Warning and a prophecy.
  BREWE 10:3901
Wilson, J.
  In vindication of the colonies.
  POC:308
Zubly, J. J.
  Law of liberty. POC:611

---- ---- See also Boston Massacre, 1770; Boston Tea Party,
  1773; Great Britain - Colonies

---- ---- CONFEDERATION
Barlow, J.
  Unfinished revolution.
  ANN 3:90
Witherspoon, J.
  Public credit under the Con-
  federation. BREWE 10:3912

---- ---- WAR OF 1812
Brougham and Vaux, H. P. B.
  Against Pitt and war with
  America. BREWE 2:661
Clay, H.
  Free trade and seamen's
  rights. BREWE 4:1264
  On the War of 1812.
  ANN 4:327
German, O.
  Unprepared for war with Eng-
  land. ANN 4:319
Grundy, F. and others
  Debate over war with England.
  ANN 4:291

Madison, J.
 Fifth annual message.
  STAT 1:122
 Fourth annual message.
  STAT 1:115
 Seventh annual message.
  STAT 1:133
 Sixth annual message.
  STAT 1:129
 War message. ANN 4:314
Quincy, J., 1772-1864
 Against conquest of Canada.
  BREWE 9:3274
Rush, R.
 Fourth of July oration,
  1812. HAW:16
Webster, D.
 Against conscription.
  ANN 4:355

---- ---- WAR WITH MEXICO
Cadwell, D.
 Oration. HAW:319
Corwin, T.
 War with Mexico.
  BREWE 4:1405; HOW:203
Dayton, W. L.
 Arraigning President Polk.
  BREWE 5:1676
Polk, J. K.
 Fourth annual message.
  STAT 1:731
 Second annual message.
  STAT 1:664
 Third annual message.
  ANN 7:374; STAT 1:699

---- ---- CIVIL WAR
Adams, C. F.
 States and the Union.
  BREWE 1:25
Adams, C. F., Jr.
 Battle of Gettysburg.
  BREWE 1:31
Allen, E.
 Call to arms (1861).
  BREWE 1:150
Beecher, H. W.
 Liverpool speech, October
  16, 1863. LINS:229
 Raising the flag over Fort
  Sumter. BREWE 1:347
 Success of American democ-
  racy (anniversary of attack
  on Fort Sumter). OLIS:191
Bell, J.
 Against extremism, North
  and South. BREWE 1:384

Benjamin, J. P.
 Farewell to the Union.
  BREWE 1:399
Brownlow, W. G.
 Grape shot and hemp.
  BREWE 2:690
Campbell, J. P.
 Give us equal pay and we will
  go to war. FON:300
Choate, R.
 Preservation of the Union.
  HURH:80
Cobb, H.
 Speech of Howell Cobb, at
  Atlanta, Georgia, May 22.
  ECH:182
Colfax, S.
 Confiscation of rebel property.
  BREWE 4:1361
Davis, H. W.
 Reasons for refusing to part
  company with the South.
  BREWE 5:1642
Davis, J.
 Against Clay and compromise.
  BREWE 5:1660
 Final exhortation to the Con-
  federate people. ANN 9:557
 Speech of President Davis at
  Richmond, June 1st, 1861.
  ECH:146
Dickinson, D. S.
 Rebuking Senator Clemens of
  Alabama. BREWE 5:1844
Doolittle, J. R.
 Attitude of the West in the
  Civil War. BREWE 5:1891
Douglas, S. A.
 Issues of 1861.
  BREWE 5:1929
 John Brown raid.
  BREWE 5:1926
Douglass, F.
 "Men of color, to arms!"
  OE:49
 The mission of the war.
  FON:283
Drake, C. D.
 Against "Copperheads."
  BREWE 5:1936
Garfield, J. A.
 Revolution and the logic of
  coercion. BREWE 6:2226
Garrison, W. L.
 At Charleston, South Caro-
  lina, 1865. BREWE 6:2241
 Beginning a revolution.
  BREWE 6:2237

Union and slavery.
BREWE 6:2240
Green, A. M.
Let us take up the sword.
FON:249
Hill, B. H.
Little personal history.
BREWE 7:2507
Houston, S.
Sam Houston's speech at
Independence, Texas, May
10. ECH:174
Johnson, A.
Presidential plan of Recon-
struction. CUR:8;
STAT 2:1112
King, T. S.
The two declarations of in-
dependence: 1776 and 1861.
HAW:260
Lincoln, A.
First annual message.
STAT 2:1054
Fourth annual message.
STAT 2:1097
"A house divided against it-
self cannot stand."
ANN 9:1; BAS:100 (outline
only); BREWE 7:2777;
FRIP:197; HURH:88
Message to Congress, July
5, 1861. ANN 9:268
Second annual message to
Congress. BOORA 1:396;
STAT 2:1068
Third annual message.
ANN 9:473; STAT 2:1084
Mason, J. M.
Speech of J. M. Mason,
at Richmond, Va., June
8, 1861. EDH:166
Phillips, W.
Under the flag. MDT:119
Schurz, C.
The irrepressible conflict
(1860). DAVF:130
Seward, W. H.
Irrepressible conflict.
ANN 9:32; BREWE 9:3394;
HURH:99
Stephens, A. H.
On the Confederate Consti-
tution. ECH:77
Speech of Hon. A. H.
Stephens at Atlanta, Ga.,
April 30, 1861. ECH:157
Speech of Hon. A. H.
Stephens at Richmond, Va.,

April 22, 1861. ECH:191
Speech of Hon. A. H.
Stephens, delivered in the hall
of the House of Representa-
tives of Georgia, Nov. 14,
1860. ECH:7
Stevens, T.
Concerning wartime taxes in
the North. ANN 9:335
Toombs, R.
Robert Toombs' address, to
the people of Georgia.
ECH:103
Territorial acquisition and
Civil War. BREWE 9:3641
Vallandigham, C. L.
Centralization and the revolu-
tionary power of federal
patronage. BREWE 10:3674
Plea to stop the war.
ANN 9:409
Voorhees, D. W.
Opposition argument in 1862.
BREWE 10:3700
Wise, H. A.
Speech of ex-governor Henry
A. Wise. ECH:150
Wood, F.
Proposal for the secession of
New York City. ANN 9:233

---- ---- ---- See also Confederate
States of America; Recon-
struction; Slavery in the
United States

---- ---- ---- CAUSES
Buchanan, J.
Fourth annual message.
ANN 9:209; STAT 1:1025
Crittenden, J. J.
On the Crittenden Compromise.
ANN 9:221
Union at any price.
ANN 9:246
Davis, J.
Inaugural address in 1861.
ANN 9:238; BREWE 5:1656;
ECH:137
Message to Congress, April
29, 1861. ANN 9:259
On withdrawing from the Un-
ion. BAS:71 (outline only);
BREWE 5:1651; ECH:72;
HURH:109
Stephens, A. H.
Sanctity of the Union.
ANN 9:199

Toombs, R.
"Let us depart in peace."
ANN 9:192; BREWE 9:3646
Wade, B. F.
On secession and the state
of the union.   ANN 9:220

---- ---- WAR OF 1898
Clinton, D.
Against the military spirit.
BREWE 4:1309
McKinley, W.
Second annual message.
STAT 2:1881
Third annual message.
STAT 2:1922
War message, April 11,
1898.   ANN 12:173
Putnam, F.
The Negro's part in new na-
tional problems.   FON:629

---- ---- EUROPEAN WAR,
1914-1918 See European
War, 1914-1918

---- ---- WORLD WAR, 1939-
1945 See World War,
1939-1945 - United States

---- IMMIGRATION See Immigration and emigration

---- LIBRARY OF CONGRESS
Boorstin, D. J.
Beginnings.   BA 1976-77:138

---- NATIONAL CHARACTER-
ISTICS See National characteristics, American

---- NAVY
Bayard, J. A.
Commerce and naval power.
BREWE 1:262
Cheves, L.
In favor of a stronger navy.
BREWE 3:1101
Middendorf, J. W.
World sea power: United
States vs. USSR.
LINRST:234
Roosevelt, F. D.
Navy Day address on the
attack on the destroyer
Kearney.   ANN 16:90
Roosevelt, T.
Seventh annual message.

STAT 3:2240
Sixth annual message.
STAT 3:2194
Talmage, T. D.
On Admiral Dewey and the
American Navy.
BREWE 9:3584
Truman, H. S.
Navy Day speech on foreign
policy.   ANN 16:393

---- NEUTRALITY
Hutchins, R. M.
Drifting into suicide.
ANN 16:66
Lindberg, C. A.
Independent policy.
ANN 16:72; HURH:254;
ROD:290
Roosevelt, F. D.
This nation will remain neu-
tral.   ROD:274
Taft, R. A.
Opposition to the Roosevelt
war policies.   ANN 16:94
Thomas, N.
America and the war.
HURH:261
Thompson, D.
Hitler's plans for Canada and
the United States.   HURH:257
Wilson, W.
Neutrality message to the
Senate, August 19, 1914.
ANN 13:491

---- ---- See also United States -
Foreign Relations

---- POLITICS AND GOVERNMENT
Barnard, D. D.
American experiment in gov-
ernment.   ANN 6:353
The social system.   HOW:106
Blair, A.
Military government.
BREWE 2:504
Calhoun, J. C.
Self-government and civiliza-
tion.   BREWE 3:924
Choate, R.
Necessity of compromise in
American politics.
BREWE 3:1127
Clay, H.
Dictators in American politics.
BREWE 4:1224
Cleaver, E.

Political struggle in America.
SMHR:166
Clinton, D. W.
Federal power and local
rights. BREWE 4:1306
Conkling, R.
Stalwart standpoint.
BREWE 4:1369
Door, T.
People's right to remake
their constitution. ANN 7:56
Eisenhower, D. D.
Faith in the individual.
CAPG:31
Hoover, H. C.
Against the proposed New
Deal (October 31, 1932).
ANN 15:188
Humphrey, H. H., Jr.
American system. CAPG:21
Kennedy, J. F.
History will be our judge.
LINS:371
Lincoln, A.
Perpetuation of our political
institutions (1837).
ANN 6:424; MOP:368
Lippmann, W.
Rise of personal govern-
ment in the United States.
BAD:97
McGovern, G. S.
American politics: a per-
sonal view. BA 1972-73:22
Mathias, C. M.
Truth in government.
BA 1972-73:60
Moynihan, D. P.
The middle of the journey.
BA 1970-71:29
Reagan, R.
Time for choosing.
CAPG:48
Rogers, W. P.
A brief assessment of where
we stand today.
BA 1974-75:54
Roosevelt, F. D.
Call for federal responsibil-
ity (October 13, 1932).
ANN 15:185
Root, E.
Proper pace of political
change. ANN 13:436
Thoreau, H. D.
Civil disobedience.
BOORA 1:318
Wriston, W. B.

Long view of the short run.
BA 1968-1969:89

---- PUBLIC LANDS
Jackson, A.
Fourth annual message.
STAT 1:358
Marshall, T. R.
National power and the Amer-
ican peace policy (on public
land sales, 1841).
BREWE 8:2964
Van Buren, M.
First annual message.
STAT 1:472

---- SOCIAL CONDITIONS
Barnard, D. C.
The social system. HOW:106
Chisholm, S.
It is time to reassess our na-
tional priorities.
BA 1968-69:68
Clark, K. B.
Beyond dilemma.
BA 1969-70:168
Fulbright, J. W.
Great Society is a sick soci-
ety. LAA:10
Johnson, L. B.
Great Society (commencement
address at University of
Michigan). ANN 18:216;
CAPG:15; MDV:108; MUS:135
King, Mrs. M. L., Jr.
We need to be united.
FON:1169
Long, H. P.
Every man a king. BEN:80
Smith, M. C.
Declaration of conscience--
twenty years later.
BA 1969-70:133
Wilson, Woodrow
What is progress? BEN:62
Wriston, W. B.
Long view of the short run.
BA 1968-69:89

---- SOCIAL POLICY
Abernathy, R. D.
The Kerner Report, promises
and realities. FON:1145
Humphrey, H. H., Jr.
American system. CAPG:21
Johnson, L. B.
Second annual message.
STAT 3:3161

Third annual message.
STAT 3:3171
Spottswood, S. G.
The Nixon administration's
anti-Negro policy.
FON:1173

---- SUPREME COURT
Black, H. L.
United States v. Lovett,
Watson, and Dodd: opinion
for the court. ANN 16:404
---- and others
Korematsu v. United States:
opinion for the court and
dissenting opinion.
ANN 16:234
Bradley, J. P. and others
Civil rights cases: opinion
for the court and dissenting
opinion. ANN 10:577
Brandeis, L. D.
Ashwander rules.
ANN 15:350
Danger of inaction: dissenting
opinion for the Supreme
Court on New State Ice Co.,
v. Liebmann, 1931. ROD:73
Brennan, W. J., Jr.
Baker v. Carr: opinion for
the Supreme Court.
ANN 18:130
---- and others
Ginzburg et al v. United
States: opinion for the court
and dissenting opinion.
ANN 18:350
Brewer, D. J.
In Re Debs: opinion for the
court. ANN 12:18
Brown, H. B. and others
Plessy v. Ferguson: opinion
for the court and dissenting
opinion. ANN 12:92
Burges, T.
Supreme Court.
BREWE 2:729
Clark, T. C.
Sheppard v. Maxwell, warden:
opinion for the court.
ANN 18:402
Davis, D.
Ex parte Milligan, 1866;
opinion for the court.
ANN 10:31
Field, D. D.
In re Milligan--martial law
as lawlessness.

BREWE 6:2147
In the case of McCardle--
necessity as an excuse for
tyranny. BREWE 6:2155
Frankfurter, F.
The judicial process and the
Supreme Court, April 22,
1954. FRIP:345
Fuller, M. W. and others
United States v. E. C.
Knight Company, 1895:
opinion for the Supreme Court
and dissenting opinion.
ANN 12:23
Hallett, B.
Sovereignty of the people
(Luther v. Borden case).
ANN 7:410
Harlan, J. M. and others
Northern Securities Company
v. United States, 1904: opin-
ion for the court and dissent-
ing opinion. ANN 12:576
Holmes, O. W., Jr.
Dissenting opinion on Abrams
v. United States.
ANN 14:244; BOORA 2:666
Lochner v. New York, 1905:
dissenting opinion for the
Supreme Court.
BOORA 2:662
Nixon v. Herndon: opinion
for the court. ANN 14:534
Hughes, C. E.
National Labor Relations
Board v. Jones and Laughlin
Steel Corporation, 1937:
opinion for the Supreme
Court. ROD:207
Schechter Poultry Corporation
v. United States, 1935:
opinion for the Supreme
Court. ANN 15:301; ROD:186
Small step toward racial
equality: opinion for the
Supreme Court on Mitchell
case, 1941. ROD:224
Jackson, R. H.
Court broadens the rights of
citizens: the Second Flag
Salute Case, 1943. ROD:214
---- and others
West Virginia Board of Educa-
tion et al v. Barnette et al:
opinion for the court and dis-
senting opinion. ANN 16:148
Jenner, W. E. and others
Proposal to limit the power of

Republic). ANN 10:231
Hoar, G. F.
Lust of empire. ANN 12:248
Sumner, C.
Against annexation (of the
Dominican Republic).
ANN 10:233

UNIVERSAL NEGRO IMPROVE-
MENT ASSOCIATION
Garvey, M.
The principles of the Uni-
versal Negro Improvement
Association. FON:748;
OE:103

UNIVERSE
Lardner, D.
Plurality of worlds.
BREWE 7:2716
Lovell, B.
Our present knowledge of
the universe. MDYG:239

UNIVERSITIES AND COLLEGES
See Colleges and univer-
sities, e.g. Harvard
University

UNIVERSITY OF CALIFORNIA
Kerr, C.
Perspectives on the prophets
of doom. HOR:34

UNIVERSITY OF MALAYA
Abdul Rahman, T.
Our university; pledge to
nation (installation speech
as Chancellor of University
of Malaya). MONS:28
Tan Chee Khoon
Monstrous piece of legisla-
tion (Internal Security Act--
Malaysia). MONS:190

UNIVERSITY OF PENANG
Hamzah Sendut
Some new approaches to
university education.
MONSA:168

UNKNOWN SOLDIER
Fosdick, H. E.
Unknown soldier. LINS:312

UNVEILING SPEECHES See
Dedication speeches

URANIUM
Hahn, O.
From the natural transmutations of uranium to its artificial fission. NOLC 3:51

URBAN LEAGUE
Jordan, V. E., Jr.
Survival. BA 1971-72:49

URBANIZATION - MALAYSIA
Muhammad Ghazali bin Shafie
Strategy for the future: role
of youths in national development. MONSA:129

Urey, Harold Clayton
Science and society (at 100th
anniversary Academic Con-
vocation of Cooper Union for
the Advancement of Science
and Art). ARS:78
Some thermodynamic properties
of hydrogen and deuterium
(Nobel Lecture for 1934, Feb.
14, 1935). NOLC 2:339

UREY, HAROLD CLAYTON
Palmaer, W.
Presentation [of the Nobel
Prize for Chemistry for 1934
to Harold Clayton Urey, Feb.
14, 1935]. NOLC 2:333

URSULINE COLLEGE
Gannon, A. I.
A Catholic college, yesterday
and tomorrow. HOR:78

UTAH
Buchanan, J.
First annual message.
STAT 1:942
Second annual message.
STAT 1:969

Uvnäs, B.
Presentation [of the Nobel Prize
for Physiology or Medicine to
Daniel Bovet, Dec. 11, 1957].
NOLM 3:549
Presentation of the Nobel Prize
for Physiology or Medicine
to Julius Azelrod, Ulf Von
Euler, and Bernhard Katz,
Dec. 12, 1970. NOLM 4:441

- V -

V-J DAY See World War, 1939-
1945 - Japan - Surrender

VALEDICTORY ADDRESSES
Binney, B.
Valedictory oration.
POC:51

Vallandigham, Clement L.
Centralization and the revolu-
tionary power of federal
patronage. BREWE 10:3674
Plea to stop the war.
ANN 9:409

Vallotton, Henry
Acceptance [of the Nobel Prize
for Literature for Hermann
Hesse, 1946]. NOB 9:237;
NOL:416

Van Buren, Martin
Against government aid for
business losses.
ANN 6:314
First annual message.
STAT 1:472
Fourth annual message.
STAT 1:543
Inaugural address.
USINAU:61; USINAUG:61
Second annual message.
STAT 1:494
Third annual message.
STAT 1:517

---- See also Sanford, N., jt.
auth.

Vance, Cyrus R.
Human rights and the foreign
policy (Athens, Ga.,
April 30, 1977).
BA 1976-77:127

Vandenberg, Arthur H.
Sovereignty and the United
Nations. ANN 16:331

Vander Jagt, Guy
Bonn report. SCHW:162
John Marshall. SCHW:201
Price of the best. SCHW:59

Vander Werf, Nathan
Mistaken enemy. SCHW:171

Vane, Sir Henry
Against Richard Cromwell.
BREWE 10:3684
At his trial for high treason.
BREWE 10:3685
Speech for duty in contempt of
death. Same as his At his
trial for high treason

Van Engen, Bernice
Casual approach to war.
SCHW:195

Van Tatenhove, Jane E.
Echo or a voice? SCHW:115

Van't Hoff, Jacobus Henricus See
Hoff, Jacobus Henricus Van't

Van Voorst, Bruce
Clock. SCHW:74

Vanzetti, Bartolomeo
Last statement in court See
Sacco, N. and Vanzetti, B.
Proclaim their innocence

Vargas, Jorge B.
The role of the army (Baguio,
March 13, 1937). CURM:98

Varnum, James Mitchell and others
(W. Williams)
Disputation on "Whether British
America can under present
circumstances consistent with
good policy, affect to become
an independent state." POC:14

VENEREAL DISEASES
Bjorklund, J.
Nice people. EHN:158;
MOPR:246
Wayman, M. K.
Unmentionable diseases.
LINR:224; LINRS:200

Vergniaud, Pierre Victurnien
Reply to Robespierre.
BREWE 10:3692
To the camp. BREWE 10:3690

VERRES, GAIUS
Cicero, M. T.

First oration against Verres.
BREWE 3:1174

Vest, George Graham
Eulogy to the dog.   Same as
  his Man's best friend--his
  dog
"He guards the sleep of his
  pauper master as if he were
  a prince. " Same as his
  Man's best friend--his dog
Man's best friend--his dog.
  (Washington, 1903).
  ALA:45; HURH:161

VETERANS
Brandli, W.
  Taps and reveille.
  SCHW:30

---- See also Pensions, Military

---- EDUCATION
Hines, F. T.
  G.I. Bill of Rights.
  ANN 16:215

VETERANS' DAY
Willkie, W. L.
  Loyal opposition.   GRG:63;
  HURH:243

VETO - UNITED STATES See
  Executive power - United
  States

VIETNAMESE WAR, 1957-1975
Ball, G. W.
  Issue in Vietnam.
  BA 1965-66:43
Barger, R. N.
  Theology and amnesty.
  BA 1973-74:177
Bilheimer, R. S.
  Christian conscience and
  the Vietnam War. VI:15
Brooke, E. W.
  Report on Vietnam and East
  Asia. BA 1966-67:23
Church, F.
  Foreign policy and the gener-
  ation gap. BA 1970-71:49
  War without end.
  BA 1969-70:27
Connor, J. T.
  Impact on the American
  economy of the Vietnamese
  program. BA 1969-70:47

Fulbright, J. W.
  Arrogance of power.
  ANN 18:362
  Great Society is a sick society.
  LAA:10
  Two Americas.
  BA 1965-66:115
Galbraith, J. K.
  On history, political economy,
  and Vietnam. BA 1975-76:78
Gruening, E.
  United States policy and action:
  in Vietnam. BA 1965-66:23
Hatfield, M. O.
  Reconciliation and peace.
  BA 1972-73:91
Humphrey, H. H., Jr.
  Campaign speech, Salt Lake
  City, Utah, September 30,
  1968. SIN:380
  Guns and butter are tied to-
  gether. LAA:207
Johnson, L. B.
  A president defends his policies
  by argument from authorities.
  JEF:331; JEFF:316
  Remarks to the nation (declining
  nomination to Presidency).
  ANN 18:613; BA 1967-68:63
  Speech at a joint session of the
  Tennessee State Legislature.
  BA 1966-67:11
  Speech before the National
  Legislative Conference.
  BA 1967-68:11
  Third annual message.
  STAT 3:3171
  Vietnam: the struggle to be
  free (on accepting National
  Freedom Award).
  BA 1965-66:11
  Why must we take this painful
  road? LAA:185
Kennan, G. F.
  Statement on Vietnam.
  BA 1965-66:56
Kennedy, J. F.
  Vietnam--illusion and reality.
  ANN 18:599
Kerry, J. F.
  Vietnam veterans against the
  war. LINRS:244
King, M. L., Jr.
  A time to break silence.
  FON:1048
Lindsay, J. V.
  Vietnam moratorium address.
  AND:153

McCarthy, E. J.
  Address on Viet Nam (February 1, 1967).   REIR:117
Mansfield, M. J.
  Assessment in Vietnam.
  BA 1967-68:49
Nixon, R. M.
  Cambodia.   LINRS:236
  Pursuit of peace.
  BA 1969-70:9; ERP:145
Paul VI
  Key to peace.   BAS:150
  (outline only)
Rostow, E. V.
  Choice in foreign policy.
  ANN 18:605
Rowe, J. N.
  An American prisoner of war in South Vietnam.
  LINRS:45
Udall, M. K.
  United States and Vietnam--what lies ahead.
  BA 1967-68:21
Wald, G.
  Generation in search of a future.   BA 1968-69:33
Westmoreland, W. C.
  Vietnam--the situation today (1967).   BAS:59 (outline only)

---- MORAL AND RELIGIOUS
     ASPECTS
Aubert, J.
  Vietnam and world peace.
  VI:104
Blake, E. C.
  Ecumenism and peace.
  VI:132
Coffin, W. S., Jr.
  Vietnam: a sermon.
  VI:64
Davis, G. R.
  Vietnam War: a Christian perspective.   VI:46
Evans, T. H., Jr.
  Application of love.   VI:90
Hall, R. O.
  Fear and faith.   VI:98
King, M. L., Jr.
  Declaration of independence from the war in Vietnam.
  VI:115
Payne, J. R.
  Australia and the Vietnam War.   VI:75
Ramsey, R. P.
  Counting the costs.   VI:24

Reeves, R. A.
  Journey to Hanoi.   VI:83

---- NEW ZEALAND
Holyoake, K. J.
  A military contribution in Vietnam, 1965.   MACS:398 sel.

Vigneaud, Vincent Du
  A trail of sulfur research: from insulin to oxytocin (Nobel Lecture, Dec. 12, 1955).
  NOLC 3:446

VIGNEAUD, VINCENT DU
Fredga, A.
  Presentation [of the Nobel Prize for Chemistry to Vincent du Vigneaud, Dec. 12, 1955].
  NOLC 3:443

Vincent, John
  Churchill's early achievements.
  MDYG:50

Vinzons, Wenceslao Q.
  Defects in the draft of the Constitution (Manila, Nov. 10, 1934).   CURM:304

VIOLENCE
Edwards, G.
  Murder and gun control.
  BA 1971-72:101
Fulbright, J. W.
  Violence in the American character.   ANN 18:206

VIRGINIA
Marshall, J.
  Cohens v. Virginia, 1821: opinion for the Supreme Court.
  ANN 5:1

Virtanen, Artturi Ilmari
  The biological fixation of nitrogen and the preservation of fodder in agriculture, and their importance to human nutrition (Nobel Lecture, Dec. 12, 1945).   NOLC 3:74

VIRTANEN, ARTTURI ILMARI
Westgren, A.
  Presentation [of the Nobel Prize for Chemistry to Artturi Ilmari Virtanen, Dec. 12, 1945].   NOLC 3:71

VIRUSES
  Lwoff, A.
    Interaction among virus, cell,
    and organism. NOLM 4:186
  Stanley, W. M.
    The isolation and properties
    of crystalline tobacco mosaic.
    NOLC 3:137

VITAMIN C
  Haworth, W. N.
    The structure of carbohydrates
    and of vitamin C.
    NOLC 2:414

VITAMIN K
  Dam, H.
    The discovery of vitamin K,
    its biological functions and
    therapeutical application.
    NOLM 3:8

VITAMINS
  Hopkins, Sir F. G.
    The earlier history of vitamin
    research. NOLM 2:211
  Karrer, P.
    Carotenoids, flavins and
    vitamin A and B2.
    NOLC 2:433
  Szent-Györgyi, A.
    Oxidation, energy transfer,
    and vitamins. NOLM 2:440

Vogel, Julius
  Colonization by public works
  and immigration (Budget
  speech, June 28, 1870).
  MACS:42 sel.

VOLTAIRE, FRANÇOIS MARIE
    AROUET DE
  Hugo, V. M.
    On the centennial of Voltaire's
    death. BREWE 7:2550

Von Braun, Wernher
  Earth benefits from space and
  space technology (Washington, D.C., March 13, 1972).
  BA 1971-72:111

VON BRAUN, WERNHER
  Sevareid, E.
    Eulogy for Wernher Von
    Braun. EHN:373

Von Euler, Ulf
  Adrenergic neurotransmitter

functions (Nobel Lecture, Dec.
12, 1970). NOLM 4:470

VON EULER, ULF
  Uvnäs, B.
    Presentation [of the Nobel
    Prize for Physiology or Medi-
    cine to Julius Axelrod, Ulf
    Von Euler, and Bernhard Katz,
    Dec. 12, 1970]. NOLM 4:441

Voorhees, Daniel W.
  Opposition argument in 1862.
  BREWE 10:3700
  Speech in the Tilden convention.
  BREWE 10:3697

VOTING See Elections; Blacks -
    Politics and suffrage; Woman
    Suffrage

VOTING RIGHTS LAW OF 1965
  Johnson, L. B.
    Voting Rights Law of 1965--a
    victory for freedom. CAPG:97

                - W -

Waals, Johannes Diderik van der
  The equation of state for gases
  and liquids (Nobel Lecture,
  Dec. 12, 1910).
  NOLPH 1:254

WAALS, JOHANNES DIDERIK VAN
    DER
  Montelius, O.
    Presentation [of the Nobel
    Prize for Physics to Johannes
    Diderik Van der Waals, Dec.
    12, 1910]. NOLPH 1:251

Wade, Benjamin Franklin
  On secession and the state of the
  union. ANN 9:220
  Opposition to compromise. Same
  as his On secession and the
  state of the union

WAGES
  Sutherland, G. and others
    Adkins v. Children's Hospital:
    opinion for the court and dis-
    senting opinion. ANN 14:391

Wagner, Ralph B.
  Public relations. ANN 16:285

Pump-priming--it is necessary
for business recovery.
BAD:44
To feed the hungry.   ROD:77

Wagner-Jauregg, Julius
The treatment of dementia
paralytica by malaria in-
oculation (Nobel Lecture,
Dec. 13, 1927).
NOLM 2:159

WAGNER-JAUREGG, JULIUS
Wernstedt, W.
Presentation [of the Nobel
Prize for Physiology or
Medicine to Julius Wagner-
Jauregg, Dec. 12, 1927].
NOLM 2:155

Wah-shee, James
A land settlement--what does
it mean? (Ottawa, May 24,
1974). MAES:45

Waite, Morrison Remick and
others (S. J. Field)
Munn v. Illinois, 1876: opinion
for the court and dissenting
opinion. ANN 10:377

Wakefield, Edward Gibbon
The demand for responsible
government (Auckland,
June 2, 1854). MACS:86
Extending the 'frontier' of New
South Wales (Parliamentary
Select Committee on the
Disposal of Land in Colonies,
June 27, 1836). MACS:3

Waksman, Selman Abraham
Streptomycin: background,
isolation, properties, and
utilization (Nobel Lecture,
Dec. 12, 1952).
NOLM 3:370

WAKSMAN, SELMAN ABRAHAM
Wallgren, A.
Presentation [of the Nobel
Prize for Physiology or
Medicine to Selman Abraham
Waksman, Dec. 12, 1952].
NOLM 3:365

Walbert, Richard B.
Introduces Albert L. Cole,

president of Reader's Digest
Association.   PRS:96
Introduces Bruce Catton, histori-
an.   PRS:87
Introduces Clinton S. Sanders,
chairman of the American
Trucking Association.   PRS:89
Introduces Dr. Ernest L. Wilkin-
son, president of Brigham
Young University.   PRS:44
Introduces Dr. Norman Vincent
Peale.   PRS:112
Introduces George Meany, presi-
dent of the AFL-CIO.   PRS:59
Introduces J. Paul Austin, president,
the Coca-Cola Company.
PRS:19
Introduces Jervis Langdon, Jr.
PRS:16
Introduces Mark O. Hatfield,
governor of Oregon.   PRS:91
Introduces Senator Thurston B.
Morton.   PRS:97
Introduces William G. Cole,
president of Lake Forest Col-
lege.   PRS:51
Introduces William W. Scranton,
governor of Pennsylvania.
PRS:109

Wald, George
Generation in search of a future.
BA 1968-69:33
The molecular basis of visual
excitation (Nobel Lecture,
Dec. 12, 1967).
NOLM 4:292

WALD, GEORGE
Bernhard, C. G.
Presentation [of the Nobel
Prize for Physiology or Medi-
cine to Ragnar Granit, Haldan
Keffer Hartline, and George
Wald, Dec. 12, 1967].
NOLM 4:251

Walker, Alan
Why I am a Christian pacifist.
MCA:204

Walker, David
We must have unity (Boston, 1828).
SMHV:11

Walker, Harold Blake
The future of the past (Washing-
ton, D.C., Sept. 20, 1970).
BA 1970-71:63

Walker, Robert J.
  Address to the people of Kansas.
    ANN 8:452

Wallace, George C.
  Address on law enforcement
    (Miami, Fla., Aug. 29, 1967).
    MAC:271; MACR:312
  Civil Rights Bill: fraud, sham,
    and hoax. MDV:175

Wallace, Henry Agard
  Declaration of interdependence.
    ANN 15:220
  Economic bill of rights.
    ANN 16:268
  Is American foreign policy
    leading to war?
    ANN 16:370
  New Farm Act--balanced
    abundance for farm and
    city. BAD:37
  Pigs and pig iron. ANN 15:336
  Price of peace. Same as his
    Is American foreign policy
    leading to war

Wallach, Otto
  Alicyclic compounds (Nobel
    Lecture, Dec. 12, 1910).
    NOLC 1:178

WALLACH, OTTO
  Montelius, O.
    Presentation [of the Nobel
    Prize for Chemistry to Otto
    Wallach, Dec. 12, 1910].
    NOLC 1:175

Wallack, Morton A.
  And thou shalt choose life.
    WALE: 197
  Living presence. WALE:194

Waller, Edmund
  Tyrant's plea, necessity (im-
    peaching Justice Crawley).
    BREWE 10:3709

Waller, Helen H.
  Presents Bertrand Russell.
    LYI:94
  Presents Estes Kefauver.
    LYI:230

Waller, I.
  Presentation [of the Nobel Prize
    for Physics to Alfred

Kastler, Dec. 12, 1966].
    NOLPH 4:183
Presentation [of the Nobel Prize
    for Physics to Eugene P.
    Wigner, Maria Goeppert
    Mayer and J. Hans D. Jen-
    sen, Dec. 12, 1963].
    NOLPH 4:3
Presentation [of the Nobel Prize
    for Physics to Hideki Yukawa,
    Dec. 12, 1949].
    NOLPH 3:125
Presentation [of the Nobel Prize
    for Physics to Lev Davidovic
    Landau, 1962]. NOLPH 3:607
Presentation [of the Nobel Prize
    for Physics to Max Born and
    Walther Bothe, Dec. 11, 1954].
    NOLPH 3:253
Presentation [of the Nobel Prize
    for Physics to Murray Gell-
    Mann, 1969]. NOLPH 4:295
Presentation [of the Nobel Prize
    for Physics to Robert Hof-
    stadter and Rudolf Ludwig
    Mossbauer, Dec. 11, 1961].
    NOLPH 3:555
Presentation [of the Nobel Prize
    for Physics to Sin-Itiro Tomon-
    aga, Julian Schwinger, and
    Richard P. Feynman, Dec. 11,
    1965]. NOLPH 4:123
Presentation [of the Nobel Prize
    for Physics to Sir John Douglas
    Cockcroft and Ernest Thomas
    Sinton Walton, Dec. 11, 1951].
    NOLPH 3:163
Presentation [of the Nobel Prize
    for Physics to Willis Eugene
    Lamb and Polykarp Kusch,
    Dec. 12, 1955]. NOLPH 3:283
Presentation [of the Nobel Prize
    for Physics for 1945 to Wolf-
    gang Pauli, Dec. 13, 1946].
    NOLPH 3:25

Wallgren, A.
  Presentation [of the Nobel Prize
    for Physiology or Medicine to
    Selman Abraham Waksman,
    Dec. 12, 1952]. NOLM 3:365

Walpole, Horace, 4th Earl of Orford
  Debate in 1741 on wages of
    sailors. BREWE 10:3717;
    BRYH:176
  Debate with Pitt in 1741. Same
    as his Debate in 1741 on wages
    of sailors

---- See also Walpole, R., jt.
auth.

Walpole, Sir Robert, 1st Earl of
Orford
On patriots (at motion to dismiss him from Council).
BREWE 10:3724
Remarkable debate in the House
of Commons on the Bill for
encouraging seamen and
manning the fleet. Same
as his Debate in 1741 on
wages of sailors

---- and others
Debate in 1741 on wages of
sailors. BRYH:176

WALPOLE, SIR ROBERT 1ST
EARL OF ORFORD
Wyndham, W.
Attack on Sir Robert Wal-
pole. BREWE 10:3925

Walters, Alexander and others
(B. T. Washington)
Two contrasting Black voices
(April, 1899). FON:611

Walton, Ernest Thomas Sinton
The artificial production of
fast particles (Nobel Lecture, Dec. 11, 1951).
NOLPH 3:187

WALTON, ERNEST THOMAS
SINTON
Waller, I.
Presentation [of the Nobel
Prize for Physics to Sir
John Douglas Cockcroft and
Ernest Thomas Sinton Wal-
ton, Dec. 11, 1951].
NOLPH 3:163

Wamper, Cloud
Responds to introduction.
PRS:128

Wanamaker, John
On the department store.
BOORA 2:632

Wang, Gung Wu
Tribute to Dr. Zakir Husain
(presenting him with Doctor
of Laws degree). MONS:277

WAR
Buisson, F. E.
Changes in concepts of war and
peace (Nobel Lecture, 1927,
May 31, 1928). NOLP 2:35
Chalmers, T.
War and truth. BREWE 3:1024
Crittenden, J. J.
Against warring on the weak.
BREWE 4:1477
DeVries, C.
Standards that stand. SCHW:15
Ducommun, E.
The futility of war demon-
strated by history (Nobel Lec-
ture for 1902). NOLP 1:17
Fosdick, H. E.
Unknown soldier. LINS:312
Gaustad, E. S.
The beginning of wisdom.
CAPG:370
Geren, P.
The lie of war. CAPG:359
Hains, J.
New day dawns. SCHW:140
Ingersoll, R. G.
Vision of war, 1876 speech.
BREWE 7:2582
Inozemstev, N. N.
Alternative to war. MDV:69
Levai, B.
Broken sword. SCHW:144
Loula, L. A.
Drunken orgy. SCHW:149
Roosevelt, F. D.
Quarantining the aggressors.
ANN 15:502; BEN:93;
BOORA 2:847; BRYF:474;
ROD:263
Sumner, C.
War system of the Common-
wealth of Nations. ANN 7:548
Vander Jagt, G.
Bonn report. SCHW:162
Van Engen, B.
Casual approach to war.
SCHW:195
Wallace, H. A.
Is American foreign policy
leading to war? ANN 16:370

---- See also Army; Disarmament;
Peace; United States - Neutrality. Also Names of wars,
e.g. World War, 1914-1918;
World War, 1939-1945

WAR AND EDUCATION See
Veterans - Education

WAR AND MORALS
  Bennett, J. C.
    Issue of peace: the voice of
    religion. BA 1965-66:142
  Fosdick, H. E.
    Christian conscience about
    war. OLIS:237

---- See also Vietnamese War,
  1957-1975 - Moral and religious aspects

WAR OF 1812 See United
  States - History - War of
  1812

WAR ON POVERTY See Poverty

Warburg, Otto Heinrich
  The oxygen-transferring fer-
    ment of respiration (Nobel
    Lecture, Dec. 10, 1931).
    NOLM 2:254

WARBURG, OTTO HEINRICH
  Hammarsten, E.
    Presentation [of the Nobel
    Prize for Physiology or
    Medicine to Otto Heinrich
    Warburg, Dec. 10, 1931].
    NOLM 2:251

Ward, Edward John
  Petrov case. MCA:196

Ward, Sir Joseph
  Advances to settlers, 1894
    (New Zealand House of
    Representatives, Sept. 14,
    1894). MACS:207
  New Zealand support for the
    Royal Navy, 1891-1908
    (New Zealand House of
    Representatives, Dec. 8,
    1909). MACS:254
  The 1928 election (Auckland,
    Oct. 16, 1928). MACS:311

Ward, Samuel R.
  Speech on the Fugitive Slave
    Bill (Boston, March 25,
    1850). FON:93

Warner, A. J. and others (H. C.
  Baldwin)
  The British plot to enslave the
    world (2nd National Silver
    Convention, Washington,
    May, 1892). DAVF:192

Warren, Earl
  Brown et al v. Board of Educa-
    tion of Topeka et al: opinion
    for the court. ANN 17:253;
    BOORA 2:904
  Federal court congestion.
    ANN 17:487
  Perez v. Brownell: dissenting
    opinion. ANN 17:499

---- and others (B. R. White)
  Miranda v. Arizona: opinion
    for the court and dissenting
    opinion. ANN 18:427

WARREN, EARL
  Pepper, G. W.
    Presents Earl Warren.
    LYI:121

Warren, Joseph
  Against a British Army in the
    Colonies. Same as his Boston
    Massacre
  Boston Massacre (March 5, 1772).
    ANN 2:211; POC:237
  Constitutional liberty and arbitrary
    power. BREWE 10:3727
  Oration on the Boston Massacre,
    March 5, 1775. POC:245

WARREN, JOSEPH
  Morton, P.
    Oration at the reinterment of
    Warren. POC:320

Warren, Patricia
  Bring forth the children.
    BRYF:485; MOPR:368

Washington, Booker T.
  Address at the opening of the
    Atlanta Exposition (Sept. 18,
    1895). ANN 12:9; BAPRR:255;
    BAS:77 (outline only); BRYF:492;
    FON:577; LINS:263; OE:82;
    SMHV:94
  Address delivered at the Harvard
    Alumni dinner in 1896 (Boston,
    Mass., June, 1896).
    HURH:144
  "The country demands that every
    race measure itself by the
    American standard." Same as
    his Address at the Opening of
    the Atlanta Exposition
  Road to Negro progress. Same
    as his Address at the opening
    of the Atlanta Exposition

Speech at the Cotton States ex-
position. Same as his Ad-
dress at the Opening of the
Atlanta Exposition
There is still much to be done
(New Haven, Conn., Oct.
25, 1915). FON:707
We must be a law-abiding and
law-respecting people (Afro-
American Council in New
York, Oct. 11, 1906).
FON:652

---- See also Walters, A., jt.
auth.

Washington, George
Acceptance of military com-
mission. POC:164
Acceptance of the command of
the Continental Armies.
Same as his Acceptance of
military commission
Address to the officers of the
army. ANN 2:598
Eighth annual address.
ANN 3:604; STAT 1:31
Farewell address (Philadelphia,
Sept. 19, 1796).
ANN 3:606; BEN:18;
BOORA 1:194; BREWE 10:3740;
HURH:44
Fifth annual address.
STAT 1:17
First annual address.
STAT 1:2
First inaugural address.
ANN 3:344; BOORA 1:172;
BREWE 10:3737;
USINAU:1; USINAUG:1
Fourth annual address.
STAT 1:12
National university. Same as
his Eighth annual address
Second annual address.
STAT 1:4
Second inaugural address.
USINAU:5; USINAUG:5
Seventh annual address.
STAT 1:27
Sixth annual address.
STAT 1:21
Third annual address.
STAT 1:7
"Tis our true policy to steer
clear of permanent alliances
with any portion of the for-
eign world." Same as his
Farewell address

WASHINGTON, GEORGE
Addams, J.
Washington's birthday.
HURH:163
Clay, C. M.
The man died, but his memory
lives. BLY:109
Daniel, J. W.
Dedication of the Washington
Monument. BREWE 4:1608
Fuller, Z.
Tree of liberty (George Wash-
ington birthday address).
ANN 5:355
Lee, H.
Funeral oration on Washington.
BREWE 7:2744
Phillips, C.
Dinas Island speech on Wash-
ington. BREWE 8:3176
Potter, H. C.
Washington and American
aristocracy (100th anniversary
of Washington's first inaugura-
tion). BREWE 8:3225

WATER - POLLUTION
Campbell, B.
On the banks of the Wabash.
KEO:226; STOT:266
Palovesik, S.
Ripples of hope. BREWW:179
Ransley, M.
The life and death of our
lakes. LINRS:63

WATERGATE
Aiken, G. D.
Either impeach ... or get off
his back. BA 1973-74:66
Cox, A.
Creativity in law and govern-
ment. BA 1973-74:49
Ford, G. R.
First presidential address.
BA 1974-75:50
Gallagher, W.
Free just free.
BA 1973-74:132
Huffman, J. A.
Retrospect '73--Biblical les-
sons we can learn from
Watergate. TAC:221
Jordan, B. C. and others
Hearings on articles of im-
peachment by the Committee of
the Judiciary of the House of
Representatives.
BA 1974-75:15

Nixon, R. M.
Our long national nightmare
is over--speech of resigna-
tion. BA 1974-75:43
Press conference (Watergate).
BA 1973-74:24
The Watergate case.
BA 1972-73:50
Richardson, E. L.
Vulnerability and vigilance.
BA 1973-74:13
Rogers, W. P.
A brief assessment of where
we stand today.
BA 1974-75:54
Sargent, F. W.
The computer and civil
liberties. BA 1973-74:141
Weicker, L. P.
The Watergate investigation.
BA 1973-74:40

WATERSIDE STRIKE, 1913, NEW
ZEALAND
Holland, H.
The 1913 Waterside Strike.
MACS:230 sel.

Watkins, Ferre C.
Introduces Cloud Wampler,
chairman of the board,
Carrier Air Conditioning.
PRS:126

Watkins, William J.
Our rights as men (Boston,
Legislative Committee on
the Militia, Feb. 24, 1853).
FON:130

Watson, Arthur K.
Presents William W. Scranton.
LYI:201

Watson, James Dewey
The involvement of RNA in the
synthesis of proteins (Nobel
Lecture, Dec. 11, 1962).
NOLM 3:785

WATSON, JAMES DEWEY
Engström, A.
Presentation [of the Nobel
Prize for Physiology or
Medicine to Francis Harry
Compton Crick, James
Dewey Watson, and Maurice
Hugh Frederick Wilkins,
Dec. 11, 1962]. NOLM 3:751

Watson, Thomas J., Jr.
Medical care (Rochester, Minn.,
Nov. 19, 1970).
BA 1970-71:115; BAPR:359;
BAPRR:266

Watterson, Henry
The compromises of life.
BLY:158

WATTERSON, HENRY
Root, E.
Introducing H. Watterson to
New England Society of New
York. LYI:111

WAUGH, EVELYN
Sykes, C. and others
Evelyn Waugh--the man.
MDYG:11

Wauters, Charles C. M. A.
Acceptance [of the Nobel Prize
for Literature for Maurice
Maeterlinck, 1911]. NOL:114

WAVE MECHANICS
Schrodinger, E.
The fundamental idea of wave
mechanics. NOLPH 2:305

Way, Peggy See Brown, Joan

Wayman, Mary Katherine
Unmentionable diseases.
LINR:224; LINRS:200

WEALTH
Dewey, O.
Rust of riches. BREWE 5:1823
Long, H. P.
Every man a king. BEN:80
Sharing our wealth (January,
1935 radio speech).
ANN 15:318; BAD:109
Morris, W.
Art, wealth, and riches.
BRYH:422
Newman, J. H.
Property as a disadvantage.
BREWE 8:3093
Rogers, W.
Education and wealth.
HURH:200
Young, J.
Property under the common
law (Coster v. Lorillard case).
ANN 6:181

---- See also Money

WEALTH, ETHICS OF See
    Ethics

Wears, Isaiah C.
    The Ku Klux of the North (Phila-
        delphia, 1871). FON:378
    Lincoln's colonization proposal
        is anti-Christian (Philadel-
        phia, Aug. 15, 1862).
        FON:259

WEATHER
    Clemens, S. L.
        New England weather.
        HURH:128

Weatherford, William, Creek chief
    To General Jackson.
        BREWE 7:2570

Weaver, Andrew Thomas
    Responds to an introduction.
        PRS:137

Weaver, Robert C.
    Negro as an American.
        MDV:162; SMHV:129

Weaver, Warren
    Presents Sir Charles Percy
        Snow. LYI:171

Webb, James E.
    From Runnymede to Ganymede.
        BA 1967-68:194

Webb, Walter Prescott
    Presents Harry S. Truman.
        LYI:193

Webster, Daniel
    Against conscription.
        ANN 4:355
    Basis of the Senate.
        ANN 4:634
    Bunker Hill monument (Boston,
        June 17, 1825).
        BREWE 10:3828; HURH:62;
        LINS:145
    Contracts and corporate
        charters. Same as his
        Dartmouth College case
    Dartmouth College case.
        ANN 4:477; BREWE 10:3860
    Dartmouth College versus
        Woodward--on the obligation

of contracts. Same as his
    Dartmouth College case
Eulogy on Adams and Jefferson.
    BREWE 10:3848
Exordium in the Knapp murder
    case. Same as his Knapp
    White murder case
For a uniform bankruptcy law.
    ANN 6:561
For reform of the naturalization
    laws. ANN 7:168
For the Bank Renewal Bill.
    ANN 5:535
Fourth of July oration, 1800.
    (Dartmouth College, July 4,
    1800). HAW:1
Knapp White murder case.
    BREWE 10:3865
Laying the corner-stone of Bunker
    Hill Monument. Same as his
    Bunker Hill Monument
Liberty and Union. Same as his
    Reply to Hayne
"Mind is the great lever of all
    things." Same as his Bunker
    Hill monument
On the Clay Compromise.
    ANN 8:24
- Plea for harmony and peace.
    Same as his On the Clay
    Compromise
Plymouth oration. BREWE 10:3846
Progress of the mechanic arts.
    BREWE 10:3856
Property and political power.
    Same as his Basis of the
    Senate
Railroad in New Hampshire (open-
    ing Northern Railroad).
    ANN 7:388
Reception at Madison, Indiana.
    OLIS:36
Reply to Hayne (U. S. Senate,
    Jan. 26, 1830). ANN 5:347;
    BEN:35; BREWE 10:3758;
    BRR:23; HOW:53
Supporting the Compromise of
    1850. BREWE 10:3868
Technical progress and prosperity.
    ANN 6:266

---- and others (J. Randolph)
    Debate on the Greek Revolution.
    ANN 5:108

WEBSTER, DANIEL
    Parker, T.
        Discourse on the death of

Daniel Webster.
BREWE 8:3137

Weicker, Lowell P., Jr.
Be a flake ... on behalf of
somebody or something
(Greenwich, Conn., June 15,
1979). BA 1979-80:187
Televised debates (Washing-
ton, Sept. 10, 1976).
BA 1976-77:61
The Watergate investigation
(New Haven, Conn., Nov.
26, 1973). BA 1973-74:40

Weinberger, Solomon
Cheerful spirit. WALE:198

Weinstein, Jacob J.
One of the thirty-six.
WALE:200

Weisensel, Kathy
David: and a whole lot of
other neat people.
LINRST:71

Welch, Robert
More stately mansions (Chi-
cago, June 5, 1964).
DAVF:327

WELCOMING ADDRESSES
Boy and his Dad (welcome
address on Father's Day).
HNWM:12
Children on Children's Day
(welcome address).
HNWM:15
Downing, G. T.
May Hungary be free.
FON:102
Forgotten man (welcome ad-
dress on Father's Day).
HNWM:10
Four examples of short wel-
come speeches to a group.
BNH:48
Garran, R. R.
Royal visit. MCA:191
Girls' auxiliary (or similar
girls' missionary group).
HNWM:24
He's somebody special (wel-
come address on Father's
Day). HNWM:11
Holy motherhood (welcome ad-
dress on Mother's Day).

HNWM:8
Howdy, pardner (outline of speech
to welcome Dr. Gifford Win-
gate as new Chairman of the
Drama and Speech Department
at Texas Western College).
CUB:66
Love in search of a word (wel-
come address on Mother's
Day). HNWM:6
Men's brotherhood (for laymen's
group). HNWM:23
Pictures of mother (welcome ad-
dress on Mother's Day).
HNWM:7
Suggestions for preparation of
speech of welcome. MILS:11
Suggestions for preparation of
speeches of welcome.
(Teacher welcoming two busi-
ness men to her classroom).
With examples of. PAE:180
Welcome and introduction of coach
of athletic team at awards ban-
quet. HNWM:34
Welcome to a delegation of for-
eign students. HNWM:48
Welcome to a Fire Chief as
speaker to a civic club.
HNWM:42
Welcome to a freshman class.
HNWM:50
Welcome to a new educational di-
rector (2 examples). BNH:50
Welcome to a new pastor and
family (2 examples). BNH:49
Welcome to a State Attorney
General as speaker at a civic
club. HNWM:42
Welcome to a visiting pastor's
wife. BNH:51
Welcome to adult choir members.
HNWM:30
Welcome to All-sports church
banquet. HNWM:33
Welcome to Baptist Training
Union officers (Christian En-
deavor, etc.). HNWM:27
Welcome to Boy Scout troop (or
Boys' Brigade). HNWM:49
Welcome to Chief of Police as
speaker at a civic club.
HNWM:41
Welcome to children's choir mem-
bers. HNWM:31
Welcome to church officials (Dea-
cons, Stewards, Elders, etc.).
HNWM:26

Welcome to civic affairs
(Arbor Day).   HNWSN:53
Welcome to civic affairs
(Chamber of Commerce).
HNWSN:50
Welcome to civic affairs
(Christmas Tree Lighting).
HNWSN:52
Welcome to civic affairs
(Civic Club).   HNWSN:47
Welcome to civic affairs
(Dedication of historical
museum).   HNWSN:58
Welcome to civic affairs
(Dedication of park).
HNWSN:55
Welcome to civic affairs
(Dedication of the school).
HNWSN:54
Welcome to civic affairs
(Fourth of July).
HNWSN:56
Welcome to civic affairs
(Groundbreaking).
HNWSN:46
Welcome to civic affairs (In-
auguration of club officers).
HNWSN:47
Welcome to civic affairs (In-
auguration of public official).
HNWSN:48
Welcome to daughters at
Mother-Daughter banquet.
HNWM:36
Welcome to fathers at Father-
Son banquet.   HNWM:37
Welcome to Four H Club mem-
bers.   HNWM:49
Welcome to Girl Scouts (or
Pioneer Girls, etc.).
HNWM:50
Welcome to guest speaker at
a stewardship banquet (3
examples).   HNWM:60
Welcome to guest speaker at
a stewardship banquet (3
examples).   HNWM:60
Welcome to husbands at Ladies
Civic Club.   HNWM:45
Welcome to military personnel.
HNWM:25
Welcome to minister as speaker
at a civic club (3 examples).
HNWM:43
Welcome to missionary ap-
pointee (3 examples).
HNWM:57
Welcome to mothers: Mother's

Day, a day of remembrance.
HNWM:5
Welcome to mothers at Mother-
Daughter banquet.   HNWM:35
Welcome to mothers on Children's
Day.   HNWM:7
Welcome to new Christians (3
examples).   HNWM:62
Welcome to new church member
by transfer.   HNWM:63
Welcome to new church members
(new Christians).   HNWSN:11
Welcome to new church members
(transfers from other churches).
HNWSN:14
Welcome to new members in civic
club (3 examples).   HNWM:46
Welcome to new members of
church staff and family.
HNWM:64
Welcome to newspaper editor as
speaker at a civic club.
HNWM:44
Welcome to old friends (2 exam-
ples).   BNH:52
Welcome to parents and ladies of
the Woman's Missionary Soci-
ety on Education Day.
HNWM:21
Welcome to parents at vacation
Bible school commencement.
HNWM:19
Welcome to public official as
speaker at a civic club.
HNWM:41
Welcome to returning missionary
(3 examples).   HNWM:55
Welcome to Royal Ambassadors
(or similar Boys' Missionary
group).   HNWM:23
Welcome to sons at Father-Son
banquet.   HNWM:38
Welcome to students on Education
Day.   HNWM:20
Welcome to Sunday school offi-
cers.   HNWM:28
Welcome to teachers on Education
Day.   HNWM:18
Welcome to teachers on Teacher
Appreciation Day.   HNWM:17
Welcome to various new church
members.   HNWM:64
Welcome to visitors (Ladies'
weekly meeting).   HNWSN:22
Welcome to visitors (Men-of-the-
Church dinner).   HNWSN:23
Welcome to visitors (New church
member class).   HNWSN:24

(National Negro Conference,
May 31, 1909). FON:687

WENDT, GERALD
Schnadig, E. L.
Presents Gerald Wendt.
LYI:186

Wentworth, Peter
Liberty of the Commons (House
of Commons, Feb. 7, 1576).
BRYH:79; CLAYP:1
Speech in behalf of the liberties
of the Parliament. Same as
his Liberty of the Commons

Wentworth, Thomas, 1st Earl of
Strafford See Strafford,
T. W.

Wentworth, William Charles
For the University Bill.
MCA:17

Werner, Alfred
On the constitution and configuration of higher-order compounds (Nobel Lecture, Dec.
11, 1913). NOLC 1:256

WERNER, ALFRED
Nordström, T.
Presentation [of the Nobel
Prize for Chemistry to
Alfred Werner, Dec. 11,
1913]. NOLC 1:253

Wernstedt, W.
Presentation [of the Nobel Prize
for Physiology or Medicine
to Julius Wagner-Jauregg,
Dec. 12, 1927]. NOLM 2:155
Presentation of the Nobel Prize
for 1926 to Johannes Andreas
Grib Fibiger, Dec. 12, 1927].
NOLM 2:119

Wesley, John
On dressing for display.
BREWE 10:3880
Poverty of reason.
BREWE 10:3874
Sacra fames auri.
BREWE 10:3877
Use of money. BRYH:191

Wessén, E.
Presentation [of the Nobel Prize

for Literature to Halldor Kiljan
Laxness, 1955]. NOB 12:3;
NOL:505

West, Dick
Cultural differences: a base.
MAES:120

West, Samuel
Election--sermon. POC:578

WEST, THE
Beecher, L.
A plea for the West. HOW:133
Billington, R. A.
Cowboys, Indians, and the land
of promise: the world image
of the American frontier.
BA 1975-76:176
Thoreau, H. D.
Walking westward. ANN 8:125

WEST POINT
MacArthur, D.
Farewell to the cadets (accept-
ing Sylvanus Thayer award for
service to his nation).
LINR:264; MDV:20; MUS:332
Pierce, F.
Military academy. ANN 6:273

Westgren, A.
Presentation [of the Nobel Prize
for Chemistry to Arne Wilhelm
Kaurin Tiselius, Dec. 13,
1948]. NOLC 3:191
Presentation [of the Nobel Prize
for Chemistry to Artturi Ilmari
Virtanen, Dec. 12, 1945].
NOLC 3:71
Presentation [of the Nobel Prize
for Chemistry to Edwin Mattison
McMillan and Glenn Theodore
Seaborg, Dec. 12, 1951].
NOLC 3:309
Presentation [of the Nobel Prize
for Chemistry for 1943 to
George De Hevesy, Dec. 12,
1944]. NOLC 3:5
Presentation [of the Nobel Prize
for Chemistry for 1944 to Otto
Hahn, Dec. 13, 1946].
NOLC 3:47
Presentation [of the Nobel Prize
for Chemistry to Petrus
Josephus Wilhelmus Debye,
Dec. 12, 1936]. NOLC 2:379
Presentation [of the Nobel Prize

for Chemistry to Willard
Frank Libby, Dec. 12, 1960].
NOLC 3:589

Westmoreland, William C.
Vietnam--the situation today
(1967). BAS:59 (outline only)

Weyforth, B. Stuart, Jr.
Introduces Barry Goldwater,
Senator from Arizona.
PRS:39
Introduces Boris Morros.
PRS:66
Introduces Cornelia Otis Skinner.
PRS:53
Introduces General Mark W.
Clark, president of the
Citadel. PRS:64
Introduces George A. Smathers,
United States Senator from
Florida. PRS:36
Introduces Mrs. Ivy Baker
Priest, Treasurer of the
United States. PRS:28
Introduces Mural Deusing.
PRS:63
Introduces Nikolai Khokhlov,
former Soviet intelligence
officer. PRS:68
Introduces Robert C. Tyson,
chairman of the finance
committee, United States
Steel Corporation. PRS:15

WHALEN, GROVER A.
Nizer, L.
Presents Grover A. Whalen.
LYI:65

Wheeler, Alfred
Product of labor. ANN 11:113

Wheeler, Burton K.
Menace of Lend-Lease.
ANN 16:46

WHIG PARTY
Sumner, C.
Antislavery duties of the
Whig Party. HOW:218

Whipper, William
Eulogy on William Wilberforce
(Philadelphia, Dec. 6, 1833).
FON:49

Whipple, George Hoyt
Hemoglobin regeneration as

influenced by diet and other
factors (Nobel Lecture, Dec.
12, 1934). NOLM 2:346

WHIPPLE, GEORGE HOYT
Holmgren, I.
Presentation [of the Nobel
Prize for Physiology or Medi-
cine to George Hoyt Whipple,
George Richards Minot, and
William Parry Murphy, Dec.
12, 1934]. NOLM 2:335

WHISKEY INSURRECTION, 1794
Washington, G.
Sixth annual address.
STAT 1:21

White, Byron R. See Warren, E.,
jt. auth.

White, Edward Douglas and others
(J. M. Harlan)
Standard Oil Company of New
Jersey v. United States, 1911:
opinion for the court and dis-
senting opinion. ANN 13:310

WHITE, EDWARD H.
Sevareid, E.
Eulogy for the astronauts.
MOP:189

White, George H.
Defense of the Negro race (Washington, D.C., Jan. 29, 1901).
FON:635
I raise my voice against one of
the most dangerous evils in our
country (Washington, Jan. 20,
1900). FON:624

White, Richard
The educated man in the age of
Aquarius (Wabash College,
June 7, 1970). BAAE:271

White, Samuel
Opposition to the Louisiana Purchase. ANN 4:175

White, Walter F.
"Work or fight" in the South
(1918). FON:724

White, William Allen
Speaking for the consumer (Wash-
ington, Sept. 20, 1937).
HURH:234

"This is a middle-class country
and the middle-class will
have its will and way."
Same as his Speaking for
the consumer

WHITE HOUSE CONFERENCE ON
  CHILDREN
  Nixon, R. M.
    Remarks at the White House
    Conference on Children.
    BA 1970-71:37

Whitefield, George
  Abraham's offering up his son
    Isaac. OLIS:6
  Kingdom of God.
    BREWE 10:3885

Whitehead, Alfred North
  Technical education and its re-
    lation to science and litera-
    ture (London, Jan. 5, 1917).
    MCB:403

WHITEHEAD, W. E.
  Erickson, D. J.
    Presents W. E. Whitehead.
    LYI:63

Whitemen, Henrietta V.
  Spiritual roots of Indian suc-
    cess. MAES:377

Whitney, Andrew Griswold
  Oration (Detroit, July 4, 1818).
    HAW:329

Whitney, Asa
  Railroad to the Pacific.
    ANN 7:272

Whitney, Frank L.
  Total redevelopment of cities.
    ANN 18:338

Wieland, Heinrich Otto
  The chemistry of the bile acids
    (Nobel Lecture for 1927,
    Dec. 12, 1928). NOLC 2:94

WIELAND, HEINRICH OTTO
  Söderbaum, H. G.
    Presentation [of the Nobel
    Prize for Chemistry for
    1927 to Heinrich Otto Wieland
    and for 1928 to Adolf Otto
    Reinhold Windaus, Dec. 12,
    1928]. NOLC 2:89

Wien, Wilhelm
  On the laws of thermal radiation
    (Nobel Lecture, Dec. 11,
    1911). NOLPH 1:275

WIEN, WILHELM
  Dahlgren, E. W.
    Presentation [of the Nobel
    Prize for Physics to Wilhelm
    Wien, Dec. 11, 1911].
    NOLPH 1:271

Wiesner, Jerome B.
  Argument against the ABM.
    BA 1968-1969:19
  Science in the affluent society
    (centennial celebration of Na-
    tional Academy of Sciences).
    ANN 18:186

Wigglesworth, Michael
  Prayse of eloquence. POC:8

Wigner, Eugene P.
  Events, laws of nature, and in-
    variance principles (Nobel Lec-
    ture, Dec. 12, 1963).
    NOLPH 4:6

WIGNER, EUGENE P.
  Waller, I.
    Presentation [of the Nobel Prize
    for Physics to Eugene P. Wig-
    ner, Maria Goeppert Mayer
    and J. Hans D. Jensen, Dec.
    12, 1963]. NOLPH 4:3

Wilberforce, William
  Horrors of the British slave trade
    in the eighteenth century.
    BREWE 10:3891

WILBERFORCE, WILLIAM
  Whipper, W.
    Eulogy on William Wilberforce.
    FON:49

WILBUR, RAY LYMAN
  Merriam, J. C.
    Presents Ray Lyman Wilbur.
    LYI:82

Wilkes, John
  Denies the right of the House of
    Commons to reject duly elected
    members. STRM:39
  Motion to redress. Same as his
    Denies the rights of the House
    of Commons to reject duly

elected members
Warning and a prophecy.
BREWE 10:3901

WILKES, JOHN
Mansfield, W. M.
In the case of John Wilkes.
BREWE 8:2943

Wilkins, Maurice Hugh Frederick
The molecular configuration
of nucleic acids (Nobel
Lecture, Dec. 11, 1962).
NOLM 3:754

WILKINS, MAURICE HUGH
FREDERICK
Engström, A.
Presentation [of the Nobel
Prize for Physiology or
Medicine to Francis Harry
Compton Crick, James
Dewey Watson, and Maurice
Hugh Frederick Wilkins,
Dec. 11, 1962].
NOLM 3:751

Wilkins, Roy
The conspiracy to deny equality
(National Association for the
Advancement of Colored Peo-
ple, August, 1955).
FON:892; SMHV:120
Keynote address to the NAACP
annual convention, Los
Angeles, July 5, 1966.
AND:101; BOSC:89; OE:166
Sail our NAACP ship-keynote
address. Same as his Key-
note address to the NAACP
annual convention, Los Ange-
les, July 5, 1966

Wilkinson, Howard C.
How separate should government
and God be? LINR:98

Willcox, William R.
Introducing G. W. Goethals to
the Economic Club of New
York, March 5, 1914.
LYI:183

William I (the Conqueror of England)
Speech to his troops before the
battle of Hastings. BRYH:27

Williams, Francis
Duty of colored men in the present
national crisis. (Allegheny
City, Pa., 1864). FON:281

Williams, Peter
Abolition of the slave trade.
Same as his Oration on the
abolition of the slave trade
Oration on the abolition of the
slave trade (New York, Janu-
ary 1, 1808). FON:20
Slavery and colonization (St.
Philip's Protestant Episcopal
Church, July 4, 1830).
FON:43
A tribute to Captain Paul Cuffe
(New York African Institution,
Oct. 21, 1817). FON:28

Williams, William See Varnum,
J. M., jt. auth.

Willkie, Wendell L.
Acceptance speech. ANN 16:27;
SIN:171
Campaign speech, St. Louis,
Missouri, October 17, 1940.
SIN:183
Consensus established. ROD:174
Education determines civilization;
the importance of liberal edu-
cation policies. CROCK:93
Loyal opposition (National radio
address, Nov. 11, 1940).
GRG:63; HURH:243
"Our American unity must be
forged between the ideas of the
opposition and the practices
and the policies of the adminis-
tration." Same as his Loyal
opposition
Private enterprise--we have gone
far enough down the road to
federal control. BAD:69

Willstätter, Richard Martin
On plant pigments (Nobel Lecture
for 1915, June 3, 1920).
NOLC 1:301

Wilson, Charles Thomson Rees
On the cloud method of making
visible ions and the tracks of
ionizing particles (Nobel Lecture, Dec. 12, 1927).
NOLPH 2:194

WILSON, CHARLES THOMSON
    REES
    Siegbahn, K. M. G.
        Presentation [of the Nobel
        Prize for Physics to Arthur
        Holly Compton and Charles
        Thomson Rees Wilson, Dec.
        12, 1927]. NOLPH 2:169

Wilson, Dick
    Real Indian leaders condemn
        A. I. M. MAES:63

Wilson, Edward Foss
    Introduces Wilbur M. Brucker,
        then Secretary of the Army.
        PRS:41

Wilson, James
    In vindication of the colonies.
        POC:308
    Speech to the convention of the
        Pronvince of Pennsylvania.
        Same as his In vindication
        of the colonies
    Study of law in the United States.
        ANN 3:380

WILSON, JOSEPH
    Stanley, J.
        Tribute to a fallen Black
        soldier. FON:268

Wilson, Logan
    Education for adequacy (Univ. of
        Houston, June 3, 1967).
        HOR:16

Wilson, Orlando W.
    Police arrest privileges in a
        free society. ANN 18:36

Wilson, Warren H.
    Interaction of country and city.
        ANN 14:4

Wilson, Woodrow
    Appeal for neutrality. Same
        as his Neutrality message
        to the Senate, August 19,
        1914
    Appeal for support of the
        League of Nations (Omaha,
        Nebraska speech). ANN 14:187
    Appeal to the voters to return
        a Democratic Congress.
        ANN 14:166
    Commission city government.

ANN 13:269
Eighth annual message.
    STAT 3:2608
"Eyes of the people opened. "
    STAT 3:2580
Fear of monopoly. ANN 13:356
Fifth annual message. Same as
    his "Eyes of the people
    opened. "
First annual message.
    STAT 3:2544
First inaugural address.
    ANN 13:412. USINAU:199;
    USINAUG:199
For the League of Nations (Des
    Moines, Iowa speech).
    LINS:300
Fourteen points (Washington, Jan.
    8, 1918). BOORA 2:773;
    FRIP:291; GRG:42; HURH:180;
    OLIS:228
Fourth annual message.
    STAT 3:2575
League of Nations. Same as his
    Speech at Peace Conference at
    Paris (Session February 15,
    1919)
The nature of democracy in the
    United States (Owl Club in
    Hartford, Conn., May 17,
    1889). FRIP:270
Neutrality message to the Senate,
    August 19, 1914. ANN 13:491
New call to duty. ALA:77
"Only a peace between equals can
    last. " Same as his Peace
    without victory
Peace Conference at Paris: Ses-
    sion, January 25, 1919.
    HURH:185
Peace without victory (Washington,
    D.C., Jan. 21, 1917).
    ANN 14:65; FRIP:286; HURH:173
"The program of the world's
    peace, therefore, is our pro-
    gram. " Same as his Fourteen
    points
Responding to the new call of
    duty. Same as his New call
    to duty
Second annual message.
    STAT 3:2551
Second inaugural address.
    USINAU:203; USINAUG:203
Seventh annual message.
    STAT 3:2598
Sixth annual message.
    STAT 3:2587

Speech at Peace Conference
at Paris (Session February
15, 1919). ANN 14:180
Speech opening campaign for
fourth liberty loan (Sept.
27, 1918). FRIP:295
Tampico incident.
ANN 13:468
Third annual message.
STAT 3:2560
"... to make permanent ar-
rangements that justice shall
be rendered and peace maintained. " Same as his Peace
Conference at Paris: Session, January 25, 1919
War message to Congress,
April 2, 1917. ANN 14:77;
HURH:177; LINS:291
"... we will not choose the
path of submission and suffer
the most sacred rights of our
nation and our people to be
ignored and violated. " Same
as his War message to Congress
What is progress? BEN:62

WILSON, WOODROW
Connally, T. T. and others
Censure of Senator Nye.
BRR:69
Johnsen, A.
Remarks [presenting the
Nobel Prize for Peace to
Thomas Woodrow Wilson,
1919, Dec. 10, 1920].
NOLP 1:293
Olney, R.
Presents Woodrow Wilson.
LYI:215
Schmedeman, A. G.
Acceptance [of the Nobel
Prize for Peace for Woodrow
Wilson, 1919, Dec. 10,
1920]. NOLP 1:294

Windaus, Adolf Otto Reinhold
Constitution of sterols and
their connection with other
substances occurring in
nature (Nobel Lecture, Dec.
12, 1928). NOLC 2:105

WINDAUS, ADOLF OTTO REIN-
HOLD
Söderbaum, H. G.
Presentation [of the Nobel

Prize for Chemistry for 1927
to Heinrich Otto Wieland and
for 1928 to Adolf Otto Reinhold
Windaus, Dec. 12, 1928].
NOLC 2:89

Winnington, Thomas See Walpole,
R. , jt. auth.

Winter, Robert A.
This I believe. SCHW:87

Winthrop, John
"Liberty is the proper end and
object of authority. " Same as
his Little speech on liberty
Little speech on liberty (Plymouth
Colony, 1645). HURH:17;
POC:135
Modell of Christian charity.
BOORA 1:10

Winthrop, Robert C.
Oregon question. ANN 7:317

Wirsén, C. D. af
Presentation [of the Nobel Prize
for Literature to Bjørnstjerne
Martinus Bjørnson, 1903].
NOL:14; NOB 3:77
Presentation [of the Nobel Prize
for Literature to Christian
Matthias Theodor Mommsen,
1902]. NOL:7; NOB 13:235
Presentation [of the Nobel Prize
for Literature to Frédéric
Mistral and José de Echegaray
y Eizaguirre, 1904].
NOL:23; NOB 13:119
Presentation [of the Nobel Prize
for Literature to Giosué
Carducci, 1906]. NOB 5:3;
NOL:48
Presentation [of the Nobel Prize
for Literature to Henryk
Sienkiewicz, 1905]. NOL:36;
NOB 17:173
Presentation [of the Nobel Prize
for Literature to Maurice
Polydore Marie Bernhard
Maeterlinck, 1911].
NOB 12:139; NOL:107
Presentation [of the Nobel Prize
for Literature to Paul Johann
Ludwig Heyse, 1910].
NOB 7:279; NOL:100
Presentation [of the Nobel Prize
for Literature to Rudyard

Kipling, 1907]. NOB 11:89;
NOL:58
Presentation [of the Nobel Prize
for Literature to Sully Prud-
homme, 1901]. NOL:2;
NOB 16:303

Wirt, William
Burr and Blennerhasset (at
trial of Burr).
BREWE 10:3908
Death of Jefferson and Adams.
BREWE 10:3905
Genius as the capacity of work.
BREWE 10:3910

Wirtz, W. Willard
Address at the Catholic Univer-
sity of America.
BA 1966-67:177
Economic Opportunity Act of
1964. CAPG:165

Wise, Henry A.
Speech of ex-Governor Henry
A. Wise. ECH:150

Wise, Stephen Samuel
Abraham Lincoln, man and
American (Springfield, Ill.,
Feb. 12, 1914). HURH:169
"Lincoln is become for us the
test of human worth." Same
as his Abraham Lincoln,
man and American

WIT AND HUMOR
Hazlitt, W.
On wit and humor.
BREWE 7:2449

---- See also After-dinner
speeches; Satiric speeches

Witherspoon, John
On eloquence. POC:44
Public credit under the Con-
federation. BREWE 10:3912

Witter, Jean
Statement [before the] Subcom-
mittee on Constitutional
Amendments of the Committee
on the Judiciary of the U.S.
Senate. (May 5-7, 1970).
BOST:203

Wittstock, Laura Waterman
Native American women in the

feminist milieu. (Palo Alto,
Calif., March 21-22, 1975).
MAES:373

Wivell, Cathy A.
World hunger: a question of
rights. BREWW:119

WOLBERG, IRVING
Kosman, M.
Eulogy for Irving Wolberg.
JAM:44

Wolcott, Oliver
Address at state line between
Southwick, Massachusetts and
Granby, Connecticut, July 4,
1825. HAW:122

Wolfe, Helen B.
The backlash phenomenon (Middle
Atlantic Regional Conference,
June, 1976). LINRST:85

WOMEN
Abzug, B. S.
A new kind of Southern strat-
egy. BA 1971-72:37
Bates, D.
Bride-price. MDYG:59
Burke, Y. B.
"Aspirations ... unrequited."
BA 1974-75:143
Carpenter, L.
Faces and voices of American
women. BA 1977-78:184
Chisholm, S.
Women in politics.
BA 1972-73:79
Clemens, S. L.
"The ladies." BEN:201
Depew, C. M.
Woman. HURH:125
Dunbar, R.
Women's liberation: where the
movement is today and where
it's going. STOT:311
Feldmann, M.
Of mice and women. SCHW:64
Horner, M. S.
Opportunity for educational
innovation. BA 1972-73:184
Introduction for housewives (5
examples). BNH:33
Lim, P. G.
Women's role in national de-
velopment. MONS:339
Nies, N.
Warrior and the woman.

SCHW:10
Peterson, M.
In these present crises.
BA 1970-71:73
Schroeder, P.
You can do it.
BA 1972-73:86
Spain, J. B.
A woman could be President.
VER:249
Steinem, G. and others
Meet the press.
BA 1972-73:65
Steinem, G.
Speech at the U. S. Naval
Academy. JAM:46
Thibeault, M. L.
The hazards of equity.
VERD:265
Tribute to a pastor's wife (2
examples). BNH:77
Trotter, V. Y.
A shift in the balance.
BA 1974-75:148
Truth, S.
When woman gets her rights
man will be right. FON:345
Woman's rights. FON:100
Welcome to wives of civic club
members (on Ladies Day).
HNWM:44

---- BLACK
Crummell, A.
The Black woman of the
South: her neglects and her
needs. FON:479
Davis, A.
I am a Black revolutionary
woman. FON:1177
Terrell, M. C.
The progress of colored
women. FON:643

---- EDUCATION See Education
of women

---- EMPLOYMENT
Furay, M.
Statement before the Sub-
committee on Constitutional
Amendments of the Com-
mittee on the Judiciary of
the U. S. Senate.
BOST:219

---- LEGAL STATUS, LAWS, ETC.
Clay, L.

Laws of the states affecting
women. BLY:199
Pankhurst, E. G.
Speech at the Bow Street
Police Court. BRYF:499;
BRYH:455

---- SUFFRAGE
Anthony, S. B.
Enfranchisement of women.
HURH:123
Catt, C. C.
Political parties and women
voters. BRYF:506
Douglass, F.
Woman suffrage. FON:517
May, S. J.
Enfranchisement of women.
ANN 7:342
Pankhurst, E. G.
Importance of the vote.
BRYH:442
Speech at the Bow Street
Police Court. BRYF:499;
BRYH:455
Stanton, E. C.
Natural rights of civilized
women. ANN 9:151

WOMEN AUTHORS
Yalow, R. S.
"Let us join hands, hearts and
minds." BA 1977-78:181

WOMEN IN AGRICULTURE
Ferguson, V.
Women in agriculture.
BREWW:122

WOMEN'S RIGHTS
Brown, J.
Liberation struggle generates
tension on race, sex issues.
BOST:265
Buckley, J.
The Equal Rights Amendment:
the legislative aspect.
LINRST:271
Chisholm, S.
In support of the Equal Rights
Amendment. BOST:243;
EHN:364; MOPR:372
Goldman, E. and others
Statement [before the] Subcom-
mittee on Constitutional Amend-
ments of the Committee on the
Judiciary of the U. S. Senate.
BOST:215

Green, E.
  Representative Edith Green
  speaks in support of the
  Equal Rights Amendment.
  BOST:237
Griffiths, M. W. and others
  House debates the Equal
  Rights Amendment.
  BOST:230
Holtzman, E.
  Women and equality under
  the law. BA 1976-77:80
Springen, P. J.
  The dimensions of the op-
  pression of women.
  LINRS:109; LINRST:130
Witter, J.
  Statement [before the] Sub-
  committee on Constitutional
  Amendments of the Committee
  on the Judiciary of the
  U. S. Senate. BOST:203
Wolfe, H. B.
  The backlash phenomenon.
  LINRST:85

Wong, Lin Ken
  Intelligentsia in a nation of im-
  migrants (Singapore).
  MONS:476

Wong Lin Ken See Wong, Lin Ken

Wood, Fernando
  Proposal for the secession of
  New York City. ANN 9:233

Woodmason, Charles
  You are to take these free
  booters and desperadoes.
  POC:548

Woodward, George W. See
  Butler, B. F., jt. auth.

Woodward, Robert Burns
  Recent advances in the chemistry of natural products
  (Nobel Lecture, Dec. 11,
  1965). NOLC 4:100

WOODWARD, ROBERT BURNS
  Fredga, A.
  Presentation of the Nobel
  Prize for Chemistry to
  Robert Burns Woodward,
  Dec. 11, 1965. NOLC 4:97

Woolsey, John M.
  Opinion December 6, 1933
  (Ulysses case--freedom of
  reading). ANN 15:236
  United States v. One book called
  Ulysses. Same as his Opinion
  December 6, 1933 (Ulysses
  case--freedom of reading)

Worden, George J.
  Publican. SCHW:92
  Person to person. SCHW:174

WORK
  Furuset, A.
  Work is worship. ANN 14:561
  Wirt, W.
  Genius as the capacity of work.
  BREWE 10:3190

WORKINGMEN'S PARTY OF THE
    UNITED STATES
  Clark, P. H.
  Socialism: the remedy for
  the evils of society. FON:451

WORLD COURT See Permanent
  Court of International Justice

WORLD FOOD CONFERENCE,
    ROME, 1974
  Kissinger, H. A.
  Address before the World Food
  Conference. BA 1974-75:62

WORLD POLITICS, 1945-
  McNamara, R. S.
  Address before the American
  Society of Newspaper Editors.
  BA 1966-67:160

WORLD WAR, 1939-1945
  Chapuisat, E.
  The activity of the International
  Committee of the Red Cross
  during the War, 1939-1945
  (Nobel Lecture for 1944, Dec.
  11, 1945). NOLP 2:295
  Churchill, W. L. S.
  Address to the Congress, De-
  cember 26, 1941. ALS:223;
  AND:120; ARN:301; BRR:51;
  CROCK:29; JEF:190; JEFF:184
  Hoover, H. C.
  War comes to Europe. GRG:61
  Mote, C. H.
  The ruling oligarchy wants to

engage in a foreign war
(1941). DAVF:255
Randolph, A. P.
A call for mass action.
FON:822
Roosevelt, F. D.
Acceptance speech via radio
to convention, Washington,
D.C., July 19, 1940.
SIN:156
Taft, R. A.
Opposition to the Roosevelt
war policies. ANN 16:94
Vander Jagt, G.
Price of the best. SCHW:59
Willkie, W. L.
Campaign speech, St.
Louis, Missouri, October
17, 1940. SIN:183

---- AERIAL OPERATIONS
Churchill, W. L. S.
Parliament in the air raids
(September 17, 1940 speech).
STRM:481

---- AUSTRALIA
Curtin, J.
We are fighting mad.
MCA:154

---- CAMPAIGNS - WESTERN
FRONT
Eisenhower, D. D.
Order of the Day to the
Allied troops invading
France. GRG:74
Patton, G. S.
"Flanks are something for
the enemy to worry about."
HURH:274

---- CHINA
Chiang, Mei-Ling
Japan is first U.S. foe.
CROCK:46

---- CIVILIAN ACTIVITIES
Roosevelt, F. D.
Message to Congress, Janu-
ary 7, 1943.
STAT 3:2867

---- GREAT BRITAIN
Bevan, A.
Change the direction of the
war. MCB:524
Churchill, Sir W. L. S.

Be ye men of valour.
MCB:495
"Blood, sweat and tears."
ALA:99; MCB:493
Dunkirk. MCB:498
Never in the field of human
conflict. MCB:514
Solemn hour (May 19, 1940
broadcast). BRYH:534
"Their finest hour." MCB:506

---- GREECE
Menzies, R. G.
Greece and the Anzac spirit.
MCA:138

---- ITALY
Roosevelt, F. D.
Italy enters this war.
ANN 16:8

---- JAPAN
Chiang, Mei-Ling
Japan is first U.S. foe.
CROCK:46

---- ---- SURRENDER
MacArthur, D.
Hope of all mankind.
ALA:105
Remarks and final speech at
Japanese surrender.
ANN 16:339

---- NAVAL OPERATIONS
Roosevelt, F. D.
Navy Day address on the at-
tack on the destroyer Kearney.
ANN 16:90

---- NEW ZEALAND
Savage, M. J.
New Zealand's war aims,
1939. MACS:365 sel.

---- UNITED STATES
Chiang, Mei-Ling
Japan is first U.S. foe.
CROCK:46
Roosevelt, F. D.
Address at the annual gather-
ing of the White House Cor-
respondents' Association,
February 12, 1943.
ANN 16:130
Fireside chat (December 9,
1941). ANN 16:105
First war address before

Congress. HURH:269;
STAT 3:2861
Message to Congress, January 7, 1943.
STAT 3:2867
Message to Congress, January 11, 1944. ANN 16:211;
ROD:337; STAT 3:2875
Message to Congress on the state of the nation, January 6, 1945. STAT 3:2882
Navy Day address on the attack on the destroyer Kearney. ANN 16:90
Opening campaign speech at dinner of International Brotherhood of Teamsters.
LINS:330
This nation will remain neutral. ROD:274
War address (Washington, Dec. 8, 1941). ANN 16:103;
CUB:88 (outline); GRG:71;
HURH:265; LINS:327;
MAC:242; MACR:282;
MOPR:377; ROD:306
Truman, H. S.
Announcement of the first use of the atomic bomb.
ANN 16:334
First annual message.
STAT 3:2900

---- ---- AID TO GREAT BRITAIN
Roosevelt, F. D.
Address to White House Correspondents' Association dinner, March 15, 1941.
CROCK:11
Preservation of American independence. HURH:246;
OLIS:249

---- WAR AIMS
Chiang, Mei-Ling
Japan is first U.S. foe.
CROCK:46

---- WAR CRIMINALS
Taft, R. A.
Equal justice under law.
BEN:100

WORSHIP
Tyndale, W.
Use and abuse of images and relics. BREWE 9:3660

WOUNDED KNEE
Bellecourt, V.
American Indian Movement.
MAES:66
Wilson, D.
Real Indian leaders condemn A.I.M. MAES:63

Wright, Frances
Of existing evils and their remedy. ANN 5:290

Wright, Frank Lloyd
Art and the machine.
ANN 12:409
"A new integrity of human life."
Same as his On architecture
On architecture (London, May, 1939). HURH:241

Wright, John S. See Severeid, E., jt. auth.

Wright, Theodore S.
Prejudice against the colored man (Utica, N.Y., New York State Anti-Slavery Society, Sept. 20, 1837). FON:61

Wright, Tom
"Viva la Huelga." BREWW:174

Wriston, Walter B.
Long view of the short run.
BA 1968-1969:89
Risk and other four-letter words (Chicago, Oct. 25, 1979).
BA 1979-80:191

WRITS OF ASSISTANCE
Otis, J.
Writs of Assistance, February, 1761. ANN 2:74;
BREWE 8:3125; POC:90

Wulfstan
Sermon of the Wolf to the English when the Danes persecuted them most, which was in the year 1014 from the incarnation of our Lord Jesus Christ.
BRYH:21

Wycliffe, John
Concerning a grain of corn.
BREWE 10:3924
Good lore for simple folk.
BREWE 10:3920

Mercy to damned men in Hell.
BREWE 10:3922
Rule for decent living.
BREWE 10:3918
Sermon for the Sunday within
the week of the twelfth day
after Christmas, January
6--on meaning.
BRYH:38

Wydler, John W.
Science and the public trust
(Schenectady, N. Y. , Oct.
18, 1979).
BA 1979-80:139

Wyndham, Sir William, Bart
Attack on Sir Robert Walpole.
BREWE 10:3925
Royal prerogative delegated
from the people (Army
Bill, 1734).
BREWE 10:3927

- X -

Xavier S. Thani Nayagam See
Thani Nayagam, Xavier S.

X-RAYS
Bragg, W. L.
The diffraction of x-rays by
crystals. NOLPH 1:370
Compton, A. H.
X-rays as a branch of optics.
NOLPH 2:174
Laue, M. V.
Concerning the detection of
x-ray interferences.
NOLPH 1:347

- Y -

YALE UNIVERSITY
Eliot, C. W.
Harvard and Yale.
HURH:130

Yalow, Rosalyn S.
"Let us join hands, hearts and
minds" (Stockholm, Dec.
10, 1977).
BA 1977-78:181

Yamzon, Victoriano
The lawyer shall never retreat
(Manila, Oct. 22, 1937).
CURM:323

Yang, Chen Ning
The law of parity conservation
and other symmetry laws of
physics (Nobel Lecture, Dec.
11, 1957). NOLPH 3:393

YANG, CHEN NING
Klein, O. B.
Presentation [of the Nobel
Prize for Physics to Chen
Ning Yang and Tsung Dao Lee,
Dec. 11, 1957]. NOLPH 3:389

YANKEES See National characteristics, American

Yazzie, Ethelou
Navajo wisdom, 4th International
Conference, Tarrytown, N. Y. ,
November 1975. MAES:261
Navajo wisdom as found in Navajo
oral history. MAES:263
Special problems of Indian women
in education (Window Rock,
Ariz. , Sept. 24-25, 1975).
MAES:360

Ybarra, Barry
The wheel of poverty (Chabot
College, 1971). BAPR:356;
BAPRR:266

Yeang, C. H.
The building of peaceful bridge
the rotary way (Penang, Sept.
27, 1970). MONSA:218

Yeats, William Butler
Acceptance [of the Nobel Prize
for Literature, 1923].
NOB 18:263; NOL:199
The Irish dramatic movement
(Nobel Lecture, Dec. 15, 1923).
NOL:201

YEATS, WILLIAM BUTLER
Hallström, P.
Presentation [of the Nobel
Prize for Literature to Wil-
liam Butler Yeats, 1923].
NOB 18:275; NOL:194

YELLOW FEVER
  Theiler, M.
    The development of vaccines
    against yellow fever.
    NOLM 3:351

Yonge, Sir William See Walpole,
  R., jt. auth.

Youle, Clinton
  Introduces Charles B. Thornton.
    PRS:100
  Introduces Don Whitehead,
    chief of the Washington
    bureau of the New York
    Herald Tribune.   PRS:65
  Introduces Percy Brundage,
    then director of the Federal
    Budget.   PRS:31
  Introduces Stanley C. Hope,
    president, National Associa-
    tion of Manufacturers.
    PRS:15
  Introduces W. Randolph Bur-
    gess, United States per-
    manent representative on the
    North Atlantic Council.
    PRS:30
  Presents S. Clarke Beise,
    president of the Bank of
    America.   PRS:15

Young, John
  Property under the common
    law (Coster v. Lorillard
    case). ANN 6:181

Young, Owen D.
  How we meet ourselves (semi-
    centennial of Hendrix Col-
    lege, Conway, Ark., Nov.
    20, 1934). HURH:227
  "You must fuse at white heat
    the several particles of
    your learning." Same as
    his How we meet ourselves

Young, Whitney M., Jr.
  Can the city survive? Same
    as his Crisis of the city:
    the danger of the ghetto
  Crisis of the city: the danger
    of the ghetto (54th annual
    Fall Conference of the Na-
    tional Association of Bank
    Loan and Credit Officers,
    Oct. 28, 1968).
    BA 1966-67:82; OE:177;

SMHV:160
The social revolution: challenge
  to the nation (National Urban
  League, 1963). FON:961
A strategy for the seventies:
  unity, coalition, negotiation
  (New York, National Urban
  League Conference, July 19,
  1970). STOT:331

YOUNG, WHITNEY M., JR.
  Cheek, J. E.
    A promise made, a promise
    to keep: Whitney Young and
    the nation. BA 1970-71:131

YOUNG DEMOCRATIC CLUBS OF
    AMERICA
  Roosevelt, F. D.
    Address to Young Democratic
    Clubs of America, August 24,
    1935. FRIP:304

YOUNG MEN'S CHRISTIAN ASSOCI-
    ATION
  Johari, M. K.
    Malaysian Brothers (diamond
    jubilee of Y.M.C.A. of Kuala
    Lumpur). MONS:150

Youngdahl, Luther
  United States v. Lattimore.
    ANN 17:300

YOUTH
  Abbott, R. S.
    A message to youth. FON:778
  Ferrell, D.
    Young men with visions.
    CAPG:385
  Harper, P. C.
    What's happening, baby?
    JEF:232; JEFF:202; KEO:252
  Hutchins, R. M.
    Message to the younger gener-
    ation. MDV:198
  Kennedy, R. F.
    Address to the Free University
    of Berlin. MDV:95
    Special message to the Con-
    gress on the nation's youth.
    THOMS:34
  Lee Kuan Yew
    Problems of leadership.
    MONS:371
  Lim Kim San
    Youth leadership. MONSA:310
  Little, M.

To young people.   FON:1004
Pontier, G.
  Plea for understanding.
  SCHW:136
Roosevelt, F. D.
  Address to Young Democratic
  Clubs of America, August
  24, 1935.   FRIP:304

---- ADULT RELATIONSHIP
Berson, A.
  Open letter to my middle-
  aged father.   REIR:215
Church, F.
  Foreign policy and the gener-
  ation gap.   BA 1970-71:49
Horn, F. H.
  The student revolt, a defense
  of the older generation.
  HOR:49
Perkins, J. A.
  Bridging the generation gap,
  how the New Deal became
  today's establishment.
  HOR:56
Read, D. H. C.
  Is God over thirty? Religion
  and the youth revolt.
  BA 1966-67:129
Walker, H. B.
  The future of the past.
  BA 1970-71:63

---- RELIGIOUS LIFE
Read, D. H. C.
  Is God over thirty? Religion
  and the youth revolt.
  BA 1966-67:129

YOUTH WEEK
  Youth for Youth Week.
  HNWM:16

YUCATAN
  Niles, J. and others
  Debate on the Yucatan Bill.
  ANN 7:426

Yukawa, Hideki
  Meson theory in its developments (Nobel Lecture, Dec.
  12, 1949).   NOLPH 3:128

YUKAWA, HIDEKI
  Waller, I.
  Presentation [of the Nobel
  Prize for Physics to Hideki
  Yukawa, Dec. 12, 1949].
  NOLPH 3:125

- Z -

Zeeman, Pieter
  Light radiation in a magnetic
  field (Nobel Lecture for 1902,
  May 2, 1903).   NOLPH 1:33

ZEEMAN, PIETER
  Theel, Hj.
  Presentation [of the Nobel
  Prize for Physics to Hendrik
  Antoon Lorentz and Pieter
  Zeeman, 1902].   NOLPH 1:11

Zellner, Leon R.
  What can we prove about God?
  (Pennsylvania State University,
  March 7, 1965).   ARN:337;
  ARS:187

Zernike, Frits
  How I discovered phase contrast
  (Nobel Lecture, Dec. 11,
  1953).   NOLPH 3:239

ZERNIKE, FRITS
  Hulthén, E.
  Presentation [of the Nobel
  Prize for Physics to Frits
  Zernike, Dec. 11, 1953].
  NOLPH 3:237

Ziegler, Karl
  Consequences and development of
  an invention (Nobel Lecture,
  Dec. 12, 1963).   NOLC 4:6

ZIEGLER, KARL
  Fredga, A.
  Presentation [of the Nobel
  Prize for Chemistry to Karl
  Ziegler and Giulio Natta, Dec.
  12, 1963].   NOLC 4:3

Zimbardo, Philip
  Puerto Ricans and the neighbor-
  hood: a persuasive interview.
  STOT:305

Zimmerman, Ralph
  Mingled blood.   ARS:98;
  LINR:199

Zola, Emile
  Appeal for Dreyfus.   BAS:110
  (outline only); BREWE 10:3931
  Honor of France.   Same as his
  Appeal for Dreyfus

Zsigmondy, Richard Adolf
  Properties of colloids (Nobel
    Lecture for 1925, Dec. 11,
    1926).   NOLC 2:45

ZSIGMONDY, RICHARD ADOLF
  Söderbaum, H. G.
    Presentation [of the Nobel
    Prize for Chemistry for
    1925 to Richard Adolf Zsig-
    mondy, Dec. 11, 1926].
    NOLC 2:41

Zubly, John Joachim
  Law of Liberty.   POC:611

Zumwalt, Elmo
  Introduction to Edmund G.
    Brown, Jr.   (August 12,
    1976).   JAM:33

Zwerling, Jeffrey C.
  Federal government should con-
    tinue its present housing
    program for low-income
    groups rather than change
    to the proposed rent subsidy
    plan.   BAS:196 (outline only)

SELECTED LIST OF TITLES

EXPLANATION

Titles listed in the Selected List of Titles can be located by referring back to the Speech Index proper under the name of the author which follows each title.

Included in this list are the titles which the compiler thought would be difficult to locate for the user who does not know the name of the author, or if the meaning in the title bears no resemblance to the topic discussed, or if there are no key words in the title to guide the user to the proper subject entry. Examples of such titles are: "Acres of diamonds"; "Green parrot"; and "The strangler."

This list does not include titles which obviously may be located readily by subject or type of speech. "Liberty or death" can be found under LIBERTY.

Many titles of war speeches delivered by war leaders or by civilians are included in this list because the entry is usually under the name of a specific war rather than WAR in general.

By excluding the numerous titles under such types of speeches as INTRODUCTIONS; RESPONSES; INAUGURAL ADDRESSES; ACCEPTANCE SPEECHES, etc., much repetition was avoided, and the list kept simple enough to be quickly scanned for vaguely remembered titles, variant titles, and titles of speeches where the author is not known.

SELECTED LIST OF TITLES

Abilities and possibilities of our
race - Douglass, F.
Abolition of slavery - Paul, N.
Abolition of the provinces, 1876,
The - Atkinson, H.
Abolitionism is equivalent to
revolution - Otis, H. G.
Abraham's offering up his son
Isaac - Whitefield, G.
Acceleration or direction -
Benezet, L. T.
Acres of diamonds - Conwell,
R. H.
Action challenged - Landon, A. M.
Action defended - Roosevelt, F. D.
Activity of the International Com-
mittee of the Red Cross during
the War, 1939-1945, The -
Chapuisat, E.
Activity of the nerve fibres, The
- Adrian, E. D.
Adams and Jefferson - Everett, E.
Address at Harvard University -
Marshall, G. C.
Address at the Catholic University
of America - Wirtz, W. W.
Address at the centennial anniver-
sary of the Pennsylvania Soci-
ety for Promoting the Abolition
of Slavery - Harper, F. E. W.
Address at the memorial service
for Sir Winston Churchill -
Stevenson, A. E.
Address at the opening of the
Atlanta Exposition - Washing-
ton, B. T.
Address at University of Penn-
sylvania - Roosevelt, F. D.
Address before the American So-
ciety of Newspaper Editors -
McNamara, R. S.
Address before the Midwest Re-
gional Republican Committee -
Agnew, S.
Address delivered at the Harvard
Alumni dinner in 1896 -
Washington, B. T.

Address in honor of Robert E. Lee
- Stanley, A. O.
Address of the United States Anti-
Masonic Convention (1830) -
Freemasons
Address on Constitution Day -
Roosevelt, F. D.
Address on constitutionality of Alien
and Sedition Laws - Marshall, J.
Address on law enforcement - Wal-
lace, G. C.
Address on the King's speech -
Fox, C. J.
Address to Congress - Churchill,
W. L. S.
Address to Nero - Seneca, L. A.
Address to the Free University of
Berlin - Kennedy, R. F.
Address to the General Assembly,
Frankfort, Kentucky, April 20,
1936 - Chandler, A. B.
Address to the Humane and benevol-
ent inhabitants of the city and
county of Philadelphia - Forten, J.
Address to the people of color -
Johnstone, A.
Address to the people of England -
Lee, R. H.
Address to the slaves of the United
States of America - Garnet,
H. H.
Address to the throne concerning
affairs in America, November 18,
1777 - Pitt, W., 1708-1778
Address to the unknown loyal dead
- Douglass, F.
Address to Young Democratic Clubs
of America - Roosevelt, F. D.
Adkins v. Children's Hospital -
Sutherland, G.
Administration of Chips - Churchill,
R. H. S.
Adoption of the Statute of Westmin-
ster, The - Fraser, P.
Adrenergic neurotransmitter func-
tions - Von Euler, U.

Fear and hysteria: the Japanese
relocation, etc. - Stones, H. F.
Feast or famine: the key to
peace - Butz, E. L.
Federal Court orders must be up-
held - Eisenhower, D. D.
Federal experiments in history
- Monroe, J.
Federal judiciary - Bayard, J. A.
Federal power and local rights -
Clinton, D. W.
Federal support of science and
medicine - Califano, J. A.
Feeding the hungry world - Rush,
W.
Fermentation of sugars and fer-
mentative enzymes - Euler,
H. V.
Fervent appeal for free silver -
Fitch, T.
Festival of the Supreme Being -
Robespierre, M.
"Fifty-four forty or fight" -
Cobb, H.
Fifty years of trade-union activity
in behalf of peace - Jouhaux,
L.
Fight for Merdeka - Abdul Rah-
man, T.
Filipinos of today and Filipinos
of yesterday - Quezon, M. L.
Financial reform - Churchill,
R. H. S.
Finding America - Hartzog, G.
B., Jr.
Fine structure of the hydrogen
bomb - Lamb, W. E.
Finish the good work of uniting
colored and white workingmen
- Myers, I.
Fireside chat on party primaries
- Roosevelt, F. D.
Fireside chat: unity on U. S.
goals - Carter, J.
First Amendment, The: freedom
and responsibility - Mathias,
C. M.
First Olynthiac oration - Demos-
thenes
First oration against Catiline -
Cicero, M. T.
First oration against Verres -
Cicero, M. T.
First Philippic - Demosthenes
First step in nation building -
Lee Kuan Yew
First war address before Con-
gress - Roosevelt, F. D.

Five hundred miles south - Slabach,
D.
"Flanks are something for the enemy
to worry about" - Patton, G. S.
Flash photolysis and some of its ap-
plications - Porter, F.
Folle epoque, La - Buckley, F. R.
Food--a world crisis - Stratton,
R. D.
Foolish exchange - Taylor, J.
For a vigorous prosecution of the
war - Clay, H.
For a white Australia - Deakin, A.
For federal government by the peo-
ple - King, R.
For ratification of treaties with
Panama - Rusk, D.
For the encouragement of learning -
Dering, E.
For the Federal Constitution -
Deakin, A.
For the nomination of Gerald R.
Ford - Percy, C. H.
Force Bill - Calhoun, J. C.
Foreign-born children in the primary
grades - Addams, J.
Foreign policy--old myths and new
realities - Fulbright, J. W.
Forgiveness of injuries - Cranmer,
T.
Forward defence--from the Middle
East to Malaya, 1955 - Holland,
S.
Four faces of peace, The - Pearson,
L. B.
Four good signs - Lipis, P. L.
Four human freedoms - Roosevelt,
F. D.
Four ways of looking at a speech -
Lee, I. G.
Fourteen points - Wilson, W.
Fourth Philippic - Cicero, M. T.
Frankenstein in the making -
Seenivasagam, D. R.
Fraternity among nations - Branting,
K. H.
Freaks for Jesus' sake - Elson,
E. L. R.
"Free by '63" - Patterson, W. L.
Free Huey - Seale, B.
Free just free - Gallagher, W.
Free land and the supply of labor -
Sutherland, J.
Free people - Grattan, H.
Free speech and fundamental rights
- Erskine, T.
Freedom and individual security -
Lehman, H. H.

God's promise to his plantations
- Cotton, J.

Golden rule for foreign affairs
- Fillmore, M.

Good lore for simple folk - Wycliffe, J.

Good neighbor policy - Roosevelt,
F. D.

Good news from a far country -
Chauncy, C.

Good time is at hand - Purvis, R.

Goodwill in industry - Baldwin,
S. B.

Gospel-covenant, The - Bulkeley,
P.

Government is determined to take
drastic measures if ... -
Rahman, D. I. B. A.

Government of the tongue -
Butler, J.

Government policy - Churchill,
W. L. S.

Government spending is sound -
Eccles, M. S.

Governments for the people and
not the people for governments
- Sidney, A.

Grand alternatives - Skidelsky, R.

Grape shot and hemp - Brownlow,
W. G.

Great American institution - Gale,
J.

Great institution - Lee, H. H. S.

Great migration north - DuBois,
W. E. B.

Great society - Johnson, L. B.

Great society is a sick society
- Fulbright, J. W.

Greatest thing in the world -
Drummond, H.

Greatness of a plain American -
Emerson, R. W.

Green parrot - Carlat, J.

Green revolution, peace, and
humanity, The - Borlaug,
N. E.

Grievances and oppressions
under Charles I - Bristol,
G. D.

Guided tour of gobbledygook, A
- Ashley, L. R. N.

Guide-lines and strategies for
achieving national unity -
Muhammad Ghazali bin Shafie

Guns and butter are tied together - Humphrey, H. H., Jr.

- H -

Hand that held the dagger - Roosevelt, F. D.

Happiness of a people in the wisdom
of their rulers directing and in
obedience of their brethren attending unto what Israel ought to
do - Hubbard, W.

Harmony--from where the sun now
stands - Trimble, C.

Harvard and Yale - Eliot, C. W.

Has one government the right to
intervene in the internal affairs
of another - Chateaubriand, F.
A. R.

Has TV made the public speaker
obsolete? - Braden, W. W.

Hate in politics - Canning, G.

Have faith in Massachusetts -
Coolidge, C.

Haven of the defeated - Karos, P. A.

Hazards of equity - Thibeault,
M. L.

He cannot be replaced - Milgrom, J.

He died climbing - Minda, A. G.

He stood up and drank the toast and
joined in the applause! - Sandosham, A. A.

Healthier than healthy - Menninger,
K.

Healthy heresies - Gunsaulus, F. W.

Heap of trouble, A - Hall, C.

Heavenly footman - Bunyan, J.

Heavenly glow - Simon, E. Y.

Hemoglobin regeneration as influenced by diet and other factors
- Whipple, G. H.

Heroes of faith - Chrysostom, J.

Heroic in history - Carlyle, T.

Higher education begins the seventies - Hesburgh, T. M.

Higher law than the Constitution -
Seward, W. H.

Highest attainment - Garsek, I.

Highest form of expression -
Robertson, F. W.

Highest manhood - Hughes, T.

His sovereignty under his hat -
Curtis, G. W.

History of Singapore's struggle for
nationhood, 1945-1959 - Marshall,
D. S.

Hitler's plans for Canada and the
United States - Thompson, D.

Holy crusade for liberty - Hoover,
H. C.

- O -

- X -

- Y -

- Z -